A

DICTIONARY FOR

ARACHNOLOGY

Other books by Tim Williams
(available via www.Lulu.com)

A Dictionary of the Roots and Combining Forms of Scientific Words

A Check List and Synonym Key for the Phylum Porifera

A Dictionary for Invertebrate Zoology

A Dictionary for Vertebrate Zoology

A Dictionary for Entomology

Front Cover: the 66th plate from Ernst Haeckel's *Kunstformen der Natur* (1904).

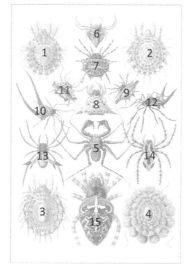

1. *Tegeocranus hericius* 0.6mm Dornkronen-Moosmilbe (Nymphe) Europa
2. *Tegeocranus latus* 0.9mm Stachelkranz-Moosmilbe (Nymphe) Europa
3. *Tegeocranus cepheiformis* 0.62mm Gefiederte Moosmilbe (Nymphe) Europa
4. *Leiosoma palmicinctum* 1.0mm Blattgürtel-Moosmilbe (Nymphe) Europa
5. *Phrynus reniformis* (natural size) Nierenförmiger Geißelskorpion, Eastindia
6. *Arkys cordiformis* (2x) Herzförmige Arkysspinne, America
7. *Gasteracantha cancriformis* (3x) Krabbenförmige Stachelspinne, Brasil
8. *Gasteracantha acrosomoides* (5x) Dreieckige Stachelspinne, Madagascar (now *Acrosomoides acrosomoides*)
9. *Gasteracantha geminata* (3x) Doppeldornige Stachelspinne, Eastindia
10. *Gasteracantha arcuata* (2x) Bogendornige Stachelspinne, Java (is now *Macracantha arcuata*)
11. *Acrosoma hexacanthum* (4x) Sechsspitzige Stachelspinne, Brasilien (now *Gasterocantha cancriformis*)
12. *Acrosoma spinosum* (2x) Dickdornige Stachelspinne, Southamerika (now *Micrathena schreibersi*)
13. *Acrosoma bifurcatum* (4x) Zweigabelige Stachelspinne, Brasilien (now *Micrathena furcata*)
14. *Oxyopes variegatus* (3x) Bunte Springspinne, Germany (now *Oxyopes heterophthalmus*)
15. *Epeira diadema* (3x) Fromme Kreuzspinne, Germany (now *Araneus diadematus*)

A

DICTIONARY FOR

ARACHNOLOGY

An essential reference source for every Zoology and Arachnology student. This work also includes many commonly encountered terms from the fields of Anatomy, Animal Behavior, Genetics, Ecology, Taxonomy and Zoogeography, as well as many terms covering sizes, shapes, colors, forms and textures.

Compiled by Tim Williams Ph.D.

timwilliams@asia.edu.tw

Paperback ISBN 978-1-716-17701-9

Second edition published in 2021 by Lulu.com
Set in Palatino & Symbol type. Composition and design by Tim Williams.
Printed in the United States of America by Lulu.com

Although the author and publisher have made a considerable effort to ensure the accuracy of the information contained in this publication, we accept no responsibility for any loss, injury or inconvenience sustained by anyone using this book. Notification of factual errors, typing errors and suggestions for improvement will be gratefully received by the author at timwilliams@asia.edu.tw

CONTENTS

Introduction

Arachnids are a large group of invertebrates that are mainly terrestrial, have eight legs and a variable number of eyes. A few inhabit fresh water, a few have modified legs and a few have no eyes. This group includes the well known spiders, scorpions, ticks, mites and harvestmen as well as several less well known orders. As well as having eight legs, which easily distinguishes them from the insects, the have two more appendages at the front end which have become variously modified for sensory perception, feeding or defense. There are also some adult forms of mites with only six or four legs. Arachnids also never have antennae or wings and their bodies are organized into two sections or 'tagmata', known as the prosoma (or cephalothorax) and opisthosoma (or abdomen). The prosoma results from a fusion of the head (cephalon) and the thorax and is normally covered by a single unsegmented carapace. The abdomen may be segmented in the primitive forms, although this is only clearly visible in scorpions.

Most people regard spiders as being predatory, but although that is popularly seen to be the case, what is not so often seen, probably because it is not so dramatic, is that many spiders feed on a variety of foods. For example, the jumping spider *Bagheera kiplingi* gets over 90% of its food from plant material produced by acacias as part of a mutually beneficial relationship with a species of ant (Meehan et al. 2008)

Laboratory studies have found that spiderlings in some families, for example Anyphaenidae, Corinnidae, Clubionidae, Thomisidae and Salticidae feed on plant nectar. Apparently they do so intentionally and over long periods. It has also been found that these spiders prefer sugar solutions to plain water, which indicates that they are seeking nutrients. Because many spiders are nocturnal and thus their habits are difficult to observe, the extent of nectar consumption may be under-estimated. Nectar of course is not just sugar, it also contains amino acids, lipids, vitamins and minerals, and studies have shown that some spider species live longer when nectar is available (Jackson et al. 2001). Feeding on nectar is a good strategy as it avoids the potential risks of damage from struggling with prey and the metabolic costs of producing venom and digestive enzymes.

Various species are known to scavenge on dead arthropods, web silk and their own shed exoskeletons. Pollen caught in webs may also be eaten, and some research has shown that young spiders have a better chance of survival if they have the opportunity to eat pollen. In captivity, several spider species are also known to feed on bananas, marmalade, milk, egg yolk and sausages.

The material for this book has been compiled from many sources, most of which are listed in the bibliography. The original material has been re-written in a style appropriate for a dictionary and, in the light of rapid advances and changing concepts, checked for accuracy.

In general each entry is structured in the following way: the main term is followed by spelling variations and synonyms (if they exist), then comes the etymology of the term, showing its Latin, Greek or other language roots. Next is the description of the term and at the end of an entry there is direction to other, related entries; should they exist. The descriptions of animals include all the taxonomic categories down to the level of family in most cases. Each animal entry includes the two higher taxonomic categories; so that the entry on (for example) the Chthoniidae, a family of Pseudoscorpiones, mentions the superfamily Chthonioidea, and the order Heterosphyronida, each of which are of course entered in the dictionary. Thus one could 'walk up' through the text from the lower taxonomic level to the highest, and vice versa.

At present the systematics of some taxa is in a state of flux and seems like it will be for some time to come as new information is continually being added and older ideas are discarded. Also, there are many erroneous publications, both in spelling and context, especially on the internet. I have endeavored to use current terminology but inevitably there will be some disagreement about which categories are relevant. The taxonomic hierarchies presented here are the ones which seem to be most widely accepted at present; accepted competing ideas have been noted.

Finally, no work of this nature can ever be as complete as could be desired. No doubt many terms which should have been included have been omitted and many terms which may profitably have been excluded have been retained. New terms are being added every day to the scientific vocabulary and the temptation to carry on including information has to be realistically constrained by publishing timetables. The proof-reading of this work has been a major task in itself and any errors or omissions that remain are exclusively my own.

A brief introduction to scientific Latin and Greek

Most of the words used in zoology are derived from Greek or Latin; many more from the former than from the latter. One of the major problems for any scientist is the understanding of the technical terms of their field. Many natural historians and biologists, although conversant with the Latin names of species and the Greek-derived technical terms, are unable to explain the meaning behind them. In this dictionary an attempt is made to remedy this by providing the word roots. Thus, for example, the entry **Halacaridae** (a family of marine, brackish and fresh-water mites) is given as being derived from the Greek αλιος (halios) 'of the sea', and ακαρι (acari), a 'mite'. The name describing their most distinctive characteristic at the time of their original description: they live in the sea. Similarly, knowing that *ortho-* is from the Greek for *straight* (oρθος) and *-gnatha* is from the Greek for *jaw* (-γναθος), being **Orthognathous** means that the axis of the head is at right angles to the body or, in terms of spiders, refers to type of chelicerae that project forward with fangs articulating along the longitudinal (vertical) axis.

Not only does an awareness of the roots of a scientific name bring that particular name to life, in many cases it also helps to form a useful mental picture. Many such roots are common to many scientific terms, and once the meaning of these roots is understood their occurrence in words subsequently encountered will immediately suggest the meanings of the new words.

Transliteration

Transliteration is the process of rendering the letters and sounds of one language into those of another. The recommended transliteration of the classic Greek alphabet of twenty four letters plus diphthongs into Latin and ultimately into English is demonstrated as follows.

Vowels and Consonants

	Greek		English	Pronunciation
Alpha	A, α	=	A, a	as in hat
Beta	B, β	=	B, b	as English
Gamma[1]	Γ, γ	=	G, g	as in got
Delta	Δ, δ	=	D, d	as English
Epsilon	E, ε	=	E, e	as in pet
Zeta	Z, ζ	=	Z, z	as in sd/z (wisdom)
Eta[2]	H, η	=	E, e	as in hair
Theta	Θ, θ	=	Th, th	as in thigh
Iota[3]	I, ι	=	I, i (sometimes J, j)	as in pit
Kappa[4]	K, κ	=	K, k, C, c	as English
Lambda	Λ, λ	=	L, l	as English
Mu	M, μ	=	M, m	as English
Nu	N, ν	=	N, n	as English
Xi	Ξ, ξ	=	X, x	as English
Omicron	O, o	=	O, o	as in pot
Pi	Π, π	=	P, p	as English

Rho[5]	P, ρ	=	R, r	as English
Sigma[6]	Σ, σ, ς	=	S, s	as in sing
Tau	T, τ	=	T, t	as English
Upsilon[7]	Y, υ	=	U, u, Y, y	as in p*u*t
Phi	Φ, φ	=	F, f	as English
Chi	X, χ	=	Ch, ch	as in lo*ch*
Psi	Ψ, ψ	=	Ps, ps	as in la*ps*e
Omega[8]	Ω, ω	=	O, o	as in s*aw*

[1]Gamma becomes *n* before γ, κ, ξ, χ:
γγ = *ng*, as in στρογγυλος (strongylus), γαγγλιον (ganglion)
γκ = *nc*, as in σφιγκτηρ (sphincter), εγκεφαλος (encephalus)
γξ = *nx*, as in φαλανξ (phalanx), σαλπιγξ (salpinx)
γχ = *nch*, as in κογχη (concha), ρυγχος (rhynchus)

[2]Epsilon and eta are not distinguished in transliteration, nor is there any way of deciding from a transliterated word which letter is meant. However, eta at the end of most nouns becomes *a*, as in Ανδρομεδη (Andromeda), κομη (coma), θεκη (theca), but there are exceptions, e.g. ψυχη (psyche), νικη (nike).

[3]It is common now to use *i* before a consonant, as in *Ichneumon, icon*, and in almost all instances (exceptions: *major, majestas*) before a vowel in a post-initial syllable (*socialis, vaccinium*); and a J before an initial vowel (*janitor, justitia*). The initial *i* is kept if the word is still essentially Greek and has an *i* sound as an initial syllable, e.g. ιον (ion).

[4]Kappa is retained in many English words (*karyotype, keratin, ketone, krypton, plankton, skeleton*, etc.)

[5]In compound words the initial r of the second term is doubled after a vowel, as in αιμορραγια (haemorrhage), καταρριν (catarrhin, hook-nosed), πλατυρρινος (platyrrhinos, broad-nosed) but remains single after a diphthong, as in ευρις (eurhis - with a good nose), χιμαιρα (chimaera / chimera). In some words the double ρρ results from the euphonic assimilation of ν to ρ in the prefixes αν- (an-) and συν- (syn-). initial ρ = rh, medial ρρ = rrh

[6]The final '*s*' is always ς. Initial σ, medial σ and final ς are not distinguished in transliteration.

[7]Upsilon (ypsilon or hypsilon) is normally transliterated as '*y*', but in some cases it has been maintained as '*u*' (μυραινα - muraena - moray, τυμβος - tumba - tomb). It is kept as '*u*' in the diphthongs *au, eu, ou*. Initial υ = Y

[8]Omicron and omega are not distinguished in transliteration, nor is there any way of deciding from a transliterated word which letter is meant except sometimes in the final ον, ος, ων, ως.
ον = *um*, as in χρυσανθεμον (chrysanthemum), αρον (arum) and = *on*, as in νευρον (neuron), γαγγλιον (ganglion), μικρον (micron).
ος = *us*, as in ιπποος (hippus), ποταμος (potamus) and = *os*, as in κοσμος (cosmos), λογος (logos).
ων = *on*, as in σιφον (siphon), χιτων (chiton).
ως = *os*, as in ερως (eros), ρινοκερως (rhinoceros).

Diphthongs and other double letters.

A diphthong consist of two vowels written together and pronounced as a single vowel. In some older texts *ae* and *oe* may be represented as Æ, æ, Œ and œ.

Greek	Transliteration	Pronunciation
αι	ai, ae, e (preferably e)	as in h*i*gh
αυ	au	as in h*ow*
ει/ηι	ei or i (preferably i)	as in h*ei*ght

εv/ηv	eu	as in feud ('e-oo')
οι/ωι	oe, oi, e (preferably oe)	as in boy
ου	ou, u (preferably u)	as in too
υι	yi	as in suite
αη	ae (not a diphthong)	
γγ	ng	as in finger
ov	final ov = um	
ος	final ος = us	

When changing a Greek word to a corresponding Latin, or Latinized form, the ending of the word is usually changed to the corresponding Latin ending in the nominative of the same gender. The Latin pleural is also used.

Masculine ending: Greek -ος, Latin -us. As in δακτυλος = dactylus (a finger). Pl. *dactyli*.

Feminine ending: Greek -η, Latin -a. As in θηκη = theca (case). Pl. *thecae*.

Neuter ending: Greek -ov, Latin -um. As in κροταλov = crotalum (rattle). Pl. *crotali*.

General rules for pronunciation of scientific names

Vowels. All vowels are pronounced. At the end of a word the pronunciation is long (*e* as in meet, *i* as in mite, *o* as in rope, *u* as in cute) except *a*, which has an *uh* sound, as in idea. The vowel in the final syllable has a short sound (*a* as in flat, *e* as in let, *i* as in hit, *o* as in slot, *u* as in put) except *es*, which is pronounced *ease*.

Diphthongs.   As above.

Consonants.   When derived from Greek, Ch as k (as in chameleon), when derived from other languages, Ch as in church.
C has a soft sound (s as in lice) when it is followed by *ae, e, oe, i* or *y*. It has a hard sound (k, as in cat) when followed by *a, o, oi*, or *u*.
G has a soft sound (j as in gin) when followed by *ae, e, i, oe*, or *y*; and a hard sound (g as in go) when followed by *a, o, oi*, or *u*.
The initial consonant is not pronounced in words beginning with *ps, pt, ct, cn, gn*, or *mn*. However, when these combinations occur within a word the first letter is pronounced.
An initial *x* is pronounced as *z*, and as *ks* when it occurs elsewhere in the word.
A double c followed by *i* or *y* is pronounced *ks*.

Accent   The accented syllable is either the penultimate syllable (one before the end) or the antepenultimate syllable (one before the one before the end). In long words there may well be a secondary accent on a syllable near the beginning of the word.

For a detailed, entertaining and excellent discussion of the composition of scientific words see Brown, R.W. (1956). *Composition of Scientific Words*. Smithsonian.

Abbreviations

AFr. - Anglo-French
AL - Anglo-Latin
alt. - alternative
Ar. - Arabic
AS. - Anglo Saxon
Br. - Brazilian
ca. - circa, approximately
Carib. - Caribbean
cf. - confer ('compare')
chem. - chemical
cogn. - cognate with
comp. - comparative
Da. - Danish
den. - denoting
dim. - diminutive
deriv. - derived from/derivation.
Du. - Dutch
e.g. - exempli gratia (for example)
erron. - erroneous/erroneously
etc. - et cetera (and so forth)
fem. - feminine
Fr. - French
Gallo-Rom. - Gallo-Roman
Ger. - German
Gmc. - Germanic
Gr. - Greek
Hind. - Hindu
Ice. - Icelandic
i.e. - id est (that is)
IE. - Indo-European
imit. - imitation/imitative
ind. - indicating
It. - Italian
L. - Latin
LG. - Low German
LL. - Late Latin
L.OE. - Late Old English
Mal. - Malaysian
Malag. - Malagasy
masc. - masculine
MdfL. - Modified Latin
MDu - Middle Dutch
ME. - Middle English
medic. - medical
MedL. - Medieval Latin
metaph. - metaphorical
Mex. - Mexican

MD. - Middle Dutch
MG. - Middle German
Mongl. - Mongolian
MHG - Middle High German
ML. - Modern Latin
MLG. - Middle Low German
Mod.L. - Modern Latin
myth. - mythology/mythological
NL. - New Latin
Norw. - Norwegian
obs. - obsolete
OE. - Old English
OFr. - Old French
OHG. - Old High German.
ON. - Old Norse
opp. - opposite
orig. - original
perh. - perhaps
Pers. - Persian.
pert. - pertaining to
pl. - plural
poet. - poetical/poetically
Pr. - Provençal
prec. - preceding
pref. - prefix
prob. - probably
Rom. - Roman, Romance
Rus. - Russian
SAm. - South American
SAm.Sp. - South American Spanish
Sc. - Scottish
Skr. - Sanskrit
Sp. - Spanish
Sin. - Sinhalese
sing. - singular
spec. - specifically
suf. - suffix
super. - superlative
Sw. - Swedish
Tp. - Tupi (SAm. native language)
Turk. - Turkish
uncert. - uncertain
unkn. - unknown
var. - variation
VL. - Vulgar Latin
† - Extinct taxon

External features of a typical female spider

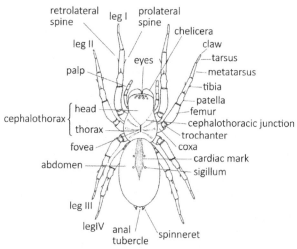

retrolateral spine — leg I — prolateral spine — chelicera — claw — tarsus — metatarsus — tibia — patella — femur — cephalothoracic junction — trochanter — coxa — cardiac mark — sigillum

leg II — eyes — palp — head — cephalothorax — thorax — fovea — abdomen — leg III — legIV — anal tubercle — spinneret

dorsal aspect

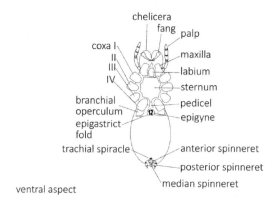

chelicera — fang — palp — coxa I, II, III, IV — maxilla — labium — sternum — branchial operculum — pedicel — epigyne — epigastrict fold — trachial spiracle — anterior spinneret — posterior spinneret — median spinneret

ventral aspect

External features of a typical mesostigmatid mite.

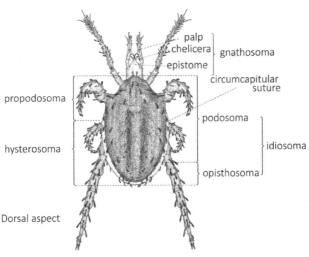

palp
chelicera ⎱ gnathosoma
epistome

circumcapitular
    suture

propodosoma

podosoma ⎱

hysterosoma

idiosoma

opisthosoma ⎭

Dorsal aspect

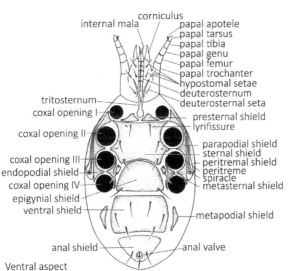

corniculus
internal mala
papal apotele
papal tarsus
papal tibia
papal genu
papal femur
papal trochanter
hypostomal setae
deuterosternum
deuterosternal seta
tritosternum
presternal shield
coxal opening I
lyrifissure
coxal opening II

parapodial shield
sternal shield
peritremal shield
peritreme
spiracle
metasternal shield
coxal opening III
endopodial shield
coxal opening IV
epigynial shield
ventral shield

metapodial shield

anal shield
anal valve

Ventral aspect

Typical examples of the sixteen orders of arachnids, not to scale, and there is much variation within many orders.

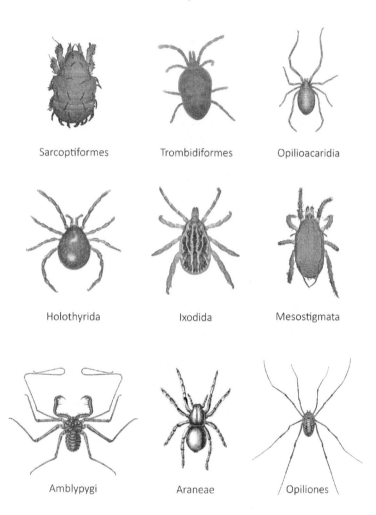

Sarcoptiformes   Trombidiformes   Opilioacaridia

Holothyrida   Ixodida   Mesostigmata

Amblypygi   Araneae   Opiliones

Typical examples of the sixteen orders of arachnids, not to scale, and there is much variation within many orders.

Palpigradi

Pseudoscorpiones

Ricinulei

Schizomida

Scorpiones

Solifuge

Uropygi

THE DICTIONARY

A

A-, Ab-. Latin prefix meaning; off, from, apart, away, out, etc. For example, *ab*actinal, *ab*oral: away from the actinal/oral surface. (Also *ab*normal etc.).

A-, An-. Greek prefix meaning; not, there is not, without. Occurs in words having a Greek base, but coming mainly through late and modern Latin as *a*branchiate, *a*cephalous, *a*septic, *a*symmetry etc., as well as from terms derived from other bases, e.g. *a*sexual, *a*caulous.

ABAXIAL. [L. *ab*, from; *axis*, axle]. A surface that is remote to, or turned away from, the axis (midline). E.g. the lateral (outer) face of a chelicera. Opposite: adaxial.

ABDOMEN. [L. *abdomen*, belly]. The posterior of the two major divisions of the arachnid body in which the segments are similar to each other and which contain most of the digestive tract, the gonads and the genital openings. See Opisthosoma.

ABDOMERE. [L. *abdomen*, belly; Gr. μερος. part]. An abdominal segment.

ABDOMINAL. [L. *abdomen*, belly]. Of structures and organs situated in, or closely related to, the abdomen.

ABDUCENT. [L. *abducere*, to lead away]. Drawing out or drawing away from.

ABDUCT/ABDUCTION. [L. *abducere*, to lead away]. To move a part of the body away from the mid-line. Opposite: Adduct/Adduction.

ABDUCTOR MUSCLE. [L. *abducere*, to lead away]. A muscle which draws any part of the body away from its normal (resting) position or away from the median line. See also Adductor Muscle, Muscle Terminology.

ABERRANT. [L. *aberrare*, to stray]. Of characters not in general accordance with those of the species, type, etc.

ABIENCE (ABIENT). [L. *abire*, to depart]. The withdrawal or retreat from a stimulus and thus the avoidance of reaction. Opposite: Adience.

ABIOCOEN. [Gr. α-, not/un-; βιος, life; κοινος, in common]. The totality of the abiotic parts of an environment.

ABJUGAL FURROW. [L. *ab*, from; *jugum*, yoke]. In ticks and mites: the line separating the aspidosoma (prodorsum) and the podosoma.

ABLATION. [L. *ablatus*, taken away]. The removal of a part by excision or amputation.

ABORIGINE. [L. *ab*, from; *origo*, beginning]. The original biota of a region.

ABRUPT. [L. *abrumpere*, to break off]. Cut off or broken at an extremity, or appearing so.

ABRUPT SPECIATION. [L. *abrumpere*, to break off, *species*, particular kind]. See Speciation,

ABSCISED. [L. *abscissus*, cut off]. Cut off squarely; with a straight margin.

ABSCISSION. [L. *abscissus*, cut off]. The separation of parts. Abscission zone: the region where separation occurs.

ABSCONDITUS. [L. *absconditus*, hidden/concealed]. Hidden, concealed. Retracted into another.

ABSOLUTE ABUNDANCE. The exact number of individuals of a particular taxon in a particular region.

ABUNDANCE. [L. *abundare*, to abound]. The total number of individuals of a taxon in a particular area.

ABUNDISMUS. [L. *abundare* to overflow]. Incomplete melanism resulting from a relative increase in the number of black pigment spots within non-black areas of a color pattern.

ACANTHA (AKANTHA). [Gr. ακανθα, thorn]. A spine, prickle or thorn.

ACANTHACEOUS. [Gr. ακανθα, thorn; L. *-aceous*, of the nature of]. Bearing spines or prickles.

2

ACANTHION. [Gr. ακανθιον, small thorn]. The most prominent point on a spine.

ACANTHODION, ACANTHOIDES. [Gr. ακανθωδης, thorny]. In ticks and mites: a tarsal seta containing extensions of a sensory basal hair. See also Eupathidion.

ACANTHOID. [Gr. ακανθα, thorn; ειδος, form]. Resembling a spine, thorn or prickle.

ACANTHUS. [Gr. ακανθα, thorn]. A spine, spur or prickle.

ACARI (ACARINA). [LL. *acarus*, mite. Gr. ακαρι, mite or tick]. The terms Acari and Acarina have both been previously used for a taxon composed of the arachnid subgroups Acariformes, Opilioacariformes, and Parasitiformes. Because of the great morphological diversity and relatively few unifying features, this taxon of around 32,000 described species is considered to be an unnatural polyphyletic grouping; the phylogeny is disputed and several taxonomic schemes have been proposed for their classification. These groups of ticks and mites are now classed as superorders (class Euchelicerata, subclass Arachnida), and together form one of the most ubiquitous and diverse groups in the animal kingdom, ranging from polar regions to desert regions. Mostly minute (average 1 mm or less in length for mites but some ticks may attain 3 cm in length), they have a rounded body without divisions and four pairs of legs without gnathobases. Most are either scavengers or ectoparasites, but some are herbivores and others are detritivores. The blood-sucking ticks usually have an elongated proboscis, whilst the free-living mites have mouth parts which are clawed or sensory. Superorders: Acariformes, Opilioacariformes, Parasitiformes.

ACARIASIS (ACARIOSIS, ACARIDIASIS). [Gr. ακαρι, mite or tick; -ιασις, diseased condition]. Infestation with ticks or mites, or any resulting diseased condition.

ACARIDIA (ACARIDEI). [Gr. ακαρι, mite or tick]. In a previous classification; an infraorder (or parvorder) of 'biting' mites (order Sarcoptiformes, suborder Astigmata) that united the superfamilies: Acaroidea, Canestrinioidea, Glycyphagoidea, Hemisarcoptoidea, Histiostomatoidea, Hypoderoidea, Schizoglyphoidea.

ACARIFORMES (ACTINOTRICHIDA). [LL. *acarus*, mite, *forma*, shape]. The large superorder of mites (class Euchelicerata, subclass Arachnida) containing about 351 families, including plant parasites, chiggers, hair follicle mites, velvet mites, water mites, fur, feather, dust and human itch mites, etc. Orders: Sarcoptiformes, Trombidiformes.

ACARINA. [LL. *acarus*, mite]. See Acari.

ACARINARIUM, ACARINIUM. [LL. *acarus*, mite; -*arium*, a place where something is kept]. Any location that regularly serves as an abode for mites. In old world carpenter bees (Xylocopinae, **Apidae**): a small pouch on the abdomen which provides protection for their symbiotic mites (*Dinogamasus*, **Laelapidae**).

ACAROCECIDIUM. [Gr. ακαρης, tiny; κεκιδιον, little nut]. The gall caused by gall-mites (Eriophyidae).

ACARODOMATIUM (ACARODOMATIA, DOMATIA). [LL. *acarus*, mite; domatium, dwelling]. Plant structures that serve as refugia for mites. E.g. At the junction of two veins on the ventral surface of the leaves of some plants that are inhabited by predatory or fungivorous mites.

ACAROIDEA. [Gr. ακαρι, mite or tick]. A superfamily of 'biting' mites (suborder Astigmata, parvorder Acaridia). Families: **Acaridae, Gaudiellidae** (syn. **Platyglyphidae**), **Glycacaridae, Lardoglyphidae, Sapracaridae, Scatoglyphidae, Suidasiidae.**

ACAROLOGY. [Gr. ακαρης, tiny; LL. *acarus*, mite; Gr. λογος, discourse]. The scientific study of ticks and mites.

ACARONYCHOIDEA. [Gr. ακαρι, mite or tick; ονυξ, talon]. A small monotypic superfamily of mites (suborder Oribatida, infraorder Palaeosomata). Family: **Acaronychidae.**

ACAROPHILOUS. [LL. *acarus*, mite; Gr. φιλος, loving]. Living well in association with ticks and mites.

ACAROPHYTISM. [LL. *acarus*, mite; Gr. φυτον, a plant]. A symbiotic relationship between plants and mites.

ACAUDATE (ECAUDATE). [Gr. α-, without; L. *cauda*, tail]. Without a tail.

3

ACCELERATION, LAW OF. The theory that the sequence of development of organs is directly related to their importance to the organism.

ACCELERATOR (NERVE or MUSCLE). [L. *accelerare*, to quicken]. A nerve or muscle which increases the rate of an action.

ACCESSORIUS (MUSCLE). [L. *accedere*, be added to]. Any muscle aiding the action of another. See also Muscle Terminology.

ACCESSORY. [L. *accedere*, be added to]. Additional: employed especially of those parts of a sense organ which have the function of making the reception of stimuli more efficient.

ACCESSORY CLAW. [L. *accedere*, be added to; AS. *clawu*, claw]. In some spiders: claw-like bundles of setae or bristles, which are serrated and greatly thickened, below the true claws.

ACCESSORY SETA. [L. *accedere*, be added to; *seta*, bristle]. The opisthosomal seta h1 in the Eriophyoidea. See Grandjean System.

ACCIDENTAL. Of an animal or plant found in an area in which it does not normally occur.

ACCIDENTAL HOST. A host in which a pathogenic parasite is not commonly found.

ACCLIMATION. [L. *ad*, to; Gr. κλιμα, climate]. A phenotypic reversible adaptation to environmental fluctuations. Acclimatization to an artificial environment.

ACCLIMATISE. [L. *ad*, to; Gr. κλιμα, climate]. To become used to a certain environment as a result of natural change, for example, seasonal changes.

ACCLIVOUS. [L. *acclivis*, ascending]. Sloping upwards. Opposite: Declivous.

ACCRETION. [L. *accrescere*, to increase]. Growth or increase by external addition. See also Intussusception.

-ACEOUS. Latin suffix meaning 'of the nature of', as in 'predaceous ' - of the nature of a predator.

ACERATA. [Gr. α, without; κερας, horn]. In a previous classification: a class which united the Merostomata and Arachnida.

ACERATE. [L. *acer*, sharp]. Needle-shaped.

ACEROSE. [L. *acer*, sharp]. Narrow or slender. Having a sharp, rigid point.

ACERVATE. [L. *acervare*, to amass]. Clumped, heaped together.

ACERVULINE. [LL. diminutive of *acervus*, heap]. Irregularly clumped or heaped together. Resembling small clumps.

ACETABULIFORM. [L. *acetabulum*, vinegar cup; *forma*, shape]. Shaped like a shallow saucer with more or less incurved sides.

ACETABULUM. [L. *acetabulum*, vinegar cup]. Any cup-shaped cavity or organ. The concave portion of a ball and socket joint. The genital sucker in ticks and mites. In armored mites (Brachypylina): the cavities where the trochanter articulates with the coxae. In acariform mites the genital opening and papillae are contained within an acetabulum.

ACHAETOUS. [Gr. α-, without: χαιτη, hair]. Without chaetae.

ACHATINE, ACHATINUS. [L. *achates*, name of a river in Sicily where agate is found]. Of lines resembling those of an agate, i.e. in bands of more or less concentric circles.

ACHELATE. [Gr. α-, without; χηλη, claw]. Without claws or pincer-like organs.

ACHELIIDAE (AMMOTHEIDAE). [Gr. α-, without; χηλη, claw]. A cosmopolitan family of sea spiders (suborder Eupantopodida, superfamily Ascorhynchoidea) in which the body is compacted and imperfectly segmented. Chelifores are small, the proboscis is fusiform and movably connected to the cephalon. The palps well developed with 4-9 segments. Ovigerous legs present in both sexes, with 7-10 segments, without a terminal claw while the ambulatory legs have auxiliary claws.

ACHILARY. [Gr. α, without; χειλος, lip]. Lacking a lip.

4

ACHIPTERIOIDEA. [Gr. αρχι-, first; πτερον, wing]. A superfamily of mites (suborder Oribatida, infraorder Brachypylina - section Poronoticae). Families: **Achipteriidae** (**Austrachipteriidae**), **Epactozetidae**, **Tegoribatidae**.

ACHROMATIC/ACHROIC. [Gr. α, without; χρωμα, color]. Uncolored. Achroos.

ACHROMIC. [Gr. α, without; χρωμα, color]. Unpigmented.

ACHROOS. [Gr. αχροματος, without color]. Unpigmented, colorless.

ACICULA (ACICULIFORM). [L. *aciculum*, a small needle]. A slender needle-like body such as the spines or prickles of some animals and plants, or some crystals.

ACICULAR. Pointed or needle shaped.

ACICULATE. Of a surface that appears as if scratched with a needle. See also Exsculpate.

ACIDURIC. [L. *acidus*, sour; *durus*, hardy]. Of organisms tolerating acid environments.

ACIFORM. [L. *acus*, needle; *forma*, shape]. Needle-shaped.

ACINACEOUS. [L. *acinus*, berry]. Consisting of acini, formed like a blackberry or raspberry. See Acinus.

ACINACIFORM. [L. *acinaces*, short sword; *forma*, shape]. Shaped like a scimitar or sabre.

ACINARIOUS. [L. *acinarius*, of grapes]. Having globose vesicles resembling grapes.

ACINIFORM. [L. *acinus*, berry; *forma*, shape]. Grape or berry-shaped, commonly applied to the silk-gland in spiders.

ACINOSE/ACINOUS. [L. *acinus*, berry]. Containing acini.

ACINUS (pl. ACINI). [L. *acinus*, a berry]. A racemose gland, the blind end of a duct of a several-lobed secreting gland.

ACONDYLOUS. [Gr. α-, without; κονδυλος, knuckle]. Without joints or nodes.

ACOUSTIC. [Gr. ακουειν, to hear]. Of organs or structures associated with the sense of hearing.

ACQUIRED CHARACTER (TRAIT). A permanent functional structural change or modification induced in an organism by use or disuse of an organ, disease or trauma, or some environmental influence.

ACQUISITION. The stage during which a new response is learnt and gradually strengthened.

ACRIDOPHAGOUS. [Gr. ακρις, locust; -φαγος, -eating]. Feeding on grasshoppers (**Acrididae**).

ACRODENROPHILOUS. [Gr. ακρος, tip; δενδρον, tree; φιλος, loving]. Living in tree-top habitats.

ACRONOMIC. [Gr. ακρος, summit; νομος, custom]. An animal that dwells in high places (treetops, cliffs, etc.).

ACROPHILOUS. [Gr. ακρος, tip; φιλειν, to love]. Preferring high altitude regions.

ACROPODIA. [Gr. ακρος, tip; πους, foot]. A digit.

ACROPSOPILIONIDAE. [Gr. ακρος, tip; ωψ, eye; +*Opilio*, a genus of the Phalangiidae]. A small family of harvestmen (suborder Dyspnoi, superfamily Acropsopilionoidea).

ACROPSOPILIONOIDEA. [Gr. ακρος, tip; ωψ, eye; +*Opilio*, a genus of the Phalangiidae]. A monospecific superfamily of harvestmen (order Opiliones, suborder Dyspnoi). Family: **Acropsopilionidae**.

ACROSCOPIC. [Gr. ακρος, tip; σκοπειν, to view]. Looking towards the apex. Opposite, Basiscopic.

ACROTARSUS (APICOTARSUS). [Gr. ακρος, tip; ταρσος, sole of the foot]. The distal subdivision of the tarsus, usually of tarsus I (not the pretarsus).

ACTIC. [Gr. ακτιτης, shore dweller]. The rocky zone between high and low tides.

ACTINAL. [Gr. ακτις, a ray]. Star-shaped.

ACTINEDIDA. [Gr. ακτις, ray]. A little-used alternative name for the Prostigmata.

ACTINIFORM. [Gr. ακτις, ray; L. *forma*, shape]. Star-shaped. Of the cheliceral appendages of some Uropodoidea.

ACTINOCHITIN. [Gr. ακτις, ray; χιτων, tunic]. An optically active form of chitin which exhibits birefringence in polarized light. It is present on the Acariformes, but lacking in the Parasitiformes. See also Actinopilin.

ACTINOPILIN. [Gr. ακτις, ray; L. *pilus*, single hair; *-in*, chem. suf.]. In acariform mites: an optically active component of the core of birefringent setae; it is surrounded by an outer isotropic layer. Actinopilin may occur in true setae (mechanoreceptors, trichobothria) as well as eupathidia and famuli which have a protoplasmic core. Solenidia lack actinopilin. See also Actinochitin.

ACTINOPODIDAE. [Gr. ακτις, ray; -πους, -foot]. A family of trapdoor spiders (infraorder Mygalomorphae, superfamily Avicularioidea) from Australia, South and Central America. This family includes *Missulena*, the venomous mouse spiders.

ACTINOTRICHIDA. [Gr. ακτις, ray, θριξ, hair]. Those mites having setae containing actinopilin, i.e. the Acariformes.

ACTIUM. [Gr. ακτιος, of, or on, the sea-beach]. A rocky-shore community.

ACTOPHILOUS. [Gr. ακτιτης, shore dweller; φιλος, loving]. Living on rocky shores.

ACUATE. [L. *acus*, needle]. Needle-shaped, sharp pointed, sharpened.

ACUITY. [LL. *acuitas*, sharpness or acuteness]. Sharpness, resolving power, applied particularly to sensory perception of low intensity stimuli (relative to the sensitivity of the sense organ).

ACULEATE-SERRATE. [L. *aculeatus*, stinging; *serratus*, toothed like a saw]. Armed with saw-like teeth inclined in one direction.

ACULEIFORM. [L. *aculeus*, a prickle; *forma*, shape]. Thorn-shaped.

ACUMINATE. [L. *acumen*, point]. Tapering to a long point.

ACUMINIFEROUS. [L. *acumen*, point; *ferre*, to bear]. Bearing pointed tubercles.

ACUMINOSE. [L. *acumen*, point]. Nearly acuminate.

ACUMINULATE. [L. *acuminulus*, little point]. Minutely acuminate. Having a very sharp tapering point.

ACUPUNCTATE. [L. *acus*, needle; *punctus*, a pricking]. Of fine, superficial punctures. Pin-pricks.

ACUTANGULATE. [L. *acutus*, sharpened; *angulus*, angular]. Forming, or meeting in an acute angle.

ACUTE. [L. *acutus*, sharpened]. 1. Ending in a sharp point (opp = obtuse). 2. Of limited duration.

ACYCLIC PARTHENOGENESIS. See Parthenogenesis.

ACYCLIC. [Gr. α, without; κυκλος, circle]. Not arranged in circles or whorls. Not Cyclical.

AD. In acariform mites: the adanal segment. See Anamorphosis, Grandjean System.

AD 1-3. In the Mesostigmata: the designations for the setae on the anterior dorsal surface of a leg or palp segment. See Evans Leg Chaetotactic System. In the Acariformes: the designations for the setae of the adanal segment. See Grandjean System.

ADACTYL, ADACTYLE. [Gr. α, without; δακτυλος, finger]. Without claws.

ADAMYSTOIDEA [Gr. αδαμας, unconquerable]. A monotypic superfamily of mites (suborder Oribatida, infraorder **Anystina**). Family: **Adamystidae**.

6

ADANAL. [L. *ad*, near; *anus*, anus]. Being located near the anus.

ADANAL PLATE / REGION/SHIELD. [L. *ad*, near; *anus*, anus]. The sclerites or sclerotized regions on the ventral surface and laterad to the anal region. They bear adanal setae and are important in oribatid mite taxonomy.

ADANAL SEGMENT. [L. *ad*, near; *anus*, anus]. In the order Acariformes: segment XIV plus one of the paraproctal segments.

ADANAL SETAE. [L. *ad*, near; *anus*, anus; *seta*, bristle]. In acariform mites: the setae on the adanal plate or region. The paranal setae in the Mesostigmata.

ADAPTATION. [L. *adaptare*, to fit to]. The process of modifying so as to suit new conditions. **Divergent**: adaptation to different kinds of environmental influence that results in a change from a common ancestral form. **Evolutionary**: the development of any characteristics of living organisms which are related to their environment and generally are seen as improving their chances of survival and thus ultimately of leaving descendants. **Phenotypic**: changes in behavior in response to environmental changes. **Physiological**: changes in an organism as a result of exposure to certain environmental conditions or stimuli; usually which allow the individual to react more favorably to these (new) conditions. **Sensory**: changes in the response of a sense organ as a result of continuous stimulation so that a stimulation of greater intensity is needed to elicit the same response.

ADAPTIVE BEHAVIOR. [L. *adaptare*, to fit to]. Behavior that allows an animal to adjust to its variable environment.

ADAPTIVE CONVERGENCE. [L. *adaptare*, to fit to]. A superficial similarity between different species due to similarity of habitats, or sometimes due to developing a protective resemblance to some other species. Several species of spiders (e.g. the ant-mimic jumping spider *Myrmarachne*: **Salticidae**) have developed a protective resemblance to ants. See also Mimicry.

ADAPTIVE ORIENTATION. [L. *adaptare*, to fit to]. A trait shown by many animals of standing or resting in such an attitude as to make the best possible use of their protective coloration.

ADAXIAL. [L. *ad*, to; *axis*, axle]. Situated on the side, or facing toward an axis (midline). Turned upwards towards the axis. Opposite: abaxial. See also Paraxaial.

ADDORSAL. [L. *ad*, near; *dorsum*, back]. Near to the middle of the dorsum.

ADDUCT / ADDUCTION. [L. *ad*, to; *ducere*, to lead]. To move a part of the body towards the mid-line. Opposite Abduct, Abduction.

ADDUCTOR MUSCLE. [L. *ad*, to; *ducere*, to lead]. Any muscle that brings parts into apposition. See also Muscle Terminology.

ADECIDUATE. [L. *a*, away from; *decidere*, to fall down]. Not falling away.

ADELOMORPHIC, ADELOMOPHOUS. [Gr. αδελος, concealed; μορφη, shape]. Indefinite in shape.

ADELPHOGAMY. [Gr. αδελφος, brother; γαμος, marriage]. Brother-sister mating.

ADELPHOPARASITE. [Gr. αδελφος, brother; παρα, beside; σιτος, food]. A parasite parasitic on a closely related host.

ADENIFORM. [Gr. αδην, a gland; L. *forma*, shape]. Gland-like. Resembling the shape of a gland.

ADENOCYTE. [Gr. αδην, a gland; κυτος, a hollow vessel]. A secretory cell of a gland.

ADENOID. [Gr. αδην, a gland; ειδος, form]. A structure resembling a gland or lymphoid tissue.

ADENOSE. [Gr. αδην, a gland]. Glandular.

ADENOTAXY. [Gr. αδην, a gland; ταξις, an arranging]. In ticks and mites: the number and distribution of the openings of the tegumentary glands.

ADESMATIC. [Gr. α, without; δεσμος, ligament]. Of a segment of an appendage, or the articulation between segments of an appendage, lacking its own tendons and muscles.

7

ADGENITAL SCLERITE/PLATE (INGUINAL PORE PLATE). [L. *ad*, at; *genitalis*, of generation or birth]. In the Mesostigmata: a pair of small sclerites that bears the inguinal glands gv2. They are located in the posterior corners of the genital shield and parapodals IV.

ADHERENT. [L. *adhærere*, stick to]. Attached or clinging to.

ADHESIVE GLAND. [L. *adhærere*, stick to]. Any invertebrate gland that secretes a sticky substance.

ADIAPHANOUS, ADIAPHANUS. [Gr. α, without; διαφανης, transparent]. Impervious to light; opaque.

ADIENCE (ADIENT). [L. *adire*, to approach]. The advance towards a stimulus. Opposite: Abience.

ADIPOSE BODY. [L. *adeps*, fat]. Fat cells.

ADIPOSE TISSUE. [L. *adeps*, fat]. Fatty tissue. Connective tissue in which there are large cells containing stored droplets of fat.

ADITUS. [L. *aditus*, entrance]. Any anatomical structure forming the approach or entrance to any part of the body or organ.

ADIVERTICULATE. [Gr. α, without; L. *divertere*, to turn away]. Lacking diverticula.

ADJACENT. [L. *adjacere*, lie near]. Of structures next to one another, contiguous as opposed to separated.

ADJACENTLY SYMPATRIC. [L. *adjacere*, lie near]. Populations that are geographically separated for most of their border but in contact at some point(s), so that gene flow between them is possible.

ADMEDIAL (ADMEDIAN). [L. *ad*, towards; *medius*, middle]. Near the middle.

ADNATE. [L. *ad*, near; *natus*, born]. Of some structure being united or fused to another organ or structure, normally of unlike parts.

ADNEXAE. [L. *ad*, near; *nectere*, to bind]. Of the spermathecae and ducts forming the internal reproductive organs of the female spider.

ADORAL. [L. *ad*, to; *os*, mouth]. In acariform mites: of the setae distal on the subcapitulum (designations ao1, ao2).

ADPRESSED (APPRESSED). [L. *ad*, to; *pressus*, pressed]. Pressed together without being united.

ADRECTAL. [L. *ad*, to; *rectum*, rectum]. Near to, or associated with the rectum.

ADSORPTION. [L. *ad*, near; *sorbere*, to suck in]. The adhesion of dissolved substances, liquids or gases, to the surfaces of solid bodies with which they come into contact.

ADSPERSE, ADSPERSUS. [L. *adspursus*, a sprinkling]. Having closely spaced small spots.

ADSPERSED. [L. *ad*, to; *spergere*, to strew]. Widely distributed.

ADSTERNAL. [L. *ad*, near; Gr. στερνον, chest]. Situated next to the sternum.

ADULT. [L. *adultus*, full grown]. The stage when an animal is sexually mature and ready to reproduce normally.

ADUNCATE (ADUNCOUS). [L. *aduncus*, bent inwards]. Hooked - formed in the shape of a hook.

ADUST(O)US. [L. *adustus*, sunburnt]. Of scorched appearance - browned.

ADVEHENT. [L. *advehere*, to carry to]. Afferent, going in the direction of an organ.

ADVENTITIOUS. [L. *adventitius*, extraordinary]. Acquired, accidental, additional, occurring in abnormal places, ectopic.

ADVENTIVE. [L. *advenire*, to arrive]. Not native.

ADYNAMANDROUS. [Gr. α-, not/un-; δυναμις, power; ανηρ, male]. 1. Incapable of self-fertilization. 2. Having non-functioning male reproductive organs.

ADYNAMOGYNOUS. [Gr. α-, not/un-; δυναμις, power; γυνη, female]. Having non-functioning female reproductive organs.

AEDEAGUS (ADEAGUS). [Gr. αιδοια, genitals, αγος, leader]. The male intromittent organ, especially when it is sclerotized. e.g. in Tetranychoidea, Raphignathoidea. Often used interchangeably with 'penis'.

AENEOUS, AENEUS. [L. *aeneus*, of bronze]. Bright brassy or golden green.

AENESCENT. [L. *aeneus*, of bronze]. Becoming or appearing bronzed or brassy.

AENICTEQUOIDEA (erron **AENICTEGUOIDEA**). [Gr. αινικτηρ, one who speaks darkly]. A superfamily of mites (suborder Trigynaspida, infraorder Antennophorina). Families: **Aenictequidae, Euphysalozerconidae, Messoracaridae, Ptochacaridae.**

AEOLIAN. [L. *Aeolus*, god of the winds]. Wind-borne, as, for example, in some spiders.

AEOLIAN DEPOSITS. [L. *Aeolus*, god of the winds]. Wind-blown sediments, consisting of sand and dust.

AEQUILATUS. [L. *aequale*: equal]. Of equal breadth throughout.

A.E.R. The Anterior Eye Row: usually consisting of the anterior median and anterior lateral eyes.

AEROPLANKTON. [Gr. αηρ, air; πλαγκτος, wandering]. Aerial plankton. Anemoplankton. Minute organisms drifting freely suspended in the air and dispersed by wind (together with pollen, spores, bacteria, etc.).

AEROPYLE. [Gr. αηρ, air; πυλη, gate]. A structure on, or just below, the surface of many eggs that mediates the transfer of gasses between the egg and the atmosphere. A small pore, see Peritreme.

AEROSCEPSY. [Gr. αηρ, air; σκεψις, inquiry]. The perception of air-borne sound, chemical stimuli or atmospheric changes.

AEROSTATS. [Gr. αερ, air; στατος, placed]. Air sacs in the body.

AEROTAXIS. [Gr. αηρ, air; ταξις, disposition]. Directed movement either towards (positive) or away from (negative) an air-liquid interface or a concentration gradient of dissolved oxygen.

AERUGINOUS, AERUGINOSE, AERUGINUS. [L. *aerugo*, copper rust]. Of the nature or color of copper-rust or verdigris (green).

AESTHESIA, ESTHESIA. [Gr. αιστθητες, perceiver]. Sense perception.

AESTHESIS. [Gr. αισθησις, sensation]. Sense perception.

AESTHETE, ESTHETE. [Gr. αισθητης, perceiver]. Any invertebrate sense organ. Usually applied to sensory nerve endings, but also used for sensory hairs and bristles.

AESTIVAL. [L. *aestus*, summer]. One of the terms for the six part division of the year commonly used in ecology, especially with reference to terrestrial and fresh-water communities. The six parts are: prevernal (early spring), vernal (late spring), aestival (early summer), serotinal (late summer), autumnal (autumn) and hibernal (winter).

AESTIVATE. [L. *aestivus*, of summer]. To spend the summer, or any hot dry season, in a state of torpor superficially resembling hibernation.

AFFERENCE. [L. *ad*, near; *ferre*, to bear]. Impulses from the external sense organs of an animal due to events in the environment. See also Reafference.

AFFERENT. [L. *afferre*, to bring]. Conducting inwards, centripetal. Of vessels which convey blood towards a particular organ. **Afferent Fiber.** A nerve fiber carrying impulses from a receptor to the central nervous system. **Afferent Nerve.** A nerve that conducts impulses from the periphery towards a nerve center; the axon of a sensory neuron between a receptor and the central nervous system. **Afferent Neuron(e).** A sensory neuron that conveys inward impulses received or perceived by a sense organ from external sources.

AFFERENT NEURONAL INHIBITION. [L. *afferre*, to bring; Gr. νευρον, nerve; L. *inhibere*, to restrain/prevent]. When an animal is attending to a stimulus: the inhibiting or filtering out of other sensory inputs by peripheral 'gating' mechanisms in the sensory pathways.

AFFINIS (AFF., AFFIN). [L. *affinis*, related/adjacent]. Related to, or similar in structure or development.

ag. aggenital or pregenital setae in the Acariformes. See Grandjean System, Pritchard & Baker System.

AGAMEON. [Gr. α, without; γαμος, marriage; ον, being]. A species reproducing exclusively by apomixis. See also Parthenogenesis.

AGASTRIC. [Gr. α-, without; γαστηρ, stomach]. Having no distinct alimentary canal.

AGELENIDAE. [Gr. αγελαιος, of a herd]. The cosmopolitan family (infraorder Araneomorphae, superfamily Entelegynae) of sheet-web spiders, funnel-web spiders, funnel weavers. They construct tubular-web refuges from which extends either a small collar of silk, or a small to large sheet, which may be slightly funnel-shaped. These spiders are elongate, with a flattened thorax and a wide sternum which is heart-shaped and may project between the fourth coxa. The chelicerae are usually convex, toothed and nearly vertical, the outer margin having three teeth whilst the inner margin has two to eight teeth. The uniformly sized eyes are usually arranged in two short rows. The majority of species bear two-segmented posterior spinnerets which are distinctly longer than the anterior ones. All species catch their prey on the upper surface of the sheet web. The water spider (*Argyroneta aquatica*), the only arachnid to live permanently below water is sometimes included in this family; otherwise in its own family: **Argyronetidae.**

AGELENOIDEA. [Gr. αγελαιος, of a herd]. In a previous classification, a superfamily of sheet-web, funnel-web and funnel weaver spiders (suborder Opisthothelae, infraorder Araneomorphae) that united the families **Agelenidae, Amphinectidae** (the **Neolanidae,** genus *Neolana,* was recently included here). The **Amphinectidae** has been recently merged with the **Desidae.**

AGENASIA (AGENESIS). [Gr. α-, not/un-; γενεσις, origin]. A failure to develop. An inability to produce offspring.

AGGENITAL. [L. *ad*, to; *genitalis*, genitalia]. In ticks and mites: pertaining to the area on both sides of the genital region.

AGGLUTINATION. [L. *agglutinare*, to glue on]. A sticking or clumping together.

AGGREGATE. [L. *ad*, to; *gregare*, to collect into a flock]. To form a group or cluster. A group of animals that forms when individuals are attracted to a resource or in response to an environmental stimulus. The term does not imply social organization.

AGGREGATION PHEROMONE. [L. *ad*, to; *gregare*, to collect into a flock]. See Pheromone.

AGGRESSIN. [L. *aggressus*, attacked]. Any toxic substance produced by micro-organisms that is pathogenic in animals. Aggressin may inhibit a defensive reaction in the host organism.

AGGRESSION. [L. *aggressus*, attacked]. Behavior involving threat or attack, usually to protect a family, offspring, a resource, territory or to establish dominance. Aggressive behavior is not associated with predation.

AGGRESSIVE MIMICRY (PECKHAMMIAN MIMICRY). [L. *aggressus*, attacked; Gr. μιμικος, imitating]. See Mimicry.

AGONIST. [Gr. αγωνιστης, champion]. A primary muscle responsible for the movement of a part or appendage.

AGONISTIC BEHAVIOR. [Gr. αγωνιστης, champion]. All behavior (ritualized or not) relating to conflict or contest. Thus it includes not only aggressive behavior but also defense against, or flight from, an aggressive opponent, or the showing of any sort of submissive behavior.

AGORISTENIDAE. [Gr. αγορα, assemblage; στενος, scanty]. A family of neotropical harvestmen or daddy longlegs (suborder Laniatores, superfamily Gonyleptoidea) endemic to the Greater Antilles and northern South America.

10

AGRIOTYPE. [Gr. αγριος, wild; τυπος, pattern]. The wild or ancestral type.

AGROPHILOUS. [Gr. αγρος, field; φιλος, loving]. Living in cultivated soils.

AHELIOTROPISM. [Gr. α-, without; ηλιος, the sun; τροφη, nourishment]. See Apheliotropism.

AIGIALOPHILOUS. [Gr. αιγιαλος, seashore; φιλος, loving]. Living in beach habitats.

AIPHYLLOPHILUS. [Gr. αειφαλλης, ever-green; φιλος, loving]. Living in evergreen woodland.

AITIOGENIC. [Gr. αιτιος, causing; γενναω, generate]. Reactions induced by an external stimulus.

AKANTHA. See Acantha.

AKTOLOGY. [Gr. ακτη, the coast; λογος, discourse]. The study of shallow, inshore ecosystems.

al 1-2. In the Mesostigmata: designations for the setae on the anterior lateral surface of a leg or palp segment. See Evans Leg Chaetotactic System.

ALA. [L. *ala*, wing]. Any wing-like bony projection.

ALAR. [L. *alaris*, of the wing]. Of a wing, or wing-shaped.

ALARM PHEROMONE. [Gr. φερειν, to bear; hor*mone* (Gr. ορμαινω, excite)]. A pheromone which, when released, causes a fright response in other members of the same species. See also Pheromone.

ALARM RESPONSE. Any signal emitted by an animal that warns others (of the same species or not) of a perceived danger. These signals may be visual, aural or olfactory.

ALARY. [L. *ala*, wing]. Of or pertaining to the wing.

ALARY (ALIFORM) MUSCLES. [L. *ala*, wing; *musculus*, little muscle]. A series of small triangular or fan-shaped muscles attached to the pericardial wall. The contraction of these muscles causes blood to circulate from the perivisceral cavity into the pericardium and so, via ostia (small openings) to the long, dorsal tubular heart.

ALASSOSTASY. [Gr. αλλασσειν, to change; στασις, standing]. In the Chelicerata: an orthostasic stage in the life cycle which involves secondary changes in number and / or shape of stases and number of molts. See also Orthostasy.

ALATATE. [L. *ala*, wing]. Possessing lateral wing-like expansions.

ALATE, ALATUS. [L. *alatus*, winged]. Winged, or with auricles. Alae or wing-like expansions, similar to wings in appearance though not necessarily similar in function.

ALBI, ALBUS. [L. *albus*, white]. White.

ALBICANS. [L. *albicans*, to be white]. Formed or made of white.

ALBIDUS. [L. *albidus*, whitish]. White with a dusky tinge.

ALBINIC. [Sp. *albino*: white]. Of the character of an albino.

ALBINO, ALBINISM. [Sp. *albino*; white]. An animal having an inborn error of metabolism in the form of an autosomal recessive trait concerning either a deficiency in, or a defect of, the enzyme tyrosinase. This trait precludes the production of pigment.

ALBUMEN, ALBUMIN. [L. *albumen*, egg white]. The characteristic protein forming the white of an egg. The name is also used of any similar protein; as for instance one of those found in blood serum, muscles and other tissues.

ALBUMINOID. [L. *albumen*, egg white]. Like albumen.

A.L.E. The Anterior Lateral Eyes.

ALEATORY. [L. *alea*, a game of chance]. Of organs that are existing or lacking, depending on chance.

11

ALECITHAL. [Gr. α-, without; λεκιθος, yolk]. An egg with very little or no yolk. See also Centrolecithal, Heterolecithal, Macrolecithal, Mediolecithal, Meiolecithal, Mesolecithal, Microlecithal, Oligolecithal, Polylecithal, Telolecithal.

ALEPIDOTE. [Gr. α-, without; λεπιδοτος, scaly]. Without scales.

ALGESIS. [Gr. αλγησις, sense of pain]. The sense of pain.

ALGICOLOUS. [L. *alga*, seaweed; *colere*, to inhabit]. Living on or amongst algae.

ALGIVOROUS/ALGOPHAGOUS. [L. *alga*, seaweed; *vorare*, to devour/Gr. -φαγος, -eating]. Feeding on algae.

ALIFORM. [L. *ala*, wing; *forma*, shape]. Wing shaped.

ALIMENTARY (ENTERIC) CANAL. [L. *alimentarius*, pert. to sustenance]. The gut: essentially a tube or passage concerned with the transfer, digestion and absorption of food. In some animals e.g. flatworms (Platyhelminthes) and hydras (Coelenterata) it has only one opening but in most animals it has an opening (mouth) into which food is taken, and another opening (anus) from which waste is expelled. It may consist of a number of regions such as esophagus, stomach, intestines, etc. but usually the actual digestion takes place only in the central part, known as the mid-gut or mesenteron, which is lined with cells of endodermal origin. The foregut (or stomodeum) and hindgut (or proctodeum) are ectodermal. See Feeding.

ALIMENTARY CASTRATION. [L. *alimentarius*, pert. to sustenance; *castrare*, to castrate/prune]. Of an individual which suffers suppression of gonadal development as a consequence of being deprived of sufficient nourishment in the larval form. See also Phasic Castration.

ALIMENTARY SYSTEM. [L. *alimentarius*, pert. to sustenance]. The alimentary canal with all its associated glands, organs etc.

ALIZARINE (ALIZARIN). [prob. Fr. *alizarine*]. A transparent, orange red.

ALKALIPHILIC. [Ar. *al*, the; *qali*, ash; Gr. φιλος, loving]. Living in an alkaline environment.

ALKALODURIC. [Ar. *al*, the; *qali*, ash; L. *durare*, to endure]. Tolerant of highly alkaline conditions.

ALLAESTHETIC. [Gr. αλλος, other; αισθητης, perceiver]. Characters which are only effective when perceived by other organisms.

ALLANTOID. [Gr. αλλαντοειδης, sausage-like]. Sausage-shaped.

ALLEE'S EFFECT (LAW). [*Warder Allee*, American ecologist]. The law that states that the density of a population varies according to the spatial distribution of the individuals.

ALLELOCHEMIC (XENOMONE). [Gr. αλληλων, one another; χημεια, a transmutation]. A substance produce by an organism that has an effect, often inhibitory, on the growth, behavior or population dynamics of another species. These substances are sometimes divided into four subgroups based on whether the emitter, the receiver, or both benefit from the interaction: Allomones, Apneumones, Kairomones, Synomones.

ALLELOMIMETIC. [Gr. αλληλων, one another; μιμητικος, imitative]. Behavior that involves imitating another animal, usually of the same species.

ALLELOPATHIC SUBSTANCE. [Gr. αλληλων, one another; παθος, suffering]. A chemical substance (an Allelochemic), often a waste product, that has an inhibitory or regulatory effect on other organisms.

ALLELOPATHY. [Gr. αλληλων, one another; παθος, suffering]. The chemical inhibition of one organism by another.

ALLESTHETIC TRAIT. [Gr. αλλος, other; αισθετικος, perceptive]. Any individual character that has an adaptive function only as a result of interaction with the nervous system of another individual. E.g., displays of color patterns, mating calls, odor, etc.

ALLIGATUS, ALLIGATE. [L. *alligare*, to tie]. United, fastened or suspended by a thread.

ALLOBIOSIS. [Gr. αλλος, another; βιωσις, manner of life]. The change in the response of an organism to a changed environment - internal or external.

12

ALLOCHEIRAL. [Gr. αλλος, another; χειρ, hand]. Reversed symmetry. Having the left and right sides reversed.

ALLOCHORE. [Gr. αλλος, other; χορειν, to spread]. Any organism occurring in two different habitats in the same geographic region.

ALLOCHRONIC. [Gr. αλλος, another; χρονος, time]. Existing at different times, not contemporary. Of species living, growing or reproducing at different times of the year.

ALLOCHRONIC SPECIATION. [Gr. αλλος, another; χρονος, time]. See Speciation.

ALLOCHRORIC. [Gr. αλλος, another; χρως, color]. Able to change color.

ALLOCHTHONOUS. [Gr. αλλος, different; χθων, the ground]. Not aboriginal, exotic.

ALLOCRYPTIC COLORATION. [Gr. αλλος, different; κρυπτος, hidden]. The accidental or casual use of any available material by an animal in order to conceal itself.

ALLOIOMETRON. [Gr. αλλοιος, different; μετρον, measure]. Within a species or race; measurable changes in physiological proportions or intensity of development, e.g. in limb, head, etc. proportions.

ALLOKINESIS. [Gr. αλλος, another; κινησις, movement]. Passive or involuntary movement. Passive movement - as in drifting.

ALLOKINETIC. See Autokinetic.

ALLOMERISTIC. [Gr. αλλος, other; μερος, part]. Of any animal differing in the number of parts of any organ from that which is customary in the group.

ALLOMETRIC COEFFICIENT. [Gr. αλλος, another; μετρον, a measure]. The ratio of relative growth rates. See Allometry.

ALLOMETRIC (HETEROGONIC) GROWTH. [Gr. αλλος, different; μετρον, a measure]. See Allometry.

ALLOMETROSIS. [Gr. αλλος, other; μητρο–, mother]. Having different species or races living in an organized group.

ALLOMETRY. [Gr. αλλος, different; μετρον, a measure]. The study of relative growth rates within an individual. If an organ grows relatively faster or slower than the body as a whole then its proportions will obviously differ in animals of differing adult size. Allometric change is used as a means of investigating the proportions of an organ throughout a growth period as well as between adults throughout an evolutionary sequence. **Allometric (Heterogonic) Growth** or **Ontogenetic Allometry**: differential rates of growth wherein the sizes of certain parts of the body are a constant exponential function of the size of the whole animal. **Static Allometry**: the shifts in proportion between a series of related taxa of different size. **Evolutionary Allometry**: the gradual shift in proportions as size changes within an evolutionary lineage.

ALLOMONE. [Gr. αλλος, different; hormone (Gr. ορμαινω, excite)]. A chemical substance released by one species in order to communicate with another species. See also Allelochemic.

ALLOMORPHIC EVOLUTION. [Gr. αλλος, another; μορφη, shape]. A rapid increase in specialization.

ALLOMORPHOSIS. [Gr. αλλος, another; μορφη, shape]. Evolution with a rapid increase in speciation.

ALLOPARAPATRIC SPECIATION. [Gr. αλλος, another; παρα, besides; πατρη, native land]. See Speciation.

ALLOPARASITE. [Gr. αλλος, different; παρα, beside; σιτος, food]. An organism parasitic on an unrelated host.

ALLOPARENT. [Gr. αλλος, another; L. parens, parent]. An individual that assists the parents in the care of the offspring.

ALLOPATRIC. [Gr. αλλος, different; πατρη, native land]. Of species that occupy different and mutually exclusive geographical regions. See also Parapatric, Sympatric, Speciation.

13

ALLOPATRIC INTROGRESSION. See Introgression.

ALLOPATRIC SPECIATION. [Gr. αλλος, different; πατρη, native land]. See Speciation.

ALLOPATRY. [Gr. αλλος, different; πατρη, native land]. The occurrence of species in different geographical regions, and separated by distance alone or some geographical barrier.

ALLOSCUTUM. [Gr. αλλος, another; L. *scutum*, shield]. In larval ticks, the dorsal region, behind the scutum, which bears numerous fine striations denoting superficial folds in the cuticular surface. In the mid-dorsal region are paired structures containing numerous tiny pores (the foveae dorsalis or foveal pores). These structures are most evident in females and may have a role in pheromone secretion and mating. They sometimes also occur in males (although absent in *Ixodes*).

ALLOSEMATIC COLOR. [Gr. αλλος, another; σημα, signal]. See Sematic.

ALLOSEMATIC PROTECTION. [Gr. αλλος, another; σημα, signal]. A method of protection in which an animal regularly associates itself with another which is dangerous, distasteful or poisonous.

ALLOTANAUPODOIDEA. [Gr. αλλος, another; ταναος, stretched; πους, foot]. A monotypic superfamily of mites (suborder Prostigmata, infraorder Anystina). Family: **Allotanaupodidae**.

ALLOTHERM. [Gr. αλλος, another; θερμη, heat]. An organism in which the body temperature is determined mainly by the ambient temperature.

ALLOTHETIC. [Gr. αλλος, another; θετος, set]. Of information from the external spatial environment that is used by an animal to determine its orientation. See also Idiothetic.

ALLOTOPIC. [Gr. αλλος, another; τοπος, a place]. Of species or populations that inhabit different microhabitats.

ALLOTRIOMORPHIC. [Gr. αλλοτριος, strange; μορφη, shape]. Displaying an abnormal or unexpected shape.

ALLOTROPHIC. [Gr. αλλος, another; τροφη, nourishment]. Obtaining nourishment from another organism.

ALLURING COLORATION. [L. *ad*, near; *leurre*, to lure]. Aggressive mimicry. Patterns or colorings adapted by predators that attract other species.

ALLURING GLANDS. [L. *ad*, near; *leurre*, to lure]. Glandular structures that disperse an odor attractive to the opposite sex; usually sex pheromones.

ALPINE, ALPESTRINE. [L. *alpinus*, of or like high mountains]. Of organisms occurring in high mountain meadows.

A.L.S. The Anterior Lateral Spinnerets: large in the Araneomorphae but absent in most Mygalomorphae.

ALSOCOLOUS/ALSOPHILOUS. [Gr. αλσος, grove; L. *colere*, to inhabit/Gr. φιλος, loving]. Living/thriving in woody groves.

ALTERNATING CALYPTOSTASY. [L. *alternatus*, one after the other; Gr. καλυπτος, covered; στασις, standing]. In the Parasitengona, **Pterygosomatidae**, and some other prostigmatans, the alternation of calyptostatic and elattostatic developmental stages. But see Parasitengona. See also Calyptostasic, Elattostase, Protelattosis.

ALTERNES. [L. *alternus*, one after another]. Two or more communities alternating with each other in a particular area.

ALTRICIAL. [L. *altrix*, nourisher]. Having young at hatching or birth that require postnatal care.

ALTRUISM. [L. *alter*, the other]. Of behavior that is disadvantageous to the individual, but benefits other individuals of the species.

ALTUS. [L. *altus*, high]. Above. Of a part raised above the usual level.

ALUTACEOUS. [L. *aluta*, soft leather; *-aceous*, of the nature of]. Tan-colored, leathery and appearing to have minute cracks.

ALVEOLA. [L. *alveolus*, small pit or cavity]. A small cavity or pit on the surface of an organ.

ALVEOLAR. [L. *alveolus*, small pit or cavity]. Any small sac terminating a glandular duct.

ALVEOLATE. [L. *alveolatus*, pitted]. Honeycombed.

ALVEOLUS (pl. **ALVEOLI**). [L. *alveolus*, small pit or cavity]. A small cavity, pit, or depression. In spiders: a cavity in the cymbium, from which the palpal bulb arises. The receptacle for the haematodocha. A setal socket.

ALYCOIDEA. [Gr. α-, not; λυκος, wolf]. In some classifications, a superfamily of mites (suborder Endeostigmata, infraorder Bimichaeliida). Families: **Alycidae, Nanorchestidae, Proterorhagiidae.**

AMAUROBIIDAE. [Gr. αμαυρος, obscure; βιος, life]. A cosmopolitan family of night-active cribellate spiders (infraorder Araneomorphae, superfamily Entelegynae) known as tangled-nest spiders, night spiders, hacklemesh weavers. All species (*Amaurobius*) are quite large with firm legs and may live for several years. The female produces about 40 eggs and spins a closed breeding chamber in which she stays. The spiderlings hatch, consume the remaining egg yolk, and then eat their mother before emerging. Previously in the superfamily Amaurobioidea.

AMBIENT. [L. *ambire*, to go round]. Surrounding.

AMBILATERAL. [L. *ambo*, both; *latus*, side]. Of both sides.

AMBITUS. [L. *ambitus*, going round]. The outer margin.

AMBIVALENT. [L. *ambi-*, on both sides; *valere*, be strong]. Confused behavior arising from concurrent conflicting impulses e.g. to fight or flee.

AMBLYPYGI (PHRYNICIDA). [Gr. αμβλυς, dull; πυγη, rump]. An order of tropical and semi-tropical dark-colored arachnids (class Euchelicerata, subclass Arachnida) of nocturnal and secretive habit known as 'tail-less whip-scorpions' or 'whip-spiders'. They have a flattened body and a pair of powerful raptorial pedipalps, the final two segments of which may be almost chelate (pincer-like) and with which they capture and tear apart their insect prey. The first pair of legs are modified as long antenna-like (whip-like) appendages provided with a variety of different types of receptors. They walk sideways with a crab-like gait and one of the long tactile legs is always pointed towards the direction of movement. Suborders: Euamblypygi, Paleoamblypygi.

AMBOSEXUAL. [L. *ambo*, both; *sexus*, sex]. Common to both sexes.

AMBULACRUM. [L. *ambulacrum*, a place for walking]. The claws and empodium of the apotele or pretarsus.

AMBULATORIAL. [L. *ambulare*, to walk]. Adapted for walking.

AMBULATORY. [L. *ambulare*, to walk]. To move by walking. Formed for walking.

A.M.E. The Anterior Median Eyes (primary eyes). These are morphologically distinct from the other eyes and are commonly reduced or absent. See Eye.

AMENSALISM. [Gr. α-, not; L. *mensa*, table]. An interspecific interaction in which toxins produced by, but not affecting, one population, effectively inhibit another population.

AMERISTIC. [Gr. αμεριστος, undivided]. Undivided, unsegmented, undifferentiated, undeveloped.

AMEROBELBOIDEA. [Gr. αμερος, gentle; +*Belba*, a genus of mite in the Damaeidae]. A superfamily of mites (suborder Oribatida, infraorder Brachypylina - section Pycnonoticae). Families: **Ameridae, Amerobelbidae, Basilobelbidae, Ctenobelbidae, Damaeolidae, Eremobelbidae, Eremulidae, Heterobelbidae, Oxyameridae, Platyameridae, Spinozetidae, Staurobatidae.**

AMERONOTHROIDEA. [Gr. αμερος, gentle; νωθρος, slothful]. A superfamily of mites (suborder Oribatida, infraorder Brachypylina - section Pycnonoticae). Families: **Ameronothridae, Fortuyniidae, Selenoribatidae.**

AMETABOLIC. [Gr. α-, without; μεταβολη, change]. Without metamorphosis.

15

AMETABOLOUS. [Gr. α-, without; μεταβολη, change]. Not changing in form.

AMETHYSTINE. [Gr. αμεθυστος, not drunk]. Of, or resembling amethyst, a bluish-violet color.

AMETOECIOUS. [Gr. α-, without; μετοικιη, change of abode]. Being parasitic on one host during one life cycle.

AMMOPHILOUS. [Gr. αμμος, sand; φιλος, loving]. Living in, or frequenting, sand.

AMMOTHEIDAE. [Gr. αμμος, sand; NL, *thea*, lesser]. See **Acheliidae**.

AMMOTRECHIDAE. [Gr. αμμος, sand; τρεχω, run]. A large family of sun spiders (subclass Arachnida, order Solifugae) known as sand-runners; from South America, the southern United States and the Caribbean Islands. The pedipalps have pairs of lateroventral spines, and the males bear an immovable flagellum on the mesal face of each chelicerum.

AMMOXENIDAE. [Gr. αμμος, sand, ξενις, guest]. A small family of spiders (infraorder Araneomorphae, superfamily Entelegynae) from south Africa and Australia, known as termite hunters.

AMNIOS. [Gr. αμνιον, fetal membrane]. The cuticular covering of an embryo that is shed before or very shortly after hatching.

AMNIOTIC CAVITY. [Gr. αμνιον, fetal membrane]. In many animals: the cavity between the amnion and the embryo in the developing egg.

AMNIOTIC FLUID. [Gr. αμνιον, fetal membrane]. The liquid surrounding the embryo while it is in the egg.

AMNIOTIC PORE. [Gr. αμνιον, fetal membrane]. An opening to the amniotic cavity during embryonic development.

AMORPHOUS. [Gr. α-, without; μορφη, shape]. Having no determinate shape.

AMPHECLEXIS. [Gr. αμφι-, both; εκλεξις, choice]. Sexual selection.

AMPHEROTOKY. See Amphitoky.

AMPHIAPOMICT. [Gr. αμφι-, both; απο, away; μικτος, mixed]. Biotypes that propagate facultatively, i.e. amphimictally and parthenogenetically.

AMPHIARTHROSIS. [Gr. αμφι-, both; αρθρον, joint]. A slightly movable joint.

AMPHIBIOTIC. [Gr. αμφι-, both; βιοτικος, of life]. Of an organism that can be either parasitic or symbiotic on a particular host.

AMPHIBIOUS. [Gr. αμφι-, both; βιος, life]. Capable of living in both water and on land.

AMPHIBOLIC. [Gr. αμφι-, both; βολη, a throw]. Capable of turning both forwards and backwards.

AMPHICOELOUS. [Gr. αμφι-, both; κοιλος, hollow]. See Biconcave.

AMPHICYRTIC. [Gr. αμφι-, both; κυρτος, curved]. Having both sides curved, biconvex.

AMPHIGEIC (AMPHIGEAN, AMPHIGAEAN). [Gr. αμφι-, both; γεα, earth]. Of both the Old World and the New World.

AMPHIGONIC. [Gr. αμφι-, both; γονη, seed]. Of organisms that produce male and female gametes in different individuals.

AMPHIGONY (AMPHIGENESIS). [Gr. αμφι-, both; γονος, offspring]. Sexual reproduction.

AMPHILEPSIS. [Gr. αμφι-, both; λεπσις, a receiving]. Inheritance of characters from both parents.

AMPHIMICT. [Gr. αμφι-, both; μικτος, mixed]. An obligate sexual organism.

AMPHIMIXIS. [Gr. αμφι-, both; μιξις, a mingling]. True sexual reproduction in which male and female gametes fuse.

AMPHIPLEXUS. [Gr. αμφι-, around; L. *plexus*, interwoven]. A sexual embrace.

AMPHITOKY (AMPHEROTOKY). [Gr. αμφι-, both; τοκος, birth]. Production of both males and females parthenogenetically.

AMPHOGENIC. [Gr. αμφω, both of two; –γενης, producing]. Producing both male and female offspring.

AMPHOTROMBIOIDEA. [Gr. αμφω, both of two; + Trombidiidae]. A monospecific superfamily of mites (suborder Prostigmata, infraorder Anystina). Family: **Amphotrombiidae.**

AMPLIFICATUS. [L. *amplificatus*, enlarged]. Dilated. Enlarged.

AMPULLA. [L. *ampulla*, a flask]. Any membranous vesicle.

AMPULLACEAL (AMPULLACEOUS). [L. *ampulla*, a flask]. Flask-shaped. In arachnids: of the spinning glands which provide the silk.

AMPULLARY. [L. *ampulla*, a flask]. Resembling an ampulla.

AMPULLIFORM. [L. *ampulla*, a flask; *forma*, shape]. Flask-shaped.

AMPULLULA. [L. *ampullula*, a small flask]. A small ampulla.

A.M.S. The Anterior Median Spinnerets. They are present only in some Mesothelae; are absent in the Mygalomorphae and represented by the cribellum or colulus in the Araneomorphae.

AMYGDALIFORM. [Gr. αμυγδαλη, almond; L. *forma*, shape]. Almond-shaped.

AN. In acariform mites: the anal segment that is added on the protonymph. See Anamorphosis, Grandjean System.

ANABIOTIC, ANABIOSIS, (CRYPTOBIOTIC, CRYPTOBIOSIS). [Gr. αναβιωσις, recovery of life]. The contracted, desiccated state in which some animals exist during periods of dry weather. When water is again available, the animal swells and becomes active within a few hours.

ANACANTHOUS. [Gr. ανα, not; ακανθα, prickle]. Without spines.

ANACHORESIS. [Gr. αναχωρησις, retiring]. Of an animal living in holes or crevasses.

ANACTINOTRICHIDA. [Gr. ανα, not; ακτις, ray, θριξ, hair]. Of those mites that do not have setae containing actinopilin. See also Actinotrichida, Parasitiformes.

ANAGOTOXIC. [Gr. αν, without; αγον, contest; τοξικον, poison]. Having the ability to counter the effects of a poison.

ANAL. [L. *anus*, anus]. Of, or in the neighborhood of the anus. Of, or attached to, the last segment of the abdomen.

ANAL APERTURE (ANUS). [L. *anus*, anus; L. *aperire*, to open]. The posterior exit of the alimentary canal. The anus is situated in the median line posterior to the coxae and includes the external anal apparatus consisting of two laterally moving valves (plates). In some **Ixodidae** species the aperture is bordered by two anal valves and surrounded by a cuticular ring.

ANAL GROOVE. [L. *anus*, anus; OE *græf*, ditch/grave]. In the Prostriata group of the genus *Ixodes* (**Ixodidae**), a groove adjacent to the anus which originates on or near the posterior body margin and surrounds the anus anteriorly. In some species the groove are not continuous anteriorly, while in others the grooves fuse in a semicircle in front of the anus, in others they form an ogive (ogival, like a gothic arch). In the other **Ixodidae** group (Metastriata) the anal groove is smaller and lies posterior to the anus. In most cases they run forwards and outwards towards the genital grooves. In some cases they are continuous with a postero-median groove from which they fork anteriorly.

ANAL LOBE. [L. *anus*, anus; LL. *lobus*, lobe]. In the Eriophyoidea (herbivorous mites): the most posterior region of the body (segment PS); it contains the anal opening and often functions as an adhesive disk to anchor the body during feeding.

ANAL ORIFICE. [L. *anus*, anus]. See Anal Aperture.

17

ANAL PEDICEL. [L. *anus*, anus; *pediculus*, little foot]. In the deutonymphs of the **Sejidae** and Uropodina: a stalk produced from a cement-like secretion from the anal opening. It is used to attach to a phoretic host.

ANAL SETA. [L. *anus*, anus; *seta*, bristle]. Any seta on an anal valve or ascribed to the anal region. True anal setae may be present in acariform mites that add segment AN. In spider mites: pseudanal setae ps1-3.

ANAL SHIELD. [L. *anus*, anus]. In the Mesostigmata: a ventral shield bearing the anal opening and circumanal setae (po, pa), but without any ventral setae or lyrifissures (pores). See also Ventrianal Shield.

ANAL SUCKER PLATE. [L. *anus*, anus; OE. *sucan*, to suck]. In the Astigmata: the complex attachment organ on the posterior venter of a hypopus.

ANAL SUCKERS. [L. *anus*, anus; OE. *sucan*, to suck]. In the male Astigmatina: a pair of modified setae near the anal opening act as suckers for holding onto females during precopula and mating.

ANAL TUBERCLE. [L. *anus*, anus, *tuberculum*, small hump]. A small projection, located dorsal to the spinnerets, which bears the anal opening.

ANAL VALVE. [L. *anus*, anus; *valva*, folding door]. A shield protecting the anal opening.

ANALGOIDEA. [Gr. αναλγης, painless]. A superfamily of scab- and mange-producing fur mites (order Sarcoptiformes, suborder Astigmata). Eighteen families.

ANALOGOUS ORGANS. [Gr. αναλογια, analogy]. 1. Organs which, although they may occur in different species (and thus may have quite different evolutionary origins), perform the same functions. Possession of analogous organs does not imply a close evolutionary relationship, just a similar adaptation to similar conditions. 2. May also be used of organs with similar function(s), whether or not the organs are homologous.

ANALOGOUS VARIATION. [Gr. αναλογια, analogy]. A phenomenon first noted by Darwin in which two groups of closely related animals tend to resemble one another not only in their typical appearance and structure, but also in the kind of variation amongst them.

ANALOGUES. [Gr. αναλογια, analogy]. Organs of different origin in different animals, but of similar function.

ANALS. [L. *anus*, anus]. In acariform mites; the pseudanal setae ps1-3 in the Pritchard & Baker System.

ANAMIDAE. [derive.uncert. but possibly "a name"]. A family of mygalomorph spiders (infraorder Mygalomorphae, superfamily Avicularioidea).

ANAMORPHIC DEVELOPMENT, ANAMORPHOSIS. [Gr. ανα, again; μορφωσις, shaping]. Development in which the young gradually become more like the adult in body form after each ecdysis, as opposed to metamorphosis. In the Acariformes additions occur behind the anal opening (pseudanal segment in the larva); anal (AN) in the protonymph; adanal (AD) in the deutonymph; peranal (PA) in the tritonymph. See also Epimorphic Development.

ANAPIDAE. [Gr. αν-, not/without; L. *apis*, a bee]. A cosmopolitan family of very small spiders (infraorder Araneomorphae, superfamily Entelegynae) encompassing fifty-eight genera. The previous families **Holarchaeidae**, **Micropholcommatidae** are recognized as synonyms and thus included here.

ANARTHRIC/ANARTHROUS. [Gr. αν, without; αρθρον, joint]. Having no distinct joints. See also Diarthric, Stenarthric.

ANASTOMOSIS. [Gr. αναστομωσις; formation of a network]. Intercommunication between two vessels, channels or branches by a connecting cross branch. Originally used to describe the cross connections between the arteries and veins etc., but now used of any branching system.

ANAUTOGENOUS. [Gr. αν, not; αυτος, self; -γενης, producing]. Of a female that must feed if her eggs are to develop.

ANAUXOTROPHE. [Gr. αν, not; αυξη, growth; τρεφω, nourish]. A nutritionally independent organism.

ANAXIAL. [Gr. αν, without; L. *axis*, axle]. Asymmetrical, without a distinct axis.

ANCHYLOSIS (ANCHYLOSED). [Gr. αγκυλος, crooked; –οσις, suf. of condition]. The formation of a stiff joint by consolidation of the articulating surfaces.

ANCIPITAL, ANCEPS. [L. *anceps*, with two edges]. Being flattened and having two edges. Ensiform.

ANCISTROID (ANKISTROID). [Gr. ανκιστρον, a hook; ειδος, shape]. Hook-shaped; barbed.

ANCOCOLOUS. [Gr. αγκος, valley; L. *colere*, to live]. Living in canyons.

ANCOPHILOUS. [Gr. αγκος, valley; φιλος, loving]. Thriving in canyons.

ANCYLOID. [Gr. ανκυλος, hooked; ειδος, shape]. Limpet-shaped.

ANDRIC. [Gr. ανηρ, male]. Male. (Gynic = female).

ANDROGENESIS (PATROGENESIS). [Gr. ανδρο–, of a man; γενεσις, descent]. Male parthenogenesis. Development in which, due to failure of the nucleus of the female gamete, the embryo contains only paternal chromosomes. See also Parthenogenesis.

ANDROGENIC. [Gr. ανδρο–, of a man; γενναω, produce]. Of hormones and tissues capable of masculinization - stimulating male characters.

ANDROGENOUS. [Gr. ανδρο–, of a man; γενος, descent]. Producing only male offspring.

ANDROID. [Gr. ανηρ, male; ειδος, form]. Resembling a male.

ANDROMORPHIC. [Gr. ανδρο–, of a man; μορφη, shape]. Having a morphological resemblance to the male.

ANDROPHILOUS. [Gr. ανδρο–, of a man; φιλος, loving]. Thriving in proximity to man.

ANDROSYNHESMIA. [Gr. ανδρο–, of a man; συν, with; εσμος, swarm]. A group of males gathered together during mating season. See also Swarm (Synhesmia), Gynosynhesmia.

ANEBOUS. [Gr. ανηβος, before manhood]. Immature. Prepubertal.

ANECDYSIS. [Gr. αν, not; εκδυσις, an escape]. A passive period between two molts. During this period there may not appear to be any preparation for the next molt.

ANELYTROUS. [Gr. αν, without; ελυτρον, a sheath]. Without an elytra or sheath.

ANEMOCHOROUS. [Gr. ανεμος, wind; χορειν, to spread]. Dispersed by the wind.

ANEMOPHILOUS. [Gr. ανεμος, wind; φιλος, loving]. Dispersed by wind.

ANEMOPLANKTON. [Gr. ανεμος, wind; πλαγκτος, wandering]. Wind-borne organisms. See Aeroplankton.

ANEMORECEPTOR. [Gr. ανεμος, wind; L. ρεχιπερε, to receive]. A sensory receptor of air currents. See also Trichobothrium.

ANEMORRHIA (ANEMORHIA). [Gr. ανεμος, wind; ρεω, flow]. Dispersal by air, as in spider mites and eriophyoid mites.

ANEMOTAXIS. [Gr. ανεμος, wind; ταξις, a disposition]. Movement towards or away from wind or an air current.

ANENTEROUS (ANENTERIC). [Gr. αν, without; εντερον, gut]. Without an alimentary tract.

ANFRACTOSE. [L. *anfractus*, bending]. Sinuous, wavy.

ANGULATE. [L. *angulus*, angular]. Forming an angle: i.e. when two margins meet in an angle.

ANGULOSE. [L. *angulus*, angular]. Having angles.

19

ANGUSTATUS. [L. *angustare*, to make narrow]. Narrowed. Narrowly drawn out.

ANHYDROBIOSIS. [Gr. αν, without; υδρο-, water; βιωσις, living]. A state of dormancy in various invertebrates due to low humidity or desiccation.

ANHYDROUS. [Gr. αν, without; υδρο-, water]. Being completely without water.

ANIDIAN. [Gr. αν, without; ειδος, form]. Without shape, formless.

ANISOCHELA. [Gr. ανισο-, unequal; χηλη, claw]. A claw with the two parts unequally developed.

ANISOMORPHIC. [Gr. ανισο-, unequal; μορφη, shape]. Differing in structure, shape or size.

ANKYROID. [Gr. αγκυλος, hooked; ειδος, form]. Hook-shaped.

ANNECTENT. [L. *annectere*, to bind together]. An intermediate species or genus.

ANNIDATION. [Gr. αν, without; L. *nidus*, nest]. The situation wherein a mutant organism survives in a population due to being able to utilize an ecological niche that the normal (or parental) organism cannot use.

ANNUAL. [L. *annus*, year]. Occurring once a year, or lasting for one year.

ANNUATION. [L. *annuus*, yearly]. Fluctuations in behavior or abundance resulting from annual changes in one or more environmental factors.

ANNULAR. [L. *annulus*, ring]. Of being ring-shaped or marked with rings or bands.

ANNULATE. [L. *annulatus*, furnished with a ring]. Composed of, or furnished with, ring-like bands (annuli). This may refer to structural bands or colored bands.

ANNULATIONS. [L. *annulatus*, ringed]. Deep, transverse cuticular striae occurring at intervals (usually regular) giving the body a segmented appearance. Rings of pigmentation around the leg segments.

ANNULET. [L. *annulus*, ring]. A small ring into which a segment is divided by complete transverse constrictions, crenulations, or plicae.

ANNULI. [L. *anulus*, little ring]. The transverse wrinkles, or rings, on an epigynal scape.

ANNULIFORM. [L. *anulus*, little ring; *forma*, shape]. In the form of rings or segments.

ANNULUS (ANNULI). [L. *anulus*, little ring]. Any ring-like structure.

ANOGENITAL. [L. *anus*, anus; *gignere*, to beget]. Of the region of the body containing the genitals and the anus. In oribatid mites: the ventral region encompassing the anal, adanal, genital, and aggenital sclerites.

ANOMALOUS. [Gr. ανωμαλος, irregular]. Unusual: departing greatly from the usual type.

ANOPHTHALMIC. [Gr. αν, without; οφθαλμος, the eye]. Eyeless.

ANSA. [L. *ansa*, handle]. A loop or loop-like structure.

ANSIFORM. [L. *ansa*, handle; *forma*, shape]. Looped, loop-shaped.

ANT- ANTE- Latin prefix carrying the idea of before/in front of.

ANT- ANTI- Greek prefix [αντι-] carrying the idea of against/in opposition to/opposite/before.

ANTAGONISM. [Gr. ανταγωνιστης, adversary]. 1. The interference with or inhibition of growth and/or development of one organism by another through the creation of unfavorable environment(s). 2. Of hormones, drugs, etc. producing opposing effects. 3. Of muscles: producing opposite movements at the same time so that the contraction of one is accompanied by the relaxation of the other (reflexes usually accomplish this).

ANTAGONISTIC SYMBIOSIS. [Gr. συμβιωναι, to live with]. A symbiotic association in which one symbiont seeks to establish domination over the other. See also Parasitism.

ANTEAL. [L. *ante*, before]. Being in front or forward.

ANTENNIFORM. [NL. *antenna*, feeler; L. *forma*, shape]. Having the shape or form of an antenna; typically used of long slender legs that often lack an apotele, as in the modified first pair of walking legs in the whip scorpions (Uropygi), or for palps that resemble antennae; as in the **Bdellidae**.

ANTENNOPHORINA. [NL. *antenna*, feeler; Gr. -φορα, -carrying]. An infraorder of mites (order Mesostigmata, suborder Trigynaspida). Superfamilies: Aenictequoidea, Antennophoroidea, Celaenopsoidea, Fedrizzioidea, Megisthanoidea, Paramegistoidea, Parantennuloidea.

ANTENNOPHOROIDEA. [NL. *antenna*, feeler; Gr. -φορα, -carrying]. A monotypic superfamily of mites (suborder Trigynaspida, infraorder Antennophorina). Family: **Antennophoridae**.

ANTEPISEMATIC. [L. *ante-*, before; Gr. επι, upon; σημα, signal]. See Sematic.

ANTERGISM. [L. *ante-*, before; Gr. εργον, work]. Simultaneous contraction of opposing muscles.

ANTERIAD. [L. *ante-*, before; *-ior*, comp. suf.; *-ad*, toward]. Pointing forward. Op. Posteriad.

ANTERIOR. [L. *ante-*, before; *-ior*, comp. suf.]. Situated at, relatively near to, or concerning or facing the front. Usually the end directed forwards when the animal is moving normally.

ANTERIOR DORSAL SETA. [L. *ante-*, before; *-ior*, comp. suf.]. In the Mesostigmata: setae on the anterior dorsal surface of a leg or palp segment. See AD 1-3.

ANTERIOR EYE. [L. *ante-*, before; *-ior*, comp. suf.]. The more anterior of a pair of lateral ocelli.

ANTERIOR HYPOSTOMAL (HYPOSTOMATIC) SETAE. [L. *ante-*, before; *-ior*, comp. suf.; Gr. υπο, under; στομα, mouth]. In the Mesostigmata: the most anterior (h1) of the three pairs of hypostomatic setae. They are present in the larva.

ANTERIOR PARA-ANALS. [L. *ante-*, before; *-ior*, comp. suf.; Gr. παρα, near; L. *anus*, anus]. Setae h3 in the Pritchard & Baker System.

ANTERIOR PROJECTION. [L. *ante-*, before; *-ior*, comp. suf.; ML. *proiectum*, something thrown forth] In the **Argasidae** (hard ticks): an extension of the body that renders the capitulum invisible from the dorsal aspect.

ANTERIOR SHIELD SETA. [L. *ante-*, before; *-ior*, comp. suf.; *seta*, bristle]. In the Eriophyoidea (herbivorous mites): the unpaired median internal vertical seta vi (single anterior shield seta) or the paired external vertical setae ve.

ANTERO. [L. *antero*, anterior]. To the front: Anteriorly.

ANTERODORSAL. [L. *antero*, anterior; *dorsum*, back]. Toward the front and the top or upper side.

ANTEROLATERAL. [L. *antero*, anterior; *latus*, side]. Of the anterior end and the side.

ANTEROLATERAL SETA. [L. *antero*, anterior; *latus*, side; *seta*, bristle]. In the Mesostigmata: either of the setae (al 1-2) on the anterior lateral surface of a leg or palp segment.

ANTEROLATERALS. [L. *antero*, anterior; *latus*, side]. On the tarsi of acariform mites: a pair of ventral setae between the subunguinal seta and the primiventrals.

ANTEROMEDIAL SETA. [L. *antero*, anterior; *medius*, middle]. In the Mesostigmata: the palpgenual seta al1.

ANTEROMESAL. [L. *antero*, anterior; Gr. μεσος, middle]. Of the anterior end and the midline.

ANTEROPOSTERIOR AXIS. [L. *antero*, anterior; *posterior*, behind]. The longitudinal axis, from head to tail.

ANTEROVENTRAL. [L. *antero*, anterior; *venter*, belly]. In the front on the lower side.

ANTEROVENTRAL SETA. [L. *antero*, anterior; *venter*, belly; *seta*, bristle]. In the Mesostigmata: a seta (av 1-3) on the anterior ventral surface of a leg or palp segment.

ANTHROPOCENTRIC. [Gr. ανθρωπος, a man; κεντρον, center]. 1. Interpreting the activities of organisms in relation to human values. 2. Assuming humans to be of central importance in the universe or the end point of creation. 3. Attributing human characteristics to non-human organisms.

ANTHROPOCHORY. [Gr. ανθρωπος, a man; κωρεω, to spread abroad]. Dispersal by man.

ANTHROPOGENIC. [Gr. ανθρωπος, a man; –γενης, producing]. Caused by or produced by man.

ANTHROPOMORPHISM. [Gr. ανθρωπος, a man; μορφη, shape]. The ascription of human traits, attributes or personality to non-human entities. A cardinal sin!

ANTIAPOSEMATIC. [Gr. αντι-, in opposition to; απο, away; σημα, signal]. See Sematic.

ANTIAXIAL (ABAXIAL). [Gr. αντι-, in opposition to; L. *axis*, axle]. Away from the axis (midline) of the body. The outer or lateral face of a chelicera.

ANTIAXIAL LYRIFISSURE. [Gr. αντι-, in opposition to; L. *axis*, axle; ridge between two furrows, lyre; *fissura*, crack]. In the Mesostigmata: the lyrifissure on the outer face of the chelicera.

ANTIBIOSIS. [Gr. αντι-, in opposition to; βιοσις, manner of life]. An association between two organisms in which one secretes a substance which destroys or inhibits the other.

ANTICLINAL. [Gr. αντι-, in opposition to; κλινω, incline]. Radial. Inclining in opposite directions. At right angles to the surface of a part.

ANTICOAGULANT. [Gr. αντι-, in opposition to; L. *coagulum*, rennet]. A substance which prevents the coagulation (or clotting) of blood, e.g. heparin. See also Saliva.

ANTICOAGULIN. [Gr. αντι-, in opposition to; L. *coagulare*, to curdle]. A secretion of some parasitic species that prevents or delays the coagulation of the host's blood.

ANTICRYPTIC COLORATION. [Gr. αντι-, in opposition to; κρυπτος, hidden]. The protective coloration of a predator that facilitates the attack or capture of prey. See also Homochromy.

ANTICUS. [L. *anticus*, foremost]. Anterior. Frontal. Belonging to or toward the front.

ANTIGENY. [Gr. αντι-, in opposition; γενος, generation]. Opposition or antagonism of the sexes.

ANTIMERE. [Gr. αντι-, in opposition to; μερος, part]. Of symmetrical animals: the corresponding parts, e.g. left and right limbs.

ANTIPODAL. [Gr. αντι-, in opposition to; πους, foot]. Diametrically opposite. Located on the opposite side.

ANTIROSTRUM. [Gr. αντι-, in opposition to; L. *rostrum*, beak]. The terminal segmental appendages of some mites.

ANTITROPIC. [Gr. αντι-, in opposition to; τροπη, turn]. Arranged in opposite directions, or to form bilaterally symmetrical pairs.

ANTRODIAETIDAE. [L. *antero-*, front; Gr. διαιτα, dwelling]. A small family of folding trapdoor spiders (infraorder Mygalomorphae, superfamily Atypoidea) from the western, midwest and eastern USA. Two species (*Antrodiaetus roretzi* and *A. yesoensis*) are endemic to Japan. See Trapdoor Spiders.

ANTRORSE (ANTRORSUM). [L. *antero-*, front; *versus*, towards]. Directed or bent forwards or upwards (opposite = retrose).

ANTRUM. [L. *antrum*, cavity]. 1. A hollow space or cavity. 2. A sinus.

ANUS. [L. *anus*, ring]. In most metazoans: the posterior opening of the alimentary canal.

ANYPHAENIDAE. [Gr. ανυφαινω, to weave anew]. A family of Entelegyne spiders (infraorder Araneomorphae, superfamily Entelegynae) in which the abdominal spiracle is placed one third to one half of the way anterior to the spinnerets toward the epigastric furrow on the underside of the abdomen. In most spiders the spiracle is just anterior to the spinnerets.

22

ANYSTINA. [Gr. ανυστος; to be accomplished]. An infraorder of mites (order Trombidiformes, suborder Prostigmata) that contains up to twenty-two superfamilies, many of which are disputed. Least controversial superfamilies: Anystoidea, Caeculoidea, Paratydeoidea, Pomerantzioidea.

ANYSTOIDEA. [Gr. ανυστος; to be accomplished]. A superfamily of mites (suborder Prostigmata, infraorder Anystina). Families: **Anystidae, Chulacaridae, Pseudocheylidae, Teneriffiidae.**

APATETIC COLORATION. [Gr. απατητικος, fallacious]. Protective coloration which has the effect of misleading the predator (as opposed to camouflage which 'hides' an animal from its predators; or mimicry, where a protective resemblance is assumed). In some cases the markings suggest the presence of an eye, or other organ where in fact there is none. In other cases the outline of the animal is broken up. See also Disruptive Coloration.

APERTURE (APERTURAL). [L. *aperire*, to open]. Any opening or hole, cleft, or gap.

APHANISM. [Gr. αφανης, unseen]. The loss or reduction in a descendent adult of a functioning organ that was present and functioning in both the young and adults of the ancestral stock.

APHELIOTROPISM (AHELIOTROPISM). [Gr. απο, away; ηλιος, sun; τροπη, turn]. To turn away from sunlight, or any light.

APHIDIVOROUS. [NL. *aphis*, plant-louse; L. *vorare*, to devour]. Feeding on aphids.

APHOTOTROPISM. [Gr. α-, without; φως, light τροπη, turn]. A tendency to turn away from light.

APICAD. [L. *apex*, tip; *ad*, toward]. Towards the apex.

APICAL. [L. *apex*, tip]. At or concerning the tip or furthest part of any organ.

APICAL DIVISION. [L. *apex*, tip]. The region of the genital bulb of the male palpus that consists of the conductor, embolus and associated structures.

APICOTARSUS (ACROTARSUS). [L. *apex*, summit: Gr. ταρσος, sole of the foot]. The distal subdivision of the tarsus, usually of tarsus I.

APICOTRANSVERSE. [L. *apex*, summit; *transversus*, crosswize]. Of something situated across, at, or near the tip.

APICULATE. [L. *apiculus*, little tip]. Of a short, abrupt point or points.

APICULUS. [L. *apilulus*, little summit]. A small apical termination.

APIVOROUS. [L. *apis*, honeybee; vorare, devour]. Feeding on bees.

APLASIA. [Gr. α-, without; πλασσω, form]. Arrested development. See also Hypoplasia.

APNEUMONE. [Gr. αν, without; πνευμα, air]. A substance emitted by non-living material that evokes a behavioral or physiological reaction favorable to the receiving organism, but detrimental to another species that may be found in or on the non-living material. See also Allelochemic.

APOBIOTIC. [Gr. απο, away from; βιοτικος, pert. life]. Causing the death of certain cells or tissues but not the whole body.

APOCENTRIC. [Gr. απο, away; κεντρον, center]. Deviating from the original type. See also Archecentric.

APODEMES. [Gr. απο, down from; δεμας, the living body]. In-growths of the cuticle which serve as points of attachment for the muscles.

APODERMA. [Gr. απο, away from; δερμα, skin]. In some ticks and mites: an enveloping membrane secreted during the resting stage between instars. It lacks limbs and setae. See Calyptostasic.

APOLYSIS. [Gr. απο, away; λυσις, loosen]. In arthropods: the first stage in the molting process, characterized by the detachment of the old cuticle from the underlying hypodermal (epidermal) cells. See also Ecdysis.

23

APOMICT. [Gr. απο, away from; μιξις, a mixing]. Any organism produced by apomixis.

APOMICTIC PARTHENOGENESIS. Parthenogenesis in which meiosis has been suppressed so that chromosome reduction does not occur. See Parthenogenesis.

APOMIXIS. [Gr. απο, away from; μιξις, a mixing]. A form of reproduction which has the superficial appearance of an ordinary sexual cycle but actually occurs without fertilization and/or meiosis. The ovum may develop without penetration by a male gamete (parthenogenesis) or may develop after penetration but before the nuclei have fused (pseudogamy); the act of penetration being sufficient to stimulate the ovum to undergo cleavage and develop into an embryo.

APOMORPHIC CHARACTERS. [Gr. απο, away from; μορφη, shape]. Characters that have been derived during the course of evolution as opposed to those which are primitive, or plesiomorphic. Apomorphic characters may be uniquely derived (autapomorphic) or shared-derived (synapomorphic). See also Autapomorphic Character, Phylogenetic Classification, Plesiomorphic, Synapomorphic.

APOPHYSIS. [Gr. αποφυσις, an offshoot]. A cuticular or sclerotized ingrowth of the exoskeleton, common on palpal segments, and often a site of muscle attachment.

APOSEMATIC. [Gr. απο, away from; σημα, signal]. See Sematic.

APOSEME. [Gr. απο, away; σημα, signal]. A population in which all the individuals, even though taxonomically distinct, share the same aposematic coloration.

APOSTATIC. [Gr. αποστατες, deserter]. Widely departing from the norm. Of a phenotype that differs strikingly from the search image of a predator.

APOSTATIC SELECTION. [Gr. απο, away from; στατικος, stationary]. A form of selection that acts on polymorphic prey species. Of the various morphological forms, the predation rate varies according to the relative frequency of the various forms, so, the percentage of common forms tends to decrease while the less common forms tend to increase. This form of selection can produce a stable genetic polymorphism.

APOSYMBIOTIC. [Gr. απο, away from; συμβιος, living together]. Of any organism which normally lives in symbiosis with another but which has been separated from its partner.

APOTELE (APOTELIC). [Gr. απο, away; τελος, end]. In mites: the terminal eudesmatic segment of the appendages. Generally constituting two tendons and two articulation-points. The most distal leg segment, often consisting of an empodium and a pair of claws. See also Pretarsus.

APOXYPODES. [Gr. απο, away from; οξις, sharp; -πους, foot]. A group of fossil arachnids from the Silurian. They had four pairs of legs, one pair of large pincers and, though they had no spiracles (unlike scorpions), they are thought to be intermediate between scorpions (order Scorpiones) and eurypterids (subclass Eurypterida or Gigantostraca).

APPENDAGE. [L. ad, to; pendere, to cause to hang down]. Any considerable projection from the body of an animal.

APPENDICLE. [L. ad, to; pendere, to cause to hang down]. A small appendage.

APPENDICULATE. [L. ad, to; pendere, to cause to hang down]. Bearing or forming small appendages.

APPENDIGEROUS. [L. appendix, appendage; gerere, to bear]. Bearing appendages.

APPENDIX. [L. appendix, something attached]. Any attached body or small process.

APPENDOTOMY. [L. appendix, appendage; Gr. τομη, a cutting]. The loss of appendages. See Autospasy, Autotilly, Autotomy.

APPLANATE. [L. ad, to; planatus, flattened]. Flattened.

APPRESSED (ADPRESSED). [L. ad, to; pressare, to press]. Pressed together without being joined.

AQUAMARINE. [L. aqua marina, sea water]. Blue, blue-green or green.

AQUATICOLOUS (AQUATIC). [L. *aqua*, water; *colere*, to inhabit]. Inhabiting water or aquatic vegetation.

ARACHNIDA. [Gr. αραχνης, spider]. A subclass of extremely diverse, mostly terrestrial chelicerates (subphylum Chelicerata, class Euchelicerata) that are mainly predatory and distinguished from other arthropods by having book lungs or tracheae derived from gills, indicating their aquatic ancestry, and having the body divided into two distinct regions; the prosoma and opisthosoma. The anterior prosoma (or cephalothorax) bears two pairs of prehensile and sensory appendages (the chelicerae—masticatory, and the pedipalps—manipulative) behind which there are four pairs of walking legs. The posterior abdomen, or opisthosoma bears no appendages and contains most of the internal organs and glands, and the two regions may be broadly jointed or narrowly connected by a pedicel. The prosoma has a carapace (dorsal shield) and the opisthosoma is segmented in all except the spiders and mites. There are up to twelve eyes in some scorpions but sight is generally poor and many nocturnal species have sensory hairs with which they detect their prey. In all arachnids food is pre-digested by midgut enzymes. The reproductive organs are located ventrally and courtship may be long and involve complex postural patterns, parental care is common to all. Silk and poison are common products of some orders, silk being produced from abdominal glands in spiders, from the mouth region in mites and from the chelicerae in pseudoscorpions. Poison is produced from the chelicerae of spiders, the tails of scorpions and the pedipalps of pseudoscorpions. The scorpions are considered to be the most primitive arachnids and their remains have been found in Silurian deposits. The first fossil spiders are recorded from the Devonian. Mites are probably the most specialized. There is general agreement at the higher levels of taxonomy, however, continued research, the discovery of synonyms, and differences of opinion, keep the lower levels in a state of flux. Superorders: Acariformes (orders Sarcoptiformes, Trombidiformes), Opilioacariformes (Order Opilioacarida), Parasitiformes (orders Holothyrida, Ixodida, Mesostigmata). Orders with no superorder: Amblypygi, Araneae, †Haptopoda, Opiliones, Palpigradi, †Phalangiotarbi, **Pseudoscorpiones**, Ricinulei, Schizomida, Scorpiones, Solifugae, †Trigonotarbida. †Uraraneida, Uropygi. The Xiphosura (horseshoe crabs) are sometimes included here.

ARACHNIDISM (ARACHNISM). [Gr. αραχνης, spider; -ισμος, suf. forming nouns of action]. Envenomation or poisoning by an arachnid, such as a spider, tick or scorpion.

ARACHNIDIUM. [Gr. αραχνης, spider; -ιδιον, dim. suf.]. The complete spinning apparatus of a spider.

ARACHNOID (ARACHNOIDEOUS). [Gr. αραχνης, spider; ειδος, form]. Resembling a spider or cobweb. Consisting of fine entangled hairs.

ARACHNOLOGY (ARANEOLOGY). [Gr. αραχνης, spider; λογος, discourse]. The scientific study of arachnids: spiders, ticks, scorpions, whip scorpions and others. See Arachnida.

ARANEAE. [Gr. αραχνης, spider]. The order of spiders (class Euchelicerata, subclass Arachnida), containing approximately 45,000 species in about 131 families; but more species are being discovered almost every month. Spiders range in size from 0.5 mm to about 9 cm and are ubiquitous. Typically the prosoma or cephalothorax is separated by a waist from the opisthosoma (or abdomen) which is soft, unsegmented and bears several pairs of spinnerets. The spinneret is a short conical structure bearing many spigots (the openings for the silk glands). Silk produced by these is of various kinds and is used for making webs, drag lines, egg cocoons or for trussing up victims, etc. The prosoma, which is a combination of head and thorax, bears two chelicerae which are unique among arachnids in being provided with poison glands, and two sensory organs (pedipalps) with jaw-like bases known as 'gnathobases'. The legs have seven segments of which the pretarsus (distal segment) has two comb-like claws and usually a hook-like median claw for silk manipulation. Almost all species use their eight legs for walking or rapid running and some jump by means of a sudden extension of the legs resulting from a very rapid rise in blood pressure. The convex carapace usually bears eight eyes anteriorly. In some species (e.g. the jumping spiders: **Salticidae**) vision is acute; other sensory organs include setae, trichobothria and chemical and tactile receptors on the tarsi and pedipalps. Breathing is by means of both tracheae and book lungs. Most spiders are carnivorous, they bite their prey (commonly other arthropods) with chelicerae, with which they may also hold and macerate the tissue during digestion. Probably due to their predatory habit many species of spiders have developed a highly complex precopulatory behavior in which chemical and tactile clues are of primary importance. Most species enclose their eggs in a silken cocoon and guard the eggs and young. Spiders are found in all terrestrial niches and there is one aquatic species (**Agelenidae**), some hunt on the surface film of water aided by hydrophobic tarsal hairs. The Araneae are currently divided into two suborders: Mesothelae, Opisthothelae. However, lists of spiders, such as the World Spider Catalog, currently ignore classification above the family level—although informal clade names are often used.

ARANEIDAE. [L. *araneus*, spider]. The large cosmopolitan family (ca. 175 genera) of orb-web spiders (infraorder Araneomorphae, superfamily Entelegynae). They are the most common group of spiral wheel-shaped web constructors, and have legs provided with many long spines. The chelicerae possess many teeth and in numerous species there are dwarf males. The genera of the former family **Nephilidae** are included here.

ARANEIFORM. [L. *aranea*, spider; *forma*, shape]. Spider-like in appearance.

ARANEOCLADA. [L. *araneus*, spider, Gr. κλαδος, a branch]. In a previous classifications a clade of araneomorph spiders (order Araneae, suborder Opisthothelae) that combined the superfamilies Haplogynae and Entelegynae.

ARANEOIDEA. [L. *araneus*, spider]. In a previous classification: a superfamily of spiders (order Araneae, suborder Araneomorphae) that combined the families: **Anapidae, Araneidae, Cyatholipidae, Linyphiidae, Mysmenidae, Nesticidae, Pimoidae, Symphytognathidae, Synaphridae, Synotaxidae, Tetragnathidae, Nephilidae, Theridiidae, Theridiosomatidae**.

ARANEOLOGY. [L. *aranea*, spider; Gr. λογος, discourse]. The scientific study of spiders. See also Arachnology.

ARANEOMORPHAE (LABIDOGNATHA). [L. *araneus*, spider; Gr. μορφη, shape]. The larger of two infraorders of spiders (order Araneae, suborder Opisthothelae) in which are grouped most of the extant species. Only a single pair of book lungs is present (with few exceptions) and in all species the plane of articulation of the chelicerae is at right angles to the long axis of the body and thus chelicerae act in a pincer-like fashion (cf Mygalomorphae). Previously, three groupings were generally recognized, the **Cribellate** spiders: in which there is a cribellum and calamistrum; the **Haplogyne** spiders: in which there are only six eyes, simple male palpal organs and no epigynum in the adult females, and the **Entelegyne** spiders: in which there are eight eyes, complex male palpal organs and an epigynum in the adult females. Recent investigations suggest there should be four superfamilies: Austrochiloidea, Entelegynae, Haplogynae, Hypochiloidea (may be included in the Haplogynae).

ARANEOPHAGOUS. [L. *araneus*, spider, Gr. -φαγος, -eating]. Spider-eating.

ARANIA. [L. *aranea*, spider]. An alternative name for the Araneae.

ARBOREAL. [L. *arbor*, a tree]. Living in or amongst trees.

ARBORESCENT. [L. *arborescens*, growing like a tree]. Branched like a tree. Tree-like.

ARBORICOLOUS. [L. *arbor*, a tree; *colere*, to inhabit]. Living mainly in trees or large woody shrubs.

ARBORVIRUS (ARBOVIRUS). [<u>ar</u>thropod <u>bor</u>ne <u>virus</u>]. A virus in which an arthropod is the intermediate host and a vertebrate the definitive host. There are over 200 arthropod-borne viruses which are transmitted between susceptible hosts by hematophagous (blood feeding) arthropods.

ARBUSTICLOUS. [L. *arbustum*, plantation; *colere*, to inhabit]. Living mainly on scattered shrubs and/or perennial herbs with a shrub-like habit.

ARCHAEOBUTHIDAE. [Gr. αρκαιος, ancient; + *Buthus*]. A small extinct monospecific family of scorpions (order Scorpiones, superfamily Buthoidea) known only from the Early Cretaceous amber of Lebanon.

ARCHAEIDAE. [Gr. αρκαιος, ancient]. A small family of spiders (infraorder Araneomorphae, superfamily Palpimanoidea) known as assassin spiders and pelican spiders; from South Africa and Australia. But see also Archaeoidea.

ARCHAEOIDEA. [Gr. αρκαιος, ancient]. In a previous classification: the superfamily of pelican spiders and assassin spiders (order Araneae, suborder Araneomorphae). Eight-eyed spiders South America, South Africa, Papua, Australia and New Zealand. Families: **Archaeidae, Holarchaeidae, Mecysmaucheniidae, Micropholcommatidae, Pararchaeidae**. In other classifications the families Holarchaeidae and Micropholcommatidae have been moved to the **Anapidae**; and the Archaeidae and Pararchaeidae moved to the **Malkaridae** (superfamily Entelegynae). The Mecysmaucheniidae is placed in the superfamily Palpimanoidea (infraorder Araneomorphae), but not all authorities agree.

ARCHAIC. [Gr. αρκαιος, ancient]. Ancient. No longer dominant.

ARCHALLAXIS. [Gr. αρκαιος, ancient; αλλαξις, a changing]. The addition of new attributes during an early period of embryonic development.

ARCHECENTRIC. [Gr. αρχη, origin; κεντρον, center]. Conforming to the original type. See also Apocentric.

ARCHENCEPHALON. [Gr. αρχη, beginning; κεφαλη, head]. See Archicerebrum

ARCHICEREBRUM (PROCEREBRUM). [Gr. αρχι-, first; L. *cerebrum*, brain]. The part of an arthropod brain that is formed from the fusion of the paired ganglia of the first somite together with a pair of presegmental ganglia.

ARCTACAROIDEA. [Gr. αρκτικος, northern; LL. *acarus*, mite]. A monotypic superfamily of mites (suborder Monogynaspida, infraorder Gamasina), first described from the arctic regions of North America. Family: **Arctacaridae**. In a previous classification: the suborder Arctacarina.

ARCUATE. [L. *arcuatus*, bent like a bow]. Curved like a bow or arc-shaped.

AREA EFFECT SPECIATION. Speciation that is associated with increasing differentiation between two subspecies that have incompatible gene complexes. Thus the hybrids are strongly selected against. See also Speciation.

AREA POROSAE. [Gr. πορος, channel]. Round to oval aggregations of pore-like areas of the cuticle; usually referring to the octotaxic system of the Oribatida.

AREA PUNCTATA. [L. *punctata*, punctuated/spotted]. In some Mesostigmata: the aciniform (grape-like) clusters of punctae on the sternal shields.

ARGENTATE, ARGENTEOUS. [L. *argentum*, silver]. Shining. Silvery white.

ARGILLACEOUS. [L. *argilla*, white clay; -*aceous*, of the nature of]. Containing clay, clay-like. Clayey.

ARGIOPIDAE. [Gr. αργια, leisure; -οψ, appearance]. A disused name for orb-web spiders. See **Araneidae**.

ARGYRONETIDAE. [Gr. αργυρεος, silver; νηθω, to spin (weave)]. The monotypic family of water spiders (infraorder Araneomorphae, superfamily Entelegynae) which contains the only species of spider (*Argyroneta aquatica*) known to live an almost entirely aquatic existence. A retreat is constructed among underwater vegetation and is supplied with air carried down from the surface. Once constructed, the oxygen level is maintained by diffusion from the surrounding water and small bubbles of air from aquatic plants. *Argyroneta* is an underwater hunter, preying on a range of aquatic invertebrates. It is sometimes included in the **Agelenidae**.

ARID. [L. *aridus*, parched]. Applied to regions in which the normal rainfall is insufficient to produce ordinary farm crops without irrigation and in which desert conditions prevail. See also Humid.

ARISTA. [L. *arista*, a bristle]. A bristle-like outgrowth.

ARISTATE (ATHERICEROUS). [L. *arista*, a bristle]. Bearing an arista or bristle.

ARISTIFORM. [L. *arista*, a bristle; *forma*, shape]. In the form or appearance of an arista.

ARISTULATE. [L. *aristula*, small bristle]. Bearing a short bristle.

ARKIDAE. [Gr. αρκυς, hunter's net]. A small family of ambush hunting spiders (infraorder Araneomorphae, superfamily Entelegynae). Many are brightly colored and somewhat crab-like.

ARMORED MITE. [L. *armare*, to arm]. Any mite encased in armor but especially members of the Oribatida and Uropodoidea.

ARMS RACE. A sequence of mutual counter-adaptations of two (or more) organisms coevolving. E.g. a predator and its prey.

AROLIUM (AROLIA). [NL. *arolium*, a role of cloth]. A membranous pouch-like structure. E.g. the cavity in which the empodia are situated in *Neilstigmaeus* (Prostigmata: **Stigmaeidae**).

AROMORPHOSIS. [Gr. αιρω, raise; μορφωσις, shaping]. An evolutionary increase in the degree of organization but with little increase in specialization.

ARRECT. [L. *arrectus*, upright]. Upright, erect.

ARRENUROIDEA. [Gr. αρρην, male; ουρα, tail]. A superfamily of mites (suborder Prostigmata, infraorder Anystina). Twenty families.

ARRHENOGENIC. [Gr. αρρην, male; γενος, offspring]. Producing offspring that are entirely or predominantly male. See also Thelygenic.

ARRHENOID. [Gr. αρρην, male; ειδος, form]. The exhibition of male characteristics in females whilst undergoing sex change.

ARRHENOTOKY (ARRHENOTOKOUS PARTHENOGENESIS). [Gr. αρρην, male; τοκος, birth]. The haplodiploid parthenogenesis in which males arise from unfertilized, and therefore haploid, egg cells. See Parthenogenesis.

ARTHRAL, ARTHRITIC. [Gr. αρθρον, joint]. Associated with, or in the region of joints.

ARTHRODERM. [Gr. αρθρον, joint; δηρμα, skin]. In arthropods: the outer covering of skin, or the outer body-wall.

ARTHRODIA. [Gr. αρθρωδης, well-jointed]. A type of joint that only permits gliding movements.

ARTHRODIAL. [Gr. αρθρωδης, well-jointed]. In arthropods: of articular membranes connecting the thoracic appendages to the body.

ARTHRODIAL BRUSH. [Gr. αρθρωδης, well-jointed]. In some Mesostigmata: a brush like extension of the arthrodial membrane at the articulation of the movable and fixed digits.

ARTHRODIAL CORONA/CORONET. [Gr. αρθρωδης, well-jointed; L. *corona*, crown]. In the Mesostigmata: a crown-like arrangement of fine processes from the arthrodial membrane at the juncture of the fixed and movable digits.

ARTHRODIAL MEMBRANE. [Gr. αρθρωδης, well-jointed; L. *membrana*, membrane]. The soft cuticle found at any articulation. It is often used for the juncture of the movable and fixed digits. It may have a crown-like corona of fine processes or be extended into a brush-like structure. See also Exoskeleton.

ARTHROGENOUS EVOLUTION. [Gr. αρθρο–, jointed; γενεσις, descent]. A theory of evolution that holds that there is a certain creativity in living matter that becomes prominent in response to environmental stimuli.

ARTHROMERE. [Gr. αρθρο–, jointed; μερος, part]. The body segment or somite of an arthropod.

ARTHROPLEURE. [Gr. αρθρον, joint; πλευρα, side]. In arthropods: the lateral part of a body segment.

ARTHROPODA. [Gr. αρθρο-, jointed; -πους, foot]. A vast and diverse phylum of invertebrates that first appeared in the Cambrian. At least three quarters of a million species have been described (ca. 80% of all animals described), thus making this the largest phylum in the animal kingdom in terms of number of species. The arthropod body is metameric, covered by a hard exoskeleton but with soft joints to allow movement between the skeletal plates. There is a large number of paired, jointed appendages acting as legs, jaws, gills or sense organs. Primitively, the limbs and cuticular plates correspond to the metameric segmentation of the body but in many groups there has been considerable loss and/or fusion of segments. The ventral nervous system consists of a double ventral cord with two ganglia in each segment and a collar around the pharynx. There is a dorsal heart and a high degree of cephalization which is correlated with well developed sense organs such as eyes and antennae. Many arthropod groups display complex behavior patterns. Subphyla: Chelicerata, Crustacea, Hexapoda, Myriapoda, †Trilobitomorpha.

28

ARTHROPODIN. [*Arthropod* + *-in*, chem. suf. used for neutral substances]. A water-soluble protein found in association with chitin in the exoskeleton of arthropods. It is chemically similar to seticin - the silk protein.

ARTHROPODIZATION. [Gr. αρθρο–, jointed; –πους, foot; -ιζειν, suf. ind. make/cause]. The evolutionary development of the combination of characteristics associated with arthropods, including the chitinous exoskeleton.

ARTICLE. [L. *articulus*, little joint]. In ticks: the serrated process on the chelicera. See Cheliceral Digits, Palp.

ARTICULAR. [L. *articularis*, of a joint]. Pertaining to a joint.

ARTICULAR MEMBRANE. [L. *articularis*, of a joint]. The non-sclerotized, flexible membrane between the segments of arthropods, and the joints of arthropod appendages.

ARTICULAR PAN. [L. *articularis*, of a joint]. A cup or dish-like impression into which an articulation is located.

ARTICULARIS. [L. *articularis*, of a joint]. The pretarsus.

ARTICULATE. [L. *articulus*, a small joint]. 1. To divide into significant parts. 2. To attach by a joint.

ARTICULATE FASCIA. [L. *articulus*, a small joint; *fascia*, a bundle]. A band of contiguous spots.

ARTICULATION. [L. *articulare*, to separate (meat) into joints]. A joint or point of contact between two sclerotic parts of a structure. It may or may not be moveable.

ARTIFICIAL KEY. [L. *artificialis*, of or belonging to art]. An identification key based on convenient characters and not indicating any phylogenetic relationship.

ARTIFICIAL PARTHENOGENESIS. [L. *artificialis*, of or belonging to art; Gr. παρθενος, virgin; γενεσις, birth]. Stimulating an egg, which is not normally parthenogenetic, to commence development without any contact by sperm. This may be accomplished in a variety of ways such as altering solution concentrations, adding salts, irradiating with infra-red, ultra-violet etc., and in some cases pricking with a needle.

ACSIDAE. [Gr. αοκος, a sac]. A small family of mites (infraorder Gamasina, superfamily Phytoseioidea). Some authorities consider some members of this family (*Cheiroseius*, *Lasioseius*, *Platyseius*) to be better placed in the family **Blattisociidae**.

ASCIDIAL. [Gr. ασκιδιον, little basket]. Sac-like.

ASCOIDEA. [Gr. αοκος, a sac]. A superfamily of mites (suborder Monogynaspida, infraorder Gamasina). Families: **Ameroseiidae**, **Antennochelidae**, **Ascidae**, **Melicharidae**. In some classifications this superfamily may be included in the sub-cohort Dermanyssiae.

ASCORHYNCHOIDEA. [Gr. αοκος, a sac; ρυγχος, a snout]. A superfamily of sea spiders (order Pantopoda, suborder Eupantopodida). Families: **Acheliidae** (**Ammotheidae**), **Ascorhynchidae** (**Eurycydidae**).

ASEMIC. [Gr. ασημος, without a sign]. Without markings.

ASEPTATE. [Gr. αν, without; L. *septum*, partition]. Being without a partition.

ASPECT. [L. *aspicere*, to behold]. Indicates the direction to which a surface faces or in which it is viewed: it may be dorsal, ventral, caudal, cephalic or lateral.

ASPERATE. [L. *asperum*, roughness]. Having a rough surface.

ASPERGILLIFORM. [L. *aspergillum*, a brush; *forma*, shape]. Tufted like a brush.

ASPERITY (ASPERITIES). [L. *asperare*, to roughen]. Roughness of surface. Of spine-like structures arranged in rows or confined to specific areas. Sculpturings or dot-like elevations.

ASPERSUS. [L. *asperulus*, rough]. Rough to the touch. Having very distinct elevated dots. More uneven than scabrous.

ASPERULATE (ASPERULOUS). [L. *asperum*, roughness; *-ula*, dim. suf.]. Minutely rough.

ASPIDOSOMA. [Gr. αοπις, shield; σομα, body]. In ticks and mites: the anterior dorsal region of the prosoma bordered laterally by the abjugal furrow (that may be indistinct or incomplete) posteriorly by the disjugal furrow, and anteriorly by the circumcapitular furrows.

ASPLANCHINC. [Gr. α-, without; σπλαγχνα, viscera]. Without an alimentary canal.

ASPIS. [Gr. αοπις, round shield]. A sclerotized shield over the aspidosoma.

ASSAMIIDAE. [*Assam*, Indian province]. A large family of harvestmen or daddy longlegs (suborder Laniatores, superfamily Assamioidea) with a wide range of sizes, from 2-8 mm body length and a leg length ranging from 4-40 mm. They are usually reddish brown to yellow, with black mottling and reticulate patterns.

ASSAMIOIDEA. [*Assam*, Indian province]. A superfamily of harvestmen (suborder Laniatores, infraorder Grassatores). Families: **Assamiidae, Pyramidopidae.**

ASSEMBLAGE. [L. *assimulare*, to bring together]. 1. A group of fossils occurring together at the same stratigraphic level. 2. A group of animals characteristically associated with a particular environment.

ASSEMBLY. The smallest community recognized in ecology.

ASSIMILATION. [L. *ad*, to; *similis*, like]. The absorption of digested food substances into a living organism and the building up of the complex constituents of that organism.

ASSOCIATION. [L. *ad.* to; *socius*, fellow]. 1. A group of animals in a certain environment. 2. A form of learning in which the stimulus elicits an increasingly positive response.

ASSORTATIVE MATING. Non-random mating. The phenomenon where individuals mate with similar members of the population more frequently than would be expected by chance. This process leads to a reduction in the amount of heterozygosity within a population and the consequential instability of polymorphisms. See also Disassortative Mating, Panmixia.

ASSURGENT. [L. *assurgens*, to arise]. Curving upward. Ascending.

ASTAXANTHIN. [L. *astacus*, lobster; *xanthos*, yellow]. A carotenoid red pigment that occurs naturally in a wide variety of living organisms.

ASTEGASIMOUS (ASTEGASIME). [Gr. αν, without; στεγη, roof]. Of mites when the prodorsal sclerite does not project over the chelicerae; it may be reduced or absent. See also Stegasimous.

ASTIGMATA (ASTIGMATINA). [Gr. α-, without; στιγμα, mark]. A suborder of mites (superorder Acariformes, order Sarcoptiformes) in which the tracheal system is absent and thus gas exchange occurs across the weakly sclerotized body wall. This suborder includes many species which are parasites of vertebrates, e.g. the mange and scab-producing mites (**Sarcoptidae** and **Psoroptidae**) and the storage mites (**Acaridae**). Thirteen superfamilies and 94 families, although not all authorities will agree with this arrangement.

ASTIGMATIC. [Gr. α-, without; στιγμα, mark]. Lacking stigmata; without a spiracle or breathing pore.

ASTIGMATID. Erron. for Astigmatan, the adjectival form of Astigmata.

ASTIGMATINA. [Gr. α-, without; στιγμα, mark]. In a previous classifications a suborder of the Oribatida (superorder Acariformes, order Sarcoptiformes) that contained astigmatic mites, i.e. a group of oribatid mites that are usually soft-bodied, lack bothridial sensillae and often produce a heteromorphic deutonymph (hypopus). See Astigmata.

ASTROTAXIS. [Gr. αστρον, a star; ταξις, an arranging]. The orientation of organisms sensitive to polarized skylight. I.e., bees, ants and spiders.

ASYMMETRICAL. [Gr. ασυμμετρος, disproportionate]. Structures or organs that can not be divided into two similar halves, in any plane. Having two disproportionate sides.

ATACTOTRICHY. [Gr. ατακτος, disorderly; τριχος, hair]. Chaetotaxy in which all setae are not describable in distinct patterns and arrangements. See also Primordiotrichy.

ATAVISM. [L. *atavus*, ancestor]. The occurrence of ancestral characters that were not evident in the parental generation.

ATELEBASIC RUTELLUM. [Gr. ατελης, ineffectual; L. *basis*, base; *rutellum*, little spade]. A large toothed rutellum with the apex expanded and with a paraxial lobe; as in the Holosomata and some Brachypylina. See also Pantelebasic Rutellum, Rutella.

ATELIA. [Gr. ατελης, ineffectual]. An apparently ineffectual character, generally of unknown biological significance. Incomplete or imperfect development.

ATER. [L. *ater*, black]. Black: not shining.

ATERIMUS. [L. *aterrimus*, deepest black]. The deepest black.

ATHECAL. [Gr. α, without; θηκη, case]. Without spermathecae.

ATHERICEROUS. See Aristate.

ATEMNIDAE. [Gr. α–, not; τεμνω; maim]. A family of false scorpions (suborder Iocheirata, superfamily Cheliferoidea). The subfamily Miratemninae may sometimes be classified as a distinct family: **Miratemniidae**.

ATOKOS. [Gr. ατοκος, childless]. Without offspring.

ATOMARIUS. [L. *atomos*, atom]. Having minute dots or points.

ATOPOCHTHONIOIDEA. [Gr. α–, not; τοπος, a place; χθων, the ground]. A monospecific superfamily of mites (suborder Oribatida, infraorder Enarthronota). Family: **Atopochthoniidae** (syn. Phyllochthoniidae, Pterochthoniidae).

ATOPOSPHYRONIDA. [Gr. α–, not; τοπος, a place; σφυρα, hammer]. A suborder of pseudoscorpions (subclass Arachnida, order Pseudoscorpiones) created for those species that have venom glands in the pedipalp's fingers. They are dispersed across the southern hemisphere. Families: **Feaellidae**, **Pseudogarypidae**.

ATRACHEATE. [Gr. α-, without; LL. *trachia*, windpipe]. Without tracheae. Without a visible constriction between the head and prothorax.

ATRACIDAE. [Gr. ατραξ, a town of Thessaly, but probably meaning dull black, dark]. The family of Australian funnel-web spiders (infraorder Mygalomorphae, superfamily Avicularioidea). It was previously included as a subfamily of the Hexathelidae. This family includes the deadly Sydney funnel web spider, *Atrax robustus*.

ATRETIC. [Gr. α-, without; τρητος, perforated]. Lacking an opening.

ATRIAL. [L. *atrium*, hall]. Of an atrium, cavity, pore, canal, etc.

ATRICHIC/ATRICHOUS. [Gr. α-, without; θριξ, hair]. Lacking spines or barbs.

ATRICHOSY. [Gr. α-, without; τριχος, hair]. The absence of setae due to evolutionary regression.

ATRIOBURSAL ORIFICE. [L. *atrium*, chamber; *bursa*, pouch; *os*, mouth; *facere*, to make]. The opening of the seminal receptacle of female spiders.

ATRIUM. [L. *atrium*, hall]. A cavity in the epigynal plate which contains the copulatory openings of the female, either in its floor or wall. It may be subdivided by a median septum.

ATROCOERULEUS. [L. *atro-*, terrible; *caeruleus*, azure]. A very deep blackish sky-blue.

ATROPHY (ATROPHIED). [Gr. α-, without; τροφη, nourishment]. The diminution and degeneration of a structure such as a limb, organ, tissue, etc.

ATROPURPUREUS. [L. *atro-*, terrible; *purpureus*, purple]. A dark purplish, nearly black.

ATROUS. [L. *ater*, black]. Jet black.

ATROVELUTINUS. [L. *atro-*, terrible; NL. *velutinus*, velvety]. Velvety black.

ATROVIRENS. [L. *atro-*, terrible; *virens*, green]. Dark green. Blackish-green.

ATTACHMENT DISK. The series of tiny zig zag lines or spots of silk that serve to anchor the draglines of spiders.

ATTENUATE. [L. *ad*, toward; *tenuis*, thin]. To become thin, slender, fine, extended, growing narrower, tapering.

ATTINGENT. [L. *attignus*, touching]. Touching, making contact.

ATTITUDE. [L. *aptus*, suited]. The posture or expression assumed by an organism.

ATTRACTANT. [L. *ad*, toward; *tractus*, draw]. A chemical substance causing positive behavioral responses. See also Pheromone.

-ATUS. L. suffix denoting possession of a quality or structure.

ATYPICAL. [Gr. α-, without; τυπος, shape]. Irregular; not conforming to type.

ATYPIDAE. [Gr. α- not; MedL. *typicalis*, typical]. The family of atypical tarantulas, or purse-web spiders (infraorder Mygalomorphae, superfamily Atypoidea), mainly from tropical South America. They are all less than 3 cm long, have two pairs of book lungs, six spinnerets, massive chelicerae and three tarsal claws. Their web consists of an open silk tube on the side of a tree; prey walking over the tube are attacked and impaled on the fangs and drawn in through the purse web. European species construct tubes on the ground.

ATYPOIDEA. [Gr. α- not; MedL. *typicalis*, typical]. In a recent classification, one of two superfamilies (or clades) of mygalomorph spiders (order Araneae, suborder Opisthothelae) in which abdominal segmentation, in the form of dorsal tergites, is evident. They live in subterranean burrows and use silk to construct many different types of burrow entrance. This superfamily includes the folding trapdoor spiders, atypical tarantulas or purse-web spiders, and dwarf tarantulas or sheet funnel-web spiders. The other superfamily being the Avicularioidea. Families: **Antrodiaetidae, Atypidae, Hexurellidae, Mecicobothriidae, Megahexuridae.**

AUDITORY ORGAN. [L. *audire*, to hear]. Any specialized structure capable of being stimulated by sound vibrations, such as tympanal organs and auditory hairs.

AURANTIACUS. [NL. *aurantiacus*, orange-colored]. Orange colored: a mixture of yellow and red. Chrome orange.

AURATE. [L. *auris*, ear]. Having ears or ear-like expansions.

AUREATE. [L. *aurum*, gold]. Golden yellow.

AUREOLATE. [L. *aureola*, of gold]. Having a diffused colored ring.

AUREOLE. [L. *aureola*, of gold]. A circlet of color that dissipates outwardly.

AUREOUS. [L. *aureolus*, golden]. Gold-colored.

AURICHALCEOUS. [L. *aurichalcum*, for orichalcum brass]. Brassy yellow. See also Orichalceous.

AURICLE (AURICULAR). [L. *auricula*, small ear]. In general, any ear-like appendage. An atrium or chamber of the heart.

AURICULAE. [L. *auriculae*, small ears]. paired extensions of the ventral posterior or lateral margins of the basal ring of cuticle to which the palps, chelicerae and hypostome are attached.

AURICULAR. [L. *auricula*, small ear]. Of the space or cavity surrounding the dorsal vessel.

AURICULAR VALVE. [L. *auricula*, small ear; *valva*, that which turns]. A mechanism that controls the flow of blood.

AURICULATE. [L. *auricula*, little ear]. Bearing an auricle or auricles.

AURITUS. [L. *auris*, ear]. Having two ear-like spots or appendages.

AUROREOUS. [L. *Aurora*, Roman goddess of dawn]. Red, like the aurora borealis.

AUSTRAL. [L. *australis*, southern]. Of the southern biogeographical region.

AUSTRALIAN FAUNAL REGION. [L. *australis*, southern; L. *Faunus*, god of the woods]. A zoogeographic region that encompasses Papua, Australia, New Zealand and the Pacific islands.

AUSTROCHILIDAE. [L. *australis*, southern; Gr. χειλος, a lip]. A family of small, eight-eyed spiders (infraorder Araneomorphae, superfamily Austrochiloidea) from the Andean forests of central and southern Chile and Argentina, and Tasmania.

AUSTROCHILOIDEA. [L. *australis*, southern; Gr. χειλος, a lip]. A superfamily of areneomorph spiders (order Araneae, suborder Opisthothelae). Families: **Austrochilidae, Gradungulidae.**

AUSTRODECIDAE. [L. *australis*, southern; *decus*; beauty / grace]. A small family of sea spiders (order Pantopoda, suborder Stiripasterida). May contain only *Austrodecus*, or include *Pantopipetta.*

AUTAPOMORPHIC CHARACTER. [Gr. αυτος, self; απο, away from; μορφη, shape]. A derived character unique to a particular species or other monophyletic group. See also Apomorphic Characters, Phylogenetic Classification, Plesiomorphic, Synapomorphic.

AUTECOLOGY (AUTOECOLOGY). [Gr. αυτος, self; οικος, house; λογος, discourse]. The study of individual species, as opposed to communities, in relation to the environment.

AUTOCHTHON. [Gr. αυτοχθων, aboriginal]. An indigenous species.

AUTOCHTHONOUS. [Gr. αυτος, self; χθων, the ground]. Aboriginal, indigenous, inherited or hereditary, native, originating within an organ (as in the continued beating of an excised heart).

AUTOECIOUS (MONOXENOUS). [Gr. αυτος, self; οικος, house]. Of a parasite that passes different stages of its life cycle in the same host.

AUTOECOLOGY. See Autecology.

AUTOGROOMING. Self-grooming.

AUTOINFECTION. [Gr. αυτος, self; L. *inficere*, to taint]. The direct re-infection of a host by the larval offspring of an existing parasite.

AUTOKINETIC. [Gr. αυτος, self; κινεω, move]. Moving by its own action.

AUTOLOGOUS. [Gr. αυτος, self; λογος, discourse]. Referring to something obtained or derived from an individual organism.

AUTOMICTIC PARTHENOGENESIS. [Gr. αυτος, self; μιξις, mingling; παρθενος, virgin, γενεσις, descent]. See Parthenogenesis.

AUTOMIMICRY. [Gr. αυτος, self; μιμητικος, imitative]. See Mimicry.

AUTONOMIC. [Gr. αυτονομος, independent]. Self-governing. Of the movements due to development or induced by internal stimuli, such as growth, unfolding, etc. See also Choronomic, Paratonic.

AUTOPARASITE. [Gr. αυτος, self; παρασιτος, parasite]. A parasite's parasite.

AUTOPARTHENOGENESIS. [Gr. αυτος, self; παρθενος, virgin; –γενσις, descent]. The chemical or physical stimulation necessary for the development of unfertilized eggs. See also Parthenogenesis.

AUTOPHAGY. [Gr. αυτος, self; φαγειν, to eat]. The eating of an appendage shed from the body by autotomy or other process.

AUTOPLOID. [Gr. αυτος, self; απλοος, onefold; ειδος, form]. See Ploidy.

AUTOPOLYPLOID. [Gr. αυτος, self; πολυς, many; απλοος, onefold; ειδος, form]. See Ploidy.

AUTOPOTAMIC. [Gr. αυτος, self; ποταμος, river]. Thriving in streams.

AUTOSPASY. [Gr. αυτος, self; σπαω, pluck off]. Self-amputation. The loss of appendages by breaking them at a predetermined locus of weakness when pulled by an outside force. This is frequent in spiders and other arachnids. See also Appendotomy, Autotomy, Autotilly.

AUTOTILLY. [Gr. αυτος, self; τιλλω, tear]. Self amputation; usually in response to predator attack, as seen in certain spiders (e.g. **Lycosidae, Agelenidae**). A preformed breakage plane between the coxa and trochanter allows breakage of the joint, by a muscular reflex, followed by rapid closure of the wound. See also Appendotomy, Autospasy, Autotomy.

AUTOTOKY. [Gr. αυτος, self; τοκος, birth]. The production of progeny by a single organism, including hermaphroditism and parthenogenesis.

AUTOTOMY (AUTOTOMIZE). [Gr. αυτος, self; τομη, cutting]. The ability to break off part of the body when threatened or seized by a predator. Severance always takes place at a pre-formed breakage plane. See also Appendotomy, Autospasy, Autotilly.

AUTOTOXIN. [Gr. αυτος, self; τοξικον, a poison]. Any substance produced by an organism that is toxic to itself.

AUTOXENOUS. [Gr. αυτος, self; ξενια, hospitality]. Of a parasite that passes through the different stages of its life cycle in the same host.

AUTUMNAL. [L. *autumnus*, autumn]. In the autumn. One of the terms for the six part division of the year commonly used in ecology, especially with reference to terrestrial and fresh-water communities. The six parts are: prevernal (early spring), vernal (late spring), aestival (early summer), serotinal (late summer), autumnal (autumn) and hibernal (winter).

AUXESIS. [Gr. αυξησις, growth]. Growth in size due to an increase in cell volume without cell division.

AUXILARY STYLETS (INNER INFRACAPITULAR STYLETS). [L. *auxilium*, assistance; *stylus*, pricker]. In the Eriophyoidea: a pair of stylets in the bundle of 7-9 stylets.

av 1-3. In the Mesostigmata: the designations for the setae on the anterior ventral surface of a leg or palp segment. See Evans Leg Chaetotactic System.

AVERSIVE. [L. *avertere*, to avert]. Stimuli which evoke a fear and avoidance behavioral response.

AVESICULATE. [Gr. α-, without; L. *vesicula*, small bladder]. Of a genital system lacking seminal vesicles.

AVICULAR. [L. *avicula*, little bird]. Beak-like.

AVICULARIOIDEA. [L. *avicula*, little bird]. In a recent classification, one of two superfamilies (or clades) of mygalomorph spiders (order Araneae, suborder Opisthothelae) in which the vestiges of abdominal segmentation, in the form of dorsal tergites, are lacking. The other superfamily being Atypoidea. Twenty-six families.

AVICULOID. [L. *avicula*, little bird; Gr. ειδος, form]. Having wing-like projections.

AXIAL. [L. *axis*, axle]. Of an axis.

AXIS. [L. *axis*, axle]. The central line of symmetry of an organ or organism.

AZURE. [L. *azure*, blue]. Clear sky-blue.

AZYGOUS/AZYGOS. [Gr. α-, without; ζυγον, yoke]. Of an unpaired structure such as a muscle, artery, etc.

B

BACCIFORM (BACCATE). [L. *bacca*, berry, *forma*, shape]. Berry-shaped.

BACILLARY. [L. *bacillum*, little stick]. Rod-shaped, or consisting of rod-shaped structures.

BACILLARY LAYER. [L. *bacillum*, little stick]. See Brush Border.

BACILLIFORM. [L. *bacillum*, little stick; *forma*, shape]. Rod-shaped.

BACK. [AS. *bæc*, back, backwards, behind]. The dorsal or upper surface.

BACULIFORM. [L. *baculum*, a staff; *forma*, shape]. Rod-shaped.

BADIUS. [L. *badius*, reddish-brown]. Liver-brown: lighter than castaneous.

BALANOID. [Gr. βαλανος, acorn; ειδος, form]. Acorn-shaped.

BALLOONING. A method of transportation/dispersal used by the spiderlings of many species as well as the adults of some of the smaller species. The spider climbs to the top of a twig or blade of grass and releases a strand of silk. As soon as the air currents are sufficient to produce a tug on the strand the spider releases its grip on the perch and is carried away.

Ballooning spiders have landed on ships several hundred kilometers off-shore and have been collected by airplanes at 10,000 ft. However, desiccation and lack of food would make successful long distance travel unlikely.

BAND. [AS. *bindan*, band]. A transverse marking broader than a line.

BARAESTHESIA. [Gr. βαρος, weight; αισθησις, sensation]. The sensation of pressure.

BARB. [L. *barba*, beard]. A hooked hair-like bristle. A spine with teeth pointing backward.

BARBATE, BARBATED (BRUSH-LIKE). [L. *barbatus*, bearded]. Bearded. Brush-like.

BARBELLATE. [L. *barba*, beard]. Having stiff, hooked bristles.

BAROCEPTOR, BARORECEPTOR. [Gr. βαρος, pressure; L. *capere*, to take]. An organ that perceives changes in pressure.

BAROGNOSIS. [Gr. βαρος, pressure; γνωσις, recognizing]. The ability to detect changes in pressure.

BAROPHILIC. [Gr. βαρος, pressure; φιλος, loving]. Living in (or preferring) high pressure environments - such as those found in the depths of the oceans.

BAROTAXIS. [Gr. βαρος, pressure; ταξις, a disposition]. The reaction of an organism to a pressure stimulus.

BAROTROPISM. [Gr. βαρος, pressure; τροπη, turning]. An orientation response to a pressure stimulus.

BARYCHELIDAE. [Gr. βαρυς, heavy, χηλη, claw]. The family of brushed trapdoor spiders (infraorder Mygalomorphae, superfamily Avicularioidea) from the tropics worldwide. They have a digging rake on the front surface of their chelicerae and some species can stridulate. Previously in the now abandoned monospecific superfamily Barycheloidea.

BASAD. [Gr. βασις, base; L. *ad*, towards]. Towards the base.

BASAL. [Gr. βασις, base]. At the base of, or forming the basis upon which something rests.

BASAL ARTICLE. [L. *basis*, base; *articulus*, a part]. In arachnids: the most basal of the three cheliceral segments. They are often obscure or absent in the Acariformes.

BASAL DIVISION. [L. *basis*, base]. The part of the bulb of the male palpus. It comprises the subtegulum and associated structures.

BASE. [L. *basis*, base]. The part of any appendage that is nearest the body. The portion of the thorax that is nearest the abdomen.

BASIFEMORAL RING. [L. *basis*, base; *femur*, thigh]. In ticks and mites: the suture in the basal segment of the femur, that separates the basifemur and telofemur of the leg.

BASIFEMUR. [L. *basis*, base; *femur*, thigh]. In ticks and mites: the proximal segment of the femur - between the trochanter and the telofemur.

BASILAR. [L. *basis*, base]. Related to or situated at the base.

BASILAR PIECE. [L. *basis*, base]. In the ambulacrum of the Mesostigmata: the median internal structure with which the claws articulate.

BASILAR SCLERITE. [Gr. βασις, base; σκληρος, hard]. In some Prostigmata: a sclerotized structure which articulates with the movable cheliceral digit and to which the cheliceral muscles are attached. It is analogous to the sclerotized node in some Uropodina.

BASIS. [L. *basis*, base]. A general term for the base of any appendage.

BASIS CAPITULUM (BASIS GNATHOSOMATICA, KRAGEN). [L. *basis*, base; *capitulum*, a little head / Gr. γναθος, jaw; σωμα, body]. The sclerotized ring around the base of the capitulum in mesostigmatans and ticks. It is derived from the dorsal and ventral extensions of the palpcoxae. It bears the corniculi, internal malae, and hypostomal and palpcoxal setae ventrally and the gnathotectum (epistome) dorsally.

BASISCOPIC. [Gr. βασις, base; σκοπεω, look]. Facing towards the base.

BASITARSUS. [Gr. βασις, base; ταρσος, sole of the foot]. The metatarsus: the basal subdivision of the leg tarsus.

BASK. To hold the body in a position directly exposed to the sun.

BATATIFORM. [L. *batata*, sweet potato; *forma*, shape]. Resembling the shape of a sweet potato.

BATESIAN MIMICRY. [W. H. *Bates*, English naturalist]. See Mimicry.

BATHMOTROPIC. [Gr. βαθμος, degree; τρωπαω, a change]. Of something that affects the degree of excitability of a tissue (such as muscle).

BATHYAESTHESIA. [Gr. βαθυς, deep; αισθησις, perception]. The perception of stimuli deep within the body.

BDELLIDAE. [Gr. βδελλα, leech]. The family of snout-mites (order Trombidiformes, suborder Prostigmata). They are free-living, predaceous and capture their prey with a stringy material exuded from the mouth parts. They have a single pair of spiracles located anteriorly near the mouth parts.

BDELLOIDEA. [Gr. βδελλα, leech; ειδος, shape]. A superfamily of mites (suborder Prostigmata, infraorder Eupodina). Families: **Bdellidae, Cunaxidae**.

BELL-SHAPED. Campanulate.

BELONOID. [Gr. βελονη, needle; ειδος, form]. Needle-shaped.

BELT TRANSECT. A strip marked out across a habitat and within which species are recorded to assess their distribution and abundance.

BEMMERIDAE. [deric.uncert.]. A family of African and Asian mygalomorph spiders (infraorder Mygalomorphae, superfamily Avicularioidea)

BENTHOPOTAMOUS. [Gr. βενθος, depths of the sea; ποταμος, river]. Living on a river bed.

BESOMIFORM. [AS. *besma*, broom; L. *forma*, shape]. Broom shaped.

BI-. L. prefix, *bis*; two/twice.

BIACUMINATE. [L. *bis*, twice; *acumen*, point]. Having two tapering points.

BIANGULAR. [L. *bis*, two; *angulus*, corner]. Having two angles or double keeled.

BIANTIDAE. [*Biantes*, Myth. son of Parthenopaeus, one of the 'Seven Against Thebes']. A family of harvestmen or daddy longlegs (suborder Laniatores, superfamily Samooidea).

BIARCUATE. [L. bis, two; *arcuatus*, bent like a bow]. Twice curved.

BIARTICULATE (DIARTICULAR). [L. *bis*, twice; *articulus*, joint]. Double, or two-jointed.

BIAXIAL. [L. *bis*, two; axis, axle]. Having two axes. Permitting movement in two planes.

BICANALICULATE. [L. *bis*, two; *canalis*, a channel]. Having two channels or grooves.

BICARINATE. [L. *bis*, two; *carina*, keel]. Having two carinae or keel-like projections.

BICENTRIC. [L. *bis*, twice; Gr. κεντρον, center]. Having two centers of evolution or distribution.

BICOLOURED. [L. *bis*, two; *color*, color/hue]. With two colors that contrast to some extent.

BICONCAVE. [L. *bis*, two; *concavus*, hollow or arched inward]. Being concave on both sides. Amphicoelous. See also Amphicyrtic.

BICONDYLIC. See Dicondylar.

BICONIC. [L. *bis*, two; Gr. κονος, cone]. Being formed like two cones joined base to base.

BICONJUGATE. [L. *bis*, twice; *coniugare*, to bind together]. Having two similar sets of pairs.

BICONVEX. [L. *bis*, two; *convexus*, arched outward]. Being convex on opposite sides. Lens-shaped. See also Amphicyrtic, Amphicoelous.

BICORN. [L. *bis*, two; *cornu*, horn]. Bearing two horns. Crescent-like.

BICORNUTE. [L. *bis*, twice; *cornutus*, horned]. With two horn-like processes.

BICUSPIDATE. [L. *bis*, two; *cuspidatus*, pointed]. Being double pointed; having two cusps or points.

BIDACTYL. [L. *bis*, two; Gr. δακτυλος, finger]. An appendage, ambulacrum, apotele or claw with two lateral ungues. See also Heterodactyl, Homodactyl, Monodactyl, Tridactyl.

BIDENTATE (BIDENTAL). [L. *bis*, twice; *dens*, tooth]. Having two teeth, or two tooth-like structures.

BIDENTICULATE. [L. *bis*, twice; *denticulum*, little tooth]. Having two small tooth-like processes - as on some scales.

BIDESMATIC. [L. *bis*, two; Gr. δεσμος, bond]. Pertaining to two tendons attached at the base of the distal segment of an appendage; a eudesmatic articulation.

BIDISCOIDAL. [L. *bis*, two; Gr. δισκος, circular plate; ειδος, form]. Having two disc-shaped parts.

BIDIVERTICULATE. [L. *bis*, two; *devertere*, to turn away]. Having two diverticula.

BIEMARGINATE. [L. *bis*, two; *emarginatus*, notched at the apex]. Having two notches on the border or edge.

BIENNIAL. [L. *bis*, two; *annus*, year]. Occurring once every two years.

BIFACIAL. [L. *bis*, twice; *facies*, face]. Having similar opposite surfaces.

BIFARIOUS. [L. *bis*, two; *fariam*, in rows]. Being arranged in two rows, on either side of an axis. Being oriented or pointed in opposite directions.

BIFASCIATE. [L. *bis*, two; *fascia*, band]. With two broad well defined bands or fascia.

BIFID. [L. *bis*, twice; *findere*, to split]. Divided almost to the midline. Divided into two branches, arms, or prongs.

BIFILAR. [L. *bis*, two; *filum*, thread]. Having two filaments, threads, or fibers.

BIFLABELLATE. [L. *bis*, twice; *flabellum*, fan]. Having two fan-shaped structures. Being doubly flabellate (of pectinate antennae with long processes).

BIFLAGELLATE. [L. *bis*, twice; *flagellum*, whip]. Having two flagella. With two whip-like processes.

BIFLEX. [L. *bis*, twice; *flectere*, to bend]. Curved twice.

BIFOLLICULAR. [L. *bis*, two; *folliculus*, small sac]. Having two follicles.

BIFORATE. [L. *biforis*, having two openings]. Having two pores.

BIFORM. [L. *bis*, two; *forma*, shape]. Having two forms, or combining characteristics of two forms.

BIFURCATE. [L. *bis*, twice; *furca*, fork]. Divided into two forks, branches or peaks.

BIGEMINAL. [L. *bis*, twice; *geminus*, double]. Having some structure arranged in double pairs.

BIGUTTATE. [L. *bis*, two; *gutta*, drop]. Having two drop-like spots.

BIJUGATE. [L. *bis*, two; *jugum*, yolk]. Being yoked two together.

BIJUGUM. [L. *bis*, two; *jugum*, yoke]. In two pairs.

BILAMELLAR. [L. *bis*, twice; *lamella*, plate]. Formed from two plates or lamellae.

BILAMINAR. [L. *bis*, twice; *lamina*, thin plate]. Having two plate-like layers.

BILATERAL. [L. *bis*, two; *latus*, side]. Having two equal or symmetrical sides.

BILATERALLY SYMMETRICAL. Capable of being halved in one plane in such a way that the two halves are approximately mirror-images of each other. Usually this plane lies anterioposteriorly and dorsoventrally, thus separating right and left halves. The majority of free-living animals are bilaterally symmetrical.

BILIARY VESSELS. [L. *bilis*, gall/bile]. See Malpighian Tubules.

BILINEATE. [L. *bis*, two; *lineatus*, of a line]. Marked with two lines.

BILOBATE (BILOBED). [L. *bis*, twice; Gr. λοβος, (ear) lobe]. Having two lobes.

BILOCULAR. [L. bis, two; *loculus*, compartment]. Divided into two cells, chambers, compartments or loculi.

BIMACULTE. [L. *bis*, twice; *macula*, spot]. Having, or being marked with two spots.

BIMARGINATE. [L. *bis*, two; *margo*, border]. Having two margins.

BIMUSCULAR. [L. *bis*, two; *musculus*, muscle]. Having two muscles.

BINARY NOMENCLATURE. See Nomenclature.

BINATE. [L. *bini*, pair]. Doubled. Growing in pairs.

BINOCULAR. [L. *bini*, pair; *oculus*, eye]. Having two eyes (see **Caponiidae**).

BINODULOSE. [L. *bis*, two; *nodulus*, little knot]. Having two nodes, knobs, or swellings of small size.

BINOMEN. [L. *bis*, twice; *nomen*, name]. The two-word scientific designation of a species. The first name is the generic name (Genus) and the second the specific epithet. See Nomenclature.

BINOMIAL NOMENCLATURE. [L. *bis*, twice; *nomen*, name; *nomen*, name; *calare*, to call]. See Nomenclature.

BINOTATE. [L. *bis*, two; *nota*, mark]. Having two rounded spots.

BINUS. [L. *binus*, in pairs]. Paired. Doubled.

BIOCELLATE. [L. *bis*, twice; *ocellus*, little eye]. Having two ocelli.

BIOCOEN. [Gr. βιος, life; κοινος, common]. All of the living components of an environment.

BIOCOENOSE (BIOCENOSE). [Gr. βιος, life; κοινος, in common]. A community of organisms, both plants and animals, living together in a particular habitat or 'biotype'. The physical environment is not included but the biocoenose and the biotype form a natural unit - the 'biocoenose-biotype'. This is essentially the same as an 'ecosystem' to most biologists.

BIOGENOUS. [Gr. βιος, life; γενος, offspring]. Inhabiting another living organism, i.e. a parasite.

BIOGEOCOENOSIS. [Gr. βιος, life; γε, earth; κοινος, in common]. A community of organisms in relation to their particular habitat.

BIOGEOGRAPHICAL BARRIER. [Gr. βιος, life; γεο-, the earth; γραφιεν, to sketch]. A barrier that prevents the migration of species. Such barriers may be climatic, or consist of geographical features.

BIOGEOGRAPHICAL PROVINCE. [Gr. βιος, life; γεο-, the earth; γραφιεν, to sketch]. A biological subdivision of the earth's surface, considering both fauna and flora, and usually based on taxonomic as opposed to ecological criteria.

BIOGEOGRAPHICAL REGION. [Gr. βιος, life; γεο-, the earth; γραφιεν, to sketch]. Any geographical region characterized by a distinctive flora and or fauna. Biogeographical regions are composed of groups of biogeographical provinces - of which the following are generally recognized; Antarctic, Australasian, Ethiopian, Nearctic, Neotropical, Oceanian, Oriental and Palearctic.

BIOGEOGRAPHY. [Gr. βιος, life; γεο-, the earth; γραφιεν, to sketch]. The study of the geographic distribution of plants (phytogeography) and animals (zoogeography).

BIOLOGICAL CLOCKS. [Gr. βιος, life; λογος, discourse]. See Circadian Rhythms.

BIOLOGICAL CONTROL. [Gr. βιος, life; λογος, discourse]. The control of pests and parasites by introducing their natural enemies.

BIOLOGICAL RACE. [Gr. βιος, life; λογος, discourse]. Variants of a species that are alike morphologically but differ in some physiological aspect. For example, a parasite with some particular host requirement or a free-living organism with a particular environmental requirement. See also Race.

BIOME. [Gr. βιος, life]. A major community of plants and animals, characterized by a particular vegetation type and occupying a large geographical area.

BIOMORPHOTIC. [Gr. βιος, life; μορφη, form]. Concerning the development or change of form of a living organism by the formation of tissues.

BION (BIONT). [Gr. βιον, living]. A living individual.

BIONOMIC STRATEGY. [Gr. βιος, life; νομος, law; στρατηγια, general-ship]. The characteristic features of an organism, or population, that confer maximum fitness to the organism, or population, in its environment.

BIONOMICS. [Gr. βιος, life; νομος, law]. The study of an organism in relation to its total environment - animate and inanimate.

BIOPHAGOUS. [Gr. βιος, life; φαγειν, to eat]. Of an organism that feeds upon other living organisms.

BIORYTHMS. See Circadian Rhythms.

BIOSERIES. [Gr. βιος, life, L. *series*, row]. A continuation of changes in any single heritable character.

BIOSPELEOLOGY. [Gr. βιος, life; σπηλαιον, cave; λογος, discourse]. The study of cave-dwelling organisms.

BIOSPHERE. [Gr. βιος, life; σφαιρη, a globe]. That part of the earth and its atmosphere that is inhabited by living organisms.

BIOSTASIS. [Gr. βιος, life; στασις, a standing]. The ability of an organism to tolerate environmental change without producing adaptive changes.

BIOSYSTEM. See Ecosystem.

BIOSYSTEMATICS. [Gr. βιος, life; συστημα, an assembly]. The aspect of classification concerned with the variation and evolution of species.

BIOTA. [Gr. βιος, life]. All the flora and fauna occurring within a certain area.

BIOTIC. [Gr. βιωτικος, pertaining to life]. Of or pertaining to life.

BIOTIC COMMUNITY. [Gr. βιωτικος, pertaining to life; L. *communis*, common]. The faunal and floral community as a whole.

BIOTIC ENVIRONMENT. [Gr. βιωτικος, pertaining to life]. The fraction of an organism's environment that results from its interactions with other organisms.

BIOTICALLY SYMPATRIC. [Gr. βιωτικος, pertaining to life; συν, with; πατρη, native land]. Of populations that occupy the same habitat within the same geographical area.

BIOTOPE. [Gr. βιος, life; τοπος, place]. 1. An area that is uniform in its main climatic, soil and biotic conditions. 2. An ecological niche with suitable conditions for certain fauna and flora.

BIOTOPOGRAPHIC UNIT. [Gr. βιος, life; τοπος, a place; γραφω, to sketch]. 1. A small habitat with a distinctive form, e.g. an ant hill. 2. A distinctive micro-environment such as a windward slope, a shaded slope, etc.

BIOTROPHIC. [Gr. βιος, life; ρτοφη, nourishment]. Of a parasite obtaining nourishment from the tissue of a living host.

BIOTYPE. [Gr. βιος, life; τυπος, pattern]. 1. A naturally occurring group of individuals having the same genetic composition. 2. A physiological race, i.e. the existence within a species of a particular genetically different race or form which, although structurally indistinguishable, may show differences in biochemical or pathogenic characters.

BIPARASITIC. [L. *bis*, two; Gr. παρασιτος, one who eats at the table of another]. Being a parasite upon or in a parasite.

BIPARENTAL. [L. *bis*, two; *parentalis*, parent]. Pertaining to or derived from two parents.

BIPARENTAL INHERITANCE. [L. *bis*, twice]. The inheritance of characteristics from two parents.

BIPARIETAL. [L. *bis*, two; *paries*, wall]. Provided with two paries.

BIPARTITE. [L. *bis*, two; *partitus*, divided]. Having two distinct parts; bifid.

BIPECTINATE. [L. *bis*, twice; *pecten*, comb]. Having two margins toothed like a comb.

BIPECTUNCULATE. [L. *bis*, two; *pectunculus*, small scallop]. Minutely pectinate.

BIPELTATE. [L. *bis*, twice; *pelta*, shield]. Having, or consisting of, two shield-like structures.

BIPENNATE (BIPENNIFORM). [L. *bis*, two; *penna*, feather]. Twice pinnate.

BIPUPILLATE. [L. *bis*, two; *pupilla*, pupil of the eye]. Having two ocelli or spots that resemble two pupils.

BIRAMOUS. [L. *bis*, twice; *ramus*, branch]. Two-forked or two-branched.

BIRD SPIDERS. See **Theraphosidae**.

BISEPTATE. [L. *bis*, two; *septum*, partition]. Having two partitions.

BISERIAL (BISERIATE). [L. *bis*, twice; *series*, row]. Arranged in two rows, or subdivided into two series.

BISERRATE. [L. *bis*, two; *serra*, saw]. Having two notched or saw-teeth.

BISETOSE. [L. *bis*, two; *seta*, bristle]. Having two bristle-like appendages.

BISINUATE. [L. *bis*, two; *sinuare*, to bend]. Twice winding or bending. Having two sinuations or notches.

BISTRATE. [L. *bis*, two; *stratum*, layer]. Having two layers of tissues.

BISULCATE. [L. *bis*, twice; *sulcus*, groove]. Having two grooves.

BITUBERCULATE. [L. *bis*, two; *tuberculum*, swelling]. Having two tubercles or swellings.

BITYPIC. [L. *bis*, twice; Gr. τυπος, pattern]. Of a taxon comprising only two immediately subordinate principal taxa. E.g. a family comprised of two genera.

BIUNCINATE. [L. *bis*, two; *uncus*, hook]. Having two hooks.

BIVALVED. [L. *bis*, two; *valvae*, folding doors]. With two longitudinal plates or valve-like coverings.

BIVITTATE. [L. *bis*, two; *vitta*, band]. Having two broad longitudinal stripes or vittae.

BIVOLTINE. [L. *bis*, twice; It. *volta*, time]. Having two generations or broods in one year. See also Voltine.

BLACK WIDOW SPIDER. *Latrodectus mactans*. See **Theridiidae**.

BLADDER. [AS. *blaedre*, bladder]. A membranous or musculo-membranous bag.

BLADE. [AS. *blaed*, leaf]. Any elongate, flattened, usually stiff structure shaped like a leaf, sword or knife.

BLATTISOCIIDAE. [L. *blatta*, a cockroach; *socius*, a companion]. A small family of mites (infraorder Gamasina, superfamily Phytoseioidea). Some members of this family are considered by some authorities to be better placed in the family **Acsidae**.

BLENNOGENOUS. [Gr. βλεννυς, slime; γενναω, to produce]. Mucus producing.

BLENNOID. [Gr. βλεννυς, slime; ειδος, form]. Resembling mucus.

BLISTER MITES. Mites of the superfamily Eriophyoidea that produce blister-like galls on leaves. They typically produce flattened, subcircular swellings of the leaf surface over a cavity in the leaf lamina.

BLOOD. [AS. *blod*, blood]. A fluid contained in vessels or the spaces within endothelial walls and that is circulated through the animal by muscular activity of the vessels or specialized parts of them (heart). It usually contains respiratory pigments (haemoglobin or haemocyanin) and transports oxygen, nutritional substances, hormones, waste products, etc. Blood is present in the Annelida, Arthropoda, Brachiopoda, Chordata, Mollusca, Nemertea and Phoronida.

BLOOD SINUS. [AS. *blod*, blood; L. *sinus*, curve]. A large blood-filled cavity or enormously expanded vein.

BLOOD VESSEL. [AS. *blod*, blood; LL. *vascellum*, small vase or urn]. Any tube through which blood flows.

BLOOM. [ON. *Blomi*, flower/blossom]. A fine violet dusting similar to that on plums. See Pruinous.

BLOTCH. [OF. *bloch*, a clod of earth]. A large irregular spot or marking.

BLUMENTHAL'S TARSAL ORGANS. [*Heinz Blumenthal*, German Arachnologist]. Sense organs, which are usually pit-like, on the dorsal surface of a spider's tarsi.

BOAT-SHAPED. See Navicular, Scaphoid.

BOCHICIDAE. [*Bochica*, Muisca (from central Andean highlands) religious figure]. A family of false scorpions (suborder Iocheirata, superfamily Neobisioidea) distributed throughout the Americas as well as the Iberian Peninsula. Uniquely, the are exactly 12 trichobothria on each claw.

BODY WALL. The integument, the outer layer of many invertebrates, comprising the epidermis (hypodermis) and the cuticle.

BOMBOUS. [Fr. *bombe*, convex]. A curved or rounded surface. Blister-like.

BOOK GILL. A type of gill structure found in the Chelicerates and derived from pairs of modified appendages. They are flap-like and membranous, each pair being fused along the mid-line. The underside is formed into many leaf-like folds which provide the surface for gaseous exchange and each gill may contain approximately 150 of these lamellae, the arrangement of which gives the gill its name.

BOOK LUNG COVER. The branchial operculum: a plate covering the book lung.

BOOK LUNGS. Gas exchange organs found in some arachnids - probably a modification of book gills and an adaptation associated with the migration of the arachnids to a terrestrial environment. Book lungs occur in pairs, are situated on the ventral side of the abdomen (scorpions may have up to four pairs) and consist of a sclerotised (hardened) invagination of the ventral abdominal wall. The ventral side of this invagination is folded into a series of lamellae which are supported and separated by cross bars so that air can circulate freely. The other (dorsal) side of the invagination forms a chamber (atrium) that is continuous with the inter-lamellar spaces and that opens externally through a spiracle. There may be some ventilation due to contraction of the atrium by muscles attached to the dorsal wall, but most gas exchange is by diffusion. See also Tracheal Spiracle.

BOREAL. [L. *boreas*, north wind]. The northern biogeographical region; the Holarctic except the Sonoran (southern north America including northern Mexico).

BOREOPHTHALMI. [L. *boreas*, northern; Gr. οφθαλμος, eye]. An infraorder of harvestmen or daddy long legs (order Opiliones, suborder Cyphophthalmi). Families: **Sironidae**, **Stylocellidae**.

BOSS. [Fr. *bosse*, hump]. Any protuberant part, prominence or swelling. In spiders: a smooth lateral prominence at the base of a chelicera.

BOSSELATED. [Fr. *bosse*, hump]. Being composed of or covered with small protuberances.

BOTHRIDIAL SETA. [Gr. βοθρος, trench; -ιδιον, dim. suf.]. Variously shaped seta inserted into a bothridium.

BOTHRIDIAL SENSILLUM. [Gr. βοθρος, trench; -ιδιον, dim. suf.; L. dim. of *sensus*, sense]. An elaborately modified seta set in a cup-like base. They may be filiform, ciliate, pectinate or variously thickened or clubbed. See also Trichobothrium.

BOTHRIDIUM (BOTHRIUM). [Gr. βοθρος, trench; -ιδιον, dim. suf.]. A chitinous cavity or projecting cup in which a bothridial seta is inserted. See also Trichobothrium.

BOTHRIURIDAE. [Gr. βοθρος, trench; ουρα, tail]. A large family of scorpions (order Scorpiones, superfamily Scorpionoidea) from temperate and subtropical habitats in the southern hemisphere. *Cercophonius* has recently been discovered in the Himalayas. Uniquely, the normally pentagonal sternum is several times broader than long and consists of two transverse bars (except *Liposoma* and *Tehuankea*).

BOTRYOIDAL. [Gr. βοτρυς, bunch of grapes; ειδος, form]. In the form of a bunch or cluster of grapes.

BOTTLE-SHAPED. See Ampulla, Ampulliform, Lageniform.

BOTULIFORM. [L. *botulum*, sausage; *forma*, shape]. Sausage-shaped.

BOW-LIKE. See Arc, Arcuate.

BOX MITES. Oribatid mites that can withdraw their legs between two body regions like a penknife being closed or a box being closed. See Dichoidy, Ptychoidy, Trichoidy.

BRACHYCHTHONIOIDEA. [Gr. βραχυς, short; χθων, the ground]. A monotypic superfamily of mites (suborder Oribatida, infraorder Enarthronota). Family: **Brachychthoniidae.**

BRACHYPODOUS. [Gr. βραχυς, short; –πους, foot]. With short legs.

BRACHYPYLINA. [Gr. βραχυς, short: πυλη, gate]. An infraorder of beetle mites or armored mites (order Sarcoptiformes, suborder Oribatida) that is divided into two sections; Poronoticae (10 superfamilies, 33 families) and Pycnonoticae (23 superfamilies and 71 families).

BRACHYPYLINE. [Gr. βραχυς, short: πυλη, gate]. Having separate genital and anal plates surrounded by a large ventral plate which is composed of ag-genital and adanal elements. See also Macropyline.

BRACHYTRACHEA. [Gr. βραχυς, short; LL. *trachia*, windpipe]. In ticks and mites: an elongate, sac-like structure, sometimes branched, that functions in respiration.

BRADYAUXESIS. [Gr. βραδυς, slow; αυξη, growth]. A relatively slow growth rate. See also Heterauxesis, Isauxesis, Tachyauxesis.

BRAIN. [AS. *braegen*, brain]. The anterior part of the central nervous system, which is present in almost all bilaterally symmetrical animals. Generally it is enlarged in connection with the sense organs that are usually accumulated in the head region. To a varying degree it co-ordinates the actions of the whole body. In arachnids it consists of two cerebral ganglia connected to a pair of subesophageal ganglia by means of a circumesophageal commissure (linkage).

BRANCHED. See Ramify.

BRANCHIAL OPERCULUM (EPIGASTRIC PLATE). [L. *branchia*, gill; *operculum*, lid]. A sclerotized, hairless plate covering the book lung.

BREVIPED. [L. *brevis*, short; *pes*, foot]. Short-legged.

BREVIS. [L. *brevis*, short]. Short.

BRIDGING HOST. An intermediate host that allows a parasite to go to a previously unsuitable host.

BRISTLE. [AS. *byrst*, hair]. Any stiff coarse hairs or hair-like structures.

BROAD MITE (TEA MITE). *Polyphagotarsonemus latus* (Trombidiformes: **Tarsonemidae**), a very small plant parasite (100 - 200 μm long), that lives on the underside of leaves, tender stems, fruits, flower peduncles and flowers. Their feeding produces necrosis and deformation.

BROOD POUCH (BROOD SPOT). A pouch on the body where eggs are retained and hatched.

BROOM SHAPED. Besomiform.

BROTICOLOUS. [Gr. βροτος, a man; L. *colere*, to inhabit]. Living in close proximity to man.

BROTOCHOROUS. [Gr. βροτος, a man; χωρεω, to spread abroad]. Being dispersed by man.

BRUSH BORDER. [OE. *brusche*, brushwood]. A free epithelial surface bearing numerous microvilli, thus greatly increasing the surface area of a membrane. Brush borders may be found lining the mid-gut and Malpighian tubules of arachnids and insects.

BRUSTSTIELE. Urstigma. See Claparède's Organ.

BRYOPHILOUS. [Gr. βρυον, moss; φιλος, loving]. Thriving in a mossy environment.

BUCCAL CONE. [L. *bucca*, cheek, Gr. κωνος, cone]. In tics and mites: that portion of the mouth parts composed of hypostome and labrum.

BUCCAL FISSURE. [L. *bucca*, cheek, *fissura*, crack]. The mouth opening.

BUD MITE. Mites of the superfamily Eriophyoidea that create galls on plant buds. E.g. the Filbert big bud mites *Phytoptus avellanae* (**Phytoptidae**), *Cecidophyopsis Vermiformis* (**Eriophyidae**).

BULB. [L. *bulbus*, bulb/onion]. Any hollow globose organ. Genital Bulb = Palpal Organ. The genital structure of the male spider, which contains the sperm reservoir and is attached to the palpal tarsus. Occasionally it is fused to the tarsus, as in some **Oonopidae**.

BURSA (pl. **BURSAE**). [L. *bursa*, purse]. Any pouch or sac, a sac-like cavity. Pl. Bursae.

BURSA COPULATRIX. [L. *bursa*, pouch; *copulare*, to couple]. The female copulatory pouch. That region of the female genitalia that receives the sperm during copulation.

BURSIFORM. [L. *bursa*, purse; *forma*, shape]. Formed like a purse.

BUTHIDAE. [Gr. βυθιζω, to ruin men (metaph.), or Gr. βους, ox, hence 'ox-stinger' in ref to its powerful toxin]. A large family of 'fat-tailed', or 'bark' scorpions (order Scorpiones, superfamily Buthoidea) with a wide distribution in warmer climates (except New Zealand). Most have between two and five pairs of eyes. Some are notorious for their strong neurotoxin, and human fatalities are known.

BUTHOIDEA. [Gr. βυθιζω, to ruin men (metaph.), or Gr. βους, ox, hence 'ox-stinger' in ref to its powerful toxin]. A superfamily of thick-tailed or fat-tailed scorpions (subclass Arachnida, order Scorpiones). Families: †**Archaeobuthidae**, **Buthidae** (about 80 genera, 800 species), **Microcharmidae**, †**Palaeoburmesebuthidae**, †**Protobuthidae**.

BYSSACEOUS. [Gr. βυσσος, fine flax; L. *-aceous*, of the nature of]. Being composed of fine filaments.

BYSSOID. [Gr. βυσσος, fine flax; ειδος, form]. Resembling a byssus, or formed from fine threads.

C

c. In the Acariformes: a designation used for setae on segment C. See Grandjean System.

C. In the Acariformes: a designation used for the anterior region of the hysterosoma. See Grandjean System.

CADDOIDEA. [*Caddo*, North American indigenous culture]. A monotypic superfamily of small harvestmen (order Opiliones, suborder Eupnoi). They have a wide distribution, ranging from South Africa to Chile, North America, Australia, Japan and the Kuril Islands. Family: **Caddidae**.

CAECAL. [L. *caecus*, blind]. Ending without an outlet; as of a stomach in which the cardiac region is extended into a blind sac.

CAECULOIDEA. [L. *caecus*, blind]. A monotypic superfamily of mites (suborder Prostigmata, infraorder Anystina). Family: **Caeculidae**.

CAECUM (COECUM, CECUM). [L. *caecus*, blind]. A blind-ending branch (or diverticulum) of the gut or any other hollow organ.

CAELATE. [L. *cael*, heaven/sky/space]. A surface with plane elevations of varying forms.

CAENODYNAMISM. [Gr. καινος, new; δυναμις, power]. The replacement of complex functions with simpler ones.

CAENOGAEA (CAINOGEA). [Gr. καινος, recent; γαια, earth]. The zoogeographical region which includes the Nearctic, the Palearctic and the Oriental regions.

CAENOGENETIC (CAENOGENESIS). [Gr. καινος, recent; γενεσις, origin]. 1. Of recent origin. 2. Of those features of an embryo or larva that are particularly suited to the needs of the young but which disappear in the adult.

CAENOMORPHISM. [Gr. καινος, new; μορφη, shape]. The change in living organisms from complex forms to simpler ones.

CAERULESCENT. [L. caeruleus, azure]. With a tinge of sky-blue.

CAERULEUS (COERULEUS). [L. caeruleus, azure]. Light sky-blue.

CAESIUS (CAEOUS, CESIOUS). [L. caesius; bluish-grey]. A pale dull blue-grey.

CAESPITICOLOUS. [L. caespitis, a turf; colere, to inhabit]. Living in areas of pasture or grassy turf.

CAINOZOIC. See Cenozoic.

CALAMISTRUM, CALAMISTRA. [L. calamistrum, curling iron]. On cribellate spiders: a row of curved hairs on the metatarsus IV of the hind legs, which are used to comb out the silk produced by the cribellum.

CALCAR. [L. calcar, spur]. A spur-like projection.

CALCARATE, CALCARATUS. [L. calcar, spur]. Having a movable spur or spine-like process.

CALCARIFORM. [L. calcar, spur; forma, shape]. Spur-like.

CALCEOLATE (CALCEOLIFORM, CALCEIFORM). [L. calceus, shoe]. Slipper-shaped; oblong with a coarctate middle.

CALCITRONIDAE. [L. calcitrare, kick with the heel]. An extinct family of arachnids (order Schizomida, superfamily Hubbardioidea) known from the Pliocene of Arizona, Alaska, and the Oligocene of Shandong, China.

CALICIFORM. [Gr. καλυξ, cup; L. forma, shape]. Shaped like a cup or calyx.

CALCOSAXICOLOUS. [L. calx, lime; saxum, a rock; colere, to inhabit]. Inhabiting rocky limestone regions.

CALIOLOGY. [Gr. καλια, hut; λογος, discourse]. The study of dwellings or natural shelters utilized by animals.

CALIFORNICUS (CALIFORNIA MITE). [*California*, an imaginary realm in *Las sergas de Esplandián*, a romance by Sp. writer Garci Ordóñez de Montalvo]. The mite *Neoseiulus* (also *Amblyseius*) *californicus* (Parasitiformes: **Phytoseiidae**), a generalist predator used in a variety of cropping systems.

CALLIPALLENIDAE (PALLENIDAE). [Gr. καλλι-, beautiful; παλληνη, a peninsula of Chalcidicé]. A family of sea spiders (suborder Eupantopodida, superfamily Nymphonoidea).

CALLOSITY. [L. callus, hard skin]. A thick swollen lump, harder than its surroundings. A rather flattened elevation not necessarily harder than the surrounding tissue.

CALLOUS. [L. callus, hard skin]. Hardened. Having a callus or callosities.

CALORIGENESIS (CALORIGENIC). [L. calere, to be warm; generare, to produce]. The production of heat in the body as a result of the mechanical activity of muscle contraction or from the more ubiquitous metabolic transformations of chemical substances.

CALYCIFORM. [Gr. καλυξ, cup; L. forma, shape]. Calyx-like or goblet-shaped.

CALYCINE. [Gr. καλυξ, cup]. Cup-like. Calyx-like.

CALYCLE/CALYCULUS. [Gr. καλυξ, cup/L. caliculus, little cup]. A cup-shaped cavity or structure.

CALYPTOSTASIC, CALYPTOSTASE (NYMPHOCHRYSALIS). [Gr. καλυπτος, covered; στασις, standing]. A state in which acarine instars (ticks and mites) are subject to regressive characters from losing the use of appendages and mouthparts, due to remaining enclosed in the tegument of the preceding stage or in the egg-shell. See also Alternating Calyptostasy, Elattostase, Metelattosis, Protelattosis.

CALYPTOSTOMATOIDEA. [Gr. καλυπτος, covered; στομα, mouth]. A monotypic superfamily of mites (suborder Prostigmata, infraorder Anystina). Family: **Calyptostomatidea.**

CALYPTRA. [Gr. καλυπτειρα, a veil]. A hood or cap.

CALYX. [L. *calix*, a goblet]. Any cup-like area into which structures are set.

CAMERATION. [L. *cameratio*, vaulting]. Division into a number of chambers.

CAMEROSTOME. [L. *camera*, chamber; Gr. στομα, mouth]. In the Uropodina (Parasitiformes): a hollow in the anterior part of the podosoma that allows retraction of the chelicerae and palps; it is sealed by the subcapitulum when retracted. A recess containing the gnathosoma.

CAMOUFLAGE. [It. *camuffare*, disguise]. See Protective Coloration.

CAMPANIFORM. [LL. *campana*, bell; *forma*, shape]. Bell-shaped.

CAMPESTRAL. [L. *campester*, of fields]. Inhabiting open country and grassland.

CANALICULATE. [L. *canaliculus*, little channel]. Having longitudinal grooves, channels or sutures.

CANALICULI. [L. *canaliculus*, small channel]. Fine channels or ducts.

CANALICULUS. [L. *canaliculus*, small channel]. A minute canal.

CANALIFORM. [L. *canalis*, channel; *forma*, shape]. Canal-like.

CANESCENT. [L. *canescere*, to become hoary]. Hoary, with more white than grey.

CANESTRINIOIDEA. [L. *canestri*, baskets; *-ina*, dim.suf.; *-oideus*, resembling]. A monospecific superfamily of 'biting' mites (order Sarcoptiformes, suborder Astigmata). Family: **Canestriniidae.**

CANITIES. [L. *canus*, hoary]. Greyness or whiteness of hair.

CANNIBALISM. [Sp. *Canibales*, derived from *Caribes*, a man-eating tribe from the W. Indies]. Intraspecific predation. A special form of predation in which predator and prey are of the same species. It is known to occur in about 140 species, mostly invertebrates and commonly as a response to environmental stress or food shortage.

CANNULA. [L. *cannula*, a small tube]. A small tube.

CANOPY. [Gr. κωνωπειον, curtained bed]. The upper-most layer of branches, twigs and leaves in forest trees.

CANUS. See Canescent.

CAPILLACEOUS. [L. *capillus*, hair; *-aceous*, of the nature of]. Hair-like.

CAPILLARIS. A very slender, hair-like tube.

CAPILLARY. Long and slender like a hair.

CAPILLATE, CAPILLATUS (CORYPHATUS). [L. *capillus*, hair]. Having a covering of long slender hair.

CAPILLII. [L. *capillus*, hair]. Hairs of the head that form a cap.

CAPITATE. [L. *capitulum*, a little head]. A linear structure being abruptly enlarged with a distal swelling.

CAPITULAR APODEME. [L. *capitulum*, a little head; Gr. απο, down from; δεμας, the living body]. In ticks and mites: an apodeme separating the cheliceral frame and the infracapitulum.

CAPITULAR CAPSULE (GNATHOSOMAL CAPSULE). [L. *capitulum*, a little head]. The fused chelicerae and subcapitulum.

CAPITULAR SADDLE. [L. *capitulum*, a little head]. In ticks and mites: that area of the cervix separating the two cheliceral grooves.

CAPITULIFORM. [L. *caput*, head; *forma*, shape]. Having an enlarged terminal part, like a capitulum.

CAPITULUM (GNATHOSOMA). [L. *capitulum*, a little head]. Any small knob-like protuberance. The anterior-most part of a mite. It is composed of the cheliceral and pedipalpal segments and separated from the body (idiosoma) by a ring of soft cuticle. Sometimes known as the hypostome, infracapitulum or rostrum.

CAPONIIDAE. [deriv.uncert. ?L *caponis*; young fatted cockerel]. A family of ecribellate spiders (infraorder Araneomorphae, superfamily Haplogynae) from the USA, South America, south and west Africa. They are unusual in that most species have only two eyes. Other species have four, six or eight eyes. Sometimes the number of eyes changes from spiderling to adult. Eight eyes: *Calponia, Caponia*. Six eyes: *Caponina* (but may also have two, three, four or five eyes). Four eyes: *Nopsides, Notnops*. Two eyes: *Nops, Orthonops, Diplogena, Taintnops, Tisentnops*.

CAPONIOIDEA. In a previous classification, a superfamily of six-eyed haplogyn spiders (suborder Opisthothelae, infraorder Araneomorphae) that united the families **Caponiidae** and **Tetrablemmidae**.

CAPSULAR, CAPSULATE. [L. *capsula*, little box]. In the form of, or enclosed within a capsule.

CAPSULE. [L. *capsula*, little box]. Any membranous sac containing fluid, or investing an organ or joint; as, the capsule of the lens of the eye.

CAPSULE GLAND (CAPSULOGENOUS GLAND). [L. *capsula*, little box]. Any gland which helps to secrete, or which itself secretes, the material to form a capsule.

CAPUT. [L. *caput*, head]. 1. A head-like or knob-like protuberance. 2. The head with all its appendages.

CARABOCTONIDAE. [L. *carabus*, a crayfish; *octonus*, groups of eight]. A small family of scorpions (order Scorpiones, superfamily Iuroidea) known as hairy scorpions. The lower surface of each foot bears a single, distally bifurcating series of close-set tufts of fine hair.

CARABODOIDEA. [Carabidae, a beetle family; *-oideus*, resembling]. A superfamily of mites (suborder Oribatida, infraorder Brachypylina - section Pycnonoticae) in which the notogaster is longer than wide, and the lamellae is more-or-less parallel and confined to the edges of the prodorsum. Families: **Carabodidae, Nippobodidae**.

CARAPACE. [Sp. *carapacho*, covering]. The chitinous or bony shield covering at least part of, and commonly the whole of, the back. Any fused series of sclerites covering a portion of the body. 1. In mites and ticks: the more or less fused dorsal sclerites of the cephalothorax which cover the idiosoma. 2. In other arachnids, the upper covering of the cephalothorax.

CARBONARIUS. [L. *cabo*, coal; *-aris*, belonging to]. Coal black.

CARBONICOLOUS. [L. *carbo*, coal; *colere*, to inhabit]. Living in burnt or scorched environments.

CARCINOID. [Gr. καρκινος; a crab; ειδος, like]. Of, or resembling crabs.

CARDIAC. [Gr. καρδια, heart]. Of the heart.

CARDIAC MARK. [Gr. καρδια, heart]. In some arachnids: a lanceolate (elongate) mark on the midline of the dorsal surface of the abdomen, over the heart.

CARDIFORM. [Gr. καρδια, heart; L. *forma*, shape]. Resembling the shape of a heart.

CARINA (pl. **CARINAE**). [L. *carina*, keel]. A longitudinal ridge.

CARINATE. [L. *carina*, keel]. Ridged or keeled. Furnished with raised lines or ridges. Possessing a carina. See also Ratite.

CARINIFORM. [L. *carina*, keel; *forma*, shape]. Keel-shaped, tropeic.

CARINULA, CARINULAE. [L. *carina*, keel; *-ula*. dim. suf.]. A little carina or keel-like ridge.

CARINULATE. [L. *carina*, keel]. Of a surface bearing small and rather numerous carinae.

CARIOUS, CARIOSE. [L. *caries*, decay]. Decayed. Having surface depressions. Corroded.

CARNEOUS, CARNEUS. [L. *carnosus*, fleshy]. Resembling flesh in color or substance.

46

CARNIVORE. [L. *carno*, flesh; *vorare*, to devour]. A flesh-eating animal. This term is also applied to a few insectivorous plants.

CARNOSE. [L. *carnosus*, fleshy]. Of something that is soft and fleshy.

CAROTENE, CAROTIN. [L. *carota*, carrot]. An important hydrocarbon pigment in plants and animals.

CAROTENOPHORE. [L. *carota*, carrot; Gr. φορειν, to bear]. A pigmented stigma or eye-spot.

CARRION. [L. *caro*, flesh]. Dead, putrefying flesh.

CARRYING CAPACITY. The maximum numbers of a particular organism that a particular stable environment can support without environmental damage.

CARUNCLE. [L. *caruncula*, small piece of flesh]. Any naked fleshy outgrowth such as the adhesive disk on the tarsi in certain mites.

CARY-. See also Kary-.

CARYOPHYLLEOUS. [Gr. καρυον, nut; φυλλον, leaf]. Nut or clove brown.

CASSIDEOUS. [L. *cassis*, a helmet]. Helmet-like.

CASTANE(O)US. [L. *castanea*, chestnut]. Of the color of a chestnut. Brown. Sepia.

CAT-, See also Kat-.

CATALEPSIS. [Gr. καταληψις, seizure]. The death-feigning reflex. A state of immobilization in which the body and limbs are often plastic with muscle rigidity in the limbs retaining any unusual position into which they are placed.

CATAPHRACT, CATAPHRACTUS. [Gr. καταφρακτος, confined]. Armored with a hard callous skin, or with closely united scales.

CATAPLEXY. [Gr. καταπληξ, stricken with amazement]. Feigning death. See Catalepsis.

CATATREPSIS. See Katatrepsis.

CATENANE. [L. *catena*, chain]. A structure of two or more interlocking rings.

CATENATE. [L. *catenatus*, chained]. To convert two or more ring structures into a chain formation.

CATENOID. [L. *catena*, chain; Gr. ειδος, form]. Chain-like.

CATENULAR, CATENULATE, CATENIFORM, CATENULIFORM. [L. *catenula*, little chain]. A chain-like formation, as in color markings, etc.

CATERVATUM. [L. *caterva*: crowd/troop/flock]. In heaps.

CAUDAD. [L. *cauda*, tail]. Towards the tail. See also Cephalad.

CAUDAL. [L. *cauda*, tail]. Concerning the tail or any tail-like appendage.

CAUDAL BEND. [L. *cauda*, tail]. In most mites: the posteroventral curvature of the opisthosoma that causes the anal opening to become located ventrally. The Opilioacarida have a terminal anus (maybe a primitive condition) and others have secondarily terminal or dorsal anal openings.

CAUDAL SETA. [L. *cauda*, tail; *seta*, bristle]. In the Eriophyoidea: opisthosomal seta h2, often the longest seta on the mite and curled or whip-like.

CAUDAL VIEW. [L. *cauda*, tail]. The view from the rear or posterior.

CAUDOCEPHALAD. [L. *cauda*, tail; Gr. κεφαλη, head]. Directed towards the head from the caudal region.

CAUDOCEPHALIC. [L. *cauda*, tail; Gr. κεφαλη, head]. In a line from the head to the tail.

CAUDODORSAD. [L. *cauda*, tail; *dorsum*, back]. Directed upward and toward the tail.

CAUL. [ME. *calle*, covering]. Any investing membrane.

CAULESCENT. [L. *caulis*, stalk]. Being intermediate between sessile and stalked.

CAULIFORM. [L. *caulis*, stalk; *forma*, shape]. Stem-like.

CAULIGASTRIC. [L. *caulis*, stalk; Gr. γαστηρ, stomach]. In the Chelicerata: of those species that are narrowly joined between the prosoma and opisthosoma. See also Latigastric.

CAVATE. [L. *cavus*, hollow]. Hollowed out, cave-like.

CAVERNARIUS. [L. *caverna*, cavern; *-arium*, a place where something is kept]. Living in caves.

CAVERNICOLOUS. [L. *caverna*, cavern; *colere*, to inhabit]. Living in caves.

CAVERNOSUS. [L. *cavernosus*, chambered]. Honey-combed. Full of cavities or hollow spaces.

CELAENOPSOIDEA. [Gr. κελαινος, black/dark; οψις, appearance]. A diverse superfamily of mites (suborder Trigynaspida, infraorder Antennophorina) associated with both arthropods and reptiles. Families: **Celaenopsidae, Costacaridae, Diplogyniidae, Euzerconidae, Megacelaenopsida, Neotenogyniidae, Schizogyniidae, Triplogyniidae.**

CEMENT GLAND. [L. *caementum*, mortar]. Any gland which secretes an adhesive substance (or 'cement'), in plants and animals.

CEMENT LAYER. [L. *caementum*, mortar]. In ticks and mites: the outer layer of cerotegument. It is often produced with ornamental patterns.

CEMENT SAC. [L. *caementum*, mortar]. The region of an invertebrate oviduct that provides the egg covering.

CENTRAL NERVOUS SYSTEM (CNS). The nervous system to which the sensory impulses are transmitted and from which motor impulses are sent out. In spiders, unlike other arachnids, it is completely concentrated in the cephalothorax, and the shape of the brain, or epipharyngeal ganglion, to some extent reflects the habits of the spider. In the hunting spiders the anterior region, that is in close contact with the eyes, is larger than in web-building spiders – which are more sensitive to touch.

CENTER OF ORIGIN. The location from which a particular species has originated and radiated.

CENTRIFUGAL SPECIATION. [L. *centrum*, center; *fugere*, to flee]. See Speciation.

CENTRIPETAL. [L. *centripetus*, center-seeking]. Tending or turning towards the center of axis.

CENTROLECITHAL. [Gr. κεντρον, center; λεκιθος, yolk]. The type of egg where the nucleus is surrounded by a small area of non-yolky cytoplasm in the middle of a large mass of yolk. There is also a peripheral area of non-yolky cytoplasm. This type of egg is very common in arthropods. After fertilization the nucleus undergoes several rounds of mitotic division and the cells thus formed migrate to the periphery, ultimately forming a continuous sheath which totally encloses the yolk - the stereoblastula stage. See also Alecithal, Heterolecithal, Macrolecithal, Mediolecithal, Meiolecithal, Mesolecithal, Microlecithal, Oligolecithal, Polylecithal, Telolecithal.

CEPHALAD. [Gr. κεφαλη, head]. Towards the head or front part of an animal. See also Caudad.

CEPHALATE. [Gr. κεφαλη, head]. Having a head or head-like structure.

CEPHALIC. [Gr. κεφαλη, head]. Pertaining to the head.

CEPHALIC REGION. [Gr. κεφαλη, head]. Of, on, in, or near the head.

CEPHALIZATION. [Gr. κεφαλη, head]. The specialization of the anterior end of an animal to form a head. In this region are the feeding organs, sensory organs, nerve centers etc.

CEPHALON. [Gr. κεφαλη, head]. The head. Toward the posterior end.

CEPHALOTHORACIC JUNCTION. [Gr. κεφαλη, head; L. *thorax*, chest]. A furrow that extends forwards and to the sides from the center of the carapace. It marks the junction of the head and thoracic region, or cervical groove.

CEPHALOTHORACIC SHIELD. [Gr. κεφαλη, head; θωραξ, breastplate]. The prodorsal shield; especially in the Eriophyoidea (herbivorous mites).

CEPHALOTHORAX (PROSOMA). [Gr. κεφαλη, head; θωραξ, breastplate]. The anterior of the two major divisions of the body of a spider, which is formed by the fusion of head and thorax.

CEPHALOUS. [Gr. κεφαλη, head]. Of the head.

CEPHEID. [Gr. κεφαλη, head]. A member of the family **Cepheidae** (suborder Oribatida, infraorder Brachypylina - section Pycnonoticae), the nymphs of which often carry elaborate scalps. Cepheidae has been found to be an invalid name although the tem 'cepheid' is still used. See **Compactozetidae.**

CEPS. [NL. *ceps*, head]. Head.

CERACEOUS. [L. *cera*, wax; *-aceous*, of the nature of]. Waxy.

CERAL. [L. *cera*, wax]. Of or pertaining to wax.

CERATOZETOIDEA (LIMNOZETOIDEA). [Gr. κερας, horn; ζητες seeking]. A superfamily of mites (suborder Oribatida, infraorder Brachypylina - section Poronoticae). Families: **Ceratozetidae (Heterozetidae), Chamobatidae, Humerobatidae, Limnozetidae, Maudheimiidae, Punctoribatidae (Mycobatidae).**

CERCOMEGISTINA. [Gr. κερκος, tail; μεγιστο- greatest]. An infraorder of mites (order Mesostigmata, suborder Trigynaspida). Superfamily: Cercomegistoidea

CERCOMEGISTOIDEA. A superfamily of mites (suborder Trigynaspida, infraorder Cercomegistina). Families: **Asternoseiidae, Cercomegistidae, Davacaridae, Pyrosejidae, Saltiseiidae, Seiodidae, Vitzthumegistidae.**

CERE. [L. *cera*, wax]. To wax, or cover with wax.

CEREOUS. [L. *cereus*, waxen]. Wax-like.

CERIFEROUS. [L. *cera*, wax; *ferre*, to carry]. Wax producing.

CEROMIDAE. [Gr. κηρωμα, a wax-salve]. A family of sun spiders (subclass Arachnida, order Solifugae) from southern Africa and the Lower Cretaceous of Brazil.

CEROTEGUMENT. [L. *cera*, wax; *tegumentum*, covering]. In ticks and mites: the tegumental layers of the epicuticle, including the wax and cement layers. It is often thin and inconspicuous, but sometimes may be thick, ornamented and obscure the underlying cuticle. Thick ceroteguments often can be removed to expose a mite of very different appearance. Part of the epiostracum and part of the epicuticle. Superficial epicuticular layers. Tectostracum.

CERULEAN. [L. *caeruleus*, sky-blue]. Azure or sky-blue.

CERVICAL. [L. *cervix*, neck]. Of the neck or the cervix of an organ.

CERVICAL GROOVES. [L. *cervix*, neck; OE *græf*, ditch/grave]. In ticks and mites; the shallow groove(s) that separate the carapace into a cephalic region and a thoracic region. They may be faint, deep, shallow or absent.

CERVIX (CERVICES). [L. *cervix*, neck]. 1. A neck or any neck-like structure. 2. A constriction of the mouth of an organ. 3. In the Acariformes: the dorsal part of the infracapitulum, between the line of attachment of the cheliceral frame and the base of the *labrum*, and bounded by the lateral ridges. It encompasses the capitular saddle and cheliceral grooves. 4. In the mite sperm access system: a collar-like structure of which surrounds the base of the vesicle.

CESIOUS. [L. *caesius*]. Bluish-grey. See Caesius.

CESPITICOLOUS. [L. *caespes*, turf; *colere*, to inhabit]. Inhabiting grassy places.

CESPITOSE, CAESPITOSE. [L. *caespes*, turf]. Growing in dense clumps or tufts; matted.

CESTIFORM. [L. *cestus*, girdle; *forma*, shape]. Girdle-shaped.

CHACTIDAE. [*Chactas*, the 'noble savage' of the Natchez Indians]. A family of scorpions (order Scorpiones, superfamily Chactoidea) known from the Americas.

CHACTOIDEA (VAEJOVOIDEA). [*Chactas*, the 'noble savage' of the Natchez Indians]. A superfamily of scorpions (subclass Arachnida, order Scorpiones). Families: **Chactidae, Euscorpiidae, Superstitioniidae, Troglotayosicidae** (previously included in the Superstitioniidae), **Typhlochactidae, Vaejovidae.**

CHAERILIDAE. See Chaeriloidea.

CHAERILOIDEA. [Gr. χαιρω, to rejoice]. A monospecific superfamily of scorpions (subclass Arachnida, order Scorpiones) from southeast Asia. Family: Chaerilidae - *Chaerilus*.

CHAETAE. [Gr. χαιτη, hair]. Bristles composed largely of chitin. See also Seta.

CHAETOME. [Gr. χαιτη, hair]. A complement of setae. The arrangement of seta on a developmental stage or a body part.

CHAETOTAXY (SETATION). [Gr. χαιτη, hair; ταξις, disposition]. The arrangement of the leg spines, particularly with respect to identification and classification on the basis of differences between the structure and arrangement. See Evans Leg Chaetotactic System, Grandjean system, Lindquist-Evans system, Pritchard & Baker System, Rostral-lamellar system, Vertical-Scapular System.

CHAETIFEROUS (CHAETIGEROUS, SETIFEROUS). [Gr. χαιτη, hair; L. *ferre*, to bear]. Bearing bristles.

CHAETIGEROUS SAC. [Gr. χαιτη, hair; -γενης, producing]. See Chaetae.

CHAETOPHOROUS. [Gr. χαιτη, hair; φορα, carrying]. Bristle-bearing.

CHAGRINED. See Shagreened.

CHAIN RESPONSE. A sequence of behaviors in which each item produces a situation which invokes the next response. E.g. courtship rituals.

CHALASTOGASTROUS. [Gr. χαλαστον, chain; γαστηρ, belly]. Having the abdomen attached to the thorax by a broad base.

CHALCEOUS, CHALCEUS. [Gr. χαλκος, copper]. Brassy in color or appearance.

CHALICE. [L. *calix*, goblet]. Simple gland cells or goblet cells.

CHALLENGE DISPLAY. The highly intense aggressive display of a male to a conspecific male.

CHALYBEATE, CHALYBEATUS, CHALYBEOUS, CHALYBEUS. [Gr. χαλυβος, steel]. Metallic steel-blue, steely in appearance.

CHAMBERED. [OFr. *chambre*, a chamber / room]. A structure with discrete compartments.

CHAPARRAL. [Sp. *chaparra*, ever-green oak]. A characteristic biome of regions with a warm temperate climate but with very little summer rain. The vegetation usually consists of scattered low shrubs and drought resistant plants.

CHAPERON. [Fr. *chaperon*, protector]. The clypeus or clypeus anterior.

CHAPLET. [OF. *chapel*, hat]. 1. A small crown. 2. A terminal process in the form of a circle of hooks or similar structures.

CHARACTER. [Gr. χαρακτηρ, metaph. a distinctive mark]. Any distinguishing feature, trait or property of an organism that forms the basis for comparison. Any trait passed from parent to offspring.

CHARACTER DISPLACEMENT. [Gr. χαρακτηρ, metaph. a distinctive mark]. In sympatric populations: the exaggeration of species characteristics such as scents, mating calls, courtship rituals and other visual clues or anatomical, physiological or behavioral adaptations in comparison to allopatric populations of related species. This phenomenon is attributed to the effects of natural selection intensifying the characters used for species discrimination, or for utilizing different regions of an ecological niche and thereby avoiding direct competition.

CHARACTER DIVERGENCE. [Gr. χαρακτηρ, metaph. a distinctive mark]. A name given by Darwin to the differences developing in two or more related species in their area of sympatry resulting from selective effects of competition. See also Character Displacement.

CHARACTER GRADIENT. See Cline.

CHARASSOBATOIDEA. [Gr. χαρασσω, a pointed stake; βατης, a walker]. A superfamily of mites (suborder Oribatida, infraorder Brachypylina - section Pycnonoticae). Families: **Charassobatidae, Nosybeidae.**

CHARINOIDEA. [Gr. χαριν; for the sake of]. A monospecific superfamily of tail-less whip-scorpions (order Amblypygi, suborder Euamblypygi). Family: **Charinidae.**

CHARONTOIDEA. [Gr. Χαρων, ferryman of the Styx]. A monospecific superfamily of tail-less whip scorpions (order Amblypygi, suborder Euamblypygi). Family: **Charontidae.**

CHEEKS. [OE. *ceace*, jawbone]. In some **Argasidae:** the paired movable flap-like covers which can close medially to cover and protect the capitulum.

CHEIRACANTHIIDAE (syn. **EUTICHURIDAE**). [Gr. χειρ, hand; ακανθα, thorn]. An almost cosmopolitan family of spiders (infraorder Araneomorphae, superfamily Entelegynae) in which each species has a unique feature. In *Cheiracanthium inclusum,* the black-footed yellow-sac spider, the males have a narrow body and long legs, while *Cheiracanthium ilicis,* has an oval-shaped dorsal shield alongside small eyes arranged transversally in two rows.

CHEIRIDIIDAE. [Gr. χειρ, hand; -ιδιον, dim. suf.]. A widely distributed family of false scorpions (suborder Iocheirata, superfamily Cheiridioidea). This family may be included in the superfamily Garypoidea.

CHEIRIDIOIDEA. [Gr. χειρ, hand]. A superfamily of false scorpions (order Pseudoscorpiones, suborder Iocheirata). Families: **Cheiridiidae, Pseudochiridiidae,** (both families may be in the Garypoidea).

CHELA. [Gr. χηλη, a claw]. A pincer, as in a pseudoscorpion's distal pedipalpal segments.

CHELATE. [Gr. χηλη, a claw]. Bearing a claw. Of claws that are capable of being drawn down or back upon the last tarsal joint. Having the terminal part of an appendage in the form of a pincer, as in a crab.

CHELATE-DENTATE. [Gr. χηλη, a claw; L. *dens*, tooth]. Pincer-like chelicerae that bear teeth.

CHELATE-SERRATE (or just **SERRATE**). [Gr. χηλη, a claw; L. *serra*, saw]. Pincer-like chelicerae with a row of saw-like teeth.

CHELICERAE (MANDIBLES). [Gr. χηλη, claw; κερας, horn]. A pair of sharp or clawed appendages in front of the mouth on spiders and other arachnids. They are used for grasping, holding, tearing, crushing or piercing and are pincer-like in scorpions. The chelicerae are divided into three segments and in most orders the end segment is chelate; in spiders and amblypygids it is subchelate and in parasitic mites the chelicerae have become narrowed and reduced to form a piercing organ. The larger chelicerae are used for attacking and securing prey, they may contain a poison gland at the base. The chelicerae of ticks consist of three segments: the cheliceral bases which are located within the basis capitulum; the cheliceral shafts which extend anteriorly, originate within the basis capituli, and are surrounded by tough spinous sheaths; and the cheliceral digits that bear the denticles and, in most species, are covered by a delicate sheath (cheliceral hood).

CHELICERAL BOSS. [Gr. χηλη, claw; κερας, horn; OFr. *boce*, a hump, swelling]. In some Araneae: a tear-shaped or wedge-shaped process on the distal part of the chelicera where it comes into contact with the clypeus.

CHELICERAL DIGITS (ARTICLES). [Gr. χηλη, claw; κερας, horn; L. *digitus*, finger/toe]. In the chelicerae of ticks: structures bearing sharp denticles that are attached to the ends of the cheliceral shafts. They lie dorsal to the hypostome and bear laterally directed cutting edges. The moveable medial (internal) digit lies in a cavity of the outer digit, and is directed from side to side by tendons attached to the muscles in the internal cheliceral bases. Thus their movement result in ripping and tearing against the host skin. The inner digit bears mechanosensory and chemosensory receptors which provide information about shear forces and the chemical composition of host fluids. They may also have a role in pheromone detection.

CHELICERAL EXTENSION. [Gr. χηλη, claw; κερας, horn]. A basal, pointed projection behind the clypeus. It is conspicuous in some **Theridiidae, Nesticidae** and **Pholcidae.**

CHELICERAL FRAME. [Gr. χηλη, claw; κερας, horn]. The part of the tegument to which the chelicerae are attached.

CHELICERAL GLAND. [Gr. χηλη, claw; κερας, horn]. One of the paired glands in the dorsal part of the prosoma. The orifice is in the chelicerae.

CHELICERAL GROOVES (FANG FURROWS). [Gr. χηλη, claw; κερας, horn; OE *græf,* ditch/grave]. Paired longitudinal grooves in the dorsal surface of the infracapitulum. They receive and guide the chelicera.

CHELICERAL GUIDES (OUTER INFRACAPITULAR STYLETS). [Gr. χηλη, claw; κερας, horn]. In the Eriophyoidea: a pair of capitular processes that frame the cheliceral stylets.

CHELICERAL LAMINA. [Gr. χηλη, claw; κερας, horn; L. *lamina,* a plate]. 1. A sclertized ridge on the cheliceral margin or mesal surface. 2. A sclerite in the male palp of many **Linyphiidae.**

CHELICERAL RETAINER. [Gr. χηλη, claw; κερας, horn]. In the Eriophyoidea (herbivorous mites): the flexible spine-like structure produced by the palpcoxal base which enclose the cheliceral stylets.

CHELICERAL SETA. [Gr. χηλη, claw; κερας, horn; L. *seta,* bristle]. Any seta on the chelicera of a mite. In the Mesostigmata: the scale-like or otherwise modified seta on the dorsal surface of the chelicera.

CHELICERAL SHEATH. See Stylet Sheath.

CHELICERAL TEETH. [Gr. χηλη, claw; κερας, horn]. Serrations along the borders of the cheliceral groove.

CHELICERATA. [Gr. χηλη, a claw; κερας, horn]. A subphylum of the phylum Arthropoda comprising all the arthropods in which the first postoral appendages are chelicerae (feeding appendages), the second postoral appendages are pedipalps and there are four pairs of legs. The chelicerate body is divided into two main regions, an anterior cephalothorax or prosoma and a posterior abdomen or opisthosoma. There are no antennae. Classes: Euchelicerata, Pycnogonida. Order †Eurypterida. The Merostomata were previously included here.

CHELICERATE. [Gr. χηλη, a claw; κερας, horn]. Any member of the arthropod group Chelicerata. This includes the horseshoe crabs, scorpions, spiders, mites and their relatives.

CHELIFERIDAE. [Gr. χηλη, a claw; L. *ferre,* to bear]. A family of false scorpions (suborder Iocheirata, superfamily Cheliferoidea).

CHELIFEROIDEA. [Gr. χηλη, a claw; L. *ferre,* to bear]. A superfamily of false scorpions (order Pseudoscorpiones, suborder Iocheirata). Families: **Atemnidae, Cheliferidae, Chernetidae, Withiidae**

CHELIFEROUS. [Gr. χηλη, a claw; L. *ferre,* to bear]. Having chelae or claws.

CHELIFORM. [Gr. χηλη, a claw; L. *forma,* shape]. Claw-shaped, pincer-like.

CHELONETHIDA. See Pseudoscorpiones.

CHEMOCEPTOR. See Chemoreceptor.

CHEMOKINESIS. [Gr. χημεια, a transmutation; κινησις, movement]. Movement in response to chemical stimuli.

CHEMORECEPTOR (CHEMOCEPTOR). [Gr. χημεια, a transmutation; L. *recipere,* to receive]. A receptor cell which, by contact at the molecular level, detects and differentiates substances according to their chemical structure. E.g. the gustatory (taste) receptors which detect dissolved ions and molecules, the olfactory (smell) receptors which detect airborne molecules and the contact chemoreceptors (taste hairs). See also Receptor.

CHEMOREFLEX. [Gr. χημεια, a transmutation; L. *reflectere,* to bend back]. A reflex in response to a chemical.

CHEMOSENSATION. [Gr. χημεια, a transmutation; L. *sensus*, sense]. The ability to detect and differentiate substances according to their chemical composition.

CHEMOTAXIS. [Gr. χημεια, a transmutation; ταξυς, an arranging]. The movement of an organism towards a chemical substance, usually along a chemical gradient.

CHEMOTROPISM. [Gr. χημεια, a transmutation; τροπν, a turning]. An orienting response to a chemical stimulus. Sometimes synonymous with chemotaxis.

CHEQUERED. See Tessellate.

CHERNETES. [Gr. χερνητης, day laborer]. An alternative name for Pseudoscorpions; minute arachnids that superficially resemble scorpions.

CHERNETIDAE (syn MYRMOCHERNETIDAE). [Gr. χερνης, one who lives by his hands]. A large diverse family of false scorpions (suborder Iocheirata, superfamily Cheliferoidea). They may be found under bark, in leaf litter, in caves, and in a variety of other habitats.

CHERSOPHILOUS. [Gr. χερσος, dry land; φιλος, loving]. Living well on/in dry waste land.

CHEVRON. [Fr. *chevron*, rafter]. An arrow-headed mark or structure.

CHEYLETIDAE. [Gr. χηλη, a claw]. A family of mites (suborder Eleutherengona, superfamily Cheyletoidea) that are either free-ranging or else parasitic on birds and mammals. Members of the subfamily Cheyletinae are predatory and sometimes used in biocontrol.

CHEYLETIOSIS. [Cheyletidae + Gr. -οσις, suf. of condition]. A mange caused by mite infestation of *Cheyletiella* species (superfamily Cheyletoidea, family Cheyletidae) that live on the epidermis of small to medium sized mammals. *C. yasguri* is associated with dogs, *C. blakei* infests cats and *C. parasitivorax* parasitizes rabbits. Species of *Cheyletiella* are highly active mites and their skin-like color and rapid movement has given them their common name: 'walking dandruff'.

CHEYLETOIDEA. [Gr. χηλη, a claw]. A superfamily of mites (suborder Prostigmata, infraorder Eleutherengona) that are parasites of arthropods and vertebrates. Families: **Cheyletidae** (fur mites), **Demodecidae** (follicle mites), **Epimyodicidae**, **Harpyrhynchidae**, **Ophioptidae** (pit mites – of snakes), **Psorergatidae, Syringophilidae.**

CHIGGER. [W. Indies, *chigoe*, ? Carib./African origin, tiny mite or flea]. The parasitic larval stage of any member of the family **Trombiculidae** (infraorder Anystina, superfamily Trombiculoidea), also known as berry bugs, harvest mites, red bugs, scrub-itch mites, or aoutas. They feed on the skin of their vertebrate host, causing trombidiosis (a form of dermatitis) and some may transmit scrub typhus. Nymphs and adults feed on small arthropods and their eggs are often brightly colored and densely hairy (velvet mites).

CHILEAN PREDATORY MITE. The mite *Phytoseiulus persimilis* (superfamily Phytoseioidea, family Phytoseiidae), a commercially available and extremely efficient predator of spider mites. Also called 'persimilis' or the predatory mite. It is frequently used to control *Tetranychus urticaethe* (two-spotted spider-mites) a crop pest.

CHILUM. [Gr. χειλος, a lip]. A small sclerite at the base of the chelicera, under the clypeus.

CHITIN. [Gr. χιτων, tunic; -*in*, chem. suf. used for neutral substances]. A colorless, horny protective substance that is the principal constituent of the hard covering of arachnids and other arthropods. It consists of N-acetylglucosamine (a nitrogen-containing poylsaccharide) in beta-1,4 linkages. It is very similar to cellulose but has an acetylated amino group rather than an hydroxyl group at the C_2 position. Chitin is infiltrated by another protein, arthropodin, which can be hardened and simultaneously darkened to various degrees by tanning, a process of stabilization by cross-linking of the protein molecules.

CHITINASE. [Gr. χιτων, tunic; -*asis*, suf. used in naming enzymes]. Any of a family of enzymes capable of decomposing chitin. Found in molting fluid and as a secretion from chitinovores.

CHITINIZATION. [Gr. χιτων, tunic; -ιζειν, suf. ind. cause to be]. The process of depositing chitin, or being chitinized.

CHITINOGENOUS. [Gr. χιτων, tunic; -γενης, producing]. Of epidermal cells that secrete chitin.

CHITINOPHILUS. [Gr. χιτων, tunic; φιλος, loving]. Of micro-organisms found in association with chitin and thought to derive nourishment from it. A Chitinovore.

CHITINOUS. [Gr. χιτων, tunic]. Composed of or resembling chitin.

CHITINOVORE. [Gr. χιτων, tunic; L. *vorare*, to devour]. A micro-organism with the ability to digest chitin. See also Chitinophilus.

CHITONOSTRACUM. [Gr. χιτων, tunic; οστρακον, shell]. In ticks and mites: the thickest layer of the cuticle between epiostracum and hypodermis. See also Ectostracum.

CHITOSAN. [Gr. χιτων, tunic]. A deacetylated derivative of chitin (polymeric glucosamine) that gives a characteristic violet color with iodine. This is the most commonly used qualitative test for the presence of chitin.

CHITOSE. [Gr. χιτων, tunic]. A decomposition product of chitin; an acetyglucosamine and glucosamine salt.

CHLAMYDATE, CHLAMYDEOUS. [Gr. χλαμυς, mantle]. Bearing a cloak or mantle-like structure.

CHOANOID. [Gr. χοανη, funnel; ειδος, form]. Funnel-shaped.

CHORDOTONAL ORGANS/RECEPTORS (CHORDOTONAL SENSILLA). [Gr. χορδη, string; τονος, tension]. Receptors that are stretched between two points on the inner side of the integument, such as in the region of a joint. These receptors respond to changes in tension and are important proprioreceptors.

CHORION. [Gr. χοριον, the membrane that encloses a fetus]. The structurally complex outer layer of a spider's (and other animal's) egg. It is often externally patterned, reflecting the patterning of the follicle cells in the ovary.

CHOROLOGY. [Gr. χωρος, a place; λογος, discourse]. Biogeography. The delimitation and description of the distributional ranges of taxa.

CHORONOMIC. [Gr. χωρος, a place; νομος, law]. Externally governed. Applied to the influences of the geographical or regional environment. See also Autonomic, Paratonic.

CHROMATOCYTE (CHROMOCYTES). [Gr. χρωμα, color; κυτος, a hollow vessel]. Any pigment-containing cell.

CHROMATOTROPISM. [Gr. χρωμα, color; -τροπος, turning]. Orientation in response to a particular color.

CHROMOCYTES. [Gr. χρωμα, color; κυτος, hollow vessel]. Pigmented cells.

CHROMOGEN. [Gr. χρωμα, color; γενεσις, origin]. A substance that is converted into a pigment by, for example, oxidation.

CHROMOGENESIS, CHROMOGENIC. [Gr. χρωμα, color; γενεσις, producing]. Color production, color producing.

CHROMOLIPIDS. [Gr. χρωμα, color; λιπος, fat]. The carotenoids and related pigments.

CHROMOPHANES. [Gr. χρωμα, color; φαινειν, to show]. In general, any retinal pigments: chlorophane (green), rhodophane (red) and xanthophane (yellow).

CHROMOSOME. [Gr. χρωμα, color; σωμα, body]. The term proposed by Waldeyer in 1888 for the individual threads observed within a nucleus. These thread-shaped bodies consist largely of DNA and protein and occur, in different but definite numbers in different species, in the nucleus of every plant and animal cell, except some highly specialized cells such as mammalian erythrocytes. Normally in somatic cells they occur in pairs which are identical in appearance and are termed 'homologous'; one member of each pair being derived from each parent. Non-homologous chromosomes usually differ visibly from one another in terms of size and shape. There may be two to over 100 pairs of chromosomes per somatic cell depending on the species and most cells of most species have a set that is characteristic of that species. During meiosis (division for gamete formation) homologous chromosomes associate in a characteristic way and then separate so that the gametes ultimately contain only one member of each chromosome pair in their nuclei (i.e. half the total number present in the parent cell). Gametes are thus said to be 'haploid' whilst the parent cells are 'Diploid'. **A-chromosomes:** the 'normal' chromosomes, so called to distinguish them from **B-chromosomes (accessory chromosomes)**: supernumerary chromosomes which occur in some individuals or populations of certain species, and are usually composed entirely of heterochromatin. **X-chromosome:** a chromosome which is represented twice in the nuclei of one sex (the homogamitic sex) but only once in the nuclei of the other (the heterogamitic sex). In many animals the male is commonly the heterogamitic sex but in birds, reptiles, some fish and amphibians and lepidopterans, the female is the heterogamitic sex. **Y-chromosome:** the dissimilar chromosome represented once in a nucleus with one X-chromosome and not at all in the nuclei of the other sex; which has two X-chromosomes. During cell division a single chromosome appears as two flexible rods (arms) joined end to end at a constriction (centromere). This centromere may be mid-way along the chromosome (metacentric), displaced slightly to one end (submetacentric), displaced more towards one end (acrocentric) or at the very end of an arm (telocentric). A chromosome without a centromere is termed 'acentric' and one with two centromeres (usually one at each end) is termed 'dicentric'. See also Sex Chromosome.

CHROMOTROPIC. [Gr. χρωμα, color; τροπη, turn]. Controlling pigmentation.

CHRONIC. [Gr. χρονος, time]. Continuing permanently, or at least indefinitely.

CHRONOCLINE. [Gr. χρονος, time; κλινω, slope]. The gradual change of a character, or group of characters, over a period of geological time.

CHRONOFAUNA. [Gr. χρονος, time; L. *Faunus*, a forest god]. A geographically restricted population that maintains its basic character for a significant period of geological time.

CHRONOSPECIES. [Gr. χρονος, time; L. *species*, a particular kind]. 1. A species represented at more than one geological horizon. 2. The successive species in a phylogenetic lineage that are given ancestor and descendent status according to the geographical time sequence (horizon) in which they appear.

CHRONOTROPIC. [Gr. χρονος, time; τροπη, turn]. Affecting the rate of action, e.g. accelerating or inhibiting.

CHRYSARGYRUS. [Gr. χρυσος, gold; αργυρος, silver]. Silvery gilt.

CHTHONIIDAE. [Gr. χθονιος, beneath the earth]. A large family of false scorpions (suborder Heterosphyronida, superfamily Chthonioidea), including three species from Baltic and Dominican amber.

CHTHONIOIDEA. [Gr. χθονιος, beneath the earth]. A superfamily of false scorpions (order Pseudoscorpiones, suborder Heterosphyronida (Epiocheirata)). *Lechytia* may be include here in its own family, **Lechytiidae**, or in the Chthoniidae. Families: **Chthoniidae, †Dracochelidae** (Devonian fossil), **Pseudotyrannochthoniidae, Tridenchthoniidae**.

CHYZERIOIDEA. [deriv. uncert.]. A monotypic superfamily of mites (suborder Prostigmata, infraorder Anystina). Family: **Chyzeriidae**.

CINCT. [L. *cinctum*, girdle]. Belted, girdled or encircled.

CINEREOUS. [L. *cinereus*, ash colored]. Ash-grey, ashen, or having the color of wood ashes.

CINERESCENT. [L. *cinereus*, ash colored]. Ashen in color or appearance.

CINGULATUS (CINETUS). [L. *cingulum*, girdle]. Having a colored band.

CINGULUM. [L. *cingulum*, girdle]. Any belt-like organ.

CINNABARINE. [L. *cinnabaris*, red sulphide of mercury]. A vivid red to reddish-orange color.

CINNAMOMEOUS. [Gr. κινναμομον, cinnamon]. Cinnamon brown.

CIRCADIAN CLOCKS. [L. *circa*, round about]. Certain centers in the brain which control the release of hormones. These centers are programmed by external stimuli such as the daily length of light period, temperature and changes in the seasons as well as certain interoceptive stimuli. See also Circadian Rhythms.

CIRCADIAN RHYTHMS (DIURNAL RHYTHMS). [L. *circa*, round about]. The endogenous rhythmic changes that occur in an organism with a periodicity of about 24 hours, even when the organism is isolated from its natural environment. These rhythmic changes may be mediated by hormones released at certain well defined periods of the day or during the reproductive cycle or at certain times of the year (circannual rhythms). Circadian rhythms are considered to be a basis of photoperiodism. See also Circadian Clocks.

CIRCANNUAL RHYTHMS. See Circadian Rhythms.

CIRCINAL. [L. *circinatus*, rounded]. Spirally rolled like a watch-spring.

CIRCINATE. [L. *circinatus*, rounded]. Ring-shaped; spirally rolled.

CIRCLET. [L. *circulus*, small ring]. A small circle. A ring.

CIRCULAR OVERLAP (A RASSENKREIS). The phenomena in which a chain of contiguous and intergrading populations of one species curves back until the terminal links overlap geographically and are then found to be reproductively isolated from each other, and consequently behave as if they belong to separate species. See also Cline, Speciation.

CIRCULATORY SYSTEM. [L. *circulatio*, to be circulating]. Any system of vessels which transports a fluid (normally blood) around an organism - usually supplied with a 'pump' mechanism which may be a heart or a product of muscular movement. The system may be 'open', as in invertebrates, in which the fluid is pumped by the heart (via an artery) into an open fluid space to bathe the cells. The system may be 'closed' as in vertebrates and some invertebrates where blood flows from the arterial to the venous circulation through capillaries, where transfer of materials occurs. In all animals valves or septa determine the direction of flow.

CIRCULATUS. [L. *circulus*, small ring]. Having a cingulum or collar.

CIRCULUS (CIRCULI). [L. *circulus*, ring]. Any ring-like arrangement.

CIRCUMANAL. [L. *circum*, around; *anus*, anus]. About or surrounding the anus.

CIRCUMANAL SETAE. [L. *circum*, around; *anus*, anus; *seta*, bristle]. In the Mesostigmata: the three setae (one postanal and pair of peranal) surrounding the anal opening.

CIRCUMAUSTRAL. [L. *circum*, around; *australis*, southern]. Distributed around the high latitudes of the southern hemisphere.

CIRCUMBOREAL. [L. *circum*, around; *boreus*, northern]. Distributed around the high latitudes of the northern hemisphere.

CIRCUMCAPITULAR FURROW. [L. *circum*, around; *capitulum*, a little head]. In ticks and mites: the furrow around the base of the gnathosoma, formed from the flexible articulation that joins the capitulum (gnathosoma) to the body (idiosoma).

CIRCUMGASTRIC SCISSURE (FURROW). [L. *circum*, around; Gr. γαστηρ, stomach; L. *scissura*, a long narrow opening]. In the suborder Brachypylina (beetle mites): the flexible articulation that joins the notogaster to the ventral plate.

CIRCUMGENITAL. [L. *circum*, around; *genitalis*, belonging to birth]. Surrounding the genital pore.

CIRCUMOCULAR. [L. *circum*, around; *oculus*, eye]. Around or surrounding the eye.

CIRCUMOESOPHAGEAL. [L. *circum*, around; Gr. οισοφαγος, gullet]. Of structures or organs encircling the esophagus.

CIRCUMORAL. [L. *circum*, around; *os*, mouth]. Encircling the mouth. E.g. circumoral cilia, circumoral nerve ring, etc.

CIRCUMPEDAL. [L. *circum*, around; *pes*, foot]. Surrounding the base of a leg.

CIRCUMPOLAR. [L. *circum*, around; *polus*, end]. Of the flora and fauna of the polar regions.

CIRCUMSCISSILE. [L. *circum*, around; *scindere*, to cut]. Splitting along a circular line, as in hatching.

CIRCUMTROPICAL. [L. *circum*, around; Gr. τροπη, turning]. Encircling the earth in an area between 22.5° north and 22.5° south.

CIRCUMVOLUTION. [L. *circum*, around; *volvere*, to turn around]. Around an axis or center. A whorl. Rotation. Revolution.

CISTERNA. [L. *cisterna*, cistern]. Any closed membrane-limited system. It may be tubular or sac-like in form.

CITHAERONIDAE. [Gr. κιθαρα, a lyre; ερημια, desert]. A small family of pale yellowish, fast-moving spiders (infraorder Araneomorphae, superfamily Entelegynae) that hunt actively at night and rest during the day, constructing silken retreats beneath rocks. They prefer very hot dry stony places.

CITRINE. [Gr. κιτρινος, lemon-yellow]. Lemon-yellow.

CITRON SHAPED. [L. *citrus*, citron-tree]. Having the form of a large lemon.

CLADE. [Gr. κλαδος, a branch]. A monophyletic group of taxa sharing a closer common ancestry with one another than with other members of any other clade. A branch of a cladogram. A taxon consisting of a single species and its descendants—a holophyletic group. See also Nomenclature

CLADISTICS. The study of evolutionary relationships by means of applying phylogenetic systematics. Cladogenesis (the development of the cladograms used to portray these relationships) always produces, by dichotomous branching, two equal sister groups, each of which constitutes a monophyletic group with a common stem taxon unique to the group. Monophyletic groups are deduced by identifying those shared derived characteristics that were not present in their distant ancestors (synaptomorphic characters).

CLADOGRAM. [Gr. κλαδος, a branch; γραμμα, something written]. A tree-like diagram (dendrogram) that represents the evolutionary relationships between taxa in terms of their shared character states.

CLAN. [Gaelic, *clann*, offspring]. See Phratry.

CLANDESTINE EVOLUTION. [L. *clandestinus*, secret/hidden]. Evolutionary change introduced and developed in juvenile stages and incorporated into descendant adult stages by paedomorphosis.

CLAPARÈDE'S ORGAN (URSTIGMA). [É. *Claparède*, Swiss Biologist]. The oval sucker-like structures that are thought to be humidity receptors located between legs I-II in the prelarvae and larvae of many acariform mites. Serially homologous genital papillae are present in nymphs and adults whose larvae have Claparède's organ (Oudeman's Rule). Some mites (**Tydeidae**) may retain the urstigmata beyond the larval stage. See also Urstigma.

CLASPING SPINE. A type of mating spur consisting of an enlarged curved spine that articulates against the leg segment, as in **Mysmenidae**.

CLASS. [L. *classis*, a division]. One of the many different divisions of the taxonomic hierarchy used in the classification of organisms and the principle category between phylum (or division) and order. It usually consists of a number of orders, families etc. See also Nomenclature.

CLASSIFICATION. [L. *classis*, division; *-fic*, make]. The process of delimitation, ordering and ranking taxa (populations and groups of populations) at all levels by inductive procedures. See also Nomenclature.

CLAVA. [L. *clava*, club]. Any club-shaped structure. The ventral mouth part of ticks. Pl. Clavae.

CLAVATE (CLAVIFORM). [L. *clava*, a club]. Club-shaped. With the distal end swollen.

CLAVUS. [L. *clavis*, key]. In spiders: a projection (or crotchet) from the scape.

CLAW (APOTELE, UNGUIS). [AS. *clawu*, claw]. The epidermal claws, often toothed, present on the legs or female's palp. See also Limb.

CLAW DENTITION. [AS. *clawu*, claw; L. *dens*, tooth]. Of the comb-like (pectinate) ventral surface of most claws, arranged in either a single (uniserial) or double (biserial) row of teeth.

CLAW TEETH. [AS. *clawu*, claw; *toth*, tooth]. The teeth, varying in numbers, lining the curve of the true claws.

CLAW TUFTS. [AS. *clawu*, claw]. The pair of dense tufts of adhesive hairs present below the paired claws at the tip of the tarsi of many spiders.

CLEFT. [AS. *cleofian*, split]. Split or forked. Of coleopteran claws so divided that the parts lie one above the other.

CLEPTOBIOSIS (erron. for Kleptobiosis). See Symbiosis.

CLEPTOPARASITE (erron. for Kleptoparasite). See Parasite.

CLIMAX COMMUNITY. [Gr. κλιμαξ, ladder]. The concept of a stable and permanent community of organisms that has reached the end of its ecological sequence of succession under the prevailing climatic and edaphic conditions. A mature and stabilized stage of a biotic community extending over a vast geographic area.

CLINAL. [Gr. κλινω, incline]. The gradual varying of characteristics.

CLINAL SPECIATION. [Gr. κλινω, incline; *species*, particular kind]. See Cline, Speciation.

CLINE. [Gr. κλινω, incline]. The gradual change in the character(s) of an organism correlated with its geographical and / or ecological distribution. The change is usually very gradual so that each community (of plants or animals) differs but very little from the neighboring one, and so interbreeding is possible. However, at the extreme ends of the cline the differences may be very great, sometimes so great that an individual from one 'end' of the cline is reproductively isolated from an individual at the other 'end'. Obviously this situation creates problems with the concept of species. See also Circular Overlap, Speciation.

CLINTHERIFORM. [Etymology obscure; L. *forma*, shape]. Shaped like a plate.

CLOACAROIDEA. [L. *cloaca*, sewer; LL. *acarus*, mite]. A monotypic superfamily of parasitic mites (suborder Prostigmata, infraorder Eleutherengona) found in the cloaca of two species of North American aquatic turtles (*Chelydra serpentine, C. picta*). Family: **Cloacaridae.**

CLOUD FOREST. A moist high-altitude forest characterized by dense undergrowth and an abundance of mosses, ferns, orchids and other plants on the trunks and branches of trees.

CLUBBED. [ON. *klubba*, club]. Having the distal part or segment enlarged.

CLUBIONIDAE. [ON. *klubba*, club; βιουν, to live]. A cosmopolitan family of spiders (infraorder Araneomorphae, superfamily Entelegynae) known as 'sac spiders'. They are wandering predators that construct silken retreats, or sacs, on foliage, under bark, or under rocks. Some males have huge palps.

CLUB SHAPED. See Clavate.

CLUNALS. [L. *clunes*, buttocks]. The 5th dorsocentral setae (dc5 = h1 or f3) of the Prichard & Baker System.

CLUNAL SETAE. [L. *clunes*, buttocks; *seta*, bristle]. In the Mesostigmata: setae J5, which are usually the most posterior pair of median opisthonotal setae in the Prichard & Baker System.

CLYPEAL. [L. *clypeus*, shield]. Of or pertaining to the clypeus.

CLYPEATE. [L. *clypeus*, shield]. Shaped like a shield. Having a clypeus.

CLYPEIFORM. [L. *clypeus*, shield]. Clypeate.

CLYPEUS. [L. *clypeus*, shield]. The anterior tagma between the eyes and the anterior edge of the carapace.

COACERVATE. [L. *coacervare*, to heap up]. Piled up. Collected into a crowd; densely clustered.

COACTUS. [L. *coactus*, compress]. Pertaining to a short stout form; condensed.

COADUNATE. [L. *coadunare*, to unite with]. Combined or joined together.

COAGULATION. [L. *coagulare*, to curdle]. The change from a liquid to a viscous or solid state.

COALESCE. [L. *coalitus*, united]. To come together into one. To fuse or blend.

COALESCENT. [L. *coalitus*, united]. A growing together, uniting.

COALITE. [L. *coalitus*, united]. To unite or associate.

COBWEB SPIDERS. See **Theridiidae.**

COCHLEA. [Gr. κοχλιας, a snail]. In some **Linyphiidae**: a pit at the tip of the epigynal scape.

COCHLEATE (COCHLEIFORMIS). [Gr. κοχλιας, a snail]. Spiral. Screw-like. Snail-shell like.

COCOON. [Pr. *coucoun*, egg-shell]. The protective covering for the eggs of spiders. A silken case spun by some acariform mites in which molting occurs.

COECAL. [L. *caecus*, blind]. Ending blindly, or in a closed tube or pouch.

COECUM. See Caecum.

COE - For words not found here see **CE-** or **CAE-**.

COECUM, COECA. See Caecum.

COELOCONOID (EXTRACONIC). [Gr. κοιλος, hollow; κωνος, cone; ειδος, form]. Approaching conical but with concave sides. See Conoid, Cyrtoconoid.

COELOMIC CAVITY. [Gr. κοιλωμα, a hollow]. That area between the viscera and the body wall.

COELOMIC FLUID. [Gr. κοιλωμα, a hollow]. Lymph or similar fluid filling the coelom.

COELOMODUCT. [Gr. κοιλωμα, a hollow; L. *ducere*, to lead]. A duct formed from the lining of the coelom (i.e. from mesoderm) and leading from the coelom to the exterior, for example the oviduct and the excretory ducts of many animals.

COELOMOSTOME. [Gr. κοιλωμα, a hollow; στομα, mouth]. The inner opening of a coelomoduct or coelomopore.

COENOSIS. [Gr. κοινος, common; -οσις, suf. of condition]. A group of organisms having similar ecological preferences.

COENOSITE. [Gr. κοινος, common; σιτος, food]. A commensal. Any organism that usually shares food with another organism.

COENOTROPIC BEHAVIOR (COENOTROPE). [Gr. κοινος, common; τροπη, change]. Behavior common to all members of a group or species. It may be regarded as the product of original nature and a shared environment, or alternatively, common behavior that results from common social motives.

CO-EVOLUTION. [L. *cum*, with; *evolvere*, to unroll]. The related and complementary evolution of two species, e.g. host/parasite, predator/prey, flowering plant/pollinator. See also Counter Evolution.

COHABITANTS. [L. *cum*, together; *habitare*, to dwell]. Organisms that dwell with others.

COHORT. [L. *cohors*, enclosure]. 1. An indefinite taxonomic group that is used in different ways by different authorities. It may be used as a rank above superorder, a rank between class and order, or for a group of related families. 2. A group of individuals of the same age.

COLD-BLOODED ANIMALS. See Poikilotherm.

COLIFORM. [L. *colum*, sieve; *forma*, shape]. Sieve-like. Cribriform.

COLLAR. [ME. *coler*, collar]. In ticks and mites: a circular line or ridge at the place of epiostracal attachment of setae, ungues, and rutellum.

COLLAR TRAECHAE. An obsolete term used for a peritreme.

COLLATERAL. [L. *cum*, with; *latera*, sides]. A subsidiary. Indirect. A lateral branch of an axon.

COLLICULOSE, COLLICULATE. [L. *colliculus*, small hill]. Having small elevations. Having raised, rounded and reticulate-like ornamentation on shields. In the Mesostigmata especially: having a pattern resembling fish scales.

COLLICULUM. [L. *colliculum*, little hill]. A small elevation.

COLLIGATE. [L. *cum*, with; *ligare*, to bind]. To tie or bind together.

COLULATE. [L. *colus*, small distaff]. Having a colulus.

COLULUS. [L. *colus*, small distaff]. The slender or pointed structure immediately in front of the spinnerets in some spiders; in others it may be greatly reduced or seemingly missing. A homologue of the anterior median spinnerets or cribellum.

COMATE, COMATUS. [L. *comatus*, with long hair]. Having hair. Hairy.

COMB CLAWS. The bipectinate or biserrate claws or empodia, as for example in the Teneriffiidae (Prostigmata).

COMB-FOOTED SPIDERS. See **Theridiidae**.

COMB SETA. [L. *seta*, bristle]. Pectinate setae on the palps of cheyletid mites (Prostigmata)

COMB SHAPED. Pectinate.

COMMENSAL (COMMENSALISM). [L. *cum*, with; *mensa*, table]. Of members of different species that live in close association and share the same food but without much mutual influence. A type of symbiotic relationship in which one species benefits and the other species is neither benefited nor harmed. See also Parasitism, Symbiosis.

COMMINUTE. [L. *comminutus*, shattered]. To grind up finely. To reduce to minute particles.

COMMISSURAL INDURATION. [L. *commissura*, a seam; *induratio*, hardness of heart.]. In mites: a sclerotized thickening along the inner part of a commissural line to support the lip walls.

COMMISSURAL LINE. [L. *commissura*, a seam]. In arachnids: the union between two lips. In ticks and mites there are three or four, two superior and one or two inferior.

COMMUNICATION. [L. *communis*, common]. 1. Action on the part of one organism that alters the pattern of behavior in another organism. 2. Sending of signals that influence the behavior or development of others.

COMMUNITY. [L. *communis*, common]. An ecological term for any naturally occurring group of different organisms that inhabit a common environment and interact with each other, especially through food relationships. The communities may be of varying sizes and a larger one may contain smaller ones.

COMMUNITY ECOLOGY. [L. *communis*, common; Gr. οικος, household]. An approach to the study of ecology which places emphasis on the living components of an ecosystem and usually involves the analysis of interactions between community members by making use of classification and ordination.

COMOSE. [L. *comosus*, hairy]. Having hair. Hairy. Ending in a tuft. Comate.

COMPANION SETA. [L. *seta*, bristle]. A seta that is strongly associated with a solenidion, sometimes sharing the same location.

COMPASS ORIENTATION. The ability to proceed in a particular direction without reference to landmarks.

COMPETITION. The interaction between individuals of the same species (intraspecific competition), or between different species (interspecific competition) for a particular resource. The usual result of interspecific competition is that the growth and survival of one species is adversely affected and may lead to the replacement of one species by another, if it has a competitive advantage. Competition favors the separation of closely related or similar species and separation may be achieved temporally, spatially or ecologically by (e.g.) behavioral or morphological adaptations. The separation of species in this way is known as the competitive-exclusion principle.

COMPETITIVE ASSOCIATION. The relationship between coexisting groups whose boundaries are defined by competition for space or resources.

COMPETITIVE EXCLUSION PRINCIPLE. The principal that groups (or individuals) competing for identical ecological requirements cannot coexist indefinitely. See Competition.

COMPLANATE. [L. *complanatus*, flattened]. Flattened. Level.

COMPLICATE. [L. *cum*, with; *plicare*, to fold]. Folded longitudinally. Folded together or in an irregular manner.

COMPOUND OCELLUS. [L. *ocellus*, little eye]. Any ocellate spot containing three or more circles of color.

COMPOUND PHANERE. [Gr. φανερος, manifest]. In phanerotaxy, composed of two different elements, one basal and one distal.

COMPRESSED. [L. *comprimere*, to compress]. Of body form: flattened from side to side as if by a lateral force, as opposed to depressed - which is flattened vertically.

COMPRESSOR. [L. *compressus*, pressed together]. A muscle that serves to compress.

CONCAMERATION. [L. *cum*, with; *camera*, chamber]. Divided into chambers or cavities.

CONCATENATE. [L. *cum*, together; *catena*, chain]. To join or link together. To connect in a series or chain. Having a series of points placed in regular order.

CONCHATE/CONCHIFORM. [L. *concha*, shell; *-atus*, provided with/*forma*, shape]. Shell-shaped.

CONCINATE, CONCINNE. [L. *concinnus*, well-arranged]. Neat, elegant.

CONCOLOUR. [L. *concolour*, colored uniformly]. Of uniform color.

CONCOLOUROUS. [L. *concolour*, of the same color]. Of the same color, of uniform color.

CONCRESCENCE. [L. *concrescere*, to grow together]. The growing together of parts.

CONCRETE. [L. *concretus*, grown together]. Grown together to form a single structure.

CONCRETION. [L. *cum*, together; *crescere*, to grow]. A massing together of parts or particles.

CONCURRENT. [L. *cum*, together; *currere*, run]. Meeting or coming together. Acting in conjunction, as a joint or vein.

CONDUCTOR. [L. *conducere*, to lead together]. In male spiders: an accessory projection at the base of the embolus (a penis-like projection). This structure, along with others (depending on the family) and in association with the sclerotized configurations of the female epigynum, aid in the orientation of the palp and in the insertion of the embolus into the female opening.

CONDUPLICATE. [L. *cum*, together; *duplicare*, to double]. Doubled or folded together; folded together lengthwise.

CONDYLE. [Gr. κονδυλος, knuckle]. A knob-like process that forms the fulcrum for joint movement.

CONDYLOPHORE. [Gr. κονδυλος, knuckle; -φορα, -carrying]. In the Acariformes: a pair of internal sclerotized structures concerned with the articulation of the empodial and lateral claws.

CONE SHAPED. Cyrtoconic.

CONFAMILIAL. [L. *cum*, together; *familia*, family]. Belonging to the same taxonomic family.

CONFERTED, CONFERTIM. [L. *confertus*, pressed together]. Densely assembled or packed. Crowded.

CONFLECT. [L. *cum*, with; *flectere*, to turn/alter one's course]. Crowded. Clustered. The opposite of sparse.

CONFLICT. [L. *confligere*, to strike]. The situation in which an animal is motivated to perform more than one activity at a time. This may lead to one motivation becoming dominant, or to unresolved ambivalent behavior, or to irrelevant behavior.

CONFLUENT. [L. *confluere*, flowing together]. Flowing together. Merging. Running together as confluent spots without marked lines of distinction.

CONFUSED. [L. *confusus*, indistinct/disordered]. Of a marking with indefinite outlines. Of a running together as of lines and spots without definite pattern.

CONGENER. [L. *congener*, of the same race]. A species belonging to the same genus.

CONGENERIC. [L. *congener*, of the same race]. Belonging to the same race.

CONGENETIC. [L. *cum*, with; Gr. γενεσις, descent]. Having the same origin.

61

CONGENITAL. [L. *congenitus*, born along with]. Of some trait, physical or otherwise, that is present at birth.

CONGESTED. [L. *congerere*, to bring together]. Heaped together. Crowded.

CONGLOBATE. [L. *conglobatus*, formed into a ball]. Gathered together in a ball or sphere. The action of rolling up into a ball.

CONGLOMERATE. [L. *conglomerare*, to entangle together]. Bunched together.

CONICO-ACUMINATE. [L. *conus*, cone; *acumen*, point]. Shaped like a long, pointed cone.

CONICULUS. [L. *coniculus*, little cone]. In mites: the malapophyses and lips enclosing the preoral cavity. The rostrum.

CONIFEROUS. [L. *conus*, cone; *ferre*, to bear]. Bearing a cone-like process.

CONISPIRAL. [L. *conus*, cone; *spira*, coil]. With a spire projecting as a cone.

CONJOINED. [L. *cum*, together; *jungere*, to join]. United or joined together.

CONJUNCTIVE. [L. *cum*, together; *jungere*, to join]. Conjoining, connecting or connective.

CONNATE. [L. *connatus*, born together]. Originating together. Fused together or immovably united.

CONNECTING DUCTS. [L. *ducere*, to lead]. Ducts in the female genitalia which connect the copulatory pores to the spermathecae.

CONNECTIVE. [L. *connexus*, join]. A longitudinal cord of nerve fibers connecting successive ganglia.

CONNIVENT. [L. *connivere*, to close the eyes]. Arching over so as to meet. Gradually converging.

CONOID. [Gr. κωνος, cone; ειδος, form]. Cone-like.

CONOID DISCS. [Gr. κωνος, cone; ειδος, form]. The two pairs of structures on the ventral sucker plate of astigmatan deutonymphs. See Hypopus.

CONSANGUINOUS MATING. [L. *consanguineus*, related by blood]. Mating between genetically closely related individuals, e.g. siblings, cousins.

CONSCUTUM. [L. *cum*, with; *scutum*, shield]. In some ticks: the dorsal shield which is formed by the union of the scutum and alloscutum.

CONSIMILAR. [L. *consimilis*, entirely similar]. Similar in all respects.

CONSPECIFIC. [L. *cum*, together with; *species*, particular kind]. Of individuals belonging to the same species.

CONSPERSE. [L. *conpersus*, besprinkled]. Thickly and irregularly scattered with minute markings.

CONSPURCATUS. [L. conspurcatus, pollute/defile]. Confusedly sprinkled with discolored or dark spots.

CONSTRICTED. [L. *constrictus*, drawn together]. Narrowed medially and dilated toward the extremities.

CONSTRICTOR. [L. *constrictus*, drawn together]. A muscle that compresses or constricts a cavity, orifice, or organ.

CONSUTE. [L. *consuere*, to sew together]. With stitch-like markings.

CONTRACTILE. [L. *cum*, with; *trahere*, to move by pulling]. That which may be drawn together or contracted or which has the power of contracting.

CONTERMINOUS. [L. *cum*, together; *terminus*, boundry]. Touching at the boundry, contiguous.

CONTIGUOUS. [L. *contiguus*, touching together]. Touching but not actually united.

CONTINUOUS BREEDER. An animal that may breed at any time of the year.

CONTINUOUS VARIATION (QUANTITATIVE INHERITANCE). Variation within a species that shows a gradual change from one state to another and fluctuates about a mean.

Variations of height and color are common examples and, if treated statistically, exhibit graphically a 'normal' curve. This phenomenon is due to the interaction of a large number of genes (polygenes/multiple allelomorphs).

CONTORTED. [L. *contortus*, twisted together]. Twisted or straining out of shape or place.

CONTRACTILE BULBILS. [L. *cum*, with; *trahere*, to draw together; *bulbus*, bulb]. Pulsating swellings, sometimes containing valves, in some of the principle arteries of animals which have no true heart.

CONTRALATERAL. [L. *contra*, opposite to; *latus*, side]. Pertaining to the other side. Opposite: Ipsilateral.

CONUS. [L. *conus*, cone]. Any cone-shaped structure.

CONVERGENCE (CONVERGENT EVOLUTION, EPHARMONIC CONVERGENCE). [L. *convergere*, to incline together]. Evolutionary changes whereby animals from different groups come to produce increasingly similar characteristics due to similar environments or habits.

CONVERGENT. [L. *convergere*, to incline]. Tending to approach.

CONVEX. [L. *convexus*, arched]. The outer curved surface of a segment of a sphere.

CONVOLUTE. [L. *cum*, together; *volvere*, to wind]. Rolled together, as for example in shells in which the outer whorls overlap the inner.

CO-OPERATION. [L. *cooperationem*, a working together]. Mutually beneficial behavior that may involve several individuals of the same species or group, e.g. in pack hunting, care of young, predator detection. Co-operation between different species is termed symbiosis.

CO-OPERATIVE BREEDING. [L. *cooperationem*, a working together]. Mutually A breeding system in which parents are assisted in the care of the young by other adults or *sub*-adults.

COPARASITISM. [L. *cum*, together; Gr. παρασιτος, one who eats at the table of another]. The parasitization of a host by more than one parasite.

COPULATE. [L. *copulare*, to couple]. To unite in sexual intercourse.

COPULATION. [L. *copulare*, to tie/connect]. The act of sexual intercourse between two animals, *in copula*, sometimes written incorrectly as *in copulo*.

COPULATORY BURSA. [L. *copulare*, to tie/connect; *bursa*, purse]. See Bursa Copulatrix.

COPULATORY DUCTS. [L. *ducere*, to lead]. The paired tubes that lead inwards from the copulatory openings of the female to the spermathecae, and receive the embolus of the male.

COPULATORY ORGAN. [L. *copulare*, to tie/connect]. Any organ, such as a palpal organ, that enables the male to inseminate the female.

COPULATORY SAC. [L. *copulare*, to tie/connect]. See Bursa Copulatrix, Spermatheca.

CORD. [Gr. χορδη, cord]. Any chord-like structure.

CORDATE, CORDIFORM. [L. *cor*, heart]. Heart-shaped.

CORE TEMPERATURE. The body temperature of an animal measured near to or at the center of the body.

COREMIFORM. [Gr. κορημα, a broom; L. *forma*, shape]. Broom-shaped.

CORIACEO-RETICULATE. [L. *corium*, leather; *reticulum*, little net]. Having impressed reticulations giving a leather-like appearance.

CORIACEOUS. [L. *corium*, leather; *-aceous*, of the nature of]. Tough and leathery. Having a leathery texture.

CORIARIOUS. [L. *corium*, leather; *arium*, a place where something is kept]. Leather-like in sculpture or texture.

CORINNIDAE. [Gr. Κοριννα, an Ancient Greek poet/or 'maiden']. The cosmopolitan family of corinnid sac spiders (infraorder Araneomorphae, superfamily Entelegynae). Some genera appear to be mimics of ants and velvet ants, and others are ant-like.

CORINNOIDEA. [Gr. Κοριννα, an Ancient Greek poet/or 'maiden']. In a previous classification: the large, cosmopolitan, superfamily of dark sac and liocranid sac spiders (infraorder Araneomorphae, superfamily Entelegynae) that unified the families: **Corinnidae, Liocranidae.**

CORNEOUS. [L. *corneus*, of horn]. Resembling horn. Having a hornlike texture.

CORNICULATE. [L. *corniculum*, little horn]. Having small horns or small horn-like structures.

CORNICULUS (CORNICULI). [L. *corniculum*, little horn]. In some mites: a horn-shaped infracapitular seta on the malapophysis that supports the salivary styli. It may be toothed, bifurcate, trifurcate, spine-like, spatulate or membranous.

CORNIFORM. [L. *cornu*, horn; *forma*, shape]. A long mucronate or pointed process similar to the horn of an ox.

CORNU (CORNUA). [L. *cornu*, horn]. A horn or horn-shaped structure.

CORONAL PLANE (FRONTAL PLANE). [L. *corona*, crown]. A plane of view that cuts a body or organ squarely and vertically from left to right, thus dividing the body into anterior and posterior portions.

CORONA. [L. *corona*, crown]. A region of minute denticles at the anterior end of the ventral mouth-parts of ticks.

CORONARY. [L. *corona*, crown]. Crown-shaped or crown-like. Encircling.

CORPORA. [L. *corpora*, bodies]. Plural of Corpus.

CORPORA ADIPOSA. [L. *corpora*, bodies; *adeps*, fat]. A mass of fatty tissue.

CORPUS. [L. *corpus*, body]. The body as a whole.

CORPUS ADIPOSUM. [L. *corpus*, body; *adeps*, fat]. Fat bodies.

CORRIDOR DISPERSAL ROUTE. A migration route that allows more or less unhindered exchange of organisms between locations. An ancient dispersal corridor exists between western Europe and China, via central Asia.

CORRUGATED (CORRUGATE). [L. *corrugare*, to wrinkle]. Wrinkled; contracted into alternate ridges and furrows.

CORTEX. [L. *cortex*, bark]. An outer layer of any organ.

CORTICAL. [L. *cortex*, bark]. Relating to the cortex or outer skin.

CORTICATE. [L. *cortex*, bark]. Having a special cortex, or external layer.

CORTICIFORM. [L. *cortex*, bark; *forma*, shape]. Sculptured or textured like bark.

CORTICINUS. [L. *cortex*, bark]. Bark-like in sculpture, texture or color.

CORTICOLOUS. [L. *cortex*, bark; *colere*, to inhabit]. Inhabiting bark.

CORVINUS. [L. *corvus*, crow]. Deep, shining black.

COSCINOID. [Gr. κοσκινον, a sieve; ειδος, form]. Sieve-like.

COSMETIDAE. [Gr. κοσμεω. metaph. to adorn]. A diverse family of harvestmen or daddy longlegs (suborder Laniatores, superfamily Gonyleptoidea) from Argentina to the southern USA. Many have elaborate white/yellow/green/orange/red spots and stripes on the dorsal scutum, and strongly compressed pedipalps.

COSMIOTAXY. [Gr. κοσμιος, regular; ταξις, an arranging]. Secondary formation of recognizable and simple organs.

COSMOCHTHONIOIDEA. [Gr. κοσμος, world; χθονιος, beneath the earth]. A superfamily of mites (suborder Oribatida, infraorder Enarthronota). Families: **Cosmochthoniidae, Haplochthoniidae, Pediculochelidae, Sphaerochthoniidae.**

COSMOPOLITAN. [Gr. κοσμος, world; πολιτης, citizen]. Of world-wide, or pandemic, distribution.

COSMOTROPICAL. [Gr. κοσμος, world; τροπικος, of a turn or change]. Occurring throughout most of the tropics.

COSTATE. [L. *costa*, rib]. With longitudinal ribs or ridges.

COSTELLA (COSTELLAE). [L. *costella*, little rib]. A small costa or rudimentary rib.

COSTELLATE. [L. *costella*, little rib]. Bearing costellae.

COSTIFORM. [L. *costa*, rib; *forma*, shape]. Shaped like a costa or raised rib.

COSTULA. [L. *costula*, little rib]. On the prodorsum of some oribatid mites: a longitudinal ridge or set of ridges that are similar to lamellae but without a projecting edge or cusp.

COSTULATE, COSTULATUS. [L. *costula*, little rib]. Being less prominently ribbed than costate.

COTERMINOUS. [L. *cum*, with (the same); *terminous*, boundary]. Of organisms having the same distribution.

COTYLA. [Gr. κοτυλη, cup]. The cup or socket of a ball and socket joint.

COTYLIFORM, COTYLOID. [Gr. κοτυλη, cup; L. *forma*, shape]. Cup-shaped.

COTYLOID. [Gr. κοτυλη, cup; ειδος, form]. Shaped like a cup.

COUNTER EVOLUTION. The evolution of certain characteristics within a population in response to adverse interactions with another population.

COUNTER SHADING. A coloring strategy in which the animal is darker dorsally and lighter ventrally. Thus when viewed from below (when the lighting is from above) the animal appears inconspicuous. See also Cryptic Coloration, Obliterative Coloration.

COURTSHIP. [L. *cortem*, enclosed yard]. The elaborate patterns of specialized instinctive behavior exhibited by almost all animals prior to mating. This includes **Courtship Feeding** in which food, or food-like objects are presented by a male to the female during courtship. The gift may be of nutritional significance but commonly the presentation is an act of appeasement and may be ritualized.

COWLED. [L. *cucullus*, hood]. Shaped like a hood. Hooded.

COXA, COXAE. [L. *coxa*, hip]. The uppermost, or proximal, segment of a leg, often firmly attached to the body. It articulates with the thorax proximally and the trochanter distally. The coxal musculature originates within the thorax. Coxae are numbered I, II, III and IV from anterior to posterior and in some males are greatly enlarged and cover most of the ventral surface. They may bear two spurs and be deeply incised (described as bifid) or may be trenchant and have a knife-like margin. See also Coxapodite, Limb.

COXA CAVA. See Coxal Cavity.

COXAL CAVITY. [L. *coxa*, hip]. The cavity in which the coxa articulates. An acetabulum.

COXAL FIELDS. [L. *coxa*, hip]. In acariform mites: the venter where the coxae have fused to the body wall and thus cover the sternal region.

COXAL GLANDS. [L. *coxa*, hip]. In arachnids and other chelicerates: the thin-walled spherical glands found along the side of the prosoma (cephalothorax). These glands (of which there are never more than four pairs) collect wastes from the surrounding blood. The wastes are then transported to the outside by a long convoluted duct which opens onto the coxa of the appendages. Some arachnids may posses both coxal glands and malpighian tubules.

COXAPODITE (COXOPODITE). [L. *coxa*, hip; Gr. –πους, foot]. The coxa of arachnids. See Limb.

COXISTERNAL PLATE. [L. *coxa*, hip; Gr. σταρνον, chest]. A sclerotized plate in the coxisternal region.

COXISTERNAL SETA. [L. *coxa*, hip; Gr. σταρνον, chest; *seta*, bristle]. A seta in or between the coxisternal plates and numbered from coxa I-IV e.g. 1a-c, 2a-c, 3a-c, 4a-c.

COXISTERNUM. [L. *coxa*, hip; Gr. σταρνον, chest]. The floor of the podosoma that supports the legs. It is composed of the fused coxae (epimera I-IV).

COXOTROCHANTERAL JOINT. [L. *coxa*, hip; Gr. τροχαντηρ, runner]. One of the two primary bendings of a typical arthropod leg. Of the joining of the coxa and the trochanter. See also Femorotibial Joint.

CRANAIDAE. [Gr. κρανσος, rugged, also myth. a king of Attica]. A family of neotropical harvestmen or daddy longlegs (suborder Laniatores, superfamily Gonyleptoidea).

CRENA. [L. *crena*, notch]. A notch, cleft or indentation.

CRENATE. [*to furnish with a battlement* (from L. *crena*, notch)]. Having a scalloped or toothed margin. Indented. Notched.

CRENATION. [L. *crena*, notch]. One of a series of rounded projections forming the edge of an object or structure.

CRENATURE. [L. *crena*, notch]. A rounded projection; the indentation as between crenations.

CRENEL(L)ATIONS. [*to furnish with a battlement* (from L. *crena*, notch)]. In tick and mites: small hypostomal ridges or denticle-like structures often found in non-feeding males of some species. They may also occur beyond the denticulate zone in species in which the hypostome bears prominent denticles.

CRENICOLOUS. [Gr. κρεηνη, a spring; L. *colere*, to inhabit]. Living in springs.

CRENOPHILOUS. [Gr. κρεηνη, a spring; φιλος, loving]. Thriving in springs.

CRENULATE. [L. *crenula*, little notch]. With minutely scalloped edges.

CREPERA. [L. *crepera*, dark]. A ray of paler color on a dark background.

CREPUSCULAR. [L. *crepusculum*, dusk]. Of the twilight: principally of animals active at dusk, and sometimes including those active just before dawn. See also Diurnal, Nocturnal.

CRESCENT, CRESCENTIC, CRESCENTIFORM. [L. *crescere*, to grow]. Crescent-shaped. Sickle shaped.

CREST. [L. *crista*, crest]. A ridge or linear prominence on any part of the head or body. See Cristate, Carinate.

CRIBELLATE. [L. *cribellum*, little sieve]. Of spiders which have a cribellum: a plate through which a particular type of silk is produced. This silk is combed out by the small curved bristles on the calamistrum and mixed with ordinary silk from the spinnerets to make a bluish lace-like composite strand. The fibers are so small in diameter that prey insects easily become entangled in them, without any adhesive.

CRIBELLUM. [L. *cribellum*, little sieve]. A sieve-like transverse plate, usually divided by a delicate keel into two equal parts, located in front of the spinnerets; the modified anterior median spinnerets.

CRIBRATE. [L. *cribrum*, sieve]. Pierced with closely set, small holes.

CRIBRIFORM / CRIBROSE. [L. *cribrum*, sieve; *forma*, shape]. Sieve-like. Cribrose.

CRIBRUM. [L. *cribrum*, sieve]. In the Mesostigmata: the spiculate area posterior to and often lateral to the anal opening on the shield bearing the anal opening and circumanal setae.

CRIOCONE. [Gr. κριος, ram; κωνος, a pine cone]. In the shape of an uncoiled spiral (such as a ram's horn).

CRISPATE. [L. *crispus*, curly]. Having a wrinkled or fluted margin; ruffled; irregularly twisted.

CRISTA. [L. *crista*, crest]. Any ridge or crest.

CRISTA METOPICA. [L. *crista*, ridge; Gr. μετωπιον, forehead]. The propodosomal plate of adult mites (Prostigmata).

CRISTATE, CRISTIFORM. [L. *cristatus*, crested]. Crest-shaped.

CRISTIFORM. [L. *crista*, ridge; *forma*, shape]. In the form of a sharp ridge or crest.

CRISTULA. [L. *crista*, ridge; *-ula*, dim.suf.]. A small crest.

CRISTULATE. [L. *cristula*, crest]. Having a small crescent-like ridge or crest.

CROCEOUS, CROCUS. [Gr. κροκωτος, saffron-yellow]. Saffron-yellow.

CROCHET (CROTCHET). [Fr. *crochet*, small hook]. A distal joint (unguis) of the chelicerae.

66

CRONISM. [Gr. Κρονος, Saturn]. The attempted or successful eating of moribund or dead infants by their parents.

CROOK. [ON. *krokr*, crook]. A hook; recurved tip; bend or curve.

CROTCHET. [Fr. *crochet*, small hook]. See Crochet.

CROTONIOIDEA (NOTHROIDEA). [Gr. κροτων, a tick (*Ixodes ricinus*)]. A superfamily of mites (suborder Oribatida, infraorder Holosomata). Families: **Crotoniidae (Camisiidae)**, **Malaconothridae, Nothridae, Trhypochthoniidae.**

CRUCIATO-COMPLICATUS. [L. *crux*, cross; *cum*, with; *plicare*, to fold]. Folded crosswise.

CRUCIFORM. [L. *crux*, cross; *forma*, shape]. Resembling a cross; cross-shaped.

CRURA, CRUS. [L. *crura / crus*, legs / leg]. Any leg or leg-like appendage.

CRUSTA. [L. *crusta*, shell]. Any hard covering.

CRYOPHILIC. [Gr. κρυος, frost; φιλος, loving]. Thriving in low temperatures.

CRYPSIS. [Gr. κρυπτος, hidden]. The ability to be hidden or camouflaged.

CRYPT. [Gr. κρυπτος, hidden]. Any simple glandular tube or cavity.

CRYPTIC. [Gr. κρυπτος, hidden]. Concealing; stillness; silence; death-feigning; protective coloration.

CRYPTIC COLORATION. [Gr. κρυπτος, hidden]. Any coloration which helps concealment, either by resembling the surroundings or by breaking up the body outline. See also Counter Shading, Obliterative Coloration.

CRYPTO-. [Gr. κρυπτος, hidden]. Hidden, concealed.

CRYPTOBIOSIS. [Gr. κρυπτος, hidden; βιωσις, a living]. See Anabiotic.

CRYPTOFAUNA (PHYTALFAUNA). [Gr. κρυπτος, hidden; L. *Faunus*, a god of the woods]. Animals that live in concealed places such as rock cervices.

CRYPTORHESIS. [Gr. κρυπτος, hidden; ρεω, flow]. The process of internal secretion.

CRYPTOSPHERE. [Gr. κρυπτος, hidden; σφαιρα, sphere]. The habitat of cryptozoans.

CRYPTOSTIGMATA. [Gr. κρυπτος, hidden; στιγμη, a mark]. See Oribatida.

CRYPTOZOA. [Gr. κρυπτος, hidden; ζωη, life]. Invertebrates which are large enough to be visible yet small enough to live between the litter and the soil. See also Patobionts, Patocoles, Patoxenes, Phanerozoa.

CRYPTOZOIC. [Gr. κρυπτος, hidden; ζωον, animal]. Inhabiting cervices, spaces under stone, leaves, etc. Living in concealment.

CRYPTOZOOLOGY. [Gr. κρυπτος, hidden; ζωον, animal; λογος, discourse]. The scientific study of cryptozoa.

CRYPTS. [Gr. κρυπτος, hidden]. Minute secretory follicles or cavities.

CRYSTALLINE. [Gr. κρυσταλλινος, crystalline]. Transparent, like crystal.

CRYSTALLOID. [Gr. κρυσταλλος, ice; ειδος, form]. Crystal-like.

CTENIDAE. [Gr. κτεις, a comb]. The family of wandering spiders (infraorder Araneomorphae, superfamily Entelegynae). They are highly defensive and venomous nocturnal hunters with a distinctive longitudinal groove on the top-rear of their oval carapace, similar to those of the **Amaurobiidae.**

CTENIDIA. [Gr. κτεις, a comb]. In some **Dictynidae** (Araneae): structures on the male palpapl tibia consisting of a short process bearing diminutive stout spines.

CTENIFORM. [Gr. κτεις, a comb; L. *forma*, shape]. Comb-shaped.

CTENIZIDAE. [Gr. κτενιζω, to comb]. The family of cork-lid trapdoor spiders (infraorder Mygalomorphae, superfamily Avicularioidea). Several genera of this primitive family use a comb-like rake on the chelicerae to excavate a burrow, sometimes as deep as 1 m (~3 feet). The burrow and lid are lined with thick silk and an opening is cut, leaving one side of a snugly-fitting door still attached. The spider uses its large, downward-facing fangs to hold the hinged door shut until it feels the vibrations of an approaching meal; it then dashes out, pounces on its prey and pulls it back inside the burrow. They can distinguish between potential prey with amazing accuracy and also hold the door tightly shut against predators. Previously in the monotypic superfamily Ctenizoidea.

CTENOID. [Gr. κτεις, a comb; ειδος, form]. Comb-like. Having a margin of small teeth.

CTENOSE. [Gr. κτεις, comb]. Comb-like.

CUCULLUS. [L. *cucullus*, hood]. In the Ricinulei (an order of small arachnids): a hinged plate attached to the carapace and covering the mouth parts.

CUIRASS. [F. *cuirasse*, leather breastplate]. A protective covering such as a cuticle, plates, scales or shells.

CULTELLATE. [L. *cultellus*, knife]. Knife-like.

CULTRATE (CULTRIFORM). [L. *cultratus*, knife-shaped]. Shaped like a pruning knife. Cultriform.

CULUS. [L. *culus*, fundament]. The anus.

CUMULATE. [L. *cumulatus*, heap up]. To accumulate in groups or heaps.

CUMULUS (CUMULI). [L. *cumulus*, heap]. An accumulation; a group or heap.

CUNAXID. [*Cunaxa*, an ancient town in Babylonia, near the Euphrates]. A predatory mite (**Cunaxidae**: Prostigmata). Some are bright red and have large raptorial palps, others are pale red to brownish and have short palps. Both types usually have a distinctive neck between the capitulum and idiosoma.

CUNEATE, CUNEIFORM. [L. *cuneatus*, wedge-shaped; *forma*, shape]. Wedge-shaped.

CUP SHAPED. Cupuliform. Cyathiform.

CUPOLA ORGAN. [L. *cupula*, a little tub]. See Sensillum Campaniformium.

CUPREOUS. [L. *cupreus*, of copper]. Copper colored, coppery.

CUPULATE. [L. *cupula*, a little tub]. Cup-shaped.

CUPULE. [L. *cupula*, a little tub]. A small sucker or acetabulum.

CUPULIFORM. [L. *cupula*, tub; *forma*, shape]. Cup-shaped. Cyathiform.

CURSORIAL. [L. *cursor*, runner]. Adapted for running.

CURVATE. [L. *curvatus*, bend]. Curved.

CUSP. [L. *cuspis*, point]. Any sharp-pointed structure.

CUSPIDATE. [L. *cuspidare*, to make pointed]. Terminating in a point, as in teeth, leaves, etc.

CUSPULES. [L. *cuspis*, point]. In the Mygalomorphae: small spines on the endites and labium.

CUSTODITE. [L. *custodis*, guardian]. Guarded, as an enclosed larva.

CUTANEOUS. [L. *cutis*, skin]. Of the skin.

CUTICLE. [L. *cuticula*, thin skin]. The superficial non-cellular layer of horny material secreted by and covering the epidermis of many animals. It is present in most invertebrates and is mainly made of a collagen-like material or of chitin. It is secreted by an underlying layer of epidermal cells and in arthropods can be a thick three-layered structure (outer epicuticle, exocuticle, inner endocuticle) firm enough to function as a skeleton (hardened by lime-salts in crustaceans) or a thin, even, elastic structure in wings and leg hinges. It can be colored for camouflage or warning, permeable for aquatic gas exchange or have a thin waterproof covering of wax (epicuticle) to prevent excessive water loss. These properties can exist in different parts of the same individual. The cuticle commonly contains specialized gland cells that secrete pheromones and defensive chemicals as well as various types of sensory receptors. See also Chitin.

CUTICULAR. [L. *cuticula*, thin skin]. Of or pertaining to the cuticle.

CUTICULAR LOBES. [L. *cuticula*, thin skin]. In the cuticles of many mites: the pattern of minute raised processes that ornament the plicate ridges.

CUTICULAR ORNAMENTATIO. [L. *cuticula*, thin skin]. A mark or sculpture of any type on the cuticle of an animal.

CUTICULAR PORES. [L. *cuticula*, thin skin]. Minute pores opening at the surface of the cuticle.

CUTICULARIZATION. [L. *cuticula*, thin skin]. The process of cuticle formation.

CUTICULIN. [L. *cuticula*, thin skin; *-in*, chem. suf.]. In mites: the epiostracum.

CYANEOUS. [Gr. κυανος, dark-blue]. Dark blue.

CYANESCENT. [Gr. κυανος, dark-blue; L. *escens*, become]. Having a deep bluish tinge or shading. See also Cerulean.

CYANIC. [Gr. κυανος, dark blue]. Blue or bluish.

CYANOGENIC. [Gr. κυανος, dark-blue; -γενης, producing]. 1. Production of the blue color. 2. Used to describe pungent and irritating vapors emitted by certain arthropods.

CYANOPHIL. [Gr. κυανος, blue; φιλος, loving]. Having an affinity for blue stains.

CYATHIFORM. [L. *cyathus*, cup; *forma*, shape]. Cup-shaped.

CYATHOLIPIDAE. [Gr. κυαθος, cup; λιπος, grease/fat]. A family of spiders (infraorder Araneomorphae, superfamily Entelegynae) that live in a wide range of habitats from humid montane forests to dry savannahs.

CYBAEIDAE. [Gr. κυβαια, a kind of merchant ship]. The small family of diving-bell spiders, (infraorder Araneomorphae, superfamily Entelegynae).

CYCLAMEN MITE. [*Cyclamen*, plant genus - family Myrsinaceae]. *Phytonemus* (*Steneotarsonemus*) *pallidus* a plant parasite mite (Prostigmata: family **Tarsonemidae**).

CYCLICAL VARIATION. [Gr. κυκλος, circle]. A periodic fluctuation in any animal or plant population in a particular locality. This can be correlated with (for example) periodic climatic variation or the periodic abundance of food.

CYCLOCTENIDAE. [Gr. κυκλος, circle; κτεις, a comb]. A small family of spiders (infraorder Araneomorphae, superfamily Entelegynae).

CYCLOPEAN, CYCLOPIC. [Gr. κυκλωψ, round-eye]. A single median eye developed under certain artificial conditions, or a mutation in place of the normal pair.

CYDARIFORM. [L. *cydarum*, a kind of ship; *forma*, shape]. Globose or orbicular, but truncated at opposite ends.

CYLINDRACEOUS. [Gr. κυλινδρος, cylinder; L. *-aceous*, of the nature of]. Of, or like, a cylinder.

CYLINDRICAL. [Gr. κυλινδρος, cylinder]. Round, cylinder-like with parallel sides.

CYLINDROCONIC. [Gr. κυλινδρος, cylinder; κωνος, cone]. Having the shape of a cylinder terminating in a cone.

CYMBAEREMAEOIDEA (EREMELLOIDEA). [Gr. κυμβη, small boat; ερημια, desert]. A superfamily of mites (suborder Oribatida, infraorder Brachypylina - section Pycnonoticae). Families: **Adhaesozetidae**, **Ametroproctidae**, **Cymbaeremaeidae**, **Eremellidae**.

CYMBIFORM. [Gr. κυμβη, small boat; L. *forma*, shape]. Boat-shaped. Navicular. Scaphoid.

CYMBIUM. [Gr. κυμβιον, small boat]. In some spiders: the boat-shaped tarsus of the pedipalps to which the palpal bulb is attached. See also Paracymbium.

69

CYPHOPHTHALMI. [Gr. κυφος, stooping; οφθαλμος, the eye]. A small suborder of harvestmen or daddy long legs (subclass Arachnida, order Opiliones) from Africa, Asia and southern Europe. They are characterized by having small prehensile palps, short legs and a reduced sternum. Infraorders: Boreophthalmi, Scopulophthalmi, Sternophthalmi.

CYRTAUCHENIIDAE. [Gr. κυρτος, curved; αυχενιος, of the neck]. The family of wafer trapdoor spiders (infraorder Mygalomorphae, superfamily Avicularioidea) from the United States, Mexico, South America, Africa central and southeast Asia. They lack the thorn-like spines on tarsi and metatarsi I and II (the two outermost leg segments) found in true trapdoor spiders. Previously in the monotypic superfamily Cyrtauchenioidea.

CYRTOCONIC. [Gr. κυρτος, curved; κωνος, a cone]. Cone shaped.

CYRTOCONOID. [Gr. κυρτος, curved; κωνος, a cone; ειδος, like]. Approaching a cone in shape, but with convex sides. See also Conoid, Coeloconoid.

D

d. In the Acariformes: a designation used for setae on segment D, e.g. d1-2. See Grandjean System.

D. In the Acariformes: a designation used for the second region of the hysterosoma. See Grandjean System.

D1-5; DC1-5. See Pritchard & Baker System.

DACRYOID. [Gr. δακρυον, a tear; ειδος, form]. Tear-drop shaped.

DACTYL. [Gr. δακτυλος, finger]. In scorpions: a terminal ventral projection of the clawed distal segment of the leg (the praetarsus).

DACTYLOID. [Gr. δακτυλος, finger; ειδος, form]. Finger-like.

DACTYLOPODITE. [Gr. δακτυλος, finger; πους, foot]. The metatarsus and tarsus of spiders.

DADDY-LONGLEGS. 1. Arachnids of the order Opiliones - also known as Harvestmen. They can be recognized by having the anterior and posterior regions fused together and surmounted by a characteristic tubercle. Typically all the limbs are extremely long except in soil living species. 2. Craneflies, dipterans of the family **Tipulidae**.

DAESIIDAE. [deriv.uncert.]. A large family of sun spiders (subclass Arachnida, order Solifugae) from southern Europe, central Asia, the Middle East, Africa, and South America.

DAGGER MARK. A marking in the form of the Greek letter Psi (ψ).

DAMAEOIDEA. [L. damae, fallow / red-deer]. A superfamily of fungivorous mites (suborder Oribatida, infraorder Brachypylina - section Pycnonoticae) that live mainly in plant litter and organic soil layers. They have a regulatory effect of the density of fungi that are plant-pathogenic. Families: **Damaeidae, Hungarobelbidae.** Some authorities consider the Hungarobelbidae to be a synonym for the Damaeidae.

DE NOVO. [L. de novo, anew]. Arising anew.

'DEAR ENEMY' PHENOMENON. The recognition of, and reduced aggression towards territorial neighbors, with a resulting increase in aggression towards strangers.

DEATH FEIGNING (TONIC IMMOBILITY, THANATOSIS). A state of total stillness characteristically elicited in many species in response to particular stimuli perceived as dangerous. It is usually employed when escape is impossible and is particularly successful against predators that only kill living prey.

DEATH POINT. The level of an environmental variable (e.g. temperature) above or below which organisms can not exist.

DEAURATE. [L. de, away from; auratus, golden]. Having a gold color that appears rubbed or worn.

DECAMEROS. [Gr. δεκα, ten; μερος, part]. With parts arranged in 10s.

DECIDUOUS. [L. *decidere*, to fall off]. To fall away at the end of a period of growth, or at maturity.

DECLINATE. [L. *de*, away; *clinare*, to bend]. To bend aside, to curve away with the apex downward.

DECLIVOUS (DECLIVITY, DECLIVITOUS). [L. *de*, away from; *clivis*, hill]. Sloping downward; gradually descending. Opposite: Acclivous.

DECOLLATE. [L. *de*, away from; *collum*, neck]. Cut or broken off.

DECORTICATE. [L. *de*, away from; *cortex*, bark]. To divest of the exterior coating; deprived of the cortex or outer coat.

DECREPITANS. [L. *decrepitus*, worn out (with age)]. Crackling.

DECUMBENT. [L. *decumbere*, to lie down]. Bending downward. Upright at the base and bending down at the tip.

DECURRENT. [L. *de-*, down; *currere*, to run]. Closely attached to and running down the body.

DECURVED. [L. *de*, down; *curvus*, bent]. Curved or bent downwards.

DECUSSATE, DECUSSATION. [L. *decussare*, to cross]. X-like. Crossing over from one side to another; as when bristles alternately cross each other.

DEDIFFERENTIATION. [L. *de*, away; *differentia*, difference]. The loss of specialized cellular features and the consequent returning to a more generalized condition. This phenomenon is characteristic of regeneration.

DEFAECATION. [L. *defaecare*, to defecate]. The egestion of feces from an animal.

DEFERENT. [L. *deferre*, to carry away]. Conveying away from; e.g. of ducts. Opposite: Efferent.

DEFICIENT. [L. *deficiens*, disappoint/fail]. Of setae that are reduced from a supposed holotrichous number.

DEFINITIVE HOST. [L. *definire*, to limit]. The final host of the adult parasite. See also Intermediate Host.

DEFINITIVE RESERVOIR. [L. *definire*, to limit]. A host or location in which a natural supply of the terminal stage (frequently sexual) of a parasite occurs.

DEFLECTED. [L. *de*, away from; *flectere*, to bend]. Bent backward or to one side or downward.

DEFLEX. [L. *deflectere*, to turn aside]. To bend downwards.

DEGENERATE. [L. *degenerare*, to degenerate]. To become less specialized or less complex or smaller, either within a life-cycle or during evolution.

DEGENERATION. [L. *degenerare*, to degenerate]. The progressive lowering of the efficiency of an organ or organs during life or during evolution. The evolutionary loss of structure and function leading to a vestigial organ.

DEHISCENCE. [L. *dehiscere*, to split open]. The cracking, splitting or tearing of an opening in an organ or structure along lines of weakness.

DEIMATIC (DYMANTIC) BEHAVIOR. [Gr. δειματοω, frighten]. Posturing intended to intimidate or frighten. It may be a bluff or it may precede attack.

DEINOPIDAE (erron. **DINOPIDAE**). [Gr. δεινος, frightful; -ωψ, appearance]. The family of ogre-eyed, ogre-faced, gladiator or net-casting spiders (infraorder Araneomorphae, superfamily Entelegynae). Cribellate spiders that capture prey by hanging upside down on a thread and holding a small square of web between the anterior four legs. The web is not adhesive but the strands are very elastic and combed into many loops. As prey passes underneath, the spider stretches out the net and drops it onto the insect, the loops catch on the insect's hairs and entangle it. They have highly developed eyesight.

DELAMINATION. [L. *de*, away from; *lamina*, a thin plate]. Split or divided into layers.

DELETERIOUS. A trait, mutation or characteristic that impairs survival.

DELIMITATION. [L. *de*, away from; *limes*, boundary]. Setting or marking a boundary.

DELIQUESCE. [L. *deliquescere*, to melt away]. To turn to water. To become liquid.

DELITESCENCE. [L. *delitescere*, to lie hidden]. The incubation period of a pathogenic organism. The latent period of a poison.

DELOMORPHIC. [Gr. δελος, visible, μορφα, shape]. Of definite form.

DELTOID. [Gr. Δ-delta; ειδος, form]. Having a general triangular shape.

DEME. [Gr. δημος, the people]. An interbreeding group in a population. A local population.

DEMERSAL. [L. *demergere*, to plunge]. Living on or near the bottom of the sea or of a lake.

DEMODICIDAE. [Gr. δημος, fat; δηξ, wood-worm]. The family of follicle mites (infraorder Eleutherengona, superfamily Cheyletoidea). Worm-like mites that live in the hair follicles of mammals and spend their entire life cycle attached to the host.

DEMOID. [Gr. δημωδης, popular]. Abundant.

DENATANT. [L. *de*, down; *natare*, to swim]. Migrating, swimming or drifting with the current.

DENDRITIC/DENDRIFORM/DENDROID. [Gr. δενδρον, tree; L. *forma*, shape]. Tree-like or branching.

DENDROCOLOUS. [Gr. δενδρον, tree; L. *colere*, to inhabit]. Living in or on trees.

DENDROID/DENDRITIC/DENDRIFORM). [Gr. δενδρον, tree; ειδος, form/ L. *forma*, shape]. Tree-like or branching.

DENDROPHILOUS. [Gr. δενδρον, tree; φιλος, loving]. Thriving in trees or orchards.

DENS. [L. *dens*, tooth]. A tooth or tooth-like process.

DENTATE. [L. *dens*, tooth]. Toothed. Having teeth or tooth-like projections.

DENTATE-LIRATE. [L. *dens*, tooth; *lira*, ridge between two furrows]. Having teeth and fine raised lines or grooves.

DENTATE-SERRATE. [L. *dens*, tooth; *serra*, saw]. Teeth with serrated dentations on the edges.

DENTATE-SINUATE. [L. *dens*, tooth; *sinus*, curve]. Teeth with a wavy indented margin.

DENTICLE. [L. *denticulus*, little tooth]. Any small tooth-like structure.

DENTICULATE. [L. *denticulus*, little tooth]. Bearing very small tooth-like projections.

DENTIFORM. [L. *dens*, tooth; *forma*, shape]. Formed or appearing like a tooth.

DENTIGEROUS RIDGES. [L. *dentes*, teeth; *gerere*, to bear]. Elevations bearing small teeth or tooth-like projections.

DENTITION. [L. *dentes*, teeth]. In ticks and mites: of the arrangement of denticles on the hypostome. E.g 2/2 refers to 2 longitudinal files of denticles on either side of the hypostomal midline.

DENUDATE. [L. *nudus*, naked]. Without covering: destitute of scales or hair.

DENUDE. [L. *nudus*, naked]. To free from covering: to rub so as to remove the surface covering of scales, hair or other vestiture.

DEPAUPERATE. [L. *de*, away from; *pauper*, poor]. Impoverishing or exhausting. Falling short of the natural size or development due to being impoverished or starved.

DEPENDENT. [L. *dependere*, hang down from]. Hanging down.

DEPLANATE, DEPLANATUS. [LL. *deplanatus*, make level]. Level off, make level, make even.

DEPRESSED. [L. *deprimere*, to keep down]. Of body form: flattened from top to bottom as if by a vertical force, as opposed to compressed - which is flattened laterally.

DEPRESSOR MUSCLE. [L. *de*, away from; *pressus*, bear down]. Any muscle that lowers or depresses any appendage.

DEPURATION. [L. *de*, away from; *puratus*, cleanse]. The act of cleansing. Of being free of impurities.

DERIVED CHARACTER. A character not present in the ancestral stock.

DERMA, DERMIS (CORNIUM). [Gr. δερμα, skin]. The layer of the cuticle beneath the epidermis.

DERMAL. [Gr. δερμα, skin]. Relating to the skin or outer covering.

DERMAL BRANCHIAE. [Gr. δερμα, skin; βραγχια, gills]. The respiratory processes formed as outgrowths from the skin in many aquatic animals.

DERMAL GLANDS. Unicellular glands which secrete wax, cement, pheromones, etc.

DERMANYSSIAE. [Gr. δερμα, skin; νυσσω, to stab]. In some classifications: a sub-cohort of mites (suborder Monogynaspida, infraorder Gamasina) that unites the superfamilies Ascoidea, Dermanyssoidea, Eviphidoidea, Rhodacaroidea, Veigaioidea.

DERMANYSSIDAE. [Gr. δερμα, skin; νυσσω, to stab]. A family of mites (infraorder Gamasina, superfamily Dermanyssoidea). They have a pair of tracheal spiracles next to each coxae of the third pair of legs and the body is covered with numerous brown plates. They are economically important parasites on birds (red mites) and mammals.

DERMANYSSINA. [Gr. δερμα, skin; νυσσω, to stab]. In a previous classification: a suborder of mites (superorder Parasitiformes, order Mesostigmata) defined by the possession of a secondary sperm access system in the female and a spermatodactyl in the male. The superfamilies previously grouped here (Ascoidea, Dermanyssoidea, Eviphidoidea, Rhodacaroidea, Veigaioidea) are now included in the infraorder Gamasina.

DERMANYSSOIDEA. A superfamily of mites (suborder Monogynaspida, infraorder Gamasina) which are mainly parasitic on vertebrates, but some (e.g. species of *Varroa*, *Tropilaelaps*) are parasites of honeybees or other insects. Twenty families. In some classifications this superfamily may be included in the sub-cohort Dermanyssiae.

DERMATOID. [Gr. δερμα, skin; ειδος, form]. Skin-like or functioning as skin.

DERMATOSKELETON. [Gr. δερμα, skin; σκελετος, hardened]. See Exoskeleton.

DERMATOZOON (DERMOZOON). [Gr. δερμα, skin; ζωον, animal]. A skin parasite.

DERMECOS. [Gr. δερμα, skin; οικος, house]. The habitat limited to the spaces between the hairs of a mammal's skin, in which ectoparasites live.

DERMOSKELETON. [Gr. δερμα, skin; σκελετος, dried]. See Exoskeleton.

DERMOZOON. See Dermatozoon.

DESCLEROTIZATION. [L. *de*, away from; Gr. σκληρος, hard]. A reduction of sclerotin in sclerotized parts or structures.

DESECTUS. [L. *desectus*, cut off]. See Truncate.

DESERTICOLOUS. [L. *desertus*, waste; *colere*, to inhabit]. Living in deserts and arid regions.

DESIDAE (AMPHINECTIDAE). [Gr. δεσις, bundling]. A family of spiders (infraorder Araneomorphae, superfamily Entelegynae). *Desis*, is a marine intertidal species that commonly lives in a barnacle shell, which is sealed with silk; thus allowing an air bubble to be maintained during high tide. Other members of the family are not intertidal.

DESMOID. [Gr. δεσμος, a band; ειδος, form]. Ligamentous. Resembling a bundle.

DESQUAMINATION. [L. *de*, away; *squama*, scale]. The shedding of cuticle or epidermis in flakes as opposed to shedding it entire.

DESTITUTUS. [L. *destitutus*, destitute]. Wanting. Being without.

DETERMINATE. [L. *determinare*, to limit]. With well-defined outlines or distinct limits.

DETONANS. [L. *detonatus*; roar out]. Exploding. A sudden noise or a puff like an explosion.

DETRITUS. [L. *detritus*, rubbed off]. The litter formed from fragments of non-living material such as dung, leaf-litter and corpses.

DETRORSE. [L. *de*, away from; *versus*, turn]. Directed downward. See also Antrorse, Retrorse.

DETUMESCENCE. [L. *de-*, down from; *tumescere*, to swell]. The subsidence of a swelling: opposite - intumescence.

DEUTOGYNE. [Gr. δευτερος, second; γυνη, woman]. An overwintering or aestivating form of eriophyoid mites (**Eriophyidae**), the female of which is morphologically different from the primogyne and has no male counterpart.

DEUTONYMPH/DEUTERONYMPH (HYPOPUS). [Gr. δευτερος, second; νυμφη, chrysalis]. In the development of ticks and mites: the second instar (nymphal stage) which may either be chrysalis-like or motile.

DEUTOSTERNAL (HYPOGNATHAL) DENTICLES. [Gr. δευτερος, second; στερνον, chest; L. *denticulus*, little tooth]. In ticks and mites: the rows of small, often irregular, tooth-like projections that run transversely across the deutosternal groove and sometimes onto the lateral faces of the subcapitulum. Sometimes reduced to a single tooth.

DEUTOSTERNAL GUTTER (DEUTOSTERNAL GROOVE, HYPOGNATHAL GROOVE, SUBCAPITULAR GROOVE). [Gr. δευτερος, second; στερνον, chest]. In parasitiform mites: the median longitudinal gutter running on the subcapitulum that receives the tritosternum.

DEUTOSTERNUM. [Gr. δευτερος, second; στερνον, chest]. In ticks and mites: the sternite of the pedipalpi-bearing segment.

DEUTOVUM. [Gr. δευτερος, second; L. *ovum*, egg]. In some ticks and mites: a stage in metamorphosis in which a secondary (deutovarial) membrane surrounds the embryo until the larval stage.

DEVELOPMENTAL HOMEOSTASIS. [Gr. ομοιος, alike; στασις, standing]. The ability to produce a normal phenotype in spite of developmental or environmental disturbances.

DEXIOTROPIC. [Gr. δεξιος, right; τροπη, turn]. Turning towards the right. Opposite - Laeotropic.

DEXTRAD, DEXTRAL. [L. *dextra*, right hand]. On, or belonging to the right side of the body, or moving towards the right side of the body. Opposite, Sinistrad, Sinistral.

DEXTRO-CAUDAD. [L. *dextra*, right hand; *cauda*, tail]. Of some structure extending obliquely between dextrad and caudad.

DEXTRO-CEPHALAD. [L. *dextra*, right hand; Gr. κεφαλη, head]. Of some structure that extends obliquely between dextrad and cephalad.

DEXTRORSE. [L. *dexter*, right handed; *vertere*, to turn]. Growing in spirals that turn from left to right, clockwise from the point of view of an observer. Opp. - Sinistrose.

DI-. Gr. prefix (δι-,). Two.

DIACTINAL. [Gr. δι-, double; ακτις, ray]. Being pointed at both ends.

DIAGNOSIS. [Gr. διαγνωσις, discrimination]. A concise description of an organism, complete with distinctive characteristics.

DIAGNOSTIC. [Gr. διαγνωσις, discrimination]. Traits or characteristics that differentiate species or genera etc.

DIAPAUSE. [Gr. διαπαυειν, to cause to cease]. A period of suspended development accompanied by greatly decreased metabolism. It may be correlated with seasonal changes such as hibernation or aestivation.

DIAPHANOUS. [Gr. διαφανης, transparent]. Showing light through its substance. Transparent. Translucent.

DIAPHRAGM. [Gr. διαφραγμα, midriff]. Any thin dividing membrane, e.g. a thin membrane separating the cavity containing the heart from the rest of the body.

DIARTHRIC. [Gr. δισ-, twice; αρθρον, joint]. Of a subcapitulum with a more or less transverse articulation that reaches the lateral margin at the base of the palp. See also Anarthrous, Stenarthric.

DIARTHROPHALLOIDEA. [Gr. δισ-, twice; αρθρον, joint; φαλλος, symbolic penis]. A monotypic superfamily of mites (suborder Monogynaspida, infraorder Uropodina). Family: **Diarthrophallidae.** This superfamily was previously included in the now-abandoned suborder Diarthrophallina.

DIARTHROSIS. [Gr. διο-, twice; αρθρον, joint]. An articulation that permits free movement.

DIARTICULAR. [Gr. δι-, two; L. *articulus,* joint]. Of, or pertaining to, two joints.

DIATROPISM. [Gr. δια-, through; τροπη, a turn]. The tendency for organs and organisms to orient themselves at right angles to the direction of a stimulus.

DIAULIC. [Gr. δισαυλος, a double pipe]. With two separate ducts open to the surface.

DIAUXIC GROWTH. [Gr. δι-, two; αυξω, to grow]. Growth in two phases separated by a period of relative inactivity.

DIAXIAL. [Gr. δι-, two; αξων, axis]. Of the chelicerae of spiders in which the paturon projects either forward or down with the fangs moving inward towards each other. See also Paraxial.

DIAXON. [Gr. δι-, two; αξων, axis]. With two axes.

DICELLATE. [Gr. δικελλα, two-pronged mattock]. Having two prongs.

DICEROUS. [Gr. δικερος, two-horned]. Having two horns.

DICHOID. [Gr. διχο-, separately; ειδος, form]. In the Acariformes: appearing to be divided between legs II-III by a flexible sejugal furrow.

DICHOIDY. [Gr. διχο-, separately; ειδος, form]. In the Acariformes: having the body articulated between legs II-III by a flexible sejugal (protero-hysterosomatic) furrow. See also Holoid, Ptychoidy, Trichoidy.

DICHOPATRIC SPECIATION. [Gr. διχο-, separately; πατρη, one's native land]. See Speciation.

DICHOPTIC. [Gr. διχο-, separately; οπτικος, of sight]. Having two distinctly separate eyes.

DICHOTOMOUS. [Gr. διχο-, separately; τομη, a cut]. Dividing into two equal branches.

DICHOTOMY. [Gr. διχο-, separately; τομη, a cut]. Classification into two groupings on the basis of the presence or absence of a certain characteristic, or by paired opposites.

DICRANOLASMATIDAE. [Gr. δι-, two; L. *cranium,* skull; Gr. ελασμα, metal plate]. A small family of short-legged harvestmen (suborder Dyspnoi, superfamily Troguloidea) in which most parts f the body are encrusted with soil particles.

DICHROISM. [Gr. δι-, two; χρως, color]. The property of showing two very different colors, one by transmitted light and the other by reflected light, or of some dyes which stain different tissues different colors.

DICHROMATIC. [Gr. δι-, two; χρωμα, color]. 1. Having two color varieties. 2. Seeing only two colors.

DICHROMATISM. [Gr. δι-, two; χρωμα, color]. The condition in which members of a species show one of two distinct color patterns.

DICOELOUS. [Gr. δι-, two; κοιλος, hollow]. Having two cavities.

DICONDYLAR. [Gr. δι-, two; κονδυλος, knuckle]. Having a double articulation.

DICTYNIDAE. [Gr. δικτυον, a hunting net]. A family of small cribellate spiders (infraorder Araneomorphae, superfamily Entelegynae) that exhibit social behavior; large numbers living together without territoriality, aggression or cannibalism and feeding simultaneously on prey caught in large communal webs.

DICTYNOIDEA. [Gr. δικτυον, a hunting net]. In a previous classification: a superfamily of araneomorph spiders (order Araneae, suborder Araneomorphae) that united the families: **Anyphaenidae, Cybaeidae, Desidae, Dictynidae, Hahniidae, Nicodamidae**. These families are now grouped in the superfamily Entelegynae.

DIDACTYL. [Gr. δι-, two; δακτυλος, digit]. Having two claws.

DIDUCTOR MUSCLE. [Gr. δι-, double; L. *ducere*, to lead]. A muscle that causes two parts of the body to separate.

DIDYMOUS. [Gr. διδυμος, twin]. Growing in pairs.

DIECDYSIS. [Gr. δι-, double; εκδυσις, an escape]. The (usually) short period in the molting cycle, between metecdysis and proecdysis.

DIECIOUS. See Dioecious.

DIEL. [L. *dies*, day]. Occurring in a 24 hour period.

DIFFRACTED. [L. *dis*, twice; *frangere*, to break]. 1. Bent in different directions. 2. Separated into parts.

DIFFRACTION COLORS. Colors produced by unevenness on the surface of an organism - as opposed to colors produced by pigmentation.

DIFFUSE. [L. *diffusus*, spread out]. Not sharply distinct at the edge or margin. Widely spread; extended.

DIFFUSE SENSITIVITY. [L. *diffusus*, spread out]. Response to stimuli which affects the whole surface of an organism.

DIFFUSION TRACHEAE. [L. *diffusus*, spread out; LL. *trachia*, windpipe]. Cylindrical tracheae which are not subject to collapse. See also Ventilation Tracheae.

DIGAMETIC. [Gr. δι-, twice; γαμετης, spouse]. Having two types of gamete, one that produces females and one that produces males.

DIGENY. [Gr. διο-, double; -γενες, production]. Sexual reproduction.

DIGEST. [L. *digerere*, to digest]. To break down ingested food into soluble matter which can be absorbed through the wall of the gut.

DIGESTION. [L. *digestio*, digestion]. The enzymic breaking down of the large and complex molecules of foodstuffs into simpler compounds which can readily be absorbed and incorporated into metabolism. This may occur extracellularly by excreting enzymes from salivary glands, glands in the gut wall or from other glands into the gut cavity.

DIGESTIVE TRACT. [L. *digestio*, digestion]. The alimentary canal as a whole, or more specifically that portion behind the crop, in which assimilation takes place.

DIGITATED. [L. *digitus*, finger]. Divided into finger-like processes.

DIGITIFORM. [L. *digitus*, finger / toe; *forma*, shape]. Finger-shaped.

DIGITULE. [L. *digitulus*, little finger]. Any small finger-like processes. The small finger-like processes on tarsi.

DIGITUS (DIGITI). [L. *digitus*, finger]. A digit.

DIGITUS FIXUS. [L. *digitus*, a finger / toe; *fixus*, immovable]. See Fixed Digit.

DIGUETIDAE. [deriv.uncert.]. The small family of cone-web spiders (infraorder Araneomorphae, superfamily Haplogynae) that construct in tangled webs with a cone-like central retreat where they hide and lay eggs. It is sometimes considered to be subfamily of the **Plectreuridae**

DILACERATE. [L. *dis*, apart; *lacera*, torn]. To tear to pieces. To tear apart.

DILATE. [L. *dilatare*, to enlarge]. To swell or enlarge in volume.

DILATOR. [L. *dilatare*, to enlarge]. Any muscle that expands an organ.

DIMERIC (DIMEROUS). [Gr. δις-, two; μερος, part]. Bilaterally symmetrical. Having two parts. Having a two-jointed tarsus.

DIMIDIATE. [L. *dimidiare*, to halve]. Divided into two.

DIMORPHISM. [Gr. δι-, two; μορφη, shape]. The existence of two distinct forms within a species. Sexual dimorphism is the existence of marked morphological differences between males and females; such as body size or plumage. See also Monomorphism, Polymorphism.

DIOECIOUS. [Gr. δι-, two; οικος, house]. Unisexual, bisexual, i.e. the male and female reproductive organs being borne on different individuals (applied to plants and animals).

DIESTRUS. [Gr. δι-, two; οιστρος, gadfly]. See Anestrus.

DIONYCHA. [Gr. δι-, two; ονυξ, talon]. A grouping of spiders in which there are two claws on the end of the tarsus. Members of this group are usually hunting spiders and many have a dense tuft of hairs known as a 'claw-tuft' at the end of the tarsus. These hairs are split into thousands of fine cuticular extensions and facilitate walking upside down on smooth surfaces, such as the undersides of leaves. See also Scopula, Trionycha.

DIONYCHOPODES. [Gr. δι, two; ονυξ, talon; πους, foot]. In an older classification: a suborder (subclass Arachnida, order Scorpiones) containing some living scorpions and some fossil members from the Carboniferous period.

DIONYCHOUS. [Gr. δι-, two; ονυξ, talon]. Having two claws, as on the tarsi of hunting spiders. See Dionycha.

DIOPTRATE. [Gr. δι-, two; ωψ, eye]. Having the eyes or ocelli separated by a narrow line.

DIOPTRIC. [Gr. δι-, two; ωψ, eye]. Refractive. Vision by refraction of light.

DIPHYGENETIC. [Gr. διφυης, two-fold; γενετης, the begotten]. Producing embryos of two different types.

DIPLOCENTRIDAE. [Gr. διπλοος, double; κεντρον, center]. A large family of scorpions (order Scorpiones, superfamily Scorpionoidea) that are mainly from the New World, plus *Nebo* (subfamily Nebinae) from the Middle East. Recent work suggest that this family should be a subfamily (Diplocentrinae) of the Scorpionidae, but even more recent work has re-established the family.

DIPLOE. [Gr. διπλοη, fold]. The tail of a scorpion.

DIPLOID. [Gr. διπλοος, double; ειδος, form]. See Ploidy.

DIPLOID PARTHENOGENESIS. See Parthenogenesis.

DIPLOSTICHOUS. [Gr. διπλοος, double; στιχος, row]. Arranged in two series or rows.

DIPLURIDAE. [Gr. διπλοος, double; ουρα, tail]. The family of curtain-web spiders, or funnel-web tarantulas (infraorder Mygalomorphae, superfamily Avicularioidea) from tropical and sub-tropical regions. Rastella are lacking, the carapace in the head region is not higher than the thoracic region and they have a thoracic groove that is a circular pit. Their anterior spinnerets are much shorter than their posterior spinnerets, which have three segments of about equal length. They construct funnel-shaped webs then lie in wait at the narrow end. Previously in the monotypic superfamily Dipluroidea.

DIPNEUMONOUS. [Gr. δι-, two,πνευμων, lung]. Of spiders which have two book lungs. See also Tetrapneumonous.

DIRECT COMPETITION. The exclusion of one individual or species from a resource by the direct aggressive behavior of another.

DIRECT EYES. The anterior median pair of eyes in spiders.

DIRECTIONAL SENSE. The sense or senses that permit an animal to locate its position in its environment and move towards the source of a stimulus or to evade it as necessary. One of the most important directional senses in the animal kingdom is sight but this may be supplemented or supplanted by sound reception (subsonic - which may be vibrational, sonic and ultrasonic), chemical reception, weak electric fields (in many fish) infra-red sensors (in rattlesnakes), magnetic field receptors and gravity field receptors (as in ears). There may also be other senses of which we are not yet aware.

DIRECTIVE COLORATION. Marks or colors which tend to divert the attention of an enemy from more vital parts.

DISARTICULATE. [L. *dis*, separate; *articulus*, joint]. To separate at a joint.

DISASSORTATIVE MATING. The phenomenon where individuals in a population mate with dissimilar members of the population more frequently than would be expected by chance. See also Assortative Mating, Panmixia.

DISCIFORM. [L. *discus*, a disc; *forma*, shape]. Having the shape of a plate or disc; discoid.

DISCLERITOUS. [Gr. δις, double; σκλερος, hard]. Of tergites and sternites which are distinct and separate. See also Synscleritous.

DISCODACTYLOUS. [Gr. δισκος, a disc; δακτυλος, digit]. With a sucker at the end of a digit.

DISCOID. [Gr. δισκος, a disc; ειδος, form]. Flat and circular. Disciform.

DISCOLOUR, DISCOLOUR. [L. *discolour*, of different colors]. A change of color. More than one color.

DISCREPANT. [L. *discrepantia*, discordancy]. Discordant, disagreeing, different.

DISCRETE. [L. *discretus*, separated]. Well separated. Applied to distinct parts.

DISCRIMINATION. The perception of difference, or differential response, or the ability to perceive slight differences. The time taken to discriminate between two or more stimuli before reacting is the discrimination time.

DISEROTIZATION. [Gr. διο-, separate; ερως, love]. Inhibition of copulation due to low temperature.

DISJUGAL FURROW/PLANE. [Gr. διο-, separate; L. *jugum*, yoke]. In mites: of the furrow separating the prosoma and opisthosoma.

DISJUNCT. [L. *disiunctus*, separated]. 1. Having body regions separated by a deep constriction. 2. Any discontinuity.

DISJUNCTUS. [L. *disiunctus*, separated]. Separated. Standing apart.

DISLOCATE. [L. *dis*, without; *locus*, place]. To move out of its proper place, as when stria, bands or lines are in discontinuity.

DISPERSAL. [L. *dispergere*, to disperse]. The spread or distribution of the offspring of an organism, or of some chemical produced by it. Dispersal from the birth site is natal dispersal and from the breeding site, breeding dispersal.

DISPERSAL BARRIER. [L. *dispergere*, to disperse]. An ecological barrier. A region of unsuitable habitat that separates regions of suitable habitat, e.g. large stretches of water in the case of terrestrial organisms and regions of (cultivated) cereal monocultures in the case of woodland organisms.

DISPERSAL MECHANISM. [L. *dispergere*, to disperse]. An adaptation specifically for dispersal, which constitutes part of the reproductive strategy of many sessile or slow-moving animals. In general, any means by which a species is aided in extending its range.

DISPERSES. [L. *dispergere*, to disperse]. With scattered markings, punctures or other small sculptures.

DISPLACEMENT BEHAVIOR. Behavior - usually in a situation of conflict - which may seem irrelevant to the situation at hand.

DISPLAY. A stereotyped pattern of behavior involved in communication between animals. It may be for mating, warning, territorial dominance, etc.

DISRUPTIVE COLORATION. A form of animal camouflage in which patches of light and dark, or patches of color, serve to break up the body outline and thus deceive the potential predator.

DISRUPTIVE SELECTION. See Selection.

DISSECTED. [L. *dissecare*, to cut open]. Divided into parts. Cut into parts. Cut open with the internal parts displayed.

DISSEMINULE. [L. *dis*, away from; *seminare*, to sow]. One who originates colonization.

DISSEPIMENT. [L. *dissaepire*, to separate]. A partition wall.

DISSILIENT. [L. *dissilire*, to burst asunder]. Bursting or springing open.

DISSIMULATION. [L. *dissimulare*, feigned]. Feigning.

DISTAD. [L. *distare*, to stand apart]. Away from the base, body or point of attachment.

DISTAL. [L. *distare*, to stand apart]. Away from the center. Away from the body (as of a limb or appendage); away from a defined point on or within the body (opposite - Proximal).

DISTANCE RECEPTOR. An exterior receptor responding to stimuli (e.g. sound/light) that allows the animal to orient itself to the source of the stimuli.

DISTICH. [Gr. διστιχος, of two rows]. Two vertical rows.

DISTITARSUS. [L. *distare*, be distant; Gr. ταρσος, sole of foot]. The metatarsus; the distal subdivision of the tarsus.

DISTOMESAD. [L. *distare*, be distant; *medius*, middle]. Farthest from the base.

DISTOMESAL. [L. *distare*, be distant; Gr. μεσος, middle]. Of the tip and midline.

DISTYCHUS. [Gr. διστιχος, of two rows]. Bipartite. Separated into two parts.

DISUSE HYPOTHESIS. A hypothesis that states that visual disuse leads to the loss of the ability of visual inputs to stimulate the cortical cells.

DITREMATOUS. [Gr. δι-, two; τρημα, opening]. Having the anal and genital openings separate.

DITYPIC. [Gr. δι-, two; τυπος, type]. Having marked sexual dimorphism. Having two distinct types.

DIURNAL. [L. *diurnus*, of the day]. 1. Active during the day. 2. At daily intervals. See also Nocturnal, Crepuscular.

DIURNAL EYES. [L. *diurnus*, of the day]. In spiders: eyes that are dark in color.

DIURNAL RHYTHM. [L. *diurnus*, of the day]. Having a 24 hour periodic cycle. See Circadian Rhythms.

DIVARICATE. [L. *divaricatus*, spread apart]. Forked or divided into branches. Diverging.

DIVARICATOR. [L. *divaricatus*, spread apart]. A muscle which causes parts to open.

DIVARICATORS. [L. *divaricatus*, stretched apart]. Forked. Bifid. Widely diverging.

DIVERGENT. [L. *diversus*, different]. Becoming more separated distally; extending in different directions from the same origin.

DIVERGENT ADAPTATION. See Adaptation.

DIVERSE. [L. *diversus*, turned different ways]. Of a community or taxon that includes numerous, widely differing species.

DIVERSITY INDEX. A mathematical expression of the number of species and number of individuals of each species that are present in a particular habitat.

DIVERTICULUM. [L. *diverticulum*, a by-way]. A blind-ending tubular or sac-like outgrowth branching off from a canal, usually the alimentary canal.

DIVIDED DORSAL SHIELD. [L. *dorsum*, back]. In the Mesostigmata: the two, usually subequal dorsal shields, in adult mites.

DIVISIONS OF YEAR. The six division of the year commonly used in ecology, especially with reference to terrestrial and fresh-water communities: prevernal (early spring), vernal (late spring), aestival (early summer), serotinal (late summer), autumnal (autumn) and hibernal (winter).

DIXENOUS. [Gr. δι-, two; ξενος, host]. Of a parasite using two hosts during its life cycle. See also Autoecious.

DOLABRIFORM (DOLABRATE). [L. *dolabra*, pick-axe; *forma*, shape]. Axe-shaped.

DOLICHOCYBOIDEA. [Gr. δολιχος, long; κυβη, head (of mushroom)]. A superfamily of mites (suborder Prostigmata, infraorder Eleutherengona). Families: Crotalomorphidae, Dolichocybidae.

DOLIFORM (DOLIIOFORM). [L. *dolium*, wine-cask; *forma*, shape]. Barrel-shaped.

DOMAIN (SUPERKINGDOM). [L. *dominus*, master]. A classification level higher than a Kingdom. There are three Domains: 1. **Bacteria**, which contains most of the known Prokaryotes. In this grouping are the Proteobacteria (nitrogen-fixing bacteria), Cyanobacteria (blue-green bacteria), Eubacteria (true gram-positive bacteria), Spirochetes (spiral bacteria) and Chlamydiae (intracellular parasites). 2. **Archaea**, Prokaryotes from extreme environments, Kingdoms: Crenarchaeota (Thermophiles), Euryarchaeota (Methanogens and Halophiles) and Korarchaeota (some hot-spring forms known only from 16s rRNA gene sequences obtained from samples from high temperature hydrothermals). 3. **Eukarya**, containing the Kingdoms Protista, Fungi, Plantae and Animalia. See also Nomenclature.

DOMATIUM. [Gr. δωματιον, small house]. In some plants: a hollow or crevice in which mites (and insects) take refuge. See also Acarodomatium.

DORSAD. [L. *dorsum*, the back; *ad*, to]. In the direction of the back or dorsal surface.

DORSAL. [L. *dorsum*, the back]. On or in the region of the back of an animal. The back of an animal is that part of the body normally directed upwards with reference to gravity.

DORSAL ASPECT. [L. *dorsum*, the back]. The view of the back of an animal. See Dorsal.

DORSAL GROOVE. [L. *dorsum*, the back; OE *græf*, ditch/grave]. A median furrow, or groove, on the carapace that marks the presence of an ingrowth of the body wall on which the dilator muscles of the sucking stomach are attached.

DORSAL HEXAGON. [L. *dorsum*, the back; Gr. εξαγονια, six-cornered]. In many mesostigmatans: a notional hexagonal area defined by setal pairs j5, z5 and j6 in the podonotal region. See Lindquist-Evans System.

DORSAL LYRIFISSURE. [L. *dorsum*, the back; *lyra*, ridge between two furrows; *fissura*, crack]. In the Mesostigmata: the dorsal lyrifissure posterior to the cheliceral seta.

DORSAL PLATE. [L. *dorsum*, the back]. On the larvae in many ticks in the family **Argasidae**: a smooth surface, usually elongated or subcircular, on the dorsum.

DORSAL SCAPE. See Parmula.

DORSAL SETA. [L. *dorsum*, the back; *seta* bristle]. Any seta on the dorsum.

DORSAL SHIELD. [L. *dorsum*, the back]. A carapace that covers the prosoma.

DORSAL VESSEL. [L. *dorsum*, the back]. The heart.

DORSAL VIEW. [L. *dorsum*, the back]. Viewed from above.

DORSIFEROUS. [L. *dorsum*, back; *ferre*, to carry]. Carrying young or eggs upon the back.

DORSIGEROUS. [L. *dorsum*, the back; *gerere*, to bear]. Of animals that carry their young on their back.

DORSILATERAL. [L. *dorsum*, the back; *latus*, side]. Of the back and both sides.

DORSIMESON. [L. *dorsum*, the back; Gr. μεσος, middle]. The middle of the upper surface.

DORSIVENTRAL. [L. *dorsum*, the back; *venter*, belly]. Of the back and belly.

DORSOCAUDAD. [L. *dorsum*, back; *cauda*, tail]. Toward the dorsal surface and caudal end of the body.

DORSOCENTRAL. [L. *dorsum*, back; *centralis*, midpoint]. Of the mid-dorsal surface.

DORSOLATERAL. [L. *dorsum*, the back; *latus*, side]. Towards the sides of the dorsal (upper) surface.

DORSOMEDIAN. [L. *dorsum*, back; *medius*, middle]. Of the true middle line on the dorsum of an individual.

DORSOMESAL. [L. *dorsum*, back; Gr. μεσος, middle]. Being at the top and along the midline.

DORSOMESON. [L. *dorsum*, back; Gr. μεσος, middle]. Where the midline of the body (meson) meets the dorsal surface of the body.

DORSOPLEURAL LINE. [L. *dorsum*, back; Gr. πλευρον, side]. The line of separation between the dorsum and the limb bases of the body, often marked by a fold or groove.

DORSO-SEJUGAL SUTURE/GROOVE. [L. *dorsum*, the back; *seiugo*, separate; *sutura*, seam/OE *græf*, ditch/grave]. A suture that marks the fusion of the prodorsum and notogaster. The anterior portion of the circumgastric scissure. This term is commonly misapplied to a flexible juncture or furrow.

DORSOVENTRAL. [L. *dorsum*, the back; *venter*, belly]. Running from the dorsal (upper) surface to the ventral (lower) surface.

DORSOVENTRAL (DORSIVENTRAL). [L. *dorsum*, back; *venter*, belly]. In the axis or direction from the dorsal toward the ventral surfaces.

DORSULUM. [L. *dorsum*, the back]. The mesonotum before the scutellum, with the wing sockets. Also the mesoscutellum.

DORSUM. [L. *dorsum*, the back]. The upper side or back of an animal.

DRACOCHELIDAE. [Gr. δρακων, dragon; χηλη, claw]. An monospecific extinct family of false scorpions (suborder Heterosphyronida, superfamily Chthonioidea) known from the mid-Devonian of New York State.

DRAG LINE. The thread of silk laid out by spiders, that acts as a safety line. This line of dry silk is laid out behind them as the spiders move around and, at intervals, fasten it to the substratum with adhesive silk.

DRAW-THREAD. The silk-producing gland.

DREPANIFORM/DREPANOID. [Gr. δρεπανη, a sickle; L. *forma*, shape/Gr. ειδος, form]. Sickle-shaped.

DRYMUSIDAE. [Gr. δρυμος, oak coppice]. A small family of long-legged spiders (infraorder Araneomorphae, superfamily Haplogynae) known as 'false violin spiders', from the Caribbean, Costa Rica, South America, and South Africa.

DROMOTROPIC. [Gr. δρομος, race-course; τροπη, turn]. Bent in a spiral.

DUCT. [L. *ducere*, to lead]. Any tube which conducts a fluid or other substance. Usually a tube formed from living cells attached to one another to form an epithelium that is wrapped into a tube with the apical epithelial surface lining the lumen and the basal surface facing outwards.

DUCTUS DEFERENS. [L. *ducere*, to lead; *defero*, to carry away]. An alternative name for the vas deferens, the tube along which sperm travel from the testis to the ampulla adjacent to the prostate gland.

DUCTUS EJACULATORIUS (EJACULATORY DUCT). [L. *ducere*, to lead; *eiaculor*, to throw out]. The duct through which seminal fluid is transferred from the male genitalia to the exterior.

DUPLEX SETAE. [L. *duplex*, two-fold; *seta*, bristle]. A pair of setae, or a seta and a solenidion that share the same insertion.

DUPLICITY. [L. *dupliciter*, doubly]. Being two-fold. Principally applied to the theory that (in the eye) rods are the brightness receptors (scotopic receptors) and cones are the color receptors (photopic receptors).

DUPLIVINCULAR. [L. *duplex*, two-fold; *vinculum*, a band]. Of a ligament formed from alternate bands of hard and soft tissue.

DURUS. [L. *durus*, hard]. Hard.

DUTY FACTOR. The amount of time a foot spends on the ground during locomotion. For example, a walking man may have a duty factor of 0.6 for each foot, thus implying that for 0.2 of the time both feet are on the ground simultaneously.

DUSKY. [OE. *dox*, dark from the absence of light]. Somewhat darkened: pale fuscous.

DWARF MALES (PIGMY (PYGMY) MALES). [ON. *dverge*, dwarf]. Males which are considerably smaller than the females.

DYMATIC COLORATION. [Gr. δειματοω, to frighten]. Coloration designed to startle an attacker.

DYSDERIDAE. [Gr. δυσ-, mis-; δερη, neck]. The family of woodlouse hunting spiders (infraorder Araneomorphae, superfamily Haplogynae). Six-eyed spiders found primarily in Eurasia, extending into North Africa, with a few species occurring in South America and one (*Dysdera crocata*) introduced into many regions of the world.

DYSDEROIDEA. [Gr. δυσ-, mis-; δερη, neck]. In a previous classification, a cosmopolitan superfamily of haplogyne, six-eyed spiders (suborder Opisthothelae, infraorder Araneomorphae) that united the families: **Dysderidae, Oonopidae, Orsolobidae, Segestriidae**. These families are now grouped in the larger superfamily Haplogynae.

DYSPNOI. [Gr. δυσ, mis; πνεω, breathe]. A small suborder of harvestmen (subclass Arachnida, order Opiliones). Superfamilies: Acropsopilionoidea, Ischyropsalidoidea, Troguloidea.

DYSTROPHIC. [Gr. δυσ-, mis-; τροφη, nourishment]. Inadequately or wrongly nourished. Inhibiting appropriate nourishment, as in lakes with an excess of undecomposed organic matter. See also Eutrophic, Oligotrophic.

E

Σ. [Gr. letter epsilon]. In some acariform mites: a designation for the famulus on the tarsi.

e. In the Acariformes: a designation used for setae on segment E; e.g. e1-2. See Grandjean System.

E. In the Acariformes: a designation used for the third region of the hysterosoma. See Grandjean System.

EARTH MITES. Mites of the family **Penthaleidae** (suborder Eupodina, superfamily Eupodoidea). This includes some major plant pests such as the red-legged earth mite (*halotydeus destructor*), the blue oat mites (*Penthaleus* spp.), and the winter grain mite (*Penthaleus major*).

EBENINE. [Gr. εβενος, ebony]. Black, like ebony.

EBURNEAN, EBURNEOUS. [L. *eburneus*, ivory-colored]. Made of, or like ivory; ivory white.

ECALCARATE, ECALCARATUS. [L. *ex*, out of; *calcar*, spur]. Lacking a spur or spur-like process.

ECARINATE. [L. *ex*, without; *carina*, keel]. Without a keel or keel-like structure.

ECAUDATE. [L. *ex*, without; *cauda*, tail]. Without a tail.

ECBOLIC. [Gr. εκβολη, a throwing out]. Thrown out.

ECCRINE. [Gr. εκκρινειν, to secrete]. Of glands that secrete their product without disintegrating.

ECCRITIC TEMPERATURE. [Gr. εκκρινειν, to select]. The preferred body temperature. Used of poikilothermic animals that warm up to around 35 °C by absorbing solar energy and then maintain this body temperature by changing posture. See also Ectotherm, Poikilotherm, Temperature Regulation.

ECDEMIC. [Gr. εκδημος, abroad]. Not native. Opposite - Endemic.

ECDYSIAL. [Gr. εκδυσις, an escape]. Of the fluid found between the old and new layers of cuticle during the molting period. Of glands (Verson's Glands) secreting this 'molting fluid'. See also Ecdysis.

ECDYSIAL CLEAVAGE LINE. [Gr. εκδυσις, an escape]. See Epicranial Suture.

ECDYSIS. [Gr. εκδυσις, an escape]. Molting (molting): the periodic shedding of the outer cuticle in arthropods. It is mediated by the hormone Ecdysone, released from 'molting glands' and all but the lining of the finest trachea are shed. The inner part of the old cuticle is absorbed, the rest splits at a predetermined line of weakness and the animal crawls out. Ecdysis does not usually occur in adults. Four stages are recognized in the molting cycle: **Proecdysis** - a time of preparation for molt during which food reserves are accumulated and blood calcium level rises, possibly due to reabsorption of the old cuticle. New cuticle is laid down and the old one becomes detached. **Ecdysis** - the actual shedding of the old cuticle, which is commonly eaten to regain calcium salts. **Postecdysis** - the endocuticle is secreted and calcified. During this time the animal remains hidden and does not eat. **Intermolt** - the period between molts. See also Apolysis, Verson's Glands.

ECDYSONES. [Gr. εκδυσις, an escape]. Endocrine hormones that mediate molting and puparium formation in arthropods.

ECDYSOTROPHIC CYCLE. [Gr. εκδυσις, an escape; τροφη, nourishment]. Alternation of blood feeding and molting in mites, ticks, and hemimetabolous insects.

ECHINATE. [Gr. εχινος, hedgehog]. Having spines or bristles.

ECHINULE. [Gr. εχινος, spine]. Having small spines.

ECLOSION. [L. e-, out; clausus, shut]. The hatching of an egg.

ECOLOGICAL BARRIER. See Dispersal Barrier.

ECOLOGICAL NICHE. [Gr. οικος, household; λογος, discourse; L. nidus, nest]. The specific role of a particular species in its habitat.

ECOLOGICAL PRESSURE. [Gr. οικος, household; λογος, discourse]. The totality of all environmental pressures or factors that act as agents of natural selection.

ECOLOGICAL SYSTEM. See Ecosystem.

ECOLOGY (OECOLOGY, OIKOLOGY). [Gr. οικος, household; λογος, discourse]. The scientific study of the interrelations, distribution and abundance of organisms.

ECOPARASITE (ECOSITE, OECOPARASITE). [Gr. οικος, household; παρασιτος, parasite]. A parasite that can invade a healthy and uninjured host, i.e. most parasites.

ECOSTATE. [L. e, without; costa, rib]. Without costae.

ECOSYSTEM. [Gr. οικος, household; συστημα, organized whole]. Any interacting living community of plants and animals together with their physical environment. An ecosystem consists of autotrophic organisms, mainly green plants (producers) and heterotrophic organisms, mainly animals (consumers) plus bacteria and fungi (decomposers). The food chains and chemical cycles created lead to the same elements being used over and over again. Thus the whole planet could be considered as one ecosystem.

ECOTONE. [Gr. οικος, household; τονος, tension]. The transition zone, or boundary line, between two diverse communities. Ecotones arise naturally, e.g. at land-water interfaces but may also be the result of human manipulation of the environment, e.g. cleared areas of forest.

ECRIBELLATE. [L. ex, out of; cribellum, little sieve]. Of spiders that lack a cribellum.

ECTAD. [Gr. εκτος, outside; L. ad, towards]. Towards the exterior. Externally.

ECTADENIA. [Gr. εκτος, outside; αδενα, gland]. Ectodermal accessory glands in the male ejaculatory tract.

ECTAL. [Gr. εκτος, outside]. External, outer.

ECTALLY. [Gr. εκτος, outside]. Near to or towards the body wall. See also Ental.

ECTAL MARGIN. [Gr. εκτος, outside]. In the Mygalomorphae: the outer margin of the cheliceral furrow.

ECTAL VIEW. [Gr. εκτος, outside]. From the outside. Commonly referring to a point of view, e.g. male palps are often observed in the ectal view, i.e. away from the midline of the body.

ECTENDOTROPHIC. [Gr. εκτος, outside; ενδον, within; τροφη, nourishment]. Of a parasite that feeds from both the exterior and interior of its host.

ECTOBATIC. [Gr. εκτος, outside; βαινειν, to go]. Leading away from. Efferent. Exodic.

ECTOCRINE. [Gr. εκτος, outside; κρινειν, to separate]. An environmental hormone that is released from a decaying body and which influences the activity of other organisms.

ECTOENTAD. [Gr. εντος, within; L. ad, towards]. Moving or directed inwards from the outside.

ECTOGENOUS. [Gr. εκτος, outside; γενος, birth]. Having origins outside the organism.

ECTOHORMONES. [Gr. εκτος, outside; ορμαω, set in motion]. An old term for the chemical messengers used in external communication. This has now been superseded by the term 'pheromone'.

ECTOPARASITE. [Gr. εκτος, outside; παρασιτος, parasite]. See Parasite.

ECTOPARASITOIDS. [Gr. εκτος, outside; παρασιτος, parasite; ειδος, form]. Parasitoids that develop externally on the host, usually feeding through a lesion produced by the larva. Most ectoparasitoids complete their development on the animal originally attacked due to the female parasitoid paralysing the host prior to laying her eggs, and also because the larvae grow very rapidly. Parasitoids tend to be host-specific.

ECTOPHAGOUS. [Gr. εκτος, outside; φαγειν, to eat]. Feeding on the outside of a food source. Opposite: Entophagous.

ECTOPIC. [Gr. εκ, out of; τοπος, place]. Of an organ or structure not in its normal place. Anything occurring in an abnormal place or manner. Opposite = Entopic.

ECTOSITE. See Ectoparasite.

ECTOSKELETAL. [Gr. εκτος, outside; σκελετος, hard]. Referring to the outside or exoskeleton.

ECTOSTRACUM. [Gr. εκτος, outside; οστρακον, shell]. 1. In the exoskeleton of acarids: the outer primary layer of exocuticle. 2. The middle layer of integument of arachnids.

ECTOSYMBION(T). [Gr. εκτος, outside; συμβιωναι, to live with; ον, being]. A symbiont that lives on or among its hosts. See also Endosymbiont.

ECTOSYMBIOSYS. [Gr. εκτος, outside; συμβιωναι, to live together]. A form of symbiosis in which both symbionts are external, neither living within the body of the other.

ECTOTHECAL. [Gr. εκτος, outside; θηκη, case]. Not being enclosed by a theca.

ECTOTHERM. [Gr. εκτος, outside; θερμη, heat]. An animal whose internal body temperature is totally dependent on external heat sources - primarily solar radiation, but also hot rocks, geysers and springs. See also Eccritic Temperature, Poikilotherm, Temperature Regulation.

ECTOTRACHEA. [Gr. εκτος, outside; LL. trachia, windpipe]. A layer of epithelium on the outer side of the trachea.

ECTOTROPIC. [Gr. εκτος, outside; -τροπος, turning]. To curve outwards.

ECTOZOON. [Gr. εκτος, outside; ζωον, animal]. An alternative for Ectoparasite.

ECUMENICAL. [Gr. οικουμενη, the whole habitable globe]. Cosmopolitan. Pandemic.

EDAPHIC. [Gr. εδαφος, ground]. Relating to, or belonging to, the soil or substratum.

EDAPHIC FACTORS. [Gr. εδαφος, ground]. Environmental or ecological factors that are determined by the physical chemical and biological characters of the soil.

EDAPHIC RACE. [Gr. εδαφος, ground]. A race that is affected by edaphic factors rather than other environmental factors.

EDAPHON. [Gr. εδαφος, ground]. The organisms found living in the soil, i.e. the soil flora and fauna.

EDENTATE (EDENTULOUS). [L. ex, without; dens, tooth]. Being devoid of teeth or folds. Lacking chelicerae

EDGE EFFECT. The tendency for the variety and density of organisms to increase in the region of a boundary zone between communities.

EDGE SPECIES. Species that live mainly, most frequently, or numerously at the edges of communities.

EFFECTED. [L. effectus, brought about/accomplished]. Somewhat angularly bent outward.

EFFERENT. [L. ex, out of; ferre, to carry]. Leading away from. A term used of any nerve or blood vessel leading away from any organ or part of the body. Opposite: Deferent.

EFFETE. [L. effetus, exhausted]. No longer capable of fertility. Barren.

EFFODIENT. [L. effodere, to dig up]. Having the habit of digging.

EFFUSE. [L. effusus, poured out]. Spreading thinly.

EFLECTED. [L. ex, out of; flectere, to bend]. Bent outward somewhat angularly.

EGEST. [L. egestus, discharged]. To eliminate solid material from a cell or from the enteron.

EGESTA. [L. egestus, discharged]. The totality of substances (liquid and solid) discharged from the body. Opposite - Ingesta.

EGESTION. [L. egestus, discharged]. The removal of feces or unwanted or unused food from the body.

EGG. [AS. aeg, egg]. 1. The term usually used to denote an ovum or egg-cell with much yolk and surrounded by several membranes, possibly albumin, and a shell. 2. By definition, the non-motile and usually larger reproductive unit - the counterpart of sperm.

EGLANDULAR. [L. ex, out of; glandula, small acorn]. Without glands.

EICHLER'S RULE. See Host-Parasite Associations.

EILOID. [Gr. ειλεω, roll up; ειδος, form]. Coil-shaped.

EJACULATE. [L. ex, out of; jacere, to throw]. Emitted seminal fluid. Ejected fluid from the body.

EJACULATORY DUCT. [L. ex, out of; jacere, to throw]. The terminal portion of the male sperm duct.

ELABRATE. [L. ex, out of; labrum, lip]. Without a labrum.

ELAIODOCHON (ELAEODOCHON). [Gr. ελαιοδοχος, oil-containing]. An oil gland.

ELATE. [L. elatus, high]. Elevated.

ELATTOSTASE. [Gr. ελαττον, smaller; στασις, position]. In the Chelicerata: a rare condition in a prelarva or larva in which the mouthparts are subject to regression thus, though the mouthparts are intact, they are unable to function. Or there is a lack of chelicerae and palps, closure of the mouth and regression of the pharynx. See also Alternating Calyptostasy, Calyptostasic, Protelattosis.

ELECTROMAGNETIC SENSE. [Gr. ελεκτρον, amber; L. magneta, a loadstone]. The sensory system with which many invertebrates are able to orient themselves either within a self-generated electric field or by detecting disturbances in the Earth's electric or magnetic fields.

ELECTROTAXIS (GALVANOTAXIS). [Gr. ελεκτρον, amber; ταξις, a disposition]. Orientative movement in response to an electric field.

ELECTROTROPISM. [Gr. ελεκτρον, amber; τροπη, turning round]. The response of an organism to an electric field.

ELEUTHERENGONA (ELEUTHERENGONIDA, ELEUTHERENGONINA). [Gr. ελευθερος, free, γονη, seed]. An infraorder of mites (order Trombidiformes, suborder Prostigmata) that includes many important plant parasites. Superfamilies: Cheyletoidea, Cloacaroidea, Dolichocyboidea, Heterocheyloidea, Myobioidea, Pterygosomatoidea, Pyemotoidea, Raphignathoidea, Scutacaroide, Tarsocheyloidea, Tarsonemoidea, Tetranychoidea, Trochometridioidea.

ELEUTHEROZOIC. [Gr. ελευθερος, free; ζωη, life]. Free-living.

ELEVATE, ELEVATUS. [L. *elevatus*, raised up]. Of a part higher than its surroundings.

ELUTE. [L. *ex*, out; *lutus*, washed]. With barely distinguishable marking.

EMARGINATE. [L. *e*, out of; *marginare*, to delimit]. With a distinct notch or indentation.

EMASCULATION. [L. *e*, away from; *masculus*, male]. The removal of the male reproductive organs, or the inhibition of male reproductive capacity.

EMBOLE/EMBOLIC. [Gr. εμβολη; a throwing in]. Invagination./Ingrowing, or pushing in.

EMBOLIC DIVISION. [Gr. εμβολη; a throwing in]. In the **Linyphiidae**: the terminal portion of the palpal bulb. It consists of the radix, embolus and various accessory sclerites and is attached to the suprategulum by a narrow stalk.

EMBOLOBRANCHIATA. [Gr. εμβολος, a wedge; βραγχια, gills]. An informal grouping of terrestrial arachnids that use book lungs or trachea, or both. This group includes mites and ticks, spiders (Aranea), scorpions (Scorpiones) and phalangids (Opilones).

EMBOLUS. [Gr. εμβολος, a wedge]. The penis-like structure for the transmission of sperm in male spiders. The copulatory organs of these males are not connected to the sperm duct opening but are located at the end of the pedipalps as a modification of the tarsal segment. Each palp consists of a bulb-like reservoir extending into an ejaculatory duct which leads to the embolus. During copulation regions of the tarsal segment (hematodocha) become engorged with blood causing the reservoir and embolus to extend; the embolus being inserted into one of the female reproductive openings and the sperm discharged. In primitive spiders this organ remains simple but in the more advanced families the palps become very complex by the addition of many accessory parts. The structural constancy of these accessory parts between species is of fundamental importance in classification.

EMBOSSED. [ME. *embossen*, to hide]. Ornamented with a raised pattern.

EMERGENT. [L. *emergere*: rise out/up]. Projecting. Rising above.

EMERIT'S GLAND. [M. *Emerit*, French Arachnologist]. Oval cuticular glands found on the tibia and patellae of many spiders, e.g., **Cybaeidae**, **Leptonetidae**, **Telemidae**. They are thought to be repugnatorial.

EMERY'S RULE. See also Host-Parasite Associations.

EMIGRATION. [L. *e*, out of; *migratio*, migration]. The migration of an individual or group out of an area or population.

EMINENCE. [L. *eminens*, projecting]. A ridge or projection on a surface.

EMITTED BEHAVIOR. [L. *emittere*, to send out]. The random behavior shown by an animal as it explores a new environment.

EMPODIUM (EMPODIA). [Gr. εν, in; -πους, -foot]. An unpaired structure located between the tarsal claws. It may take the form of pad-like to claw-like and commonly bears structures such as tenent hairs or dense setulae. It may also take the form of a feather-claw. See also Arolium, Digitule

ENANTIOMORPHIC. [Gr. εναντιος, opposite; μορφη, form]. Contraposed, as of mirror images.

ENARTHRONOTA. [Gr. εν, in; αρθρον, joint; νωτον, back]. An infraorder of beetle mites or armored mites (order Sarcoptiformes, suborder Oribatida). Superfamilies: Atopochthonioidea,

Brachychthonioidea, Cosmochthonioidea, Heterochthonioidea, Hypochthonioidea, Lohmannioidea, Mesoplophoroidea, Protoplophoroidea.

ENARTHROSIS. [Gr. εν, in; αρθρον, joint]. An articulation. A ball and socket joint.

ENAULOPHILUS. [Gr. εναλιος, of the sea; φιλος, loving]. Thriving in sandy dunes.

ENCAPSULATION. [Gr. εν, in; L. *capsa*, box]. 1. Enclosed in a capsule or membrane. 2. The result of a host surrounding and walling off internal parasites. Capsules often involve blood cells, or melanin formation.

ENCEPHALON. [Gr. εγκεφαλος, brain]. The brain.

ENCYST. [Gr. εν, 'to put in a state of'; κυστις, bladder]. To surround by a cyst, shell, coat or capsule.

ENDEMIC. [Gr. ενδημος, native]. Confined to a particular region, e.g. an island or country, and in some cases originating from there. Opposite: Ecdemic. See also Epidemic, Pandemic.

ENDEOSTIGMATA. [Gr. ενδεης, in need of a thing; στιγμα, mark]. A suborder of mites (superorder Acariformes, order Sarcoptiformes) that are mainly fungivores, algivores or feed on minute soft-bodied invertebrates such as nematodes. The taxonomy of this group is in a state of confusion. Infraorders: Alicorhagiida, Bimichaeliida, Nematalycina, Terpnacarida. Alternatively, superfamilies: Alicorhagioidea, Alycoidea, Nematalycoidea, Oehserchestoidea, Terpnacaroidea. (Adjective = endeostigmatic, not the commonly used incorrect endeostigmatid.)

ENDITE (GNATHOBASE, GNATHOCOXA, MAXILLA). [Gr. ενδον, within]. The expanded plate borne by the coxa of the pedipalps of most spiders. It is situated laterally to the labium and used to crush prey.

ENDOBIOTIC. [Gr. ενδον, within; βιωτικος, life]. Living within another organism.

ENDOCARDIUM. [Gr. ενδον, within; καρδια, heart]. The membrane lining the inner surface of the heart.

ENDOCHROME. [Gr. ενδον, within; χρωμα, color]. Any pigment within a cell.

ENDOCRINE CELLS. [Gr. ενδον, within; κρινειν, to separate]. Cells that release their secretory products towards the blood stream. Endocrine secretions always include hormones.

ENDOCUTICLE. [Gr. ενδον, within; L. *cutis*, little skin]. The flexible inner layer of the arthropod cuticle. It is composed of chitin and protein bound together to form a complex glycoprotein. During each molt it is digested by enzymes produced from epidermal glands and recycled. See also Ecdysis, Epicuticle, Exocuticle, Mesocuticle.

ENDOGASTRIC. [Gr. ενδον, within; γαστηρ, belly]. Within the stomach.

ENDOGEAN. [Gr. ενδον, within; γαια, the earth]. Interstitial soil dwellers. See also Epigean, Hypogeal.

ENDOGENOUS. [Gr. ενδον, within; -γενης, producing]. Originating from within.

ENDOGENOUS PHASE. [Gr. ενδον, within; -γενης, producing]. The parasitic phase of a life cycle as opposed to the exogenous (free-living) phase.

ENDOGENOUS RHYTHM. [Gr. ενδον, within; -γενης, producing; ρυθμος, measured motion]. A metabolic or behavioral rhythm that originates and is maintained within an animal, but usually regulated by external stimuli such as light or temperature (the '*zietgeber*' [Ger.] = time giver). If the rhythm is synchronized to an exact 24 hour cycle then such external control is known as 'Entrainment'. If the rhythm length is not strictly controlled by external stimuli (e.g. the circadian rhythm, which varies between 23 and 25 hours) it is said to be free-running.

ENDOGYNAL (ENDOGYNIAL, PERIGYNUM) PROCESSES. [Gr. ενδον, within; γυνη, female]. In Mesostigmatans such as the **Parasitidae**, Trigynaspida and **Zerconidae**: sclerotized structures that lie beneath the genital shield. They may be simple or elaborated. See also Vaginal Sclerites.

ENDOGYNUM. [Gr. ενδον, within; γυνη, female]. The endogynal processes. The internal, sclerotized genital characters.

ENDOLITHIC. [Gr. ενδον, within; λιθος, a stone]. Growing or living between stones.

ENDOPARASITE (ENTOPARASITE, ENDOSITE). [Gr. ενδον, within; παρασιτος, parasite]. See Parasite.

ENDOPHAGOUS (ENTOPHAGOUS). [Gr. νενδον, within; φαγειν, to devour]. Feeding from within a food source. Opposite: Ectophagous.

ENDOPHAGY. [Gr. ενδον, within; φαγειν, to eat]. The internal feeding of endoparasites.

ENDOPLICA. See Implex.

ENDOPODAL SHIELD. [Gr. ενδον, within; πους, foot]. In the Mesostigmata: the narrow strap-like angular to subtriangular sclerites around the bases of the coxae. The anterior endopodal shields (I, II) are often fused to the sternal shield.

ENDOSCLERITE. [Gr. ενδον, within; σκληρος, hard]. Any sclerite (chitinous plate/spicule) of the exoskeleton.

ENDOSITE. [Gr. ενδον, within; σιτος, food]. An alternative for endoparasite.

ENDOSKELETON. [Gr. ενδον, within; σκελετος, dried body]. A skeleton or internal supporting structure of the body or anapodemes for muscle attachment. See also Exoskeleton.

ENDOSPINE. [Gr. ενδον, within; L. *spina*, a spine]. See Papilla.

ENDOSTERNITES (ENTOSTERNITES). [Gr. ενδον, within; στερνον, chest]. Ingrowths (apodemes) from the ventral cuticular plates. They are used for the attachment of muscle and connective tissue.

ENDOSYMBION(T). [Gr. ενδον, within; συμβιωναι, to live together]. An internal symbiont. See also Ectosymbiont.

ENDOSYMBIOSIS. [Gr. ενδον, within; συμβιωναι, to live together]. A relationship of mutual benefit between an invading organism and the host.

ENDOTHERMIC. [Gr. ενδον, within; θερμη, heat]. Absorbing and utilising heat energy.

ENDOTOKY. [Gr. ενδον, within; τοκος, birth]. A form of reproduction in which the eggs develop within the body of the mother. See also Exotoky.

ENDOTRACHEA. [Gr. ενδον, within; LL. *trachia*, windpipe]. The innermost chitinous lining of the trachial tubes.

ENDOZOIC. [Gr. ενδον, within; ζωη, life]. Living within, or passing through, the body of an animal.

ENDYSIS. [Gr. ενδυσις, putting on]. The development of new skin structures: the opposite of ecdysis.

ENGRAVED (EXSCULPTATE). [OF. *engraver*, cut]. Having superficial irregular, impressed lines.

ENGORGED. [Fr. *engorger*; to block up]. Swollen, usually from feeding, as in a tick or chigger.

ENSATE. [L. *ensis*, sword]. Sword-shaped. Ensiform.

ENSIFORM (XIPHOID, GLADIATE). [L. *ensis*, sword, *forma*, shape]. Sword-shaped.

-ENSIS. Latin adjectival suffix indicating origin or place. Belonging to.

ENTAD. [Gr. εντος, within; L. *ad*, toward]. Inwards: towards the interior.

ENTAL. [Gr. εντος, within]. Interior. Away from the body wall, towards the center of the body. See also Ectal.

ENTANGIAL. [Gr. εντος, within; αγγειον, a vessel]. Within a vessel.

ENTELEGYNAE. [Gr. εντελης, full-grown; γυνη, female]. A superfamily of spiders (suborder Opisthothelae, infraorder Araneomorphae) in which there are eight eyes, complex male palpal organs which are expanded and moved by hemolytic pressure alone, and in adult females there are two separate copulatory openings by which sperm is injected to the spermathecae. These opening are usually surrounded by the epigynum. This grouping contains both cribellate and ecribellate spiders in sixty-nine families.

ENTELEGYNE. [Gr. εντελης, fullgrown; γυνη, female]. Of spiders in which there are eight eyes, complex male palpal organs and an epigynum in the adult females. See also Haplogyne.

ENTERIC CANAL. [Gr. εντερον, gut]. An alternative name for the alimentary canal.

ENTERON. [Gr. εντερον, gut]. The digestive cavity of multicellular animals.

ENTEROZOA. See Entozoa.

ENTEROZOON. [Gr. εντερον, gut; ζωον, animal]. Any animal parasite inhabiting the gut.

ENTHETIC. [Gr. ενθετος, implanted]. Implanted, introduced.

ENTIRE. [L. *intergrum*, complete]. Without emargination. Having a smooth margin.

ENTOECTAD. [Gr. εντος, within; εκτος, without; L. *ad*, towards]. Coming from within, outwards.

ENTOPARASITE. [Gr. εντος, within; παρασιτος, parasite]. See Endoparasite.

ENTOPHAGOUS (ENDOPHAGOUS). [Gr. εντος, within; φαγειν, to devour]. Feeding from within a food source. Opposite: Ectophagous

ENTOPIC. [Gr. εν, in; τοπος, place]. In the normal position. Opposite - Ectopic.

ENTOPTIC. [Gr. εντος, within; οψις, sight]. Having visual sensations caused within the eye by some stimulus other than light.

ENTORETINA. [Gr. εντος, within; L. *rete*, a net]. The retina proper. The inner or neural part of the retina.

ENTOSTERNITE. See Endosternites.

ENTOZOA. [Gr. εντος, within; ζωη, life]. Internal parasites.

ENTRANCE DUCTS. The paired tubes leading inwards from the copulatory openings of the female to the spermathecae. They receive the embolus of the male during copulation.

ENTRAINMENT. See Endogenous Rhythm.

ENTYPESIDAE. [derive.uncert.]. A family of African mygalomorphae spiders (infraorder Mygalomorphae, superfamily Avicularioidea).

ENVIRONMENT. [Fr. *environ*, surroundings;]. All the biotic and abiotic factors that surround and affect an individual organism at any time in its life cycle.

ENVIRONMENTAL HORMONE. [Fr. *environ*, surroundings; Gr. ορμαινω, excite]. An external chemical substance that influences biological systems or processes.

ENVIRONMENTAL SEX DETERMINATION. [Fr. *environ*, surroundings]. Offspring sex determination as a result of environmental factors, commonly temperature. See also Sex Determination.

ENVIRONMENTAL VARIANCE. [Fr. *environ*, surroundings]. The amount of phenotypic variation due to, or attributed to, differences in the environment to which the individuals of a population have been exposed.

EOTROGULIDAE. [Gr. ηως, early; +Trogulidae]. An extinct family of harvestmen (suborder Dyspnoi, superfamily Troguloidea) known from Carboniferous of Commentry in northern France.

ep. In acariform mites: the epicoxal of the palpcoxa.

ep1. In acariform mites: the epicoxal seta of coxa I.

EPALPATE. [L. *e-*, without; *palpus*, palp]. Without palpi (palps).

EPAPILLATE. [L. *e-*, without; *papilla*, nipple]. Without papillae.

EPAXIAL. [Gr. επι, upon; L. *axis*, axle]. Above the axis, i.e. dorsal.

EPECTINATA. [L. *e-*, without; *pecten*, comb]. A grouping of arachnids which have a short undivided abdomen without a tail-like termination. This grouping includes the spiders (Aranea), ticks and mites and related orders but not the scorpions (Scorpiones).

EPEDANIDAE. [Gr. ηπεδανος, weak]. A large family of harvestmen or daddy longlegs (suborder Laniatores, superfamily Epedanoidea) that are endemic to Asia. The chelicerae are heavy and bear strong teeth and the pedipalps are long and strong, with powerful spines lining the inside of the claw.

EPEDANOIDEA. [Gr. ηπεδανος, weak]. A superfamily family of harvestmen or daddy longlegs (suborder Laniatores, infraorder Grassatores). Families: **Epedanidae, Petrobunidae, Podoctidae, Sandokanidae** (incl. **Oncopodidae**), **Tithaeidae.**

EPEDAPHIC. [Gr. επι, upon; εδαφος, ground]. Depending on climatic conditions.

EPHARMONIC CONVERGENCE. [Gr. επι, towards; αρμονια, harmony]. See Convergence.

EPHARMONY. [Gr. επι, towards; αρμονια, harmony]. Gradual adaptation to a changing environment.

EPHARMOSIS. The method of adaptation of organisms to a new environment.

EPHEBIC STATE. [Gr. εφεβος, grown up youth]. The adult stage. Between the neanic and gerontic stage. The winged adult stage.

EPHEMERAL. [Gr. εφημεριος, lasting for one day]. Short-lived, or occurring only once.

EPIANDRUM. [Gr. επι, upon; ανηρ, male]. In the Holothyrida: a large concave intercoxal region containing the male genital opening.

EPIANDROUS GLANDS. [Gr. επι, upon; ανηρ, male]. In the Chelicerata: a group of glands found in most male spiders that add to the sperm web a small white mat on which a drop of sperm is deposited.

EPIBIONT. See Epicole.

EPIBIONTIC. [Gr. επι, upon; βιος, life]. Living attached to another organism but without either benefit or detriment to the host.

EPIBIOSIS. [Gr. επι, upon; βιος, life]. A symbiotic relationship in which one organism lives on the outer surface of another.

EPIBIOTIC. [Gr. επιβιοναι, to survive]. 1. Endemic species that are relicts of former fauna. 2. Growing on the surface of other animals. See also Hypobiotic.

EPICNEMIS. [Gr. επι, upon; κνημη, leg]. A tibial accessory joint of arachnids.

EPICOLE (EPIBIONT). [Gr. επι, upon; L. *colere*, to inhabit]. An animal that lives on the surface of another animal and neither harms nor helps that animal.

EPICOXAL SETA. [Gr. επι, upon; L. *coxa*, hip; *seta*, bristle]. In some acariform mites: a minute peg-like seta on the dorsal face of the palpcoxa (ep) or coxae of legs I (ep1).

EPICRIINA. [Gr. επκριον, yard-arm]. In a previous classification: a suborder of mites (superorder Parasitiformes, order Mesostigmata). This suborder has been abandoned in favor of suborder Monogynaspida.

EPICRIOIDEA. [Gr. επκριον, yard-arm]. A superfamily of mites (suborder Monogynaspida, infraorder Gamasina). Families: **Dwigubskyiidae, Epicriidae.**

EPICRINE. [Gr. επικρινω, give judgement upon]. Of glands that do not disintegrate when they discharge.

EPICUTICLE. [Gr. επι, upon; L. *cuticula*, little skin]. The thin outermost layer of the arthropod cuticle. Made of proteins and lipids which, in terrestrial arthropods, commonly contains a waxy waterproofing layer and usually a tough protective cement layer. See also Endocuticle, Exocuticle, Mesocuticle.

EPIDEICTIC DISPLAY. [Gr. επιδεικτικος, displayed as a sample]. Behavior used to define the territory of an animal or group of animals and to warn off potential invaders or encroachers from neighbouring territory.

EPIDERMIS. [Gr. επι, upon; δερμος, skin]. The outer layer of the skin: derived from embryonic ectoderm and forming a continuous epithelium over the whole body. It is generally one cell-layer thick and often secretes a cuticle.

EPIDIDYMIS. [Gr. επι, upon; διδυμος, testicle]. The coiled part of the vas deferens.

EPIGAMITIC CHARACTERS. [Gr. επι, upon; γαμος, marriage]. 1. Characters that serve to attract and/or stimulate individuals of the opposite sex during courtship, such as the semaphore signaling of spiders. 2. Secondary sexual characters developed as a result of hormonal action. For example, body coloration.

EPIGAMIC SELECTION. [Gr. επι, upon; γαμος, marriage]. Sexual selection.

EPIGASTRIC FOLD. [Gr. επι, upon; γαστηρ, belly]. A fold and groove separating the anterior region of the ventral abdomen (containing epigyne and book lungs) from the posterior region.

EPIGASTRIC FURROW. [Gr. επι, upon; γαστηρ, belly]. A transverse groove on the ventral side of the abdomen of female spiders. The reproductive openings for the reception of the male copulatory organs are located in the middle of the groove and the spiracles of the book lungs are on either side of it. See also Epigynum.

EPIGASTRIC PLATE (BRANCHIAL OPERCULUM). [Gr. επι, upon; γαστηρ, belly]. See Branchial Operculum.

EPIGASTRIUM. [Gr. επι, upon; γαστηρ, belly]. The anterior ventral portion of the opisthosoma of arachnids.

EPIGEAL. [Gr. επι, upon; γε, earth]. Of animals inhabiting exposed land surfaces, as distinct from underground.

EPIGEAN, EPIGAEN. [Gr. επι, upon; γη/γαια, earth/a country]. Living on or above the ground. See also Endogean, Hypogeal.

EPIGENOUS. [Gr. επι, upon; γενος, descent]. Growing, or developing on the surface.

EPIGYNIAL PLATE. [Gr. επι, upon; γυνη, woman]. See Epigynum.

EPIGYNUM, EPIGYNIUM. [Gr. επι, upon; γυνη, woman]. In most female spiders: a sclerotized plate on the ventral surface of the abdomen, just in front of the epigastric furrow, on which are located the reproductive openings for the reception of the male copulatory organ. In mites this structure may also be referred to as an epigynial plate or genital plate. See also Epigastric Furrow.

EPILOHMANNIOIDEA. [Gr. επι, upon; *H. Lohmann*, German? biologist]. A monotypic superfamily of mites (suborder Oribatida, infraorder Mixonomata - section Dichosomata). Family: **Epilohmanniidae.**

EPIMEGETIC. [Gr. επι, upon; μεγας, large]. Being the largest in a series of polymorphic forms. See also Hypomegetic.

EPIMELETIC. [Gr. επιμελεια, care]. Of animal behavior relating to the care of others.

EPIMERAL PLATES. [Gr. επι, upon; μερος, part]. In males of the genus *Ixodes*: the paired ventral plates which are situated laterally and posteriorly to the spiracular plates.

EPIMERE/EPIMERON. [Gr. επι, upon; μερος, part]. In oribatid mites: a sclerotized coxal field. In the Astigmata: the anterior coxal apodeme.

EPIMERITE. [Gr. επι, upon; μερος, part]. In the Astigmata: the posterior coxal apodeme.

EPIMORPHIC DEVELOPMENT. [Gr. επι, upon; μορφη, shape]. Development in which the young display the full complement of segments when hatched, i.e. the juvenile hatches with adult morphology. See also Anamorphic Development.

EPINEUSTON. [Gr. επι, upon; ναυστος, floating]. Organisms living on the surface film of a body of water. See also Neuston.

EPIOCHEIRATA. [Gr. επι, upon; ιοχεαιρα; shooter of arrows]. See Heterosphyronida.

EPIOSTRACUM. [Gr. επι, upon; οστρακον, shell]. In ticks and mites: the thin cuticle or epicuticle that covers the exocuticle or ectostracum.

EPIPARASITE. [Gr. επι, upon; παρασιτος, parasite]. See Parasite.

EPIPROSOMA. [Gr. επι, upon; προ, before; σομα, body]. In ticks and mites: a body division consisting of the gnathosoma and aspidosoma.

EPISEMATIC. [Gr. επι, upon; σημα, signal]. See Sematic.

EPISEME. [Gr. επι, upon; σημα, signal]. A recognition mark or color.

EPISITE. [Gr. επι, upon; σιτος, food]. An ectoparasite.

EPISKELETAL. [Gr. επι, upon; σκελετος, hardened]. Exterior to the endoskeleton.

EPISTOME (EPISTOMA, EPISTOMIS, EPISTOMUM). [Gr. επι, upon; στομα, mouth]. In ticks and mites: a sub-cheliceral plate. An outgrowth of the body wall at the base of the labrum which partly covers the preoral cavity in front. It is thought to be the morphological equivalent of the insect clypeus.

EPITHET (SPECIFIC EPITHET). [Gr. επιθετος, added]. The second name in a binomial. See Nomenclature.

EPIZOIC. [Gr. επι, upon; ζωον, animal]. Living on, or attached to the body of an animal.

EPIZOITE. [Gr. επι, upon; ζωον, animal]. A non-parasitic plant or animal living on another for the purpose of anchorage, protection or dispersal.

EPIZOOCHOROUS. [Gr. επι, upon; ζωον, animal; χωρειν, to spread abroad]. Dispersed by being attached to the surface of an animal.

EPIZOOETIC. [Gr. επι, upon; ; ζωον, animal]. Living or parasitic on animals from the outside or on the surface.

EPIZOON. [Gr. επι, upon; ζωον, animal]. An ectoparasite, an animal living on the exterior of another.

EPIZOOTIC. [Gr. επι, upon; ζωον, animal]. A disease or affliction affecting a large number of animals at the same time. This corresponds to 'epidemic' for human diseases.

EPLICATE. [L. explicaturos, to unfold]. Not folded.

EPULOSIS. [Gr. επι, over; ουλη, scar]. Scar formation.

EPUPILLATE. [L. ex, out of; pupilla, pupil of eye]. Of ocellate spots that have a colored margin, but lack a pupil or central spot.

EQUIBIRADIATE. [L. aequus, equal; bis, twice; radius, ray]. Having two equal rays.

EQUIDISTANT. [L. aequus, uniform; distantia, remoteness]. Equally spaced from any two or more points.

EQUIFACIAL. [L. aequus, equal; facies, face]. Having equal or equivalent surfaces.

EQUILIBRATING. [L. aequus, uniform; libra, balance]. Balancing equally.

EQUIPEDAL. [L. aequus, uniform; pes, foot]. Possessing pairs of equal feet.

EQUITANT. [L. equitans; ride (horseback)]. Laminated. Overlapping or folding one upon the other.

ERADIATE. [L. ex, out of; radiatus, rayed]. To radiate. To shoot forth as rays of light.

ERECTILE. [L. erigere, to raise up]. Capable of being raised or erected.

ERECTOR MUSCLE. [L. erigere, to raise up]. A muscle which raises up an organ or structure.

EREMAEOIDEA. [Gr. ερημια, desert]. A superfamily of mites (suborder Oribatida, infraorder Brachypylina - section Pycnonoticae). Families: **Aribatidae, Caleremaeidae** (incl. **Megeremaeidae), Eremaeidae, Kodiakellidae, Oribellidae.**

EREMELLOIDEA. [Gr. ερημια, desert; L. -*ella*, dim. suf.]. See Cymbaeremaeoidea.

EREMIC. [Gr. ερημος, of the desert]. Living in deserts.

EREMOBIC. [Gr. ερημος, solitary; βιος, life]. Living in isolation.

EREMOBATIDAE. [Gr. ερημια, desert; βατης, walker]. A family of sun spiders (subclass Arachnida, order Solifugae) from north and central America.

EREMOPHILOUS. [Gr. ερημια, desert; φιλος, loving]. Desert-loving: of animals that live in deserts or arid regions.

EREYNETAL ORGAN. [Gr. ερημια, desert; νηθω, spin]. In some **Ereynetidae:** a solenidion in a pouch-like recess in the tibiae.

ERESIDAE. [*Eresus*, A city of Lesbos]. The family of ladybird spiders and velvet spiders. Large, robust, cribellate spiders (infraorder Araneomorphae, superfamily Entelegynae) with a massive domed head carrying four median eyes and four lateral eyes. The abdomen is round to oval; the legs are short and stout and the cribellum is situated ventrally just anterior to the spinnerets. *Stegodyphus* is plant-living, all other eresids are terrestrial and live within a silk-lined subterranean tube, above which is a roof of cribellate silk. Their common name is derived from the pattern of spots on the male abdomen. Previously in the superfamily Eresoidea.

ERESOIDEA. [*Eresus*, A city of Lesbos]. In a previous classification: a superfamily of entelegyne spiders (order Araneae, suborder Araneomorphae) that united the families: **Eresidae, Hersiliidae, Oecobiidae.**

ERICETICOLOUS. [Gr. ερικη, heath; L. *colere*, to inhabit]. Inhabiting a heath or similar environment.

ERINEUM (ERINEA). [Gr. εριον, wool]. In the Eriophyoidea: the open, fleece-like galls produced by some mites.

ERINOSE MITE. [Gr. εριον, wool]. In the Eriophyoidea: mites that produce galls that resemble dense aggregations of fleece-like hairs.

ERIOCOMOUS. [Gr. εριον, wool; κομη, hair]. Having woolly, fleece-like hair.

ERIOPHYID (ERIOPHYOID). [Gr. εριον, wool; φυη, growth]. Of or relating to mites of the family **Eriophyidae.** Minute worm-like and quadripod mites that cause erinae, galls, and other damage to plants.

ERIOPHYIDAE. [Gr. εριον, wool; φυη, growth]. A family of minute gall mites (infraorder Eupodina, superfamily Eriophyoidea) in which there is a single pair of spiracles anterior to the mouth parts. They are widely distributed, sap-sucking, plant parasites.

ERIOPHYOIDEA (TETRAPODILI). A superfamily of herbivorous mites (suborder Prostigmata, infraorder Eupodina) in which the post-embryonic instars lack the third and fourth pairs of legs, and there is no respiratory system. Families: **Diptilomiopidae, Eriophyidae, Nalepellidae, Pentasetacidae, Phytoptidae.**

ERYTHRAEINA. [Gr. ερυθρος, red]. In some classifications: a clade of mites (suborder Prostigmata, infraorder Anystina) that unites the superfamilies: Calyptostomatoidea, Erythreoidea.

ERYTHREAN INVASION. [Gr. Ερυθρα Θαλασσα, Erythrà Thálassa, an ancient name for the Indian Ocean]. See Lessepsian Migration.

ERYTHRAEOIDEA. [Gr. ερυθρος, red]. A superfamily of mites (suborder Prostigmata, infraorder Anystina) known as chiggers. Families: **Erythraeidae, Smarididae.**

ERYTHRINUS. [Gr. ερυθρος, red]. The red of arterial blood. A dilute carmine.

ESCADABIIDAE. [Escada, type location in Brazil; Gr. βιος, life]. A small family of neotropical harvestmen or daddy longlegs (suborder Laniatores, superfamily Zalmoxoidea), that are endemic to Brazil.

ESEPTATE. [L. *ex*, without; *septum*, partition]. Lacking septa.

ESODIC. [Gr. εισοδος, a way in]. Afferent. Centripetal. In an inward direction. Opposite - Exodic.

ESOPHAGUS. See Esophagus .

ESOTERIC. [Gr. εσωτερικος, arising within]. Originating within an organism.

ESTIVATE. See Aestivate.

ETHEOGENESIS. [Gr. ηθεος, a youth; γενεσις, descent]. Male producing parthenogenesis. The development of a male gamete in the absence of fertilization.

ETHIOPIAN FAUNAL REGION. [Gr. αιθιοψ, burnt-face; L. *Faunus*, god of the woods]. The zoogeographical region that includes Africa south of the Sahara and southern Arabia.

ETHOLOGICAL BARRIERS (ISOLATION). [Gr. εθος, custom; λογος, discourse]. Barriers between potential mates caused by behavioral incompatibilities.

ETHOLOGY. [Gr. εθος, custom; λογος, discourse]. The study of an animal's behavior in its natural environment, i.e. its natural behavior.

ETHOSPECIES. [Gr. εθος, custom; L. *species*, one of a kind]. Species defined as such by behavioral traits.

EU-. Greek prefix meaning: well, good, genuine, true, easily. Used to indicate those members of a group which are most typical, and excluding those which are considered primitive. Also used in many ecological terms to denote richness/abundance, e.g. eutrophic (nutrient-rich), euphotic (light-rich).

EUAGRIDAE. [Gr. ευ-, good/true; αγρωστης, a type of spider]. A family of mygalomorph spiders (infraorder Mygalomorphae, superfamily Avicularioidea). They have very long spinnerets which are use to construct elaborate funnel-like retreats which are the hub of large silk curtains and platforms. They feed upon a variety of invertebrate prey including snails.

EUAMBLYPYGI. [Gr. ευ-, good/true; + Amblypygi]. A suborder of tail-less whip scorpions or whip spiders (subclass Arachnida, order Amblypygi). Superfamilies: Charinoidea, Charontoidea, Phrynoidea.

EUANAL SETAE. [Gr. ευ-, true; L. *anus*, anus]. In the Parasitiformes: setae borne on the anal valve.

EUCHELICERATA. [Gr. ευ-, true; χηλη, a claw; κερας, horn]. In a recent classification, a class of arthropods (phylum Arthropoda, subphylum Chelicerata) that unites the Arachnida and Xyphosura as subclasses; otherwise these are classes.

EUCTENIZIDAE. [Gr. ευ-, good/true; κτενιζω, to comb]. A family of mygalomorphae spiders (infraorder Mygalomorphae, superfamily Avicularioidea) that were previously in the Cyrtaucheniidae (subfamily Euctenizinae). They are considered to be closely related to the Idiopidae.

EUGENITAL OPENING. [Gr. ευ-, true; L. *gignere*, to beget]. See Genital Opening.

EUGENITAL SETAE. [Gr. ευ-, true; L. *gignere*, to beget]. In the Acariformes: setae originating within the genital vestibule.

EUGONIC. [Gr. ευ, good; γονος, produce]. Growing profusely.

EUHYPONEUSTON. [Gr. ευ-, well; υπο-, under; ναυστος, floating]. Organisms that normally live within the top few centimeters of water. See also Neuston.

EUKOENENIIDAE. [Gr. ευ-, true, + *Koenenia*]. A family of micro-whip scorpions (order Palpigradi, superfamily Eukoenenioidea).

EUKOENENIOIDEA. [Gr. ευ-, true, + *Koenenia*]. A superfamily of micro-whip scorpions (subclass Arachnida, order Palpigradi). Familes: **Eukoeneniidae**, **Prokoeneniidae**.

EULITTORAL. [Gr. ευ-, true; L. *litus*, beach]. Of the habitat formed on the lower shore of an aquatic ecosystem, below the littoral zone.

EULOHMANNIOIDEA. [Gr. ευ-, good / true; *H. Lohmann*, German? Biologist]. A monotypic superfamily of mites (suborder Oribatida, infraorder Mixonomata - section Dichosomata). Family: **Eulohmanniidae.**

EUNEUSTON. [Gr. ευ-, good; ναυστος, floating]. Of organisms that spend their entire existence in the neuston.

EUPATHIDION (EUPATHIDIA, ACANTHOIDES). [Gr. ευ-, good / true; παθος, suffering; - ιδιον, dim.suf.]. In many Acariformes: an optically active, hollow seta found on the palptarsus or leg I tarsus. There is a pore at the tip and it may be a chemoreceptor. Designation = zeta (ζ). See also Acanthodion.

EUPHTHIRACAROIDEA. [Gr. ευ-, good / true; φθειρ, louse; LL. *acarus*, mite]. A superfamily of mites (suborder Oribatida, infraorder Mixonomata - section Euptyctima). Families: **Euphthiracaridae, Oribotritiidae, Synichotritiidae.**

EUPLOID. [Gr. ευ-, well; απλοος, onefold; ειδος, form]. See Ploidy.

EUPNOI. [Gr. ευ-, good / true; πνεω, breathe]. A cosmopolitan suborder of harvestmen or daddy long legs (subclass Arachnida, order Opiliones) which contains many long-legged species common to northern temperate regions. The **Caddidae** have prominent eyes and spiny pedipalps. Superfamilies: Caddoidea, Phalangioidea.

EUPODINA (EUPODIDES). [Gr. ευ-, true; πους, foot]. An infraorder of mites (order Trombidiformes, suborder Prostigmata). Superfamilies: Bdelloidea, Eriophyoidea, Eupodoidea, Halacaroidea, Tydeoidea. Labidostommatoidea may be included here.

EUPODOIDEA. [Gr. ευ-, true; πους, foot]. A superfamily of mites (suborder Prostigmata, infraorder Eupodina). Families: **Cocceupodidae, Dendrochaetidae, Eriorhynchidae, Eupodidae, Pentapalpidae, Penthaleidae, Penthalodidae, Rhagidiidae, Strandtmanniidae**

EURYBIONT. [Gr. ευρυς, wide; βιον, living]. Of organisms adapted to wide variations of the environment.

EURYOECIOUS (EURYECIOUS). [Gr. ευρυς, wide; οικος, house]. Of an animal having the choice of a wide range of habitats. Opposite - Stenoecious.

EURYPHAGOUS. [Gr. ευρυς, wide; φαγειν, to devour]. Existing on a wide range of foods. Opposite - Stenophagous. See also Monophagous, Polyphagous.

EURYTHERMOUS. [Gr. ευρυς, wide; θερμη, heat]. Of animals that are adaptable to a wide range of environmental temperatures. Opposite - Stenothermous.

EURYTOPIC. [Gr. ευρυς, wide, τοπος, place]. Having a wide geographical distribution or range of environments. See also Stenotopic.

EURYVALENT. [Gr. ευρυς, wide; L. *valens*, strong] Of an organism surviving in a wide range of environmental conditions. See also Stenovalent.

EURYXENIC (EURYXENOUS). [Gr. ευ-, good / true; ξενος, stranger]. Using a broad range of habitats or hosts. A generalist.

EUSCORPIIDAE. [Gr. ευ-, good / true; σκορπιος, scorpion]. A family of scorpions (order Scorpiones, superfamily Chactoidea) with a distribution throughout the northern hemisphere.

EUTEGAEOIDEA (CEPHEOIDEA). [Gr. ευ-, good / true; τεγος, roof]. A superfamily of mites (suborder Oribatida, infraorder Brachypylina - section Pycnonoticae). Families: **Cerocepheidae, Compactozetidae** (syn. **Cepheidae**), **Eutegaeidae, Microtegeidae, Nodocepheidae, Salvidae** (syn. **Pterobatidae**), **Tumerozetidae.**

EUTROPHIC. [Gr. ευ, well; τροφιμος, nourishing]. Of lakes that are well supplied with nutrients and are highly productive in terms of organic matter. See also Dystrophic, Oligotrophic.

EVAGINATE. [L. *evaginare*, to unsheath]. To turn inside out; to evert from a sheathing structure; to produce an eversion.

EVANS LEG CHAETOTACTIC SYSTEM. [*G.O. Evans*, British Arachnologist]. In the Mesostigmata: the nomenclature for the setation of legs segments. The leg is notionally oriented dorsoventrally and at a right angle to the body midline; thus four aspects are present: dorsal, ventral, anterior lateral and posterior lateral. Setae are designated in rows for their anterior (ad), posterior dorsal (pd), ventral (av, pv) or lateral (al, pl) aspects and numbered from distal to basal.

EVERSIBLE. [L. *evertere*, to evert]. Of an organ capable of being extruded and retracted, usually by being turned inside out.

EVERT. [L. *evertere*, to evert]. To protrude by being turned inside out.

EVIPHIDOIDEA. [deriv.uncert. + Gr. ιφις, name attributed to seven individuals from Greek mythology]. A superfamily of mites (suborder Monogynaspida, infraorder Gamasina). Families: **Eviphididae, Leptolaelapidae, Macrochelidae,** Megalolaelapidae, **Pachylaelapidae, Parholaspididae.** In some classifications this superfamily may be included in the sub-cohort Dermanyssiae.

EVOLUTIONARILY DERIVED/PRIMITIVE CHARACTER. See Phylogenetic Classification.

EVOLUTIONARY ALLOMETRY. See Allometry.

EVOLUTIONARY STABLE STRATEGY (ESS). A behavioral strategy which, if adopted by most members of a species, can not be improved upon by an alternative strategy. An ESS would, therefore, eventually come to dominate the population.

EX- E-. Latin prefix and preposition meaning; out of, without, from, after, since, on account of, according to, made of.

EXAFFERENCE. [L. *ex-*, out of; *afferre* to bring to]. Stimulation as a result of external factors.

EXARTICULATE. [L. *ex*, without; *articulus*, joint]. Without distinct joints.

EXASPERATE, EXASPERATUS. [L. *exasperare*, to roughen]. Having hard, stiff, points.

EXCALCARATE. [L. *ex*, without; *calcar*, spur]. Without spurs.

EXCAVATE. [L. *ex*, out of; *cavus*, a hollow]. Hollowed out.

EXCAUDATE. [L. *ex*, without; *cauda*, tail]. Ecaudate, lacking a tail.

EXCENTRIC. [L. *ex*, away from; *centrum*, center]. Off center, unequally developed.

EXCISION. [L. *excosio*, excision]. The action or process of cutting out or cutting off.

EXCLUSION PRINCIPLE. [L. *ex*, out of; *claudere*, shut]. The principle that states that two species can not co-exist in the same locality at the same time if they both have identical ecological requirements.

EXCREMENTACEOUS, EXCREMENTITIOUS. [L. *excrementum*, a discharge; *-aceous*, of the nature of]. Resembling, or made of, excrement.

EXCRESCENCE. [L. *excrescere*, grow out or up]. An outgrowth; usually abnormal. In the Trigynaspida and some **Microgynidae**: brush-like, dendritic or otherwise ornamented processes produced from openings in the movable digit.

EXCRETA. [L. *excretum*, separated]. The waste material eliminated from the tissues or the body.

EXCRETION. [L. *ex*, out of; *cernere*, to sift]. The removal of the waste products of metabolism (water, carbon dioxide, nitrogenous substances) either by storing them in an insoluble form or by removing them from the body. The main organs of excretion being the Malpighian tubes.

EXCRETORY. [L. *ex*, out of; *cernere*, to sift]. Of those structures concerned in ridding the body of waste products.

EXCURVATE, EXCURVED. [L. *ex*, out of; *curvare*, to curve]. Curved outwards from the center.

EXINGUINAL. [L. *ex*, away from; *inguen*, the groin]. Of the second joint of the arachnid leg.

EXOCHORION. [Gr. εξο, outside; χοριον, skin]. The thicker outer layer of the chorion ('shell') of an egg.

EXOCRINE GLANDS. [Gr. εξο, outward; κρινειν, to separate]. Glands which release their product through an opening or duct.

EXOCUTICLE. [Gr. εξο, outside; L. *cuticula*, dim. of *cutis*, skin]. The middle cuticular layer of the arthropod exoskeleton, above the endocuticle and below the epicuticle. It is usually thick and composed of chitin and other proteins bound together in a matrix to form a complex, tanned, glycoprotein; i.e. with the participation of phenols its molecular structure is stabilized by the formation of many cross-links. Exocuticle is absent from joints and along the line where the exoskeleton will rupture when molting. See also Endocuticle, Epicuticle, Mesocuticle.

EXODIC. [Gr. εξοδυς, way out]. Efferent. In an outward direction. Opposite - Esodic.

EXOGENOUS. [Gr. εξο, outside; -γενης, producing]. Originating from outside the organism.

EXOGENOUS RHYTHM. [Gr. εξο, outside; -γενης, producing; ρυθμος, rhythm]. A behavioral or metabolic rhythm synchronized by some external influence. The rhythm ceases when the influence is removed.

EXOPARASITE. [Gr. εξο, outside; παρασιτος, parasite]. See Ectoparasite.

EXOPODAL SHIELD. [Gr. εξο, outside; πους, foot]. In the Mesostigmata: narrow strap-like sclerites, sometimes broad, produced around the lateral bases of the coxae. They are sometimes fused to the peritrematal shield.

EXOSKELETON (DERMATOSKELETON, DERMOSKELETON). [Gr. εξο, outside; σκελετος, hard]. Any skeleton covering the outside of the body or situated within the skin layer. In arthropods: a complex structure, commonly formed of chitin impregnated with calcium compounds, and thus very hard. The exoskeleton is secreted by the hypodermis (an underlying cellular layer) and is composed of a thin outer epicuticle which is covered with wax or grease. Below this are the outer exocuticle and inner endocuticle; both these layers are composed of chitin and protein bound together to form a complex glycoprotein. The exocuticle is further stabilized by phenolic tanning and cross linking. The exocuticle and endocuticle layers are jointly the procuticle, until the separation of the layers becomes obvious due to tanning or sclerotization. Below the procuticle is Schmidt's layer (or subcuticle), which may represent the endocuticle in the process of formation. Below Schmidt's layer is the basement membrane, an amorphous, granular layer which forms a continuous sheet and, at points where muscles are attached, is continuous with the sarcolemma. The presence and nature of these layers varies from species to species as well as from place to place in the exoskeleton of an individual. Cuticle is rigid, relatively impermeable to water and has a high strength to weight ratio. Consequently, as the animal grows the exoskeleton has to be shed (ecdysis) from time to time and a new one formed. Ingrowths of the cuticle (apodemes) provide muscle attachment points and the cuticle is divided into separate plates to facilitate movement: the plates are connected by an arthrodial membrane (or intersegmental membrane) of thin, flexible, untanned cuticle.

EXOTHERMIC. [Gr. εξο, outside; θερμη, heat]. Releasing heat. See also Poikilotherm.

EXOTIC. [Gr. εξοτικος, foreign]. Non-endemic, introduced.

EXOVATION. [L. *ex*, out of; *ovum*, egg]. The act of hatching.

EXPLANATE. [L. *explanare*, to make level]. Having a flat extension. Spread out flat.

EXPLICATE. [L. *explicatus*; unfolded]. Unfolded. Open. Without folds or plica.

EXPLORATION. [L. *explorare*, to explore]. The pattern of behavior seen when an animal starts to investigate new surroundings. This behavior often involves latent learning and, to continue, must be rewarding in some way, which leads to an increased rate of change of the stimulation interacting with the animal's sense organs.

EXPLOSIVE BREEDERS. [L. *explodere*, to explode]. A species in which the breeding season is very short.

EXSCULPATE. [L. *ex*, out; *sculpere*, to carve]. Having the surface marked with regular raised lines with grooves between. See also Aciculate.

EXSERTED. [L. *exsertus*, projecting]. Protruding or projecting from the body.

EXSERTILE. [L. *exsertus*, projecting]. Capable of being exerted or extruded.

EXSERTION. [L. *exsertus*, projecting]. A protrusion. An extension of a line or other ornamentation beyond its ordinary course.

EXSHEATH. [L. *ex*, out of; AS. *sceath*, case]. To escape from the residual membrane (egg shell) of a previous developmental stage.

EXSICCATE. [L. *exsiccare*, to dry up]. To dry up.

EXSTROPHY. [Gr. εξo-, outwards; στροφη, turning]. Eversion. Of a normal or anomalous projection of luteal tissue to the exterior of the ovary.

EXTANT. [L. *ex(s)tare*, prominent/visible]. Existing at the present time - not extinct.

EXTENSILE. [L. *ex*, out of; *tendere*, to stretch]. Capable of being extended, stretched or spread.

EXTENSOR MUSCLE. [L. *ex*, out; *tendere*, to stretch]. A muscle which acts to open out a joint (a flexor muscle closes a joint). See also Unguitractor.

EXTENUATE. [L. *ex*, out of; *tenuis*, thin]. To make or become thin or slender; to diminish.

EXTERIOR MARGIN. The outer margin; sometimes the costal margin.

EXTERNAL GENITALIA. [L. *gignere*, to beget]. The organs involved with sexual mating and the deposition of eggs.

EXTERNAL HYPOSTOMAL (HYPOSTOMATIC) SETAE. [Gr. υπo, under; στομα, mouth]. In larval Mesostigmata: the most lateral (h2) of the three pairs of hypostomatic setae.

EXTERNAL MALAE. [L. *mala*, cheek]. See Corniculus.

EXTERNAL RESPIRATION. The process of gaseous exchange between an organism and its environment.

EXTERNAL SCAPULAR SETA. [L. *scapula*, shoulder]. In the Acariformes: the prodorsal seta sce (also se or s2).

EXTERNAL SECRETION. Any secretion to the outside of the body or into the cavity of the enteron.

EXTERNAL VERTICAL SETA. In the Acariformes: the prodorsal seta ve (also se or s2).

EXTEROCEPTORS. [L. *exter*-, outside; *capere*, to take]. Sensory structures of the skin and other sense organs that detect stimuli originating from outside the animal. See also Interoceptor, Proprioceptor, Receptor.

EXTINCT. [L. *ex*, out; *stinguere*, to quench]. No longer existing - not extant.

EXTOGENOUS. See Exogenous.

EXTRACONIC. [L. *extra*, outside; Gr. κονoς, cone]. See Coeloconoid.

EXTRACORPOREAL. [L. *extra*, outside; *corpus*, body]. Occurring outside of the body.

EXTRACORPOREAL DIGESTION. [L. *extra*, outside; *corpus*, body]. A mode of feeding in which some parasites and predators release oesophageal or salivary secretions into the host or prey that predigests their internal contents.

EXTRADOS. [L. *extra*, outside; Fr. *dos*, the back]. The exterior curve of an arch. Opposite: Intrados.

EXTRAORAL. [L. *extra*, outside; *os*, mouth]. Away from or beyond the mouth.

EXTRATROPICAL. [L. *extra*, outside; *tropicus*, solstice]. Outside the tropics.

EXTRAVENTRICULAR. [L. *extra*-, beyond; *ventriculus*, little belly]. Arising beyond a ventricle.

EXTREMITY. [L. *extremitas*, limit]. The distal portion of a limb, limb-like structure, or any external structure that grows away from the main body.

EXTRINSIC. [L. *extrinsecus*, on the outside]. 1. External. Not in or a part of a body or congregation. 2. Of environmental influences on a population. See also Intrinsic.

EXTRINSIC ARTICULATION. [L. *extrinsecus*, on the outside; *articulus*, joint]. Articulation in which the articulating surface is outside the skeletal parts. See also Intrinsic Articulation.

EXTRINSIC FACTORS. [L. *extrinsecus*, on the outside]. Factors that come from outside the animal, and over which it has no control, i.e. weather, disease, catastrophe, etc.

EXTRINSIC MUSCLES. Muscles which move an organ (leg, etc.), but that originate outside of it. See also Intrinsic Muscles.

EXTRORSE. [L. *extrorsus*, in an outward direction]. Turning or facing outwards. Towards the outside. See also Introrse.

EXTRUDE. [L. *ex*, out of; *trusus*, thrust]. To turn. To force out. Extrusion.

EXUDATE. [L. *exudare*, to sweat]. A substance discharged from a cell or organ through a membrane, incision, pore or gland.

EXUDE. [L. *exsudo*, discharge by sweating]. To ooze moisture or other liquids through minute openings.

EXUVIAE. [L. *exuere*, to strip off]. The cast parts of the cuticle. The cuticle shed at a molt. This term is usually used only in the plural.

EXUVIAL GLANDS. [L. *exuere*, to strip off]. Epidermal glands associated with the molting fluid during ecdysis.

EXUVIAL SPACE. [L. *exuere*, to strip off]. An area between the epidermis and the cuticle into which the molting enzymes are secreted after apolysis.

EXUVIATE. [L. *exuere*, to strip off]. To cast-off or shed a skin.

EXUVIATION. [L. *exuere*, to strip off]. The act of molting.

EXUVIUM. [L. *exuere*, to strip off]. The cast off outer shell or skin of an arthropod, or sometimes any animal. Plural, Exuviae.

EYE. [AS. *eage*, eye]. A receptor organ sensitive to light and communicating directly with the central nervous system (or the equivalent). Most spiders have eight simple eyes (ocelli) as opposed to compound eyes and sight is normally poor but some species, such as the jumping spiders (**Salticidae**) and the ogre-eyed or net-casting spiders (**Dinopidae**), have highly developed eyesight. AME, Anterior Median Eyes or 'direct' eyes; they appear darker than the other eyes and in some are differentially sensitive to the orientation of polarization in linearly polarized light. **ALE**, Anterior Lateral Eyes; **PLE**, Posterior Lateral Eyes; **PME**, Posterior Median Eye - all are indirect eyes and usually have a layer of light reflecting crystals, the tapetum, behind the light sensitive retina, giving these eyes a silvery appearance. Thus, indirect eyes are adapted for seeing at low light intensities and they often have enlarged lenses, giving good vision. **Reflector Eyes**: eyes with well-developed tapeta. **Search-Light Eyes**: the enormously enlarged rear eyes (PME) of the net-casting spider *Deinopis* (**Deinopidae**).

EYE FORMULA. A representation of eye distribution starting with the anterior row. Thus, 4-2-2 = 4 eyes in the anterior row, 2 eyes in the middle row, 2 eyes in the posterior row.

EYE TUBERCLE. [L. *tuberculum*, small hump]. In the Mygalomorphae: the eye turret. The eyes grouped together on a turret.

EYLAOIDEA. [Gr. ευλαιγξ poet for ευλιθος, goodly stone]. A superfamily of mites (suborder Prostigmata, infraorder Anystina). Families: **Apheviderulicidae, Eylaidae, Limnocharidae, Piersigiidae.**

F

f. In the Acariformes: a designation used for setae on segment F, e.g. f1-2. See Grandjean System.

F. In the Acariformes: a designation used for the fourth region of the hysterosoma. See Grandjean System.

FACE (FACIES). [L. *facies*, countenance]. The surface of anything.

FACULTATIVE. [L. *facultas*, capability]. The ability to live under different conditions. See also Obligate.

FACULTATIVE AGENTS. [L. *facultas*, faculty]. Agents such as parasitism, disease and starvation which exert a severe restraint on the population density of a species as the population tends to increase. Other controlling influences are known as catastrophic agents.

FACULTATIVE MUTUALISM (PROTOCO-OPERATION). [L. *facultas*, faculty; *mutuus*, borrowed; *-ism*, suf. forming nouns of action from verbs]. Interaction between individuals of different species in which both organisms benefit, but in which neither is dependent on the relationship. See also Mutualism.

FACULTATIVE PARASITE. [L. *facultas*, faculty; Gr. παρασιτος, parasite]. See Parasite.

FACULTATIVE PARTHENOGENESIS. [L. *facultas*, faculty; Gr. παρθενος, virgin; γενεσις, descent]. The ability of some animals, that normally reproduce sexually, to produce offspring from unfertilized eggs (i.e. in the absence of males). The offspring are thus clones of the mother.

FACULTATIVE SYMBIONT. [L. *facultas*, faculty; Gr. συμβιωναι, to live together]. A symbiont that establishes a relationship with a host only if the opportunity presents itself. See also Obligate Symbiont.

FACULTATIVE SYMBIOSIS (PARAMUTUALISM). [L. *facultas*, faculty; Gr. συμβιος, living together]. The ability of an organism (the symbiont) to live either self-dependently or symbiotically.

FACULTATIVE THERMOPHILE. [L. *facultas*, faculty; Gr. θερμη, heat; φιλος, loving]. An organism that requires a temperature of between 50 °C and 65 °C for optimum growth, but which can also live at a lower temperature.

FACULTY. [L. *facultas*, faculty]. The ability, natural or acquired, to perform a certain task.

FECAL (FAECAL) SESTON. [L. *fæces*, dregs; Gr. σεσις, sifting]. Particulate fecal material suspended in water. See also Seston.

FECES (FAECES). [L. *fæces*, dregs]. The indigestible remains of food together with dead gut bacteria, dead cells, mucous and bile pigments that are egested from the alimentary canal through the anus.

FAHRENHOLZ'S RULE. [*Heinrich Fahrenholz*, German Biologist]. See Host-Parasite Associations.

FALCATE. [L. *falx*, sickle]. Sickle-shaped or hooked.

FALCES. [L. *falx*, sickle]. The chelicerae of arachnids.

FALCIFORM. [L. *falx*, sickle; *forma*, shape]. Sickle-shaped.

FALCULATE. [L. *falcula*, little hook]. Sickle-shaped with a sharp point.

FALLACIS. [L. *fallacis*, deceitful]. The mite *Neoseiulus* (*Amblyseius*) *fallacis*. An extremely effective spider mite predator, used in a variety of cropping systems.

FALSE SCORPIONS. Very small (ca. 5 mm or less) arachnid predators (Pseudoscorpiones) that superficially look like scorpions in having the pedipalps modified as claws, but lack the recurved 'tail'. They are commonly known to attach themselves to the hairs of larger animals for the purpose of dispersal. See also Phoresis.

FALSE SPIDER MITE/FLAT MITE. Mites of the family **Tenuipalpidae** (infraorder Eleutherengona, superfamily Tetranychoidea), such as *Brevipalpus*. They have a similar stylophore and whip-like stylets to spider mites, but are usually protected by sclerotized plates and are often dorsoventrally flattened.

FALSE SPIDERS. Large ferocious arachnids that feed on anything up to a small lizard. They grow up to 5 cm long, the body is completely covered with long sensitive hairs and they have formidable biting apparatus. See Solifugae.

FAMILY. [L. *familia*, household]. One of the sub-divisions used in classifying organisms. It may be divided into subfamilies, but consists basically of a number of genera of assumed common phylogenetic origin. Similar families are grouped in superfamilies, suborders and an order. In zoology the standard family name is suffixed with -idae. (In Botany and Bacteriology; -aceae). See also Nomenclature.

FAMULUS. [L. *famulus*, attendant]. In some mites: micro-sensory seta found on the genu, tibia and tarsi.

FANG. [AS. *fang*, grip]. A tooth or other appendage, such as the chelicerae of spiders, modified for injecting poison.

FANG FURROW. See Cheliceral Groove.

FARCATE/FARCTUS. [L. *farctus*, stuffed]. Stuffed, filled, not hollow.

FARINACEOUS (FARINOSE). [L. *farina*, flour; -*aceous*, of the nature of]. Mealy. Powdery. Flour-like.

FASCIATE. [L. *fascia*, a bundle]. Banded transversely.

FASCICLE, FASCICULUS. [L. *fasciculus*, small bundle]. A small bundle or tuft. A surface when covered with bundles of long hair.

FASCIOLA. [L. *fasciola*, small bandage]. A narrow colored band.

FASCIO-MACULATA. [L. *fasciola*, small bandage; *macula*, spot]. Having spots arranged in bands.

FASCIO-PUNCTATE. [L. *fasciola*, small bandage; *punctum*, a spot]. Ornamented with colored points arranged in bands.

FASTIGALS. [L. *fastigium*, gable end]. In acariform mites: the most basal pair of the dorsal setae on the tarsi.

FASTIGIATE. [L. *fastigium*, gable end]. Arranged into a conical bundle.

FATAL FLATULENCE. [L. *flatus*, a breaking wind]. The (possibly mythical) ability of some Parasitiformes to discharge a paralyzing gas from their anal opening when hunting springtails.

FAT BODY. The aggregated cells that store food reserves.

FAT CELL. See Lipocyte.

FATISCENT. [L. *fatiscere*, to crack]. Gaping open, cracked.

FAUNAL PROVINCE. [L. *Faunus*, god of the woods]. A zoogeographical region containing a distinct fauna, and isolated from other regions by migratory barriers.

FAUNAL REGION (FAUNAL ZOOGEOGRAPHIC KINGDOM). [L. *Faunus*, god of the woods]. An area characterized by a particular group (or groups) of animals. The degree of distinctiveness may vary as a reflection of the climate and the existence of barriers to migration. Six zoogeographic regions are recognized: Australian, Ethiopian, Nearctic, Neotropical, Oriental and Palearctic. In defining a region, great emphasis is place on the mammal fauna.

FAVEOLATE. [L. *faveolus*, little honeycomb]. Honeycombed.

FAVEOLUS. [L. *faveolus*, little honeycomb]. A small depression or pit.

FAVOID. [L. *favus*, honeycomb; Gr. ειδος, form]. Resembling a honeycomb.

FAVUS. [L. *favus*, honeycomb]. A cell like that of a honeycomb.

FEAELLIDAE. [*Leonardo Fea*, Italian naturalist; L. -*ella*, dim.suf.]. A monospecific family of pseudoscorpions (suborder Atoposphyronida, superfamily Feaelloidea) in which there is a carapace with multiple frontal lobes, a dorsoventrally flattened and heavily sclerotized body, and pedipalps that are stout, heavily armed and without a venom gland in both fingers. Genus *Feaella*.

FEAELLOIDEA. [*Leonardo Fea*, Italian naturalist; L. -*ella*, dim.suf.]. A superfamily of false scorpions (order Pseudoscorpiones, suborder Atoposphyronida). Families: **Feaellidae**, **Pseudogarypidae**.

FEATHER CLAW. [ME. *fether*, feather]. The highly divided bipectinate empodial claw found in the Eriophyoidea.

FEATHER MITE. [ME. *fether*, feather]. Any member of the Astigmata that lives on bird feathers.

101

FECULA. [L. *fæces*, dregs]. In insects: excrement.

FECUND. [L. *fecundus*, fertile]. Fertile: capable of producing offspring.

FECUNDATE. [L. *fecundare*, to make fruitful]. To fertilize or pollinate.

FECUNDITY. [L. *fecunditas*, fruitfulness]. The reproductive potential of an organism as measured by the number of reproductive units (eggs, sperms, asexual reproductive structures) produced over a defined period.

FEDRIZZIOIDEA. [*Giacento Fedrizzi*, Italian entomologist]. A diverse superfamily of strongly sclerotized mites (suborder Trigynaspida, infraorder Antennophorina) associated with passalid beetles (**Passalidae**). Families: **Fedrizziidae, Klinckowstroemiidae.**

FEEDING. All behavior that involves the obtaining, manipulation and ingestion of food. See also Foraging. In spiders: when the prey is caught venom, which contains digestive enzymes, is injected and thus the internal contents of the victim are broken down and digestion begins external to the spider. The liquefied contents are drawn into the alimentary canal by a sucking stomach that is located in the cephalothorax. Particles in the food are efficiently filtered out by the hairs around and in the mouth. From the sucking stomach the food is transferred via the intestine to the midgut which is located in the abdomen where secretory cells release more digestive enzymes. The midgut finally ends in the cloacal chambers where the feces are stored.

FEELER. [AS. *felan*, to feel]. A tactile organ of many invertebrates.

FEMALE. [L. *femina*, woman]. An individual whose reproductive organs (usually) contain only non-motile gametes. Sexually opposite of male. Symbol ♀.

FEMALE DUCTS. See Gonoduct, Oviduct.

FEMINIZATION. [L. *femina*, woman]. The development of female characteristics in males, usually as a result of hormonal changes.

FEMORAL SPOT. [L. *femur*, thigh]. In some spiders: a sclerotized spot of unknown function that is located ventrally and subapically on femur I and sometimes on femur II, usually on females but it can be present on males, as in the Mysmenidae.

FEMOROGENU. [L. *femur*, thigh; *genu*, knee]. In mites: a leg segment resulting from the fusion of the femur and genu.

FEMOROTIBIAL JOINT. [L. *femur*, thigh; *tibia*, shin]. In arthropods: one of the two primary bendings of a typical leg. Of the femur and the tibia. See also Coxotrochanteral Joint.

FEMUR. [L. *femur*, thigh]. 1. In spiders: the thigh, normally the stoutest segment, articulating with the body through the trochanter and coxa and bearing the patella and remaining leg segments at the distal end. 2. In mites: a segment of palp and legs, between the trochanter and genu; sometimes divided into femur 1 (proximal) and femur 2 (distal). See also Limb.

FENESTRA, FENESTRAE. [L. *fenestra*, window]. An opening in an otherwise continuous surface.

FENESTRATE. [L. *fenestra*, window]. Having small perforations or transparent spots.

FERAL. [L. *fera*, wild animal]. Wild, not domesticated or cultivated.

FERRALLITIC SOIL. [L. *ferrum*, iron]. The deep red acidic soils found on freely draining sites in humid tropical regions.

FERREOUS. [L. *ferreus*, of iron]. A metallic grey color.

FERRUGINO-TESTACEOUS. [L. *ferruginus*, rusty; *testaceus*, brick-colored:]. A mixture of rusty red with a dull yellow brown.

FERRUGINOUS. [L. *ferruginus*, rusty]. Having a rusty-brown color tinged with orange.

FERTILE. [L. *fertilis*, fertile]. Capable of producing offspring.

FERTILITY RATIO. [L. *fertilis*, fertility]. The number of offspring in a population in relation to the number of adult females.

FERTILITY. [L. *fertilis*, fertile]. The actual rate of reproduction of an individual based on the number of viable offspring produced.

FERTILIZATION. [L. *fertilis*, fertility]. The union of two specialized cells (gametes) in the process of sexual reproduction, the result of the union being a zygote. Fertilization may be internal (as in most land animals) or external as in many aquatic species. There are two main phases, (a) the fusion of two haploid nuclei either from two distinct individuals (cross fertilization) or from one (self fertilization) and (b) the initiation of development of a new individual. (In parthenogenesis the latter phase commences without the former).

FERTILIZATION DUCTS. [L. *fertilis*, fertility]. Passages leading from the female's spermathecae, through which the stored sperm is passed to fertilize the eggs.

FESTIVUS. [L. *festivus*, holiday]. Having a variety of colors.

FESTOON. [Fr. *feston*, garland]. The margin of the integument of ticks when there are rectangular divisions.

FESTOONED. [It. *festone*, a festive ornament]. Arranged in loops as if hung from nails.

FIBRIL. [L. *fibrilla*, small band]. Any minute thread-like structure.

FIBROIN. [L. *fibra*, thread]. The major protein of silk fibers, produced from fibroinogen.

FIBROUS. [L. *fibra*, band]. Composed of fibers.

FICKERT'S GLAND. [C. *Fickert*, Polish (?) Arachnologist]. In some **Linyphiidae**: a swelling of the sperm duct within the embolus.

FILAMENT. [L. *filum*, a thread]. Any long thread-like structure. A thread-like structure at the end of an antenna.

FILIFORM. [L. *filum*, thread; *forma*, shape]. Thread-like; long and narrow.

FILIGEROUS. [L. *filum*, a thread; *gerere*, to carry]. With thread-like outgrowths of flagella.

FILISTATOIDEA. [L. *filum*, a thread; Gr. στατος, standing]. In a previous classification, a monospecific superfamily of cribellate spiders (suborder Opisthothelae, infraorder Araneomorphae) known as 'crevice spiders'. They are relatively large and produce a distinctive flat, tangled web. These spiders exhibit a great degree of sexual dimorphism with the females being a dark charcoal grey to almost black while the males are khaki to amber and have very long, slender legs and palpi. Family: **Filistatidae**.

FILLETS. [L. *filum*, thread]. Bands of fibers. Any raised rib.

FILOSE. [L. *filum*, a thread]. Slender and thread-like.

FIMBRIA. [L. *fimbria*, fringe]. Any fringe-like border of an opening.

FIMBRIATE. [L. *fimbriatus*, fringed]. Fringed at the margin, as in some tubes, ducts and antennae.

FIMICOLOUS. [L. *fimus*, manure; *colere*, to inhabit]. Growing in or on dung.

FINAL HOST. In a parasite's life cycle, the host which harbors the sexually mature parasite. The young stage resides in the intermediate host. See also Host.

FIRST SEGMENT. A segment of any segmented appendage which is nearest the body at the point of attachment.

FISH SPIDER. See **Pisauridae**.

FISSATE. [L. *fissus*, cleft]. Cleft or split. Having fissures or cracks.

FISSIDENTATE. [L. *fissus*, cleft; *dens*, tooth]. Having teeth with multiple points.

FISSILE. [L. *fissus*, cleft]. Capable of being divided, separated into layers or divided into parallel lamellae.

FISSIPHALLIIDAE. [L. *fissus*, cleft; Gr. φαλλος, penis]. A small family of neotropical harvestmen or daddy longlegs (suborder Laniatores, superfamily Zalmoxoidea) from the central and eastern Amazon Rainforest and at elevations of around 3,500 meters in Colombia.

FISSURE. [L. *fissura*, split]. A deep groove or furrow dividing an organ into lobes, or subdividing and separating areas of the lobes.

FISSUS. [L. *fissus*, cleft]. Longitudinally divided nearly to base.

FITNESS. The probability of survival of a genotype relative to an arbitrary standard genotype, whose fitness is expressed as unity. A measure of the ability of a population to survive natural selection. The number of offspring that reach reproductive age.

FIXATION MUSCLES. [L. *figere*, to fix / fasten; *musculus*, muscle]. Muscles that maintain the general body equilibrium.

FIXATION. [L. *figere*, to fix / fasten]. A stereotyped behavioral response shown by an animal regardless of whether it is accompanied by positive or negative reinforcement.

FIXED DIGIT. [L. *figere*, to fix / fasten; *digitus*, finger]. The distal extension of the middle article of the chelicera. It commonly bears teeth and a distal hook and, in chelate-dentate forms, is opposed to the movable digit. In the Mesostigmata the fixed digit may bear the pilus dentilis.

FIXED HAIRS. See Macrotrichia, Microtrichia.

FIXED JAW. In ticks and mites: the distal (fixed) part of the cheliceral segment.

FLABELLUM (BOUTON). [L. *flabellum*, fan]. Any fan-shaped organ or structure.

FLAGELLUM. [L. *flagellum*, whip]. An external structure on the basal joint of the chelicera in Pseudoscorpiones.

FLAMMATE, FLAMMATEUS. [L. *flammula*, blaze]. Flaming or fiery red.

FLAMMAULES. [L. *flammula*, blaze; Gr. αυλη, court or quadrangle]. Having spots of color resembling a small flame; reddish, tinged with red.

FLASH COLORATION. The brightly colored parts of an animal's body which are normally covered but are suddenly exposed to frighten and / or confuse a predator.

FLAT MITE. See False Spider Mite.

FLAVESCENT. [L. *flavescere*, to turn yellow]. Growing or turning yellow.

FLAVID (FLAVOUS, FLAVUS). [L. *flavus*, yellow]. Golden yellow. Sulfur yellow.

FLAVO-TESTACEOUS. [L. *flavus*, yellow; *testaceous*, shell-like]. Light yellow-brown.

FLAVO-VIRENS. [L. *flavus*, yellow; *virens*, green]. Green verging upon yellow.

FLEX. [L. *flectere*, to bend]. To bend: especially of movements of the limbs.

FLEXILE, FLEXILIS. [L. *flectere*, to bend]. Flexible. Capable of being bent at an angle without breaking.

FLEXION REFLEX. [L. *flectere*, to bend]. The commonest type of response to stimulation of the skin. Also known as 'nociceptive' or 'defensive' reflex, it occurs in response to painful stimulation and evokes a marked contraction (flexion) of the limb away from the source of stimulation.

FLEXOR MUSCLE. [L. *flectere*, to bend]. Any muscle that, when it contracts, causes a limb, or any part of a limb to bend.

FLEXOR SURFACE. [L. *flectere*, to bend]. A surface brought closer when a jointed structure is bent at a joint.

FLEXUOUS, FLEXUOSE. [L. *flectere*, to bend]. Curving in a zig-zag manner.

FLEXURE. [L. *flectere*, to bend]. A curve, bend, kink or fold.

FLOCCOSE. [L. *floccus*, a lock of wool]. Covered with wool-like tufts.

FLOCCULATION. [L. *floccus*, a lock of wool]. The clumping together of fine particles.

FLOCCULENT. [L. *floccus*, a lock of wool]. Covered with a soft, waxy substance which often resembles wool. Clinging together in bunches.

FLOCCUS. [L. *floccus*, a lock of wool]. Any tuft-like structure.

FLOSS. [OFr. *flosche*, down]. Any downy or silky substance. The loose piece of silk in a cocoon.

FLUMINEOUS. [L. *fluare*, to flow]. Pertaining to running water.

FLUTED. [OFr. *flaute*, flute]. A channeled or grooved area.

FLUVIATILE. [L. *fluviatilis*, of a river]. Pertaining to, or inhabiting rivers.

FLUVIOMARINE. [L. *fluvius*, a stream; *mare*, sea]. Pertaining to, or inhabiting rivers and seas.

FLUVIOTERRESTRIAL. [L. *fluvius*, a stream; *terra*, land]. Pertaining to, or inhabiting streams and the land beside them.

FOLDS. In the Argasidae: conspicuous cuticular ridges on the ventral or marginal surface of the body.

FOLIOSE. [L. *folium*, leaf]. Leaf-like. Commonly of a flattened, oval to rectangular setae that may or may not have other ornamentation.

FOLIUM. [L. *folium*, leaf]. A pigmented design or pattern on the abdominal dorsum of some spiders.

FOLIVEROUS. [L. *folium*, leaf; *vorare*, to devour]. Leaf-eating.

FOLLICLE. [L. *folliculus*, small sac]. A small cavity or sheath.

FOLLICLE MITES. [L. *folliculus*, small sac; OHG. *miza*, gnat]. See **Demodicidae**.

FOLLICULAR. [L. *folliculus*, small sac]. Pertaining to or having follicles.

FOLLICULATE. [L. *folliculus*, small sac]. Having, consisting of, or enclosed in a follicle or follicles.

FOOT. [AS. *fot*, foot]. A general name for virtually any structure used for ground locomotion or anchoring in animals.

FORAGING. [OFr. *fuerre*, straw]. Searching for food, and all behavior associated with the acquisition and consumption of food.

FORNICATE(D). [L. *fornicatus*, vaulted]. Arched, concave inside, convex outside.

FOSSA. [L. *fossa*, ditch]. Any pit or trench-like depression.

FOSSORIAL. [L. *fossor*, digger]. Adapted for digging.

FOSSULA. [L. *fossula*, little ditch]. A small pit or trench-like depression.

FOSSULATE. [L. *fossula*, little ditch]. Having small hollows or grooves.

FOSSULET. [L. *fossulet*, little ditch]. A long, narrow depression.

FOVA PEDALES (PEDOFOSSA). [L. *fovea*, depression; *pedales*, measuring a foot]. In some Mesostigmata, particularly the **Uropodidae**: a pit in the cuticle into which the legs can be withdrawn.

FOVEA. [L. *fovea*, depression]. Any small depression, pit or fossa. A short median groove on the thoracic part of the carapace which marks the location of the internal attachment of the gastric muscles.

FOVEATE. [L. *fovea*, depression]. Marked with small pits or depressions.

FOVEOLA. [L. *foveola*, small depression]. A small pit, cavity or depression.

FOVEOLATE. [L. *foveola*, small depression]. Having small regular depressions.

FOWL MITE. [OE. *fugel*, bird]. Any member of the superfamily Dermanyssoidea (suborder Monogynaspida, infraorder Gamasina) parasitic on birds, especially the northern fowl mite or starling mite *Ornithonyssus sylviarum*, poultry red mite *Dermanyssus gallinae*, or the tropical fowl mite *Ornithonyssus bursa*.

FRACTATE. [L. *fractus*, broken]. Displaced, bent at an angle.

FRACTUS. [L. *fractus*, broken]. Broken. Also of a geniculate antenna.

FRATRICIDE. [L. *frater*, brother; *-cidere*, to kill]. The killing of siblings by siblings.

FREE. [Skr. *prijas*, dear - from *pri*, to love]. Unattached, motile, distinct, separate.

FREE-LIVING. Not parasitic or symbiotic. Not attached to a substrate.

FREE RUNNING. An endogenous rhythm unaffected by any external influence. See also Circadian Rhythms.

FREE-SWIMMING. Swimming about; not sessile.

FREEZE RESPONSE. See Death Feigning.

FREYANOIDEA. [deriv.uncert. maybe a name (Freyana) in Old Persian]. A superfamily of scab- and mange-producing feather mites (suborder Astigmata, infraorder Psoroptidia). Families: **Caudiferidae, Freyanidae, Vexillariidae**. In other classifications these families are included in the superfamily Pterolichoidea.

FRIABLE. [L. *friare*, to crumble into small pieces]. Easily powdered.

FRIGOFUGE. [L. *frigus*, cold; *fugere*, to flee]. A non-cold tolerant organism.

FRINGE. [L. *fimbria*, fringe]. Hair, scales or other processes extending beyond the margin, usually of equal length.

FRONDOSE. [L. *frondis*, of leaves]. More or less divided into leaf-like expansions.

FRONTAL. [L. *frons*, forehead]. Applied to organs and structures in the region of the forehead or front end of an animal. A plane at right angles to the medial longitudinal or sagittal plane.

FRONTAL SETA. [L. *frons*, forehead; *seta*, bristle]. In the Eriophyoidea: the unpaired median internal vertical seta, vi.

ft. In acariform mites: a designation for the fastigials; the most basal pair of dorsal tarsal setae on the tarsi.

FUGACIOUS. [L. *fugax*, fleeting; *-aceous*, of the nature of]. Of a structure that withers or falls very rapidly.

FUGITIVE SPECIES. [L. *fugitivus*, fleeing]. Species which colonize temporary habitats, reproduce, and leave quickly before the temporary habitat disappears, or competition from other organisms overpowers them.

FULCRAL. [L. *fulcrum*, support]. Of or pertaining to a fulcrum.

FULCRUM. [L. *fulcrum*, support]. Any structure that props or supports another.

FULGID, FULGIDUS. [L. *fulgidus*, shining]. Appearing red with bright metallic reflections.

FULIGEROUS. [L. *fuligo*, soot; *-igerous*, in use always]. Sooty in color.

FULIGINOUS, FULIGINOSUS. [L. *fuliginosus*, sooty]. Sooty or smoky brown.

FULVOAENEOUS. [L. *fulvus*, tawny]. Brazen, with a touch of brownish yellow.

FULVOUS. [L. *fulvus*, tawny]. Tawny or yellowish brown.

FUMAGINOUS. [L. *fumus*, smoke]. Smoky-colored.

FUMATE, FUMATUS. [L. *fumus*, smoke]. Smoky grey.

FUMOSE. [L. *fumus*, smoke]. Smoky.

FUNCTIONAL RESPONSE. A change in behavior in response to a change in circumstances.

FUNDAMENTAL. [LL. *fundamentalis*, of the foundation]. Of a seta or other structure present in the larval stage.

FUNDIFORM. [L. *funda*, sling; *forma*, shape]. Sling-shaped, looped.

FUNDUS. [L. *fundus*, bottom]. The base of an organ.

FUNGICOLOUS. [L. *fungus*, mushroom; *colere*, to inhabit]. Living in or on fungus.

FUNGIFORM. [L. *fungus*, mushroom; *forma*, shape]. Shaped like the fruit-body of an agaric fungus (i.e. the 'typical' mushroom shape).

FUNICLE. [L. *funiculus*, thin rope]. Any strand or cord of connective tissue holding an organ in place. A strand of nerve fibers.

FUNICULAR. [L. *funiculus*, thin rope]. Consisting of a cord or small band.

FUNICULATE. [L. *funiculus*, thin rope]. Having or forming a funiculus.

FUNIFORM. [L. *funis*, rope; *forma*, shape]. Rope-shaped.

FUNNEL SHAPED. See Infundibulum.

FUNNEL-WEB SPIDERS. See Dipluroidea.

FURCAL. [L. *furca*, two-pronged fork]. Forked.

FURCATE. [L. *furca*, fork]. Branching, like the prongs of a fork. Having two divergent branches from a common base.

FURCIFEROUS. [L. *furcifer*, fork-bearer]. Having a forked appendage.

FURCIPULATE. [L. *forceps*, pincers]. Pincer-like.

FURFURACEOUS. [LL. *furfuraceus*, bran-like]. Covered with bran-like or scurf-like particles.

FUR MITES. [OFr. *forrer*, to sheath/encase; Gmc. *miton*, gnat]. Parasitic scab and mange producing mites of mammals (**Psoroptidae** and **Sarcoptidae**). See also Astigmata.

FURRED. Covered with dense hair resembling fur.

FURROW. [AS. *furh*, trench]. A groove separating parts, divisions or segments of an invertebrate body. A short median groove on the thoracic part of the carapace that is situated just above the internal attachment of the gastric muscles.

FUSCESCENT. [L. *fuscus*, dusky]. Having a dusky or somber hue. With a brown shading.

FUSCO-FERRUGINOUS. [L. *fuscus*, dusky; *ferruginus*, rusty]. Brownish rust red.

FUSCOUS. [L. *fuscus*, dusky]. Brownish black; dark brown, approaching black, dusky.

FUSED. [L. *fundere*, to pour/melt]. Of being united, blended or run together.

FUSED CHELICERAE. [Gr. χηλη, claw]. In some Haplogynae: chelicerae that are joined mesally, at least along the base.

FUSEO-PICEOUS. [L. *fuscus*, dusky; *piceus*, pitch black]. Pitch black with a brown tinge or admixture.

FUSEO-RUFUS. [L. *fuscus*, dusky; *rufus*, red]. Red-brown, approaching liver brown.

FUSEO-TESTACEOUS. [L. *fuscus*, dusky; *testaceus*, brick-colored]. Dull reddish brown.

FUSI. [L. *fusus*, spindle]. In spiders: organs composed of two retractile processes which issue from the mammulae, and form threads.

FUSIFORM. [L. *fusus*, spindle; *forma*, shape]. Spindle-shaped, torpedo-shaped, streamlined.

FUSOID. [L. *fusus*, spindle; Gr. ειδος, form]. Somewhat fusiform or spindle-shaped.

FUSULUS, FUSULAE (SPOOLS). [L. *fusulae*, little spindle]. In spiders: the cylindrical projections of the spinnerets, each of which contains numerous minute tubules from which the silk is secreted.

G

g. A designation used for genital setae.

GABELZHAN. [Ger. *gabel*, fork; *zahn*, tooth]. In the Mesostigmata: the offset and commonly most distal tooth on the fixed digit.

GALEA. [L. *galea*, helmet]. In arachnids such as Pseudoscorpiones: horn-like processes on the moveable part (finger/digit) of the chelicerae. It is used to spin silken cocoons for protection during molting, hibernation, or the brooding of eggs.

GALEIFORM/GALEATE. [L. *galea*, helmet, *forma*, shape]. Helmet-shaped.

GALEODIDAE. [L. *galeo*, cover with a helmet]. A large family of sun spiders (subclass Arachnida, order Solifugae) from northern Africa southeaster Europe and Asia. They have microsetae on the tarsal claws of legs II to IV, a characteristic that does not occur on any other group of solifuges. Some *Galeodes* species are able to stridulate. Females deposit their eggs in a burrow and, in some species, guard them.

GALERIFORM. [L. *galerum*, a hide cap]. Cap-shaped.

GALLERY. [ML. *galilaea*, gallery]. A passage or corridor made by an animal.

GALLIENIELLIDAE. [*Joseph Simon Gallieni*, French colonial administrator; L. *-ella*, dim.suf.]. A small family of spiders (infraorder Araneomorphae, superfamily Entelegynae) that may be specialized in preying on ants (Formicidae).

GALL MITE. [OE. *gealla*; painful swelling]. Any mite that produces galls on plants, commonly species of the superfamily Eriophyoidea.

GALUMNOIDEA. [L. *galumna*, a cover]. A superfamily of mites (suborder Oribatida, infraorder Brachypylina - section Poronoticae). Families: **Galumnellidae, Galumnidae.**

GALVANOTAXIS. [L. *Galvani*, Italian physiologist; Gr. ταξις, an arranging]. A directed reaction or change in direction in response to an electrical current.

GALVANOTROPISM. [L. *Galvani*, Italian physiologist; Gr. -τροπος, turning]. An orientation response to an electrical current.

GAMASIDA. [L. *gamasus* agile]. In some classifications: a superfamily (or order, or suborder, or infraorder, or family **Gamasidae**) of insect-parasitizing mites (superorder Parasitiformes, order Mesostigmata). Families: **Laelaptidae, Macronyssidae.** Otherwise these families are in the superfamily Dermanyssoidea. Gamasida may also be a synonym for Mesostigmata.

GAMASINA. [L. *gamasus* agile]. In infraorder (order Mesostigmata, suborder Monogynaspida) of free-living predatory mites associated with soil and leaf litter and which have an influence on population growth of other organisms and control the abundance of springtails, soil-dwelling mites, larvae and eggs of insects as well as nematodes and enchytraeids. Superfamilies: Arctacaroidea, Ascoidea, Dermanyssoidea, Epicrioidea, Eviphidoidea, Heatherelloidea, Parasitoidea, Phytoseioidea, Rhodacaroidea, Veigaioidea, Zerconoidea.

GAMETOTOKY. [Gr. γαμετης, spouse; τοκος, birth]. Parthenogenesis in which unfertilized eggs develop into either sex. See Parthenogenesis.

GAMODEME. [Gr. γαμος, marriage; δημος, population]. A group of individuals that form a relatively isolated interbreeding population.

GAMOSEMATIC. [Gr. γαμος, marriage; σημα, signal]. Behavior or appearance that helps one of a pair of animals communicate with the other.

GANGLION. [Gr. γαγγλιον, little tumor]. A small compact mass of neuron cell bodies and connective tissue, that gives rise to nerve fibers.

GARYPIDAE. [derive.uncert. but may be: Garypus as a modification of grypos (Gr. γρυπος, hook-nosed or curved) referring to the strongly curved chelal fingers]. A family of false scorpions (suborder Iocheirata, superfamily Garypoidea)

GARYPINOIDEA. [see Garypidae]. A superfamily of false scorpions (order Pseudoscorpiones, suborder Iocheirata). Families: **Garypinidae, Larcidae.**

GARYPOIDEA. [see Garypidae]. A superfamily of false scorpions (order Pseudoscorpiones, suborder Iocheirata). Families: **Garypidae, Geogarypidae, Hesperolpiidae, Menthidae, Olpiidae.**

GAS TRANSPORT. The movement of gasses within the body, between the respiratory surface and the cells, usually involving a respiratory pigment.

GASEOUS PLASTRON. See Plastron.

GASTER. [Gr. γαστηρ, belly]. An abdomen, especially the part of the abdomen which lies behind the 'waist' in a spider.

GASTRAEUM. [Gr. γαστηρ, stomach]. The ventral side of the body.

GASTRAL (GASTRIC). [Gr. γαστηρ, stomach]. Of the stomach region.

GASTRIC. [Gr. γαστηρ, stomach]. Of or belonging to the belly or to the stomach.

GASTRIC GLAND (PRINCIPLE GLAND). [Gr. γαστηρ, stomach]. A simple or compound, tubular, gastric juice and mucous secreting gland in the wall of the fundic end of the stomach.

GASTRIC JUICE. [Gr. γαστηρ, stomach]. The secretions of the glands of the stomach.

108

gdj, gds, gdz. Various designations for the podonotal glands that are associated with particular setal rows. See Krantz & Redmond, 1987 and Johnston & Moraza 1991.

gdJ, gdS gdZ. Various designations for the opisthonotal glands that are associated with particular setal rows. See Krantz & Redmond, 1987 and Johnston & Moraza 1991.

GENA. [L. *gena*, cheek]. The cheek or side part of the head.

GENACERORE. See Wax Glands.

GENATASINUS. See Genital Pouch.

GENERA. Plural of Genus.

GENERAL PROCRYPSIS. [Gr. προ-, before; κρυπσις, concealment]. Having a color that generally helps to conceal an animal in the variety of habitats in which it lives. Not a specific cryptic color pattern.

GENERIC. [L. *genus*, race]. Common to all species of a genus.

GENERIC NAME. [L. *genus*, race]. The first name of a binomen or trinomen. E.g. in the name *Loxosceles devia* (Texas recluse spider - **Sicariidae**) '*Loxosceles*' is the generic name and '*devia*' is the specific epithet. See also Nomenclature.

GENE'S ORGAN. [*C.G. Gene*, Italian Zoologist]. In female ticks: a complex subscutal or cephalic gland that secretes a viscous waxy substance that is used to provide a waterproofing layer during oviposition. This organ develops in synchrony with oogenesis and oviposition.

GENICULATE. [L. *geniculum*, little knee]. Bent like a knee joint. Commonly applied to chelicerae in which the basal segment (paturon) extends beyond the clypeus, thus giving the chelicerae the appearance of being bent.

GENICULUM. [L. *geniculum*, little knee]. A sharp bend.

GENITAL. [L. *genitalis*, of generation or birth]. Of the region of the reproductive organs and applied to corpuscles, glands ridges, tubercles, veins, etc.

GENITAL ACETABULUM. [L. *genitalis*, of generation or birth; *acetabulum*, vinegar cup]. In the Hydrachnida: an invagination containing the genitalia. Also, the genital papillae.

GENITAL APERTURE. [L. *genitalis*, of generation or birth]. The genital opening. In ticks and mites it is located approximately in the midline between the coxae. In females the aperture appears as a posteriorly directed U- or V-shaped groove with prominent marginal folds. The shape of the female genital pore varies greatly and is useful in taxonomy. In males of the Metastriata subdivision of the **Ixodidae** the genital pore is covered by a moveable plate which can be elevated when a spermatophore is to be passed. See also Metastriata, Prostriata.

GENITAL ARMATURE. [L. *genitalis*, of generation or birth; *armatura*, armor]. Those portions of the reproductive system directly involved in copulation.

GENITAL DISC. See Genital Papillae.

GENITAL DUCT. See Gonoduct.

GENITAL BULB. [L. *genitalis*, of generation or birth]. On the male palp: the copulatory apparatus lying within the alveolus of the cymbium.

GENITAL GROOVE. See Epigastric Furrow.

GENITAL LAMELLA. [L. *genitalis*, of generation or birth; *lamella*, thin plate]. In male **Parasitidae** (Mesostigmata): a small process that may cover the base of the tritosternum.

GENITALIA. [L. *genitalis*, of generation or birth]. The organs of reproduction, the associated gonads and any accessory organs.

GENITAL LOCK. [L. *genitalis*, of generation or birth]. The temporary inability of copulating partners to separate.

GENITAL OPENING. [L. *genitalis*, of generation or birth]. In ticks and mites: a transverse slit or trifid orifice associated with segment eight. In many species it is located in the progenital chamber, and then it is termed the eugenital opening.

GENITAL OPERCULUM. [L. *genitalis*, of generation or birth; *operculum*, a lid]. In some arachnids: a soft rounded cleft median lobe of the sternum of the first pre-abdominal segment. The opening of the genital duct is at its base.

GENITAL ORIFICE. [L. *genitalis*, of generation or birth; *os*, mouth; *facere*, to make]. The male genital opening. In the Mesostigmata the genital orifice has 1-2 valves, is usually subcircular and is situated in the intercoxal region, often at the base of the tritosternum.

GENITAL PAPILLA / PAPILLAE. [L. *genitalis*, of generation or birth; *papilla*, nipple]. In the acariform mites: 1-3 pairs of extrusible projections that may be finger-like or button-like and that are commonly retracted into the genital vestibule. They sometimes form sessile disks (genital suckers) around the genital opening. As they are modified and dispersed over the body of many freshwater mites, they are thought to have an osmoregulatory function. Genital papillae are absent in the larva, but may be added ontogenetically: protonymphs have one pair, deutonymphs two pairs, and tritonymphs (and adults) three pairs. Although the tritonymphal pair is often lost. Claparède's organ is usually present in both the larvae and prelarvae of mites exhibiting genital papillae in nymphs and adults (Oudeman's Rule).

GENITAL POUCH. [L. *genitalis*, of generation or birth]. Any recess acting as an adjunct to the genital aperture.

GENITAL SEGMENTS. [L. *genitalis*, of generation or birth]. Body segments that bear copulatory organs.

GENITAL SETA. [L. *genitalis*, of generation or birth; *seta*, bristle]. In the Mesostigmata: a seta on a genital shield or valve; seta st5. In spider mites: the genitals g1-g2. In the Eriophyoidea: the coxisternal seta 3a.

GENITAL SHIELD. [L. *genitalis*, of generation or birth]. A shield, or shields, covering the genital opening. In female Mesostigmata this shield is usually called the epigynal (epigynial) shield.

GENITAL SUCKER. See Genital Papilla.

GENITAL TRACHEAE. [L. *genitalis*, of generation or birth; LL. *trachia*, windpipe]. In ticks and mites: the tracheae from the progenital chamber. It resembles gland ducts and often ends in caecae. There may be a respiratory function.

GENITAL VALVES. [L. *genitalis*, of generation or birth; *valvae*, folding doors]. The small sclerites that cover the genital opening. The larger sclerites are usually known as shields or plates.

GENITAL VESTIBULE. [L. *genitalis*, of generation or birth; *vestibulum*, porch]. The ventral chamber which contains the genital papillae and genital opening, and is closed by a pair of genital valves.

GENITIVENTRAL SHIELD (OPISTHOGENITAL SHIELD). [L. *genitalis*, of generation or birth; *venter*, belly; Gr. οπισθο-, behind]. In the Mesostigmata: an epigynal shield that extends back over the ventral region but is separate from the anal shield (as in *Pseudoparasitus*: Laelapidae).

GENITO-VENTRAL. [L. *genitalis*, of generation or birth; *venter*, belly]. In some ticks and mites: of the plate formed by the fusion of epigynial and ventral sclerites.

GENU. [L. *genu*, knee]. Any knee-like bend. In some ticks and mites: a segment between the tibia and the femur.

GENUS. [L. *genus*, race]. A taxonomic grouping consisting of closely related species of (presumably) common phylogenetic origin. Genera are grouped into families. The names of genera are singular nouns, printed in italics (or underlined if written) and with a capital initial letter, e.g. *Eriophyes*, (a genus of mite), *Centruroides*, (a genus of scorpion). See also Nomenclature.

GEOGARYPIDAE. [Gr. γεω-, earth; + *Garypus*]. A small monospecific family of false scorpions (suborder Iocheirata, superfamily Garypoidea) containing on genus: *Afrogarypus*.

GEOTAXIS. [Gr. γεω-, earth; ταξις, a disposition]. The locomotor response to gravity.

GEOTONUS. [Gr. γεω-, earth; τονος, tension]. The normal position in relation to gravity.

GEOTROPISM. [Gr. γεω-, earth; τροπη, a turn]. Movement in relation to a gravitational field, usually either towards to ground (positive geotropism) or away (negative geotropism).

GERALINURIDAE. See Thelyphonoidea.

GERONTOGAEOUS (GERONTOGEOUS/GERONTOGEIC). [Gr. γερων, old man; γεα, earth]. Of, or originating in the Old World. See also Neogeic.

GIBBA. [L. *gibbus*, hump]. A rounded protuberance or prominence.

GIBBOUS (GIBBOSE). [L. *gibbus*, hump]. Inflated, pouched, humped. Of a macula when it resembles a moon more than half full.

GIBBUS. [L. *gibbus*, hump]. When the whole surface forms a hump or obtuse cone.

GILL/GILL BOOK. [cogn. Gr. χειλος, lip]. See Book Gill.

GILVUS. [L. *gilvus*, pale yellow]. Pale yellow. Flavus.

GIMPED. [?Du. an ornamental flat braid or round cord used as a trimming]. Crenate. With scalloped edges.

GINGLYMOID. [Gr. γιγγλυμος, a hinge; ειδος, form]. Constructed like a hinge-joint.

GINGLYMUS. [Gr. γιγγλυμος, a hinge]. A joint in which the articulating surfaces can only move in one plane.

GLABROUS. [L. *glaber*, smooth]. Smooth, hairless.

GLADIATE. [L. *gladius*, sword]. Ensiform. Sword-shaped.

GLAND. [L. *glandula*, gland of the throat, tonsil]. A single cell, or a mass of cells specializing in the secretion of a specific substance (or substances) that exercise an important influence on the body. Glands can generally be divided into two groups; duct glands and ductless glands (or endocrine glands).

GLAND ORIFICE. Any external opening for gland secretion.

GLANDIFORM. [L. *glans*, an acorn; *forma*, shape]. Acorn-shaped.

GLANDILEMMA. [L. *glans*, an acorn; Gr. λεμμα, skin]. The outer covering of a gland.

GLANDULAR. [L. *glandula*, small acorn]. Having or bearing a gland or gland cell, i.e., hair, spines, etc.

GLANDULAR BRISTLES/HAIRS. [L. *glandula*, small acorn]. Stout and rigid glandular setae.

GLANDULAR EPITHELIUM. [L. *glandula*, a little acorn; Gr. επι, upon; θηλη, nipple]. The epithelial tissue of glands, composed of either columnar, cubical or polyhedral cells whose protoplasm contains or modifies the material being secreted.

GLANDULARIUM (GLANDULARIA). [L. *glandula*, a little acorn; -*arium*, a place where something is kept]. In water mites (within the infraorder Anystina): the gland complex on the surface that consists of the gland openings and associated trigger hairs. It is often borne on a small sclerite.

GLANDULAR RESPONSE. The change in the secretory activity of glands in response to either internal or external stimulation.

GLAREAL. [L. *glarea*, gravel]. Living in or growing on gravely ground.

GLAUCESCENT. [L. *glaucus*, sea-green/blueish green]. Somewhat blueish-green.

GLAUCOUS. [L. *glaucus*, sea-green/blueish green]. Blueish-green. Covered with a pale green bloom.

GLENOID. [Gr. γληνη, socket; ειδος, form]. Like a socket.

GLENOID CAVITY. [Gr. γληνη, socket; ειδος, form]. In ticks and mites: part of a condylar articulation.

GLOBOID (GLOBATE, GLOBOSE, GLOBULAR). [L. *globus*, globe; Gr. ειδος, shape]. Spherical.

GLOBULE. [L. *globulus*, small globe]. Any minute, spherical body.

GLOBULOSE. [L. *globulus*, small globe]. Consisting of small globules.

GLOCHIDIATE. [Gr. γλωχιδιον, small arrow point]. Covered with barbed hairs. Inuncate.

GLOCHIS. [Gr. γλωχις, arrow-point]. A barbed hair, bristle, spine or point.

GLOMERATE. [L. *glomus*, ball]. Massed or compacted into a cluster.

GLOMERULATE. [L. *glomus*, ball]. Bearing glomerules. Arranged in clusters.

GLOMERULUS, GLOMERULE. [L. *glomerulus*, small ball-shaped mass]. A tuft or cluster of blood vessels or nerve fibers.

GLOMUS. [L. *glomus*, ball]. A number of glomeruli run together.

GLYCYPHAGOIDEA. [Gr. γλυκυς, sweet; φαγειν, to eat]. A superfamily of 'biting' mites (order Sarcoptiformes, suborder Astigmata). Families: **Aeroglyphidae, Chortoglyphidae, Echimyopodidae, Euglycyphagidae, Glycyphagidae, Pedetropodidae, Rosensteiniidae.**

GNAPHOSIDAE (incl. **PRODIDOMIDAE**). [Gr. γναφος, the prickly teasel]. A world-wide family of ground-running nocturnal hunting spiders (infraorder Araneomorphae, superfamily Entelegynae), which feed mainly on other spiders. They are dark-colored and often with silvery eyes.

GNAPHOSOIDEA. [Gr. γναφος, the prickly teasel]. In a previous classification, a superfamily of mainly eight-eyed araneomorph spiders (order Araneae, suborder Araneomorphae) that united the families: **Ammoxenidae, Cithaeronidae, Gallieniellidae, Gnaphosidae, Lamponidae, Prodidomidae** (now in the **Gnaphosidae**), **Trochanteriidae.** All are now in the superfamily Entelegynae.

GNATHOBASE (GNATHOCOXA, MAXILLA). [Gr. γναθος, jaw; L. *basis*, base]. The expanded lobe of the palpal coxa, located laterally to the labium.

GNATHOCOXA. [Gr. γναθος, jaw; *coxa*, hip]. See Gnathobase.

GNATHOSOMA (CAPITULUM). [Gr. γναθος, jaw; σωμα, body]. In ticks and mites: the head region carrying the mouth parts. It is separated from the body (idiosoma) by a ring of soft cuticle.

GNATHOSOMAL CAPSULE. [Gr. γναθος, jaw; σωμα, body]. The fusion of the chelicerae and subcapitulum (gnathosomal elements) into a single structure; as seen in some prostigmatans.

GNATHOTECTUM (EPISTOME, TECTUM). [Gr. γναθος, jaw; L. *tectum*, roof]. In the Mesostigmata: a membranous dorsal projection of the anterior margin of the basis capitulum. It is often diagnostic at the family, genus or species levels.

GOBLET CELLS. [OFr. *gobelet*, little cup]. Mucous secreting epithelial cells having a flask shaped cavity.

GOBLETS. [OFr. *gobelet*, little cup]. Stigmatal plate markings of certain hard ticks (**Ixodidae**). Small cavities within the cuticle of the spiracular plate which appear as subcircular structures when viewed from the external surface

GOFFERED. [Fr. *gaufrer*, from *gaufre*, honeycomb]. Reticulated. A surface with regular impressions, closely set, and separated by narrow ridges.

GONA. Dead.

GONAD. [Gr. γονη, seed]. Either an ovary, testis or ovotestis.

GONAPOPHYSIS. [Gr. γονη, seed; απο, from; φυω, make to grow]. Any genital appendages.

GONDWANA (GONDWANALAND). [Skr. *Gondvana*, forest of Gond (an Indian kingdom]. A vast southern-hemisphere land mass formed from what is now South America, Africa, India, Australia and the Antarctic and separated from Eurasian land areas by the east-west Tethys sea. The existence of Gondwana was first postulated to account for the similarities in the fossil records occurring in these continents. The break up of the land mass started during the Late Jurassic and Early Cretaceous, and of course continues to the present day. See also Laurasia, Pangaea.

GONODUCT. [Gr. γονος, offspring; L. *ductus*, led]. In any reproductive system: the principle duct providing for the transport of sperm or eggs.

GONOPODY. [Gr. γονος, begetting; –πους, foot]. A type of internal fertilization whereby the male sperm is transferred by an appendage to the female genital organs. See also Podospermia, Tocospermia.

GONOPORE. [Gr. γονος, offspring; πορος, channel]. The external reproductive opening, located in the middle of the epigastric furrow.

GONOTREMA. [Gr. γονος, offspring; τρημα, hole]. A genital opening, as in arachnids.

GONYLEPTIDAE. [Gr. γονυ, the knee; λεπτος, small/delicate]. A very large neotropical family of harvestmen or daddy longlegs (suborder Laniatores, superfamily Gonyleptoidea). Most species inhabit dense tropical, subtropical and temperate forests, some occur in open vegetation and a few live in caves.

GONYLEPTOIDEA. [Gr. γονυ, the knee; λεπτος, small/delicate]. A superfamily of harvestmen (suborder Laniatores, infraorder Grassatores). Families: **Agoristenidae, Cosmetidae, Cranaidae, Gonyleptidae, Manaosbiidae, Metasarcidae, Stygnidae, Stygnopsidae, Tricommatidae.**

GONYTHECA. [Gr. γονυ, knee; θηκη, case]. An articulating surface of the femur to which the tibia is joined.

GOSSAMER. [ME. *gossomer, gos* (goose) + *somer* (summer)]. Of the light film of spider's silk, often enhanced by dew; or groups of strands floating through the air.

GOSSYPINE. [L. *Gossypium*, generic name of cotton]. Cotton-like.

GRACILE. [L. *gracilis*, slender]. Gracefully slender or thin.

GRADUATED. [L. *gradus*, step]. Becoming longer or shorter by steps.

GRADUNGULIDAE. [L. *gradus*, step; *unguis*, claw]. A small family of medium to large three-clawed haplogyne spiders (infraorder Araneomorphae, superfamily Austrochiloidea) that have two pairs of book lungs (as in the Mygalomorphae). They are endemic to southern and western Australia and New Zealand.

GRAINED. [L. *granum*, grain]. Dotted with small tubercules.

GRAMINACEOUS. [L. *gramen*, grass; *-aceous*, of the nature of]. Grass-colored.

GRAMINICOLOUS. [L. *gramen*, grass; *colere*, to dwell]. Living on grasses or in a grassy habitat.

GRAMINIVOROUS. [L. *gramen*, grass; *vorare*, to eat]. Grass-eating.

GRAMMATE. [Gr. γραμμη, line]. Striped or marked with lines or slender ridges.

GRAMMINEUS. [L. *gramen*, grass]. Grass-Green.

GRANDJEAN SYSTEM. [*F. Grandjean*, French Arachnologist]. In the Acariformes: the main system for the designation of hysterosomal setae. Hypothesized segments (anterior to posterior) are C, D, E, F, H, PS (pseudanal), AD (adanal), AN (anal) and PA (peranal). 'G' is absent to avoid confusion with the genital segment, which is treated separately. Setae are designated from the midline to the sides, for example, in segment 'C' the setae are: c1 (midline), c2, c3, c4 (also cp). See also Anamorphosis.

GRANIVOROUS. [L. *granum*, grain; *vorare*, to devour]. Seed or grain-eating.

GRANOSE. [L. *granum*, grain]. Like a chain of grain.

GRANULAR, GRANULOSE, GRANULATE. [L. *granum*, grain]. Consisting of grains, covered with grains, or having a grain-like appearance.

GRANULATED. [L. *granulum*, small grain]. Covered with grains or small tubercles.

GRASSATORES. [L. *grassator*, footpad/highway robber]. An infraorder of harvestman (order Opiliones, suborder Laniatores) that are short-legged, hard-plated and spiny with a robust body. Superfamilies: Assamioidea, Epedanoidea, Gonyleptoidea, Phalangodoidea, Samooidea, Zalmoxoidea.

GRAVIPERCEPTION. [L. *gravis*, heavy; *percipere*, to feel]. The ability to feel (or sense) gravity.

GREGARIOUS. [L. *grex*, flock; *-arius*, connected with]. Of animals that live together or nest in groups, but which do not co-operate, i.e. they are not social.

GRESSORIAL. [L. *gressorius*, a stepping]. Adapted for walking.

GROWING MOLT (MOULT). [L. *mutare*, to change]. A molt that results in a larger size, but no changes in characters or form. See also Repetition Molt.

GROWTH FORM. The morphology of an animal, especially as reflected in its physiological adaptations to its environment.

GROWTH HORMONE. [Gr. ορμαινω, excite]. Any of various growth promoting hormones.

GROOVE. [MD. *groeve*, furrow, ditch]. Any channel, furrow, or linear depression. In ticks and mites: a deep linear depressions in the cuticle, usually on the ventral surface.

GUASINIIDAE. [derive. uncert.]. A small family of harvestmen or daddy longlegs (suborder Laniatores, superfamily Zalmoxoidea) from Venezuela and Brazil. All described species in this family are anophthalmic (completely eyeless).

GULLET. [L. *gula*, gullet]. The esophagus.

GUSTATION. [L. *gustare*, to taste]. The sense of taste. The chemoreception of ions and molecules in solution by specialized epithelial receptors.

GUSTATORY. [L. *gustare*, to taste]. Of the sense of taste; usually applied to cells, hairs, pores, nerves, stimuli, etc.

GUSTATORY RECEPTORS. [L. *gustare*, to taste; *recipere*, to receive]. Chemoreceptors which detect dissolved ions and molecules.

GUSTAVIOIDEA. [quote from original paper: "*named Gustavia sol because of its radiant hairs*"]. A superfamily of mites (suborder Oribatida, infraorder Brachypylina - section Pycnonoticae). Families: **Astegistidae, Ceratoppiidae, Gustaviidae, Liacaridae, Multoribulidae, Peloppiidae** (syn. **Metrioppiidae**), **Tenuialidae, Xenillidae.**

GUT. [AS. *gut*, gut]. The intestinal tract. The alimentary canal, or part of.

GUTTA. [L. *gutta*, drop]. A small spot of color on an animal's body surface.

GUTTATE. [L. *gutta*, a drop]. Having drop-like markings.

GUTTIFORM. [L. *gutta*, a drop or spot; *forma*, shape]. Drop-shaped.

GUTTULA. [L. *guttula*, a small drop]. A small, drop-shaped spot.

GYLIPPIDAE. [Gr. γυλιππος, Spartan commander.]. A family of sun spiders (subclass Arachnida, order Solifugae) from southern Africa and central Asia.

GYMNOBISIIDAE. [Gr. γυμνος, uncovered + *Obisium*.]. A small family of false scorpions (suborder Iocheirata, superfamily Neobisioidea) from South Africa, the Falkland Islands and South America.

GYMNODAMAEOIDEA. [Gr. γυμνος, uncovered; + Damaeidea]. A superfamily of mites (suborder Oribatida, infraorder Brachypylina - section Pycnonoticae). Families: **Aleurodamaeidae, Gymnodamaeidae.**

GYNANDROMORPH (GYANDER). [Gr. γυνη, woman; ανηρ, man; μορφη, shape]. An adult form which is a genetic mosaic in terms of having different sex chromosome constituents in different parts of its body. I.e. it is typically male in certain regions and typically female in others (but not hermaphrodite). The male and female components develop normally.

GYNANDRY. [Gr. γυνη, woman; ανηρ, man]. The tendency in a female towards a male body form.

GYNIC. [Gr. γυνη, woman]. Female. (Andric = male).

GYNOSYNHESMIA. [Gr. γυνη, woman; συν, together; εσμος, a swarm]. A group of females gathering together during mating season. See also Androsynhesmia, Swarm.

GYRAL, GYRATE. [L. *gyrus*, circle]. To move in a circular or spiral fashion.

GYRATORY. [L. *gyrare*, to turn about]. Moving in a circle; circular or rotary motion.

GYRE. [L. *gyrare*, to turn about]. Coiling.

GYROSE. [L. *gyrare*, to revolve]. Sinuous. Curving. With undulating lines.

H

h. In the Acariformes: a designation used for setae on segment H , e.g. h1-3. In the Mesostigmata: a designation used for the hypostomal (hypostomatic) setae (h1-3). See Grandjean System.

H. 1. In the Acariformes: a designation used for the fifth region of the hysterosoma in Acariformes. 2. In spider mites: the humeral seta in the Pritchard & Baker system. H = c3 in the Grandjean System.

HABIT. [L. *habitus*, appearance]. The regular or normal behavior of an animal.

HABITAT. [L. *habitare*, to live, inhabit, dwell]. The totality of any particular environment inhabited by a particular organism. This environment comprises the whole complex of flora, fauna, edaphic and climatic features to which the organism has become adapted.

HABITAT SELECTION. [L. *habitare*, to live, inhabit, dwell]. The ability of a dispersing individual to select a particular (species-specific) environment.

HABITUATION. [L. *habitus*, appearance]. The progressive reduction in response to a stimulus due to continued repetition of the stimulus, without reward or punishment. An important process in learning to ignore insignificant stimuli.

HABITUS (HABITUDE). [L. *habitus*, appearance]. The general appearance or conformation characteristic of an animal (or plant).

HACKLED BAND. [ME. *hackle*, a flax comb]. In cribellate spiders: the composite threads spun by the cribellum and combed by the calamistrum setae.

HAEM- For words of Greek origin related to blood (Gr. αιμα, blood) the correct transliteration could be either haem- or hem-. *Haem-* is common in British English and *Hem-* is common in American English. In older works æ is often used.

HAHNIIDAE. [*Carl Wilhelm Hahn*, German zoologist]. The cosmopolitan family of dwarf sheet spiders (infraorder Araneomorphae, superfamily Entelegynae). Very small spiders (ca. 2 mm) that build extremely delicate webs in the form of a sheet that, unlike many spiders, does not lead to a retreat.

HAIR FOLLICLE MITE. See **Demodicidae.**

HALACARIDAE. [Gr. αλιος, of the sea; ακαρι, a mite]. A family of marine, brackish and fresh-water mites (infraorder Eupodina, superfamily Halacaroidea). Some are predatory, some algivorous, and some appear to be parasitic (e.g. *Astacopsiphagus* on the gills of the crayfish *Euastacus spinifer*).

HALACAROIDEA. [Gr. αλιος, of the sea; ακαρι, a mite]. A superfamily of marine water-mites (suborder Prostigmata, infraorder Eupodina). Families: **Halacaridae, Pezidae.**

HALF-TERETE. [L. *teres*, rounded]. Flat on one side, rounded on the other.

HALIOTOID. [Gr. αλι- sea, ους, ear; ειδος, like]. Ear shaped.

HALITUOUS. [L. *halitus*, breath]. Of the nature of breath, vaporous.

HALLER'S ORGAN. [G. *Haller*, German Zoologist]. On the dorsal aspect of tarsus I of ticks and mites: a chemoreceptor within one or more pits.

HALONOPROCTIDAE. [Gr. αλων, a disk; πρωκτος, hind quarters]. A family of medium to large spiders (infraorder Mygalomorphae, superfamily Avicularioidea) that construct burrows with some form of trapdoor, either wafer-like or cork-like. They have recently been split off from the **Ctenizidae.**

HAMATE/HAMULOSE/HAMIFORM. [L. *hamatus*, hooked]. Hook-shaped. See also Aduncate.

HAMIROSTRATE. [L. *hamus*, a hook; *rostrum*, beak]. Having a hooked beak.

HAMULA. See Hamulus.

HAMULATE. [L. *hamulus*, little hook]. Having small, hook-like processes.

HAMULOSE (HAMATE). [L. *hamatus*, hooked]. Hook-shaped.

HAMULUS, HAMULI. [L. *hamulus*, little hook]. Any hook-shaped appendage.

HAPLOGYNAE (SYNSPERMIATA). [Gr. απλοος, simple; γυνη, woman]. A superfamily of spiders (suborder Opisthothelae, infraorder Araneomorphae) in which there are only six eyes (in most species), simple male palpal organs and no sclerotized epigynum in the adult females. Some members in the family **Caponiidae** have four eyes whiles members of the **Plectreuridae** have eight. Seventeen families.

HAPLOGYNE. [Gr. απλοος, simple; γυνη, woman]. Of spiders: in which there are usually only six eyes, simple male palpal organs and no epigynum in the adult females. See also Entelegyne.

HAPLOID. [Gr. απλοος, simple; ειδος, form]. See Ploidy.

HAPLOID PARTHENOGENESIS. [Gr. απλοος, simple; ειδος, form; παρθενος, virgin; γενεσις, origin]. The development of a haploid individual from a female gamete that has undergone meiotic division but has not been fertilized. See Parthenogenesis.

HAPTIC. [Gr. απτειν, to touch]. Relating to stimuli and reactions.

HAPTOTROPISM. [Gr. απτειν, to touch; τροπη, a turn]. The response by curvature to make contact with the source of a stimulus.

HARMONIC GROWTH. See Przibram's Rule.

HARMOSIS. [Gr. αρμονια, concord]. Adaptation in response to a stimulus.

HARPACTOPHAGOUS. [Gr. αρπακτηρ, robber; -φαγος, eating]. Feeding by preying on other animals.

HARVESTMEN (HARVEST SPIDERS). [*harvest*, derived from Gr. καρπος, fruit]. Round bodied, short, and (the more familiar) long legged spiders (subclass Arachnida, order Opiliones) that lack the characteristic narrow waist of arachnids. There are about 4,500 species worldwide.

HASTATE/HASTIFORM. [L. *hasta*, spear]. Spear-shaped. More or less triangular with divergent basal lobes.

HATCHED. [Fr. *hacher*, to chop]. Closely marked with numerous short, transverse lines.

HAWKED. Curved like a hawk's beak.

HEAD. [OE. *heafod*, top of the body]. The specialized anterior part of an animal in which (by definition) are the mouth and principle sense organs. The head is often enlarged to accommodate the principle ganglia and brain. In arachnids: the cephalothorax anterior to the cephalothoracic junction.

HEART. [AS. *heorte*, heart]. A hollow muscular pump which, by continuous rhythmic contraction, causes the blood to circulate the body. The heart generally consists of an enlarged region of a blood vessel with a varying number of chambers and at least two non-return valves. The chamber that receives the blood being the auricle (or atrium) and that which expels the blood, the ventricle.

HEART CHAMBER. [AS. *heorte*, heart; OFr. *chambre*, a chamber/room]. One of the segmental swellings of the dorsal blood vessel.

HEATHERELLOIDEA. [*Heather Proctor*, Canadian Arachnologist; L. *-ella*, dim. suf.]. A monospecific superfamily of mites (suborder Monogynaspida, infraorder Gamasina). Family: **Heatherellidae**. In a previous classification: suborder Heatherellina.

HEBETATE. [L. *hebes*, blunt/dull]. Blunt ended.

HEBETIC STAGE. [Gr. εβετικος, juvenile]. A juvenile stage.

HEDERIFORM. [L. *hedera*, ivy; *forma*, shape]. Shaped like an ivy leaf.

HEDONIC. [Gr. ηδονη, pleasure]. Of factors that act to stimulate sexual activity.

HELIC. [Gr. ελος, marsh]. Of marshes or marsh communities.

HELICAL. [Gr. ελιξ, spiral]. Arranged spirally, like a corkscrew.

HELICINE. [Gr. ελιξ, spiral]. Spiral, convoluted.

HELICOID. [Gr. ελιξ, spiral; ειδος, form]. Spiral-like. Coiled like a snail's shell.

HELICIFORM. [Gr. ελιξ, spiral; L. *forma*, shape]. In the form of a spiral snail shell; applied to the cases of some trichopterans.

HELIOPHIL. [Gr. ηλιος, sun; -φιλ, loving]. Adapted to a relatively high intensity of light.

HELIOPHOBIC. [Gr. ηλιος, sun; φοβος, fear]. Avoiding bright sunlight.

HELIOTACTIC. [Gr. ηλιος, sun; ταξις, an arranging]. Light loving. Of species that live in the open in daylight.

HELIOTAXIS. [Gr. ηλιος, sun; ταξις, an arranging]. Movement in response to sunlight. See also Phototaxis, Skototaxis.

HELIOTHERMIC. [Gr. ηλιος, sun; θερμη, heat]. Of animals that maintain a relatively high body temperature by basking.

HELIOTROPISM. [Gr. ηλιος, sun; -τροπος, turning]. Orientation in response to sunlight.

HELIX (HELICES). [Gr. ελιξ, spiral]. A spiral. A coiled structure.

HELMINTHOID. [Gr. ελμινθ, a worm; ειδος, form]. Shaped like a worm.

HELOBIUS. [Gr. ελος, marsh; βιος, life]. Living in marshes.

HELVOLUS, HELVBEOLUS. [L. *helvus*, yellowish]. Tawny or dully reddish yellow.

HELVUS. [L. *helvus*, yellowish]. Honey yellow.

HEM- For words of Greek origin related to blood (Gr. αιμα, blood) the correct transliteration could be either haem- or hem-. *Haem-* is common in British English and *Hem-* is common in American English. In older works æ is often used.

HEMAL, HEMATAL. [Gr. αιμα, blood]. Of blood.

HEMAPOIESIS. See Hematopoiesis.

HEMATOCHROMES (HEMOCHROMES). [Gr. αιμα, blood; χρωμα, color]. Respiratory pigments. Oxygen-carrying pigments formed from compounds of iron or copper combined with protein molecules. E.g. hemoglobin (haemoglobin), the red iron-containing compound; hemocyanin (haemocyanin), the blue copper-containing compound.

HEMATOCRYAL. [Gr. αιμα, blood; κρυος, frost/ice]. Cold-blooded.

HEMATOCYANIN. See Hemocyanin.

HEMATOCYTE (HEMACYTE, HEMOCYTE, HAEMACYTE, HAEMOCYTE). [Gr. αιμα, blood; κυτος, a hollow vessel]. A general name for a blood corpuscle. More particularly, a blood corpuscle in insects and other arthropods. Classification is difficult as these cells have very different appearances under different conditions, but there are generally agreed to be four main types. 1. Cystocytes (coagulocytes): which have a small, sharply defined nucleus and pale, hyaline cytoplasm containing dispersed black granules. 2. Granular hematocytes: which are phagocytic and carry acidophilic granules in the cytoplasm. 3. Plasmatocytes: variable in form, phagocytic and with basophilic cytoplasm. 4. Prohematocytes (Hemocytoblast, Prohaemocytes): small rounded cells with relatively large nuclei in strongly basophilic cytoplasm that divide at frequent intervals and develop into hemocytes.

HEMATODOCHA (HAEMATODOCHA). [Gr. αιμα, blood; δοχη, receptacle]. In male spiders: fibro-elastic regions of the tarsal segment (base) of the male pedipalp which, during mating, becomes engorged with blood thus causing the embolus (a penis-like projection) to be extended prior to being inserted into one of the female reproductive openings.

HEMERECOLOGY. [Gr. ημερος, tame; οικος, household; λογος, discourse]. The study of the ecology of cultivated land.

117

HEMEROPHILIC. [Gr. ημερος, cultivated; φιλος, loving]. Having the ability to withstand cultivation and human interference with the environment.

HEMEROPHOBIC. [Gr. ημερος, cultivated; φοβος, fear]. Lacking the ability to withstand cultivation and human interference with the environment.

HEMI. [Gr. ημι-, half]. Prefix: half.

HEMICTENATA. [Gr. ημι, half; κτενος, comb]. In some classifications, a monotypic infraorder of false scorpions (order Pseudoscorpionida, suborder Iocheirata). Superfamily: Neobisioidea. Not all authorities agree with this scheme.

HEMISARCOPTOIDEA. [Gr. ημι, half; + Sarcoptidae]. A superfamily of 'biting' mites (order Sarcoptiformes, suborder Astigmata). Families: **Algophagidae, Carpoglyphidae, Chaetodactylidae, Hemisarcoptidae, Hyadesiidae, Meliponocoptidae, Winterschmidtiidae.**

HEMISCORPIIDAE (syn Ischnuridae, Liochelidae). [Gr. ημι-, half; σκορπιος, scorpion]. A monospecific family of scorpions (order Scorpiones, superfamily Scorpionoidea) that have flat, broad bodies in association with their principal habitat of tight rock crevices.

HEMIZYGOID PARTHENOGENESIS. [Gr. ημι-, half; ζυγον, yoke; ειδος, form; παρθενος, virgin; γενεσις, birth]. The development of an individual from an unfertilized haploid egg. See Parthenogenesis.

HEMOCOEL (HAEMOCOEL). [Gr. αιμα, blood; κοιλος, hollow]. An expanded part of the blood system. A large, blood filled body cavity or sinus which surrounds most of the internal organs in arthropods, molluscs and many other invertebrates. Unlike the coelom, it never communicates with the exterior and never contains germ cells. Blood from the arteries empties directly into the hemocoel rather than passing into capillaries, so that every organ is bathed in it. Blood returns to the heart via the pericardial sinus and thence through ostia (small openings in the heart wall).

HEMOCYANIN (HEMATOCYANIN). [Gr. αιμα, blood; κυανος, dark blue]. A dark blue copper-containing respiratory pigment found in the plasma (as opposed to being cellular) in many molluscs and arthropods.

HEMOLYMPH. [Gr. αιμα, blood; L. lympha, pure water]. The organ-bathing fluid found in the coelom of many invertebrates and considered to be the equivalent of blood and lymph in higher organisms. Hemolymph consists of a fluid plasma in which proteins, carbohydrates, fats, various enzymes, organic acids and nucleated cells are suspended.

HEMOPOIESIS, HEMATOPOIESIS, HAEMATOPOIESIS, HAEMOPOIESIS. [Gr. αιμα, blood; ποιησις, creating/forming]. The formation of blood cells.

HEMOSTATIC. [Gr. αιμα, blood; στατικος, causing to stand]. In some arthropods: applied to the membrane that crosses the joint between the trochanter and the femur in autotomy of the limb. Also, any agent that stops bleeding.

HEMOSTATIC DIAPHRAGM/MEMBRANE. [Gr. αιμα, blood; στατικος, causing to stand; διαφραγμα, midriff]. In some arthropods: an obstruction device between the femur and trochanter that prevents fluid loss after autotomy. An occlusive diaphragm.

HEPATICOLOUR. [Gr. ηπαρ, the liver; L. color, pigment]. Liver-brown (dragon's blood).

HEPTAMEROUS. [Gr. επτα, seven; μερος, part]. Having seven parts.

HERCOGAMY. [Gr. ερκος, barrier; γαμος, marriage]. The situation in which self fertilization is impossible.

HERMANNIELLOIDEA. [Jean-Frédéric Hermann, French Arachnologist; L. -ella, dim. suf.]. A monospecific superfamily of mites (suborder Oribatida, infraorder Brachypylina - section Pycnonoticae). Families: **Hermanniellidae, Plasmobatidae.**

HERMANNIOIDEA. [Jean Frédéric Hermann, French Arachnologist]. A monospecific superfamily of mites (suborder Oribatida, infraorder Brachypylina - section Pycnonoticae). Family: **Hermanniidae (Galapagacaridae).**

HERSILIIDAE. [*Hersilia*, Roman wife of Romulus]. The cosmopolitan family of tree-trunk spiders (infraorder Araneomorphae, superfamily Entelegynae). There are two prominent spinnerets that are almost as long as the entire abdomen, so they sometimes known as "two-tailed spiders". They do not make a web, but lay a light layer of threads over an area of tree bark and, being well camouflaged, wait nearby for an insect to become entangled. They then direct their spinnerets toward their prey and immobilize it by circling while casting silk.

HESPEROLPIIDAE. [Gr. εσπερα, the west; + *Olpium*]. A family of false scorpions (suborder Iocheirata, superfamily Garypoidea) with a distribution covering America, Africa, Asia and southern Europe.

HETERAUXESIS. [Gr. ετερο-, different; αυξησις, growth]. The relation of the growth rate of a part of a developing organism to the growth rate of another part of the organism, or the whole organism. If the part grows more rapidly than the organism as a whole, it shows tachyauxesis, if slower then bradyauxesis. The term heterauxesis was proposed by Neeham and Lerner (1941) to supersede the term allometry, which is reserved for comparison of relative proportions in different types of animals. See also Bradyauxesis, Isauxesis, Tachyauxesis.

HETERO-. [Gr. ετερο-, different]. As a prefix: unequal, different from.

HETEROCHEYLOIDEA. [Gr. ετερο-, different; χελωνη, tortoise/turtle]. A monotypic superfamily of mites (suborder Prostigmata, infraorder Eleutherengona). Family: **Heterocheylidae.**

HETEROCHROME. [Gr. ετερο-, different; χρωμα, color]. Having different colors. See also Homochrome.

HETEROCHRONISM. [Gr. ετερο-, different; χρονος, time]. In development: a departure from the typical temporal sequence in the formation of organs. Organs (or other factors) thus maturing at earlier or later growth stages can lead to paedomorphosis or recapitulation.

HETEROCHROSIS. [Gr. ετερο-, different; χρως, coloring]. Abnormal coloration.

HETEROCHTHONIOIDEA. [Gr. ετερο-, different; χθωνιος, beneath the earth]. A superfamily of mites (suborder Oribatida, infraorder Enarthronota). Families: **Arborichthoniidae, Heterochthoniidae, Nanohystricidae, Trichthoniidae.**

HETERODACTYL. [Gr. ετερο-, different; δακτυλος, finger]. In the Chelicerata: having claws, apoteles or ungues differing from each other. See also Bidactyl, Homodactyl, Monodactyl, Tridactyl.

HETERODYNAMIC LIFE CYCLE. [Gr. ετερο-, different; δυναμις, power]. 1. A life cycle in which there is a period of dormancy. 2. A life cycle that includes a rest period not caused by environmental conditions. See also Homodynamic Life Cycle.

HETEROFACIAL. [Gr. ετερο-, different; L. *facies*, face]. Having regional differentiation.

HETEROGAMY. [Gr. ετερο-, different; γαμος, offspring]. 1. The alternation of reproduction by parthenogenesis and bisexual reproduction. 2. The preference of an individual to mate with another of dissimilar phenotype or genotype. See also Homogamy.

HETEROGONIC GROWTH. [Gr. ετερο-, different; γονος, produce]. See Allometry.

HETEROGONIC LIFE CYCLE. [Gr. ετερο-, different; γονος, produce]. A life cycle involving alternation of parasitic and free-living generations. See also Homogonic Life Cycle.

HETEROGONY. [Gr. ετερο-, different; γονος, seed]. 1. Study of relative growth. Allometry. 2. Alternation of generations. See Heterogamy. 3. Having both males and females present in a colony. 4. See Parthenogenesis: Cyclic Parthenogenesis.

HETEROLECITHAL. [Gr. ετερο-, different; λεκιθος, yolk]. Having unequally distributed deutoplasm (yolk). See also Alecithal, Centrolecithal, Macrolecithal, Mediolecithal, Meiolecithal, Mesolecithal, Microlecithal, Oligolecithal, Polylecithal, Telolecithal.

HETEROMEROUS. [Gr. ετερο-, different; μερος, part]. Having unequal numbers of parts. Having a different number of tarsal segments on different legs. See also Homoeomerous.

HETEROMORPHIC. [Gr. ετερο-, different; μορφη, form]. Having different morphological forms, either within a particular life stage or in a developmental stage, that differs radically from other stages.

HETERONYCHIA. [Gr. ετερο-, different; ονυξ, claw]. In the Chelicerata: one or more legs with a different number of claws than the other legs.

HETEROPARTHENOGENESIS. [Gr. ετερο-, different; παρθενος, virgin; γενεσις, birth]. Parthenogenesis producing either offspring that reproduce parthenogenetically or offspring that reproduce sexually. See Parthenogenesis.

HETEROPLOID. [Gr. ετερο-, different; απλοος, onefold, ειδος, form]. Organisms with a genetic complement of one basic set of chromosomes are haploid, those with two sets are diploid, the rest are heteroploid. See also Ploidy.

HETEROPODIDAE. [Gr. ετερο, different; ποδ, foot]. See **Sparassidae**.

HETEROSPHYRONIDA (EPIOCHEIRATA). [Gr. ετερο-, different; σφυρα, hammer] A suborder of false scorpions (subclass Arachnida, order Pseudoscorpiones). Superfamily: Chthonioidea.

HETEROSTIGMATA (HETEROSTIGMATINA). [Gr. ετερο-, different; στιγματα, marks]. In a previous classification: a section or infraorder of mites (order Trombidiformes; suborder Prostigmata) that united the superfamilies Dolichocyboidea, Heterocheyloidea, Pyemotoidea, Pygmephoroidea, Tarsocheyloidea, Tarsonemoidea, Trochometridioidea. These superfamilies are now in the infraorder Eleutherengona, except the Pygmephoroidea, which has been abandoned as a junior synonym for the Scutacaroidea.

HETEROSTROPHY. [Gr. ετερο-, different; στροφη, turning/twisting]. Being coiled in the opposite direction to normal.

HETEROTHERM. [Gr. ετερο-, different; θερμη, heat]. See Poikilotherm.

HETEROZERCONOIDEA. [Gr. ετερο-, different; + Zerconidae]. A superfamily of mites (order Mesostigmata, suborder Sejida). Families: **Discozerconidae, Heterozerconidae**.

HEXAPOD. [Gr. εξ, six; πους, foot]. 1. Having three pairs of legs. 2. In larval mites: having or using three pairs of legs.

HEXATHELIDAE. [Gr. εξ, six; θηλη, nipple]. A superfamily of medium to large, venomous funnel-web tarantulas (infraorder Mygalomorphae, superfamily Avicularioidea) in which the body is typically three times longer than it is wide and the eyes are close together. They are darkly colored, ranging from black to brown, with a glossy carapace covering the front part of the body. They generally have long spinnerets. They were previously included as a subfamily of the **Dipluridae** and previously in the superfamily Hexatheloidea.

HEXISOPODIDAE [Gr. εξ, six; ισος, equal; πους, foot]. A family of sun spiders (subclass Arachnida, order Solifugae) from southern Africa. They lack of claws on the fourth pair of legs.

HIBERNAL. [L. *hibernus*, wintry]. One of the terms for the six part division of the year commonly used in ecology, especially with reference to terrestrial and fresh-water communities. The six parts are: prevernal (early spring), vernal (late spring), aestival (early summer), serotinal (late summer), autumnal (autumn) and hibernal (winter).

HIBERNATE. [L. *hibernare*, to be in winter quarters]. To pass the winter in a dormant condition.

HIRSUTE. [L. *hirsutus*, rough, shaggy]. Bearing coarse hairs or hair-like processes.

HISPID. [L. *hispidus*, bristly]. Having bristles or short, stiff hairs.

HISPIDULOUS. [L. *hispidus*, bristly]. Minutely hispid.

HISTIOID (HISTOID). [Gr. ιστιον, a web; ειδος, form]. Web-like, arachnoid.

HISTIOSTOMATOIDEA. [Gr. ιστιον, a web; στομα, mouth]. A superfamily of 'biting' mites (order Sarcoptiformes, suborder Astigmata). Families: **Guanolichidae, Histiostomatidae**.

HOARY. [AS. *hor*, grey/old]. Greyish white, usually due to a fine pubescence.

120

HOLODORSAL SHIELD. [Gr. ολος, whole; L. *dorsum*, back]. Any shield that covers the dorsum. In the Mesostigmata: it is thought to result from the fusion of the podonotal and opisthonotal shields; a suture between these regions is often evident.

HOLOGASTRIC SHIELD. [Gr. ολος, whole; γαστηρ, stomach]. In the Mesostigmata: a shield that covers the genital, ventral and anal regions. It may be formed from a ventrianal shield that incorporates the metapodal elements and is fused to the epigynal shield.

HOLOID. [Gr. ολος, whole; ειδος, form]. In the Acariformes: lacking a flexible cuticle between legs II-III. See also Dichoidy, Ptychoidy, Trichoidy.

HOLOPELTIDA. [Gr. ολος, whole; πελτη, shield]. In a previous classification: a group of arachnids (class Euchelicerata, subclass Arachnida), known as whip-scorpions, in which the prosoma is covered with a single, thick, chitinous plate. This group is sometimes considered to be an order in its own right, or sometimes included within the Uropygi (whip scorpions).

HOLOSOMATA (DESMONOMATA, NOTHRONATA). [Gr. ολος, complete, σομα, body]. A monotypic infraorder of beetle mites or armored mites (order Sarcoptiformes, suborder Oribatida). Superfamily: Crotonioidea (Nothroidea).

HOLOTHYRIDA (TETRASTIGMATA). [Gr. ολος, whole; θυροειδης, door-like]. An order of large, predatory mites (subclass Arachnida, superorder Parasitiformes) from Australia, New Zealand and the Indo-Pacific region. They have a sclerotized, non-segmented body and possess two pairs of spiracles, one pair by the third coxa and one pair behind the fourth coxa. Families: **Allothyridae, Holothyridae, Neothyridae.**

HOLOTRICHY. [Gr. ολος, complete; θριξ, hair]. Possessing all the setae normally present in their natural group. Having the complete complement of setae thought to have been present in the ancestor group See also Hypertrichy, Neotrichy.

HOLOVENTRAL SHIELD. [Gr. ολος, whole; L. *venter*, belly]. In male mesostigmatans: a shield that covers the entire venter, including the intercoxal region (where it bears the genital aperture), the ventral and anal regions.

HOLOZOIC. [Gr. ολος, whole; ζωον, animal]. A method of feeding in which nutrients are obtained by consuming other organisms, i.e. the method employed by the majority of animals.

HOMALONYCHIDAE. [Gr. ομαλος, average; ονυξ, claw]. A monospecific family of spiders (infraorder Araneomorphae, superfamily Entelegynae) containing three species. They do not build webs, and are typically found under rocks or dead vegetation. The two North American species have specialized setae which allow them to attach sand and fine soil particles to themselves as camouflage; they also partially bury themselves.

HOMEO-. [Gr. ομοιος, alike]. Prefix: the same, similar. For definitions not found here, see **HOMO-.**

HOMEOCHRONOUS, HOMOECHRONOUS. [Gr. ομοιος, alike; χρονος, time]. Variation occurring at the same age in offspring as in the parent.

HOMEOMEROUS. See Homoeomerous.

HOMEOMORPHS. [Gr. ομοιος, alike; μορφη, form]. Two unrelated taxa that are superficially alike.

HOMEOSIS. See Homoeosis.

HOMING. The return to a particular location that is used for resting or breeding. Homing can apply to a daily return, or to seasonal or annual returns.

HOMO-. [Gr. ομος, uniform]. Prefix: the same, similar.

HOMOCHROME. [Gr. ομος, uniform; χρωμα, color]. Having one color or hue. See also Heterochrome.

HOMOCHROMY. [Gr. ομος, uniform; χρωμα, color]. Of the same or uniform color. A phenomenon in which certain animals tend to have a general resemblance to the prevailing color of the environment. See also Anticryptic Coloration.

HOMODACTYL. [Gr. ομος, uniform; δακτυλος, finger]. In the Chelicerata: of a claw similar in shape to the lateral claws (ungues). See also Bidactyl, Heterodactyl, Monodactyl, Tridactyl.

HOMODONT (ISODONT). [Gr. ομος, uniform; οδων, tooth]. Having all the teeth alike.

HOMODROMOUS. [Gr. ομος, uniform; δραμεν, to run]. Moving in the same direction.

HOMODYNAMIC LIFE CYCLE. [Gr. ομος, uniform; δυναμις, power]. 1. A life cycle in which there is continuous development; i.e. not interrupted by a diapause. 2. A life cycle in which dormancy can only be caused by adverse environmental conditions. See also Heterodynamic Life Cycle.

HOMODYNAMOUS. [Gr. ομος, uniform; δυναμις, strength]. Direct development without a resting stage.

HOMOECIOUS. [Gr. ομοιος, shared in common; οικος, dwelling]. Occupying the same host throughout the life cycle.

HOMOEOCHROME. [Gr. ομοιος, alike; χρωμα, color]. Of the same color. See also Heterochrome.

HOMOEOMEROUS, HOMEOMEROUS, ISOMEROUS. [Gr. ομοιος, alike; μερος, part]. Having the same number of tarsal segments on all legs. See also Heteromerous.

HOMOEOMORPHIC. [Gr. ομοιος, alike; μορφη, shape]. Of structures or organisms that exhibit convergence.

HOMOEOSIS (HOMEOSIS). [Gr. ομοιωσις, likeness]. The development of one structure into the likeness of another structure.

HOMO-. [Gr. ομος, uniform]. Prefix: the same, similar. For definitions not found here, see **HOMEO-.**

HOMOGENEOUS. [Gr. ομος, the same; γονος, produce]. Of the same kind or nature or similar in texture or parts.

HOMOGENETIC. [Gr. ομος, the same; γενεσις, descent]. Having the same origins.

HOMOGENY, HOMOGENOUS. [Gr. ομος, the same; γενος, race]. Having analogous parts or organs due to descent from the same ancestral type. See also Homoplasy.

HOMOGONIC LIFE CYCLE. [Gr. ομος, the same; γονος, produce]. A life cycle in which all generations are free-living or all are parasitic. There is no (or little) alternation of the two. See also Heterogonic Life Cycle.

HOMOIOMEROUS. [Gr. ομοιος, alike, μερος, part]. Of uniform structure. Composed of cells of the same type.

HOMOLATERAL. [Gr. ομος, the same; L. latus, side]. On, or of, the same side.

HOMOLOGOUS. [Gr. ομολογος, agreeing]. Of an organ, structure or chromosome of one animal that is thought to have the same evolutionary origins as a similar organ, structure or chromosome of another animal, although the functions may be very different. Homology is usually deduced from the combined fields of embryology, comparative anatomy and paleontology.

HOMOLOGY. [Gr. ομολογια, agreement]. Having the same phylogenetic origin but not necessarily the same final structure or function.

HOMOMORPHIC. [Gr. ομος, uniform; μορφη, shape]. Being similar in appearance or form.

HOMOMORPHOSIS. [Gr. ομος, the same; μορφωσις, shaping]. Having a newly regenerated part like the part removed.

HOMONOMIC. [Gr. ομος, the same; νομος, law]. Having the same functional behavior.

HOMOPHYLIC. [Gr. ομος, the same; φυλη, race]. Resembling one another due to common ancestry.

HOMOPLASY. [Gr. ομος, the same; πλαστος, molded]. The appearance of similar structures in different evolutionary lineages, i.e. not due to inheritance from a common ancestor. This term covers the concepts of convergence and parallel evolution. See also Homogeny, Phylogenetic Classification.

HOMOTENE, HOMOTENOUS. [Gr. ομος, the same; L. *tenere*, to hold]. Retaining the primitive form.

HONEYBEE TRACHEAL MITE. The mite *Acarapis woodi* (**Tarsonemidae**), that lives parasitically in the tracheae of honeybees (**Apidae**) and is associated with the development of Isle of Wight Disease. Other *Acarapis* species are external parasites of bees.

HOOD. [AS. *hod*, hood]. Any color marking or expansion suggesting a hood. In beetle mites (Oribatida): the dorsal wall of the camerostome that extends over the capitulum.

HOODED. [AS. *hod*, hood]. Having head coloration conspicuously different from the rest of the body.

HOOK, HOOKLETS. See Hamulus.

HORMONES. [Gr. ορμαω, rouse]. Complex chemical regulators or messengers produced by specialized tissues (endocrine glands) within an organism. They are secreted into the interstitial fluids and blood and act upon distant target tissues within the same organism. The interaction of the hormone with the appropriate cell surface receptor molecule initiates a series of steps that influences one or more aspects of the physiology or chemistry of those cells. Hormones are classified into three groups (1) amines, (2) steroids and (3) polypeptides and proteins. There are also three very general classes of actions: (1) Kinetic effects - pigment migration, muscle contraction and glandular secretion. (2) Metabolic effects - changes in the rate and balance of reactions and concentrations of tissue constituents. (3) Morphogenic effects - associated with growth and differentiation. Hormones often have multiple effects and there are certainly many still to be discovered.

HORN. [AS. *horn*, horn]. A stiff, pointed, unbranched cuticular process.

HOST. [L. *hospes*, host]. Any organism within or upon which a parasite lives. The **paratenic host** is an intermediate host, which acts as a vector and in which the reproductive stage of the parasite can live, but not reproduce. The **intermediate host** is any host (maybe one or several) in which the juvenile stage of the parasite lives before proceeding to the **final host/definitive host**, which is the host in which the parasite reproduces sexually.

HOST-PARASITE ASSOCIATIONS. **Eichler's rule:** groups of hosts that show more variation are parasitized by more species than taxonomically more uniform groups. **Emery's rule:** a generalization that species of social parasites are very similar to their host species and are therefore presumed to be closely related to them phylogenetically. **Fahernholz's rule:** a general rule that states that there is usually a considerable degree of parallelism between the phylogenetic development and speciation of a host group and its associated parasite group. **Manter's rules:** (1) parasites evolve more slowly than their hosts, and (2) the longer the association within a particular host group, the greater the specificity exhibited by the parasite. **Szidat's rule:** the more primitive the host, the more primitive the parasites which it harbors.

HOST SELECTION PRINCIPLE. [L. *hospes*, host]. A theoretical hypothesis that a female parasite that breeds on two or more hosts will return to the host on which she was reared to reproduce.

HOST SPECIFICITY. [L. *hospes*, host]. The degree to which a parasite is able to mature in one or more host species.

HOUSE SPIDER. See **Agelenidae.**

HUB. [ME. *hubbe*, lump]. The center platform of an orb web.

HUBBARDIIDAE (SCHIZOMIDAE). [*H.G. Hubbard*, American Arachnologist]. A family of short-tailed whipscorpions (order Schizomida, superfamily Hubbardioidea) with a wide distribution.

HUBBARDIOIDEA. [*H.G. Hubbard*, American Arachnologist]. The superfamily of schizomids. Families: †**Calcitronidae, Hubbardiidae, Protoschizomidae.**

HUMERAL PROCESS (PROJECTION). [L. *humerus*, shoulder]. Any fixed projection in the humeral region.

HUMERAL SETA. [L. *humerus*, shoulder; *seta*, bristle]. In the Mesostigmata: a seta in the humeral region that often projects at a right angle to the body; usually seta r3 (rarely r4). In the Acariformes: H or c3 (rarely c4 = cp).

HUMICOLOUS (HUMICOLE). [L. *humus*, soil; *colere*, to inhabit]. Soil or humus-inhabiting.

HUMID. [L. *humidus*, moist]. Of regions in which the normal rainfall is sufficient to produce ordinary farm crops without irrigation. See also Arid.

HUMOR. [L. *humor*, moisture]. Any body fluid.

HUNTING SPIDERS. See **Lycosidae**.

HUTTONIIDAE. [Captain F.W. *Hutton*, New Zealand Biologist]. A monospecific family of spiders (infraorder Araneomorphae, superfamily Palpimanoidea) from New Zealand and containing a single species *Huttonia palpimanoides* (although there are others waiting to be described).

HUXLEY'S POWER LAW. [*T.H. Huxley*, English Zoologist]. $y = bx^{\alpha}$ where y = weight or size of the organ; x = the body weight or size; b = initial growth index; α = growth rate. For allometric growth; this relationship expresses, in its simplest form, the growth of an organ compared to the growth of the whole body - with time eliminated. When both organ and body retain the same ratio, $\alpha = 1$ and the adult looks like the infant. Usually the head grows more slowly than the body, and then $\alpha < 1$.

HYACINTHINE. [Gr. υακινθος, the hyacinth]. The purple blue of the hyacinth (between mauve and lilac).

HYALINE. [Gr. υαλος, glass]. Translucent. Resembling glass.

HYALOID. [Gr. υαλοειδης, glass-like]. Transparent, glassy.

HYDATID. [Gr. υδατις, a watery vesicle]. Generally, any vesicle or sac filled with clear watery fluid.

HYDRACARINA (HYDRACHNELLIDA, HYDRACHNIDA). [Gr. υδρο-, water; LL. *acarus*, mite]. In a previous classification: a cosmopolitan grouping (clade) of water mites (order Prostigmata, suborder Parasitengona) in which there is a single pair of spiracles located anteriorly near the mouth parts. Marine water mites (**Halacaridae**) live mainly in shallow waters and are frequently encountered on algae, bryozoans, hydroids and sponges. The freshwater mites (**Hydrachnellidae, Unionicolidae**) are often bright red and many are active swimmers. Larval stages may be parasitic on the gills of freshwater clams or aquatic insects. Superfamilies: Arrenuroidea, Eylaoidea, Hydrachnoidea, Hydrovolzioidea, Hydryphantoidea, Hygrobatoidea, Lebertioidea, Sperchontoidea, Stygothrombioidea. These superfamilies are now included in the infraorder Anystina (suborder Prostigmata) and the Hydracarina grouping has been abandoned, but may still be used as a term of convenience.

HYDRACHNOIDEA. [Gr. υδρο-, water; αραχνης, spider]. A monospecific superfamily of aquatic mites (suborder Prostigmata, infraorder Anystina). Family: **Hydrachnidae**.

HYDRIC. [Gr. υδρο-, water]. Relating to an abundance of moisture.

HYDRO-. [Gr. υδρο-, water]. Prefix: relating to water.

HYDROBIONT. [Gr. υδρο-, water; βιον, living]. An organism living chiefly in water.

HYDROCHORIC. [Gr. υδρο-, water; χωρισις, separation]. Dispersed by water.

HYDROCOLE. [Gr. υδρο-, water; L. *colere*, to inhabit]. A general term for any animal living in water.

HYDROFUGE HAIRS. [Gr. υδρο-, water; L. *fugere*, to flee]. Unwettable hairs.

HYDROPHANOUS. [Gr. υδρο-, water; φαινειν, to show]. Becoming transparent when immersed in water.

HYDROPHILIC, HYDROPHILOUS. [Gr. υδρο-, water; φιλος, loving]. Of something attracted to water, or attracting water, either at the molecular or macromolecular scale.

HYDROPHILOUS (HYGROPHILOUS). [Gr. υδρο-, water; φιλος, loving]. Moisture-loving.

124

HYDROPHOBIC. [Gr. υδρο-, water; φοβος, fear]. Of something repelled by water, or repelling water, either at the molecular or macromolecular scale. E.g. the hydrophobic tarsal hairs of some water-surface hunting spiders.

HYDROTAXIS. [Gr. υδρο-, water; ταξις, an arranging]. Movement in response to the stimulus of water.

HYDROVOLZIOIDEA. [Gr. υδρο-, water; *Walter Volz*, Arachnologist]. A monotypic superfamily of mites (suborder Prostigmata, infraorder Anystina). Family: **Hydrovolziidae.**

HYDROZETOIDEA. [Gr. υδρο-, water; ζητετης, seeker]. A monotypic superfamily of mites (suborder Oribatida, infraorder Brachypylina - section Pycnonoticae). Family: **Hydrozetidae.**

HYDRYPHANTOIDEA. [Gr. υδρο-, water; φαντες, voices from heaven]. A superfamily of mites (suborder Prostigmata, infraorder Anystina). Families: **Ctenothyadidae, Hydrodromidae, Hydryphantidae** (incl. Eupatrellidae), **Malgasacaridae, Rhynchohydracaridae, Teratothyadidae, Thermacaridae, Zelandothyadidae.**

HYGRIC. [Gr. υγρος, moist]. Relating to moisture.

HYGROBATOIDEA. [Gr. υγρος, moist; βατης, walker]. A superfamily of mites (suborder Prostigmata, infraorder Anystina) from North America. Thirteen families.

HYGROKINESIS. [Gr. υγρος, moist; κινεσις, movement]. Orientation due to differences in humidity.

HYGROMETABOLISM. [Gr. υγρος, moist; μεταβολη, change]. The influence of humidity on metabolism.

HYGROPHILIC (HYGROPHYLOUS). [Gr. υγρος, moist; φιλος, loving]. Inhabiting moist, humid or marshy places.

HYGROPHILOUS. [Gr. υγρος, moist; φιλος, loving]. See Hydrophilous.

HYGRORECEPTOR. [Gr. υγρος, moist; L. *recipere*; receive]. A sensory receptor sensitive to changes in humidity.

HYGROSCOPIC. [Gr. υγρος, moist; σκοπειν, to regard]. Sensitive to moisture.

HYGROTAXIS. [Gr. υγρος, moist; ταξις, an arranging]. Movement in response to humidity or moisture.

HYIDAE. [derive. uncert.]. A family of false scorpions (suborder Iocheirata, superfamily Neobisioidea) from south-east Asia, Sri Lanka, India, north-western Australia, and Madagascar.

HYLEA. [Gr. υλη, a forest]. A primeval forest, especially a tropical forest.

HYMEN. [Gr. υμην, membrane]. A thin plain membrane serving as a partition.

HYMENIFEROUS. [Gr. υμην, membrane; L. *ferre*, to carry]. Having a hymen.

HYOID. [Gr. υοειδης, Y-shaped]. Y-shaped.

HYPERFEMINIZATION. [Gr. υπερ, above; L. *femina*, woman; *-ization*, suf. forming nouns of action]. An unusual degree of feminization in structure and function, or behavior, especially in castrated males in which female gonads have been implanted.

HYPERGAMESIS. [Gr. υπερ, above; γαμος, marriage]. The process of absorption, in the female, of excess spermatozoa.

HYPERMASCULINIZATION. [Gr. υπερ, above; L. *masculus*, male; *-isation*, suf. forming nouns of action]. An unusual degree of masculinization in structure and function, or behavior, especially in castrated females in which male gonads have been implanted.

HYPERMORPHOSIS. [Gr. υπερ, above; μορφωσις, shaping]. The development of extra characters in an organism, when in comparison with the adult ancestral type.

HYPERPARASITE. [Gr. υπερ, above; παρασιτος, parasite]. See Parasite.

HYPERPHORESY. [Gr. υπερ, above; φορευς, a carrier]. A phoretic mite carried on another phoretic organism.

HYPERSENSITIVITY. [Gr. υπερ, above; L. *sentire*, to feel]. The condition of being unusually sensitive to stimuli.

HYPERTELY (HYPERTELIA). [Gr. υπερ, above; τελος, end]. Excessive, or over-development of some characteristic.

HYPERTRICHY. [Gr. υπερ, above; τριχος, hair]. Possessing greater numbers of setae than those present in their natural group. See also Holotrichy, Neotrichy.

HYPERTROPHY. [Gr. υπερ, above; τροφη, nourishment]. Excessive growth in a tissue or organ.

HYPISTOMA. See Hypopharynx.

HYPOBIOSIS. [Gr. υπο, under; βιοσις, living]. Dormancy.

HYPOBIOTIC. [Gr. υπο, under; βιωναι, to live]. Of organisms living under objects or projections.

HYPOCHILOIDEA. [Gr. υπο, under; χειλος, a lip]. In some classifications: a monospecific superfamily of long-legged spiders (suborder Opisthothelae, infraorder Araneomorphae) known as 'lampshade spiders' due to the structure of their web, which they construct under overhangs and in caves. In the United States they inhabit the Appalachian, Rocky and California Mountains, while the monospecific genus *Ectatosticta* is found in central China. They are among the most primitive of araneomorph spiders and, like mygalomorphs, they have two pairs of book lungs but like araneomorphs they have intersecting fangs. Family: **Hypochilidae**. They may be included in the superfamily Haplogynae.

HYPOCHTHONIOIDEA. [Gr. υπο, under; χθων, the ground]. A superfamily of mites (suborder Oribatida, infraorder Enarthronota). Families: **Eniochthoniidae, Hypochthoniidae, Psammochthoniidae.**

HYPOCRATERIFORM. [Gr. υπο, under; L. *crater*, bowl; *forma*, shape]. Salver-shaped.

HYPODEROIDEA. [Gr. υπο, under; δερη, neck]. A monotypic superfamily of 'biting' mites (order Sarcoptiformes, suborder Astigmata). Family: **Hypoderidae**.

HYPOGEAL, HYPOGEAN. [Gr. υπο, under; γη, earth]. Of animals that live underground.

HYPOGENESIS. [Gr. υπο, under; γεννησις, a producing]. Development that occurs without an alternation of generations.

HYPOGEOUS. [Gr. υπο, under; γη, earth]. Growing or developing beneath the soil surface.

HYPOGNATHAL DENTICLES. [Gr. υπο, under; γναθος, jaw; L. *denticulus*, little tooth]. See Deutosternal Denticles.

HYPOGNATHAL GROOVE. [Gr. υπο, under; γναθος, jaw]. See Deutosternal Gutter.

HYPOGRAPHOUS. [Gr. υπογραφω, sketch out]. Shaded. Of a fascia that becomes gradually darker.

HYPOKINESIS. [Gr. υπο, under; κινεσις, movement]. Reduced vigor of movement or motor response.

HYPOLITHIC. [Gr. υπο, under; λιθος, stone]. Of an organism living beneath stones.

HYPOMEGETIC. [Gr. υπο, under; μεγας, large]. Of the smallest in a series of polymorphic organisms. See also Epimegetic.

HYPONASTY. [Gr. υπο, under; ναστος, close-pressed]. Growth in a flattened structure in which the lower surface grows more vigorously than the upper surface.

HYPOPHARYNX (HYPISTOMA). [Gr. υπο, under; φαρυγξ, pharynx]. In spiders: a chitinous plate on the surface of the labium.

HYPOPHLOEODAL. [Gr. υπο, under; φλοιος, bark]. Living under bark.

HYPOPLASIA. [Gr. υπο, under; πλασις, a forming]. Underdevelopment or incomplete development of a tissue or organ. See also Aplasia.

HYPOPUS/HYPOPODE (HYPOPI). [Gr. υπο, under; πους, foot]. In the Astigmata: the heteromorphic deutonymph, usually at a phoretic stage and bearing a large ventral sucker plate. Hypopi lack functional mouthparts, the capitulum is reduced and bears a pair of processes. Some may feed by absorbing fluids through the cuticle.

HYPOSCLERITIC. [Gr. υπο, under; σκλερος, hard]. In mites: a region that is only partially sclerotized.

HYPOSKELETAL. [Gr. υπο, under; σκελετος, dried]. Lying beneath the endoskelton.

HYPOSTOMA (HYPOSTOME). [Gr. υπο, under; στομα, mouth]. In ticks: the ventral mouth-parts.

HYPOSTOMAL (HYPOSTOMATIC) SETAE. [Gr. υπο, under; στομα, mouth]. In the Mesostigmata: the three pairs of setae on the hypostome. The anterior (h1) and external hypostomal (h2) setae are present in the larva, while the internal hypostomal seta (h3) develops in the protonymph.

HYPOSTOMAL DENTICLES (RETRORSE TEETH). [Gr. υπο, under; στομα, mouth; L. *denticulus*, little tooth]. In ticks and mites: the backwardly directed tooth-like projections on the elongate hypostome that are used to anchor the capitulum to the host's skin while feeding.

HYPOSTOMAL GROOVE (GUTTER). [Gr. υπο, under; στομα, mouth; OHG. *gruoba*, ditch]. median longitudinal depression on the ventral gnathosoma in Mesostigmata.

HYPOSTOME, HYPOSTOMA. [Gr. υπο, under; στομα, mouth]. In ticks and mites: the median ventral extension of the basis capituli, between the palps and the chelicerae, and forming the ventral-median wall of the gnathosoma. It is fused with the pedipalps in most groups but in ticks there is a toothed structure between the pedipalps. It is with recurved teeth on its ventral surface; with a pronounced pre-oral canal (hypostomal gutter) on the dorsal surface. The dentition is indicated by figures on either side of a vertical line. Thus 3 | 3 means 3 longitudinal files of teeth on each half of the hypostome. It may be pointed, rounded or distally emarginated and may bear teeth from tip to base, or only bear teeth along part of its length. An unarmed, protruding median ridge, which broadens basally, may run down the length of the hypostome, starting near the tip. A coronal hypostome bears a number of very minute denticles at the tip.

HYPOTRICHOUS. [Gr. υπο, under; τριχος, hair]. Having fewer than the number of setae normally found in their group.

HYSTERODEHISCENCE. [Gr. υστερος, later; L. *dehiscere*, to split open]. In ticks and mites: dehiscence or splitting of the cuticle in the posterior part of the body. During hatching the animal moves backwards.

HYSTEROGENIC. [Gr. υστερος, later; γενος, birth]. Of later development or growth.

HYSTEROSOMA. [Gr. υστερος, after; σωμα, body]. In ticks and mites: the region of the body posterior to the proterosoma (cephalothorax), comprising the metapodosoma (the body region between the third and fourth pairs of legs) and opisthosoma ('abdomen').

HYTHER. [Gr. υδωρ, water; θερμη, heat]. The combined effect of temperature and moisture on an organism.

I

ia. In the Acariformes: a designation for the anterior-most pair of cupules. They are typically lateral and associated with the border of segments C-D. In the Mesostigmata: the antiaxial lyrifissure on the chelicera.

iad. In the Acariformes: a designation for the posterior-most pair of cupules. They are typically ventral and associated with segment AD.

ICALEPTIDAE. [*Ica*, a Chibchan people; *Gonyleptes* (Gonyleptidae)]. A small family of neotropical harvestmen or daddy longlegs (suborder Laniatores, superfamily Zalmoxoidea).

127

Only two species, in which the fourth pair of legs are ventrally inserted, giving them a flea-like appearance.

id. In the Mesostigmata: a designation for the dorsal lyrifissure on the chelicera.

idj, ids, idz. Designations for podonotal lyrifissures associated with particular setal rows: Krantz & Redmond 1987 and Johnston & Moraza 1991.

idJ, idS idZ. Designations for opisthonotal lyrifissures associated with particular setal rows. Krantz & Redmond 1987 and Johnston & Moraza 1991.

-IDAE. [Gr. -ιδες, a patronymic suffix]. A standard suffix in zoology used to indicate a family in the recognized codes of classification. Thus 'Idiopidae' is a family of tarantula-like spiders. (In botanical nomenclature: the ending of a name of a subclass). See Nomenclature.

IDEAL PARASITE. An imaginary parasite which (1) 'recognizes' a suitable host, (2) maintains its position there, (3) is adapted to the physico-chemical conditions of the host, (4) utilizes the host's nutrients in a manner compatible with the survival of the host and (5) presents a surface with a molecular configuration such that the host's immune response is absent or minimized.

IDEORONCIDAE. [Gr. ιδιος, peculiar to oneself; derive.uncert.]. A family of false scorpions (suborder Iocheirata, superfamily Neobisioidea).

IDIONOTAL. [Gr. ιδιος, one's own; νωτον, the back]. On the dorsum of the body (idiosoma).

IDIONYMIC. [Gr. ιδιος, one's own; ονομα, name]. Of structures or stages that differ in discontinuous surface characters.

IDIOPIDAE. [Gr. ιδιος, one's own; σωμη, body]. The family of tarantula-like spiders (infraorder Mygalomorphae, superfamily Avicularioidea), known as armored trapdoor spiders, from tropical and southern subtropical regions worldwide. Some construct burrows and some species close these with a trapdoor. In some species the males have a spur on their legs, which they show if provoked. They were previously in the monotypic superfamily Idiopoidea.

IDIOSOMA. [Gr. ιδιος, peculiar to oneself; σωμα, body]. Of ticks and mites: the body, prosoma and opisthosoma.

IDIOTHETIC. [Gr. ιδιος, peculiar to oneself; θετος, placed]. Of information concerning orientation in an environment that is obtained by the animal by reference to a previous orientation of its body, i.e. without external spatial clues. See also Allothetic.

idJ, idS idZ. Designations for opisthonotal lyrifissures associated with particular setal rows, based on the works of Krantz & Redmond (1987)

-IFORMES. [L. *forma*, shape]. A suffix commonly used when a name of an order, superorder, or suborder of animals is derived from the name of an included family or genus. See Nomenclature.

IGNITUS. [L. *ignitus*, make red-hot]. Fire-red.

ih. In the Acariformes: a designation for a pair of cupules; typically lateral and associated with segment H.

im. In the Acariformes: a designation for second anterior-most pair of cupules; typically lateral and associated with segment E.

IMAGO. [L. *imago*, image]. An adult sexually mature insect or acarid the develops after metamorphosis.

IMAGOCHRYSALIS. [L. *imago*, image; Gr. χρυσαλλις, chrysalis]. In the chigger mite (**Trombiculidae**) life cycle: a quiescent stage between the nymph and adult in which a calyptostatic cuticle is formed within the deutonymphal cuticle.

IMBRICATE. [L. *imbricare*, to tile]. Having parts overlapping, as of scales and plates.

IMBRICATE PLATES. [L. *imbricare*, to tile]. Overlapping plates.

IMBRICATION LINES. [L. *imbricare*, to tile]. Parallel growth lines.

128

IMITATIVE. [L. *imitari*, to imitate]. Of form, color, habitat, etc. assumed for protection or aggression, or of the behavior of an animal when it repeats the actions of another.

IMMACULATE. [L. *in-*, not; *macula*, spot]. Without spots or markings of a different color.

IMMARGINATE. [L. *in-*, not; *margo*, edge]. Without a distinct margin.

IMMATURE. [L. *immaturus*, unripe]. Of the developmental stage of an individual before sexual maturity.

IMMATURES. [L. *immaturus*, unripe]. Any developmental stage preceding the adult form.

IMMERSED, IMMERSUS. [L. *in*, not; *mergere*, to dip]. Inserted, imbedded or hidden, either as a part, or organ.

IMPLEX. [L. *implescus*, plaited]. An in-folding of the integument for muscle attachment.

IMPLICATE. [L. *implicare*, to entangle]. To in-fold or twist together.

IMPREGNATION. [L. *imprægnare*, to fertilize]. The transference of sperm from the male to the female.

IMPRESSED, IMPRESSUS. [L. *in*, on; *premere*, to press]. Produced by pressure, as of depressed areas or markings.

IMPUBERAL. [L. *impubes*, under age]. Sexually immature.

IMPUNCTATE. [L. *in*, not; *punctum*, puncture]. Without marks, pits, spots or holes.

-INAE. [L. *-inae -inæ*, -ine; indicating a relationship of position, possession, origin]. A suffix used to denote a subfamily. See Nomenclature.

INAEQUALIS. [L. *inaequalis*, uneven / unequal]. Unequal.

INANITION. [L. *inanis*, empty]. 1. The state of being empty; inane. 2. Exhaustion from lack of nutrients; the physical condition resulting from insufficient nutrients.

INAPPENDICULATE. [L. *in-*, not; *appendicula*, little appendage]. Without appendages.

INARTICULATE. [L. *in-*, not; *articulatus*, jointed]. Not jointed, not segmented. Lacking distinct body segments.

INAURATE, INAURATUS. [L. *inauratus*, gild]. Golden yellow.

INBORN BEHAVIOR. See Species-Specific Behavior.

INCANUS. [L. *incanus*, hoary]. Hoary.

INCERTAE SEDIS. [L. *incertus*, uncertain; *sedis*, seat]. Of uncertain affinity: used of a taxonomic category of uncertain taxonomic position.

INCEST. [L. *incestus*, impure]. Mating between members of the same family unit, either between parent and offspring or between siblings.

INCISAL. [L. *incidere*, to cut into]. A cutting edge, as of a tooth or similar biting structure.

INCISED. [L. *incisus*, cut into]. With a deeply notched margin.

INCISIFORM. [L. *incisus*, cut into; *forma*, shape]. Incisor-shaped.

INCISION. [L. *incisus*, cut into]. Any cut into a margin or through a surface.

INCISOR. [L. *incisor*, cutter]. Adapted for cutting.

INCISURA, INCISURE. [L. *incidere*, to cut into]. Any cut, gash, impression line, striation, notch, indentation, depression.

INCLINATE, INCLINATUS. [L. *inclinare*, to bend]. Bent toward the midline of the body.

INCLUSUS. [L. *inclusus*, enclosed]. When one part is wholly or partially hidden in another.

INCOMPATIBILITY. [L. *in-*, not; *compatibilis*, compatible]. The genetically (and also thus morphologically) determined inability to mate successfully.

INCRASSATE. [L. *incrassare*, to thicken]. To become thicker. Swollen, particularly near a tip.

INCUBATION. [L. *incubare*, to lie on]. The action of hatching an egg by means of heat, either natural (from the body, a mound of decaying vegetation or a choice of nest site) or artificial.

INCUBATION PERIOD. [L. *incubare*, to lie on]. The time between laying an egg and hatching.

INCUBATORIUM. [L. *incubatio*, brooding; *-arium*, a place where something is kept]. A pouch in which eggs are incubated.

INCUBATORY. [L. *in*, in; *cubare*, to lie down]. Of animals that brood their young.

INCUMBENT. [L. *incumbere*, to lie upon]. Lying upon, bent downwards.

INCUNABULUM. [L. *incunabulum*, a cradle]. A cocoon.

INCURRENT. [L. *in-*, into; *currere*, to run]. Afferent, leading into.

INCURVATE. [L. *incurvus*, bent]. Inflected, incurved, curved inwards or bent back.

INCURVED. [L. *incurvus*, bent]. The state of being bowed or curved inwards.

INDENTED. [L. *in*, in; *dens*, tooth]. Notched or dented. Abruptly pressed inward. A cut or notch in a margin.

INDETERMINATE. [LL. *indeterminatus*, undefined, unlimited]. Obscure. Not defined nor well marked. Of no constant form or shape.

INDIGENOUS. [L. *indigena*, native]. Native, not imported, belonging to the locality.

INDIGOID BIOCHROME. [L. *indicum* indigo; Gr. βιος, life; χρωμα, color]. The various blues and purples derived from the metabolism of trytophan and found in plants and molluscs.

INDIGOTE. [Gr. ινδικον, a blue dye from India]. A very deep indigo blue.

INDIRECT COMPETITION. Competition for a resource in which exploitation by one individual reduces the availability of the resource to other individuals without the necessity for direct aggressive behavior.

INDUMENTUM. [L. *indumentum*, garment]. A covering of hairs, scales or tufts.

INDURATED (INDURESCENT). [L. *indurescere*, to harden]. Becoming harder, firmer.

INEQUAL. [L. *in*, not; *aequus*, equal]. Having irregular elevations or depressions.

INFERIOR. [L. *inferus*, beneath]. Applied to any structure beneath or below another structure.

INFERIOR CLAW (MEDIAN CLAW). [L. *inferus*, beneath]. The third claw (not paired). It is located apically on the tarsus and is absent from the male palpi.

INFEROMEDIAN. [L. *inferus*, beneath; *medius*, middle]. Below and in the middle.

INFRA-. [L. *infra*, below]. In classification: a group just below the level of a subgroup of the following taxon. E.g. infraclass is the group below subclass. But see also Infraorder and Nomenclature.

INFRABUCCAL SLIT. [L. *infra*, below; *bucca*, cheek]. In ticks and mites: the slit between the two lateral lips seen on the ventral surface of the infracapitulum.

INFRACAPITULAR GLANDS. [L. *infra*, below; L. *capitulum*, a little head]. In ticks and mites: the paired glands lying in the prosoma and emptying into the cervix.

INFRACAPITULUM. [L. *infra*, underneath; *capitulum*, small head]. The part of the gnathosoma of mites, bearing lips and palpi and containing the mouth and pharynx.

INFRACTED. [L. *infractus*, break]. Bent inward abruptly as if broken.

INFRAGENITAL. [L. *infra*, underneath; *genitalis*, belonging to birth]. Below the genital opening.

INFRAMARGINAL. [L. *infra*, below; *margo*, margin]. Beneath a margin, or marginal structure.

INFRAOCULAR. [L. *infra*, underneath; *oculus*, eye]. Below and between the eyes.

INFRAORDER. A systematic category below suborder and above superfamily. The use of this category is not obligatory and groupings are rather subjective. See Nomenclature.

INFRASOCIAL. [L. *infra*, underneath; *socius*, companion]. Leading a solitary life.

INFRASPECIFIC. [L. *infra*, below; *species*, particular kind]. Pertaining to a subdivision of a species.

INFRASPINATOUS (INFRASPINOUS). [L. *infra*, below; *spina*, thorn]. Beneath a spine.

INFRASTIGMATAL. [L. *infra*, underneath; Gr. στιγματα, marks]. Below a stigmata or spiracle.

INFRASUTURAL. [L. *infra*, underneath; *sutura*, seam]. Below a seam or suture.

INFRINGING. Encroaching upon.

INFUMATED. [L. *in*, in; *fumus*, smoke]. Clouded with a blackish color. Smoke colored.

INFUNDIBULIFORM. [L. *infundibulum*, funnel]. Funnel-shaped.

INFUNDIBULUM. [L. *infundibulum*, funnel]. In general, any funnel-shaped structure. A depression in the cuticle associated with the opening of a gland. In the laelapid type sperm access system: a swelling of the tubulus under the solenostome.

INFUSCATE. [L. *in*, into; *fuscus*, dark]. Tinged to appear dark.

INFUSEATED. [L. *infuscus*; dark-colored, dusky]. Smoky grey-brown with a blackish tinge. Roman sepia.

INGENS. [L. *ingens*, huge]. Unusually large or disproportionate in size.

INGESTA. [L. *ingestus*, taken in]. The totality of substances taken in by the body. Opposite - Egesta.

INGESTION. [L. *ingerere*, carry in]. The act of taking in food.

INGUINAL PORE PLATE. [L. *inguen*, the groin; Gr. πορος, channel]. See Adgenital Sclerite.

INHERITED BEHAVIOR PATTERNS. See Instinct.

-INI. [Gr. ινις, son or daughter]. In classification: the recommended but not mandatory suffix used to indicate a tribe of animals. See Nomenclature.

INNATE. [L. *innatus*, inborn]. Inherited.

INNATE BEHAVIOR. [L. *innatus*, inborn]. Behavior that is genetically programmed. That is, the appearance of fully formed acts in animals reared without the opportunity for learning and the ability of the developing animal to compensate for environmental deficits. See also Instinct.

INNATE RELEASING MECHANISMS (IRM). [L. *innatus*, inborn]. The mechanisms by which a fixed pattern of behavior can be elicited by one or a few key aspects of the environment. These mechanisms are thought to reside in the region of the central nervous system specific to the particular response and detect the presence of a particular configuration of stimuli and activate the appropriate response.

INNER INFRACAPITULAR STYLETS (AUXILARY STYLETS). [L. *infra*, underneath; *capitulum*, small head; Gr. στυλος, pillar]. In the Eriophyoidea: a pair of stylets of uncertain origin in the bundle of 7-9 stylets.

INNER SACRALS. [L. *sacrum*, sacred]. Setae DC4 (= f1) in the Pritchard & Baker system.

INNERVATE. [L. *in*, in; *nervus*, tendon]. To supply nerves to an organ or part.

INNOTATUS. [*in-*, not; L. *notatus*, inscribed]. Without Markings.

INOPERCULATE. [L. *in-*, without; *operculum*, lid]. Without an operculum, or lid.

INOSCULATE. [L. *in*, in; *osculari*, to kiss]. Of vessels, ducts, etc. that intercommunicate or unite.

INSEMINATION. [L. *inseminare*, to sow into]. The process by which sperm cells are introduced into the body of a female prior to fertilization of the ovum.

INSEMINATION REACTION. [L. *inseminare*, to sow into]. A type of mating barrier to prevent interspecific hybridization in which an antigenic reaction occurs, usually in the genital tract of the female and which results in immobilization and death of the sperm before it has chance to reach the eggs.

131

INSERTED. [L. *in*, in; *serere*, to join]. Joined by natural growth. Of a muscle attached to a movable part.

INSERTION. [L. *insertus*, joined]. The point of attachment of organs, muscles, etc.

INSERTUS. [L. *insertus*, joined]. A part that has its base set into another.

INSIDIATORES. [L. *insidiator*, one who lies in wait (to attack)]. See Laniatores.

IN SITU. [L. *in*, in: *situs*, placed in relation to its surroundings]. In place. In the natural or original position.

INSOLATION. [L. *in*, into; *sol*, sun]. Exposure to the sun's rays.

INSPISSATE. [L. *in*, into; *spissus*, thick, dense]. To thicken.

INSTAR. [L. *instar*, a likeness] An immature mite (or other arthropod) between molts; or from apolysis to apolysis for some authors; or between egg hatching and the first molt.

INSTINCT (INSTINCTIVE BEHAVIOR). [L. *instinctus*, impulse]. Behavior that is expressed *de novo* without the apparent opportunity for practice and learning. Such behavior patterns are commonly complex and little understood. See also Innate Behavior.

INSTITIA. [L. *institi*, take a position]. Stria or furrows of equal width throughout.

INTEGER. [L. *integer*, whole]. Entire. Of a margin without incisions.

INTEGUMENT. [L. *integumentum*, a covering]. Any outer, protective covering such as cuticle, epidermis, feathers, scales, etc.

INTER-. [L. *inter*, among/between]. Between. Among.

INTERACTIVE DEVELOPMENT. Development which is the result of both environmental and genetic factors.

INTER-ARTICULAR. [L. *inter*, between; *articularis*, of a joint]. The membranous tissue between joints or segments.

INTERCALARY. [L. *intercalaris*, inserted]. Inserted between others.

INTERCALARY SCLERITE. [L. *intercalaris*, inserted]. A sclerite located between the tegulum and the terminal apophysis and partially covered by the subtegulum.

INTERCHELICERAL GLAND. [L. *inter*, between; Gr. χηλη, claw]. In ticks and mites: the unpaired prosomatic gland that empties between the chelicerae. Their function is unknown.

INTERCOXAL. [L. *inter*, between; *coxa*, hip]. Between the coxae or proximal limb joints. In the Parasitiformes: a sternal region that lies between the bases of the legs and commonly contains one or more sternal shields and at least the anterior portion of the genital shield. In male Mesostigmata: an intercoxal shield is often known as a sternitogenital shield due to bearing the genital opening. There is no sternal region present in the Acariformes and the coxae of the legs are fused to the venter and usually meet medially; genital openings are usually postcoxal, but may intrude between the fused coxal bases.

INTERCOXAL SCLERITES. [L. *inter*, between; *coxa*, hip]. Narrow sclerites between the coxae.

INTERCRESCENCE. [L. *inter*, between; *crescere*, to grow]. Of tissues that grow into each other.

INTERFERENCE COLORS. [L. *inter*, between; *ferire*, to strike]. The colors produced by optical interference between reflections from a series of superimposed surfaces when they are separated by distances comparable with the wavelengths of light. As a result of the spacing, some of the wavelengths reflected from the successive surfaces will be in phase and so reinforced, while some will be out of phase and so cancelled. The observed (reflected) color depends on the refractive index of the material and the spacing between the reflecting surfaces. See also Iridescence.

INTERFERENCE COMPETITION. [L. *inter*, between; *ferire*, to strike]. Interaction between two species seeking the same resource such that they harm one another in the process, regardless of whether the resource is in short supply or not.

INTERFERTILE. [L. *inter*, between; *fertilis*, fertile]. Able to breed.

INTERLAMELLAR. [L. *inter*, between; *lamella*, thin plate]. Between lamellae.

INTERLAMELLAR COMPARTMENTS. [L. *inter*, between; *lamella*, thin plate]. In scorpions and spiders: the compartments of the book lungs.

INTERLOBAR. [L. *inter*, between; LL. *lobus*, lobe]. Between lobes.

INTERLOBULAR INCISIONS. See Incisura.

INTERNAL. [L. *internus*, within]. Located within the limits of the surface of something; situated on the side toward the median plane of the body.

INTERNAL FERTILITY CONTROL. [L. *internus*, within]. The increase or decrease in birth rate in response to favorable or unfavorable environmental conditions.

INTERNAL HYPOSTOMAL SETAE. [L. *internus*, within; Gr. υπο, under; στομα, mouth]. In the Mesostigmata: the most median (h3) of the three pairs of hypostomatic setae.

INTERNAL MALAE. [L. *internus*, within; *mala*, cheek]. In fluid-feeding mesostigmatans: a pair of fleshy, fimbriate processes that act as part of a filtration system.

INTERNAL RHYTHM. [L. *internus*, within]. Endogenous rhythm. See Circadian Clocks, Circadian Rhythm.

INTERNAL SCAPULAR SETA. [L. *internus*, within; *scapula*, shoulder; *seta* bristle]. In the Acariformes: the prodorsal seta sci (also si, scl or sl).

INTERNAL VERTICAL SETA. [L. *internus*, within; *vertex*, top; *seta* bristle]. In the Acariformes: the prodorsal seta vi (also vl).

INTERNUNCIAL. [L. *nuntius*, messenger]. Intercommunicating.

INTEROCEPTORS. [L. *internus*, inside; *capere*, to take]. A general name for internal sensory receptors which are excited by stimuli arising within the body. See also Exteroceptor, Proprioceptor, Receptor.

INTEROCULAR. [L. *oculus*, eye]. Located between the eyes.

INTEROSCULANT. [L. *osculari*, to kiss]. Possessing some characters common to two or more groups or species.

INTERSEX. [L. *inter*, between; *sexus*, sex]. An individual that appears to be intermediate between male and female. This may be due to an abnormality of sex chromosomes, or of sex hormones, or both. They are usually sterile.

INTERSEXUALITY. [L. *inter*, between; *sexus*, sex]. An abnormal state in adult spiders in which parts of the body and genitalia are female and parts are male. The male and female components are themselves not fully expressed or developed.

INTERSPECIFIC. [L. *inter*, between; *species*, one of a kind]. Being between distinct species.

INTERTIDAL (LITTORAL) ZONE. [L. *inter*, between; AS. *tid*, time]. The region of the shore which is alternatively inundated and exposed by the tides. The region above being the supratidal (supralittoral) zone and that below being the subtidal (sublittoral) zone.

INTERTROCHANTERIC. [L. *inter*, between; Gr. τροχαντηρ, runner]. Between trochanters. In spiders: a small segment of the leg between the coxa and the femur.

INTORTED. [L. *in*, in; *torquere*, to twist]. A turning or twisting in any direction from the vertical.

IN TOTO. [L. *totus*, whole]. In its entirety. Entirely. Altogether.

INTRA-. [L. *intra-*, within, inside; go into]. Within. Between.

INTRADEMIC SELECTION. [L. *intra-*, within; Gr. δημος, the people]. Selection occurring within a local inbreeding population.

INTRADERMAL. [L. *intra-*, within; Gr. δερμα, the skin]. Within the structure of the skin.

INTRADOS. [L. *intra*, within; Fr. *dos*, the back]. The interior curve of an arch. Opposite: Extrados.

INTRAGENERIC. [L. *intra-*, within; *genus*, race]. Between individuals of the same genus.

INTRA-GROUP COMPETITION. Competition between members of the same group for resources such as food or mates.

INTRAHEMOCOELIC, INTRAHAEMOCOELIC. [L. *intra*, within; Gr. αιμα, blood; κοιλος, hollow]. Within the hemocoel or perivisceral cavity of an invertebrate.

INTRA-OCULAR. [L. *intra-*, within; *oculus*, eye]. Situated within the eye, actually or apparently.

INTRAPULMONARY RESPIRATION. [L. *intra-*, within; *pulmo*, lung]. A type of respiration that does not involve movements of the outer body wall and is confined to the respiratory organs.

INTRASEGMENTAL. [L. *intra*, within; *segmen*, piece]. Within a segment.

INTRASEXUAL COMPETITION. [L. *intra-*, within; *sexus*, sex]. Competition between individuals of the same sex.

INTRASPECIFIC. [L. *intra-*, within; *species*, particular kind]. Within a species. Applied to aggression, selection, competition, etc.

INTRASPECIFIC AGGRESSION. [L. *intra-*, within; *species*, particular kind]. Aggression within a particular animal species, as opposed to aggression between species.

INTRASPECIFIC COMPETITION. See Competition.

INTRICATE. [L. *intricatus*, entangled]. Of markings and sculpture that are irregular or confused.

INTRINSIC. [L. *intrinsecus*, inward / on the inside]. Inherent or within. Opposite: Extrinsic.

INTRINSIC ARTICULATION. [L. *intrinsecus*, on the inside; *articulus*, joint]. A type of articulation where sclerotic prolongations within the articular membrane make contact. See also Extrinsic Articulation.

INTRINSIC MUSCLES. [L. *intrinsecus*, inward / on the inside]. Muscles which move an organ (leg, etc.) that originate within the segment. See also Extrinsic Muscles.

INTRODUCED. [L. *introducere*, to introduce]. Not native.

INTROGRESSION (INTROGRESSIVE HYBRIDIZATION). [L. *intro-*, within; *gressus*, a step]. The incorporation of genes from genetically diverging populations. If the ranges of the two populations overlap, if there are no barriers to breeding, and if fertile hybrids are produced, then back crosses with the larger population tend to be produced, resulting in a population of individuals, most of whom resemble the more abundant parents but who also possess some characters of the other parent population. This term is often used technically for gene flow occurring between closely related species (thus begging the question of taxonomic status). Introgression is not common in animals, primarily because only a small fraction of hybrids will back cross to either parental population, however it occurs very frequently in the plant kingdom. **Sympatric Introgression**. The creation of a new genotype by introgression, which then exists in the same population as the original genotype(s). **Allopatric Introgression**. The production of a new genotype by hybridization and / or backcrossing, which then exists as a separate population from the original genotype.

INTROITUS. [L. *introitus*, entry]. Any opening or orifice.

INTROMITTENT ORGAN. [L. *intro-*, within; *mittere*, to send]. The external male sexual organ.

INTRORSE. [L. *introsus*, inwards]. Turning inwards or towards the axis.

INTROVERT. [L. *introvertere*, to turn inwards]. In general, any part of an animal that can be either projected outwards (everted) or withdrawn, e.g. into its own tube (inverted).

INTRUSUS. [L. *intrusus*, thust / pushed]. Seemingly impressed with a sharp point.

INTUMESCENCE. [L. *intumescere*, to swell]. The process of swelling up: opposite - detumescence.

INTUSSUSCEPTION. [L. *intus*, within; *suscipere*, to raise]. The growth in surface extent or volume by intercalation of new materials among those already present. See also Accretion.

INUNCATE. [L. *inuncatus*, hooked together]. Covered with barbed hairs. Glochidiate.

134

INVAGINATE. [L. *in-*, into; *vagina*, sheath]. To involute or draw into a sheath.

INVAGINATION. [MedL. *invaginare*, to sheath]. An 'in-pushing' of an outer layer of an organism.

INVESTMENT. [L. *in*, in; *vestire*, to clothe]. The outer covering of an animal, or an organ.

INVOLUTE. [L. *involutus*, rolled up]. Having structures that roll under or inwards. For example, in which a later whorl surrounds an earlier ones. See also Revolute.

INVOLUTION. [L. *involutus*, rolled up]. An inward rolling.

IOCHEIRATA. [Gr. ιοχεαιρα; shooter of arrows]. A suborder of venomous pseudoscorpions (subclass Arachnida, order Pseudoscorpiones). Superfamilies: Cheiridioidea, Cheliferoidea, Garypinoidea, Garypoidea, Neobisioidea, Sternophoroidea.

ip. In the Acariformes: a designation for a pair of cupules. They are usually lateral and associated with segment F.

ips. In the Acariformes: a designation for the penultimate pair of cupules. They are usually lateral and associated with segment PS.

IPSILATERAL. [NL. *ipsi*, same; *latus*, side]. Of, or on the same side. Opposite: Contralateral.

IRIAN DIVISION. [Irian Jaya, the western half of New Guinea]. The hill and lowland division of the New Guinea biota, which includes the rain forests of the Cape York Peninsula in Australia. In these two regions almost all the animals are identical at the species level.

IRIDESCENCE. [L. *iris*, rainbow; *-escens*, becoming]. The production of fine colors on the surface of a thin film as a result of interference with light that is reflected from both the front and back of the film. See also Interference Colors.

IRIDICOLOUR. [L. *iris*, rainbow]. Of any color so broken up as to reflect the prismatic hues.

IRISED. [L. *iris*, rainbow]. With rainbow colors.

IRM. See Innate Releasing Mechanism.

IRRECIPROCAL. [L. *in*, not; *reciprocus*, going backwards]. Not reversible.

IRREGULAR. [L. *in*, not; *regularis*, according to rule]. Unequal, curved, bent.

IRREGULAR WEB. [L. *in*, not; *regularis*, according to rule; AS. *webbe*, web]. A space web of scaffold threads.

IRRITABILITY (SENSITIVITY). [L. *irritabilis*, easily roused]. The ability of an organism to respond to any change in its environment.

IRRORATE. [L. *irrorare*, to bedew]. Covered with minute droplets or dotted with minute colors.

ISABELLINE, ISABELLINUS. [named from the Spanish princess Isabella]. Pale yellow with some red and brown.

ISAUXESIS. [Gr. ισος, equal; αυξησις, growth]. Equality in growth. See also Bradyauxesis, Heterauxesis, Tachyauxesis.

ISCHNOTHELIDAE. [Gr. ισχνος, reduced; θηλη, nipple]. A family of mygalomorph spiders (infraorder Mygalomorphae, superfamily Avicularioidea).

ISCHYROPSALIDIDAE (incl. **CERATOLASMATIDAE**). [Gr. ισχυρος, strong; ψαλιδιον, a pair of scissors]. A family of harvestmen (suborder Dyspnoi, superfamily Ischyropsalidoidea) from Europe and north America.

ISCHYROPSALIDOIDEA. [Gr. ισχυρος, strong; ψαλιδιον, a pair of scissors]. A superfamily of harvestmen (order Opiliones, suborder Dyspnoi). Families: **Ischyropsalididae**, **Sabaconidae, Taracidae**.

i-series. A obsolete designation for the j-series of the Lindquist-Evans system.

ISO-. [Gr. ισος, equal]. Equal.

ISOCHROMOUS. [Gr. ισος, equal; χρωμα, color]. Uniformly colored.

ISOCHRONIC. [Gr. ισος, equal; χρονος, time]. Occurring at the same time. Having an equal duration.

ISODACTYLOUS. [Gr. ισος, equal; δακτυλος, finger]. Having all digits of equal size.

ISOFEMALE LINE. [Gr. ισος, equal; L. *femella*, little woman]. A genetic lineage that began with a single fertilized female.

ISOLATED POPULATION. [LL. *insulatus*, made into an island]. A population that is separated from other populations by any barrier, whether geographic, genetic, morphological or behavioral.

ISOLATING MECHANISMS. [LL. *insulatus*, made into an island]. Mechanisms that tend to keep populations of related species or races distinct and so provide the opportunity for divergence to become more prevalent in the course of evolution. See Isolation.

ISOLATION. [LL. *insulatus*, made into an island]. The term isolation refers to two different phenomena, spatial isolation and reproductive isolation.

ISOLECITHAL. [Gr. ισος, equal; λεκιθος, yolk]. See Homolecithal.

ISOMERE. [Gr. ισος, equal; μερος, part]. A homologous structure, region or part.

ISOMEROUS (HOMOEOMEROUS). [Gr. ισος, equal; μερος, part]. Having an equal number of parts, ridges or markings. See also Heteromerous.

ISOMETRIC GROWTH. [Gr. ισος, equal; μετρον, measure]. The growth of a part of an organism at the same rate as the growth of the whole organism. Thus relative proportions of the body parts remain constant.

ISOMETRY. [Gr. ισος, equal; μετρον, measure]. Growth of two body parts remaining constant relative to each other as body regions increase in size.

ISOMORPHIC. [Gr. ισος, equal; μορφη, shape]. Superficially alike.

ISOMORPHISM. [Gr. ισος, equal; μορφη, shape]. The apparent similarity of individuals of different race or species. See also Heteromorphic.

ISTHMIATE. [Gr. ιοθμος, neck]. Of a part connected by an isthmus-like region.

ITCH (SCABIES, MANGE) MITES. [OE. *giccan*, itch]. *Sarcoptes scabei* (Acariformes: Sarcoptidae). An ectoparasite that burrows in tunnels in the skin, thus it could be classified as both an endoparasite and an ectoparasite.

ITERALS (it). [L. *iter*, passage/path]. In the Acariformes: a pair of dorsal tarsal setae between the prorals and the tectals on the tarsi.

IURIDAE. [L. *iurus*, right/duty]. A small family of scorpions (order Scorpiones, superfamily Iuroidea) from Turkey, Iraq, Syria and Greece.

IUROIDEA. [L. *iurus*, right/duty]. A superfamily of scorpions (subclass Arachnida, order Scorpiones). Families: **Caraboctonidae** (hairy scorpions), **Iuridae**. In other classifications, these families along with the **Chaerilidae** are in the superfamily Chaeriloidea.

iv 1-5-. In the Mesostigmata: a designation for the sternal pores (lyrifissures). It is also sometimes used for the entral setae in some groups, e.g. Uropodina.

IXODIASIS. [Gr. ιξωδης, sticky]. A disease or skin lesion caused by or transmitted by ticks.

IXODIDA. [Gr. ιξωδης, sticky]. A monospecific order of ticks (subclass Arachnida, superorder Parasitiformes) that are hematophagous ectoparasites of mammals, birds, and occasionally reptiles and amphibians. They are important vectors of a number of diseases, including Lyme disease and Tick-borne meningoencephalitis. Superfamily: Ixodoidea.

IXODIDAE. [Gr. ιξωδης, sticky]. The family of hard, or wood ticks (order Ixodida, superfamily, Ixodoidea). They have a thickened shield (scutum) on top of the front of the body and prominent, well developed mouth parts with which they secure themselves to their host during feeding, which can take several days. This family is divided into two groups, the Prostriata (*Ixodes*) and the Metastriata (all other genera), based the presence or absence of anal grooves extending anterior to, or surrounding, the anus.

136

IXODIDES. [Gr. ιξωδης, sticky]. In a previous classification: a suborder of ticks that united the families **Argasidae, Ixodidae, Nuttalliellidae.** These are now placed in the superfamily Ixodoidea.

IXODOIDEA. [Gr. ιξωδης, sticky]. A superfamily of soft and hard ticks (superorder Parasitiformes, order Ixodida). Families: **Argasidae** (soft ticks), **Ixodidae** (hard ticks), **Nuttalliellidae.**

J

j-series. In the Mesostigmata: a designation for the most median longitudinal row of prodorsal setae that runs from the anterior vertical setae j1 to setae j6 at, or near, the posterior margin of the pronotal shield or region. See Lindquist-Evans System.

J-series. In the Mesostigmata: a designation for the most median longitudinal row of opisthonotal setae that runs from the anterior setae J1 to the clunal setae J5 at, or near, the posterior margin of the opisthonotal shield or region. See Lindquist-Evans System.

JACULATORY DUCT. [L. *jaculator*, javelin thrower]. A region of the vas deferens through which sperm is emitted. See Ejaculatory Duct.

JACULIFEROUS. [L. *jaculum*, a dart; *ferre*, to carry]. Bearing dart-like spines.

JANTHINA, IANTHINA. [L. *ianthinus*, violet-blue]. Violet colored.

JET EFFECT WIND. [OFr. *jeter*, throw]. An intensification of the wind as a result of funneling through a narrow canyon or mountain gap.

JIZZ. A jargon word for a combination of characters which immediately identify a creature in the field, but which may not be distinguished individually. E.g. the silhouette, shape and behavior of a spider.

JOINT. [OFr. *jointe*, joint]. 1. **Synarthrosis.** Where two structures abut one another. There is usually little, if any, movement and the connection between such elements may be formed by thin intervening sheets of cartilage or connective tissue, or by direct contact so that the lines of apposition (suture) may be obliterated in the adult. 2. **Diarthrosis.** Freely moveable joints, with their adjacent surfaces typically being covered by a film of cartilage and bound together by stout connective tissue, frequently enclosing a liquid-filled joint cavity. In arthropods: joints usually only move in one plane, so that several joints per leg are needed to give a full range of movement. The hard cuticle 'tubes' are joined by an articular membrane and fit one within the other so that when fully extended one 'locks' inside the other.

JORDAN'S LAWS. [*K. Jordan*, English zoologist]. A law stating that closely related species or subspecies are to be found immediately adjacent to each other but separated by some geographical barrier.

JORDANON (JORDAN'S SPECIES). [*K. Jordan*, English Zoologist]. See Microspecies.

JUAN FERNÁNDEZ REGION. [*Juan Fernández* (ca.1536 – ca.1604), Spanish explorer]. A subdivision of the Neotropical Region that includes two islands and an islet located 400 miles (650 km) West of Santiago, Chile. (Alexander Selkirk Island, Robinson Crusoe Island).

JUBATE. [L. *jubatus*, crested]. Fringed with long, mane-like hairs.

JUGULARIA. [L. *jugum*, yoke]. In the Mesostigmata: a pair of presternal shields bearing setae st1 and/or pores stp1. In a fused state they may be termed a tetratosternum.

JUGUM. [L. *jugum*, yoke]. In general any ridge or depression connecting two structures.

JUMPING SPIDER. See Salticidae.

JUNGLE. [Skr. *jangala*, dry ground/desert]. Dense seral vegetation, especially characteristic of tropical regions with a high precipitation level.

JUVENILE. [L. *juvenilis*, young]. A non-scientific term used to denote any stage of development prior to adulthood. It is often restricted to that stage of development immediately preceding the sexually mature adult stage. In general, the immature stages resemble the adult in general morphology except for gonadal development.

Jx. In the Mesostigmata: a designation for an extra seta in the J-series on the opisthonotum. I.e. not assignable to setae J1-5 in the Lindquist-Evans system.

K

KAIROMONE. [Gr. καιρος, fitness; hor*mone* (Gr. ορμαω, rouse)]. A chemical messenger emitted by one species and which has an effect on another species, sometimes to the detriment of the transmitter. For example, a chemical which attracts a male to a female may also attract a predator. See also Allelochemic.

KARSCHIIDAE. [*Ferdinand Anton Franz Karsch*, German Arachnologist,]. A family of sun spiders (subclass Arachnida, order Solifugae) from North Africa, the Near East and Asia.

KATHAROBIC. [Gr. καθαρος, pure, βιος, life]. 1. Of aquatic habitats that are pure and clean. See also Mesosaprobic, Oligosaprobic, Polysaprobic, Saprobic.

KEEL. [AS. *ceol*, ship]. Any prominent ridge or carina. A truncated outgrowth of the cheliceral margin.

KIMULIDAE. [derive.uncert.]. A small family of dark reddish-brown neotropical harvestmen or daddy longlegs (suborder Laniatores, superfamily Zalmoxoidea).

KIN SELECTION. [OE. *cyn*, kin]. The evolution of characters that favor the survival of close relatives (other than offspring).

KINAESTHESIS, KINESTHESIS, (PROPRIOCEPTION). [Gr. κινεω, to move; αισθησις, a sensation]. Perception of movement due to stimulation of muscles, tendons and joints.

KINAESTHETIC. [Gr. κινεω, to move; αισθησις, a sensation]. A term applied to sensory receptors or organs that detect movement or changes in their own position.

KINAESTHETIC ORIENTATION. [Gr. κινεω, to move; αισθησις, a sensation]. In the absence of sensory information: the behavior of an animal as it moves through a familiar environment, by the repetition of actions remembered from past experiences of the particular environment.

KINESIS. [Gr. κινησις, movement]. The situation in which an organism changes its rate of movement in response to the intensity of a particular stimulus. The response is unrelated to the direction of the stimulus, but related to the intensity, and continues until a better environment is attained. For example, some animals are stimulated to burrow by dry conditions and cease when they reach conditions which are sufficiently moist. See also Klinokinesis, Klinotaxis, Taxis.

KINETIC. [Gr. κινεω, to move]. Applied to the energy needed in producing a change in motion.

KINETOPHILOUS. [Gr. κινεω, to move; φιλος, loving]. An opportunistic species.

KINGDOM. [OE. *cyning*, king; *-dom*, jurisdiction]. The second to the largest of the taxonomic groupings; above being Domain, and below being Phylum. There are currently considered to be seven Kingdoms representing the greatest possible differences between known life forms. Kingdoms: Animalia, Archaea, Bacteria, Chromista, Fungi, Plantae, Protozoa. However, this is a constantly changing concept as the technology and understanding develop. See also Domain, Phylum, Nomenclature.

KINSHIP. [OE. *cyn*, kin; *sciepe*, to create]. Possession of a recent common ancestor. See also Coefficient of Consanguinity.

KLINOKINESIS (PHOBOTAXIS). [Gr. κλινιν, to slope; κινησις, movement]. A change in direction of an animal in response to a stimulus such that the rate of change is proportional to the intensity of the stimulus. See also Kinesis, Klinotaxis, Taxis.

KLINOTAXIS. [Gr. κλινιν, to slope; ταξις, an arranging]. Movement as a result of comparing stimuli from either side of the body. The animal typically moves along a sinuous path and may move either away from or towards the stimulus. See also Kinesis, Klinokinesis, Taxis.

KLEPTOBIOSIS. See Symbiosis.

KLEPTOPARASITE (erron. Cleptoparasite). [Gr. κλεπτω, to steal; παρασιτος, parasite]. A spider living in another spider's web and stealing its host's food. See also Piracy.

KNEE-SEGMENT. [AS. *cneow*, knee]. In the Chelicerata: a segment of the legs between the ascending and descending part. Known as a genu in mites and a patella in other chelicerates.

KRAGEN. [MHG. *krage*, neck]. See Basis Capitulum.

KROBYLOPHORE (SCHOPFORGANE). [Gr. κρωβυλος, tuft of hair; -φορος, -carrying]. A tuft-shaped (or flame-shaped) sense organs which reacts to chemical as well as to mechanical stimulation. They may play an important part in the sexual life of the ticks. There are three types of Krobylophore organs, which have been described as the sensilla sagittiformia, sensilla hastiformia and sensilla laterniformia. All these sense organs are duct-like structures, often of complicated shape, which penetrate the cuticle. They may play an important part in the sexual life of the ticks.

KRONISM. See Cronism.

L

L1-4. The lateral dorsal hysterosomal setae of spider mites in the Pritchard & Baker system. In the Grandjean system; L1 = c2 , L2 = d2, L3 = e2 and L4 = f2.

LABIATE. [L. *labium*, lip]. Having lips or lip-like parts or thickened margins.

LABIDOGNATHA. [Gr. λαβιδιον, a small pair of tweezers; γναθος, jaw]. See Araneomorphae.

LABIDOPHOROUS. [Gr. λαβις, forceps; φορειν, constantly to carry]. Possessing pincer-like organs.

LABIDOSTOMMATINA. [Gr. λαβιδιον, a small pair of tweezers; στομα, mouth]. A monotypic infraorder of mites (order Trombidiformes, suborder Prostigmata). Sometimes a superfamily of the infraorder Eupodina. Superfamily: Labidostommatoidea. Family: **Labidostommatidae.**

LABILE. [L. *labilis*, apt to slip]. Readily changeable, unstable, as, for example, applied to some retinal pigments.

LABIOGENAL ARTICULATION. [L. *labium*, lip; *gignere*, to beget]. A flexible junction on the venter of the subcapitulum. It permits the paired anterior sections (genae) to articulate with the base (mentum). See also Anarthrous, Diarthric, Stenarthric.

LABIOSTERNAL JUNCTION. [L. *labium*, lip; Gr. στερνον, chest]. The junction between the labium and sternum.

LABIUM. [L. *labium*, lip]. Any lip or lip-shaped structure. In the Araneae: the lower lip, lying between the maxillae and attached to the anterior border of the sternum and thus forming the floor of the mouth cavity.

LABRAL CONE (LABRAL SPUR). [L. *labrum*, lip]. In the **Anapidae** (a family of spiders): a short projection from the labrum.

LABRUM. [L. *labrum*, lip]. The 'upper' lip. It is attached to the epistome and together forms the rostrum.

LACHRIOID. [L. *lacrima*, tear; Gr. ειδος, form]. Tear-shaped.

LACHRYMIFORM (LACHRIMIFORM, LACRIMIFORM). [L. *lacrima*, tear; *forma*, shape]. Tear-shaped.

LACINIA. [L. *lacinia*, flap]. In the Mesostigmata: one of the processes borne on the stalk of the tritosternum.

LACINIATE. [L. *lacinia*, flap]. Irregularly incised.

LACINIFORM. [L. *lacinia*, flap, *forma*, shape]. Fringe-like.

LACINIOLATE. [L. *laciniolum*, little flap]. Minutely fringed.

LACUNOSE. [L. *lacuna*, cavity]. Well pitted, having many cavities.

LACUNULA. [L. *lacunula*, little cavity]. Minute space or cavity between cells.

LACUSTRINE. [L. *lacus*, lake]. Of lakes. Living beside lakes.

LAELAPID TYPE OF SPERM ACCESS SYSTEM. [Gr. λαιλαψ, furious storm]. In most Dermanyssiae (Gamasina): a secondary sperm receiving and processing system that consists of a pair of external opening (solenostomes) that usually open from the posterior intercoxal region, or on the basal segments of legs III-IV, into a small swollen area (the infundibulum) that is drawn into a long duct (tubulus). The tubulus may terminate indefinitely or join a median sacculus via a pair of horn-like rami, which it enters via a valve. The sacculus sits above the ovaries and empties via a short sperm duct. For the Phytoseioidea: see Phytoseiid Type Of Sperm Access System.

LAEOTROPIC. [Gr. λαιος, left, τροπη, turning]. Inclined, turned or coiled to the left. Opposite - Dexiotropic.

LAETE. [L. *laetus*, bright]. Bright.

LAEVIS, LAEVIGATUS. [L. *laevigatus*, smooth]. Of a surface that is smooth, shining and without elevations.

LAGENIFORM. [L. *lagena*, flask; *forma*, shape]. In the shape of a flask.

LAMELLA, LAMELLAE. [L. *lamella*, small plate]. Any thin plate or leaf-like structure. 1. In some spiders: a triangular plate on the promargin of the cheliceral fang furrow. 2. The leaves of a book-lung. 3. In many oribatid mites: a longitudinal projection on the prodorsum that protects the legs when they are retracted.

LAMELLAR CUSP. [L. *lamella*, small plate; *cuspis*, lance]. The projecting anterior portion of some lamellae.

LAMELLATE. [L. *lamella*, small plate]. Composed of or covered by thin scales, plates or layers.

LAMELLOSE. [L. *lamella*, small plate]. Composed of lamella.

LAMINA. [L. *lamina*, a plate]. Any flat, sheet-like structure, a thin plate, scale or layer.

LAMINAR. [L. *lamina*, plate]. Consisting of plates or thin layers - usually stacked.

LAMINATED. [L. *lamina*, plate]. Composed of thin plates, flat layers or leaves.

LAMINATO-CARINATE. [L. *lamina*, plate; *carina*, keel]. With an elevated ridge or keel formed of thin plates.

LAMINIFORM. [L. *lamina*, plate; *forma*, shape]. Having the form of a thin layer, or thin layers of overlapping plates or scales.

LAMMELIFEROUS. [L. *lamella*, small plate; *ferre*, to carry]. Having small plate-like structures or small scales.

LAMPONIDAE. [Gr. Λαμπος, Myth. one of the horses of Eos, Bright]. A family of spiders (infraorder Araneomorphae, superfamily Entelegynae) known as 'white tails'. Large, slender, dark spiders that are endemic to Australasia.

LANA. [L. *lana*, wool]. Wool.

LANATE, LANATUS. [L. *lana*, wool]. Woolly. Covered with short hair-like processes so giving a wool-like appearance.

LANCEOLATE. [L. *lanceola*, little lance]. Lance-shaped, tapering to a point.

LANCET. [Fr. *lancette*, small lance]. Any piercing structure.

LANCINATE. [L. *lancinare*, to tear to pieces]. To tear, lacerate, pierce or stab.

LANIARY. [L. *laniare*, to tear to pieces]. Modified for tearing.

LANIATORES (INSIDIATORES). [L. *laniare*, to tear to pieces]. A suborder of harvestman or daddy longlegs (subclass Arachnida, order Opiliones) that are typically (relatively) short-legged, hard-plated and spiny with a robust body. The palps are large and prehensile, raptorial and bear a piercing claw. They are mainly from tropical regions, principally South America where they are common under logs and stones, in leaf litter and in caves. This suborder includes the superfamilies Travunioidea and Triaenonychoidea, which were previously in the infraorder Insidiatores. Infraorder: Grassatores.

LANIFEROUS (LANIGEROUS). [L. *lana* wool. *ferre/gerere*, to bear]. Wool bearing, fleecy.

LAPIDICOLOUS. [L. *lapis*, stone; *colere*, to dwell]. Of animals that live under stones.

LAPIDROUS. [L. *lapis*, stone]. Of the nature of a stone.

LAPPET. [AS. *laeppa*, a loose hanging part]. Any loose, hanging, lobe-like structure.

LARCIDAE. [?Gr. λαρκος, a charcoal basket]. A small family (two genera) of false scorpions (suborder Iocheirata, superfamily Garypinoidea) based on the number of trichobothria on the movable chelal finger. They were previously included in the **Garypidae**.

LARVA. [L. *larva*, ghost]. An embryo which becomes independent and self-sustaining before it has assumed the characteristic features of its parent(s). It may be feeding or non-feeding. The usually active first instar in mites lacking a prelarva, and second instar in acariform mites in which there is a complete ontogenetic sequence.

LASUREUS. [L. *lasureus*, blue]. A very dark blue.

LATEBRICOLE. [L. *latebra*, hiding place; *colere*, to inhabit]. Inhabiting holes.

LATENT. [L. *latens*, hidden]. Inactive, but capable of becoming active or capable of being expressed under favorable conditions.

LATERAD. [L. *latus*, side; *ad*, towards]. Towards the side. Away from the axis.

LATERAL. [L. *latus*, side]. Situated at the side, or at a side of an axis.

LATERAL CARINA. [L. *latus*, side; *carina*, keel]. In some Ixodidae species: ridges on the lateral margins of the scutum.

LATERAL CLAWS. [L. *latus*, side]. Paired claws.

LATERAL EYES. [L. *latus*, side]. The 1-3 pairs of simple ocelli usually found on the lateral aspect of the prodorsum.

LATERAL LIPS. [L. *latus*, side]. In ticks and mites: lateroventral protuberances anterior to the mouth. They are usually joined to the labrum, and the labium when present.

LATERAL OCULAR QUADRANGLE (LOQ). [L. *latus*, side; *oculus*, eye; *quadrus*, fourfold; *angulus*, angle]. The total area occupied by the lateral eyes.

LATERAL OPISTHONOTAL GLANDS (LATERAL ABDOMINAL GLANDS, OIL GLANDS). [L. *latus*, side; Gr. οπισθο-, behind; νωτον, the back]. In the Sarcoptiformes: a pair of glands with large openings (solenostomes) on the opisthosoma. They are often surrounded by purple, red, brownish or yellow coloration if the cuticle is lightly sclerotized.

LATERAL SETA. [L. *latus*, side; *seta*, bristle]. In the Eriophyoidea: opisthosomal seta c2. See Grandjean System.

LATERAL VIEW. [L. *latus*, side]. Viewed from the side.

LATERIGRADE. [L. *latus*, side; *gradus*, step]. Walking sideways, like a crab. Or denoting the orientation of the legs of some spiders, which are rotated on their bases so that the prolateral surface is uppermost. Also the mode of locomotion of such spiders, mainly in the family **Thomisidae**.

LATERITIUS. [L. *lateris*, brick]. Yellowish-red. Yellowish brick color.

LATEROFRONTAL. [L. *latus*, side; *frons*, front]. Situated on the side but towards the front.

LATICOSTATE. [L. *latus*, broad; *costatus*, ribbed]. Broad-ribbed.

LATIGASTRIC. [L. *latus*, broad; Gr. γαστηρ, stomach]. Of those chelicerates that are broadly joined between prosoma and opisthosoma. See also Cauligastric.

LATIGYNAL (LATIGYNIAL) SHIELDS. [L. *latus*, broad; γυνη, woman]. In some female parasitiform mites: a pair of sclerites laterad the mesogynal shield that help protect the genital opening. They usually bear one or more pairs of setae and are sometimes fused to other genital or ventral elements. In the Gamasina the single female genital shield may represent a fusion of the latigynal and mesogynal shields.

LATRODECTISM. [L. *latro*, brigand; Gr. δηκτης, a biter; L. *-ism*, suf. of condition]. Envenomation of humans by *Latrodectus mactans*, the black widow spider.

141

LATTICED. [OFr. *latta*, lath]. To cross or interlace. Cancellated.

LATUS, LATERA. [L. *latus*, side]. The side of the body.

LAURASIA. [*St. Lawrence*, N. America; *Asia*]. The one-time interconnected land mass of north America, Europe, and northern Asia. First postulated to account for similar fossils occurring on these continents, now thought to have existed before continental drift moved these continents to their present positions. The break up of the land mass (Pangaea) started during the Late Jurassic and Early Cretaceous, and of course continues to the present day. See also Gondwana, Pangaea.

L.E. Lateral eyes.

LEAF VAGRANT. A mite that lives on the leaves of plants but does not form a gall or webbing.

LEBERIDOCYTES. [Gr. λεβηρις, exuvia; κυτος, hollow vessel]. In arachnid blood during molting: glycogen containing cells that develop from, and regress to, leucocytes.

LEBERTIOIDEA. [Gr. λεβηρις, exuvia]. A superfamily of mites (suborder Prostigmata, infraorder Anystina). Families: **Acucapitidae, Anisitsiellidae (Nilotoniidae), Bandakiopsidae, Lebertiidae, Oxidae, Rutripalpidae, Sperchontidae, Stygotoniidae, Teutoniidae, Torrenticolidae.**

LECHYTIIDAE. See Chthonioidea.

LEG. See Limb.

LEG FORMULA. A series of four numbers (e.g. 2143) that gives the relative leg lengths, from the longest to the shortest.

LEGIO, LEGION. [L. *legio*, legion]. An ill-defined taxonomic grouping, used in different ways by different authors.

LEG NUMBERING. The convention of numbering legs using Roman numerals, as I, II, III, IV, starting with the anterior leg; for an example, tibia II refers to the tibia of leg II.

LEIMOCOLOUS. [Gr. λειμων, meadow; L. *colere*, to dwell]. Inhabiting damp meadows.

LEMNISCATE, LEMNISCATA. [Gr. λημνισκος, a woolen ribbon]. A club-shaped organ.

LENS. [L. *lens*, lentil (because of its shape)]. The transparent covering of the eye, which focuses the light rays.

LENTIC, LENITIC. [L. *lentus*, slow]. Applied to habitats formed in very slow-moving or standing water.

LENTICULAR. [L. *lens*, lentil (because of its shape)]. Shaped like a double convex. Applied to glands, etc.

LENTICULATE, LENTIFORM. [L. *lens*, lentil; *forma*, shape]. Of some (more or less) circular structure, the upper and lower surfaces of which meet in a sharp point.

LENTICULUS. [L. *lenticulus*, little lens]. In some oribatid mites: an unpaired light receptive structure (often with a lens) at the median anterior margin of the notogaster.

LENTIGEROUS. [L. *lens*, lentil; *gerere*, to bear]. Having a lens.

LENTIGINOSE, LENTIGINOUS. [L. *lentigo*, freckled]. Freckled or speckled.

LEPTODERMOUS. [Gr. λεπτος, thin; δερμα, the skin]. Thin skinned, or thin walled.

LEPTONETIDAE. [Gr. λεπτος, slender; νηθω, spin]. A family of minute haplogyne spiders (suborder Opisthothelae, infraorder Araneomorphae) which generally have six eyes, although some are eyeless. They are commonly found in caves and similar habitats. There is a cul-de-sac spermathecae, which is essentially a diverticulum of the vagina. Seminal fluid, therefore, enters and exits through the same duct. This family includes the endangered tooth cave spider (*Neoleptoneta myopica*) of the southern United States.

LEPTONETOIDEA. [Gr. λεπτος, slender; νηθω, spin]. In a previous classification, a cosmopolitan superfamily of six-eyed araneomorph spiders (order Araneae, suborder Opisthothelae) that united the families **Leptobnetidae, Ochyroceratidae** and **Telemidae**. The

Leptonetidae and Telemidae are now in the infraorder Araneomorphae while the Ochyroceratidae has been moved to the superfamily Haplogynae.

LEPTOS. [Gr. λεπτος, slender]. Small. Fine.

LEPTOTROMBICULA. [Gr. λεπτος, slender; It. *tromba*, trumpet]. The larval stage of a trombicula - a member of the mite family Trombiculidae (chiggers), that are responsible for transmitting Tsutsugamushi disease (aka Japanese flood fever, scrub typhus).

LEPTUS. [Gr. λεπτος, small]. The six-legged larva of mites.

LESSEPSIAN MIGRATION (ERYTHREAN INVASION). [*Ferdinand de Lesseps*, French diplomat in charge of Suez Canal construction]. The migration of marine species across the Suez Canal, usually from the Red Sea to the Mediterranean Sea; rarely in the opposite direction.

LETHARGIC. [Gr. ληθαργικος, lethargic]. Of an animal that exhibits a slow or relatively slow response to a stimulus.

LETISIMULATION. [L. *lethum*, death; *similis*, like]. Feigning death. Thanatosis.

LEUCISM. [Gr. λευκος, white]. Pale coloration.

LEUCOCYTE (PLASMOCYTE). [Gr. λευκος, white; κυτος, a hollow]. A white blood cell. There are three types, present in both vertebrates and invertebrates: **Lymphocytes**, which are amoeboid non-phagocytic cells that convey or produce antibodies. **Monocytes**, which are phagocytic cells that ingest invading organisms, sometimes entering the tissue to do so. **Polymorphs**, (polymorphonuclear leucocytes, or granulocytes) which are also phagocytic.

LEVATION. [L. *levare*, to raise]. The act of raising. An upward motion such as that produced by the action of a levator muscle.

LEVATOR (ELEVATOR). [L. *levare*, to raise]. A general name for any muscle that raises an organ or part of the body.

LEVATOR TENDON. [L. *levare*, to raise]. The muscle that moves the movable digit of the chelicera. It is usually indistinct but in some Uropodidae (Mesostigmata) it has an ovoid sclerotized node that is used in identification. See also Muscle Terminology.

LEVIGATE, LEVIGATUS. [L. *levigare*, to make smooth]. To smoothen, to polish, etc. Having a smooth, somewhat shiny surface.

LICNEREMAEOIDEA. [Gr. λικνον, a winnowing-fan; ερημια, desert]. A superfamily of mites (suborder Oribatida, infraorder Brachypylina - section Poronoticae). Families: **Dendroeremaeidae, Lamellareidae, Licneremaeidae, Micreremidae, Passalozetidae, Scutoverticidae.**

LIFE EXPECTANCY. The average period of time that an organism is expected to live from any particular point in its life cycle.

LIFE FORM. The body shape an organism attains at maturity.

LIFE HISTORY. The significant features of an organism's life cycle, with particular reference to strategies influencing survival and reproduction.

LIFE SPAN. The maximum or mean life duration of an individual or population.

LIFE TABLE. A tabulation presenting complete data on the mortality schedule of a population.

LIGAMENT. [L. *ligare*, to bind]. A band or sheet of tough, fibrous tissue between parts or segments.

LIGNEOUS. [L. *lignum*, wood]. Of or like wood. Woody. Wood brown.

LIGNICOLOUS (LIGNICOLE). [L. *lignum*, wood, *colere*, to inhabit]. Living on or in wood.

LIGULATE. [L. *ligula*, little tongue]. Strap shaped.

LILACINOUS. [Pers. *lilak*, lilac]. Lilac-colored.

LIMB. [OE. *lim*, joint, main branch of a tree]. In ticks and mites (Acari) the first pair of limbs form the chelicerae (mandibles) which are used for cutting into the skin of the host, whilst the second pair of limbs forms the palps which position the capitulum for feeding. The remaining

143

four pairs of limbs form the actual legs. The typical arachnid limb is composed of eight segments. In order from the base outwards these segments are: coxa (coxapodite), trochanter, femur, patella (carpopodite), tibia (propodite), metatarsus, tarsus, claws. The limb segments are connected by soft cuticle, and in some species the femur appears superficially divided into a basifemur and a telofemur but this division is not reflected in the musculature and these subdivisions are not moveable. A similar subdivision may also be seen in the tarsus. The coxae are situated on the ventral side of the body and have very limited movement and support the articles. Of the cheliceral digits the first (trochanter) and last (tarsus) are of importance in classification as these may bear spurs, spines or teeth; and the tarsi may be tapered humped, bear ventral spurs, etc. The length of the claws in relation to the pads, or suckers (pulvillum) is also diagnostic. The tarsus of each leg bears an apotele (pre-tarsus), including the claws and the pulvillus. There is a complex sensory apparatus (Haller's organ) located on the dorsal surface of the tarsus of leg 1. This is the main organ for determining host location, and detecting host odors and pheromones etc. See also Leg Numbering, Leg Formula.

LIMBATE. [L. *limbus*, an edge]. Having a margin or limb of another color.

LIMBUS. [L. *limbus*, border]. Any distinct border; i.e. if marked off by a change in color or structure.

LIMEN (LIMINAL). [L. *limen*, threshold]. A threshold, a minimum stimulus, or a perceptible quantitative difference in stimulation. A boundary.

LIMNETIC (LIMNOPHILOUS, LIMNOBIOTIC). [Gr. λιμνη, a marshy lake]. Living in, or pertaining to, marshes or lakes.

LIMNIUM. [Gr. λιμνη, a lake]. A lake community.

LIMNOBIOS. [Gr. λιμνη, a lake; βιος, life]. The life in fresh water, animals and plants collectively.

LIMNODIUM. [Gr. λιμνωδης, marshy]. A salt-marsh community.

LIMNODOPHILOUS. [Gr. λιμνωδης, marshy; φιλος, loving]. Thriving in salt marshes.

LIMNOLOGY. [Gr. λιμνη, a lake; λογος, discourse]. The study of the biology of inland, standing waters, especially lakes.

LIMNOPHILOUS. [Gr. λιμνη, a lake; φιλος, loving]. Living in freshwater marshes.

LIMNOPLANKTON (HALOPLANKTON). [Gr. λιμνη, a lake; πλαγκτος, wandering]. The floating animal and plant life of freshwater lakes, ponds, marshes, etc.

LIMNOZETOIDEA. [Gr. λιμνη, a lake; ζητησις; seeking]. See Ceratozetoidea.

LINDQUIST-EVANS SYSTEM. [E.E. Lindquist & G.O. Evans]. A recent system of setal designations used in the Mesostigmata. Dorsally, the setae are designated with lowercase letters on the pronotum and uppercase letters on the opisthonotum representing longitudinal rows (from the midline to the lateral margin, j-J, z-Z, s-S, r-R, and an additional UR or submarginal row posteriorly) and Arabic numbers designating transverse rows from 1-6 on the pronotum and 1-5 (or higher in the UR-series) on the opisthonotum. Ventrally, idiosomal setae are treated as belonging to three regions: the sternal (intercoxal), the ventral, and the anal. Three pairs of sternal setae are present in the larva (st1-3); the genital seta st5 is added in the protonymph stage; and the metasternal seta st4 is added in the deutonymph stage. The ventral region has up to three longitudinal rows (JV, ZV, rarely SV) with 1-5 transverse row designations. The anal region has a pair of paranal setae (pa) and an unpaired postanal seta (po).

LINEA, LINEAE. [L. *linea*, line]. Linear markings or structures; usually caused by a ridge.

LINEAR. [L. *linea*, line]. Straight. In the form of a right line.

LINEAR-ENSATE. [L. *linea*, line: *ensis*, sword]. Somewhere between linear and ensiform in shape.

LINEATE. [L. *linea*, line]. Marked longitudinally with depressed parallel lines or striae.

LINEOLATE (LINEOLA). [L. *linea*, line]. Marked by fine lines or striae.

LINE TRANSECT. [L. *trans*, across; *secare*, to cut]. A straight line on the ground, defined between two points, and used as a guide from which to sample the distribution of organisms. Sampling should be confined to organisms that are actually touching the line.

LINGUA. [L. *lingua*, tongue]. A tongue or any tongue-like structure. In mites: the floor of the mouth.

LINYPHIIDAE (incl. **SINOPIMOIDAE**). [Gr. λινυφος, guild of linen-weavers]. The family of sheet-web spiders or 'money-spiders' (infraorder Araneomorphae, superfamily Entelegynae), which are among the commonest and most abundant species in the northern hemisphere. They are small, uniformly black or brown and the larger members of this family construct sheet webs, without a retreat, amongst vegetation and run upside-down on the underside of the sheet. The chelicerae have numerous teeth and the legs bear many stout setae. Many species migrate by 'ballooning' on long silken threads. The males of some species have ridges on the outer surface of the chelicerae and an opposing tooth on the inner surface of the papal femur. This is used in stridulation during courtship.

LIOCRANIDAE. [Gr. λειος, smooth; κρανιον, the head]. A family of sac spiders (infraorder Araneomorphae, superfamily Entelegynae).

LIP. [AS. *lippa*, lip]. Any lip-like part or structure. The lower lip, ventral to the mouth, lying between the maxillae and attached to the anterior edge of the sternum.

LIPHISTIIDAE. [Gr. λειπω-, lacking; ιστος, anything set upright]. A family of primitive burrowing spiders (order Araneae, suborder Mesothelae) from southeast Asia to southern Japan. They are characterized by the retention of the original segmentation of the abdomen (a primitive condition), as seen in numerous dorsal plates. There is a normal carapace covering the prosoma. They have seven or eight spinnerets, the first of which is located at the level of the second pair of book lungs. The lair is a tube, up to 60 cm deep, dug out of the substrate and the chelicerae are used to hold shut a trapdoor. Threads radiate from the tube entrance to trip prey and alert the concealed spider.

LIPHISTIOMORPHAE. [Gr. λειπω-, lacking; ιστος, anything set upright; μορφη, shape]. A previous alternative name for the Mesothelae. See Liphistiidae.

LIPOCYTE. [Gr. λιπος, fat; κυτος, a hollow]. A cell containing lipids, a fat cell.

LIPOID. [Gr. λιπος, fat; ειδος, like]. Of a fatty nature.

LIPOXENOUS. [Gr. λειπειν, to quit; ξενος, stranger]. Of a parasite that leaves the host before the completion of its (the parasite's) development.

LIRA, LIRAE. [L. *lira*, a ridge]. Fine grooves or a thread-like sculpture or ridge.

LISTROPHORIDAE. [Gr. λιστρον, tool for digging; -φορα, carrying]. The family of fur mites (suborder Asigmata, superfamily Sarcoptoidea). They have elongated bodies and mouth parts modified for grasping hairs; a tracheal system is absent and gas exchange occurs across the weakly sclerotized body wall.

LITERATE. [L. *litteratus*, educated]. Ornamented with characters like letters.

LITHODOMOUS. [Gr. λιθος, stone; δομος, house]. Living in rock holes, crevices or clefts.

LITTER LAYER. [L. *lectus*, a bed]. The layer of organic material that lies on the surface of the soil.

LITTORAL FAUNA AND FLORA. [L. *littoralis*, of the shore; *Faunus*, god of the woods]. Animals and plants of the sea shore and the shallow regions near the shore.

LITTORAL ZONE. [L. *littoralis*, of the shore]. The margins of a lake where light can reach the bottom. See also Intertidal Zone.

LITUATE. [L. *lituus*, augur's staff]. With prongs curving outwards.

LITURA, LITURATE. [L. *litura*, blot, smear]. An obscure color spot with pale margins; appearing to be daubed or blotted.

LIVID. [L. *lividus*, to be black and blue]. Black and blue. Greyish blue.

LOBAR. [Gr. λοβος, lobe]. Of a lobe or lobes.

LOBATE. [LL. *lobus*, lobe]. Divided into lobes.

LOBE. [LL. *lobus*, lobe]. Any rounded projection. A flap-like structure. A rounded outgrowth of the cheliceral margin.

LOBIFORM. [LL. *lobus*, lobe; L. *forma*, shape]. Shaped like a lobe or rounded process.

LOBULATE. Divided into small lobes or lobules.

LOBUS. [LL. *lobus*, lobe]. Any region of an organ that is delimited by septa or fissures.

LOCHMOCOLOUS. [Gr. λοχμη, thicket; L. *colere*, to inhabit]. Inhabiting thickets.

LOCHMODOPHILOUS (LOCHMOPHILUS). [Gr. λοχμη, thicket; δομος, house; φιλος, loving]. Thriving in dry thickets.

LOCOMOTION. [L. *locus*, place; LL. *motivus*, motive]. The action or power of moving from place to place. Progressive motion.

LOCULAR. [L. *loculus*, cell]. Having or containing small cavities or chambers.

LOCULUS. [L. *loculus*; compartment]. Any small chamber, cavity or compartment.

LOHMANNIOIDEA. [*H. Lohmann*, German? Biologist]. A monospecific superfamily of mites (suborder Oribatida, infraorder Enarthronota). Family: **Lohmanniidae**.

LONGITUDINAL. [L. *longitude*, length, long duration]. Lengthwise along the body or an appendage.

LONGITUDINAL SECTION. [L. *longitude*, length, long duration]. A section along or parallel to the longitudinal axis.

LONGSHORE. Of currents or water movements parallel to the shore.

LOPHIUM. [Gr. λοφιον, small crest]. A ridge community.

LOPHOPHILOUS. [Gr. λοφος, brow of hill; φιλος, loving]. Thriving on hill tops.

L.O.Q. Lateral ocular quadrangle: the total area occupied by the lateral eyes.

LORA (LORE). [L. *lorum*, thong]. In arachnids: the dorsal plate that protects the pedicle.

LORDALYCOIDEA. See Sphaerolichida.

LOTIC. [L. *lotum*, flowed over]. Living in running water such as a brook, stream or river.

LOTKA-VOLTERRA EQUATIONS (PREDATOR–PREY EQUATIONS). [*A.J. Lotka* (American mathematician) & *V. Volterra* (Italian mathematician)]. Mathematical models of competition between resource-limited species living in the same space with the same environmental requirements. This model predicts that coexistence is impossible and that one species will always be eliminated, according to the competitive exclusion principle. The models have been modified to simulate predator-prey interactions and predict cyclic variations in the predator and prey populations. An increase in the predator population leads to a decrease in the prey population which leads to a decrease in the predator population, which allows a recovery of the prey population, followed by an increase in the predator population.

LOXOSCELIDAE. [Gr. λοξος, slanting; σκελος, the leg]. See **Sicariidae**.

LUCID. [L. *lucidus*, clear]. Luminous, translucent, pellucid, shining.

LUCIFUGOUS. [L. *lux*, light; *fugere*, to flee]. Shunning light. See also Lucipetal, Phengophil, Phengophobe, Photophobic, Photophilic.

LUCIPETAL. [L. *lux*, light; *petere*, to seek]. Requiring light. See also Lucifugous, Phengophil, Phengophobe, Photophobic, Photophilic.

LUMEN. [L. *lumen*, light]. A cavity in an organ.

LUMENATE. [L. *lumen*, light]. Having a lumen.

LUNATE, LUNAR. [L. *luna*, moon]. Crescent-shaped. Falcate.

LUNULE. [L. *lunula*, small moon]. A crescent-shaped part or marking.

LUNULATE. [NL. *lunulatus*, resembling a small crescent]. Of a line made up of a series of small lunules.

146

LURE. Any means of alluring an animal.

LURID. [L. *luridus*, pale yellow]. A dirty yellowish color; dismal; dingy.

LUTEOFUSCOUS. [L. *luteus*, orange-yellow; *fuscus*, dusky]. Darkish yellow.

LUTEO-TESTACEOUS. [L. *luteus*, golden yellow; *testa*, shell; *-aceous*, of the nature of]. Dark clay yellow.

LUTEOUS. [L. *luteus*, golden yellow]. An orange or reddish yellow. Saffron.

LUTESCENT. [L. *lutescere*, become muddy]. Becoming or appearing to be clay yellow.

LUTOSE, LUTOSUS. [L. *lutosus*, muddy]. Apparently or really covered with dirt.

LYCOSIDAE. [Gr. λυκος, wolf]. The cosmopolitan family of wolf spiders, hunting spiders (infraorder Araneomorphae, superfamily Entelegynae). Medium to large, rather hairy, cursorial spiders with four large and four small eyes and with dull brown and black coloration. Some genera burrow and others construct funnel-shaped webs. In the majority of species the females carry their egg sacs attached to their circularly arranged spinnerets and the spiderlings are carried on the top of the abdomen for the first week or so after hatching.

LYCOSOIDEA. [Gr. λυκος, wolf]. In a previous classification, a superfamily of eight-eyed araneomorph spiders (order Araneae, infraorder Araneomorphae) that united the families: **Ctenidae, Lycosidae, Neolanidae** (now Stiphidiidae), **Oxyopidae, Pisauridae, Psechridae, Senoculidae, Stiphidiidae, Trechaleidae, Zoridae, Zorocratidae** (now in Zoropsidae), **Zoropsidae**. These families have been moved to the superfamily Entelegynae.

LYRATE. [L. *lyra*, lyre]. Lyre-shaped; spatulate and oblong with small lobes toward the base.

LYRE-SHAPED. [L. *lyra*, lyre]. Like a string musical instrument with two curved arms and strings attached to a yolk between the curved arms.

LYRIFISSURE. [L. *lyra*, ridge between two furrows; *fissura*, crack]. In the Chelicerata: small fissures or pores in the cuticle of the body or appendages; sometimes with an internal channel. They are thought to be proprioceptors that respond to stretching.

LYRIFORM ORGANS (SLIT SENSE ORGANS). [L. *lyra*, ridge between two furrows, *forma*, shape]. On the body and appendages of most arachnids: sense organs in the form a slit-like pit in the cuticle covered by a very thin membrane which bulges inwards. The under surface of the membrane is in contact with a hair-like process, which projects upwards from a sensory cell. These organs may occur in great numbers either individually or in groups and respond to slight changes in the tension of the exoskeleton and thus function in proprioception and in detecting (sound) vibrations, as well as kinaesthetic orientation.

M

MACROCHAETA. [Gr. μακρος, large; χαιτη, hair]. A large bristle.

MACROFAUNA. [Gr. μακρος, large; L. *Faunus*, god of the woods]. The larger animals, whose length can be measured in centimeters rather than microscopic units. See also Meiofauna, Mesofauna, Microfauna.

MACROLECITHAL. [Gr. μακρος, large; λεκιθος, yolk]. With a large amount of yolk. See also Alecithal, Centrolecithal, Heterolecithal, Mediolecithal, Meiolecithal, Mesolecithal, Microlecithal, Oligolecithal, Polylecithal, Telolecithal.

MACRONYSSID. [Gr. μακρος, large; νυσσω, stab]. Any member of the **Macronyssidae** (infraorder Gamasina, superfamily Dermanyssoidea); a family of blood-feeding parasitic mites that includes the common bird and rodent parasites in the genus *Ornithonyssus*, that often bite humans.

MACROPYLINE. [Gr. μακρος, large; πυλη, gate]. Having separate adgenital and adanal (aggenital) plates and genital and anal shields such that most of the post-coxal venter is occupied by the two paired series of shields. See also Brachypyline.

MACROSETA. [Gr. μακρος, large; L. *seta*, bristle]. Erectile seta that arise from a membranous area on the legs and palp. These are taxonomically important characters on leg IV in the **Phytoseiidae** (a family of mites that are often used as a biological control agents).

MACROTHELIDAE. [Gr. μακρος, large; θηλη, nipple]. A monospecific family of large spiders (infraorder Mygalomorphae, superfamily Avicularioidea) that construct tube-webs or funnel-webs under rocks or logs, or in crevices in the ground.

MACROTRICHIA. [Gr. μακρος, large; θριξ, hair]. The large hairs or setae of insects etc. They consist of extended epidermal cells surrounded by cuticle and may be of various types such as: 1. Simple or branching hairs covering most of the body. 2. Sensory setae with neuronal connections responding to touch, taste etc. 3. Setae which exude irritants.

MACULA. [L. *macula*, spot]. A spot or patch of color. A small pit or depression. A tubercle.

MACULATE (MACULIFEROUS, MACULOSE). [L. *macula*, spot]. Spotted.

MACULATION. [L. *macula*, spot]. The arrangement of spots on an animal or plant.

MADAGASCAN (MALAGASY) FAUNAL SUBREGION. [L. *Faunus*, god of the woods]. The endemic and insular fauna of Madagascar, the Archipelago of the Comores, the Mascarenes and the Seychelles; that includes five unique orders.

MADESCENT. [L. *madescere*, to become wet]. Becoming moist.

MAJOR DUCT. In some mesostigmatans (**Blattisociidae, Otopheidomenidae, Phytoseiidae**): a variable-length tubular duct that runs from the solenostome to the atrium of the sperm access system. See also Minor Duct.

MALACOID. [Gr. μαλακος, soft]. Soft textured.

MALA MANDIBULARIS. [L. *mala*, cheek; LL. *mandibulum*, jaw]. The grinding surface or area of a mandible.

MALA MAXILLAE. [L. *mala*, cheek; *maxilla*, upper jaw]. The lobes of maxilla: outer or galea, inner or lacinia: where only one is present, the term refers to that one.

MALAPOPHYSIS. [L. *mala*, cheek, jaw; Gr. αποφυσις, projection]. In ticks and mites: the paired anterior region of the infracapitulum.

MALAR. [L. *mala*, cheek]. Of or about the cheek region.

MALAR CAVITY. [L. *mala*, cheek]. In ticks and mites: the interior of the malapophysis that connects to the pharynx.

MALAXATION. [Gr. μαλαξις, softening]. Softening by chewing.

MALAYAN FAUNAL SUBREGION. [L. *Faunus*, god of the woods]. The zoogeographical sub-region that includes Malaya, the Philippines and Indonesia west of Wallace's Line.

MALE. [L. *mas*, male]. An individual whose reproductive organs (usually) contain only motile gametes. Sexually opposite of female. Symbol ♂.

MALE DUCTS, MALE GONODUCTS. See Sperm Ducts.

MALE PARTHENOGENESIS. See Androgenesis.

MALKARIDAE (syn. **PARARCHAEIDAE**). [*Malkara*, Australian aboriginal word for 'shield']. A small family of spiders (infraorder Araneomorphae, superfamily Entelegynae).

MALLEATE. [L. *malleus*, hammer]. Hammer-shaped.

MALLEATIONS. [L. *malleus*, hammer]. Having a hammered appearance.

MALLEOLUS. [L. *malleolus*, little hammer]. Racquet Organ. In the sun spiders (Solifugae): a sensory organ on the ventral surface of the basal segments of the fourth pair of legs, somewhat resembling a club or tennis racquet.

MALLEUS. [L. *malleus*, hammer]. Any hammer-shaped structure.

MALPIGHIAN TUBULES (MEDULLARY PYRAMIDS). [*M. Malpighi*, Italian physiologist]. In arachnids (plus insects and myriapods): the thread-like, glandular, excretory tubes that open into the posterior region of the gut, near the commencement of the hind gut. The number of these tubules varies greatly from species to species.

148

MALTHUSIAN PARAMETER. [*T.R. Malthus*, English social economist]. The rate at which a population, with a particular age distribution and birth and death rate, will increase.

MAMILLA (MAMMILAE). [L. *mamilla*, nipple]. A nipple or nipple-like structure.

MAM(M)ILLATE (MAMMIFORM, MAMMOSE). [L. *mamilla*, nipple]. Studded with small protuberances.

MAMILLATION. [L. *mamilla*, nipple]. The process of formation of nipple-like protuberances.

MAMMOSE. [L. *mammosus*, full-breasted]. Shaped like a breast or having breast-shaped protuberances.

MANAOSBIIDAE. [*Manaos*, an indigenous Amazonian people; Gr βιος, life]. A family of neotropical harvestmen or daddy longlegs (suborder Laniatores, superfamily Gonyleptoidea). Their relationship with other member of the subfamily Gonyleptoidea is unclear.

MANCHURIAN SUBREGION. [*Manchuria*, a region of northeast China]. One of four biogeographical subregions of the Palearctic, as defined by Alfred Russel Wallace. This region encompasses Mongolia, Korea, Manchuria, and Japan. The other three regions being the European, Mediterranean and Siberian.

MANDIBLES. See Chelicerae.

MANICATE, MANICATUS. [L. *manicatus*, sleeved]. Being covered with entangled hairs or matted scales.

MANIFORM. [L. *manus*, hand; *forma*, shape]. Hand-shaped.

MANTER'S RULES. See Host-Parasite Associations.

MARBLED. [Gr. μαρμαρος, marble]. Irregularly mottled, grey and white, like marble: = marmouratus.

MARCESCENT. [L. *macescere*, wither/shrivel]. Shrivelling.

MARCID. [L. *marcidus*, withered]. Withered, shrivelled.

MARGARITACEOUS. [Gr. μαργαριτης, a pearl; L. *-aceous*, of the nature of]. Pearly in texture. Nacreous.

MARGIFORM. [L. *margo*, edge; *forma*, shape]. Margin-like.

MARGIN. [L. *margo*, border]. A border or an edge.

MARGINAL GROOVE. [L. *margo*, border; OE *græf*, ditch/grave]. In the Ixodes a groove situated along the dorsal marginal; it is most distinct in females.

MARGINED, MARGINATED. [L. *margo*, border]. Having a distinct margin, either in structure or color. Bounded by an elevated or attenuated margin. Of the margin when it is edged by a flat border.

MARMOURATE, MARMOURATUS. [L. *marmour*, marble]. Having a marbled appearance.

MARSH. [ME. *mersh*, meadowland]. A region of more or less permanently wet but not peaty soil; typically found around the edges of a lake or on an undrained river flood plain.

MASTICATE. [L. *masticare*, to chew]. To chew.

MASTICATORY. [L. *masticare*, to chew]. Formed for chewing or grinding.

MASTIDIA (MASTIDION). [Gr. μαστος, breast]. Small conical nipple-like tubercles on the front of the chelicerae of small spiders.

MASTIDION. [Gr. μαστιδιον, small breast]. In some spiders: a nipple-like protuberance on the basal joint of the chelicera.

MASTOID. [Gr. μαστος, breast; ειδος, form]. Nipple-shaped.

MATING. The union of two individuals of opposite sexual type in the course of sexual reproduction.

MATING PLUG (SPERMATOPHRAGMA). A plug formed from the accessory gland secretions of the male.

MATING SPUR. In some male spiders: a rigid cuticular outgrowth, with or without apical spines, found on the anterior legs and used as a restraining structure during copulation.

MATRICLINOUS (MATRICLINAL). [L. *mater*, mother; Gr. κλινειν, to incline]. Having hereditary characteristics that are more maternal than paternal. See also Patriclinous.

MATURATION FEEDING. [L. *maturus*, ripe/timely]. The feeding required before gonads can mature to produce eggs.

MAXILLA (MAXILLAE). [L. *maxilla*, jaw]. See Gnathobase.

MAXILLIFORM. [L. *maxilla*, jaw; *forma*, shape]. Shaped like a jaw.

MAXILLOLABIAL. [L. *maxilla*, jaw; *labium*, lip]. Of the jaw and labium: applied to the dart in ticks.

M.E. Median eyes.

MEATUS. [L. *meatus*, passage]. A passage or channel.

MECHANICAL ISOLATION. Reproductive isolation due to structural incompatibility of the male and female reproductive organs.

MECHANICAL SENSE. Any of the senses that detect mechanical stimuli, i.e. touch, hearing (air vibration) and balance.

MECHANORECEPTOR. [Gr. μηχανη; contrivance; L. *recipere*, to receive]. Any specialized structure sensitive to mechanical stimuli such as sound, pressure, tension, movement, etc. See also Receptor.

MECHANOTROPISM. [Gr. μηχανη; contrivance; τροπη, turning round]. Orientation in response to a mechanical stimulus.

MECICOBOTHRIIDAE. [Mecico, *Mexico*; Gr. βοθρος, a trench/pit]. The family of dwarf tarantulas (infraorder Mygalomorphae, superfamily Atypoidea) from the western United States and southern South America. The thoracic groove is very narrow and longitudinal. There is no row of large cheliceral teeth on the retrolateral side of the closed fang and a rastellum is lacking. Many species make loose sheet webs around debris; living close to the soil in cracks or under rocks or other objects. Previously in the superfamily Mecicobothrioidea.

MECICOBOTHRIOIDEA. [Mecico, *Mexico*; Gr. βοθρος, a trench/pit]. In a previous classification: a superfamily of spiders (suborder Opisthothelae, infraorder Mygalomorphae) uniting two families: **Mecicobothriidae, Microstigmatidae**. These families have now been separated; Mecicobothriidae to superfamily Atypoidea and Microstigmatidae to superfamily Avicularioidea.

MECYSMAUCHENIIDAE. [deriv.uncert.]. A small family of spiders (infraorder Araneomorphae, superfamily Palpimanoidea) from Chile, Argentina and New Zealand. They are high-speed predators.

MEDIA. [L. *medius*, middle]. Any structure in a middle position.

MEDIAL. [L. *medius*, middle]. Situated in the middle.

MEDIAN. [L. *medius*, middle]. In the middle. Lying in the axial plane. The middle variate when variates are arranged in order of magnitude.

MEDIAN APOPHYSIS. [L. *medius*, middle; Gr. αποφυσις, an offshoot]. A sclerite that arises from, or is associated with, the tegulum and forms part of the middle division of the palpal bulb.

MEDIAN CLAW. [L. *medius*, middle; AS. *clawu*, claw]. The third claw (not paired). It is located apically on the tarsus; but is absent from male palpi.

MEDIAN LOBE. [L. *medius*, middle; LL. *lobus*, lobe]. The lobe-like protuberance along the midline of some epigyna.

MEDIAN OCULAR AREA/QUADRANGLE, MOA/MOQ. [L. *medius*, middle; *oculus*, eye]. The area delimited by the four median eyes.

MEDIAN PLATE. [L. *medius*, middle; Fr. *plate*, flat]. In male *Ixodes*: the ventral sclerotized plate between the coxae, posterior to the genital orifice.

MEDIAN SEPTUM. [L. *medius*, middle]. A raised longitudinal region on the floor of the atrium of the epigynum.

MEDIASTINAL. [MedL. *mediastinus*, medial]. Relating to the longitudinal median line or area.

MEDIODORSAL. [L. *medius*, middle; *dorsum*, back]. In the dorsal mid line.

MEDIOLECITHAL. [L. *medius*, middle; Gr. λεκιθος, yolk]. Medium-yolked. See also Alecithal, Centrolecithal, Heterolecithal, Macrolecithal, Meiolecithal, Mesolecithal, Microlecithal, Oligolecithal, Polylecithal, Telolecithal.

MEDIOPECTORAL. [L. *medius*, middle; *pectus*, breast]. Of the middle region of the sternum.

MEDIOVENTRAL. [L. *medius*, middle; *venter*, belly]. In the middle ventral line.

MEDULLA. [L. *medulla*, pith]. The central region of an organ or tissue.

MEGADICTYNIDAE. [Gr. μεγας, large; δικτυον, a hunting net]. A small family of spiders (infraorder Araneomorphae, superfamily Entelegynae) that are endemic to New Zealand.

MEGASPINE. [Gr. μεγας, large; L. *spina*, thorn]. A rigid cuticular outgrowth bearing a large apical spine.

MEGISTHANOIDEA. [Gr. μεγας, large; Θανος, death]. A diverse superfamily of mites (suborder Trigynaspida, infraorder Antennophorina) associated with passalid beetles. Families: **Hoplomegistidae, Megisthanidae**.

MEIOFAUNA. [Gr. μειον, smaller; L. *Faunus*, god of the woods]. Members of the microfauna that inhabit algae, rock fissures and the superficial layers of the muddy sea bottom. This term is often synonymous with 'interstial fauna'. See also Macrofauna, Mesofauna, Microfauna.

MEIOGYROUS. [Gr. μειον, smaller; γυρος, circle]. Slightly coiled inwards.

MEIOLECITHAL (MIOLECITHAL). [Gr. μειον, smaller; λεκιθος, yolk]. Having a small quantity of yolk. See also Alecithal, Centrolecithal, Heterolecithal, Macrolecithal, Mediolecithal, Mesolecithal, Microlecithal, Oligolecithal, Polylecithal, Telolecithal.

MEIOMERY. [Gr. μειον, smaller; μερος, part]. Having fewer than the normal number of parts.

MEIOTRICHY. [Gr. μειον, smaller; θριξ, hair]. Loss of setae in ontogenetic development or of homologous setae in natural groups.

MELANESIA. [Gr. μελας, black; νησος, island]. A geographical region comprising the continental islands of the western Pacific south of the equator. Sometimes considered to be a distinct biogeographical unit and sometimes considered to be part of Polynesia.

MELANIA. [Gr. μελας, black]. Blackness.

MELANIC. [Gr. μελας, black]. Having a blackish suffusion.

MELANIC MUTATION. [Gr. μελας, black; L. *mutare*, to change]. Any mutation that causes an animal to show an abnormal black color in comparison with others of the species.

MELANIN. [Gr. μελας, black]. A group of pigments, usually black or dark brown, found in the skin and formed in melanoblast cells from the oxidation of tyrosine by the enzyme tyrosinase, or from phenylalanine and other aromatic compounds.

MELANISM. [Gr. μελας, black; -ισμος, suf. forming nouns of action from verbs]. In an animal population: the occurrence of black individuals due to an excess of the pigment melanin. See also Albino.

MELANOBLAST. [Gr. μελας, black; βλαστος, bud]. A cell in which melanin is formed.

MELANOBLOSSIIDAE. [Gr. μελας, black; L. *Blossius*, a leading Capuan family]. A small family of sun spiders (subclass Arachnida, order Solifugae) from south Africa, Vietnam and Indonesia.

151

MELANOCYTE. [Gr. μελας, black; κυτος, a hollow vessel]. A black pigmented lymphocyte.

MELANOGENSIS. [Gr. μελας, black; γενεσις, birth]. Melanin formation.

MELANOID. [Gr. μελας, black; ειδος, form]. Looking black or dark.

MELANOIDS. [Gr. μελας, black; ειδος, form]. Black or dark brown pigments related structurally to melanin.

MELIPHAGOUS (MEL(L)IVOROUS). [Gr. μελι, honey; -φαγος, -eating]. Feeding on honey.

MEMBRANACEOUS. [L. membrana, membrane; -aceous, of the nature of]. Having the structure or consistency of a membrane. Of a pliable texture; being thin, skin-like, semi-transparent, like parchment.

MEMBRANAL. [L. membrana, membrane]. Within membranes.

MEMBRANE. [L. membrana, membrane]. A thin film or layer of tissue or skin covering or containing any region of an animal. The boundary between a cell and its environment and also between the various components of the cell. A membrane is commonly composed of lipids, proteins and some carbohydrates and functions as a selective barrier.

MEMBRANIFEROUS. [L. membrana, membrane; ferre, to carry]. Bearing, or enveloped in a membrane.

MEMBRANOID. [L. membrana, membrane; Gr. ειδος, form]. Resembling a membrane.

MEMBRANOUS. [L. membrana, membrane]. Resembling, or consisting of a membrane in being thin, pliable and semi-transparent.

MENINGOSIS. [Gr. μηνιγξ, membrane]. Attachment by means of membranes.

MENISCOIDAL. [Gr. μηνισκος, small moon, ειδος, form]. Concavoconvex, like a meniscus. Of a crescent shaped lens; i.e. one side convex and the other concave.

MENTAL SETAE. [L. mentum, chin; seta, bristle]. Setae located on the mentum ('chin').

MENTAL TECTUM. [L. mentum, chin; tectum, roof]. On some oribatid mites: a projection of the mentum.

MENTHIDAE. [L. menthe, mint]. A small family of false scorpions (suborder Iocheirata, superfamily Garypoidea) with a wide, but disjunct, distribution.

MENTUM. [L. mentum, chin]. A region at the base of the labium, between the submentum and the prementum.

MERIDIONAL. [L. meridies, noon]. Running from pole to pole along a meridian.

MERISTIC. [Gr. μερισμος, divided]. Segmented. Divided off into parts, or having a differing number of parts.

MERISTIC VARIATION. [Gr. μερισμος, divided]. A variation which involves the number of, or arrangements of, the parts of an organism.

MERITRICHY. [Gr. μερος, part; τριχος, hair]. In ticks and mites: chaetotaxy characterized by a reduction in number and size of setae from the holotrichous form.

MEROMORPHOSIS. [Gr. μερος, part; μορφωσις, shaping]. Regeneration in which the new part is less that the original.

MERON (MESEUSTERNUM). [Gr. μηρος, thigh]. The posterior region of the coxa or the sclerite between the middle and hind coxae.

MEROPARASITE. [Gr. μερος, part; παρασιτος, parasite]. A partial parasite. A parasite that can survive in the absence of its host.

MEROPODITE (MEROS, MERUS). [Gr. μηρος, thigh; πους, foot]. The femur in arachnids.

MEROSOMA (MEROSOME). [Gr. μερος, part; σωμα, body]. A somite, or body segment.

MEROSPERMY. [Gr. μερος, part; σπερμα, seed]. A condition in which the sperm penetrates the egg but the sperm nucleus does not fuse with that of the egg; development thus being parthenogenetic. See also Parthenogenesis.

MEROSTASIS. [Gr. μερος, part; στασις, standing]. The possession of a few juvenile characteristics in an otherwise adult individual.

MEROSTHENIC. [Gr. μηρος, thigh; σθενος, strength]. Having unusually developed hind limbs.

MEROTOMY. [Gr. μερος, part; τεμνειν, to cut]. Segmentation, or division into parts.

MEROTOPE. [Gr. μερος, part; τοπος, place]. A microhabitat, such as a fruit or pebble, that forms part of a larger unit.

MERTENSIAN MIMICRY. [*R. Mertens*, German Biologist]. See Mimicry.

MERUS. [Gr. μηρος, thigh]. See Meropodite.

MESAD, MESIAD. [Gr. μεσος, middle; L. *ad*, toward]. Towards the midline of the body.

MESAL, MESIAL, MESIAN. [Gr. μεσος, middle]. At or near the midline of the body. In the middle or longitudinal plane.

MESAL MARGIN. [Gr. μεσος, middle]. In the Mygalomorphae: the inner margin of the cheliceral furrow.

MESAL VIEW. [Gr. μεσος, middle]. The view from inside. Use with paired asymmetrical structures such as male palps.

MESEUSTERNUM. [Gr. μεσος, middle; ευ, well; στερνον, breast plate]. See Meron.

MESIC. [Gr. μεσος, middle]. A temperate, moist climate, neither xeric (dry) nor hydric (moist).

MESOCOLE. [Gr. μεσος, middle; L. *colere*, to inhabit]. An animal living in an environment in which there is neither an excess nor a deficiency of water.

MESOCUTICLE. [Gr. μεσος, middle; L. *cutis*, skin]. A thin region of hardened but not darkened cuticle which may exist between the sclerotized exocuticle and the inner, undifferentiated endocuticle. See also Endocuticle, Epicuticle, Exocuticle.

MESODERMAL TUBE. [Gr. μεσος, middle; δερμα, skin]. The dorsal blood vessel. The heart.

MESOFAUNA. [Gr. μεσος, middle; L. *Faunus*, god of woods]. Animals of intermediate size, i.e. from 200 μm to 1 cm. Characteristically these are Annalida, Arthropoda, Nematoda and Mollusca. See also Macrofauna, Meiofauna, Microfauna.

MESOGASTRIC. [Gr. μεσος, middle; γαστηρ, stomach]. Of the middle gastric region.

MESOGYNAL (MESOGYNIAL) SHIELD. [Gr. μεσος, middle; γυνη, woman]. In some female Parasitiformes: an unpaired median sclerite that helps to shield the genital opening. It is commonly bare and sometimes fused to other genital or ventral elements. In the Gamasina: a single female genital shield that may represent a fusion of the latigynal and mesogynal shields.

MESOLECITHAL. [Gr. μεσος, middle; λεκιθος, yolk]. Eggs with a moderate yolk content. See also Alecithal, Centrolecithal, Heterolecithal, Macrolecithal, Mediolecithal, Meiolecithal, Microlecithal, Oligolecithal, Polylecithal, Telolecithal.

MESONOTAL SCUTELLAE. [Gr. μεσος, middle; νωτον, back; L. *scutellum*, little shield]. In the Mesostigmata: the usually paired sclerites between the podonotal and pygidial shield.

MESONOTAL SHIELD. [Gr. μεσος, middle; νωτον, back]. In ticks and mites: a transverse sclerite that covers the mesonotum. It commonly lies between a podonotal and a pygidial shield.

MESOPELTIDIUM. [Gr. μεσος, middle; πελτη, a small, light shield]. See Schizopeltid.

MESOPLOPHOROIDEA. [Gr. μεσος, middle; οπλον, a tool; -φορα, -carrying]. A monotypic superfamily of mites (suborder Oribatida, infraorder Enarthronota). Family: **Mesoplophoridae.**

MESOSAPROBIC. [Gr. μεσος, middle; σαπρος, rotten; βιος, life]. Of aquatic habitats that are midway between polysaprobic and katharobic; i.e. having a reduced quantity of oxygen and a substantial amount of organic decomposition. See also Katharobic, Oligosaprobic, Polysaprobic, Saprobic.

MESOSOMA. [Gr. μεσος, middle; σωμα, body]. In arachnids: the anterior region of the opisthosoma ('abdomen').

MESOSTIGMATA. [Gr. μεσος, middle; στιγμη, mark]. A large order of parasitic and free-living mites (subclass Arachnida, superorder Parasitiformes) in which the body is covered in brown plates which vary in number and position and in which there is a pair of tracheal spiracles located behind the coxae of the third pair of legs. Suborders: Monogynaspida, Sejida, Trigynaspida and, in some classifications, the sub-cohort Dermanyssiae.

MESOSTIGMATID. Erron. for mesostigmatan, the adjectival form of Mesostigmata.

MESOTHELAE (LIPHISTIOMORPHAE). [Gr. μεσος, middle; θηλη, nipple]. A suborder of large segmented primitive spiders (subclass Arachnida, order Araneae) from southeast Asia, China and Japan. Families: †Arthrolycosidae, †Arthromygalidae, Liphistiidae.

MESOVENTRAL. [Gr. μεσος, middle; L. venter, belly]. In the middle ventral region.

METAGAMIC SEX DETERMINATION. [Gr. μετα, change of; γαμετης, spouse]. See Sex Determination.

METAGASTRIC. [Gr. μετα, after; γαστηρ, stomach]. The posterior gastric region.

METALEPTIC. [Gr. μεταληψις, participation]. Associated in a process; acting together.

METAMERIC SEGMENTATION. [Gr. μετα, after; μερος, part]. The division of an animal into a number of linear segments (metameres), each of which contains a repetition of the same organs. In annelids (such as the earthworm) this segmentation is readily apparent; in arthropods the metemeric structure may be more or less obscured in the adult, but it is clearly visible in embryos and larvae. See also Segmentation.

METAPELTIDIUM. [Gr. μετα, after; πελτη, a small, light shield]. See Schizopeltid.

METAPODAL LINE. [Gr. μετα, after; πους, foot]. In the Uropodina (Mesostigmata): a ridge running from the medial face of coxa IV postero-laterally through the metapodal region.

METAPODAL PLATES. [Gr. μετα, after; πους, foot]. Small sclerotized structures posterior to coxae IV that may denote muscle insertions. They may be circular, but more commonly are irregularly elongate and divided into two. They may be absent or incorporated into a ventrianal or holoventral shield.

METAPODAL SHIELDS. [Gr. μετα, after; πους, foot]. In the Mesostigmata: a pair of small sclerites posteriad to coxae IV in the ventral region. They may be for muscle attachments.

METAPODOSOMA. [Gr. μετα, after; πους, foot; σωμα, body]. In ticks and mites: the segment of the podosoma that bears the third and fourth pair of legs.

METAPODOSOME. [Gr. μετα, after; πους, foot; σωμα, body]. In ticks and mites: the body region between the third and fourth pairs of legs.

METASARCIDAE. [Gr. μετα, after; σαρξ, flesh]. A small family of harvestmen or daddy longlegs (suborder Laniatores, superfamily Gonyleptoidea). They were previously a subfamily (Metasarcinae) of the **Gonyleptidae**.

METASITISM. [Gr. μετα, after; σιτος, food]. Having a cannibalistic life style.

METASOMA (METASOME). [Gr. μετα, after; σωμα, body]. In general, the posterior region of the invertebrate body. In arachnids and some crustaceans: the posterior region of the opisthosoma ('abdomen') which, in scorpions for example, forms a flexible tail which bears the terminal sting.

METASOMATIC. [Gr. μετα, after; σωμα, body]. Of, or situated in the metasoma.

METASTERNAL SETAE. [Gr. μετα, after; σταρνον, chest]. In the Mesostigmata: the intercoxal setae (st4 or MS) added in the deutonymph stage. They are often borne on metasternal platelets and sometimes on the sternal shield or in soft cuticle in the adult female.

METASTERNAL SHIELD (PLATELET). [Gr. μετα, after; σταρνον, chest]. The small, usually teardrop to subtriangular shields that bear the metasternal setae (st4). They are sometimes fused to the sternal shield or the endopodal shields.

METASTERNITE. [Gr. μετα, after; σταρνον, chest]. In scorpions: a plate formed by the fusion of the sterna between the bases of the hind limbs.

METASTERNUM. [Gr. μετα, after; σταρνον, chest]. In ticks and mites: the sternum of the fourth segment of the podosoma.

METASTHENIC. [Gr. μετα, after; σθενος, strength]. Having a well developed posterior region.

METASTIGMATA. [Gr. μετα, after; στιγμη, mark]. In a previous classification: a suborder of large parasitic 'soft' and 'hard' ticks (subclass Arachnida, superorder Parasitiformes) in which the mouth bears recurved teeth modified for piercing. A tracheal spiracle is located behind the third or fourth pair of coxae. The members of this grouping are now distributed between the orders Ixodida and Mesostigmata.

METASTIGMATE. [Gr. μετα, after; στιγμη, mark]. In mites: having posterior tracheal openings or stigmata.

METASTOMA (METASTOME). [Gr. μετα, after; στομα, mouth]. In general: any organ or region behind the mouth.

METASTRIATA. [Gr. μετα, after; L. *stria*, furrow]. One of two subdivision of the **Ixodidae** based on the presence or absence of anal grooves extending anterior to, or surrounding, the anus. The Metastriata (absence) contains all genera except *Ixodes*, which is in the subdivision Prostriata (presence).

METATARSUS. [Gr. μετα, after; ταρσος, sole of foot]. In spiders: the first dactylopodite or basitarsus, between the tibia and the tarsus. See also Limb.

METELATTOSIS. [Gr. μετα, after; ελαττων, smaller]. In the Chelicerata: the occurrence of inhibition at any level of the ontogeny, other than the first. See also Calyptostasic.

METOPION. [Gr. μετωπιον, the forehead]. The point where the mid-sagittal plane intersects with an imaginary line connecting the frontal eminences.

MICANS. [L. *micans*, flashing/gleaming]. Shining. Also of a surface of which only parts are shining.

MICROARTHROPOD. [Gr. μικρος, small; + Arthropod]. A minute arthropod, typically used to refer to soil-inhabiting arthropods with bodies under some arbitrary length (e.g. 1 cm, 5 mm). Part of the Microbiota.

MICROBIOTA. [Gr. μικρος, small; βιωναι, to live]. The organisms of microscopic size in a community or region, especially in the soil. See also Mesobiota, Macrobiota.

MICROCHAETA. [Gr. μικρος, small; χαετη, hair]. A small bristle.

MICROCHARMIDAE. [Gr. μικρος, small; χαρμη, lust for battle]. A small family of scorpions (order Scorpiones, superfamily Buthoidea) from Central Africa, Madagascar, and caves of France, Spain, and Ecuador. Members of this family were previously in the Buthidae

MICROCLIMATE. [Gr. μικρος, small; κλιμα, slope]. The climate of a very small (or micro-) habitat.

MICROENDEMIC. [Gr. μικρος, small; ενδημος, dwelling in]. Restricted to a very small region.

MICROFAUNA. [Gr. μικρος, small; L. *Faunus*, god of the woods]. Animals less than 200 μm long (the limit of comfortable vision of the unaided human eye). See also Macrofauna, Meiofauna, Mesofauna.

MICROGYNIOIDEA. [Gr. μικρος, small; γυνη, woman]. A superfamily of mites (suborder Monogynaspida, infraorder Uropodina). Families: **Nothogynidae, Microgyniidae.** This superfamily was previously included in the now-abandoned suborder Microgyniina.

MICROHABITAT (BIOTOPE). [Gr. μικρος, small; L. *habitare*, to inhabit]. A particular location within a habitat where an individual species is normally found. The location of a parasite within a host's body. A place where organisms can survive.

MICROHEXURIDAE. [Gr. μικρος, small; εξ, six; ουρα, tail]. A monospecific family of tiny spiders (infraorder Mygalomorphae, superfamily Avicularioidea) from North America.

MICROLECITHAL. [Gr. μικρος, small; λεκιθος, yolk]. Of an egg that contains very little yolk. See also Alecithal, Centrolecithal, Heterolecithal, Macrolecithal, Mediolecithal, Meiolecithal, Mesolecithal, Oligolecithal, Polylecithal, Telolecithal.

MICRONESIA. [Gr. μικρος, small; νησος, island]. In the warmer part of the western Pacific ocean: an assemblage of many small oceanic islands that is a recognized geographical and ethnological area and which is sometimes considered to be distinct from Polynesia.

MICROPARAPATRIC. [Gr. μικρος, small; παρα beside, πατηρ, father]. Of populations that exist in adjacent habitats in the same locality so that gene flow is possible between them.

MICROPREDATOR. [Gr. μικρος, small; L. *praedator*, plunderer]. An organism that predates larger organisms, to which it attaches itself.

MICROSPECIES (JORDANON, JORDAN'S SPECIES). [Gr. μικρος, small; L. *species*, particular kind]. A true breeding unit below the level of species, i.e. subspecies, race or variety.

MICROSPLANCHNIC. [Gr. μικρος, small; σπλαγχνον, entrails]. Having a small body with long legs, as in Opiliones (daddy longlegs).

MICROSTIGMATIDAE. [Gr. μικρος, small; στιγμη, mark]. A small family of ground-dwelling spiders that make little use of silk (infraorder Mygalomorphae, superfamily Avicularioidea).

MICROSTOME. [Gr. μικρος, small; στομα, mouth]. Any small opening.

MICROSYMBIONT (MICROSYMBIOTE). [Gr. μικρος, small; συμβιοτης, companion]. The smaller of two symbiotic organisms.

MICROTHELYPHONIDA. [Gr. μικρος, small; θηλυς, female; φωνη; voice]. See Palpigradi.

MICROTRICHIA. [Gr. μικρος, small; θριξ, hair]. Small hair-like or tooth-like processes.

MICROTUBERCLE. [Gr. μικρος, small; L. *tuberculum*, small hump]. A minute tubercle or tooth-like process

MICROVILLI. [Gr. μικρος, small; L. *villus*, shaggy hair]. Small, finger-like projections which are found in large numbers on the free surfaces of many cells. They increase the surface-area-to-volume ratio and have an absorptive function, as in the brush border on the intestinal epithelium.

MICROWHIP SCORPIONS. See Palpigradi.

MICROZETOIDEA. [Gr. μικρος, small; ζητησις; seeking]. A monotypic superfamily of mites (suborder Oribatida, infraorder Brachypylina - section Poronoticae). Family: **Microzetidae.**

MIDDLE ARTICLE. [AS. *middel*, middle; L. *articulus*, a part]. In arachnids: the middle of the three cheliceral segments. In the Acariformes it is often the basal segment.

MIDDLE DIVISION. [AS. *middel*, middle]. The region of the bulb of the male palpus that comprises the tegulum and associated structures.

MIDDORSAL (DORSOMEDIAN). [AS. *middel*, middle; L. *dorsum*, back]. Of the true dorsal line of an individual.

MIGIDAE. [Gr. μιγας, mixed pell-mell]. The family of tree trapdoor spiders (infraorder Mygalomorphae, superfamily Avicularioidea) from South America, Africa and Australia, Madagascar, New Zealand and New Caledonia.

MIGOIDEA. [Gr. μιγας, mixed pell-mell]. In a previous classification: a superfamily of spiders (suborder Opisthothelae, infraorder Mygalomorphae) that united the families **Actinopodidae** and **Migidae**; which are now in the superfamily Avicularioidea.

MILIARY. [L. *milium*, millet]. Having a granular appearance or consisting of small grains or grain-like structures.

MILLEPUNCTATUS. [L. *mille*, a thousand; *punctum*, dot/spot]. Covered or studded with many dots, points, or minute depressions.

MIMESIS. [Gr. μιμησις, imitation]. Mimicry.

MIMETIC. [Gr. μιμητικος, imitative]. Exhibiting mimicry. I.e. when a species resembles another species or some other object in appearance but not in structure and other characters.

MIMETIC POLYMORPHISM. [Gr. μιμητικος, imitative; πολυς, many; μορφα, shape]. A polymorphism in which the various morphs resemble unpalatable species in order to deceive a predator. See also Mimicry.

MIMETIDAE. [Gr. μιμητικος, imitative]. A family of eight-eyed pirate spiders (infraorder Araneomorphae, superfamily Entelegynae) and bear a characteristic row of large setae on the first pair of legs. Some species may lie in wait for their prey, others actively invade webs and others lure males of prey species to their deaths by mimicking their mating rituals. Previously in the superfamily Mimetoidea.

MIMETOIDEA. [Gr. μιμητικος, imitative]. In a previous classification, a superfamily of shield spiders and pirate spiders (order Araneae, suborder Araneomorphae) that united the families: **Malkaridae**, **Mimetidae**. These families are now in the superfamily Entelegynae.

MIMIC. [Gr. μιμικος, imitating]. To assume the habits, colors or structures of another organism for protection or deceit.

MIMICRY. [Gr. μιμικος, imitating]. **Aggressive Mimicry (Peckhammian Mimicry)**. A form of mimicry in which a predator comes to resemble a non-predator and so deceives its prey. **Automimicry**. A type of protective mimicry in which palatable members of a species come to resemble unpalatable members of the same species. This is a frequency-dependent polymorphism and the unpalatable members of the species must be more abundant (hence more frequently encountered) that the palatable. **Batesian Mimicry**. A defensive strategy adopted by animals whereby a palatable and harmless species comes to resemble a harmful (i.e. poisonous, distasteful or otherwise dangerous) species, and thus is avoided by the predator. **Mertensian Mimicry**. A type of mimicry in which a fatally offensive species comes to resemble a moderately offensive species. Due to its lethality, the fatal form cannot be the model because it does not allow learning on the part of the predator. **Müllerian Mimicry**. A form of mimicry in which one distasteful or harmful species comes to resemble another similarly distasteful or harmful species. Both species gain from developing the same warning coloration since predators learn to avoid both after tasting either one. This form of mimicry was first described by Fritz Müller in relation to insects in South America. See also Sematic.

MIMOTYPE. [Gr. μιμικος, imitating; τυπος, pattern]. A form that is phenotypically, but not genotypically, similar to another and may occupy a similar niche but in a different geographical area.

MINIATE, MINIATUS. [L. *miniatus*, vermilion/scarlet]. Of the color of red lead.

MINOR DUCT. In those mesostigmatans with the phytoseiid-type of sperm access system; a fine tube originating at the atrium and usually becoming indistinct distally. See also Major Duct.

MIRATEMNIIDAE. See **Atemnidae**.

MIRE. [ME. *myre*, from Gmc. *meus*, moss]. A wetland region, especially a peaty area.

MISOGAMY. [Gr. μισειν, to hate; γαμος, marriage]. Reproductive isolation. Antagonism to mating.

MITES. See Acari.

MITURGIDAE. [Gr. μιτο–εργος, working the thread]. The family of medium to large nocturnal prowling spiders (infraorder Araneomorphae, superfamily Entelegynae). They are of agricultural importance as they are known to prey on caterpillars and various flies. In some classifications the **Zoridae** are included here as a subfamily.

MIXONOMATA. [Gr. μιξις, mixing; νωμα, brands/owner's marks]. An infraorder of beetle mites or armored mites (order Sarcoptiformes, suborder Oribatida). Superfamilies in Section Dichosomata: Epilohmannioidea, Eulohmannioidea, Nehypochthonioidea, Perlohmannioidea. Superfamilies in Section Euptyctima: Euphthiracaroidea, Phthiracaroidea.

MOA. Median Ocular Area.

MODIOLIFORM. [L. *modiolus*, a small measure or drinking vessel; *forma*, shape]. Of a structure in the form of the hub of a wheel; i.e. more or less globular with truncated ends.

MOLAR. [L. *mola*, mill]. Adapted for grinding.

MONEY SPIDERS. See **Linyphiidae**.

MONKEY SPIDERS. See Mygalomorphae.

MONOCHROMATIC. [Gr. μονος, single; χρωμα, color]. Having only one color, or being color blind.

MONOCHRONIC. [Gr. μονος, single; χρονος, time]. Occurring only once.

MONOCYCLIC PARTHENOGENESIS. [Gr.μονος, single; κυκλος, circle; παρθενος, virgin; γενεσις, birth]. See Parthenogenesis.

MONODACTYL, MONODACTYLE, MONODACTYLOUS. [Gr. μονος, single; δακτυλος, finger]. Of any appendage, ambulacrum or claw with only one unguis. See also Bidactyl, Heterodactyl, Homodactyl, Tridactyl.

MONODESMATIC. [Gr. μονος, single; δεσμος, a band]. In the Chelicerata: of an articulation between two segments of an appendage where one tendon is inserted at the base of the distal segment.

MONOGAMY, MONOGAMOUS. [Gr. μονος, single; γαμος, marriage]. Mating of a pair with no other sexual partners. See also Polygamy.

MONOGONEUTIC. [Gr. μονος, single; γονευειν, to produce]. Breeding once a year.

MONOGYNASPIDA. [Gr. μονος, single; γυνη, woman; ασπις, shield]. In some classifications: a suborder (superorder Parasitiformes, order Mesostigmata) of parasitic and free-living mites that are characterized by having a single genital shield in the adult female that usually bears one pair of setae (st5) or may be bare. This group is divided into four cohorts: Gamasina, Heatherellina, Microgyniina, Uropodina. In more recent classifications the suborder Monogynaspida is divided into two infraorders: Gamasina, Uropodina.

MONOMENISCOUS. [Gr. μονος, single; μηνισκος, small moon]. Of an eye with only one lens.

MONOMERI. [Gr. μονος, single, μερος, part]. Having one-jointed tarsi.

MONOMERIC. [Gr. μονος, single, μερος, part]. Of one segment or being derived from one part.

MONOMEROUS. [Gr. μονος, single, μερος, part]. Having only one joint or part.

MONOMIAL. [Gr. μονος, single; L. *nomen*, name]. In taxonomy: a name or designation that consists of only one term. See also Nomenclature.

MONOMORPHIC. [Gr. μονος, single; μορφη, form]. Being the same as other members of the species, either morphologically, biochemically or in terms of DNA. See also Polymorphous.

MONOMORPHIC POPULATION. [Gr. μονος, single; μορφη, form]. A population in which only one trait of a potentially variable set is expressed due to fixation of that one allelic form.

MONOMORPHISM. [Gr. μονος, single; μορφη, form]. 1. A population that exhibits a single form. See also Polymorphism. 2. Of species that contain only the female sex. See also Dimorphism.

MONONEMIC. [Gr. μονος, single; νημα, thread]. Single-stranded.

MONONT. [Gr. μονος, single; ov, being]. An individual that reproduces without conjugation.

MONONYCHOUS. [Gr. μονος, single; ονυξ, claw]. Having a single or uncleft claw.

MONOPARENTAL. [Gr. μονος, single; L. parens, progenitor]. Having, or being derived from, a single parent.

MONOPHAGOUS. [Gr. μονος, single; φαγος, -eating]. Existing on only one kind of food or source of nourishment. See also Euryphagous, Polyphagous, Stenophagous.

MONOPHYLETIC (MONOPHYLY). [Gr. μονος, single; φυλη, tribe]. Of a group of taxa which share a common ancestry and are ultimately derived from a single interbreeding (Mendelian) population. For example, the families in an order would all be monophyletic if they were all descended from the same family or lower taxonomic unit, or more strictly from a single species. See also Phylogenetic Classification.

MONOPLACID. [Gr. μονος, single; πλαξ, flat plate]. Bearing only one plate.

MONOSCUTIDAE. [Gr. μονος, single; L. scutum, shield]. A family of small harvestmen or daddy longlegs (suborder Eupnoi, superfamily Phalangioidea) from Australia and New Zealand. Most species are colored in shades of brown to black, and the male chelicerae are enormously enlarged.

MONOSTICHOUS. [Gr. μονος, single; στιχος, row]. Arranged in one row or along one side of an axis.

MONOSTIGMATOUS. [Gr. μονος, single; στιγμα, mark]. Having one stigma only.

MONOSY. [Gr. μονος, alone]. The separation of parts that are normally fused.

MONOSYMMETRICAL. [Gr. μονος, single; συμμετρια, symmetry]. See Zygomorphic.

MONOTAXIC. [Gr. μονος, single; ταξις, an arranging]. Belonging to the same taxonomic group.

MONOTHALAMOUS. [Gr. μονος, single; θαλαμος, chamber]. Unilocular. Single chambered.

MONOTHECAL. [Gr. μονος, single; θηκη, case]. Having one chamber or loculus.

MONOTHELY, MONOTHELIOUS. [Gr. μονος, single; θηλυς, female]. Of one female mating with more than one male. Polyandry.

MONOTROPHIC. [Gr. μονος, single; τροφη, nourishment]. Existing on only one kind of food.

MONOTYPIC. [Gr. μονος, single; μονος, single]. Of a taxon that contains only one immediately subordinate taxon. Thus a monotypic superfamily would contain only one family.

MONOVALENT ARTICULATION. [Gr. μονος, single; L. valere, to be strong; articulus, joint]. Articulation permitting movement in one mode only; forward and backward, but not up and down, etc.

MONOVARIAL. [Gr. μονος, single; L. ovum, egg; arium, a place where something is kept]. Having one ovary.

MONOXENOUS. [Gr. μονος, single; ξενος, guest]. See Autoecious.

MONTANE. [L. mons, mountain]. Of mountains and the coniferous forests of mountains.

MONTICOLOUS. [L. mons, mountain; colere, to inhabit]. Inhabiting mountainous regions.

MOOR. [ME. *mor*, moor]. An acidic upland, usually peat, community which is often dominated by low-growing heaths and heathers with some areas dominated by grasses and sedges.

MOR. [Da. *mor*, humus]. An acid humus of cold wet soils composed of several layer of organic matter in various stages of decomposition. Animal and plant remains are visible and there is very little microbial activity except by fungi.

MORES. [L. *mores*, customs/habits]. Groups of organisms that prefer the same habitat, have the same reproductive season and agree in their general reactions to the physical environment. See also Mune.

MORIBUND. [L. *moribundus*, dying]. Dying. Near to death.

MORIFORM. [L. *morum*, mulberry; *forma*, shape]. Shaped like a mulberry.

MORPH. [Gr. μορφη, form]. One of the members of a polymorphic population.

MORPHALLAXIS. [Gr. μορφη, form; αλλαξις, exchange]. Regeneration. Transformation of one part into another. Gradual growth or development into a particular form.

MORPHISM. See Polymorphism.

MORPHOMETRY. [Gr. μορφη, form; μετρειν, to measure]. The analysis of measurements of external dimensions and structures.

MORPHOSIS. [Gr. μορφωσις, form]. The manner of the development of tissues or part of an organism.

MORPHOSPECIES. [Gr. μορφη, form; L. *species*, particular kind]. A group of individuals that differ in some morphological respect from all other groups or are considered to belong to a particular species on morphological grounds only.

MOTTLED (MACULATED, BLOTCHED). [AFr. *motteley*, diversified in color]. Spotted with different colors.

MOLT, MOLTING. [L. *mutare*, to change]. See Ecdysis.

MOLTING GLANDS (ECDYSIAL GLANDS). [L. *mutare*, to change]. Glands in the skin which exude a liquefying enzyme that breaks down the endocuticle, thus facilitating the shedding of the two outer layers (exocuticle and epicuticle). See also Ecdysis.

MOLTING HORMONE. See Ecdysones.

MOUND NEST. A nest or part of one built above ground.

MOUTH PARTS (OF ARTHROPODS). The modified appendages that are used in feeding. They may be modified to form a piercing stylet or a sucking proboscis. The blood-sucking ticks usually have an elongated proboscis, whilst the free-living mites have mouth parts which are clawed or sensory. See also Chelicerae, Feeding, Gnathosoma, Hypostoma et seq., Infracapitulum, Labium, Lingua, Mystax, Palp, Prechelicerae, Promuscidate, Prostomiate, Rima, Siphonostomatous, Stenostomatous, Stomatogenesis.

MOVABLE DIGIT. The most distal article of the chelicera, the cheliceral apotele. It usually bears teeth and a distal hook and, in chelate-dentate forms, is opposed to the fixed digit. When the fixed digit is regressed the movable digit may be saw-like, knife-like or needle-like.

MOVABLE FINGER. The dactyl of the chela.

M.S. 1. In the Araneae: median spinnerets. The typical small, innermost pair of spinnerets. 2. In ticks and mites: metasternal seta (st4).

MUCID. [L. *mucidus*, mucus-like]. Moldy, slimy.

MUCIFIC (MUCIPAROUS). [L. *mucus*, mucus; *facere* to make]. Mucus-secreting.

MUCIFORM. [L. *mucus*, mucus; *forma*, shape]. Resembling, or behaving like mucus.

MUCIGEN (MUCINOGEN). [L. *mucus*, mucus; -γενης, producing]. In mucus glands: the granules or globules from which mucus is produced.

MUCILAGES. [L. *mucus*, mucus]. The sticky or slimy substances produced by many animals and plants. They are usually complex heterosaccharides and are capable of absorbing water to become swollen and slimy but become hard on drying. On hydrolysis they produce mixtures of hexoses, pentoses and uronic acids.

MUCILAGINOUS. [L. *mucus*, mucus]. Composed of, containing or resembling mucilage. Applied to various joints, cells, ducts, glands, canals, etc.

MUCIN. [L. *mucus*, mucus]. A general name for any of a group of widely distributed mucoproteins secreted by mucus producing cells or glands.

MUCINOGEN. See Mucigen.

MUCIPAROUS. [L. *mucus*, mucus; *parere*, to beget]. See Mucific.

MUCOREOUS. [L. *mucor*, mold]. Appearing to be moldy. Of a surface covered with small fringe-like processes.

MUCOSA. See Mucous Membrane.

MUCOUS GLANDS. [L. *mucus*, mucus]. Any of many of the glands that secrete mucus.

MUCOUS MEMBRANE (MUCOSA). [L. *mucus*, mucus]. In general; any moist membrane consisting of an epithelium, commonly ciliated, underlain by connective tissue.

MUCRO (MUCRON). [L. *mucro*, sharp]. Any stiff or sharp point that terminates an organ.

MUCRONIFEROUS (MUCRONATE). [L. *mucro*, sharp; *ferre*, to bear]. Of some organ abruptly terminated by a sharp point.

MUCRONULATE. [L. *mucro*, sharp]. Ending with a small, sharp point.

MUCULENT. [L. *mucus*, mucus]. Mucus-like, or containing mucus.

MUCUS. [L. *mucus*, mucus]. A slimy substance, rich in mucin or other viscous substances, that is produced by the goblet cells of a mucous membrane or by the mucous glands of a cell which are usually located in epithelial structures. A similar slimy secretion produced by the external body surface of many animals.

MÜLLERIAN ASSOCIATION. [*F. Müller*, German Naturalist]. A grouping of different species at a particular location, all of which display aposematic coloration.

MÜLLERIAN MIMICRY. [*F. Müller*, German Naturalist]. See Mimicry.

MULTIARTICULATE (POLYARTHRIC). [L. *multus*, many; *articulus*, joint]. Having many articulations. Many jointed.

MULTIAXIAL (MULTAXIAL). [L. *multus*, many; *axis*, axis]. Of several axes that permit movement in many planes.

MULTICAMERATE. [L. *multus*, many; *camera*, chamber]. Having many chambers.

MULTICARINATE. [L. *multus*, many; *carina*, keel]. Having many ridges or carinae.

MULTICOSTATE. [L. *multus*, many; *costa*, rib]. Having many ridges.

MULTIFARIOUS. [L. *multifarius*, many and various]. Arranged in several rows. See Polystichous.

MULTIFASCICULI. [L. *multus*, many; *multifasiculus*, many small bundles.]. Containing many fasciculi.

MULTIFID. [L. *multus*, many; *multifidus*, cloven into many parts]. Having many clefts or divisions.

MULTIGYRATE. [L. *multus*, many; *gyrus*, ring]. Having many gyri (circles, circular structures). Tortuous.

MULTILAMINATE. [L. *multus*, many; *lamina*, plate]. Constructed of several to many laminae (layers).

MULTILOBATE (MULTILOBAR). [L. *multus*, many; *lobus*, lobe]. Composed of several to many lobes.

MULTILOBULATE. [L. *multus*, many; *lobus*, lobe]. Bearing several to many lobes.

MULTINODAL (MULTINODATE). [L. *multus*, many; *nodus*, knot]. Having many nodes or node-like structures.

MULTINOMIAL. [L. *multus*, many; *nomen*, name]. Of a name or designation composed of several names or terms. See also Trinomial, Nomenclature.

MULTIOCULAR. [L. *multus*, many; *oculus*, eye]. Having many eyes.

MULTIPARASITISM. [L. *multus*, many; Gr. παρασιτος, parasite]. The concurrent parasitism of an organism by two or more parasites of different species.

MULTIPAROUS. [L. *multus*, many; *parere*, to beget]. 1. Producing several or more offspring at one time. 2. Having produced more than one previous brood. See also Parity, Pluriparous.

MULTIPARTITE. [L. *multus*, many; *partitis*, divided]. Divided into many parts.

MULTIPERFORATE. [L. *multus*, many; *perforare*, to bore through]. Having several to many perforations.

MULTIPLICATE. [L. *multiplicare*, to make many]. Consisting of many folds or plicae.

MULTIPOROUS. [L. *multus*, many; Gr. πορος, passage]. Having several to many pores.

MULTIRADIATE. [L. *multus*, many; *radius*, ray]. Many-rayed.

MULTIRAMOUS. [L. *multus*, many; *ramus*, branch]. Many branched.

MULTISEPTATE. [L. *multus*, many; *septum*, partition]. Having several to many divisions or septa.

MULTISERIAL. [L. *multus*, many; *series*, a row]. Having many series or rows.

MULTISERIATE (MULTISERIAL). [L. *multus*, many; *series*, row]. Arranged in many rows.

MULTISETIFEROUS. [L. *multus*, many; *seta*, bristle; *ferre*, to bear]. With many setae.

MULTISPINOSE. [L. *multus*, many; *spina*, thorn]. With many spines.

MULTISPIRAL. [L. *multus*, many; *spira*, a coil]. With numerous whorls.

MULTISTRIATE. [L. *multus*, many; *stria*, furrow]. With many striations. With numerous thread-like lines, grooves or scratches.

MULTISULACTE. [L. *multus*, many; *sulcus*, furrow]. Greatly furrowed.

MULTITUBERCULATE. [L. *multus*, many; *tuberculum*, small swelling]. Having several to many small protuberances, or prominences.

MULTIVOLTINE. [L. *multus*, many; It. *volta*, time]. Of an animal that produces more than one brood per year. See also Voltine.

MUMMUCIIDAE. [L. *Mummius Plancus*, a Roman commander who destroyed and looted Corinth]. A small family of sun spiders (subclass Arachnida, order Solifugae) from South America.

MUNE. [L. *munus*, function]. A group of organisms with a shared characteristic behavioral response. See also Mores.

MURAL LACUNA. [L. *murus*, wall; *lacuna*, cavity]. A Pustule. A blister-like prominence.

MURICATE. [L. *muricatus*, having sharp points]. Of some structure formed with sharp points or covered with sharp outgrowths.

MURIFORM. [L. *murus*, wall; *forma*, shape]. Resembling a brick wall.

MURINE, MURINUS. [L. *muris*, a mouse or rat]. Mouse-colored.

MUSCICOLINE. [L. *muscus*, moss; *colere* to inhabit]. Living among mosses.

MUSCLE. [L. *musculus*, muscle]. A fibrous cellular tissue arranged as sheets or bundles and which is capable of contraction. There are three general types of muscle: voluntary (striated), involuntary (smooth) and cardiac (heart). **Smooth muscle** lacks sarcomeres and is derived from embryonic mesenchyme and develops in association with connective tissue cells and (for example) lines the gut, trachea, and circulatory vessels. Histologically the muscle fibers appear smooth and there is no cross banding as seen in striated muscle. **Striated muscle** is derived in the main from the myotomes of the embryo and in general attaches to and moves limbs. The muscle fiber surface is covered by the sarcolemma and each cell is innervated by a nerve fiber ending in close contact. Striated muscle cells are arranged in parallel to form muscles, and connective tissue fibers run between the muscle fibers, bind them together, form sheaths of fiber bundles (fascicles) and form an external sheath (the perimysium) for the muscle as a whole. Striated muscles are able to contract rapidly and are particularly associated with voluntary movements. **Cardiac muscle** is unique to the heart. Embryologically it is a special type of smooth musculature but there are no separate fibers; instead the whole heart musculature is a continuous network of dividing and recombining strands. See also Muscle Terminology.

MUSCLE COUPLES. [L. *musculus*, muscle]. Pairs of muscles that act in opposition such that when one contracts the other relaxes and vice versa.

MUSCLE TERMINOLOGY. [L. *musculus*, muscle]. **Abductor**, draws a segment outwards. **Accessorius**, any muscle aiding the action of another. **Adductor**, draws a segment inwards. **Aponerosis** or **Fascia**, the flat sheet of connective tissue which terminates a muscle and forms the connection with the anchor point. **Belly**, the fleshy mass of a muscle. **Depressor**, lowers a structure. **Dilator**, opens a structure. **Extensor**, acts to open out a joint (absent in arachnids). **Flexor**, acts to close a joint. **Levator**, raises a structure. **Occlusor**, closes a structure (such as an operculum). **Phasic**, a general term for muscles which cause movement by a lever system, as in limb muscles. **Pronator**, rotates the distal region of a limb towards a prone position, i.e. with the undersurface down. **Protractor**, extends a part or draws it out or away from the body. **Retractor**, withdraws by contraction, bringing the part attached to it towards the body. **Retrahens**, draws a part backwards. **Rotator**, twists a limb segment. **Sphincter** or **Constrictor**, contracts to close an orifice, such as the entrance and exit to the stomach. **Supinator**, rotates the distal region of a limb towards a supine position, i.e. with the undersurface up. **Tendon**, the connective tissue that connects muscle to its anchor point.

MUSCULARIS. [L. *musculus*, muscle]. A muscular sheath surrounding the alimentary canal.

MUSCULATURE. [L. *musculus*, muscle]. The system or arrangement of muscles as a whole.

MUTICATE (MUTICOUS). [L. *muticus*, curtailed]. Without defensive structures.

MUTILOUS. [L. *mutilus*, harmless]. Without defensive structures such as claws, teeth, horns etc.

MUTUALISM. [L. *mutuus*, reciprocal]. Any interaction between two species that benefits both. In a strict sense, obligatory mutualism in which neither can survive under natural conditions without the other.

MYGALOMORPHAE (ORTHOGNATHA). [Gr. mugalh, field mouse; morfh, form]. An infraorder of spiders (order Araneae, suborder Opisthothelae) in which there are two pairs of book lungs, two pairs of coxal glands, three-segmented posterior spinners and the plane of articulation of the fangs is the same as the long axis of the body; thus at rest they are folded along this axis and many species use them for digging burrows (*c.f.* Araneomorphae). Most of the larger species are commonly, but incorrectly, known as tarantulas; some have hairs which produce a urtica-like (nettle-like) rash and some are venomous but less dangerous than is generally believed. Most species occur in Australia. Superfamilies: Atypoidea, Avicularioidea.

MYOBIOIDEA. [Gr. μυς, a mouse]. A monotypic superfamily of mites (suborder Prostigmata, infraorder Eleutherengona). Family: **Myobiidae**.

MYRMECOMORPHS. [Gr. μυρμηξ, ant; μορφα, form]. Ant-mimicking spiders, e,g, *Myrmarachne plataleoides* – **Salticidae**. Many species mimic ants commonly for predator evasion, occasionally for preying on ants.

MYRMECOPHILOUS. [Gr. μυρμηξ, ant; φιλος, loving]. Of ant-mimicking spiders that thrive in association with ants.

MYRMOCHERNETIDAE. See **Chernetidae**.

MYSTACINE. [Gr. μυσταξ, moustache]. Bearded. Having tactile hairs or vibrissae.

MYSMENIDAE. [Gr. μυσις, closing; μηνα, the moon]. A cosmopolitan family of small (ca. 0.75-3 mm) orb-weaving spiders (infraorder Araneomorphae, superfamily Entelegynae).

MYSTAX. [Gr. μυσταξ, moustache]. A group of hairs above the mouth.

N

NAIL. [AS. *naegel*, nail]. A tarsal claw. An unguis.

NAKED. [AS. *nacod*, nude]. Lacking the usual covering.

NAMATIUM. [Gr. ναματιον, little stream]. A brook or stream community.

NAMATOPHILUS. [Gr. ναμα, stream; φιλος, poet. -loving]. Thriving in brooks and streams.

NANANDER. [Gr. νανος, dwarf; ανηρ, male]. A dwarf male.

NANHERMANNIOIDEA. [Gr. νανος, dwarf; *Jean-Frédéric Hermann*, French Arachnologist]. A monotypic superfamily of mites (suborder Oribatida, infraorder Brachypylina - section Pycnonoticae). Family: **Nanhermanniidae.**

NANOID. [Gr. νανωδης, dwarfish]. Dwarf-like.

NARIFORM. [L. *nares*, nostrils; *forma*, shape]. Nostril-shaped.

NASO. [L. *nasus*, nose]. In ticks and mites: an acronal protuberance at the anterior of the body which overhangs the chelicerae.

NATAL. [L. *natalis*, pert. birth]. Of birth or birth place.

NATAL DISPERSAL. See Dispersal.

NATALITY. [L. *natalis*, pert. birth]. Birth rate. The number of offspring produced per female or head of population per unit time.

NATANT. [L. *natare*, to swim]. Floating on the surface of water.

NATATORIAL. [L. *natare*, to swim]. Adapted for swimming.

NATATORY. [L. *natare*, to swim]. Swimming habitually.

NAVICULAR. [L. *navicula*, small ship]. Boat-shaped. Cymbiform. Scaphoid.

NEALOGY. [Gr. νεαλης, youthful; λογος, discourse]. The scientific study of young animals.

NEARCTIC FAUNAL REGION. [Gr. νεος, new; αρκτικος, northern; L. *Faunus*, god of the woods]. The zoogeographical region comprising America north of the northern edge of the Mexican tropical rain forest, including Greenland, and having borders with the Arctic Ocean to the north, the Bering Strait and Pacific Ocean to the west and the Atlantic Ocean to the east. Thus it extends from about 20°N to about 83°N.

NECROTIC ARACHNIDISM. [Gr. νεκροσις, becoming dead; αραχνης, spider]. The result of envenomation by a spider such as *Loxosceles* spp., in which the toxin attacks the body tissues.

NEHYPOCHTHONIOIDEA. [Gr. νεος, new; χθων, the earth]. A monotypic superfamily of mites (suborder Oribatida, infraorder Mixonomata - section Dichosomata). Family: **Nehypochthoniidae.**

NEMASTOMATIDAE. [Gr. νημα, thread; στομα, mouth]. A family of harvestmen (suborder Dyspnoi, superfamily Troguloidea) in which the pedipalps are very elongated and thin in some groups.

NEMASTOMOIDIDAE. [Gr. νημα, thread; στομα, mouth]. An extinct family of harvestmen (suborder Dyspnoi, superfamily Troguloidea) known from Carboniferous of Commentry in northern France, and Illinois (USA).

NEMATALYCOIDEA. [Gr. νημα, thread; λυκος, wolf]. A superfamily of mites (suborder Endeostigmata, infraorder Nematalycina). This superfamily is sometimes included in the infraorder Eupodina: Families: **Micropsammidae, Nematalycidae, Proteonematalycidae.**

NEMATOID (NEMEOUS). [Gr. νημα, thread; ειδος, form]. Thread-like, filamentous.

NEMESIIDAE. [Gr. Νεμεσις, Greek myth. the impersonation of divine wrath]. A family of trap door spiders (infraorder Mygalomorphae, superfamily Avicularioidea) from South America, South Africa, Asia and Australia. They are relatively large, brown, elongated spiders with robust legs, and the female *Atmetochilus* can attain over 4 cm in body length. They were formerly included in the **Dipluridae** and the superfamily Nemesioidea.

NEMOROSE (NEMORICOLE, NEMORICOLOUS). [L. *nemorosus*, sylvan]. Inhabiting open woodlands.

NEOBISIIDAE. [Gr. νεος, new; deriv. uncert.]. A family of false scorpions (suborder Iocheirata, superfamily Neobisioidea) from Africa, the Americas and Eurasia. Their pedipalps are very long, and contrary to most other pseudoscorpions the venom gland and duct are located in the immobile finger of each pedipalp, rather than in the moblie one. They usually have four eyes, but some cave-dwelling have two, or none.

NEOBISIOIDEA. [Gr. νεος, new; deriv. uncert.]. A superfamily of false scorpions (order Pseudoscorpiones, suborder Iocheirata). Families: **Bochicidae, Gymnobisiidae, Hyidae, Ideoroncidae, Neobisiidae, Parahyidae, Syarinidae.**

NEOGEIC. [Gr. νεος, new; γαια, earth]. Belonging to the Western Hemisphere or New World. See also Gerontogaeous.

NEOGOVEIDAE. [Gr. νεος, new + Ogoveidae]. A family of small eyeless harvestmen (suborder Cyphophthalmi, infraorder Scopulophthalmi) from the tropical regions of South American and West Africa. They often have a solea on the first pair of tarsi.

NEOLIODOIDEA. [Gr. νεος, new; λειος, smooth]. A monotypic superfamily of mites (suborder Oribatida, infraorder Brachypylina - section Pycnonoticae). Family: **Neoliodidae.**

NEOMORPHOSIS. [Gr. νεος, new; μορφωσις, change]. A type of regenerative process in which the new part is significantly different from any other structure in the body.

NEONATAL (NEONATE). [Gr. νεος, new; L. *natus*, born]. Newly born or recently hatched.

NEOPILIONIDAE. [Gr. νεος, new' + Opiliones]. A family of harvestmen or daddy longlegs (suborder Eupnoi, superfamily Phalangioidea) from Australia, South Africa, and South America. Unusually, some species have a blue pigmentation.

NEORICINULEI. See Ricinulei.

NEOSOMY (NEOSOMIC). [Gr. νεος, new; σωμα, body]. In some acarines: the external transformations that occur during the formation of new cuticle.

NEOSPERMY. [Gr. νεος, new: σπερμα, seed]. In the Mesostigmata: having the derived ribbon-like sperm characteristic of some gamasinans and the **Parasitidae.**

NEOTENY (ENOTEINIA, NEOTEINY, PALAEOGENESIS). [Gr. νεος, young; τεινειν, to extend]. 1. The retention of larval or juvenile characteristics beyond the normal period. 2. The appearance of adult characteristics in the larvae. As the juvenile stages of many organisms are less specialized than the corresponding stage in the adult, such changes in development allow the organism to switch to new evolutionary pathways.

NEOTRICHY. [Gr. νεος, new; τριχος, hair]. In ticks and mites: the secondary formation of setae by multiplication of primary setae in a given area. See also Holotrichy, Hypertrichy.

NEOTROPICAL FAUNAL REGION (NEOTROPICS, NEOGAEA, NEOTROPICAL REALM). [Gr. νεα, new; τροπικος, of the tropics; L. *Faunus*, god of the woods]. South from the coastal area of Baja California and Sinaloa flanking the Gulf of California, to Tierra del Fuego (except the southernmost archipelago), including all the continental shelf islands, the West Indies and the Galapagos Islands. It is one of the six major biogeographic areas of the world defined on the basis of its characteristic animal life, and is divided into forty-seven provinces.

NEPHROID. [Gr. νεφρος, kidney; ειδος, shape]. Kidney-shaped, reniform.

NEPIONIC. [Gr. νηπιος, infant]. Of the postembryonic developmental phase of an individual.

NERITIC ZONE. [Gr. νηριτης, sea-snail]. The marine biological region of an ocean that extends from the low-tide line on the shore to the edge of the continental shelf.

NERITIC. [Gr. νηριτης, sea-snail]. Living only in coastal waters.

NERVATE. [L. *nervus*, sinew]. Having nerves or veins.

NERVATION. [L. *nervus*, sinew]. The arrangement of nerves and veins.

NERVE. [L. *nervus*, sinew]. One of the many fibrous, stimuli-transmitting structures that connect the central nervous system (CNS) with the parts of the body.

NERVOUS SYSTEM. [L. *nervus*, sinew]. The totality of nerves and all their branches. In all multicellular animals except sponges (Porifera) there is a network of nerve cells (neurons) linked together by thread-like branching processes (dendrites) whose endings lie in close proximity to one another and separated by narrow gaps (synapses). The stimulation of a receptor sends an electro-chemical impulse along a nerve fiber to a synapse where it produces a neurotransmitter that initiates an impulse in the neighboring nerve, and so on until the impulse reaches its destination. This is the means by which all the activities of an animal are co-ordinated. In complex animals the cell bodies of the neurones are usually concentrated in a central nervous system but in many simpler animals there is only a network of neurons with no definite center of activity.

NESTICIDAE. [Gr. νεστικος, for spinning]. A family of spiders (infraorder Araneomorphae, superfamily Entelegynae) which construct a web of fine criss-cross threads in dark, damp locations. The main prey seems to be crawling insects.

NEST ROBBING. Kleptobiosis. See Symbiosis.

NETTED. See Reticulate.

NETTED-VEINED. Having veins in the form of a network.

NEURAL. [Gr. νευρον, nerve]. Of something being closely connected with nerves, nervous systems or nervous tissues.

NEUROTOXIC. [Gr. νευρον, nerve; τοξικον, poison]. Of some toxin that attacks nervous tissue, e.g. *Latrodectus* toxin (several widow spiders).

NEUSTON. [Gr. νευστος, floating]. Organisms that float or swim on (epineuston) or under (hyponeuston) the surface film of water.

NICHE. [Fr. *niche*, from It. *nicchia*, a recess in a wall]. The ecological position of an organism in its environment: comprising the habitat, the time it is active there and the resources it obtains there. This term is sometimes used loosely as the equivalent of microhabitat.

NICODAMIDAE. [Gr. νικοδημος, victory of the people]. A small family of small to medium-sized spiders (infraorder Araneomorphae, superfamily Entelegynae) that construct small sheet-webs near the ground in eucalyptus forests.

NIGER. [L. *niger*, black]. Black. Glossy black.

NIGERRIMA. [L. *niger*, black; *-rimus*, superlative ending]. Very black.

NIGRESCENT. [L. *nigrescere*, to turn black]. Blackish, or turning black.

NIGRICANS. [L. *nigrans*, shadowy]. Black, tinged with grey.

NIGROPUNCTATE. [L. *niger*, black; *punctum*, a spot]. With black spots.

NIPHOCEPHEOIDEA. [Gr. νιφας,, snow flake; κεφαλη, head]. A monotypic superfamily of mites (suborder Oribatida, infraorder Brachypylina - section Pycnonoticae). Family: **Niphocepheidae**.

NIPPONONYCHIDAE. [*Nippon*, Japan; Gr. ονυξ, claw]. A small family of harvestmen or daddy longlegs (suborder Laniatores, superfamily Travunioidea) that are endemic to Japan.

NIPPONOPSALIDIDAE. [*Nippon*, Japan; Gr ψαλιδιον, a pair of scissors (from *Ischyropsalis*]. A small family of harvestmen (suborder Dyspnoi, superfamily Troguloidea) from east Asia. They have a domed carapace, with a large low ocularium, and large eyes. The chelicerae are heavily sclerotized and longer than the body, and both the pedipalps and legs are very long and slender.

NITID (NITIDOUS). [L. *nitidus*, shining]. Shiny, glossy, lustrous.

NIVEOUS. [L. *niveus*, snowy]. Resembling the color of snow.

NIVICOLOUS. [L. *nivis*, snow: *colere*, to inhabit]. Living in snow or snow-covered habitats.

NOMENCLATURE. [L. *nomen*, name; *calare*, to call]. The process of creating and defining distinguishing names for animals and plants. The Codes of Nomenclature require that all scientific names be Latin in form, written in the Latin alphabet and subject to the rules of Latin grammar even if, as is often the case, they are derived from other languages. **Binomial (Binary) Nomenclature.** The present method of naming plants and animals scientifically in which they are given two names. The first name (the generic name) designates the Genus to which the plant or animal belongs and the second name (the specific epithet) is particular to the species. The generic name is always capitalized and the specific epithet not, regardless of the derivation of the word; and both names are Latinized. The complete name being italicized in normal text, or underlined in handwritten text. Thus the fat-tailed scorpion *Androctonus amoreuxi* is one species and *Androctonus australis* is another species of the same genus. Strictly, the name of the author responsible for describing the species should be appended, e.g. *Androctonus amoreuxi* (Audouin, 1826), and *Androctonus australis* (Linnaeus, 1758). **Trinomial Nomenclature.** Where subspecies or varieties have been described a trinomial system is commonly used, the third name indicating the subspecies. For example *Heteroscodra crassipes latithorax*, a subspecies of Central African tarantulas. These and other rules form the International Rules of Zoological Nomenclature, with separate rules: the International Code of Nomenclature, for algae, fungi, and plants.
The main **RANKS** are domain (dominus) kingdom (regnum), phylum or division (divisio), class (classis), order (ordo), family (familia), genus and species. Further divisions in the hierarchy are made by prefixes such as sub-, super-, infra-, etc.
-ACEA. [L. *-aceus*, suffix: belonging to]. Used to form the names of classes or orders of animals, as in 'Crustacea' etc.
-IFORMES. [L. *forma*, shape]. A suffix commonly used when a name of an order or suborder of animals is derived from the name of an included family or genus; earlier use favored '-morphae'. Usually a family or genus typical of the order or suborder. E.g. Sarcoptiformes, an order of the Arachnida containing mites and ticks. Nomenclature above the level of superfamily is not governed by the International Code of Zoological Nomenclature.
-OIDEA. [L. *-oideus*, resembling]. In taxonomy: a recommended but not mandatory suffix used to indicate a superfamily of animals (the World Spider Catalogue currently ignores classification above the family level), e.g. Thelyphonoidea, the superfamily that includes the whip scorpions (family Thelyphonoidae).
-OIDEI. [L. *-oideus*, resembling]. Used to form taxonomic names of fish at the level of suborder. E.g. Zeioidei, the suborder of dories (order Zeiformes).
-IDAE. [Gr. -ιδες, a patronymic suffix]. A standard suffix in zoology used to indicate a family. Thus 'Austrodecidae' is a family of sea spiders. (In botanical nomenclature: the ending of a name of a subclass).
-INAE. [L. *-inae -inæ, -ine*; indicating a relationship of position, possession, origin]. A suffix used to denote a subfamily, e.g. Spartaeinae, a subfamily jumping spiders (family Salticidae).
-INI. [Gr. ινις, son or daughter]. In classification: the recommended but not mandatory suffix used to indicate a tribe of animals. For example, family Salticidae (jumping spiders); subfamily Spartaeinae; tribe Myrmarchnini (ant-like jumping spiders).

NOCICEPTIVE. [L. *nocere*, to hurt; *capere*, to take]. Of stimuli which tend to cause pain or injure tissue.

NOCICEPTOR. [L. *nocere*, to hurt; *capere*, to take]. A receptor that is sensitive to pain.

NOCTURNAL. [L. *nocturnus*, by night]. Of the night: principally of animals active during the hours of darkness. See also Crepuscular, Diurnal.

NOCTURNAL EYES. [L. *nocturnus*, by night]. The pearly-white eyes of arachnids.

NODE. [L. *nodus*, knob]. A knob or swelling.

NODIFEROUS. [L. *nodus*, knob; *fero*, bear]. Having or bearing nodes.

NODIFORM. [L. *nodus*, knob; *forma*, shape]. In the form of a knob or knot.

NODOSE, NODOSUS. [L. *nodus*, knob]. Having swellings; knotted or with knots.

NODULAR. [L. *notula*, little mark]. Having small knobs or nodule-like projections.

NODULE. [L. *nodus*, knob]. Any knob-like structure.

NODULOSE, NODULOSUS, NODULATE. With small nodes or nodules. Of a surface sculpture of knots or links connected by an undulating line.

NONCLAVATE. [L. *non-*, not; *clava*, a club]. Not club-shaped.

NON-HOMOLOGOUS. [L. *non-*, not; Gr. ομολογος, agreeing]. Of any structures or traits that do not share a common ancestry. See also Homologous.

NORTHERN FOWL MITE. See Fowl Mite.

NOTAL. [Gr. νωτον, the back]. Dorsal. Of the back.

NOTATE. [L. *nototus*, marked]. Being marked with lines or spots.

NOTCHED. [ME. *nock*, a notch]. Nicked or indented; usually of a margin.

NOTCHED TROCHANTER. [ME. *nock*, a notch]. A trochanter with a shallow to deep ventro-apical excavation.

NOTOCEPHALON. [Gr. νωτον, back; κεφαλη, head]. In some ticks and mites: a dorsal shield on the leg-bearing segments.

NOTOGASTER (OPISTHOSOMATAL PLATE). [Gr. νωτον, back; γαστηρ, belly]. In some ticks and mites: a posterior dorsal shield.

NOTOSTIGMATA. [Gr. νωτον, back; στιγμη, mark]. See Opilioacariformes.

NOTUM. [Gr. νωτον, back]. The dorsal idiosoma.

NUDE, NUDUS. [L. *nudus*, naked]. Naked. A surface devoid of hair, scales or other vestiture.

NUPTIAL APPAREL. [L. *nuptialis*, of marriage]. The morphological changes that occur in an animal, commonly a male, during the mating season.

NURSERY-WEB SPIDERS. See **Pisauridae.**

NUTANT. [L. *nutare*, to nod]. Nodding, drooping, having the apex hanging down.

NUTRIENT. [L. *nutrire*, to nourish]. Any food substance.

NUTRITION. [L. *nutrire*, to nourish]. The ingestion, digestion and assimilation of food.

NUTRITIVE. [L. *nutrire*, to nourish]. Concerned with the function of nutrition; applied to plasma, polyps, yolk, zooids, etc.

NUTRITIVE CHAMBER. [L. *nutrire*, to nourish]. An enlarged section of an ovarian tube which is filled with granular nutritive material used in developing the egg cells.

NYCTOPERIOD. [Gr. νυκτος, by night; περιοδος, circuit]. The daily period of exposure to dark.

NYMPH. [Gr. νυμφη, chrysalis]. In mites: the juvenile form.

NYMPHA, NYMPHAE. [Gr. νυμφη, bride]. In mites: a pair of sclerites beneath the epigynal plates.

NYMPHAL PHASE. [Gr. νυμφη, bride]. In the Chelicerata: the second or third phase of postembryonic development. In ticks and mites with six stases: the third phase, comprised of proto-, deuto- and tritonymphs.

NYMPHIPAROUS (NYMPHIPARA). [Gr. νυμφη, bride; L. *parere*, to produce]. Giving birth to offspring at the nymphal stage of development.

NYMPHOCHRYSALIS. [Gr. νυμφη, chrysalis; χρυσαλλις, gold-colored sheath of butterflies]. In some mites: a developmental resting stage between the larval and nymphal forms.

NYMPHOID. [Gr. νυμφη, , bride; ειδος, form]. In the Chelicerata: the nymphal phase instars that cannot be homologized with nymphal instars of other species.

NYMPHOPHAN ORGANS. [Gr. νυμφη, chrysalis; φαινω, to show]. See Genital Papilla.

NYMPHOSIS. [Gr. νυμφη, chrysalis]. The process of changing into a nymph or pupa.

O

OB-. L. prefix: inversely.

OBCOMPRESSED. [L. *ob*, towards; *comprimere*, to compress]. Flattened in a vertical direction.

OBCONIC/OBCONICAL. [L. *ob*, against; *conus*, cone]. Cone shaped and attached at its apex. Inversely conical.

OBCORDATE (OBCORDIFORM). [L. *ob*, against; *cor*, heart]. Inversely heart-shaped.

OBCURRENT. [L. *ob*, against; *currere*, to run]. Converging and attached at the point of contact.

OBDELTOID. [L. *ob*, against; Gr. Δ, delta; ειδος, shape]. More-or-less triangular with the apex as the point of attachment.

OBESE. [L. *obesus*, fat]. Distended. Enlarged. Corpulent.

OBEX (pl. **OBICES**). [L. *obex*, an obstacle]. Any barrier separating populations. A limiting factor.

OBLANCEOLATE. [L. *ob*, inverse; *lanceolatus*, spear-like]. Inversely lanceolate.

OBLATE. [L. *oblatus*, spread out]. Flattened. Flattened at the poles. Of a spheroid in which the diameter is shortened at two opposite ends.

OBLIGATE. [L. *obligatus*, bound]. Applied to animals limited to one mode of life, as in obligate parasites, obligate parthenogenesis, obligate anaerobe, obligate thermophile, etc. See also Parasite.

OBLIGATE BROOD REDUCTION. [L. *obligatus*, bound]. A type of behavior in which the older, and usually stronger, offspring kill off their younger, and usually weaker siblings.

OBLIGATE PARASITE. [L. *obligatus*, bound; Gr. παρασιτος, parasite]. See Parasite.

OBLIGATE SYMBIONT. [L. *obligatus*, bound; Gr. συμβιωναι, to live with]. An organism that is physiologically dependent upon a symbiotic relationship with another. See also Facultative Symbiont.

OBLIQUE. [L. *obliquus*, slanting]. Slanting.

OBLIQUUS. [L. *obliquus*, slanting]. Any oblique muscle.

OBLITERATE. [L. *obliteratus*, erased]. Of body markings that are diffuse or indistinct.

OBLITERATIVE COLORATION (OBLITERATIVE SHADING). [L. *obliteratus*, erased]. A type of coloration in which the animal is shaded more darkly on those surfaces of its body that are exposed to the most intense light, usually the dorsal surface, and there is a gradual shading off to the ventral surface. When exposed to light from above, the gradation of coloring often exactly counter-balances the fact that the ventral region of the animal is in shadow. Thus the animal blends with its background more effectively. See also Counter Shading, Cryptic Coloration.

OBOVATE. [L. *ob*, inverse; *ovate*, egg-shaped]. Inversely egg-shaped, with the narrower end downwards.

OBOVOID. [L. *ob*, against; *ovum*, egg; Gr. ειδος, shape]. More-or-less egg-shaped.

OBPYRIFORM. [L. *ob*, inverse; *pyrum*, pear; *forma*, shape]. Inversely pear-shaped.

OBSCURE. [L. *obscurus*, dark/secret/vague]. 1. Dark. A dark color; dim. 2. Remote. Hidden. 3. Not well defined.

OBSITE, OBSITUS. [L. *obsitus*, covered (with)]. Of a surface covered with equal scales or other objects.

OBSOLETE. [L. *obsolescere*, to wear out]. Of any structure that is becoming less and less functional with passing generations.

OBTECT, OBTECTED. [L. *obtectus*, covered over]. Covered. Enclosed within a hard covering.

OBTURATOR. [L. *obturare*, to close]. A structure which closes off a cavity.

OBTUSE. [L. *obtusus*, blunt]. Blunt. Of an angle greater than a right angle. Opposite = acute.

OBUMBRATE. [L. *obumbrare*, to over-shadow]. Having a structure overhanging and partly concealing the region beneath.

OBVERSE. [L. *obvertere*, to turn round]. Of some structure in which the base is narrower than the apex.

OCCLUSAL. [L. *occludere*, to shut in]. In contact with the opposite surface.

OCCLUSION. [L. *occludere*, to shut in]. The closure of a structure, duct, etc.

OCCLUSOR MUSCLE. [L. *occludere*, to shut in]. See Muscle Terminology.

OCCULT, OCCULTUS. [L. *occulere*, to hide]. Hidden from sight.

OCEANIA. [Gr. Ωκεανος, myth. god of the river encircling the earth]. The islands of the Pacific and surrounding seas.

OCEANIC ISLAND. [Gr. ωκεανος, ocean]. A volcanic island that has arisen from the sea, as opposed to a continental island which arises as a consequence of a land mass being cut off from the main land.

OCELLATE. [L. *ocellus*, little eye]. Of markings that resemble an eye.

OCELLATED (OCELLIFEROUS). [L. *ocellus*, little eye]. Having eye-like spots or markings.

OCELLIGEROUS. [L. *ocellus*, little eye; *gerere*, to carry]. Bearing ocelli.

OCELLUS. [L. *ocellus*, little eye]. A simple eye or eye spot or any eye-like marking.

OCHRACEOUS. [Gr. ωχρος, yellow: L. *-aceous*, of the nature of]. Ochre-colored. Brownish-yellow.

OCHROLEUCOUS. [Gr. ωχρος, yellow; λευκος, white]. Yellowish-white.

OCHROPHORE. [Gr. ωχρος, yellow; -φορα, -carrying]. A pigment cell bearing a yellow-pigmented inclusion.

OCHYROCERATIDAE. [Gr. οχυρος, firm/stout; κερας, horn] A family of haplogyne spiders (infraorder Araneomorphae, superfamily Haplogynae) that build small, irregular sheet-webs in dark, damp places around leaves, sticks and logs, and typically carry their eggs in their chelicerae until they hatch. At least one species, *Theotima minutissima*, (0.9 mm long) is parthenogenetic.

OCTOTAXIC SYSTEM. [Gr. οκτω, eight; ταξις, an arranging]. In the Brachypylina (Oribatida): the set of four pairs of porose or sacculate dermal glands on the notogaster.

OCULAR. [L. *oculus*, eye]. Of the eye, or perceived by the eye.

OCULAR QUADRANGLE, O.Q. [L. *oculus*, eye; *quadrus*, fourfold; *angulus*, angle]. The area enclosed by certain groups of eyes; e.g., the median ocular quadrangle of spiders with eyes in two rows is the area enclosed by the anterior median eyes and posterior median eyes.

ODONTOID. [Gr. οδων, tooth; ειδος, shape]. Tooth-like.

ODONTOPHORE. [Gr. οδων, tooth; -φορα, -carrying]. Any organ bearing teeth.

ODOR TRAIL. [L. *odor*, smell]. A chemical trace (pheromone) deposited by one animal for another to follow.

OECO-. See also Eco-

OECOBIIDAE. [Gr. οικος, house; βιος, living]. The cosmopolitan family of disc web spiders (infraorder Araneomorphae, superfamily Entelegynae). Small spiders (~ 2mm) than construct tiny flat webs close to a surface, commonly a ceiling in homes.

OECOLOGY. [Gr. οικος, household; λογος, discourse]. See Ecology.

OECOPARASITE. [Gr. οικος, household; παρασιτος, parasite]. See Ecoparasite.

OEHSERCHESTOIDEA. [Gr. οιησις, a false impression; ορχηστης a dancer/pantomimic dancer]. A superfamily of mites (suborder Endeostigmata, infraorder **Terpnacarida**). Families: **Grandjeanicidae, Oehserchestidae.**

OERUGINOUS, OERUGINUS. See Aeruginous.

ESOPHAGUS. [Gr. οισοφαγος, gullet]. The region of the alimentary canal between the pharynx and the stomach.

OGOVEIDAE. [river *Ogooué* in The Congo]. A family of harvestmen (suborder Cyphophthalmi, infraorder Scopulophthalmi) from equatorial West Africa. They lack eyes, their body is covered with distinct granulations, and they possess a compressed pedipalpal femur that allows the pedipalps to fold over the chelicerae.

OGOVEOIDEA. [river *Ogooué* in The Congo]. In a previous classification: a superfamily of harvestmen (order Opilones, suborder Cyphophthalmi) that united the families **Neogoveidae** and **Ogoveidae**. These families are now in the infraorder Sternophthalmi, and the superfamily Ogoveoidea is abandoned.

-OIDEA. [L. *-oideus*, resembling]. In taxonomy: a recommended but not mandatory suffix used to indicate a superfamily of animals. See Nomenclature.

OIKE. [Gr. οικεω, inhabit]. Habitat.

OIKOLOGY. [Gr. οικος, household; λογος, discourse]. See Ecology.

OIKOSITE. [Gr. οικος, house; σιτος, food]. A stationary or attached commensal or parasite.

OIL GLANDS. See Lateral Opisthonotal Glands.

OLFACTORY CONE. [L. *olfacere*, to smell]. See Sensillum Basiconicum.

OLFACTORY ORGANS/RECEPTORS. [L. *olfacere*, to smell]. The chemosensory organs responsive to airborne molecules.

OLIGACANTHOUS. [Gr. ολιγος, few; ακανθα, spine]. Bearing only a few spines.

OLIGOGYRAL. [Gr. ολιγος, little; L. *gyrus*, circle]. See Paucispiral.

OLIGOLECITHAL. [Gr. ολιγος, little; λεκιθος, yolk]. An egg with a small amount of yolk. See also Alecithal, Centrolecithal, Heterolecithal, Macrolecithal, Mediolecithal, Meiolecithal, Mesolecithal, Microlecithal, Polylecithal, Telolecithal.

OLIGOLOBATE. [Gr. ολιγος, few; LL. *lobus*, lobe]. Divided into a small number of lobes.

OLIGOMERIZATION. [Gr. ολιγος, few; μερος, part]. An evolutionary trend in which there is a reduction in the number of body segments.

OLIGOMEROUS (OLIGOMERY). [Gr. ολιγος, few; μερος, part]. Having fewer parts or organs than other related forms.

OLIGOSAPROBIC. [Gr. ολιγος, few; σαπρος, rotten; βιος, life]. Of an aquatic environment in which there is a high content of dissolved oxygen and little organic decomposition. See also Katharobic, Mesosaprobic, Polysaprobic, Saprobic.

OLIGOTOKOUS. [Gr. ολιγος, few; τοκος, offspring]. Having only a few offspring per brood.

OLIGOTRICHY. [Gr. ολιγος, few; θριξ, hair]. Having few or weakly developed setae.

OLIGOTROPHIC. [Gr. ολιγος, little; τροφη, nourishment]. 1. Of lakes that are deficient in organic matter and thus have a low level of nutrient minerals. See also Dystrophic, Eutrophic. 2. Of any organism that requires only a small nutrient supply, or a restricted range of nutrients.

OLIGOXENOUS. [Gr. ολιγος, few; ξενος, host]. Of parasites which are adapted to life in only a few host species.

OLIGOZOIC. [Gr. ολιγος, few; ζωον, animal]. Having a few species or a small number of animals in a particular habitat.

OLIVACEOUS. [L. *oliva*, olive: *-aceous*, of the nature of]. Resembling or having an olive green color.

OLIVIFORM. [L. *oliva*, olive; *forma*, shape]. Oval. Resembling an olive shape.

OLPIIDAE. [Gr. ολπη, a leathern oil-flask]. A family of false scorpions (suborder Iocheirata, superfamily Garypoidea), mainly from xeric habitats.

OLPIOIDEA. [Gr. ολπη, a leathern oil-flask]. In a previous classifications, a superfamily of false scorpions (order Pseudoscorpiones, suborder Iocheirata) that united the families **Menthidae** and **Olpiidae**. Otherwise these families are in the superfamily Garypoidea.

OMEGA Ω/ω A designation for the solenidion on the tarsus of acariform mites. See also Φ/φ (phi) on the tibia, and Σ/σ (sigma) on the genu.

OMMATOIDS. [Gr. ομμα, eye; ειδος, shape]. In some arachnids: two or four light-colored spots on the last opisthosomal segment. Their function is not yet clear.

OMMOCHROMES (OMMACHROMES, OMMATOCHROMES). [Gr. ομμα, eye; χρωμα, color]. A group of yellow, red or brown pigments that are derived from (are metabolites of) the amino acid tryptophan and were first isolated from the eye although they are now known to exist in the body as well.

OMNIVOROUS (PANTOPHAGOUS). [L. *omnis*, all; *vorare*, to devour]. Eating both plants and animals. Such an organism being an omnivore (or diversivore).

OMPHALOID. [Gr. ομφαλος, the navel; ειδος, shape]. Shaped like a navel.

ONCOPHYSIS. [Gr. ογκος, swelling; φυσις, growth]. In the Chelicerata: any extension of an arthrodial membrane, that is usually in the form of a hyaline intumescence. See also Trägårdh's Organ.

ONCOPODIDAE. See **Sandokanidae**.

ONTOGENETIC ALLOMETRY. [Gr. ον, being; γενεσις, birth; αλλος, another; μετρον, a measure]. The measurement of differential growth rates of different body parts. See Allometry.

ONTOGENETIC MIGRATION. [Gr. ον, being; γενεσις, birth; L. *migrare*, to transfer]. The occupation of different habitats at different stages of an animal's development.

ONTOGENY (ONTOGENESIS, ONTOGENETIC). [Gr. ον, being; γενεσις, birth/descent]. The history of the development and growth of an individual.

ONYCHES. [Gr. ονυξ, claw]. See Tarsal Claw.

ONYCHIUM, ONYCHIA. [Gr. ονυξ, claw]. In some spiders: a false articulation at the end of the tarsus, that bears claws. This is prominent in the haplogyne families **Oonopidae** and **Ochyroceratidae**.

ONYCHOGENIC. [Gr. ονυξ, claw; -γενης, producing]. Being capable of producing a nail or nail-like substance.

OOID. [Gr. ωον, egg; ειδος, form]. Egg-shaped.

OONOPIDAE. [Gr. ωον, egg; οψ, looks like (oval eyes)]. The cosmopolitan family of goblin spiders (infraorder Araneomorphae, superfamily Haplogynae), in which there are generally six eyes, but some species have four, some have two and some cave-dwelling species are completely eyeless, as are some species which are exclusively found in termite nests. Some species may be parthenogenetic.

OPACUS. [L. *opacus*, shady]. Opaque. A surface without any luster.

OPALINE. [L. *opalus*, opal]. Opalescent. Bluish or milky white with an iridescent luster.

OPAQUE. [L. *opacus*, shady]. Not transparent or translucent.

OPERCULATE (OPERCULIFEROUS). [L. *operculum*, lid]. Having a lid-like covering.

OPERCULIFORM. [L. *operculum*, lid; *forma*, shape]. Lid-like.

OPERCULIGENOUS. [L. *operculum*, lid; Gr. -γενης, producing]. Producing an operculum.

OPERCULIGEROUS. [L. *operculum*, lid; *gerere*, to bear]. Having an operculum.

OPERCULUM, OPERCULA, (OPERCLE). [L. *operculum*, lid]. In general, any lid-like covering. In some arachnids: a small plate covering the opening to the book lung.

OPHTHALMIC. [Gr. οφθαλμος, the eye]. Of the eye.

OPILIOACARIFORMES (NOTOSTIGMATA). [L. *opilionis*, a shepherd; Gr. ακαρι, mite or tick; L. *forma*, shape]. A monospecific superorder of large, leathery, primitive mites (class Euchelicerata, subclass Arachnida) that have a segmented abdomen, four pairs of spiracles located behind the fourth coxa, and six pairs of eyes. They are brightly colored and resemble the harvestmen (Opiliones). Order Opilioacarida, family: **Opilioacaridae.**

OPILIONES (PHALANGIDA). [L. *opilionis*, a shepherd]. An order of long-legged spiders (class Euchelicerata, subclass Arachnida) known as 'daddy-long-legs' or harvestmen. The prosoma is broadly jointed to the short, externally segmented abdomen but without a constriction between the two divisions. They lack silk glands, the chelicerae are three-jointed and bear pincers and the pedipalps are leg-like. Leg autotomy is an important means of defense but there is no regeneration. They live in both temperate and tropical climates and prefer a humid habitat. Some species are less than 1 mm in length while at the other extreme some tropical species attain a body length of 20 mm with a leg length of 160 mm. The taxonomy of this order is in a state of flux and some confusion. Suborders: Cyphophthalmi, Dyspnoi, Eupnoi, Laniatores. The Palpatores were formerly included here but have recently been distributed between the Dyspnoi + part Eupnoi.

OPISTHOCYRT. [Gr. οπισθο-, behind; κυρτος, curved]. Arched backward.

OPISTHODORSAL. [Gr. οπισθο-, behind; L. *dorsum*, the back]. Of the rear posterior.

OPISTHOGASTRIC SHIELD. [Gr. οπισθο-, behind; γαστηρ, stomach]. In the Mesostigmata: a shield that covers all of the venter behind legs IV including the anal region. A ventrianal shield that incorporates the metapodal and usually the exopodal elements.

OPISTHOGENESIS. [Gr. οπισθο-, behind; γενεσις, origin]. The development of segments or markings that proceeds forwards from the posterior region.

OPISTHOGENITAL SHIELD (GENITIVENTRAL SHIELD). [Gr. οπισθο-, behind; L. *genitalis*, of generation]. In the Mesostigmata: an epigynal shield that extends back over the ventral region but is separate from the anal shield.

OPISTHONOTAL. [Gr. οπισθο-, behind; νωτον, back]. The dorsal opisthosoma.

OPISTHOTNOTAL GLANDS. [Gr. οπισθο-, behind; νωτον, back]. See Lateral Opisthonotal Glands.

OPISTHONOTAL SHIELD. [Gr. οπισθο-, behind; νωτον, back]. In the Mesostigmata: the posterior shield with divided dorsal shields.

OPISTHOSOMA. [Gr. οπισθο-, behind; σωμα, body]. The posterior region of the body. In primitive arachnids it consists of thirteen segments and a telson, but tends to become shortened and more variable in the more specialized forms. In the Araneae it has become a more-or-less spherical and apparently unsegmented abdomen, while in scorpions it forms a segmented tail bearing a sting.

OPISTHOSOMAL GLANDS. [Gr. οπισθο-, behind; σωμα, body]. See Lateral Opisthonotal Glands.

OPISTHOSOMATAL PLATE. [Gr. οπισθο-, behind; σωμα, body]. See Notogaster.

OPISTHOSOMATIC APPENDAGES. [Gr. οπισθο-, behind; σωμα, body]. In the Chelicerata: vestigial appendages present on the ventral regions of segments VII-XIII, such as genital papillae or valves.

OPISTHOSOMATIC SCISSURE. [Gr. οπισθο-, behind; σωμα, body; L. *scissura*, a long narrow opening]. In ticks and mites: a narrow band of skin between sclerotized plates. It is often transverse on the opisthosoma.

OPISTHOTHELAE. [Gr. οπισθο, behind; θηλη, nipple]. A general term to describe modern spiders, in which the spinnerets are located at the end of the abdomen. In recent classifications this group is a suborder of the Araneae, with the Araneomorphae (Labidognatha) and Mygalomorphae (Orthognatha) being infraorders.

OPISTOSOMA. Erron. for Opisthosoma.

OPPIOIDEA. [Proto-Finnic, *oppidak*, to check (a trap, etc.) as part of hunting vocabulary]. A superfamily of mites (suborder Oribatida, infraorder Brachypylina - section Pycnonoticae). Sixteen families.

OPSIBLASTIC. [Gr. οψι, late; βλαστη, growth]. 1. Of eggs that have a period of dormancy prior to hatching. 2. Of embryos that exhibit delayed cleavage. See also Tachyblastic.

OPSIGENES. [Gr. οψι, late; -γενης, born]. Structures that form or become functional long after birth.

OPTIC. [Gr. οψις, sight]. Pertaining to sight.

OPTIMUM FORAGING THEORY. [L. *optimus*, best; Anglo-Latin *foragium*, fodder]. The theory that selection favors foraging strategies that involve decisions which maximize the net rate of food intake.

OPTIMUM YIELD (MAXIMUM SUSTAINED YIELD). [L. *optimus*, best; OE. *gield*, payment]. The theoretical point at which the size of a population produces a maximum rate of increase, equal to half the carrying capacity.

O.Q. See Ocular Quadrangle.

ORA. [L. *ora*, shore / coast]. A border.

ORAD. [LL. *oralis*, mouth; *ad*, to]. In the direction of the mouth or the region of the mouth.

ORAL. [LL. *oralis*, mouth]. Of, or belonging to, the mouth. On the same side as the mouth.

ORAL CAVITY. [LL. *oralis*, mouth]. The mouth. The buccal cavity.

ORAL STYLET. [LL. *oralis*, mouth; Gr. στυλος, pillar]. In the Eriophyoidea: the unpaired stylet in the bundle of stylets.

ORB, ORBICULAR. [L. *orbis*, circle]. A circle or globe.

ORBICULARIS. [L. *orbis*, orb]. Of a muscle whose fibers surround an opening.

ORBICULATE. [L. *orbiculatus*, rounded]. Almost circular in outline.

ORB WEB. [L. *orbis*, circle]. A two-dimensional web that is more-or-less circular in design (and therefore not an orb!) with the silk threads radiating from a central hub. These threads are then overlaid with a spiral of silk, running from the periphery almost to the hub.

ORB-WEB SPIDERS. See **Araneidae.**

ORDER. [L. *ordo*, order]. The principle taxonomic grouping above the level of family and below that of class. See also Nomenclature.

ORDINAL. [L. *ordin*, methodical arrangement]. Belonging or pertaining to an order.

ORDINATE. [L. *ordinatus*, arranged]. Having body markings arranged in rows.

ORDINATOPUNCTATE. [L. *ordinatus*, arranged; *punctum*, a prick]. Having dots etc. arranged in serial rows.

ORGAN. [Gr. οργανον, implement]. Any part of a structure adapted for a particular function.

ORGANOGENESIS (ORGANOGENY). [Gr. οργανον, implement; γενεσις, descent]. The formation of and development of organs.

ORGANOLEPTIC. [Gr. οργανον, instrument; λεπτικος, disposed to accept]. Capable of receiving a sensory stimulus.

ORIBATELLOIDEA. [Gr. ορεοβατες, mountain-ranging; L. *-ella*, dim.suf.]. A monospecific superfamily of mites (suborder Oribatida, infraorder Brachypylina - section Poronoticae). Families: **Ceratokalummidae, Oribatellidae.**

ORIBATIDA (CRYPTOSTIGMATA, ORIBATEI). [Gr. ορεοβατες, mountain-ranging]. A suborder of soil-living mites (superorder Acariformes, order Sarcoptiformes) known as beetle mites or armored mites. Infraorders: Brachypylina (sections Poronoticae, Pycnonoticae), Enarthronota, Holosomata, Mixonomata (sections Dichosomata, Euptyctima), Palaeosomata, Parhyposomata, and about 130 families.

ORICHALCEOUS. [L. *aurum*, gold; Gr. χαλκος, copper]. A color or luster between gold and brass. See also Aurichalceous.

ORIENTAL FAUNAL REGION (REALM). [L. *orientalis*, eastern; *Faunus*, god of the woods]. The zoogeographical region that includes the Indian subcontinent and Indo-China south to Wallace's line, including Ceylon, Sumatra, Java and the Philippines.

ORIENTATING RESPONSE. [L. *oriens*, rising of the sun]. A spontaneous reaction in which the head or body are moved so that the source of a stimulus can be more closely examined.

ORIENTATION. [L. *oriens*, rising of the sun]. The positional alteration of an animal in response to a stimulus.

ORIFICE (ORIFICIUM). [L. *os*, mouth; *facere*, to make]. The mouth or other aperture. The opening of a tube or duct.

ORIPODOIDEA (ORIBATULOIDEA). [Gr. ορει-, mountain; πους, foot]. A superfamily of mites (suborder Oribatida, infraorder Brachypylina - section Poronoticae). Seventeen families.

ORNAMENTATION. [L. *ornare*, to adorn]. Any of the sculpturing on the body or shell of an animal.

ORNITHOGAEA. [Gr. ορνις, bird; γαια, earth]. The zoogeographical region that includes New Zealand and Polynesia.

ORSOLOBIDAE. [Gr. ορσο, rouse/start/chase: LL. *lobus*, lobe]. A family of six-eyed araneomorph spiders (infraorder Araneomorphae, superfamily Haplogynae) from South America, South Africa and eastern and western Australia and New Zealand. They have recently been separated from the **Dysderidae**, and several genera were transferred from the **Oonopidae**.

ORTHOGNATHA. [Gr. ορθος, straight; γναθος, jaw]. See Mygalomorphae.

ORTHOGNATHOUS. [Gr. ορθος, straight; γναθος, jaw]. Having the axis of the head at right angles to the body. A type of chelicerae that project forward with fangs articulating along the longitudinal (vertical) axis. This can be seen in the Mesothelae and Mygalomorphae.

ORTHOGRADE. [Gr. ορθος, straight; L. *gradus*, step]. Walking with the body in a vertical position.

ORTHORRHAPHOUS. [Gr. ορθος, straight; ραφη, suture]. Straight-seamed.

ORTHOSTASY. [Gr. ορθος, straight; στασις, standing]. A stage in the chelicerate life-cycle evolution that shows only stases and no stasoids.

ORTHOTAXY. [Gr. ορθος, straight; ταξις, an arranging]. The arrangement of similar organs that have ancestral characters, and have preserved their normal position.

ORTHOTRICHY. [Gr. ορθος, straight; τριχος, hair]. In the Chelicerata: of all setae that have not disappeared but maintained their ancestral position.

ORTSTREUE. [Ger. *ortstreue*, 'local faithfulness']. Fidelity to the home region.

OS, ORA. [L. *os*, mouth]. Mouth, mouths.

OSMORECEPTORS. [Gr. ωσμος, push; L. *recipere*, to receive]. Receptor cells that are stimulated by changes in osmotic pressure.

OSMOREGULATION. [Gr. ωσμος, push; L. *regulatus*, regulated]. The regulation of osmotic pressure in the body by controlling the amount of water or the salt concentration, thus water content is maintained at a constant level by countering the tendency for it to pass in or out by osmosis.

OSSICLE. [L. *ossiculum*, little bone]. A small nodule of chitin that resembles bone.

OSTIAL. [L. *ostium*, door]. Of an ostium.

OSTIATE. [L. *ostium*, door]. Having ostia.

OSTIUM, OSTIA. [L. *ostium*, door]. Any mouth-like opening.

OTOCEPHEOIDEA. [Gr. οτο-, ear; κεφαλη, head]. A monotypic superfamily of mites (suborder Oribatida, infraorder Brachypylina - section Pycnonoticae). Families: **Dampfiellidae, Otocepheidae, Tetracondylidae, Tokunocepheidae.**

OTOPHEIDOMENIDAE. [Gr. οτο-, ear; φειδος, sparing; μηνις, wrath]. A small family of mites (infraorder Gamasina, superfamily Phytoseioidea).

OUTER INFRACAPITULAR STYLETS (CHELICERAL GUIDES). [L. *infra*, below; *capitulum*, a little head]. In the Eriophyoidea: a pair of capitular processes that frame the cheliceral stylets.

OUTER LOBE OF MAXILLA. See Galea.

OUTER SACRALS. Setae L4 (= f2) in the Pritchard & Baker system.

OVA. Plural of Ovum.

OVA GLEBATA. [L. *ovum*, egg; *gleba*, clod/lump of earth]. Eggs laid or concealed in lumps of dung.

OVA IMPOSITA. [L. *ovum*, egg; *impositus*, put upon]. Eggs laid in the substance that is to serve as food for the larva.

OVA PILOSA. [L. *ovum*, egg; *pilosus*, hairy]. Eggs that are covered with hair; that usually comes from the abdomen of the female.

OVARIAL LIGAMENT. [L. *ovarium*, ovary; *ligare*, to bind]. A ligamentous strand that attaches the terminal filaments of an ovary to the dorsal diaphragm or body wall, or maybe from the opposite side by way of a median ligament to the ventral wall of the dorsal blood vessel. It suspends the developing ovaries in the hemocoel.

OVARIAN TUBE. [L. *ovarium*, ovary]. The tubular part of an ovariole that contains the germ cells, oocytes, nurse cells, and follicle cells.

OVARIOLES (OVARIAN TUBULES). [L. *ovarium*, ovary]. The separate egg tubes or branches of the ovaries. The number of these can vary considerably.

OVARIOTESTES. [L. *ovarium*, ovary; *testis*, testicle]. The generative organ when both male and female elements are formed, as in the case of sex reversal.

OVARY (OARIUM, OVARIUM). [L. *ovarium*, ovary]. The female reproductive organ that contains eggs or egg cells (ova).

OVATE. [L. *ovatus*, egg-shaped]. Egg-shaped.

OVATELY-CONIC. [L. *ovatus*, egg-shaped; *conus*, cone]. Formed like an egg with a somewhat conic apex.

OVATE-OBLONG. [L. *ovatus*, egg-shaped; *oblongus*, oblong]. Between oval and oblong.

OVATE-SUBQUADRATE. [L. *ovatus*, egg-shaped; *sub-*, under; *quadratus*, squared]. Rounded, but somewhat four-sided.

OVERCROWDING EFFECT. A regulatory effect on population size caused by behavioral abnormalities which result from a malfunction of the endocrine glands in response to overcrowding.

OVICAPSULE. [L. *ovum*, egg; *capsula*, small box]. An egg case or ootheca.

OVIDUCAL. [L. *ovum*, egg; *ducere*, to lead]. Of an oviduct.

OVIDUCAL GLAND. [L. *ovum*, egg; *ducere*, to lead]. A gland which secretes some substance into the oviduct as, for example, that which produces the shell of an egg.

OVIDUCT. [L. *ovum*, egg; *ducere*, to lead]. The tube which transports eggs from the ovary to the uterus or from the coelom (into which the eggs are shed) to the exterior.

OVIFEROUS (OVIGEROUS). [L. *ovum*, egg; *ferre*, to carry, (*-igerous*, in use always)]. Of some structure that transports eggs.

OVIFORM. [L. *ovum*, egg; *forma*, shape]. Egg-shaped.

OVIPAROUS (OVIPARY, OVIPARITY). [L. *ovum*, egg; *parere*, to bring forth]. Egg-laying. A reproductive strategy in which there is little or no embryo development within the maternal body but eggs are laid and the embryo thus develops outside the mother's body. Most invertebrates and many vertebrates are oviparous. See also Ovoviviparous, Viviparous

OVIPOSIT. [L. *ovum*, egg; *ponere*, to lay]. To lay eggs.

OVIPOSITION. [L. *ovum*, egg; *ponere*, to place]. The act of depositing eggs.

OVIPOSITOR. [L. *ovum*, egg; *ponere*, to lay]. An extrusible organ for laying eggs. Female oribatids have a well developed ovipositor that terminates in three finger-like projections. In other mites they are less well developed or absent.

OVISAC. [L. *ovum*, egg; *saccus*, bag]. An egg capsule, egg receptacle, or a brood pouch.

OVISORPTION. [L. *ovum*, egg; *sorbere*, to suck in]. The reabsorption of oocytes.

OVOID. [L. *ovum*, egg; Gr. ειδος, form]. Egg-shaped. Ovate.

OVOVIVIPAROUS. [L. *ovum*, egg; *vivus*, living; *parere*, to bring forth]. A reproductive strategy in which an egg with a persistent membrane is produced, incubated and hatched within the maternal body. Thus giving birth to live young from an egg incubated within the maternal body but separate from it. Eggs of this type contain a considerable quantity of yolk. See also Oviparous, Viviparous.

OVULATE (OVULATION). [L. *ovum*, egg]. The emission a ripe egg, or eggs, from an ovary or ovarian follicle. The egg then passes down the oviduct.

OVUM (pl.- OVA). [L. *ovum*, egg]. A female gamete, an unfertilized egg cell. A reproductive cell consisting of a haploid nucleus, a varying amount of yolk and surrounded by a vitelline membrane. An ovum may be classified according to the quantity of yolk, thus one with a lot of yolk is megalecithal, one with a little yolk is microlecithal. If the ovum is a true egg and not just an egg cell, it may be surrounded by albumen, a number of membranes and a shell. Eggs laid in water usually lack a shell.

OXYOPIDAE. [Gr. οξυς, sharp; L. *pes*, foot]. The family of lynx spiders (infraorder Araneomorphae, superfamily Entelegynae). Long-legged, diurnal, hunting spiders which are mainly from warm climates. Many species are partly or wholly green and sit motionless on leaves in wait for prey.

OXYPHIL, OXYPHILIC. [Gr. οξυς, acid; φιλος, loving]. Tolerant of acid or acid soils.

OXYPHOBE, OXYPHOBIC. [Gr. οξυς, acid; φοβος, fright]. Not tolerant of acid soils; acidophobic.

P

φ Φ (Phi). In the Acariformes: a designation for the solenidion of the tibia. Ω (omega) on the tarsus; Σ (sigma) on the genu.

p. A pro-oral seta.

p1, p2, p3. In the Zerconidae (Mesostigmata): designations for setae on the peritrematal shield. z1, r1, r2, r3 of the Lindquist-Evans System.

P1, P2, P3. Prodorsal setae of spider mites in the Pritchard & Baker system. In the Grandjean system, P1 = v2; P2 = sc1; P3 = sc2.

pa. A designation for setae on the peranal segment in acariform mites or for the paranal setae in the Mesostigmata.

PA. In the Acariformes: a peranal segment which is added on the tritonymph stage. See Anamorphosis. See Grandjean System.

PACULLIDAE. [deriv.uncert.]. A small family of cryptic spiders (infraorder Araneomorphae, superfamily Haplogynae) from south-east Asia. They have six eyes, a rugose cuticle, and lack a cribellum.

PAD-LIKE. In the Prostigmata: of empodia that do not have a distal hook. When tenent hairs are present a 'pad-like' empodium may look more like a pincushion. In other ticks and mites: usually a simple, pad-like empodium.

PAEDOMORPHOSIS. [Gr. παιδ-, child; μορφωσις, semblance]. An evolutionary change in which primitive or embryonic structures appear (or are retained) in the adult. It may be a result of neoteny, progenesis or postdisplacement and permits an evolutionary escape from specialization. This process has been suggested for the origin of many taxa, from subspecies to phyla.

PAIRED (SUPERIOR/LATERAL) CLAWS. The claws at the tip of the leg tarsus in all spiders.

PALEA. [L. *palea*, chaff/husk]. In some male spiders: a convex and usually rugose pad at the distal end of the genital bulb of the palpus.

PALAEACAROIDEA (CTENACAROIDEA). [Gr. παλαιος, ancient; LL. *acarus*, mite]. A superfamily of mites (suborder Oribatida, infraorder Palaeosomata). Families: **Aphelacaridae, Ctenacaridae, Palaeacaridae**.

PALEARCTIC FAUNAL REGION. [Gr. παλαιος, ancient; αρκτικος, northern]. A zoogeographical region of the Holarctic which includes Europe, western Asia, Siberia, northern China and Japan. Despite the great size of this region and great range of habitats, the faunal variety is far less than that of the Ethiopian and Oriental regions to the south.

PALEACE, PALEACEOUS. [L. *paleae*, chaff: *-aceous*, of the nature of]. Chaff. Chaffy in appearance.

PALAEOBURMESEBUTHIDAE. [Gr. παλαιος, ancient, *Burma*, + *Buthus*]. A small extinct monospecific family of scorpions (order Scorpiones, superfamily Buthoidea) known from the Late Cretaceous of Burma.

PALAEOGAEA (PALAEOGEA, MEGAGAEA). [Gr. παλαιος, ancient; γαια, the earth]. The zoogeographical region comprising the Palearctic, Ethiopian, Oriental and Australian regions.

PALAEOMONTANE. [Gr. παλαιος, ancient; L. *montanus*, mountain]. Belonging to the alpine regions of the Palearctic.

PALAEOSOMATA. [Gr. παλαιος, ancient; σωμα, body]. An infraorder of beetle mites or armored mites (order Sarcoptiformes, suborder Oribatida). Superfamilies: Acaronychoidea, Palaeacaroidea (Ctenacaroidea).

PALEARCTIC. See Palearctic Faunal Region.

PALEOAMBLYPYGI. [Gr. παλαιος, ancient; + Amblypygi]. A suborder of tail-less whip scorpions or whip spiders (subclass Arachnida, order Amblypygi). Family: **Paracharontidae**.

PALINGENESIS. [Gr. παλιν, again; γενεσις, descent]. 1. The regeneration or restoration of a lost part. 2. Recapitulation: the abrupt appearance of ancestral characters.

PALLESCENT. [L. *pallescere*, to grow pale]. Becoming pale or light in color or tint.

PALLID. [L. *pallidus*, pale]. Pale or very pale.

PALLIDE-FLAVENS. [L. *pallidus*, pale; *flavus*, yellow]. Pale or whitish yellow.

PALLIDUS. [L. *pallidus*, pale]. Pale or very pale. Of a pale, cadaverous hue. A very dilute brown-pink.

PALMATE. [L. *palma*, palm]. Formed in the general shape of a hand, i.e. divided into lobes arising from a common center.

PALP, PALPUS, PALPI. [L. *palpus*, feeler]. In the Araneae: the elongate sensory structures situated near the mouth, that originate behind the chelicerae but in front of the legs. The second appendages (second pair of limbs) of the cephalothorax. The segmented appendages of the pedipalp, excluding the coxa and endite. They are simple in females but in males become a reproductive organ greatly modified for the transfer of semen. In some **Oonopidae** they are fused to the palpal tarsus, but can be differentiated by the absence of seta. In ticks and mites: the paired sensory appendages of segment 2, which maybe up to six segments long. They are normally have four segments, termed 'articles'. Article 1 articulates with the basis capituli. Articles 2 and 3 vary in length, and are almost always the longest segments of the palps, and are more flexible. Article 4 is terminal in argasid ticks, but recessed in a cavity on the ventral side of article 3 in most ixodid ticks. This is a delicate segment that can be retracted or protruded as needed and bears a sensory field numerous setae (presumed chemosensilla), on the tip. Other, frequently longer and stouter setae, occur on the ventral and medial surfaces of the palps and shield the delicate mouthparts.

PALPAL BULB/ORGAN (GENITAL BULB). [L. *palpus*, feeler]. Collectively, the structures making up the male palpal organ. They comprise groups of sclerites which are separated from each other and the cymbium by up to three haematodochae. The palpal bulb contains the semen reservoir which opens via ducts through the tip of the embolus.

PALPALAE. [L. *palpus*, feeler; *alae*, wings]. The three-serrate setae on the palp of **Harpirhynchidae** mites (Prostigmata: Cheyletoidea).

PALPATORES. [L. *palpare*, to stroke gently]. In some classifications: a large suborder of harvestmen (subclass Arachnida, order Opiliones) in which the palps are small and non-prehensile, and the body is short and wide. Superfamilies: Ischyropsalidoidea, Troguloidea, Phalangioidea. In a recent classification the Palpatores have been diversified into the suborders Eupnoi and Dyspnoi.

PALP-COXAL LOBES. [L. *palpus*, feeler; *coxa*, hip]. The paired lobes on the prolateral surfaces of the palpal coxae. They form the sides of the preoral cavity.

PALP-COXAL SETA. [L. *palpus*, feeler; *coxa*, hip]. In the Mesostigmata: the pair of palpcoxal setae (pc or pcx), the most basal setae on the subcapitulum.

PALPICORN. [L. *palpus*, feeler, *cornu*, horn]. Having long, slender, antenna-like palpi.

PALPIFEROUS, PALPIGEROUS. [L. *palpare*, to stroke; *ferre/gerere*, to bear]. Bearing a palpus.

PALPIFORM. [L. *palpare*, to stroke; *forma*, shape]. In the shape of a palp.

PALPIGRADI (PALPIGRADA, MICROTHELYPHONIDA). [L. *palpare*, to stroke; *gradus*, step]. A small, and poorly known cosmopolitan order of minute, colorless, thin skinned arachnids (class Euchelicerata, subclass Arachnida) known as micro-scorpions, or micro-whip-scorpions, mainly from southern Europe, southern USA and South America. The chelicerae are thin, three segmented and chelate with a movable lateral finger. The segmented abdomen is broadly joined to the prosoma and bears a long jointed highly mobile whip-like flagellum terminally. The pedipalps are undifferentiated and may be used as a pair of walking legs, however, the first pair of legs appear to have a sensory function and are usually held off the ground during locomotion. Sexual behavior has not been described. Eyes are lacking. Superfamily Eukoenenioidea; families: **Eukoeneniidae, Prokoeneniidae.**

PALPIMANIDAE. [L. *palpare*, to stroke, *manus*, hand]. The widely distributed family of palp-footed spiders (infraorder Araneomorphae, superfamily Palpimanoidea) in which the front legs are disproportionately powerful and heavily sclerotised. They are ground-dwelling and are not known to construct webs.

PALPIMANOIDEA. [L. *palpare*, to stroke, *manus*, hand]. An Old World superfamily of ecribellate spiders (suborder Opisthothelae, infraorder Araneomorphae) known as assassin spiders because many specialize in preying on other spiders. They have prey-catching adaptations, such as enlarged spade-like front legs, and a raised head bearing long chelicerae. Families: **Archaeidae, Huttoniidae, Mecysmaucheniidae, Palpimanidae, Stenochilidae.**

PALPOSOMA. [L. *palpus*, feeler; Gr. σωμα, body]. In the Astigmata: the reduced gnathosoma found on the heteromorphic deutonymphs (hypopi).

PALPTARSAL APOTELE (PALP APOTELE, PALPTARSAL CLAW). [L. *palpus*, feeler; Gr. ταρσος, sole of foot; απο, away; τελος, end]. The most distal segment of the palp. It is claw-like in the Opilioacarida, a subdistal, tined structure in the Mesostigmata and absent in the Acariformes.

PALPTIBIAL CLAW. [L. *palpus*, feeler; L. *tibia*, shin]. In some Prostigmata: a claw-like seta on the palptibia that forms a chelate structure with the palp tarsus, the palp thumb-claw complex.

PALPULUS. [L. *palpare*, to stroke gently]. The small palp of a feeler.

PALUDICOLE (PALUSTRAL). [L. *palus*, marsh; *colere*, to inhabit]. Living in marshes or swamps.

PALUS. [L. *palus*, stake]. Any stake-like structure.

PALUSTRAL. [L. *palus*, marsh]. See Paludicole.

PANCTENATA. [Gr. παν, all; κτενος, comb]. In some classifications, an infraorder of false scorpions (order Pseudoscorpiones, suborder Iocheirata) that unites the superfamilies: Cheliferoidea Garypoidea, Olpioidea, Sternophoroidea. Not all authorities agree with this scheme.

PANDURIFORM (PANDURATE). [L. *pandura*, a musical instrument; *forma*, shape]. Violin-shaped, oblong at the two extremities and contracted in the middle.

PANENDEMIC DISTRIBUTION. [Gr. παν-, all; ενδημος, native to somewhere]. World-wide. Cosmopolitan.

PANGAEA. [Gr. παν-, all; γαια, earth]. The supercontinent which came into being in the Late Permian and persisted for about 40 million years and from which our present day continents are thought to be derived as a consequence of breaking up followed by continental drift. This break up is thought to have started about 251 million years ago, at the beginning of the Triassic, although some authorities put the start of the break up as recent as 150 Mya. Pangaea was surrounded by the ocean of Panthalassa. See also Gondwana, Laurasia.

PANGAMIC, PANGAMY. [Gr. παν-, all; γαμος, marriage]. Indiscriminate or random mating.

PANMICTIC. [Gr. παν-, all; μικτος, mixed]. Characterized by, or resulting from matings within a randomly interbreeding population.

PANMIXIA. [Gr. παν-, all; μιξις, mixing]. Indiscriminate interbreeding; the free interchange of genes within an interbreeding population. See also Assortative Mating, Disassortative Mating.

PANNICULUS. [L. *panniculus*, a little garment]. Any thin layer of tissue.

PANNOSE. [L. *pannosus*; ragged]. Cloth-like.

PANTELEBASIC RUTELLUM. [Gr. παντελης, complete; βασις, base; L. *rutellum*, little spade]. In many Brachypylina (Oribatida): a large rutellum, in which the apex is toothed and meets medially. See also Atelebasic Rutellum, Rutella.

PANTHALASSA. [Gr. παν-, all; θαλασσα, sea]. See Pangaea.

PANTROPICAL. [Gr. παν-, all; τροπικος, turning]. Distributed throughout the tropics.

PAPILLA. [L. *papilla*, nipple]. Any conical structure, such as a nipple, the apex of a renal pyramid, etc. A glandular hair with one secreting cell above the level of the epidermis.

PAPILLARY. [L. *papilla*, nipple]. Of any structure bearing papillae.

PAPILLATE (PAPILLOSE). [L. *papilla*, nipple]. Covered by papillae, or formed like a papilla.

PAPILLIFORM. [L. *papilla*, nipple; *forma*, shape]. Shaped like a nipple.

PAPILLOSE, PAPILLOSUS. [L. *papilla*, nipple]. Pimply: a surface covered with raised dots or pimples.

PAPPIFEROUS. [L. *pappas*, down; *ferre*, to bear]. Bearing a circle or tuft of bristles or hairs (a pappus).

PAPPOSE, PAPPUS, PAPPAS. [L. *Papus*, down]. Downy. Made up or clothed with pappus.

PAPUAN. [from Papua, New Guinea]. Of a subregion of the Australian zoogeographical region that extends from New Guinea and the islands westward to Wallace's line.

PAPULOUS. [L. *papula*, pimple]. Covered with small bumps or pimples.

PAR SETAE. In the Mesostigmata: the paranal pair of seta inserted laterad to the anal opening; often designated pa.

PARABOLIC VENTRAL SUTURE. [Gr. παραβολος, deceitful; L. *venter*, belly; *sutura*, seam]. In the **Eulohmanniidae** (Oribatida): the converging ventral suture characteristic of adults.

PARACENTRAL. [Gr. παρα, near; L. *centrum*, center]. Located near the center.

PARACYMBIUM. [Gr. παρα, near; κυμβιον, small boat]. In some spiders: an accessory part of the cymbium, a genital appendage (the boat-shaped tarsus of the pedipalps). They are particularly obvious in the Linyphiidae.

PARADACTYLI (PRETARSAL OPERCULA). [Gr. παρα, beside; δακτυλος, finger]. In many of the Mesostigmata: a pair of lateral, distally toothed structures on the pretarsus. They seem to be well developed in species that live in moist environments.

PARAEMBOLAR APOPHYSIS. [Gr. παρα, beside; εμβολος, a wedge; αποφυσις, an offshoot]. In some male spiders: an apophysis on the base of the embolus.

PARAGNATHA. [Gr. παρα, beside; γναθος, jaw]. Any part or structure that lies alongside a jaw or palp.

PARAHYIDAE. [Gr. παρα, beside, + Hyidae]. A monospecific family of false scorpions (suborder Iocheirata, superfamily Neobisioidea) from Singapore and the Caroline Islands.

PARALACINIAE. [Gr. παρα, beside; L. *lacinia*, flap]. In ticks and mites: a pair of small processes on the anterior margin of the subcapitulum.

PARALIMNIC. [Gr. παρα, beside; λιμνη, lake]. Inhabiting the shores of lakes.

PARALIMNION. [Gr. παρα, beside; λιμνη, lake]. The shore area of lakes.

PARALLEL EVOLUTION. [Gr. παραλληλος, parallel; L. *evolvere*, to unroll]. The evolution of similar or identical features independently in related lineages; thought to be based on similar modifications of the same developmental pathways. See also Phylogenetic Classification.

PARALOGY. [Gr. παρα, near; λογος, discourse]. The study of similar anatomical structures that are not related by common descent or similar function.

PARAMEDIAN. [Gr. παρα, beside; L. *medius*, middle]. Along the longitudinal axis.

PARAMEGISTIDAE. [Gr. παρα, near; μεγιστος largest]. A monotypic superfamily of mites (suborder Trigynaspida, infraorder Antennophorina). Family: **Paramegistidae.**

PARAMORPH. [Gr. παρα, beside; μορφη, form]. Any variant form or variety, or a form produced as a result of environmental factors rather than genetic variation.

PARAMUTUALISM. [Gr. παρα, beside; L. *mutuus*, reciprocal]. See Facultative Symbiosis.

PARANAL. [Gr. παρα, beside; L. *anus*, anus]. At the side of, or next to, an anal structure.

PARANAL (ADANAL) SETAE. [Gr. παρα, beside; L. *anus*, anus; *setae*, bristles]. In the Mesostigmata: the pair of seta inserted laterad to the anal opening. They are usually designated pa or PAR; the anterior (= h3) and posterior (= h2) paranals in the Pritchard & Baker system.

PARANEMIC. [Gr. παρα, near; νημα, thread]. Having spirals that are not interlocked.

PARANONYCHIDAE. [Gr. παρα, near; ονυξ, claw]. A small family of armored harvestmen or daddy longlegs (suborder Laniatores, superfamily Travunioidea).

PARANTENNULOIDEA. [Gr. παρα, near; NL. *antenna*, feeler]. A superfamily of mites (suborder Trigynaspida, infraorder Antennophorina). Families: **Parantennulidae, Philodanidae, Promegistidae.**

PARAPATRIC. [Gr. παρα, beside; πατηρ, native land]. Of a distribution of species which meet in a very narrow zone of overlap. See also Allopatric, Speciation, Sympatric.

PARAPATRIC SPECIATION. [Gr. παρα, beside; πατηρ, native land]. See Speciation.

PARAPHARYNX. [Gr. παρα, beside; φαρυνξ, the throat]. See Hypopharynx.

PARAPHYLETIC. [Gr. παρα, beside; φυλον, a kind]. Of a taxon that includes some but not all the descendants of the common ancestor. See Phylogenetic Classification.

PARAPODAL SHIELD / SCLERITE). [Gr. παρα, beside; πους, foot]. In the Mesostigmata: a narrow sclerite posteriad coxa IV.

PARAPROCTS. [Gr. παρα, beside; πρωκτος, anus]. A pair of lateroventral plates located on each side of the anus.

PARARCHAEIDAE. See **Malkaridae.**

PARARECTAL. [Gr. παρα, beside; L. rectus, straight]. Of organs, structures, etc. beside the rectum.

PARASAGITTAL SECTION (PLANE). [Gr. παρα, near; L. sagitta, arrow]. A line on either side of the midline, lengthwise from front to rear. See also Sagittal Section.

PARASEMATIC. [Gr. παρα, beside; σημα, signal]. See Sematic.

PARASEME. [Gr. παρα, beside; σημα, signal]. A misleading appearance or misleading markings, as for example an eye-like marking (ocellus).

PARASIGMOIDAL. [Gr. παρα, beside; σιγμα, Σ - sigma; ειδος, form]. Curved like a reversed letter "S".

PARASITE. [Gr. παρασιτος, one who eats at the table of another]. Any organism that, at some stage in its life cycle, lives in or upon another organism of a different species (the host) and derives its food directly from the living tissues; usually to the detriment of the host. There are many adaptations for a parasitic life style, for example; the development of organs of attachment (suckers, claws, hooks), a reduction in sensory organs, adaptations of the ingestive organs and modifications in nutrition, increased reproductive capability, the development of larval stages that allow passage from one host to another, suppression of the host's immune system, etc. A parasite may have no noticeable effect on the host, or there maybe marked effects from a variety of factors. **Ectoparasite (Epiparasite)**: an organism that lives parasitically on the outside of its host. Parasites of this type are usually well developed, dorsoventrally flattened and have special structures (such as hooks and claws) to avoid being dislodged. **Endoparasite (Endosite)**: an organism that lives parasitically within another. Parasites of this type have usually lost many features but may have developed special attachment structures. **Facultative parasite**: an organism that is capable of a particular type of parasitic life-style but not dependent on it for survival. **Hyperparasite**: a parasite whose host is another parasite. **Kleptoparasite**: a parasite that steals the food or prey of another species. **Obligate parasite**: a parasite that cannot exist without a host during all or some portion of the life cycle. **Parasitoid**: strictly, an organism that is alternately parasitic and free-living, but more generally, an organism with a mode of life intermediate between parasitism and predation. It may kill its parasite host as a consequence of its own development. **Partial parasite**: a facultative parasite that lives more successfully as a parasite than it does independently. See also Commensal, Host, Mutualism.

PARASITENGONA. [Gr. παρασιτος, one who eats at the table of another; γονη, seed]. In some classifications, a large grouping of mites (order Trombidiformes, suborder Prostigmata (Actinedida / Actinotrichida)) containing the velvet mites, chiggers, and water mites. Not all authorities agree with this classification.

PARASITIFORMES (ANACTINOTRICHIDA, ONYCHOPALPIDA). [Gr. παρασιτος, parasite; L. forma, shape]. A superorder of soft-bodied, white, yellow, yellow-brown, pink or red mites (class Euchelicerata, subclass Arachnida) many of which are parasitic. Orders: Holothyrida, Ixodida, Mesostigmata.

PARASITINA. [Gr. παρασιτος, one who eats at the table of another]. In some classifications, a monotypic suborder of large, yellowish to dark brown, predatory mites (superorder Parasitiformes, order Mesostigmata). They prey on a wide range of microarthropods and nematodes. Superfamily: Parasitoidea. Family: **Parasitidae**. Otherwise a superfamily (Parasitoidea) of the infraorder Gamasina.

PARASITISM. [Gr. παρασιτος, one who eats at the table of another]. An interaction between species in which one, which is usually smaller (the parasite) lives in or on another (the host), obtaining food, shelter or other requirements. Whereas a predator kills it host (i.e. lives on the capital of its food resource) a parasite generally does not kill its host (i.e. lives on its income) although some harm may be done. The effect on the host may range from almost none to severe debilitation and eventual death, but even in the case of severe harm it does not follow that the parasite is harmful to the host species in the long term or in an evolutionary context. In fact it may even be beneficial by favoring specific adaptations in the host species population.

PARASITOID. [Gr. παρασιτος, parasite; ειδος, form]. See Parasite.

PARASITOIDEA. [Gr. παρασιτος, one who eats at the table of another]. A monospecific superfamily of mites (suborder Monogynaspida, infraorder Gamasina). Family: **Parasitidae**.

PARASYMBIOSIS. [Gr. παρα, near; συμβιος, living together]. A situation in which organisms live together without either mutual harm or benefit.

PARATELY. [Gr. παρα, near; τελος, end]. An evolutionary process resulting in a superficial but unrelated resemblance, i.e. derived by convergent evolution.

PARATENIC HOST. [Gr. παρατεινω, delay]. See Host.

PARATONIC. [Gr. παρα, beside; τονος, strain]. Of movements (tropisms and nastic movements) which are stimulated or retarded by external stimuli. See also Choronomic, Autonomic.

PARATROPHIC. [Gr. παρα, beside; τρεφειν, to nourish]. The nutritional strategy of obligate parasites.

PARATROPIDIDAE. [Gr. παρα, besides/near; τροπις, keel]. The small family of bald-legged spiders (infraorder Mygalomorphae, superfamily Avicularioidea) from northern South America.

PARATYDEOIDEA. [Gr. παρα, near; Τυδυες, a Greek hero]. A superfamily of mites (suborder Prostigmata, infraorder Anystina). Families: **Paratydeidae, Stigmocheylidae**.

PARAVERTICAL SETAE. [Gr. παρα, beside; *vertex*, top; *setae*, bristles]. In the Mesostigmata: the most anterior pair of setae in the z-series (setae z1). They are usually on the anterolateral edge of the pronotum and inserted across a lyrifissure from the vertical setae j1.

PARAXIAL. [Gr. παρα, beside; L. *axis*, axle]. Alongside the axis. To move parallel to the body axis. In spiders: of chelicerae in which the paturon projects forward with the fangs moving in a downward direction. See also Adaxial, Diaxial.

PARAXIAL ORGANS. [Gr. παρα, beside; L. *axis*, axle]. In scorpions: special gland pockets that produce the spermatophores.

PARCIDENTATE. [L. *parcus*, sparing; *dens*, tooth]. Having few teeth.

PARENTAL CARE. All the activities of an animal that are directed towards the protection, feeding and general care of its offspring, or those of a near relative, from the time of parturition or hatching to independence.

PARENTAL INVESTMENT. Any behavior by a parent towards an offspring that increases that offspring's chances of survival, maybe to the detriment of possible investment in other offspring.

PARHOMOLOGY. [L. *parilis*, similar; Gr. ομος, alike; λογος, discourse]. An apparent similarity of structure.

PARHYPOCHTHONIOIDEA. [L. *parilis*, similar; Gr. υπο–, under; χθων, the ground]. A superfamily of mites (suborder Oribatida, infraorder Parhyposomata). Families: **Elliptochthoniidae, Gehypochthoniidae, Parhypochthoniidae**.

PARHYPOSOMATA. [L. *parilis*, similar; Gr. υπο–, under; σωμα, body]. An infraorder of beetle mites or armored mites (order Sarcoptiformes, suborder Oribatida). Superfamily: Parhypochthonioidea.

PARIES, PARIETES. [L. *paries*, wall]. In general: walls or sides of a structure.

PARIETAL. [L. *paries*, wall]. Of some structure next to, or forming part of a wall. E.g. a membrane, layer, lobe.

PARITY. [L. *parere*, to give birth]. The number of times a female has given birth, regardless of the number of offspring produced at any one time. See also Multiparous, Pluriparous.

PARMULA (DORSAL SCAPE). [L. *parmula*, little shield]. In the **Linyphiidae**: the process arising from the dorsal wall of the epigynum. In some species it is dorsal to the scape. Also referred to as the dorsal scape.

PARS. [L. *pars*, part]. A part of an organ, e.g. pars glandularis, pars distalis, pars intermedia, etc.

PARS CEPHALICA. [L. *pars*, part; Gr. κεφαλη, head]. Cephalic region.

PARS PENDULA. [L. *pars*, part; *pendula*, hanging]. In some male spiders: a thin flap along the margin of the embolus.

PARS THORACIA. [L. *pars*, part; Gr. θωραξ, chest]. Thoracic region.

PARTHENOGENESIS. [Gr. παρθενος, virgin; γενεσις, birth]. The development of an individual from an egg, without fertilization by a male gamete. This reproductive strategy occurs in groups in which males may be absent. The eggs that develop in this way are usually diploid, so all offspring are genetically identical with the parent. Commonly, parthenogenesis alternates with sexual reproduction (heterogamy) which thus allows for genetic recombination. **Acyclic Parthenogenesis**: parthenogenesis in which there is no sexual phase or an alteration of generations. **Ameiotic (Apomictic) parthenogenesis**: parthenogenesis in which meiosis has been suppressed so that chromosome reduction does not occur. **Androcyclic parthenogenesis**: cyclic parthenogenesis in which a series of parthenogenetic generations is followed by the production of males as a sexual generation. **Androgenesis (Patrogenesis)**: following fusion with a normal male gamete, parthenogenetic development due to failure of the nucleus of the female gamete, or of an enucleated egg. Thus the embryo contains only paternal chromosomes. **Anholocyclic parthenogenesis**: parthenogenesis in which the sexual part of the cycle is suppressed, i.e. permanently parthenogenetic. **Arrhenotokous parthenogenesis**: haplodiploid parthenogenesis in which males arise from unfertilized and therefore haploid egg cells (this is characteristic of all hymenopterans). **Automictic parthenogenesis**, parthenogenesis in which meiosis is preserved and diploidy is reinstated either by the fusion of haploid nuclei or by the formation of a restitution nucleus. **Cyclic parthenogenesis**: reproduction by a series of parthenogenetic generations alternating with a single sexually reproducing generation. **Haploid parthenogenesis**: the development of a haploid individual from a female gamete that has undergone meiotic division but has not been fertilized. **Hemizygoid parthenogenesis**: the development of an individual from an unfertilized haploid egg. **Heteroparthenogenesis**: producing either offspring that reproduce parthenogenetically or offspring that reproduce sexually. **Holocyclic parthenogenesis**: reproduction by a series of parthenogenetic generations alternating with a single sexually reproducing generation. **Meiotic parthenogenesis (Automictic parthenogenesis)**: parthenogenesis in which meiosis is preserved and diploidy is reinstated either by the fusion of haploid nuclei or by the formation of a restitution nucleus. **Monocyclic parthenogenesis**: reproduction by a series of parthenogenetic generations alternating with one sexually reproducing generation in each annual cycle. **Paedoparthenogenesis**: parthenogenesis occurring during the larval stage. **Parthenapogamy (Ooapogamy)**: diploid or somatic parthenogenesis. **Polycyclic parthenogenesis**: reproduction involving two or more cycles of alternating parthenogenetic and sexually reproducing generations per year. **Pseudogamic parthenogenesis (Hemigamy, Merospermy)**: parthenogenetic development of an ovum after stimulation but not fertilization by a spermatozoon, which thereafter has no role in development. **Somatic (or Diploid) Parthenogenesis**: parthenogenesis in individuals in which meiosis has been suppressed so that chromosome reduction does not occur. **Thelytoky**: obligate parthenogenesis in which only diploid female offspring are produced. **Tychoparthenogenesis**: parthenogenesis which occurs in species that are normally sexually reproducing. **Zygoid parthenogenesis**: Asexual reproduction from an egg which remains diploid or undergoes diploidization during its development.

PARTIAL PARASITE (SEMIPARASITE). See Parasite.

PARTITE. [L. *partitus*, divided]. Divided nearly to the base.

PARVICELLULAR. [L. *parvus*, small; *cellula*, small cell]. Consisting of small cells.

PARVICONOID. [L. *parvus*, small; *conus*, cone]. Resembling a small cone.

PARVORDER. [L. *parvitas*, smallness; *ordo*, order]. A specific taxonomic category above superfamily and below infraorder.

PATELLA. [L. *patella*, small shallow dish]. In spiders: the fourth leg segment (also 'carpopodite'). See also Limb.

PATENT, PATENS, PATENTES. [L. *patens*, lying open]. Open. Diverging. Expanded.

PATERIFORM. [L. *patera*, flat dish; *forma*, shape]. Saucer-shaped.

PATHOGENESIS. [Gr. παθος, suffering; γεννησις, producing]. The process of disease development.

PATOBIONTS. [Gr. πατος, dirt; βιον, living]. Cryptozoans that spend their entire lives in the cryptosphere (as opposed to Patocoles and Patoxenes).

PATOCOLES. [Gr. πατος, dirt; L. *colere*, to dwell]. Cryptozoans that spend part of their life hidden in the soil but emerge to hunt and mate. See also Patobionts, Patoxenes, Phanerozoa.

PATOXENES. [Gr. πατος, dirt; ξενος, stranger]. Minute animals which, from time to time, bury themselves in the soil. See also Patobionts, Patocoles, Phanerozoa.

PATRICLINOUS (PATRICLINAL, PATROCLINOUS). [Gr. πατηρ, father; κλινειν, to incline]. Having hereditary characteristics that are more paternal than maternal. See also Matriclinous.

PATRILINEAL. [Gr. πατηρ, father]. Of the paternal line, or of some characteristic passed from the male parent to offspring.

PATRISTIC CHARACTER. [Gr. πατηρ, father]. Any character or trait inherited by all members of a group from their most recent common ancestor.

PATRISTIC DISTANCE. [Gr. πατηρ, father]. A measure of the amount of genetically determined change that has occurred between any two points of a phylogenetic tree.

PATROCLINOUS. See Patriclinous.

PATROGENESIS. [Gr. πατηρ, father; γενεσις, birth]. See Androgenesis, Parthenogenesis.

PATROGYNOPAEDIUM. [Gr. πατηρ, father; γυνη, a woman; παις, a child]. A family group in which both the parents remain with the offspring for some time.

PATRONYMIC. [Gr. πατηρ, father; ονυμα, name]. In nomenclature, a name based on that of a person.

PATULOUS. [L. *patulus*, standing open]. Spreading. Expanded. Distended. Having a wide aperture.

PATURON. [Gr. πατειν, to trample on; ουρα, rear]. In arachnids: the basal joint of the chelicerae, which is used for crushing the insect prey and extracting the body fluids.

PAUCIDENTATE. [L. *pauci*, few; *dens*, tooth]. With few teeth.

PAUCISPIRAL (OLIGOGYRAL). [L. *paucus*, few; *spira*, coil]. With relatively few whorls.

pc/pcx. In mesostigmatans: a designation used for the pair of palpcoxal setae; the most basal setae on the subcapitulum.

pd 1-3. In mesostigmatans: designations for the setae on the posterior dorsal surface of a leg or palp segment.

PEACOCK MITE, ORNATE SPIDER MITE. *Tuckerella* spp. A member of the family **Tuckerellidae** (Prostigmata).

PEARLACEOUS. [ML. *perla*, pearl; L. *-aceous*, of the nature of]. Having the appearance of a pearl.

PECKHAMMIAN MIMICRY. See Mimicry.

PECTEN. [L. *pecten*, comb]. Any comb-like structure. 1. In insects and some spiders: part of a stridulating organ. 2. In scorpions: see Pectines.

PECTINATE. [L. *pecten*, comb]. Comb-like.

PECTINES. [L. *pecten*, comb]. In scorpions: a pair of ventral, comb-like, sensory (tactile) appendages posterior to the genital plates and attached to the second abdominal segment, near the ventral midline. Each is composed of three rows of chitinous plates which form an axis that

185

projects to each side from the point of attachment. Suspended from the body of the pectine is a series of tooth-like processes. This structure is unique to scorpions.

PECTINIFERA. [L. *pecten*, comb; *ferre*, to bear]. In some classifications: a subclass of arachnids which contains all the extant groups of scorpions and a few fossil forms seen as intermediate between this group and the Eurypterida.

PECTUNCULATE, PECTUNCULOID. [L. *pecten*, comb; *-unculus*, little]. Having a row of minute appendages.

PEDAL (PODAL). [L. *pes*, foot]. Of the foot or feet.

PEDES. [L. *pes*, foot]. The feet or real legs.

PEDICEL. [L. *pediculus*, little foot]. In general, a short stalk bearing an organ or sessile organism. In the spiders: the short, narrow region of the body that connects the cephalothorax with the abdomen.

PEDIPALPS. [L. *pes*, foot; *palpare*, to feel]. The second pair of limbs in arachnids. See Palp.

PEDIPALPI. [L. *pes*, foot; *palpare*, to feel]. In an older classification: an order of arachnids (class Euchelicerata, subclass Arachnida) in which the Uropygi (scorpion-like with a terminal flagellum) and Amblypygi (spider like, tailless, whip scorpions) were often combined as suborders. All forms are strikingly flattened and have the first walking legs modified as slender whips (antenniform). The seventh body segment is constricted to form a pedicel and there are two pairs of book lungs. There are no spinnerets or poison fangs.

PEDIPALPS, PEDIPALPUS. [L. *pes*, foot; *palpare*, to feel]. In arachnids and other chelicerates: the second cephalothoracic paired appendages, that may be leg-like, pincer-like or simple. In those arachnids with large chelicerae (Araneae, Palpigrada, Solifugae, many Opilones) they have become walking legs or true palps while in the orders with small chelicerae (Amblypygi, Pseudoscorpiones, Scorpiones, Uropygi) they have often become modified to form large raptoral organs. Pedipalps are well adapted implements for killing and manipulating prey as well as for digging and defense. In all arachnids they also serve as tactile and olfactory organs. In the spiders (Araneae) they guide food to the mouth and in males the pedipalp tarsus has become modified to form a complex copulatory structure, which is often taxonomically significant. The six parts of the pedipalp are, in order from the body: coxae, trochanter, femur, patella, tibia, tarsus.

PEDOFOSSAE. [L. *pes*, foot; *fossa*, ditch]. In ticks and mites: the concavities in the podosoma into which legs II, III and IV can be tucked.

PEDOTECTUM (TECTOPEDIUM). [L. *pes*, foot; *tectum*, roof]. In some armored oribatid mites: a scale-like tectum arising around the insertion of legs I or II that covers the insertion of the leg and sometimes forms a protected space into which the legs can be withdrawn. See also Pedofossae

PEDUNCLE. [LL. *pedunculus*, little foot]. In general, any stalk or stalk-like structure.

PEDUNCULATE. [LL. *pedunculus*, little foot]. Having a peduncle.

PEG TEETH. The spine-like teeth on the chelicerae.

PELOPSIFORM. [Gr. πελοψ, Dark-face, myth. son of Tantalus; L. *forma*, shape]. In ticks and mites: having the form of the **Peloppiidae**, a family of oribatid mites.

PELTA. [Gr. πελτη, a small light shield]. A shield or shield-like structure.

PELTATE. [Gr. πελτη, a small light shield]. Shield-shaped.

PELTIDIUM. [Gr. πελτη, a small light shield]. In ticks and mites: the prodorsal shield. See also Schizopeltid.

PENESTOMIDAE. [Gr. πενης, a laborer, στομα, mouth]. A small family of spiders (infraorder Araneomorphae, superfamily Entelegynae).

PENICILLIFORM (PENICILLATE). [L. *penicillus*, painter's brush]. Having the form of a brush or pencil. Being tipped with fine hairs or fibers.

PENICILLUS, PENICILLUM. [L. *penicillus*, painter's brush]. Any brush-shaped structure; such as tufts of hair or tufts of arterioles.

186

PENIS (PHALLUS). [L. *penis*, penis]. The male copulatory organ, or paired organs which convey sperm to the female genital tract.

PENNACEOUS, PENNIFORM. [L. *penna*, feather; *-aceous*, of the nature of]. Resembling a feather in structure or marking.

PENNATE. [L. *penna*, feather]. Feathered or bearing feather-like processes.

PENTACTINAL. [Gr. πεντα-, five; ακτις, ray]. Five-rayed, five-branched.

PENTAFID. [Gr. πεντα-, five; L. *findere*, to cleave]. Divided into five lobes.

PENTAMEROUS. [Gr. πεντα-, five; μερος, part]. Composed of five parts.

PENTARADIATE. [Gr. πεντα-, five; L. *radius*, ray]. Constructed on a five-rayed plan.

PENTASTERNUM. [Gr. πεντα-, five; στερνον, chest]. In ticks and mites: the sternite of the fifth segment of the prosoma or the third segment of the podosoma.

PENTASTICHOUS. [Gr. πεντα-, five; στιχος, row]. Arranged in five rows.

P.E.R. Posterior Eye Row.

PERCURRENT. [L. *per*, through; *currere*, to run]. Continuous. Extending through the length.

PERCUTANEOUS. [L. *per*, through; *cutis*, skin]. Penetration through the skin.

PERENNATION. [L. *per*, throughout; *annus*, year]. Survival for a number of years.

PERICARDIAL (PERICARDIAC). [Gr. περι, around; καρδια, heart]. Surrounding the heart; usually applied to a cavity or septum. A region of the haemocoel surrounding the heart and from which blood flows directly into the heart via a number of ostia or valvular openings in the heart wall

PERICARDIAL CHAMBER. [Gr. περι, around; καρδια, heart]. The open space around the heart or dorsal vessel.

PERICARDIAL DIAPHRAGM. [Gr. περι, around; καρδια, heart; διαφραγμα, partition/barrier]. A delicate membranous tissue attached to the ventral surface of the heart and laterally to the body wall.

PERICARDIUM, PERICARDIAL. [Gr. περι, around; καρδια, heart]. The cavity enclosing the heart as well as membranes lining the cavity and covering the heart.

PERICENTRAL. [Gr. περι, around; L. *centrum*, center]. Around or near to the center.

PERICHAETINE. [Gr. περι, around; χαιτη, hair]. Having a ring of chaetae or setae encircling the body.

PERIDIUM. [Gr. πηριδιον, little leather pouch]. In the **Allothyridae** (Holothyrida) and some Mesostigmata: a cavity filled with cuticular processes behind coxae IV.

PERIEGOPIDAE. [Gr. περιηγητης, a guide; ωψ, appearance]. A very small monospecific family of spiders (infraorder Araneomorphae, superfamily Haplogynae) from Queensland (Australia) and New Zealand. There are only six eyes, in three widely spaced clusters of two (instead of the usual eight).

PERIGASTRIUM. [Gr. περι, around; γαστηρ, stomach]. The body cavity.

PERIGONADIAL. [Gr. περι, around; γονη, seed]. Of the cavity surrounding the gonads.

PERI-INTESTINAL. [Gr. περι, around; L. *intestinus*, intestine]. The region of the body cavity around the alimentary canal.

PERINEUM (PERINAEUM). [ML. *perinaeon*; region of the body between the anus and the genital organs]. The region between the posterior of the anus and the anterior part of the external genitalia.

PERIORAL. [Gr. περι, around; LL. *oralis*, mouth]. Of the region around the mouth.

PERIPHERAL. [Gr. περιφερης, revolving round]. Distant from the center.

PERIPHERAL ISOLATE. [Gr. περιφερης, revolving round]. A population that is isolated at the outer limits of the species' range.

PERIPHERAL NERVOUS SYSTEM. [Gr. περιφερης, revolving round]. The nervous system other than the central nervous system (CNS), or various central/co-ordinating ganglia. It consists mainly of nerves of various size which branch repeatedly after leaving the CNS to innervate sense organs and various muscles and effectors. The nerve fibers are usually continuous (i.e. no synapses) from the receptors to the CNS in the case of sensory nerves, or from the CNS to the effectors in the case of motor nerves. Within a nerve, sensory and motor nerve fibers may run side by side although they do not usually interact except via the synapses in the CNS. However, synapses do occur in some regions of the peripheral nervous system.

PERIPODOMERIC FISSURE. [Gr. περι, around; πους, foot; μερικος, particular]. In the Mesostigmata: an area of soft cuticle that marks the juncture of the basitarsus and telotarsus or the basifemur and telofemur.

PERITRACHEAL. [Gr. περι, around; LL. *trachia*, windpipe]. Surrounding the trachea.

PERITREME (PERITREMA). [Gr. περι, around; τρημα, hole]. In ticks and mites (and some insects): a small plate-like structure which is perforated by pores (aeropyles), or the opening of a spiracle. Located on the ventrolateral surface of the body caudal to coxae IV; in argasid ticks, it consists of a very small simple elevated plate (macula) and a spiracular opening next to an adjacent ridge of cuticle, all on the supracoxal fold. In the **Ixodidae** the spiracular plate is a prominent structure with may ovoid air spaces (goblets) within the cuticle which are visible externally and give this structure its distinctive appearance.

PERLATE. [ML. *perla*, pearl]. Beaded.

PERLOHMANNIOIDEA. [L. *per*, by means of/through; *H. Lohmann*, German? Biologist]. A superfamily of mites (suborder Oribatida, infraorder Mixonomata - section Dichosomata). Families: **Collohmanniidae, Perlohmaniidae**.

PERMANENT PARASITE. A parasite living its entire adult life within or on a host.

PERMEANTS. [L. *permeare*, to pass through]. Animals which move freely from one community or habitat to another.

PEROPOD. [Gr. πηρος, disabled; πους, foot]. Having rudimentary limbs.

PERSIMILIS. [L. *per*, very; *similis*, similar]. The Chilean predatory mite, *Phytoseiulus persimilis* (Ascoidea: Phytoseiidae), a commercially available and extremely efficient predator of spider mites.

PERVERSUM SIMPLEX. [L. *perversum*, to turn upside down; *simplex*, simple]. The attempted mating of one male with another male.

PERVIOUS. [L. *per*, through; *via*, way]. Perforate or open.

PES, PEDES. [L. *pes*, foot]. Any foot, foot-like structure or base.

PETALOID. [Gr. πεταλον, leaf; ειδος, form]. In the form of a petal.

PETIOLE (PODEON). [L. *petiolus*, little foot]. In spiders: a small sclerite at the base of the palpal organ. It connects the *sub*-tegulum with the alveolar wall.

PETRICOLOUS. [L. *petra*, rock; *colere*, to inhabit]. Dwelling within stones, crevices or in hard clay.

PETROBUNIDAE. [Gr. πετρα, rock; + -*bunus*, a common suffix in Opilione taxonomy]. A small, recently described, family of harvestmen or daddy longlegs (suborder Laniatores, superfamily Epedanoidea) from the Indo-Malayan region and Australasia.

PETROCOLOUS. [Gr. πετρα, rock; L. *colere*, to inhabit]. Living in rocky habitats.

PETROPHILOUS. [Gr. πετρα, rock; φιλος, loving]. Thriving in rocky habitats.

PETTALIDAE. [Gr. Myth. *Pettalus* (from Πηδασος)]. A family of small harvestmen (suborder Cyphophthalmi, infraorder Scopulophthalmi) that spend their entire life cycle in leaf litter (except for the cave-dwelling South African *Speleosiro argasiformis*). They are 2-5 mm long, and usually have an oval-shaped body.

PHACOID. [Gr. φακος, lentil; ειδος, form]. In the shape of a lentil.

PHAENO-. See also Pheno.

PHAEOCHROUS. [Gr. φαιος, dusky; χρως, color]. Dusky colored.

PHAEOMELANIN. [Gr. φαιος, dusky; μελας, black]. A brownish melanin.

PHALANGES. [Gr. φαλαγξ, a finger bone]. The segments of the tarsus. Singular - phalanx.

PHALANGIDA. [Gr. φαλαγγιον, a kind of venomous spider]. See Opiliones.

PHALANGIIDAE. [Gr. φαλαγγιον, a kind of venomous spider]. A large family of harvestmen or daddy longlegs (suborder Eupnoi, superfamily Phalangioidea).

PHALANGIOIDEA. [Gr. φαλαγγιον, a kind of venomous spider]. A superfamily of harvestmen (order Opiliones, suborder Eupnoi). Families: **Monoscutidae, Neopilionidae, Phalangiidae, Protolophidae, Sclerosomatidae, Stygophalangiidae.**

PHALANGODOIDEA. [Gr. φαλαγγιον, a kind of venomous spider]. A monotypic superfamily of harvestmen (suborder Laniatores, infraorder Grassatores) in which body length is from 1-3 mm, and the pedipalps are armed with large spines. The **Oncopodidae** was formerly included here, now in the superfamily Epedanoidea. Family: **Phalangodidae.**

PHALANX. See Phalanges.

PHALLIC GLAND. [Gr. φαλλος, penis]. A gland that secretes a substance that may be used for attaching spermatophores.

PHANERE. [Gr. φανερος, manifest]. Any prominent tegumentary formation, i.e. setae or seta-like processes. See also Phanerotaxy.

PHANERIC. [Gr. φανερος, manifest]. Applied to conspicuous coloration or other characters: i.e. those that are the opposite of cryptic.

PHANEROGENIC. [Gr. φανερος, manifest; γενος, birth]. Of known descent. Used of fossil species that have an established phylogeny from species occurring in earlier geological formations.

PHANEROTAXY, PHANEROTACTIC. [Gr. φανερος, manifest; ταξις, an arranging]. In the Chelicerata: the number and arrangements of the phaneres.

PHANEROZOA. [Gr. φανερος, manifest; ζωον, an animal]. Animals, such as spiders and mites, which have relatives among the cryptozoa but which do not live in the cryptosphere themselves. See also Patobionts, Patocoles, Patoxenes.

PHARATE. [Gr. φαρος, loose mantle]. A mite or other arthropod between apolysis and ecdysis. Of the fully formed instar prior to ecdysis, which has formed a new exoskeleton but that is still within a previous cuticle.

PHAROTAXIS. [Gr. φαρος, lighthouse; ταξις, an arranging]. The movement of an animal towards a definite place as a consequence of prior conditioning or learning. Navigation by landmarks.

PHARYNX, PHARYNGES, PHARYNXES. [Gr. φαρυγξ, the throat]. The throat. The musculo-membranous tube connecting the buccal cavity, gullet or anterior region of the alimentary canal to the esophagus. In arachnids (and insects, annelids, platyhelminths): the anterior part of the foregut, between the mouth and the esophagus .

PHASIC. [Gr. φαινειν, to appear]. Transient.

PHASIC CASTRATION. [Gr. φαινειν, to appear; L. *castrare*, to castrate/prune]. Of individuals in which the gonads are inhibited in development due to seasonal or ontogenetic conditions. See also Alimentary Castration.

PHASIC MUSCLES. See Muscle Terminology.

PHENE. [Gr. φαινειν, to appear]. A character in the phenotype that is under genetic control.

PHENGOPHIL. [Gr. φεγγος, light; φιλος, loving]. Of animals that prefer light. See also Lucifugous, Lucipetal, Phengophobe, Photophobic, Photophilic.

189

PHENGOPHOBE. [Gr. φεγγος, light; φοβος, fear]. Of animals that shun light. See also Lucifugous, Lucipetal, Phengophil, Photophobic, Photophilic.

PHENOPELOPOIDEA. [Gr. φαινειν, to appear; Πελοψ, Dark-face, myth. son of Tantalus]. A monotypic superfamily of mites (suborder Oribatida, infraorder Brachypylina - section Poronoticae). Family: **Phenopelopidea**.

PHENOTYPE. [Gr. φαινειν, to appear; τυπος, image]. The totality of the characters of an organism that appear due to the interaction between the genotype and the environment. Organisms with the same overall genotype may have many different phenotypes due to the effects of the environment and of gene interaction, or, may have the same phenotypes but different genotypes due to incomplete dominance, penetrance or expressivity.

PHENOTYPIC ADAPTATION. See Adaptation.

PHENOTYPIC SEX DETERMINATION. [Gr. φαινειν, to appear; τυπος, image]. See Sex Determination.

PHEROMONE (ECTOHORMONE, SOCIOHORMONE). [Gr. φερειν, to bear; hormone (Gr. ορμαω, rouse)]. A chemical signal given out by one animal that acts as a specific signal to another animal of the same species and elicits a particular physiological and/or behavioral response. If the pheromone produces a more or less immediate and reversible effect it is said to have a 'releaser' effect. If it triggers a chain of physiological responses, it is said to have a 'primer' effect. See also Alarm Pheromone.

Φ φ (Phi). In the Acariformes: a designation for the solenidion of the tibia. Ω (omega) on the tarsus; Σ (sigma) on the genu.

PHIALIFORM, PHIALAEFORM. [L. phiala, a bowl; forma, shape]. Cup-shaped. Saucer-shaped.

PHILODROMIDAE. [Gr. φιλος, loving; δρομειν, to run]. A large cosmopolitan family of spiders (infraorder Araneomorphae, superfamily Entelegynae) known as running crab spiders. None of the species build webs, but use their silk for draglines and egg sacs.

PHILOPATRY. [Gr. φιλειν, to love; παρτις, father]. The tendency of an organism to remain in, or return to, its home area or native locality.

PHILOPROGENETIVE. [Gr. φιλειν, to love; L. progignere, to beget]. Producing large numbers of offspring. Prolific.

PHILOTHERMIC. [Gr. φιλειν, to love; θερμη, heat]. Thriving in warm climates.

PHLOEODIC. [Gr. φλοιος, smooth or inner bark; ειδος, form]. Having the appearance of bark.

PHOBOTAXIS. See Klinokinesis.

PHOLCIDAE. [Gr. φολκος, bandy-legged]. A cosmopolitan family of small, six-eyed, haplogyne spiders (infraorder Araneomorphae, superfamily Haplogynae) which are often long-legged, resembling phalangids. They spin small webs of tangled threads in sheltered recesses, several species are responsible for household cobwebs. *Pholcus* species usually hang upside down in their open, random webs and, if disturbed, will shake and whirl their body at such high speed that they become blurred.

PHOLCOCHYROCERIDAE. [Gr. φολκος, bandy-legged; οχυρος, firm/stout; κερας, horn (spur)]. A small family of extinct spiders (infraorder Araneomorphae, superfamily Haplogynae) known from Burmese amber, from the Cretaceous of Myanmar.

PHOLCOIDEA. [Gr. φολκος, bandy-legged]. In a previous classification, a cosmopolitan superfamily of six-eyed and eight-eyed araneomorph spiders (suborder Opisthothelae, infraorder Araneomorphae) that united the families: **Pholcidae, Diguetidae, Plectreuridae.**

PHONATION. [Gr. φωνη, sound]. The production of sounds.

PHONORECEPTOR. [Gr. φωνη, sound; L. receptor, receiver]. A receptor of sound waves, e.g. certain sensillae.

PHORESIS, PHORESY, PHORESIA. [Gr. φορευς, a carrier]. Hitch-hiking. The carrying of one organism by another without parasitism. A form of symbiotic relationship when the symbiont, the phoront, is mechanically carried by its host; neither being physiologically dependent on the other. Normal behavior, e.g. feeding, reproduction, movement, ceases until some cue elicits the phoront's departure from the animal and the resumption of normal behavior. Phoresy usually results in the dispersal of populations, but may also result in reaggregation, especially for mites using highly specialized habitats (e.g. pitcher plants: Nepenthaceae & Sarraceniaceae).

PHORETIC HOST. [Gr. φορα, a carrying]. One partner in a phoretic relationship. An organism that transports another microorganism to which it is nonsusceptible.

PHORETOMORPH. [Gr. φορετος, carried; μορφη, form]. In mites: any dispersing stage, adapted especially for phoretic transport, that differs in morphology from other stages. In the previous grouping Heterostigmatina (now in Eleutherengona): a heteromorphic phoretic stage that differs from non-dispersing mites by having well developed claws on the legs.

PHOTOKINESIS. [Gr. φως, light; κινησις, motion]. The change in the speed of movement in an organism that is made in response to a change in light intensity.

PHOTOLABILE. [Gr. φως, light; L. *labare*, to waver]. Of some substance modified by light; as in some retinal pigments.

PHOTOPERIOD. [Gr. φως, light; περιοδος, circuit]. The duration of daily exposure to light, or the length of day which favors the optimum functioning of an organism.

PHOTOPERIODISM. [Gr. φως, light; περιοδος, circuit]. The response of an organism to periodic changes in either light intensity or to the relative length of a day. The onset of many animal's activities, such as breeding, feeding and migration are determined by photoperiodism. See also Circadian Rhythms.

PHOTOPHILIC. [Gr. φως, light; φιλος, loving]. Thriving in conditions of full light. See also Lucifugous, Lucipetal, Phengophil, Phengophobe, Photophobic.

PHOTOPHOBIC. [Gr. φως, light; φοβος, fear]. Intolerant of light, or avoiding full light. See also Lucifugous, Lucipetal, Phengophil, Phengophobe, Photophilic.

PHOTOPHOBOTAXIS (NEGATIVE TROPISM). [Gr. φως, light; φοβος, fear; ταξις, an arranging]. Movement involved in the avoidance of light.

PHOTOPIA. [Gr. φως, light; ωψ, eye]. Adaptation of the eye to light.

PHOTOPIGMENTS. [Gr. φως, light; L. *pingere*, to paint]. Light-sensitive pigments that are altered by the absorption of light in such a way as to change the conductance of the membrane in which they reside.

PHOTORECEPTOR. [Gr. φως, light; L. *receptus*, received]. A terminal sensory structure for receiving light stimuli. It may be a single cell or a collection of cells and contains a photoexcitable pigment associated with a receptor membrane. See also Receptor.

PHOTOTAXIS. [Gr. φως, light; ταξις, an arranging]. A change in the direction of travel by an organism in response to a change in light intensity. See also Heliotaxis, Skototaxis.

PHOTOTELOTAXIS. [Gr. φως, light; τελος, end; ταξις, an arranging]. The direct movement of an animal toward shade.

PHOTOTONUS. [Gr. φως, light; τονος, tension]. 1. Sensitiveness to light. 2. A muscle tonus stimulated by light.

PHOTOTROPISM, PHOTROPIC. [Gr. φως, light; τροπος, turn]. Movement determined by the direction of incident light.

PHRAGMOSIS. [Gr. φραγμα, fence; -οσις, suf. of condition]. The action of closing an entrance to a nest or burrow with the body.

PHRATRY (CLAN). [Gr. φρατρη, a subdivision of a tribe]. In classification: a loose term that has never been generally adopted or precisely defined, but is often used to mean subtribe.

PHTHIRACAROIDEA. [Gr. φθειρ, louse; LL. *acarus*, mite]. A monotypic superfamily of mites (suborder Oribatida, infraorder Mixonomata - section Euptyctima). Family: **Phthiracaridae (Steganacaridae).**

PHYCOPHILIC. [Gr. φυκος, seaweed; φιλος, loving]. Thriving in algae-rich habitats.

PHRUROLITHIDAE. [Gr. φουρος, watcher/guard; λιθος, stone]. The family of guardstone spiders (infraorder Araneomorphae, superfamily Entelegynae). They were previously in the Corinnidae.

PHRYNOIDEA. [Gr. φρυνος, a stone]. A superfamily of tail-less whip scorpions (order Amblypygi, suborder Euamblypygi). Families: **Phrynichidae, Phrynidae.**

PHYLA. [Gr. φυλον, race]. The plural of phylum.

PHYLETIC SPECIATION. [Gr. φυλον, race]. See Speciation.

PHYLLIFORM. [Gr. φυλλον, a leaf; L. *forma*, shape]. Leaf-shaped.

PHYLOGENETIC CLASSIFICATION. [Gr. φυλον, race; γενεσις, descent]. The study of classification from the point of view of the organism's evolutionary descent. Terminology. **Advanced**: see Derived. **Anagenesis**: change within a lineage. **Ancestral**: same meaning as primitive, but ancestral is preferred because it does not carry the meaning of better or worse. An ancestral character is one that evolved in an ancestral species and was passed down to descendant taxa. **Apomorphy**: the derived state of a character. **Autapomorphy**: the unique derived state of a character (no other taxa in the ingroup have that character state). **Character**: any morphological, behavioral, genetic, or biochemical feature or trait. **Character Polarity**: the hypothesized sequence of evolutionary transition from one character state to another. **Character State**: a character may have different states among taxa, e.g. the number of functional digits (character states = 1, 2, 3, 4 , 5 or more), or wings (character states = presence or absence). **Clade**: a monophyletic group. **Cladogenesis**: the branching of a lineage into two or more lineages; i.e. evolutionary change that results in speciation. **Cladogram (Phylogeny)**: a graphical description of evolutionary relatedness among taxa (phylogeny) constructed using cladistic principles. **Congruence**: the degree to which alternative phylogenetic trees agree. **Convergence (Homoplasy)**: taxa having similar characters or character states due to convergent evolution and not due to inheritance from a common ancestor. For example; the wings of birds and butterflies; both have wings, but they are the result of convergent evolution and not inheritance from a common ancestor. **Derived**: same meaning as advanced, but derived is preferred because it does not carry the meaning of better or worse. A derived character is one that has evolved within the taxon of interest. **Homology**: similar or identical characters or character states between taxa due to inheritance from a common ancestor. **Homoplasy**: See Convergence. **Ingroup**: the group of taxa currently under investigation. **Lineage**: a series of ancestral and descendant populations, through time. A lineage usually refers to a single evolving species, but may include several species descended from a common ancestor. **Monophyletic group**: a group of taxa in which both the ancestor taxon and all descendants of that taxon are included in one group. **Node**: a point on a phylogenetic tree that represents the splitting of two lineages. **Outgroup**: a relatively closely-related taxon that is used in comparison to the ingroup to aid construction of the phylogenetic tree. **Parallel Evolution**: the evolution of similar or identical features independently in related lineages, this is presently thought to be based on similar modifications of the same developmental pathways. **Paraphyletic Group**: a grouping that includes the common ancestor of all taxa in the group, but excludes at least one of the descendant taxa of that ancestor. **Parsimony** (Occam's Razor): a maxim (*pluralitas non est ponenda sine necessitata* - multiplicity ought not to be posited without necessity) suggesting that where several alternative hypotheses are possible, the one requiring the fewest assumptions should be chosen. In phylogenetics, it is commonly applied as 'the least number of evolutionary steps'. **Phylogeny**: see Cladogram. **Phylogenetics (Phylogenetic Tree)**: the study or the operation of using evolutionarily-related characters among taxa to derive a hypothesis of the evolutionary relatedness among those taxa. **Plesiomorphy**: an ancestral characteristic. **Polyphyletic Group**: a cladogram that includes a group of taxa, but excludes the common ancestor of those taxa. **Primitive**: see Ancestral. **Sister Group (Sister Taxa)**: two taxa that are each other's closest evolutionary relative. **Symplesiomorphy**: a shared ancestral character. **Synapomorphy**: a shared derived character. **Taxon (Taxa)**: a unit within biological classification. A taxon may be a species, genera, family, order, etc.

PHYLOGENETIC SYSTEMATICS (TAXONOMY). [Gr. φυλον, race; γενεσις, descent]. A method of classification based on the recency of common ancestors, which is assessed by recognition of shared derived characters.

PHYLOGENETIC TREE. [Gr. φυλον, race; γενεσις, descent]. A diagrammatic representation, in the form of a branching tree, that represents inferred lines of descent.

PHYLOGENY. [Gr. φυλον, race; γενναω, produce]. The history of the development of a species, or some other taxonomic group, particularly concerning the patterns of the various lines of descent.

PHYLUM (pl. **PHYLA**). [Gr. φυλον, race]. A primary division of the animal kingdom in which all the organisms included in one phyla are seen to be constructed on a similar general plan and thus thought to be related. At present there are generally held to be 37 animal phyla: Acanthocephala, Acoelomorpha, Annelida, Arthropoda, Brachiopoda, Bryozoa, Chaetognatha, Chordata, Cnidaria, Ctenophora, Cycliophora, Echinodermata, Echiura (maybe included in Annelida), Entoprocta, Gastrotricha, Gnathostomulida, Hemichordata, Kinorhyncha, Loricifera, Micrognathozoa, Mollusca, Myxozoa (maybe included in Cnidaria), Nematoda, Nematomorpha, Nemertea, Onychophora, Orthonectida, Phoronida, Placozoa, Platyhelminthes, Porifera, Priapulida, Rhombozoa, Rotifera, Sipuncula, Tardigrada, Xenacoelomorpha (Xenoturbellida + Acoelomorpha) Some phyla may be considered as subphyla or classes of other groups, depending on your point of view. In the hierarchy, phylum comes below subkingdom and above infraphylum or superclass. In botany a phylum may be called a Division. See also Nomenclature.

PHYSOGASTRY. [Gr. φυσα, bladder; γαστηρ, stomach]. A swelling of the opisthosoma to accommodate a massive numbers of eggs or developing young. Physogastry is common only in the Podapolipidae (Eleutherengona), Pyemotidae, Pygmephoridae.

PHYSOGLENIDAE. [Gr. φυσα, bladder; γληνη, socket]. A family of spiders (infraorder Araneomorphae, superfamily Entelegynae).

PHYTOBIONTIC, PHYTOBIOTIC. [Gr. φυτον, plant; βιον, living]. Of organisms that spend most of their active life on or in plants.

PHYTOSEIID TYPE OF SPERM ACCESS SYSTEM. [Phytoseiidae: Gr. φυτον, plant; σειω, shake/agitate]. In the **Phytoseiidae** (Gamasina): a sclerotized, paired secondary sperm receiving and processing system consisting of an external opening (solenostome), usually near the base of coxae III-IV, that opens into a tubular duct (major duct) of variable length which runs to a valve-like region: the atrium. A minor duct branches away from the atrium via an embolus and the major duct opens into a collar-like structure (the calyx) which empties into a vesicle. See also Laelapid Type of Sperm Access System.

PHYTOSEIIDAE. [Gr. φυτον, plant; σειω, shake/agitate]. A very large family of mites (infraorder Gamasina, superfamily Phytoseioidea) which predate thrips and other mite species. They are often used as a biological control agents. Over 2,700 documented species.

PHYTOSEIOIDEA. [Gr. φυτον, plant; σειω, shake/agitate]. A superfamily of mites (suborder Monogynaspida, infraorder Gamasina). The Phytoseiidae feed on phytophagous arthropods, including other mite species and are often used as biological control agents for managing mite pests. Families: **Blattisociidae, Otopheidomenidae, Phytoseiidae, Podocinidae.**

PHYXELIDIDAE. [Gr. φυξηλις, cowardly]. The small family of laceweb spiders (infraorder Araneomorphae, superfamily Entelegynae).

PICEOUS. [L. *piceus*, pitchy]. Pitch-black, brownish or reddish black.

PIGMENT. [L. *pingere*, to paint]. A general term for any coloring compound in an organ or plant or animal. The biological function of the compound may not be directly associated with its coloring property. **Blood pigments**: hemoglobin, hemocyanin, etc. form loosely combined compounds with oxygen and transport it around the body. **Skin pigments**: melanin, xanthophyll etc.

PIGMENT CELL. See Chromatocyte.

PIGMY (PYGMY) MALES. [Gr. πυγμαιος, dwarfish]. See Dwarf Males.

PILIFEROUS. [L. *pilus*, hair; *ferre*, to carry]. Of any structure bearing or producing hair.

PILIFORM. [L. *pilus*, hair; *forma*, shape]. Resembling hair.

PILOSE, PILOUS. [L. *pilosus*, hairy]. Hairy, downy.

PILOSITY. [L. *pilosus*, hairy]. A covering of fine, long hair.

PILUS DENTILIS (PILI DENTILIS). [L. *pilus*, hair; *dens*, tooth]. In many Mesostigmata: a seta-like or membranous sensory organ inserted ventrolaterally on the fixed digit of the chelicera.

PIMOIDAE. [*Pimoa*, 'big legs'; derived from native Gosiute language of Utah]. A small family of spiders (infraorder Araneomorphae, superfamily Entelegynae) with a patchy Holarctic distribution.

PINCERS. [M E. *pinsers*, pincers]. The chelicerae of arachnids.

PIRACY. [Gr. πιερατης, pirate]. A general term for food-stealing; also known as kleptoparasitism. Generally, food items taken by one individual (the host) are forcibly stolen by another (the pirate or kleptoparasite). The host is usually harassed, often violently and for long periods and the pirate may either snatch the food away or recover it when dropped.

PIRIFORM (PYRIFORM). [L. *pirum*, pear, *forma*, shape]. Pear-shaped.

PISAURIDAE. [L. *piscis*, fish; *aurae*, (sniffing the) air]. The family of fisher spiders or nursery-web spiders (infraorder Araneomorphae, superfamily Entelegynae). They are similar in shape to the wolf spiders (**Lycosidae**) but have longer and more robust legs. They have good vision and are active hunters around the margins of ponds, lakes and streams.

PISCIVOROUS (ICHTHYOPHAGOUS). [L. *piscis*, fish; *vorare*, to devour]. Feeding on fish.

PISTAZINUS. [L. *pistacium*, pistachio nut]. Yellowish green, with a slight brownish tinge.

PIT. [AS. *pyt*, pit]. Any depression. A short median groove on the thoracic region of the carapace, situated just above the internal attachment of the gastric muscles.

PIT CHAMBER. [AS. *pyt*, pit; OFr. *chambre*, a chamber/room]. The cavity of a bordered pit below an overarching border.

PIVOT JOINT. A joint in which movement is limited to rotation; a trochoid joint.

Pl 1-2. In the Mesostigmata: designations for the setae on the posterior lateral surface of a leg or palp segment. See Evans Leg Chaetotactic System.

PLACOID. [Gr. πλαξ, plate; ειδος, form]. Plate-like.

PLAGA. [Gr. πλαγα, a blow/stroke]. A spot, stripe or streak of color. A longitudinal spot of irregular form.

PLAGULA. [L. *plagula*, curtain]. In spiders: a ventral plate that protects the pedicle.

PLAIT. [L. *plicare*, to fold]. Folded longitudinally or laid in pleats.

PLANE OF SYMMETRY. [L. *planare* to make level; Gr. συμμετρος, even/proportionate]. The median plane that divides a bilaterally symmetrical animal into two halves that are mirror images of each other.

PLANIFORM. [L. *planus*, level; *forma*, shape]. Having a nearly flat surface.

PLASMOCYTE. [Gr. πλασμα, form; κυτος, hollow]. See Leucocyte.

PLASMOPHAGOUS. [Gr. πλασμα, form; -φαγος, -eating]. 1. Of parasites that feed on the body fluids of the host. 2. Feeding on protoplasm.

PLASTRON. [Fr. *plastron*, breast plate]. The sternum of arachnids. In the water spider (**Argyronetidae**): the film of gas or layer of gas bubbles trapped by hairs covering the abdomen and legs.

PLASTRON-LIKE. [Fr. *plastron*, breast plate]. In mesostigmatans that live in wet habitats: peritremes that are flattened and broad and serve as an incompressible plastron.

PLASTRON RESPIRATION. [Fr. *plastron*, breast plate]. A method of gas exchange with the surrounding water in which a permanent thin film of air (a plastron) is held on the outside of the body by a very dense hair pile in which the hairs resist wetting as a result of their

194

hydrofuge properties and orientation. Thus an extensive gas/water interface is present for gaseous exchange.

PLATEREMAEOIDEA. [Gr. πλατυς, flat; ερημια, desert]. A monotypic superfamily of mites (suborder Oribatida, infraorder Brachypylina - section Pycnonoticae). Family: **Licnobelbidae, Licnodamaeidae, Pheroliodidae, Plateremaeidae.**

PLATES. In male *Ixodes*: large dense armor-like chitinous structures that do not rise above the surface of the body (as for instance in e.g. *Rhipicephalus*). The plates are bounded by the ventral grooves or by soft portions of the integument. There is 1 pregential, 1 median and 1 anal plate along the median line, plus 2 adanal plates to either side of the anal plate and 2 epimeral plates with indistinct external borders extending forward outside the genital groove to near coxa IV.

PLATYTRACHEAE. [Gr. πλατυς, flat; LL. *trachia*, windpipe]. In some oribatid mites: porose lamelliform pouch-like invaginations in the cuticle.

PLECTREURIDAE. [Gr. πληκτρον, anything to strike with; ευρυς, wide]. A small family of ecribellate, eight-eyed, haplogyne spiders (infraorder Araneomorphae, superfamily Haplogynae) that are confined to the North American deserts and Cuba. They build chaotic webs under rocks and dead cacti. Little is known of their biology.

PLEOCHROIC. [Gr. πλεον, more; χρως, color]. Having various colors.

PLEOCHROMATIC. [Gr. πλεον, more; χρωμα, color]. Having different colors under different physiological or environmental conditions.

PLEOMORPHIC (PLEIOMORPHIC). [Gr. πλεον, more; μορφη, form]. 1. Being able to change shape. 2. A form of polymorphism in which distinctly different forms occur at particular stages in the individual life cycle (e.g. larva, pupa, imago, etc.).

PLEOMORPHISM, PLEIOMORPHISM. [Gr. πλεον, more; μορφη, form]. 1. Polymorphism. 2. A type of polymorphism exhibited as several different stages in a life cycle.

PLEOPHAGOUS. [Gr. πλεον, more; -φαγος, -eating]. 1. Of parasites: having several hosts. 2. Having a variety of foods.

PLEOTROPHIC. [Gr. πλεον, more; τροφη, nourishment]. Eating various kinds of food.

PLESIOMORPHIC (PLESIOMORPHOUS). [Gr. πλησιος, near; μορφη, form]. Having a similar form.

PLESIOMORPHIC CHARACTERS. [Gr. πλησιος, near; μορφη, form]. Primitive characters: i.e. those that have not been derived during the course of evolution, as opposed to those which have been (Apomorphic). See also Apomorphic Characters, Autapomorphic Character, Phylogenetic Classification, Synapomorphic.

PLEURAL. [Gr. πλευρα, side]. In general: of the side.

PLEXIFORM. [L. *plexus*, interwoven; *forma*, shape]. Network-like, entangled or complicated.

PLEXUS (RETE). [L. *plexus*, interwoven]. 1. Any network of interlacing fibers, nerves, vessels, etc. 2. A number of ganglia in close proximity or fused together.

PLICATE. [L. *plicare*, to fold]. Folded like a fan. Ridged.

PLICATION. [L. *plicare*, to fold]. A minute fold or ridge.

PLICIFORM. [L. *plicare*, to fold; *forma*, shape]. Resembling a fold.

PLOIDY. [Gr. απλοος, onefold.]. Of the number of chromosome sets present in a nucleus. **Autoploid**: having the characteristic set of chromosomes for the species. **Autopolyploid**: a polyploid in which the entire chromosome complement comes from the same individual; usually due to some accident during cell division. **Diploid**: having the chromosomes in homologous pairs so that twice the haploid number is present. Pairing of chromosomes is a characteristic of almost all animal cells except gametes and some protozoa. The diploid number is written '$2n$' to distinguish from the haploid state, which is written 'n'. **Euploid**: a situation in which each of the chromosomes of a set are present in the same number. Thus the total chromosome complement is an exact multiple of the haploid (x1) number, e.g. **diploid** (x2), **triploid** (x3), **tetraploid** (x4), etc. **Haploid**: having half the full set of chromosomes in a cell, i.e. having the number of chromosomes characteristic of the gametes for the organism.

Tetraploid: having four times (4*n*) the normal haploid number of chromosomes. **Triploid:** having three times (3*n*) the normal haploid number of chromosomes.

P.L.E. Posterior Lateral Eyes.

P.L.S. Posterior Lateral Spinnerets, typically well developed.

PLUMACEOUS (PLUMULATE). [L. *plumula*, little feather, *-aceous*, of the nature of]. Downy. With a downy covering.

PLUMATE, PLUMOSE. [L. *pluma*, feather]. Feather-like.

PLUMBEOUS. [L. *plumbeus*, leaden]. Lead colored.

PLUME. [L. *pluma*, feather]. A feather or feather-like structure.

PLUMICOME. [L. *pluma*, feather; *coma*, hair]. A spicule with plume-like tufts.

PLURIDENTATE. [L. *plus*, more, *dens*, tooth]. With many teeth.

PLURILOCULAR. [L. *plus*, more; *loculus*, little place]. With two or more loculi or compartments; multilocular.

PLURIPAROUS. [L. *plus*, more; *parere*, to bring forth]. Giving birth to, or having given birth to a number of offspring. See also Multiparous, Parity.

PLURIPARTITE. [L. *plus*, more; *partius*, divided]. Bearing many lobes or partitions.

PLURISEPTATE. [L. *plus*, more; *septum*, partition]. Bearing multiple septa.

PLURISETOSE. [L. *plus*, more; *seta*, bristle]. Bearing several seta.

PLURISTRATOSE. [L. *plus*, more; *stratum*, layer]. Arranged in a number of layers. Stratified.

PLURIVALVE. [L. *plus*, more; *valvae*, folding doors]. With several valves or valve-like appendages.

PLURIVOROUS. [L. *plus*, more; *vorare*, to devour]. 1. Feeding on several substrates. 2. Of parasites that feed on several hosts.

P.M.E. Posterior Median Eye.

P.M.S. Posterior Median Spinnerets, the innermost pair of spinnerets and typically small.

PNEUMATIZED. [Gr. πνευμα, air]. Furnished with air cavities.

PNEUMOSTOME. [Gr. πνευμα, air; στομα, mouth]. In some arachnids: a small opening to the pit which contains the book lungs (gill books).

PNEUMOTAXIS. [Gr. πνευμα, air; ταξις, an arranging]. The response of organisms towards (positive) or away from (negative) the stimulus of dissolved carbon dioxide or other gas.

PNEUMOTROPISM. [Gr. πνευμα, air; τροπη, turning round]. An orienting response to the stimulus of dissolved carbon dioxide or other gas.

po SETA. in the Mesostigmata: the unpaired median seta inserted posterior to the anal opening; usually designated po or POS.

PODAL (PEDAL). [Gr. πους, foot]. Of the foot or feet.

PODAPOLIPIDAE (PODAPOLIPODIDAE). [Gr. πους, foot; L. *polypus*, many-footed]. A family of mites (infraorder Eleutherengona, superfamily Tarsonemoidea) that are ecto- or endoparasitic in arthropods and which often display reductions in numbers of legs and gnathosomal structures. One species is associated with bees. They are the only family of arachnids to have three pairs of legs. All the other families have four pairs, except the gall mites (Eriophyidae) which have two.

PODEON (PODEUM). [Gr. ποδεων, a neck]. See Petiole.

PODEX. [L. *podex*, rump]. The region around the anus.

PODIA, PODIUM. [Gr. πους, foot]. Any foot-like structures/structure.

196

PODOCEPHALIC CANALS. [Gr. πους, foot; κεφαλη, head]. On the anterior margin of acariform mites: a pair of canals that typically run between the chelicerae posteriorly, above the insertion of the legs.

PODOCEPHALIC GLANDS. [Gr. πους, foot; κεφαλη, head]. In acariform mites (but see Acari): four glands near the base of leg I; anterior, median, coxal, and lateral glands; they are united by a common conducting duct, the podocephalic canal, which caries the product of these glands to the gnathosomatic region.

PODOCINIDAE. [Gr. πους, foot; L. -cinium suf. denoting an activity or profession]. A small family of mites (infraorder Gamasina, superfamily Phytoseioidea).

PODOCTIDAE. [Gr. πους, foot; κτεις comb/rake]. A family of harvestmen or daddy longlegs (suborder Laniatores, superfamily Epedanoidea) mainly from Southeast Asia and central Africa.

PODOGONATA. [Gr. πους, foot; γονα, seed]. See Ricinulei.

PODOMERE. [Gr. πους, foot; μερος, part]. A limb segment.

PODONOTAL. [Gr. πους, foot; νωτον, back]. In ticks and mites: relating to the dorsal podosoma, the region of the idiosoma over the legs.

PODONOTAL SHIELD. [Gr. πους, foot; νωτον, back]. In mesostigmatans with divided dorsal shields: the anterior shield.

PODONOTUM. [Gr. πους, foot; νωτον, back]. In ticks and mites: the dorsal podosoma.

PODO-OPISTHOSOMATIC ARTICULATION. [Gr. πους, foot; οπισθο-, behind; σωμα, body]. In some oribatid mites (e.g. *Elliptochthonius*): the well developed post-pedal furrow. See also Protero-Hysterosomatic Articulation and Dichoidy, Ptychoidy, Trichoidy.

PODOSOMA. [Gr. πους, foot; σωμα, body]. In ticks and mites: the body region which bears the four pairs of walking legs.

PODOSPERMIA. [Gr. πους, foot; σπερμα, seed]. A type of sperm transfer by the male chelicera (gonopod) of certain ticks and mites, to the paired orifices of the female receptaculum seminis. See also Gonopody, Tocospermia.

PODOSPERMY (POROSPERMY). [Gr. πους, foot; σπερμη, seed]. A sperm transfer system in which the spermatophore is deposited into a secondary pore-like opening. In the Dermanyssoidea (Mesostigmata), the sperm pore (solenostome) is usually located near the bases of legs III-IV, but may be elsewhere in the intercoxal region or on the coxa or trochanter of leg III or IV.

PODOUS. [Gr. πους, foot]. A walking leg.

POIKILOTHERM (COLD-BLOODED, EXOTHERM, HETEROTHERM). [Gr. ποικιλος, various; θερμη, heat]. An animal whose body temperature varies with that of the surrounding medium; commonly, but not accurately known as 'cold-blooded'. This is a characteristic of all animals except birds and mammals and optimal temperatures may be maintained by heating in the sun's radiation, muscular exercise or evaporative cooling. See also Eccritic Temperature, Ectotherm, Temperature Regulation.

POLAR. [Gr. πολος, pole]. In the region of the end of an axis.

POLITUS. [L. politus, refined/polished]. Smooth, shiny, polished.

POLYANDRY. [Gr. πολυς, many; ανηρ, male]. A mating strategy in which a female will mate with more than one male during a breeding season or a period of estrus. **Simultaneous polyandry** is when a female mates with more than one male to produce a clutch of offspring in which the individuals may be fathered by different males. **Successive polyandry** is where the female mates with one male, produces 'his' offspring which are generally cared for by the male parent; she then mates again with a different male, again leaving the offspring under paternal care. See also Promiscuity.

POLYGAMY. [Gr. πολυγαμος, often married]. The condition of a male having more than one mate at any one time. See also Polyandry, Polygyny, Promiscuity.

POLYGYNY. [Gr. πολυγυνης, having many wives]. Mating with more than one female during a breeding season.

POLYLECITHAL. [Gr. πολυς, many; λεκιθος, yolk]. Of an egg containing a relatively large amount of yolk, as in a centrolecithal egg. See also Alecithal, Centrolecithal, Heterolecithal, Macrolecithal, Mediolecithal, Meiolecithal, Mesolecithal, Microlecithal, Oligolecithal, Telolecithal.

POLYMEROUS. [Gr. πολυμερης, of many parts]. Consisting of many parts or members.

POLYMORPHISM. [Gr. πολυμορφος, multiform]. 1. The occurrence of genetically different forms of individuals within the same species or interbreeding population. The polymorphism may be transient or persist over many generations (balanced polymorphism). Polymorphisms may be cryptic and require biochemical approaches (e.g. DNA restriction analysis or sequencing) to determine them, or may be visible. See also Dimorphism, Monomorphism, Polyphenism.

POLYMORPHOUS (POLYMORPHIC, PLEOMORPHIC, PLEIOMORPHIC). [Gr. πολυμορφος, multiform]. Showing a marked degree of variation in body form, either during the life history or within a species. Having many forms or types of structure in the same species.

POLYNESIAN SUBREGION. [Gr. πολυς, many; νησος, island]. A zoogeographical region comprising the Polynesian and Micronesian Archipelagos from Fiji to the Marquesas Isles.

POLYPHAGOUS, POLYPHAGY. [Gr. πολυφαγος, eating to excess]. Eating various kinds of food. See also Euryphagous, Monophagous, Stenophagous.

POLYPHASIC. [Gr. πολυς, many; φαινειν, to appear]. Of species which are morphologically variable within a given habitat.

POLYPHENISM. [Gr. πολυς, many; φαινειν, to appear]. The occurrence of several phenotypes in a population that are not a consequence of genetic differences. See also Dimorphism, Monomorphism, Polymorphism.

POLYPHYLETIC (POLYPHYLY). [Gr. πολυφυλος, many tribes]. Combining the ancestral characters of more than one ancestral type, i.e. of members of a taxa being derived from several lines of descent. Modern phyletic taxonomy would hold that any taxon found to be polyphyletic is the result of parallel or convergent evolution and therefore an unnatural grouping, and should be disbanded. See also Phylogenetic Classification.

POLYPTEROZETOIDEA. [Gr. πολυς, many; πτερον, wing; ζητες seeking]. A superfamily of mites (suborder Oribatida, infraorder Brachypylina - section Pycnonoticae). Families: **Podopterotegaeidae, Polypterozetidae.**

POLYSAPROBIC. [Gr. πολυς, many; σαπρος, putrid; βιος, life]. Of aquatic environments in which there is heavy pollution by organic matter with little or no dissolved oxygen. There is the production of sulphides and, usually, an abundance of bacteria. See also Katharobic, Mesosaprobic, Oligosaprobic, Saprobic.

POLYSTACHYUS. [Gr. πολυσταχυς, rich in ears of corn]. With numerous spikes.

POLYSTICHOUS. [Gr. πολυστοιχος, in many rows]. Arranged in numerous rows or series.

POLYTHELIA. [Gr. πολυς, many; θηλη, nipple]. The occurrence of supernumerary nipples.

POLYTOPISM, POLYTOPIC (SUB)SPECIES, POLYTOPIC EVOLUTION. [Gr. πολυς, many; τοπος, a place]. A taxonomic anomaly in which a taxon occurs in more than one region, commonly widely separated. This may indicate parallel evolution such that two or more separated populations come to be morphologically similar, or that a more derived species or subspecies has evolved in an intervening area.

POLYTRICHOUS. [Gr. πολυτριχος, very hairy]. Having numerous hair-like outgrowths.

POLYTROPHIC. [Gr. πολυς, many; τροφη, nourishment]. 1. Nourished by more than one organism or substance. 2. Of parasites that are nourished by more than one host.

POLYVOLTINE. [Gr. πολυς, many; It. *volta*, time]. Producing several broods in one season. See also Voltine.

POLYXENOUS. [Gr. πολυξενος; visited by many guests]. Of parasites which are adapted to life in many different host species.

POMERANTZIOIDEA. [*Charles Pomerantz*, American entomologist]. A monotypic superfamily of mites (suborder Prostigmata, infraorder Anystina). Family: **Pomerantziidae**.

PONS. [L. *pons*, bridge]. Any structure connecting two parts or regions of the body.

POOL FEEDER. See Telmophage.

PORATE. [Gr. πορος, channel]. Bearing pores.

PORCATE. [L. *porca*, a ridge between two furrows]. With longitudinal ridges and furrows.

PORE. [Gr. πορος, channel]. Any minute opening or passage.

PORE CANALS. [Gr. πορος, channel]. Minute spiral tubes that pass through the cuticle, but not the outermost epicuticle.

PORIFEROUS. [Gr. πορος, channel; L. *ferre*, to bear]. Having numerous openings or pores.

POROID (PORIFORM). [Gr. πορος, channel; ειδος, form]. Having pore-like depressions or being like a pore.

PORONOTICAE. [Gr. πορος, channel; νωτον, back]. A section of the infraorder Brachypylina (order Sarcoptiformes, suborder Oribatida) in which there are typically four pairs of glandular openings (an octotaxic system) on the notogaster in the form of porose areas or saccules. Superfamilies: Achipterioidea, Ceratozetoidea (Limnozetoidea), Galumnoidea, Licneremaeoidea, Microzetoidea, Oribatelloidea, Oripodoidea (Oribatuloidea), Phenopelopoidea, Unduloribatoidea (Eremaeozetoidea), Zetomotrichoidea.

POROSE. [Gr. πορος, channel]. Having pores.

POROSE AREA. [Gr. πορος, channel]. Depressed areas on the capitulum of certain mites and ticks.

POROSPERMY. See Podospermy.

PORPHYROPHORE. [Gr. πορφυρα, purple; φορειν, to bear]. A reddish-purple pigment-bearing cell.

PORRECT. [L. *porrectus*, stretched out]. Extended outwards. Of the projecting diaxial chelicerae of some araneomorphs (e.g. **Dysderidae**) which differentiates them from the paraxial chelicerae found in the mygalomorphs.

PORRHOTHELIDAE. [Gr. πορρω, forwards/onwards; θηλη, nipple]. A monospecific family of spiders (infraorder Mygalomorphae, superfamily Avicularioidea) endemic to New Zealand. They have a small posterior sigillae and a single row of teeth on the forward-facing margin of the chelicerae.

PORTA. [L. *porta*, gate]. Any gate-like structure.

po/POS SETA. See Postanal Seta.

POSITIVE ASSORTATIVE MATING. See Assortative Mating.

POSITIVE GEOTROPISM. [Gr. γεω–, earth; τροπη, a turn]. Attraction toward the center of the earth.

POSITIVE TAXIS (POSITIVE TROPISM). [Gr. ταξις, an arranging; τροπη, turning]. The tendency to move towards, or grow towards, a source of stimulation.

POSTABDOMEN. [L. *post*; after; *abdomen*, belly]. In scorpions: the metasoma or posterior narrower five segments of the abdomen. In spiders: the anal tubercle.

POST-ANAL. [L. *post*; after; *anus*, vent]. Situated behind the anus.

POST-ANAL SETA. [L. *post*; after; *anus*, vent; *seta*, bristle]. In the Mesostigmata: the unpaired median seta inserted posterior to the anal opening. They are usually designated po or POS.

POST-BACILLARY. [L. *post*; after; *bacillum*, little staff]. In the inverted eye of spiders: having nuclei behind the sensory zone of the retinal cells. See also Prebacillary.

POST-BASCILLARY EYES. [L. *post*; after; *bacillum*, little staff]. In the Arachnida: the anterior median eyes that have the retinal nuclei behind the light-sensitive rods. See also Prebascillary Eyes.

POST-CENTRAL. [L. *post*; after; *centrum*, center]. Behind the central regions.

POST-COLON. [L. *post*; after; *colon*, colon]. In some mites: the region of the gut between the colon and the rectum.

POST-COXAL. [L. *post*; after; *coxa*, hip]. Posterior to the coxae.

POST-COXAL SETA. [L. *post*; after; *coxa*, hip; *seta*, bristle]. In the Merostigmata: the most basal seta (pc) on the subcapitulum.

POSTERIAD. [L. *post*, after; *-ad*, toward]. Directed backward. Op. Anteriad.

POSTERIOR. [L. *posterior*, following after]. Near the rear end, or towards that region in comparison, e.g. x is posterior to y.

POSTERIOR CRIBELLUM. [L. *posterior*, following after; *cribellum*, little sieve]. In the Stenochilidae: the postero-lateral spinnerets.

POSTERIOR EYE. [L. *posterior*, following after]. The more posterior of a pair of lateral ocelli. It is usually of different form from the anterior eye and may lack a distinct lens.

POSTERODORSAL SETA. [L. *posterior*, following after; *dorsum*, back; *seta*, bristle]. In the Mesostigmata: a seta (pd 1-3) on the posterior dorsal surface of a leg or palp segment.

POSTEROLATERAL, POSTEROLATERAD. [L. *posterior*, following after; *latus*, side]. Placed posteriorly and to the side.

POSTEROLATERAL SETA. [L. *posterior*, following after; *latus*, side *seta*, bristle]. In the Mesostigmata: a seta (pl 1-2) on the posterior lateral surface of a leg or palp segment.

POSTEROMEDIAL. [L. *posterior*, following after; *medius*, middle]. Placed posteriorly and medianly.

POSTEROMESAD. [L. *posterior*, following after; Gr. μεσος, middle]. Toward the posterior end and the midline.

POSTEROVENTRAL. [L. *posterior*, following after; *venter*, belly]. Placed ventrally and to the side.

POSTEROVENTRAL SETA. [L. *posterior*, following after; *venter*, belly; *seta*, bristle]. In the Mesostigmata: a seta (pv 1-3) on the posterior ventral surface of a leg or palp segment.

POST-GENITAL. [L. *post*, after; *genitalis*, of generation]. Located behind the genital segment.

POST-MATING ISOLATION. See Reproductive Isolation.

POST-OCULAR. [L. *post*, after; *oculus*, eye]. Posterior to the eye.

POST-OCULAR GLAND (PUSTULE). [L. *post*, after; *oculus*, eye]. In the Labidostommatidae (Prostigmata): a large lateral pustule directly behind the ocellus (and possibly homologous to the posterior eye).

POST-ORAL. [L. *post*, after; *os*, mouth]. Behind the mouth.

POST-PEDAL FURROW/CONSTRICTION/SUTURE. [L. *post*, after; *pes*, foot]. A constriction or articulation of the idiosoma behind legs IV. See Podo-Opisthosomatic Articulation.

POST-PELTIDIUM. See Schizopeltid.

POULTRY MITE. A member of the Dermanyssoidea (Mesostigmata) that is parasitic on birds; particularly the poultry/chicken/pigeon red mite *Dermanyssus gallinae*, the northern fowl mite or starling mite, *Ornithonyssus sylviarum*, or the tropical fowl mite *Ornithonyssus bursa*.

PRAEABDOMEN (MESOSOMA). [L. *prae*, before; *abdomen*, belly]. In scorpions: the anterior, broader region of the abdomen.

200

PRAECOXA. [L. *prae*, before; *coxa*, hip]. In arachnids: a term used instead of coxa in some groups.

PRAECRURAL. [L. *prae*, before; *crus*, leg]. On the anterior side of the leg or thigh.

PRAEMORSE (PREMORSE). [L. *praemorsus*, bitten off]. Having the end abruptly truncate, as if bitten or broken off.

PRAEOCULAR. [L. *prae*, before; *oculus*, eye]. Before the eyes.

PRAEORAL. [L. *prae*, before; *os*, mouth]. See Preoral.

PRASINOUS. [Gr. πρασινος, leek green]. The color of leeks; light green tending to yellow.

PRATINCOLOUS. [L. *pratium*, a meadow; *colere*, to inhabit]. Living in grassland and meadowland.

PRE-. See also PRAE-.

PRE-ABDOMEN. [L. *prae*, before; *abdomen*, belly]. The anterior region of the abdomen, e. g. the first seven segments of a scorpion's abdomen.

PREANAL. [L. *prae*, before; *anus*, anus]. Anterior to the anus.

PREAPICAL. [L. *prae*, before; *apex*, tip]. Before the apex.

PREBACILLARY. [L. *prae*, before; *bacillum*, little staff]. In the inverted or erect eyes of spiders: of the ocellus in which the nuclei are distal to the sensory zone of the retinal cells. See also Post-bacillary.

PRECENTRAL. [L. *prae*, before; *centrum*, center]. Anterior to the center.

PRECHELICERAE. [L. *prae*, before; Gr. χηλη, claw]. In arachnids: of a segment of the mouth region (gnathosoma) anterior to the chelicerae.

PRECHELICERAL. [L. *prae*, before; Gr. χηλη, claw; κερας, horn]. In the Chelicerata: anterior to the chelicerae; the acron and the three or four embryological segments anterior to the cheliceral segment.

PRECOXAL TRIANGLES (PRECOXAL SCLERITES). [L. *prae*, before; *coxa*, hip]. The triangular sclerotized extensions from the sternum to the coxa.

PREDACEOUS, PREDACIOUS. [L. *preda*, prey; *-aceous*, of the nature of]. Having the characteristics of a predator.

PREDATION. [L. *praedator*, hunter]. The consumption of one animal (the prey) by another (the predator).

PREDATION ANALYSIS. [L. *praedator*, hunter]. See Lotka-Volterra Equations.

PREDATION PRESSURE. [L. *praedator*, hunter]. The effects of predation on the dynamics of the prey population.

PREDATOR. [L. *praedator*, hunter]. An animal that kills other animals for food. Typically, predators are larger than their prey and the prey is usually completely consumed. Predation also includes insectivorous plants.

PREDATOR–PREY EQUATIONS. See Lotka-Volterra Equations.

PRE-EPISTOME. [L. *prae*, before; Gr. επι-, upon; στομα, mouth]. In some arachnids: a plate covering the basal portion of the epistome.

PREENING BRUSH/COMB. A transverse cluster of rigid setae at the ventral tip of the posterior metatarsus.

PREFORMATION. See Epigenesis.

PREGENITAL. [L. *prae*, before; *genitalis*, belonging to birth]. Situated anterior to the genital opening. In arachnids: of the segment behind the fourth pair of walking legs.

PREGENITALS. In ticks and mites: the ag-gential setae in the Pritchard & Baker system, = ag in the Grandjean system.

PREHENSILE. [L. *prehendere*, to seize]. Adapted for holding or grasping.

PRELARVA. [L. *prae*, before; *larva*, mask]. In ticks and mites with a four stage development: the first post-embryonic stage which usually occurs in the egg, but may be a non-feeding form after eclosion.

PREMATING ISOLATION. See Reproductive Isolation.

PREMORSE. See Praemorse.

PREOCULAR. [L. *prae*, before; *oculus*, eye]. Anterior to the eye.

PREORAL (PRAEORAL). [L. *prae*, before; *os*, mouth]. Situated in front of the mouth.

PREORAL CAVITY. [L. *prae*, before; *os*, mouth]. The mouth cavity. In ticks and mites: the space between the lips anterior to the oral commissure.

PRESEGMENTAL. [L. *prae*, before; *segmentum*, piece]. Anterior to the body segments or somites.

PRESTERNAL PLATELETS. [L. *prae*, before; Gr. σταρνον, chest]. In some Mesostigmatans: small sclerotized plates anterior to the sternal shield and laterad or posteriad to the base of the tritosternum.

PRETARSUS (PRAETARSUS). [L. *prae*, before; Gr. ταρσος, sole of foot]. In spiders (and insects): the terminal region of, or outgrowth on, the leg or claw.

PREVERNAL. [L. *prae*, before; *vernus*, spring]. One of the terms for the six part division of the year commonly used in ecology, especially with reference to terrestrial and fresh-water communities. The six parts are: prevernal (early spring), vernal (late spring), aestival (early summer), serotinal (late summer), autumnal (autumn) and hibernal (winter).

PREY. [L. *praeda*, prey]. Animals killed and eaten by predators.

PRIMARY EYES. The anterior median eyes. These are morphologically distinct from the other eyes and are often reduced or sometimes absent.

PRIMILATERALS. [L. *primus*, first; *latus*, side]. In acariform mites: the most basal pair of ventral (ventrolateral) setae on the tarsi. On the ventral tarsus behind the unguinals is the seta (s), the anterolaterals (a), primiventrals (pv), and primilaterals (pl).

PRIMIVENTRALS. [L. *primus*, first; *venter*, belly]. See Primilaterals.

PRITCHARD & BAKER SYSTEM. [*A.E. Pritchard & E.W. Baker*, American Arachnologists]. A system of setal designations of spider mites in which the setae are designated according to their location, thus: Dorsocentrals: D1 = c1; D2 = d1; D3 = e1; D4 = f1; D5 = h1; Dorsolaterals: L1 = c2; L2 = d2; L3 = e2; L4 = f2; Sublaterals: 1st sublaterals = c3; 2nd sublaterals = d3; 3rd sublaterals = e3; Humerals: H = c3; also Inner sacrals (or DC4) = f1; Outer sacrals (or L4) = f2; Clunals (or DC5) = h1 or f3; Postanals (or posterior para-anals) = h2; Anterior para-anals = h3; Anals = ps1-3; 1st genitals (or anteromedial genitals) = g1; 2nd genitals (or posterolateral genitals)= g2; Pregenitals = ag in the Grandjean system.

PROBOSCIS, PROBOSCISES. [Gr. προβοσκις, trunk]. Any extended trunk-like sucking mouth parts, e.g. as in blood-sucking ticks, etc.

PROCESS. [L. *processus*; advance/progress]. An outgrowth or projection from a surface, a margin, an appendage.

PROCRYPSIS. [Gr. προ, for; κρυπσις, hidden]. Camouflage. Any shape, pattern, coloring or behavior that tends to make an animal less conspicuous in its normal environment.

PROCRYPTIC COLORS. [Gr. προ, for; κρυπσις, hidden]. Imitative colors useful for concealment as a protection against enemies: Batesian Mimicry and Mullerian Mimicry. See Mimicry.

PROCTAL. See Anal.

PROCTODEUM (PROCTODAEUM). [Gr. πρωκτος, anus; οδος, way]. Hind-Gut.

PROCTODEAL VALVE. [Gr. πρωκτος, anus; οδος, way]. A valve ar the anterior end of the hindgut.

PROCUMBENT. [L. *pro*, forward; *cumbens*, lying down]. Lying loosely along a surface; trailing on the ground.

PROCURVED. [L. *pro*, before; *curvare*, to curve]. Used to denote the curvature of the eyes in arachnids when the lateral eyes are further forward than the median eyes. See also Recurved.

PROCUSUS. [L. *procusus*, forge/hammer out]. The retrolateral paracymbium found in the **Pholcidae**.

PROCUTICLE. [L. *pro*, before; *cuticula*, thin outer skin]. The colorless cuticle, composed of protein and chitin, prior to differentiation into endocuticle and exocuticle.

PRODEHISCENCE. [L. *pro*, before; *dehiscere*, to divide]. In ticks and mites: molting in which the splitting of the old cuticle occurs latero-frontally next to the frontal protuberance.

PRODIDOMIDAE. See Gnaphosidae.

PRODORSAL DEHISCENCE. [L. *pro*, before; *dorsum*, back; *dehiscere*, to divide]. During molting in the Chelicerata: the line of weakness following the abjugal furrow between the aspidosoma and prodosoma.

PRODORSAL SETAE. [L. *pro*, before; *dorsum*, back; *setae*, bristles]. In acariform mites: the setae on the prodorsum.

PRODORSAL SHIELD. [L. *pro*, before; *dorsum*, back]. In acariform mites: a shield on the anterior dorsal surface.

PRODORSUM. [L. *pro*, before; *dorsum*, back]. The dorsal surface of the aspidosomal tagma. It may have one or two transverse furrows.

PRODROME. [Gr. προδρομος, running before]. A preliminary process, indication or symptom.

PRODUCED. [L. *producere*, to produce]. Elongated. Extended. Projecting.

PROECDYSIS. [Gr. προ, before; εκδυσις, an escape]. See Ecdysis.

PROEPISEMATIC. [Gr. προ, before; επι, upon; σημα, signal]. See Sematic.

PROFOUND, PROFUNDUS. [L. *profundus*, deep]. Deep.

PROGAMIC SEX DETERMINATION. [Gr. προ, before; γαμετης, a spouse]. See Sex Determination.

PROGENITAL. [L. *pro*, before; *gignere*, to beget]. In ticks and mites: of the area between the primary and secondary genital opening, and the secondary opening itself.

PROGENITAL CHAMBER. [L. *pro*, before; *gignere*, to beget]. In the Acariformes: the chamber between the primary and secondary genital opening.

PROGENITAL LIPS. [L. *pro*, before; *gignere*, to beget]. In many Acariformes: the paired symmetrical valves that close the progenital chamber.

PROGENITAL VALVES. [L. *pro*, before; *gignere*, to beget]. In acariform mites: the genital valves.

PROGENITOR. [L. *pro*, before; *gignere*, to beget]. An ancestral species.

PROGENY. [L. *pro*, before; *gignere*, to beget]. Offspring.

PROGONEATE. [Gr. προ, before; γονη, generation]. Having the genital aperture to the anterior.

PROGRADE. [L. *pro*, before; *gradus*, step]. Of spiders in which the dorsal surface of the leg is uppermost. Also the mode of locomotion of such spiders.

PROGRESSIVE PROVISIONING (PROGRESSIVE FEEDING). In some spiders (and insects): feeding the young regularly during their development.

PROKOENENIIDAE. [Gr. προ, before +*Koenenia*]. A small family of micro-whip scorpions (order Palpigradi, superfamily Eukoenenioidea).

PROLATERAL. [Gr. προ, before; L. *latus*, side]. Of forward-directed spines projecting from the side of the leg. In an imaginary state of all the legs being straight out from the side; at right angles to the long axis of the body. See also Retrolateral.

PROLATEROBASAD. [L. *pro*, before; *latus*, side; Gr. βασις, base; L. *ad*, towards]. Toward the prolateral side and the base. See also Retrolaterobasad.

PROLATEROMESAD. [L. *pro*, before; *latus*, side; Gr. μεσος, middle]. Toward the prolateral side and the midline.

PROLATEROVENTRAD. [L. *pro*, before; *latus*, side; *venter*, belly, *ad*, to]. Toward the prolateral side and the venter.

PROLES. [L. *proles*, offspring]. A rather vague taxonomic grouping used in different ways by different authors.

PROLICIDE. [L. *proles*, offspring; *-cidium*, killing]. The killing of offspring.

PROLONGED. [L. *prolongare*, to extend]. Extended or lengthened beyond ordinary limits.

PROMARGIN. [L. *pro*, before; *margo*, border]. The anterior margin of the fang furrow.

PROMARGINAL. [L. *pro*, before; *margo*, border]. On the anterior margin.

PROMINENCE. [L. *prominens*, projecting]. A raised, produced or projecting area.

PROMISCUITY. [L. *promiscuus*, promiscuous]. A form of polygyny or polyandry in which a member of one sex mates with more than one member of the opposite sex. Each relationship is ephemeral and terminates soon after mating, there being no bond formation.

PROMUSCIDATE. [L. *promuscis*, proboscis]. With a proboscis or extended mouth structure.

PRONATE. [L. *pronare*, to bend forward]. Inclined.

PRO-ORALS. [L. *pro*, before; *os*, mouth]. In acariform mites: the most distal pair of dorsal setae on the tarsus.

PROPODOSOMA. [Gr. προ, before; πους, foot; σωμα, body]. In ticks and mites: the body region bearing the first and second pairs of legs.

PROPELTIDIUM. [Gr. προ, before; πελτιδιον, little shield]. In the Arachnida: the covering of the prosoma, except for plates V and VI.

PROPES. [L. *pro*, before; *pes*, foot]. See Prolegs.

PROPODITE. [Gr. προ, before; πους, foot]. In arachnids: the tibia. See also Limb.

PROPRIOCEPTION (KINAESTHESIS). [L. *proprius*, one's own]. Perception of movement due to stimulation of muscles, tendons and joints

PROPRIOCEPTOR (PROPRIORECEPTOR). [L. *proprius*, one's own; *recipere*, regain, take back]. A receptor sensitive to internal stimuli such as pressure, position and movement from muscles, tendons, exoskeleton, etc. and used to control the automatic co-ordination of movement and posture. See also Exteroceptor, Interoceptor, Receptor.

PROPRIOGENIC. [L. *proprius*, one's own; *genus*, kind]. Of effectors, other than muscles, which are both receptors and effectors.

PRORSAD. [L. *prorsus*, forwards; *ad*, to]. Forward, anteriorly.

PRORSAL. [L. *prorsus*, forwards]. Anterior.

PROSOMA (PROTEROSOMA, PROSOME). [Gr. προ, before; σωμα, body]. The anterior region of the body, especially a cephalothorax. It is not usually distinct in mites.

PROSTERNUM. [Gr. προ, before; σταρνον, chest]. In some arachnids: a ventral region of the cheliceral segment.

PROSTIGMATA (ACTINEDIDA). [Gr. προ, before; στιγμη, mark]. A large and widely distributed suborder of mites (superorder Acariformes, order Trombidiformes) in which there is a single pair of spiracles located anteriorly near the mouth parts. Many are plant parasites (e.g. **Tetranychidae, Eriophyidae**) and many are parasites of invertebrates and vertebrates (e.g. **Demodicidae, Halacaridae**). Currently, the prostigmata are divided into four infraorders: Anystina, Eleutherengona, Eupodina, Labidostommatina; although some authorities do not recognize the latter. However, the demarcation and interrelationships of these groups are entirely unclear, and whether any of these prostigmatan lineages are equally distinct remains to be determined.

PROSTIGMATID. Erron. for prostigmatan, the adjectival form of Prostigmata.

PROSTOMIATE. [Gr. προ, before; στομα, mouth]. Having a portion of the head in front of the mouth.

PROSTRATE. [L. *prostratus*, thrown down]. Lying closely along a surface.

PROSTRIATA. [Gr. προ, before; L. *stria*, furrow].]. One of two subdivision of the **Ixodidae** based on the presence or absence of anal grooves extending anterior to, or surrounding, the anus. The Metastriata (absence) contains all genera except *Ixodes*, which is in the subdivision Prostriata (presence).

PROTARRHENOTOKY. [Gr. πρωτος, first; αρρην, male; τοκος, birth]. Producing male offspring prior to producing female. See also Protothelytoky.

PROTECTIVE COLORATION (CAMOUFLAGE). The patterns or markings on an animal's body that enable it to blend into the background so that when motionless its outline becomes difficult to define.

PROTEIFORM. [Gr. Πρστευς, a changing god; L. *forma*, shape]. Assuming different forms. Variable.

PROTELATTOSIS. [Gr. πρωτος, first; ελαττων, smaller]. In ticks and mites: regression of the first instar, particularly regarding elattostase and calyptostase. See also Alternating Calyptostasy, Calyptostasic, Elattostase.

PROTELEAN. [Gr. πρωτος, first; τελειος, complete]. Of an organism that is parasitic in the juvenile stages but free-living as an adult.

PROTERODEHISCENCE. [Gr. προτερος, before; L. *dehiscere*, to divide]. In ticks and mites: splitting of the old cuticle in the anterior part of the body during molting.

PROTERO-HYSTEROSOMATIC ARTICULATION (FURROW). [Gr. προτερος, before; υστερος, after; σωμα, body]. In some acariform mites: a flexible juncture between legs II-III. See also Podo-Opisthosomatic Articulation and Dichoidy, Ptychoidy, Trichoidy.

PROTEROSOMA. [Gr. προτερος, forward; σωμα, body]. In ticks and mites: the body region comprising the gnathosoma and propodosoma.

PROTOBUTHIDAE. [Gr. πρωτος, first; + *Buthus*]. A small extinct monospecific family of scorpions (order Scorpiones, superfamily Buthoidea) known from the Early Triassic of France.

PROTOCO-OPERATION. See Facultative Mutualism.

PROTOGYNE. [Gr. πρωτος, first; γυνη, woman]. A female that resembles the male of the same species; a normal female.

PROTOLOPHIDAE. [Gr. πρωτος, first; λοφος, crest]. A monospecific family of harvestmen or daddy longlegs (suborder Eupnoi, superfamily Phalangioidea). *Protolophus* may be included in the **Sclerosomatidae** by some authorities.

PROTOMORPHIC. [Gr. πρωτος, first; μορφη, form]. Primordial; first-formed; primitive.

PROTONYMPH. [Gr. πρωτος, first; νυμφη, chrysalis]. In some ticks and mites: the first nymphal stage.

PROTOPATHIC. [Gr. πρωτος, first; παθος, feeling]. Of nerve systems concerned with the sensations of pain and large variations in temperature.

PROTOPLOPHOROIDEA. [Gr. πρωτος, first; πλοιον, floating vessel; -φορα, -carrying]. A monotypic superfamily of mites (suborder Oribatida, infraorder Enarthronota). Family: **Protoplophoroidae.**

PROTOSCHIZOMIDAE. [Gr. πρωτος, first; + Schizomida]. A family of short-tailed whip scorpions (order Schizomida, superfamily Hubbardioidea) with a wide distribution.

PROTOSOLPUGIDAE. [Gr. πρωτος, first + Solpugidae]. An extinct monospecific family of sun spiders (subclass Arachnida, order Solifugae) known from the Carboniferous of Illinois.

PROTOSTASY. [Gr. πρωτος, first; στασις, standing]. In ticks and mites: an orthostasic stage in a life cycle involving six stases. See Orthostasy.

PROTOSTERNUM. [Gr. πρωτος, first; στερνον, chest]. In ticks and mites: a sternite of the cheliceral segment of the prosoma.

PROTOTHELYTOKY. [Gr. πρωτος, first; θηλυς, female; τοκος, birth]. Producing female offspring prior to producing male. See also Protarrhenotoky.

PROTRACT. [L. pro, before; tractus, drawing out]. To extend forward or outward. To protrude.

PROTRACTOR MUSCLES. [L. pro, forth; tractus, drawing out]. A contractile muscle that extends an organ. See Muscle Terminology.

PROTRUSILE. [L. pro, before; trudo, thrust]. Capable of being protruded or withdrawn.

PROTUBERANCE. [L. protuberare, to swell]. An elevation, knob or prominence above the surface.

PROVENTRICULUS. [L. pro, before; ventriculus, little stomach]. The digestive chamber anterior to the stomach.

PROVISIONING. [L. provisto, foresight]. Providing food for young. See Progressive Provisioning.

PROXIMAD. [L. proximus, next; ad, towards]. Situated towards or placed nearest the body or base of attachment.

PROXIMAL. [L. proximus, next]. Nearest to the center. Nearest to the body (as of a limb or appendage); nearest to a defined point on or within the body (opposite - Distal).

PROXIMOCEPTOR. [L. proximus, next; recipere, to receive]. A receptor which reacts only to nearby stimuli, e.g. a contact receptor.

PROXIMOVENTRAL HAIRS. [L. proximus, next; venter, belly]. On some spider mites: the hair-like processes on the empodia. They may represent a finely divided empodium and not tenent hairs.

PRUINOSE, PRUINESCENCE. [L. pruina, hoar frost]. Covered by bloom. Covered by whitish particles or globules.

PRUINOUS, PRUINOSUS. [L. pruinosus, covered with frost]. Deep blue with a reddish tinge, like a plum.

PRZIBRAM'S RULE. [Hans Przibram, Austrian Zoologist]. A law of growth that states that as the volume increases by the cube of a number, the area increases by the square.

ps. A designation used for the setae in the PS region, e.g. ps1-2. See Grandjean System.

PS. 1. A pseudanal segment in acariform mites. The 'anal' segment in the larva. See also Anamorphosis. See Grandjean System. 2. Posterior Spinnerets, they are typically well developed.

PSAMMOFAUNA. [Gr. ψαμμος, sand; L. Faunus, god of the woods]. The animals living in a sandy region.

PSECHRIDAE. [Gr. ψηχρος, rubbed thin]. A family of large spiders (infraorder Araneomorphae, superfamily Entelegynae). They have greatly elongated legs, in which the last element is very flexible. Female Psechrus carry their egg-sac in the chelicerae, similar to their relatives, the ecribellate **Pisauridae.**

PSEUDANAL. [Gr. ψευδης, false; L. anus; anus]. In acariform mites: of the setae or other structures on segment PS.

PSEUDANAL SEGMENT. [Gr. ψευδης, false; L. anus; anus]. In ticks and mites: segment XIII and one of the paraproctal segments.

PSEUDAPOSEMATIC (PSEUDOAPOSEMATIC) COLORS. [Gr. ψευδης, false; απο, from; σημα, signal]. See Sematic.

PSEUDEPISEMATIC (PSEUDOEPISEMATIC). [Gr. ψευδης, false; επι, upon; σημα, signal]. See Sematic.

PSEUDOANNULATION (PSEUDOANNULIFORM). [Gr. ψευδης, false; L. *annulus*, ring]. Annulation involving the cuticle only; not involving the coelom.

PSEUDOAQUATIC. [Gr. ψευδης, false; L. *aqua*, water]. Thriving in wet ground.

PSEUDOARTICULATION. [Gr. ψευδης, false; L. *articulus*, joint]. An incomplete subdivision of a segment, or a groove which has the appearance of a joint.

PSEUDOCHACTOIDEA. [Gr. ψευδης, false; + Chactidae]. A monotypic superfamily of scorpions (subclass Arachnida, order Scorpiones) known from southern central and southeast Asia. Family: **Pseudochactidae.**

PSEUDOCHIRIDIIDAE. [Gr. ψευδης, false; χειρ, hand; -ιδιον, dim. suf.]. A small family of false scorpions (suborder Iocheirata, superfamily Cheiridioidea) with a wide distribution, and one species known from Miocene Dominican amber. This family may be included in the superfamily Garypoidea.

PSEUDOCOEL(E). [Gr. ψευδης, false; κοιλος, hollow]. A body cavity which is not part of the true coelom and not lined with peritoneum. The hemocoel of arthropods.

PSEUDOEPISEMATIC. Pseudepisematic. See Sematic.

PSEUDOGARYPIDAE. [Gr. ψευδης, false' + Garypidae]. A family of pseudoscorpions (suborder Atoposphyronida, superfamily Feaelloidea) endemic to Tasmania, but with species found in North America.

PSEUDOPERCULUM. [Gr. ψευδης, false; L. *operculum*, lid]. Any structure that resembles an operculum or closing membrane.

PSEUDORUTELLAR PROCESS. [Gr. ψευδης, false; L. *rutellum*, little spade]. In some Astigmata, such as feather mites: the rutellum or pseudorutellum.

PSEUDORUTELLUM. [Gr. ψευδης, false; L. *rutellum*, little spade]. The rutellum in the Astigmata.

PSEUDOSCLERITE. [Gr. ψευδης, false; σκλερος, hard]. In ticks and mites: a sclerotized area of the cuticle differing distinctly from the soft cuticle.

PSEUDOSCORPIONES (CHELONETHIDA, PSEUDOSCORPIONIDA). [Gr. ψευδης, false; σκορπιος, scorpion]. A cosmopolitan order of minute, flattened arachnids (class Euchelicerata, subclass Arachnida) which resemble scorpions in having large chelicerate pedipalps but do not possess a stinging organ and are rarely longer than 8 mm. The oval opisthoma is broadly joined to the prosoma, there are two pairs of tracheae ventrally on the third and fourth abdominal segments and one or two pairs of eyes at each anterior lateral corner of the rectangular carapace. Within the small chelicerae are several ducts leading from a pair of silk glands in the prosoma and the silk produced is used for constructing over-wintering, molting and brood chambers. They are mostly black, brown or brownish green and most species live in crevices, under bark and plant litter etc., feeding on collembola, caterpillars and ants; the prey being paralyzed or killed by poison glands in the pedipalps. Some inhabit houses. Courtship displays occur and may involve pheromones and there are indications of presocial behavior. Some disperse by phoresy. Suborders: Atoposphyronida, Heterosphyronida (Epiocheirata), Iocheirata.

PSEUDOSEMATIC. [Gr. ψευδης, false; σημα, signal]. See Sematic.

PSEUDOSTERNOGYNUM. [Gr. ψευδης, false; στερνον, chest; γυνη, female]. In the Trigynaspida (Mesostigmata): a pregenital shield that lacks pores. It may be homologous to the anterior genital shield in the Holothyrida. See also Sternogynum.

PSEUDOSTIGMA. [Gr. ψευδης, false; στιγμη, mark]. Any cup-like pit of the integument. In ticks and mites: the socket of the sensory setae.

PSEUDOSTIGMATIC ORGAN. [Gr. ψευδης, false; στιγμη, mark]. 1. In the Oribatida: one of two variously-shaped organs of sensory setae that appear from a cupule or pit located on the cephalothorax. They are thought to detect air movements and thus avoid desiccation. 2. An obsolete term for the bothridial sensillum or trichobothrium.

PSEUDOSYMMETRY. [Gr. ψευδης, false; συμμετρια, symmetry]. An approximate symmetry of a structure when split by a plane that divides the structure into halves that are less than symmetrical.

PSEUDOTAGMA. [Gr. ψευδης, false; ταγμα, corpse]. In ticks and mites: a region of a body division, such as gnathosoma, idiosoma, proterosoma and hysterosoma. See also Tagma.

PSEUDOTETRAMEROS. [Gr. ψευδης, false; τετρα, four; μερος, part]. Appearing to have four joints, where there are actually five joints or segments.

PSEUDOTRIMEROS. [Gr. ψευδης, false; τρεις, three; μερος, part]. Appearing to have three joints, when there are actually four joints or segments.

PSEUDOTYRANNOCHTHONIIDAE. [Gr. ψευδης, false; L. *tyrannus*, an absolute ruler; χθονιος, beneath the earth]. A family of false scorpions (suborder Heterosphyronida, superfamily Chthonioidea) with a wide, but discontinuous, distribution.

PSOROPTIDAE. [Gr. ψωρα, itch; οπτικος, visible]. A family of scab- and mange-producing fur mites (suborder Astigmata, superfamily Sarcoptoidea) which parasitize mammals.

PSOROPTIDIA. [Gr. ψωρα, itch; οπτικος, visible]. In a previous classification: a parvorder (or infraorder) of 'biting' mites (order Sarcoptiformes, suborder Astigmata) that united the superfamilies Analgoidea, Freyanoidea, Psoroptoidea, Pterolichoidea, Pyroglyphoidea. The constituents of these superfamilies are now distributed amongst the superfamilies of the suborder Asigmata.

PSOROPTOIDEA. [Gr. ψωρα, itch; οπτικος, visible]. In a previous classification: a superfamily of scab- and mange-producing fur mites (suborder Astigmata, parvorder Psoroptidia) that united fourteen families. These families are now in the superfamily Sarcoptoidea.

PTERATE. [Gr. πτερον, wing]. See Alate.

PTERINS (PTERIDINES). [Gr. πτερον, wing]. A group of white, yellow and red pigments which are derivatives of folic acid (pteridine ring) and were originally isolated from the wings of butterflies.

PTEROID. [Gr. πτερον, wing; ειδος, form]. Resembling a wing.

PTEROLICHOIDEA. [Gr. πτερον, wing; λιχος, greedy]. A superfamily of scab- and mange-producing fur mites (order Sarcoptiformes, suborder Astigmata). Eighteen families.

PTEROMORPHAE. [Gr. πτερον, wing; μορφη, shape]. In some ticks and mites: outgrowths from the notogaster which cover the sides of the podosoma and third and fourth pairs of legs.

PTEROTE. [Gr. πτερωτος, winged]. Having wing-like outgrowths.

PTERYGOID. [Gr. πτερυοειδης, wing-like]. Wing-like.

PTERYGOSOMATOIDEA. [Gr. πτερυξ, wing; σωμα, body]. A monotypic superfamily of mites (suborder Prostigmata, infraorder Eleutherengona). Family: **Pterygosomatidae.**

PTYCHOIDY. [Gr. πτυχη, a fold; ειδος, form]. In the Oribatida: an articulation between the prosoma and opisthosoma, allowing the legs to be concealed by a down folding of the prosoma. See also Dichoidy, Holoid, Trichoidy.

PUBERULENT. [L. *pubes*, adult]. Covered with down or fine hair.

PUBESCENT. [L. *pubescere*, to become mature]. Covered with soft hair or down.

PUBIC. [L. *pubes*, adult]. Referring to the area of the genitalia.

PUCE. [L. *pucilem*, flea]. Dark brown or purplish brown.

PULMOBRANCH(IA). [L. *pulmo*, lung; Gr. βραγχια, gills]. A gill-like organ which is adapted for air breathing conditions, as for example the book lungs of spiders.

PULVERULENT. [L. *pulverulentus*, dusty]. Powdery. Farinaceous.

PULVILLIFORM. [L. *pulvillus*, little cushion; *forma*, shape]. Shaped like a small cushion.

PULVILLUS. [L. *pulvillus*, little cushion]. In the Mesostigmata: a membranous pad-like structure associated with the claws.

PULVINAR, PULVINATE, PULVINATUS. [L. *pulvinus*, cushion]. Cushion-like.

PUNCTAE. [L. *punctum*, point]. Small pores, holes or similar marks on a surface.

PUNCTATE. [L. *punctum*, point]. Having the surface covered with small pores, holes etc., or having a dot-like appearance.

PUNCTIFORM, PUNCTIFORMIS. [L. *punctum*, point; *forma*, shape]. Having a dot-like appearance.

PUNCTULATE, PUNCTULATUS. [L. *punctulum*, little point]. Having minute pores, holes, dots, etc.

PUNCTUM. [L. *punctum*, point]. A minute pore, hole or dot.

PUNCTURE. [L. *punctura*, prick]. Any small, round surface depression.

PUNCTURED. [L. *punctura*, prick]. Marked with small, impressed dots.

PUNGENT. [L. *pungere*, to prick]. Of stimuli that strongly affect the chemical sense receptors.

PUNICEUS. [L. *puniceus*, scarlet/crimson]. Carmine red.

PUPIFORM (PUPOID). [L. *pupa*, puppet; *forma*, shape]. Shaped like a pupa; pupa-like.

PUPIL. [L. *pupilla*, pupil of the eye]. The central spot of an ocellus.

PUPILLATE. [L. *pupilla*, pupil of the eye]. Of eye markings in which there is a differently colored central spot.

PURPURASCENT. [L. *purpura*, purple]. Becoming purple.

PURPUREOUS, PURPUREUS. [L. *purpureus*, purple]. Purple, mauve.

PURSE-WEB SPIDERS. See Atypidae.

PUSTICULATE. [L. *pustula*, blister]. Ornamented with small mound-like structures. Covered with pustules.

PUSTULE. [L. *pustula*, blister]. A blister-like prominence.

pv 1-3. In the Mesostigmata: designations for the setae on the posterior ventral surface of a leg or palp segment. See Evans Leg Chaetotactic System.

PYCNONOTICAE. [Gr. πυκνος, dense/thick; νωτον, back]. A section of the infraorder Brachypylina (order Sarcoptiformes, suborder Oribatida) based on the absence of well developed downwardly-curving, or short horizontal, pteromorphae; that are present in the section Poronoticae, although this may not be a good criterion. Twenty-three superfamilies encompassing seventy families.

PYCNOTHELIDAE. [Gr. πυκνος, dense/thick; θηλη, nipple]. A family of spiders (infraorder Mygalomorphae, superfamily Avicularioidea).

PYEMOTOIDEA. [deriv.uncert.]. A superfamily of mites (suborder Prostigmata, infraorder Eleutherengona). Families: **Acarophenacidae**, **(?Bembidiacaridae)**, **Caraboacaridae**, **Pyemotidae, Resinacaridae**.

PYGAL. [Gr. πυγη, rump]. Situated at the posterior end.

PYGIDIAL SHIELD (SCLERITE). [Gr. πυγιδιον, narrow rump]. In the Mesostigmata: a shield at the back end of the idiosoma.

PYGMEPHOROIDEA. [Gr. πυγμαιος, dwarfish; -φορα, -carrying]. In a previous classification, a superfamily of mites (suborder Prostigmata, infraorder Eleutherengona) that united the families: **Microdispidae, Pygmephoridae, Scutacaridae**. These families, along with the **Neopygmephoridae** are now in the superfamily Scutacaroidea.

PYGMY (PIGMY) MALES. [Gr. πυγμαιος, dwarfish]. See Dwarf Males.

PYLORIC VALVE. [Gr. πυλωρος, gate-keeper]. A regulatory sphincter at the entrance to the intestine from the stomach. It is usually located behind the stomach in the anterior part of the proctodeum.

PYRAMIDOPIDAE. [L. *pyramis*, pyramid; Gr. -ωψ, appearance]. A family of harvestmen or daddy longlegs (suborder Laniatores, superfamily Assamioidea) known only from Africa, the Canary Islands, and recently a cave-dwelling species from Mexico.

PYRIFORM (PIRIFORM). [L. *pirum*, pear; *forma*, shape]. Pear-shaped. Applied to cells, spores, muscles, etc. In spiders: of a type of silk gland.

PYROGLYPHIDAE. [Gr. πυρο-, fire; γλυφειν, to engrave]. A family of non-parasitic mites (suborder Astigmata, superfamily Analgoidea), including the house dust mite, that may cause severe itching and a rash. Many species live in the burrows and nests of other animals where they live on the skin and feather detritus of their hosts.

PYROGLYPHOIDEA. [Gr. πυρο-, fire; γλυφειν, to engrave]. In a previous classification: a superfamily of scab- and mange-producing fur mites (suborder Astigmata, parvorder Psoroptidia) that united the families: **Pyroglyphidae, Turbinoptidae**. These families are now in the superfamily Analgoidea.

Q

QUADRAT. [L. *quadratus*, squared]. A sample area enclosed within a frame, usually one square meter. A larger quadrat of four square meters being a major quadrat. The frame itself.

QUADRICAPSULAR. [L. *quadrus*, fourfold; *capsula*, little box]. Having four capsules.

QUADRIDENTATE. [L. *quadrus*, fourfold; *dentatus*, toothed]. Having four teeth or tooth-like processes.

QUADRIFARIUM. [L. *quadrifarium*, four-fold;]. Having four rows.

QUADRIFID. [L. *quadrus*, fourfold]. Four rows. In four segments.

QUADRIGYNASPINE (QUADRIGYNASPID). [L. *quadrus*, fourfold; Gr. γυνη, a woman; L. *spina*, thorn]. Adult females of the Holothyrida, or some Trigynaspida (Mesostigmata), that are characterized by having four genital shields.

QUADRIHYBRID. [L. *quattuor*, four; *hibrida*, mongrel]. A hybrid whose parents differ in four distinct characters; therefore heterozygous for four pairs of alleles.

QUADRILATERAL. [L. *quadrus*, fourfold; *latus*, side]. Four-sided. Formed or bounded by four lines.

QUADRILOBATE. [L. *quattuor*, four; *lobus*, lobe]. Having four lobes.

QUADRIMACULATE. [L. *quattuor*, four; *macula*, spot]. Having four spots.

QUADRIPARTITE. [L. *quadrus*, fourfold; *partitus*, divided]. In four parts.

QUADRIPINNATE. [L. *quadrus*, fourfold; *penna*, feather]. Having four feather-like branches or clefts.

QUADRISERIAL. [L. *quattuor*, four; *series*, row]. Arranged in four rows.

QUADRIVOLTINE. [L. *quattuor*, four; It. *volta*, time]. Having four broods per year or per breeding season.

QUALITATIVE CHARACTER. Any inherited character that has discrete states that are not numerical or morphometric.

QUALITATIVE INHERITANCE. The inheritance of phenotypic characters that have a discontinuous variation and that tend to be controlled by one major gene or a small number of genes. E.g. gender.

QUALITATIVE MULTISTATE CHARACTER. A qualitative character that exhibits several states that cannot be arranged linearly along a single axis.

QUANTITATIVE CHARACTER. 1. Any inherited character that shows quantitative inheritance, i.e. something that can be counted. E.g. egg production. 2. Any inherited character showing continuous variation, i.e. degrees of variation between one extreme and another, and which is usually controlled by several interacting genes.

QUANTITATIVE INHERITANCE. See Continuous Variation.

QUANTITATIVE MULTISTATE CHARACTER. Any inherited character that shows several states that can be arranged linearly along a single axis.

QUANTUM EVOLUTION (QUANTUM SPECIATION). [L. *quantum*, how great an extent]. The rapid evolution of new species, usually within small peripheral populations that are isolated from the large ancestral population. Founder effect and genetic drift play important roles, particularly when the number of individuals is small and the new niche is unoccupied.

QUASISYMPATRIC SPECIATION. [L. *quasi*, as if; Gr. συμ, pref. together; πατρη, native land]. See Speciation.

QUIESCENCE (QUIESCENT). [L. *quiescere*, to become still]. The temporary cessation of development due to disadvantageous environmental conditions.

QUINCUNX, QUINCUNXES. [L. *quincunx*, arranged in diagonal rows, five-twelfths]. An arrangement of five objects in a square, with one in each corner and one in the center.

QUINQUEDENTATE. [L. *quinque*, five; *dens*, tooth]. Having five teeth.

QUINQUEFARIOUS. [L. *quinque*, five; *farius*, fold]. Arranged in five rows, ranks, or columns.

QUINQUELOCULAR. [L. *quinque*, five; *loculus*, cell]. Consisting of five cells, or five loculi.

QUINQUEPARTITE. [L. *quinque*, five; *partitus*, divided]. Divided into five parts.

R

R versus Rh. There seems to be some confusion in the literature as to whether an initial 'R' should be 'R' or 'Rh'. For example one may find both Rheophile and Reophile; Rhagidiidae and Ragidiidae. 'Rh' is correct if the word is derived from a Greek root with an initial, aspirated 'R'.

r-series. [Ger. *rand*, margin]. In the Mesostigmata: a designation for the longitudinal row of marginal prodorsal setae laterad to the s-series and running from the anterior setae r1 (commonly absent) to setae r6 at or near the posterior margin of the pronotal shield or region. See Lindquist-Evans System.

R-series. [Ger. *rand*, margin]. In the Mesostigmata: a designation for the longitudinal row of opisthodorsal setae laterad to the S-series, mesad to the UR-series, and running from the setae R1 to setae R6 (occasionally more) at or near the lateral margin of the opisthonotal region. See Lindquist-Evans System.

RACE. A particular breed. A subspecies. An interbreeding subspecific group of individuals within a species that forms a permanent variety, i.e. they are genetically distinct from members of other such groups of the same species and characterized by conspicuous physiological (physiological race), biological (biological race), geographical (geographical race) or ecological (ecological race) properties. Commonly, races are geographically isolated by, for example, mountain ranges or being island races.

RACE HISTORY. See Phylogeny.

RACEMOSE. [L. *racemus*, bunch]. A bunch or cluster, as of grapes.

RACEMOSE GLAND. [L. *racemus*, a cluster]. A type of gland formed by a simple primary invagination, forming a duct, which bears a number of secondary invaginations known as saccules or alveoli. The duct may become divided and subdivided into branches, increasing the secreting surface enormously, as in the salivary glands.

RACHIDIAN. [Gr. ραχις, a spine]. Located at or near to a rhacis (a spine).

RACHIFORM. [Gr. ραχις, a spine: L. *forma*, shape]. In the shape of a rhacis (a spine).

RACHIS (RHACHIS). [Gr. ραχις, a spine/the spine]. A spine.

RACQUET ORGAN. See Malleolus.

RADIAL APOPHYSIS. [L. *radius*, ray; Gr. απoφυας, an offshoot]. In arachnids: a process of the palp of a male, which is inserted into a grove of the epigynum of the female during mating.

RADIORECEPTOR. [L. *radius*, ray; *receptor*, receiver]. A receptor organ sensitive to light or temperature.

RADIX. [L. *radix*, root]. A point of origin. A primary source. In arachnids: the apophysis of the male copulatory organ.

RAFTING. The dispersal of terrestrial organisms (plants or animals) across water on floating objects or matter.

RAKE-LIKE. Of a limb with more or less parallel projecting setae or spines, resembling the tines of a rake.

RAIN FOREST. A tropical forest which has an annual rain fall in excess of 254 cm (100 inches).

RAMAL, RAMEAL. [L. *ramus*, branch]. Branching or branch-like.

RAMATE. [L. *ramus*, branch]. Branched.

RAMELLOSE. [L. *ramulus*, small branch]. Having small branches.

RAMIFEROUS. [L. *ramus*, branch; *ferre*, to bear]. Branched.

RAMIFICATION. [L. *ramus*, branch; *facere*, to make]. A branch of a nerve, artery, etc.

RAMIFORM. [L. *ramus*, branch; *forma*, shape]. Branch-like.

RAMIFY, RAMFIED, RAMFYING. [L. *ramus*, branch; *ficere*, to make]. To send forth outgrowths or branches.

RAMOSE. [L. *ramosus*, branching]. Branching, having lateral divisions full of branches.

RAMULIFEROUS. [L. *ramulus*, twig; *ferre*, to bear]. Bearing small branches.

RAMULOSE/RAMULOUS. [L. *ramulus*, twig]. Bearing many small branches.

RAMUS (RAMI). [L. *ramus*, branch]. Any branch-like structure.

RANDOM DISTRIBUTION. A distribution in which the outcome is the result of pure chance and thus one in which no one individual has any influence on the distribution of other individuals.

RANDOM MATING. Within a population: mating irrespective of genotype or phenotype. Thus every male gamete has an equal opportunity to join in fertilization with every female gamete.

RANDOM SAMPLE. A sample in which each individual measured or recorded is independent of all other individuals and independent of prominent features in the region being sampled.

RANDOM WALK TECHNIQUE. A sampling technique whereby the distance (e.g. number of paces) between sampling areas is determined by reference to random number tables or other source of random numbers. At each sampling area a 90 degree turn is made to determine the direction of the next area, a coin being tossed to choose left or right.

RANGIFEROID. [*Rangifer*, generic name of reindeer; Gr. ειδoς, form]. Branching like a reindeer's antlers.

RANK. In taxonomy: the position of a taxon in a hierarchy. See Nomenclature.

RAPACIOUS. [L. *rapere*, to snatch]. Feeding on prey.

RAPHÉ. [Gr. ραφη, seam]. A seam-like suture.

RAPHIGNATHAE. [Gr. ραφη, seam; γναθoς, jaw]. In a previous classification: a section or infraorder of mites (order Prostigmata, suborder Eleutherengona) that united the superfamilies Cheyletoidea, Eriophyoidea, Raphignathoidea, Tetranychoidea. The Cheyletoidea, Raphignathoidea, Tetranychoidea are now in the infraorder Eleutherengona, and the Eriophyoidea is in the Eupodina.

RAPHIGNATHOIDEA. A superfamily of mites (suborder Prostigmata, infraorder Eleutherengona). Families: **Barbutiidae, Caligonellidae, Camerobiidae, Cryptognathidae,**

Dasythyreidae, Eupalopsellidae, Homocaligidae, Mecognathidae, Raphignathidae, Stigmaeidae, Xenocaligonellididae.

RAPTATORY. [L. *raptare*, to rob]. Preying upon.

RAPTORIAL. [L. *raptor*, robber]. Adapted for snatching or robbing.

RASORIAL. [L. *radere*, to scratch]. Adapted for scratching or scraping the ground.

RASP. [OF. *rasper*, to scrape]. A roughened surface for the production of sound by friction. See also Barychelidae, Stridulating Organs.

RASSENKREIS (RHEOGAMEON). [Ger. *rasse*, breed; *kreis*, district/circle]. A species with geographical subspecies. See also Circular Overlap.

RASTELLUM. [L. *rastellus*, rake]. In some spiders: a group of teeth on the basal joint (the paturon) of the chelicerae.

RASTRATE. [L. *rastrum*, rake]. Having longitudinal scratches over the surface.

RATITE. [L. *ratis*, raft (i.e. a boat without a keel)]. Lacking a keel. Of a smooth ventral somite. Lacking ridges or raised lines. See Carinate.

RAY. [L. *radius*, ray]. One of any number of fine lines radiating from a center.

REAFFERENCE. [L. *re-*, again; *afferre*, bring to]. The stimulation of an animal as a result of the movements of its own body. See also Afference.

REALM. [OFr. *reaume*, kingdom]. A primary zoogeographical division of the earth, encompassing major climatic or physiographic zones.

REBORDED. [Fr. *rebord*, rim]. In ticks and mites: pertaining to the distal thickened and strengthened end of the labium.

RECEPTACLE. [L. *recipere*, to receive]. Any organ used as a repository.

RECEPTACULUM. [L. *receptaculum*, reservoir]. A receptacle of any type.

RECEPTACULUM SEMINIS. [L. *receptaculum*, reservoir; *semen*, seed]. See Spermatheca.

RECEPTOR. [L. *recipere*, to receive]. Specialized tissues or cells, often in a sensory organ, that are sensitive to a specific stimulus. When the stimulus exceeds a particular threshold the receptor fires an impulse into its associated nerve cells. **Exteroceptors** are those on the outside of the body. **Interoceptors** are those inside the body. **Proprioceptors** are also inside the body and are located in muscles, tendons, joints, etc. They provide information relating to position, movement, tension, etc. See also Chemoreceptor, Exteroceptors, Interoceptors, Mechanoreceptor, Photoreceptor, Proprioceptors, Stretch Receptor, Thermoreceptors.

RECESS. [L. *recessus*, withdrawn]. Any fossa, sinus, cleft or hollow space.

RECIPROCAL ALTRUISM. [L. *reciprocus*; moving backwards and forwards; It. *altrui*, somebody else]. Any mutually beneficial behavior.

RECIPROCAL ORGANS. [L. *reciprocus*; moving backwards and forwards]. Structures which exhibit secondary sexual characteristics which are of opposite size in male and female.

RECLINATE. [L. *reclinare*, to lean]. Having the apex curved downwards towards the base.

RECLINATUS. [L. *reclinatus*, reclined/bent back]. Reflexed.

RECLINING. [L. *reclinare*, to lean]. Leaning over.

RECLIVOUS, RECLIVATE. [L. *re*, back; *clivus*, slope]. Having the form of a sigmoid curve; i.e. a convex and concave line. See also Vertical.

RECONDITE. [L. *reconditus*, put away, hidden]. Concealed. Remote from ordinary or easy perception.

RECTAL. [L. *rectus*, straight]. Of the rectum.

RECTAL CAECA. [L. *rectus*, straight; *caecus*, blind]. A blind duct or diverticulum which leads off the rectum.

RECTAL GLANDS. [L. *rectus*, straight]. A term loosely applied to numerous glands adjacent to or associated with the anus. Glands which often secrete either a lubricant, silk-gum, or other specialized material such as a gelatinous matrix for the protection of eggs.

RECTAL PAPILLAE (RECTAL PADS). [L. *rectus*, straight; *papilla*, nipple]. Pads of tissue in the lining of the rectum, which are important in re-absorption of water, salts and amino acids from the urine.

RECTATE. [L. *rectus*, straight]. Straight.

RECTIGRADE. [L. *rectus*, straight; *gradus*, step]. Walking in a straight line.

RECTILINEAR. [L. *rectus*, straight; *linea*, line]. Straight; formed in—or bound by—straight lines.

RECTISERIAL. [L. *rectus*, straight; *series*, row]. Arranged in straight rows.

RECTOGENITAL. [L. *rectus*, straight; *genitalia*, genitals]. Of the rectum and genitalia.

RECTUM. [L. *rectus*, straight]. The region of the alimentary canal that leads to the anus. Feces are retained here prior to defecation.

RECTUS. [L. *rectus*, straight]. Straight.

RECUMBENT. [L. *recumbere*, to lie down]. Reclining.

RECURRENT. [L. *recurrere*, to hasten back]. Reappearing at intervals. Returning towards the origin.

RECURVED. [L. *recurvus*, bent back]. Bent upwards or backwards. Of the lateral eyes in arachnids that are farther back than the median eyes.

RECURVED OVARY. See Reflexed Ovary.

RECUTITE. [L. *recutitus*, skinned]. Lacking apparent epidermis.

RED MITES. See **Dermanyssidae**.

RED QUEEN EFFECT. An evolutionary principle, first proposed by L. Van Valen, that much of the evolution of a lineage consists of tracking environmental changes, rather than occupying or adapting to new environments. This hypothesis predicts that evolution will continue because (1) the most important component of a species' environment is other species in the community, and (2) not all species will have reached their local adaptive peaks, and thus are capable of further evolution even though the physical environment may have stabilized. Any evolutionary advance made by one species will, ultimately, have a detrimental effect on, or represent a deterioration in the biotic environment of, all other species in that same community. Consequently, these other species become subject to selective pressures to achieve evolutionary advances, just to catch up. The name is derived from Lewis Carroll's *Alice Through The Looking Glass*, in which the Red Queen had to run as fast as she could just to stay in the same place. See also Romer's Rule.

RED VELVET MITE. Any mite that has a body covered with bright red velvety hairs. Typically, the nymphal or adult stage of Parasitengonans (Prostigmata) that feed on small arthropods and their eggs.

REDINTEGRATION. [L. *redintegrare*, to make whole again]. The regeneration of an injured or lost part.

REDUCTION. [L. *reductus*, reduced]. A structural and functional development that is less complex than that of the ancestors.

REFLECTOR EYES. [L. *reflectere*, to turn back]. Eyes with well-developed tapeta, as in the four large posterior eyes of most wolf spiders (Lycosidae) which hunt in the dim light of dusk or by moonlight.

REFLECTOR LAYER. [L. *reflectere*, to turn back]. The layer of cells on the inner surface of some photogenic tissue.

REFLEX. [L. *reflectere*, to turn back]. An involuntary reaction to a stimulus.

REFLEX ACTION. [L. *reflectere*, to turn back]. A form of behavior in which a particular stimulus generates a direct and immediate response, which is automatic and often beyond conscious control. In its simplest form a nervous impulse travels along an afferent nerve to the central nervous system and then via one or more motor neurons to an efferent nerve which initiates the response, such as movement, secretion, etc.

REFLEX ARC. [L. *reflectere*, to turn back; *arcus*, a bow]. The simplest mechanism of the nervous system; consisting of a receptor, a nervous pathway (conductor) and a gland or muscle cell (effector).

REFLEX IMMOBILIZATION. See Thigmokinesis.

REFLEXED. [L. *reflectere*, to turn back]. Turned backwards.

REFLEXED OVARY. [L. *reflectere*, to turn back; *ovarium*, ovary]. An ovary that is turned back upon itself or bent abruptly back. Generally found at the junction of the ovary and oviduct.

REFRACTED. [L. *re-*, back; *frangere*, to break]. Turned backwards at an acute angle.

REFRACTIVE. [L. *re*, back; *frangere*, to break]. To turn from a direct course; turned aside.

REFRACTORY. [L. *refractarius*, obstinate]. Unresponsive. Commonly applied in the transmission of nerve impulses to the period after initial excitation during which a repetition of the stimulus fails to elicit a response.

REFRINGENT. [L. *re*, back; *frangere*, to break]. Refractive. To deflect rays of light.

REFUGIUM (REFUGIA, REFUGE). [L. *refugere*, to flee away]. A geographical region which avoids the changes which affect the surrounding regions and therefore provides a refuge for the local flora and fauna. E.g. a mountain not covered by water during an incursion by the sea, a region not covered by ice during the Pleistocene. Also, any place that offers protection from danger or predators.

REGENERATION. [L. *re-*, again; *generare*, to beget]. The renewal of a portion of the body that has been injured or lost.

REGION. [L. *regio*, district]. Any area of the world that supports a characteristic biota.

REGRESSION. [L. *regressus*, returned]. A reversal in the direction of evolution that may, sometimes, cause the progeny to revert to a less extreme condition than their parents.

REGRESSIVE CHARACTER. [L. *regressus*, returned]. A character or trait which shows a gradual loss of differentiation as a result of ageing.

REGRESSIVE EVOLUTION. [L. *regressus*, returned; *evolvere*, to unroll]. An evolutionary trend leading to a simplification of structure or a decrease in specialization. E.g. the loss of eyes in some cave-dwelling animals.

RELEASER. [L. *relaxare*, to loosen]. A type of effector device such as a structure, movement, scent or call with a very specific function, namely to provide stimuli which release (or inhibit) a response, or set of responses, in another animal of the same species. See also Sign Stimulus.

RELEASER EFFECT. See Pheromone.

RENIFORM. [L. *ren*, kidney; *forma*, shape]. Kidney-shaped.

REPAND. [L. *repandus*, turned up]. Having an undulating margin.

REPETITION MOLT (MOULT). [L. *repetere*, to seek again; *mutare*, to change]. In the Chelicerata: a molt that results in no change in characters of form or size. See also Growing Molt.

REPLACEMENT FERTILITY LEVEL. The fertility level required to maintain a population at zero growth rate.

REPLICATE. [L. *replicare*, to fold back]. Doubled over on itself.

REPRODUCTION. [L. *re-*, again; *producere*, to bring forward]. The process of producing new individuals, by either sexual or non-sexual means. It may occur by: simple or multiple fission, as in protozoans; gemmation (budding) as in cnidarians; parthenogenesis as in (for example) aphids; or sexual, the union of male and female gametes to form a zygote.

REPRODUCTIVE ISOLATION. [L. *re-*, again; *producere*, to bring forward; LL. *insulatus*, made into an island]. Any situation in which reproduction is prevented. Reproductive isolation falls into two categories: **Premating Isolation**. Ecological: two species occupying different habitats or microhabitats. Physiological: by breeding seasons being non-synchronous or members of one species being 'unattractive' to members of the other. Mechanical: by different shaped genitalia (lock and key model) or different sized genitalia. Ethological: by non-recognition of courtship rituals or inhibition in the female due to slight variations.

Postmating Isolation. Sperm transfer occurs but the egg is not fertilized (gametic mortality), the egg is fertilized but the zygote dies (zygote mortality), zygote produces an F1 hybrid of reduced viability (hybrid inviability), F1 hybrid zygote is fully viable but partially or completely sterile or produces deficient F2 (hybrid sterility), karyotype incompatibility causing the offspring to be non-viable or sterile. Many cases of reproductive isolation may arise initially from mate choice, i.e. inhibitions due to courtship rituals may be overcome in the absence of the preferred ritual. Hybrids may thus arise, and in some cases may be fertile with other hybrids and/or with either parent.

REPUGNATORIAL. [L. *repugnare*, to fight against]. Of glands and other structures which are used either defensively or offensively.

REPUGNATORIAL GLANDS. [L. *repugnare*, to fight against]. Any glands secreting noxious liquids or vapors to repel antagonists.

RESPIRATORY MOVEMENTS. [L. *respiratio*, breathing]. The movements of part of an animal which cause a flow of air or water to cross the respiratory surface at which gaseous exchange occurs.

RESPIRATORY ORGANS. [L. *respiratio*, breathing]. Any organ which accommodates an interchange of oxygen and carbon dioxide. Such organs usually have a large surface area and the main types are: external gills, internal gills, membrane gills, lungs, spiracles and tracheae, book lungs, book gills and respiratory tree.

RESPIRATORY PIGMENTS. [L. *respiratio*, breathing; *pingere*, to paint]. Complexes of proteins and metallic ions which form a loose (reversible) association with oxygen and transport it from the respiratory surface to the tissues. E.g. hemoglobin, myoglobin, hemocyanin, hemerythrin, cytochrome, chlorocruorin, etc. These pigments change color according to the degree of oxygenation (e.g. hemoglobin is bright red when oxygenated and purple when deoxygenated) and many have characteristic absorption spectra.

RESTIFORM. [L. *restis*, rope; *forma*, shape]. In the form of a rope.

RESUPINATE. [L. *resupinare*, to bend back]. Having the appearance of being inverted, reversed, or upside down.

RETE. [L. *rete*, net]. See Plexus.

RETECIOUS. [L. *rete*, net]. In the form of a network.

RETICLE. [L. *reticulum*, little net]. See Reticulum.

RETICULATE (RETICULAR, NETTED). [L. *reticulum*, little net]. Network like.

RETICULATE-FOVEATE. [L. *reticulum*, little net; *fovea*, depression]. Having a net-like ornamentation composed of irregular, rounded cells.

RETICULUM. [L. *reticulum*, little net]. In many organs: a framework of tissue.

RETIFORM (RETECIOUS, RETIARY). [L. *rete*, net; *forma*, shape]. In the form of a network, web-like.

RETINA. [L. *rete*, net]. The receptive apparatus of an eye.

RETINACULUM. [L. *retinaculum*, tether]. A connecting or retaining band.

RETINAL CELL. [L. *rete*, net]. The photosensitive neurosensory cells.

RETINAL PIGMENT CELLS. [L. *rete*, net]. The pigment cells in the retinal region of the eye.

RETINERVED. [L. *rete*, net; *nervus*, sinew]. Having reticulate nerves or veins.

RETRACTED. [L. *retractus*, withdrawn]. Drawn back. Opposite of prominent.

RETRACTILE. [L. *retractus*, withdrawn]. Of any structure, organ or part of an organ that can be drawn inwards.

RETRACTOR. [L. *retrahere*, to draw back]. Any muscle which actively draws a limb towards the body. See Muscle Terminology.

RETRAHENS. [L. *retrahere*, to draw back]. Any muscle which draws a part backwards. See Muscle Terminology.

RETRAL. [L. *retro*, backwards]. Posterior, backward.

RETROARCUATE. [L. *retro*, backwards; *arcuatus*, curved]. Curving backwards.

RETROCESSION. [L. *retro*, back; *cedere*, to go]. The act of retroceding; of moving backwards.

RETROFLECTED. [L. *retro*, backwards; *flectere*, to bend]. Bending in different directions. Bent or turned backwards.

RETROFRACT. [L. *retro*, backwards; *fractus*, broken]. Bent backwards at an angle.

RETROGRESSION (DEGENERATION, RETROGRESSIVE). [L. *retrogressus*, going back]. In an individual or race: a change from a more complex type to a simpler type.

RETROGRESSIVE (REGRESSIVE) DEVELOPMENT. [L. *retrogressus*, going back]. A developmental trend in evolution resulting in simplification of an organism, usually through the complete or partial loss of one or more structures.

RETROLATERAL. [L. *retro*, backwards; *latus*, side]. Of backward-directed spines projecting from the side of the leg. In an imaginary state of all the legs being straight out from the side; at right angles to the long axis of the body. See also Prolateral.

RETROLATERAL TIBIAL APOPHYSIS (RTA). [L. *retro*, backwards; *latus*, side, L. *tibia*, shin; Gr. αποφυσις, an offshoot]. In male spiders (Araneae): a sclerotized outgrowth or process (apophysis) on the retrolateral face of the palpal tibia. See also Tibial Apophysis, Ventral Tibial Apophysis.

RETROLATEROBASAD. [L. *retro*, backwards; *latus*, side; Gr. βασις, base; L. *ad*, towards]. Toward the retrolateral side and the base. See also Prolaterobasad.

RETROLATERODISTED. [L. *retro*, backwards; *latus*, side; L. *distare*, to stand apart]. Toward the retrolateral side and the tip.

RETROMARGIN. [L. *retro*, backwards; *marginis*, border]. The posterior margin of the fang furrow.

RETROMORPHOSIS. [L. *retro*, backwards; Gr. μορφωσις, shaping]. Development with a tendency to degenerate.

RETRORSE (RETROVERSE). [L. *retrorsum*, backwards]. Directed backwards. See also Antrorse, Detrorse.

RETRORSE TEETH. [L. *retrorsum*, backwards]. See Deutosternal Denticles.

RETROSERRATE (RUNCINATE). [L. *retro*, backwards; *serra*, saw]. With backward facing teeth.

RETROSERRULATE. [L. *retro*, backwards; *serrula*, small saw]. Having small, retrorse, teeth.

RETROVERSE (RETRORSE). [L. *retroversus*, turned backwards]. Turned backwards.

RETUSE. [L. *retusus*, blunted]. Ending in an obtuse sinus or broad, shallow notch. Terminated by an obtuse hollow.

REVERSED. [L. *reversus*, turn back]. Turned in an unusual or contrary direction; i.e. upside down or inside out.

REVERSION (ATAVISM). [L. *reversio*, turning back]. A return to an ancestral type. The return of a domesticated species to the ancestral wild type.

REVIVESCENCE. [L. *reviviscere*, to come to life again]. Emergence from hibernation or some other quiescent state.

REVOLUTE. [L. *revolvere*, to roll back]. Rolled backwards from the margin. See also Involute.

RHABDIFORM. [Gr. ραβδος, rod; L. *forma*, shape]. Rod-shaped.

RHABDITOID BURSA. [Gr. ραβδος, rod; ειδος, like]. A rod-shaped pouch, sac, or sac-like cavity.

RHABDOID. [Gr. ραβδος, rod; ειδος, like]. Of any rod-shaped body.

RHACHIDIAN. See Rachidian.

RHACHIS. See Rachis.

RHAGIDIAL ORGANS. [Gr. ραγιον, little grape/berry]. In the Eupodoidea (Prostigmata): recumbent solenidia in shallow depressions on the distal segments of legs I-II.

RHAGODIDAE. [*Rhagodes*, derived from nomenclatural change from Gr ραξ, grape]. A family of sun spiders (subclass Arachnida, order Solifugae) from Africa and south-western Asia. They are unique in having a hemispherical form to their anal segment and a ventrally located anus (terminal in all other solifuges).

RHAMPHOID. [Gr. ραμφος, beak; ειδος, form]. Beak-shaped.

RHEOGAMEON. [Gr. ρεω, flow; γαμος, marriage; ον, being]. See Rassenkreis.

RHEOPHILE (RHEOPHILIC). [Gr. ρεω, flow; φιλος, loving]. Thriving in flowing water.

RHEORECEPTOR. [Gr. ρεω, flow; L. *recipere*, to receive]. A sensory structure that signals the presence or strength of water currents.

RHEOTAXIS, REOTACTIC, RHEOTROPISM. [Gr. ρεω, flow; ταξις, an arranging]. A tactic response due to stimulation from moving fluid. **Positive rheotaxis**: migrating against the current of moving fluid. **Negative rheotaxis**: Moving with the fluid.

RHEOXENOUS. [Gr. ρεω, flow; ξενος, stranger]. Of organisms that occur infrequently in running water.

RHEXIGENOUS. [Gr. ρηξις, breaking; -γενης, producing]. Resulting from tearing or rupturing.

RHEXILYSIS. [Gr. ρηξις, breaking; λυσις, loosening]. The production of openings or cavities by rupture or fissure.

RHIGOSIS. [Gr. ριγος, cold]. The sensation of cold.

RHIPIDATE (FLABELLIFORM). [Gr. ριπις, a fan]. Fan-shaped.

RHIZOID/RHIZOMORPHOUS. [Gr. ριζα, root; ειδος, form/μορφος, shape]. Root-like.

RHODACAROIDEA. [Gr. ροδοπη-, rosy-; LL. *acarus*, mite]. A superfamily of mites (suborder Monogynaspida, infraorder Gamasina). Families: **Digamasellidae, Halolaelapidae, Laelaptonyssidae, Ologamasidae, Rhodacaridae, Teranyssidae**. In some classifications this superfamily may be included in the sub-cohort Dermanyssiae.

RHOMBOID. [Gr. ρομβος, lozenge]. Having the shape of a lozenge or rhomb, i.e. a four-sided figure in which the opposite sides and angles equal to one another but the figure is neither equilateral nor right-angled. Applied to scales, fossae, ligaments, etc.

RHOMBOID-OVATE. [Gr. ρομβος, lozenge; ειδος, form; L. *ovum*, egg]. A shape between rhomboid and oval.

RIBLET. [AS. *ribblet*, small rib]. A small or rudimentary rib. A costella.

RICINOIDIDAE. See Ricinulei.

RICINULEI (PODOGONATA). [L. *ricinus*, a kind of tick]. A small, monotypic order of tropical, eyeless arachnids (class Euchelicerata, subclass Arachnida) that inhabit leaf mold and caves in tropical Africa and America. The cuticle is very thick and heavily sculptured to warty; the abdomen is segmented and narrowed anteriorly and forms a pedicle attached to the prosoma and at the posterior forms a retractable tubercle that bears the anus. Attached to the anterior margin of the carapace is a hood-like structure that can be raised and lowered to cover the mouth and chelicerae. The chelicerae are two-segmented and in the form of pincers, the short pedipals also terminate in small pincers. They are slow-moving and feed on other small arthropods. On hatching, the spiderling is a six-legged 'larva' similar to that of ticks and mites. Suborder: Neoricinulei. Family: **Ricinoididae** (genera: *Cryptocellus, Pseudocellus, Ricinoides*).

RIMA. [L. *rima*, a crack]. The orifice of the mouth. A slit-like ostiole. A cleft or fissure.

RIMATE. [L. *rima*, a crack]. Having fissures or clefts.

RIMIFORM. [L. *rima*, a crack; *forma*, shape]. In the shape of a narrow fissure or cleft.

RIMOSE. [L. *rima*, a crack]. Having many fissures or clefts.

RIMULOSE. [LL. *rimula*, small cleft]. Having many small fissures or clefts.

RIVOSE. [L. *rivus*, groove]. Marked with irregular furrows, nonparallel furrows or canals.

ro (vi). In acariform mites: a designation for the rostral seta, the most anterior seta on the prodorsum.

ROMER'S RULE. [*A.S. Romer*, American Paleontologist]. The proposal that the effect of many important evolutionary changes is to enable organisms to continue the same way of life, rather than adapt to a new one. See also Red Queen Effect.

RORIDOUS. [L. *ros*, dew]. Covered with dew-like droplets.

RORULENTUM. [L. *rorulentum*; dewy / full of dew]. Dusty.

ROSETTE. [Fr. from L. *rosa*, rose]. A swirl of hair or hair–like structures.

ROSTEL. [L. *rostellum*, little beak]. See Rostellum.

ROSTELLAR, ROSTELLATE. [L. *rostrum*, beak]. Towards the anterior end. Towards the rostrum when anterior. Having a rostellum.

ROSTELLIFORM. [L. *rostellum*, little beak; *forma*, shape]. Shaped like a small beak.

ROSTELLUM. [L. *rostellum*, little beak]. A small rostrum or beak-shaped process.

ROSTRAD. [L. *rostrum*, beak; *ad*, toward]. Towards the anterior region of the body.

ROSTRAL. [L. *rostrum*, beak]. Of a rostrum.

ROSTRAL GUTTER. [L. *rostrum*, beak]. In the Eriophyoidea: the cheliceral sheath.

ROSTRAL GLAND. [L. *rostrum*, beak]. In spiders: the labral gland.

ROSTRAL-LAMELLAR SYSTEM. [L. *rostrum*, beak; *lamella*, thin plate]. In the Acariformes: a designation system for the prodorsal setae based on Grandjean's system as applied to the Oribatida. Each pair of setae may represent one of the six supposed prosomal segments. The designations are: rostral (ro), lamellar (le), bothridial (bo), anterior exobothridial (exa, also xa), interlamellar (in), posterior exobothridial (exp, also xp). In the Endeostigmata, the Vertical-Scapular system is more commonly used (vi, ve, sci, sce, in, exp, respectively). In the Prostigmata: the prodorsal setae are represented by the interior and exterior vertical (vi, also v1; ve, also v2) and internal and external scapular setae (sci, also s1; sce, also s2). In the Astigmata, the traditional designations follow those used in the Prostigmata.

ROSTRAL SETA. [L. *rostrum*, beak]. In the Acariformes: the anterior-most pair of prodorsal setae or an unpaired median seta. When a naso is present it often carries the rostral setae.

ROSTRAL TECTUM (ROSTRUM) . [L. *rostrum*, beak; *tectum*, roof]. In acariform mites: a prodorsal tectum that projects over at least the base of the chelicerae. It often covers most of the capitulum and possibly represents a sclerotized naso.

ROSTRATE. [L. *rostrum*, beak]. Having a rostrum or beak-like process.

ROSTRIFORM (ROSTROID). [L. *rostrum*, beak; *forma*, shape]. Having the form of a beak.

ROSTRULUM. [LL. *rostrulum*, little beak]. A small beak.

ROSTRUM. [L. *rostrum*, beak]. Any beak-like process. The combined epistome and labrum of spiders. In the Oribatida: the most anterior dorsal portion of the idiosoma, particularly when it projects over the bases of the chelicerae. See also Naso.

ROTATORY. [L. *rota*, wheel]. Of an articulation that permits a rotating motion, e.g. a ball and socket joint.

ROTATE. [L. *rota*, wheel]. Shaped like a wheel.

ROTATOR. [L. *rotatore*, rotator]. A muscle which allows a circular or twisting motion. See Muscle Terminology.

ROTATORIUM. [L. *rotare*, to cause to rotate]. A pivot joint.

ROTIFORM. [L. *rota*, wheel; *forma*, shape]. Circular.

ROTULE. See Trochantin.

ROTULIFORM. [L. *rotula*, little wheel; *forma*, shape]. Shaped like a small wheel.

ROTUNDATE. [L. *rotundus*, round]. Rounded. Nearly circular. Rounded at the angles, sides, or ends.

RTA. See Retrolateral Tibial Apophysis.

RUBEN. [L. *ruber*, red]. Red, approaching carmine.

RUBESCENT. [L. *rubescere*, to grow red]. Being reddish, or becoming red.

RUBIGINOSE (RUBIGINOUS). [L. *rubigo*, rust]. Brownish-red; rust colored.

RUBINEOUS. [L. *ruber*, red]. Ruby-like.

RUDERAL. [L. *rudus*, debris]. Living among debris, or on disturbed sites.

RUDIMENTARY. [L. *rudimentum*, first beginning]. At an early stage of development. Arrested at an early stage of development. Imperfectly developed. See also Vestigial.

RUFINISM (RUTILISM). [L. *rufus*, reddish]. The formation of a red pigmentation due to a inability to form a darker pigment.

RUFOUS, RUFESCENT (erron. RUFOS). [L. *rufus*, red]. Being reddish, red-yellowish.

RUFUS. [L. *rufus*, reddish]. Reddish-brown. Tawney.

RUGATE. [L. *rugare*, to wrinkle]. Wrinkled, ridged.

RUGOSE (RUGOUS). [L. *rugare*, to wrinkle]. Having numerous wrinkles or ridges. Corrugated.

RUGOSISSIMUS. [L. *rugosus*, full of wrinkles; *-issimus*, super. suf.]. Being extremely rugose or wrinkled.

RUGOSITY. [L. *rugosus*, full of wrinkles]. The condition of being wrinkled.

RUGULA. [L. *ruga*, wrinkle]. A small wrinkle.

RUGULOSE. [L. *ruga*, wrinkle]. Finely wrinkled.

RUNCINATE. [L. *runcina*, a plane (formerly taken to mean a saw)]. Irregularly saw-toothed. See Retroserrate.

RUPICOLOUS (RUPESTRINE, RUPICOLINE). [L. *rupes*, a rock / cliff; *colere*, to inhabit]. Living among rocks.

RUPTILE. [L. *rumpere*, to burst open]. Bursting in an irregular manner.

RUST MITES. Mites of the Eriophyoidea (Prostigmata) whose feeding causes a russet coloration on leaves.

RUTELLA (RUTELLUM). [L. *rutrum*, shovel]. In the Sarcoptiformes: the paired hypertrophied setae on the subcapitulum. They are thick, hard and dentate, and associated with ingestion of solid food. In the Astigmata the rutellum may be referred to as a pseudorutellum. See also Atelebasic Rutellum, Pantelebasic Rutellum.

RUTILANT. [L. *rutilus*, red / auburn]. Having a bright, bronze-red color.

RUTILISM. [L. *rutilus*, red / auburn]. See Rufinism.

RUTILOUS. [L. *rutilus*, red, golden red]. Of a shining bronze red color.

S

s1. In the Prostigmata: the internal scapular seta (sci, sc1, si) on the prodorsum.

s2. In the Prostigmata: the external scapular seta (sce, sc2, se) on the prodorsum.

s-series. In the Mesostigmata: a designation for the longitudinal row of prodorsal setae laterad to the z-series, mesad to the r-series, and running from the setae s1 (anterior) to setae s6 at or near the posterior margin of the pronotal shield or region. See Lindquist-Evans System.

S-series. In the Mesostigmata: a designation for the longitudinal row of opisthodorsal setae laterad to the Z-series, mesad to the R-series, and running from the setae S1 (anterior) to setae S5 at or near the postero-lateral margin of the opisthonotal shield or region. See Lindquist-Evans System.

SABACONIDAE. [Gr. Σαβακων, an Ethiopian king]. A family of harvestmen (suborder Dyspnoi, superfamily Ischyropsalidoidea) found throughout Asia, Europe and north America. The pedipalps are covered with densely plumose seta and there is a bulbous tarsus which fits closely into a tibial depression.

SABULICOLOUS. [L. *sabulo*, gravel/sand; *colere*, to inhabit]. Arenicolous. Living in sand.

SABULOUS, SABULOSE. [L. *sabulum*, sand]. Sandy, gritty.

SAC. [L. *saccus*, sack]. Any sack, bag or pouch.

SACCATE. [L. *saccus*, sack]. Pouched.

SACCIFEROUS. [L. *saccus*, sack; *ferre*, to bear]. Bearing a sac, bag or pouch.

SACCIFORM (SACCULAR). [L. *saccus*, sack; *forma*, shape]. In the form of a sack, bag or pouch.

SACCULATE. [L. *sacculus*, little bag]. Bearing a small sac, bag or pouch.

SACCULATION. [L. *sacculus*, little bag]. The process of formation of saccules.

SACCULE, SACCULUS (pl. SACCULI). [L. *sacculus*, little bag]. Any small sac, bag or pouch. Invaginated porose organs opening to the surface by a small pore. See Octotaxic System.

SACCULUS FOEMINEUS. [L. *sacculus*, little bag; *foemineus*, feminine]. In the Mesostigmata: the sack-like structure (commonly with paired swellings) in laelapid-type sperm access systems where the sperm duct originates and the tubulus annulatus enters.

SACCULUS VESTIBULUS. [L. *sacculus*, little bag; *vestibulum*, porch]. In the Mesostigmata with laelapid-type sperm access systems: the cavity in the acetabulum of the coxa or elsewhere where the tubulus annulatus originates.

SACCUS. [L. *saccus*, bag]. Any sac-like structure.

SACRALS. [LL. *os sacrum*, sacred bone]. In the Pritchard & Baker System: the Inner Sacrals (or DC4) = f1 and the Outer Sacrals (or L4) = f2;

SAGITTAL SECTION. [L. *sagitta*, arrow]. A section through a body in the median longitudinal plane, i.e. a vertical and lengthwise section from head to tail in the midline which thus divides a bilaterally symmetrical animal into two similar (right and left) halves. See also Parasagittal.

SAGITTATE (SAGITTIFORM). [L. *sagitta*, arrow]. Having the shape of an arrowhead.

SALIENT. [L. *saliens*, leaping]. Projecting outward. Prominent.

SALIVA. [L. *saliva*, spittle]. The secretion produced by the salivary glands; usually in the presence (or anticipation) of food. It also acts as a lubricant and contains various enzymes depending on the diet. In blood-sucking species it contains anticoagulants and in some species contains a local anesthetic.

SALIVARIUM. [L. *saliva*, spittle; *-arium*, a place where something is kept]. A recess in the preoral food cavity which contains the openings of the salivary ducts.

SALIVARY GLANDS (SIALADEN). [L. *saliva*, spittle]. In most animals: the glands which secrete saliva into, or near to, the mouth or buccal cavity.

SALIVARY STYLUS. [L. *stylus*, pricker]. In the Mesostigmata: tube-like external ducts protected by the corniculi.

SALPINX. [Gr. σαλπιγξ, war-trumpet]. Any trumpet-shaped structure.

SALTATORIAL, SALTATORY. [L. *saltare*, to leap]. Adapted for, or used in, leaping; e.g. the limbs of jumping spiders.

SALTICIDAE. [L. *saltare*, to leap]. The cosmopolitan, family of jumping spiders (infraorder Araneomorphae, superfamily Entelegynae), most of which are tropical although there are some northern temperate and arctic species. Medium to small spiders in which the carapace is square-fronted and there are only two tarsal claws. In association with their leaping/predatory life style the anterior median eyes are much larger than the others and members of this family have the greatest visual acuity of any arthropod. They can also distinguish color and the plane of polarized light. Leaping is accomplished by rapidly increasing the internal body pressure which extends the legs. Many species are ant mimics (Myrmecophilous) and all have very complex courtship rituals and threat displays. Previously in the monotypic superfamily Salticoidea.

SALTIGRADE. [L. *saltare*, to leap; *gradus*, step]. Moving by leaps, as in some spiders and insects.

SALT MARSH. An intertidal region of sandy mud in sheltered estuaries and sheltered coastal areas.

SAMOIDAE. [*Samoa*, in the South Pacific Ocean]. A wide-ranging family of harvestmen or daddy longlegs (suborder Laniatores, superfamily Samooidea).

SAMOOIDEA. [*Samoa*, in the South Pacific Ocean]. A superfamily of harvestmen (suborder Laniatores, infraorder Grassatores). Families: **Biantidae, Samoidae, Stygnommatidae.**

S. AMPL. Sensu Amplificato. [L. *sensus*, sense; *amplificatio*, an enlarging]. In the enlarged sense.

SANDOKANIDAE (syn **ONCOPODIDAE**). [*Sandokan*, a fictional prince-pirate]. A family of harvestmen or daddy longlegs (suborder Laniatores, superfamily Epedanoidea) from Southeast Asia and into the Himalayan region.

SANGUINE. [L. *sanguis*, blood]. Having the color of blood.

SANGUINOLENT. [L. *sanguinolentus*, bloody]. Bloody in color or appearance.

SANGUIVOROUS (SANGUINIVOROUS). [L. *sanguis*, blood; *vorare*, to devour]. Feeding on blood.

SAPPHIRINE, SAPPHYRINUS. [Gr. σαπφειρος, sapphire]. Sapphire blue.

SAPROBIC. [Gr. σαπρος, rotten; βιος life]. 1. Living on decaying organic matter. 2. Of water rich in decaying organic matter. See also Katharobic, Mesosaprobic, Oligosaprobic, Polysaprobic.

SARCOID. [Gr. σαρκωδης, fleshy]. Fleshy.

SARCOPTIDAE. [Gr. σαρξ, flesh; οπτικος, seen]. A family of mange and scab-producing fur mites (suborder Astigmata, superfamily Sarcoptoidea). Parasitic mites that pass their entire life cycle attached to the host. *Sarcoptes scabiei*, the cause of scabies, burrows into the epidermis but the irritation is caused by their secretions.

SARCOPTIFORMES. [Gr. σαρξ, flesh; οπτικος, seen; L. *forma*, shape]. An order of mites (subclass Arachnida, superorder Acariformes). Species that are mainly micro-herbivores, fungivores, and detritivores, and ingest solid food. Some (**Psoroptidae**) have become associated with vertebrates and nest-building insects. These include the house dust mites (**Pyroglyphidae**), scab mites and mange mites (**Sarcoptidae**), stored-product mites (many families), feather-mites (many families) and some fur-mites (**Cheyletidae**). Suborders: Astigmata, Endeostigmata, Oribatida.

SARCOPTOIDEA (PSOROPTOIDEA). [Gr. σαρξ, flesh; οπτικος, visible]. A superfamily of scab- and mange-producing fur mites (order Sarcoptiformes, suborder Astigmata). Twelve families.

SARCOSOMA. [Gr. σαρξ, flesh; σωμα, body]. The fleshy portion of an animal's body, as opposed to the exoskeletal portion.

SATIATION. [L. *satias*, sufficiency]. The process which leads to the termination of an activity due to a sufficient amount of that activity having occurred. This term is commonly applied to feeding behavior and may be associated with physiological changes.

SATURATION. [L. *satur*, full]. In communities: the population level at which immigration is balanced by removal (death).

SATURATION DISPERSAL. [L. *satur*, full; *dispergere*, to disperse]. The emigration of surplus individuals from a population which is near to, or at, its carrying capacity. Typically the individuals are juveniles, aged, or in poor condition.

SAVANNAH (SAVANNA). [Sp. *zavana*]. The tropical and subtropical grasslands that typically consist of drought resistant vegetation dominated by grasses and with a few scattered tall trees. Savannahs are transitional between grassland and desert or grassland and rainforest.

SAXICOLOUS. [L. *saxum*, rock; *colere*, to inhabit]. Of species that frequent rocky or stony areas.

sc1. In the Prostigmata: the internal scapular seta (sci, s1, si) on the prodorsum.

sc2. In the Prostigmata: the external scapular seta (sce, s2, se) on the prodorsum.

SCABELLUM. [L. *scabellum*, footstool]. In the Uropodina: a platform-like structure on the underside of the vertex that receives the withdrawn legs I.

SCABERULOUS/SCABROUS. [L. *scaber*, rough]. Being rough, rough-surfaced.

SCABRATE. [L. *scaber*, rough]. Covered with stiff hairs or scales.

SCABRICULOUS. [L. *scaber*, rough]. Regularly and finely wrinkled.

SCALARIFORM (SCALIFORM). [L. *scala*, ladder; *forma*, shape]. Ladder-shaped. Applied to vessels or tissues that have bars like a ladder or any structure that resembles a ladder.

SCALE. [AS. *sceala*, shell/husk]. A small, flat, plate-like, external structure.

SCALLOPED. [OF. *escalope*, shell]. Indented. Crenate. Cut at the edges into rounded hollows or segments of circles.

SCALPS. [related to ON. *skalli*, bald head]. In some oribatid mites: the retained notogastral portions of exuviae, often as a pagoda-like pile of exuviae. Scalp is also the macerated cuticle of a mite that has been cleared and mounted on a microscope slide.

SCALPELLUM, SCALPELLUS. See Lancet.

SCALPRIFORM. [L. *scalprum*, chisel; *forma*, shape]. Chisel-shaped.

SCALY. [AS. *sceala*, shell/husk]. Squamate.

SCANSORIAL. [L. *scandere*, to climb]. Adapted for climbing.

SCAPE. [Gr. σκαπος, stalk]. In some spiders: an epigynal structure which protects the vulva.

SCAPHOID, SCAPHIFORM. [Gr. σκαφη, boat; ειδος, form]. Boat-shaped.

SCAPULAE. [L. *scapula*, shoulder]. In many ixodid ticks: the shoulder-like projections on the antero-lateral edges of the scutum.

SCAPULAR SETA. [L. *scapula*, shoulder, *seta*, bristle]. In the Prostigmata: two pairs of setae (sci, sce) on the prodorsum. They are often inserted on either side of the eyes.

SCARIFIED. [L. *scarifico*, to scratch]. Scratched or cut.

SCARIOUS. [Fr. *scarieux*, membranous]. Thin, dry, membranous, scaly or scurfy.

SCAT. [Gr. σκατος (σκωρ), dung]. A fecal dropping.

SCATOLOGY. [Gr. σκατ-, dung; λογος, discourse]. The study of animal feces.

SCHIZECKENOSY. [Gr. σχιζω, to split; κενος, empty out]. In ticks and mites: a system of waste elimination in a blind-ending midgut. A lobe from the ventriculus breaks free and is expelled though a split in the posterodorsal cuticle.

SCHIZODORSAL SHIELD. [Gr. σχιζο-, split; L. *dorsum*, back]. In the Mesostigmata: a holodorsal shield that is incised laterally at about the midpoint. Also, podonotal and opisthonotal shields that are fused medially.

SCHIZOGASTRY. [Gr. σχιζο-, split; γαστηρ, stomach]. In some Prostigmata: a splitting of the cuticle to form a temporary opening to eliminate nitrogenous wastes (guanine).

SCHIZOGLYPHOIDEA. [Gr. σχιζο-, split; γλυφα, carving]. A monotypic superfamily of 'biting' mites (order Sarcoptiformes, suborder Astigmata). Family: **Schizoglyphidae.**

SCHIZOLYSIS. [Gr. σχιζειν, to split; λυσις, dissolving]. Fragmentation.

SCHIZOMIDA (SCHIZOPELTIDA, TARTARIDAE). [Gr. σχιζο, split]. An order of small tropical arachnids (class Euchelicerata, subclass Arachnida), known as short-tailed whip scorpions or micro-whip scorpions, in which the prosoma is divided into three regions, each covered dorsally by thin separate plates of chitin. The abdomen is composed of twelve conspicuous segments and bears a very short, terminal flagellum; there are no eyes but the first pair of legs are antenniform; the raptorial pedipalpi are leg-like and the two small chelicerae bear small pincers. They were previously included in the order Uropygi and are of similar habits. Superfamily: Hubbardioidea. Families: **†Calcitronidae, Hubbardiidae, Protoschizomidae.**

SCHIZOPELTID. [Gr. σχιζο-, split; πελτη, shield]. In chelicerates: the prodorsal shield (peltidium) subdivided by one or more transverse scissures. It is composed of the propeltidium, mesopeltidium and metapeltidium (or propeltidium) and postpeltidium.

SCHIZOPELTIDA. [Gr. σχιζο-, split; πελτη, a small, light shield]. See Schizomida.

SCHIZOTHECAL. [Gr. σχιζο-, split; θηκη, case]. Having scale-like, horny tarsal plates.

SCHMIDT'S LAYER. [*Adolf Schmidt*, German entomologist]. In the exoskeleton: the amorphous, granular layer between the epidermis and endocuticle (i.e. the subcuticle). It forms the membrane from which new cuticle is produced during ecdysis.

SCHOPFORGANE. [Ger. 'forelock organ']. See Krobylophore.

sci. In the Prostigmata: the internal scapular seta (sc1, s1, si) on the prodorsum. See Vertical-scapular system.

SCIENTIFIC NAME. [L. *scientia*, knowledge]. The formal Latin, or Latinized name of a taxon. See also Vernacular Name, Nomenclature.

SCISSILE. [L. *scissilis*, cleavable]. Cleavable into layers.

SCISSURE. [L. *scindere*, to cut]. A cleft or split in a body or surface. In ticks and mites: a relatively narrow band of soft skin that cuts the sclerotized cuticle into plates.

SCLERE/SCLEREID. [Gr. σκληρος, hard]. Any small, hard, skeletal structure.

SCLERIFICATION. See Sclerotization.

SCLERITE. [Gr. σκληρος, hard]. A calcareous plate or spicule. A chitinous plate. An individual plate of an exoskeleton. Sclerites are formed principally from chitin and protein (sclerotin) and commonly contain calcium salts or waxes.

SCLERITIZATION. [Gr. σκληρος, hard; L. *facere*, to make]. The formation of sclerites.

SCLERODERMITE. [Gr. σκληρος, hard; δερμα, skin]. The region of the exoskeleton over one body-segment.

SCLEROID (SCLEROUS). [Gr. σκληρος, hard; ειδος, form]. Skeletal, hard.

SCLERONODULI. [Gr. σκληρος, hard; L. *nodulus*, small knot]. Light refractile structures in the podonotal region of many Rhodacaroidea and *Protogamasellus*: Ascidae (Mesostigmata).

SCLEROSOMATIDAE. [Gr. σκληρος, hard; σωμα, body]. A large family of harvestmen or daddy longlegs (suborder Eupnoi, superfamily Phalangioidea).

SCLEROTIN. [Gr. σκληρος, hard; -*in*, chem. suf. used neutral substances]. A stable, highly resistant, quinone-tanned protein that occurs in cuticle, and in the structural proteins in many groups of invertebrates and vertebrates.

SCLEROTIZATION. [Gr. σκληρος, hard]. The hardening process which occurs in the cuticle (exoskeleton) after ecdysis.

SCLEROTIZED. [Gr. σκληρος, hard]. Hardened or horny, not flexible or membranous.

SCLEROUS. See Scleroid.

SCOBINATE. [L. *scobina*, file]. Having a rasp-like surface.

SCOBISCULAR (SCOBIFORM, SCOBISCULATE). [L. *scobiculum*, sawdust]. Resembling sawdust, granulated.

SCOLOPARIUM. See Proprioceptor.

SCOLOPIDIUM (SCOLOPOPHORE, SENSILLUM SCOLOPOPHORUM). [Gr. σκωλος, pointed stake; -ιδιον, dim.suf.]. A mechanoreceptor (part of a chordotonal organ) consisting of three cells: a sensory neuron (scolopale), an enveloping cell, and an attachment, or cap cell.

SCOLOPOPHORE, SCOLOPHORE. [Gr. σκωλος, pointed stake; φορα, a carrying]. 1. Complex sensilla consisting of a bundle of sensory cells whose endings are separated from the body by one or more accessory cells that are receptive to mechanical stimuli. 2. A sense organ perceiving continuous vibration. See also Tangoreceptor.

SCOPATE (SCOPIFEROUS). [L. *scopa*, brush]. Brush-like in having tufts of hair.

SCOPIFORM (SCOPULATE). [L. *scopa*, brush; *forma*, shape]. Brush-like.

SCOPULA. [L. *scopula*, small brush]. A small tuft of hairs. In climbing spiders: an adhesive tuft of club-like hairs on each foot, replacing the third claw. See also Dionycha, Trionycha.

SCOPULIFEROUS. [L. *scopula*, small brush; *ferre*, to bear]. Having the general form of a small, brush-like structure.

SCOPULIFORM. [L. *scopula*, small brush; *forma*, shape]. Resembling a small brush.

SCOPULOPHTHALMI. [L. *scopula*, small brush; Gr. οφθαλμος, the eye]. A monotypic infraorder of harvestmen (order Opiliones, suborder Cyphophthalmi). Family: **Pettalidae**.

SCORPAMINS. [Gr. σκορπιος, scorpion]. Toxins derived from scorpions.

SCORPIOID. [Gr. σκορπιωδες, scorpion-like]. In the form of a scorpion.

SCORPIONES. [Gr. σκορπιος, scorpion]. The order of scorpions (class Euchelicerata, subclass Arachnida). Large, primitive, secretive, nocturnal, yellow to brown or black, rarely greenish or bluish arachnids that have changed little from their aquatic ancestors of the Silurian: making them the oldest known terrestrial arthropods. Division and segmentation of the abdomen is retained, the prosoma is covered by a single carapace and broadly joins the abdomen, which is divided into a wide, seven-segmented pre-abdomen (anterior mesosoma) and a long, post-abdomen (posterior metasoma) consisting of five, narrow, ring-shaped segments terminating in a telson with a venomous sting. The chelicerae are very small and the pedipals are greatly enlarged to form a pair of large pincers. There is a pair of median eyes (except in some cave-dwelling species) and two to five pairs of lateral eyes on the carapace margin. The stinging apparatus is attached to the posterior of the last post-abdominal segment and consists of a bulbous base and a sharp, curved barb with a sub-apical opening. Most sting in defense or to subdue prey and the venom of the majority of scorpions is not harmful to man, however, members of the family **Buthidae** are dangerous to humans in having a neurotoxic venom. Mating involves deposition of a spermatophore and a lengthy and elaborate courtship which may last hours or even days; and ends with the female being pulled into position over the spermatophore. Pressure on the spermatophore lever releases the sperm mass, which is taken up into the female gonopore. All species are either ovoviviparous or truly viviparous (i.e. brooding their eggs in the reproductive tract) and there is a high degree of parental care. There is very little sexual dimorphism, most species are tropical or subtropical and all fluoresce under ultraviolet light. Superfamilies: Buthoidea, Chactoidea (Vaejovoidea), Chaeriloidea, Iuroidea, Pseudochactoidea, Scorpionoidea (Bothriuroidea). See also Pectines.

SCORPIONIDAE. [Gr. σκορπιος, scorpion]. A family of burrowing or pale-legged scorpions (order Scorpiones, superfamily Scorpionoidea) from Africa, Asia, Australia, North America, Central and Southern America. They have a pentagonal sternum and very powerful, broad pedipalps and live mainly in savannahs, humid forests and rainforests, but some are found in drier habitats. The family **Diplocentridae** was recently included here as the subfamily Diplocentrinae, and then re-established as a family.

SCORPIONOIDEA (BOTHRIUROIDEA). [Gr. σκορπιος, scorpion]. A large superfamily of scorpions (subclass Arachnida, order Scorpiones). Families: **Bothriuridae, Diplocentridae, Hemiscorpiidae** (syn. **Ischnuridae/Liochelidae**), **Heteroscorpionidae** (contentious), **Scorpionidae**.

SCORPIONS. See Scorpiones.

SCRAPER. [AS. *scrapian*, scraper]. Any structure or specialized part of a structure adapted for rasping or scraping.

SCRIPTUS. [L. *scriptus*, write]. Marked with characters resembling letters.

SCROBAL. [L. *scrobis*, ditch]. Of a pit or depression.

SCROBES. [L. *scrobis*, ditch]. Grooves for the reception or concealment of an appendage.

SCROBICULATE. [LL. *scrobiculum*, little ditch]. Ornamented with little pits or depressions.

SCROBICULUS. [LL. *scrobiculum*, little ditch]. A pit or depression.

SCROTIFORM. [L. *scrotum*, pouch; *forma*, shape]. Purse or pouch shaped.

SCULPTURE. [L. *sculptura*, carving]. The pattern or marking of impressions or elevations on the surface of an animal.

SCULPTURED. [L. *sculptura*, carving]. Of a surface marked with elevations or depressions or both when they are arranged in some definite manner.

SCUTACARID. [L. *scutellum*, little shield, +Acarid]. Turtle mites. A member of the heterostigmatan family **Scutacaridae** (Prostigmata).

SCUTACAROIDEA (PYGMEPHOROIDEA). [L. *scutum*, shield; LL. acarus, mite]. A superfamily of mites (suborder Prostigmata, infraorder Eleutherengona). Families: **Microdispidae**, **Neopygmephoridae**, **Pygmephoridae** (syn **Siteroptidae**), **Scutacaridae**

SCUTAL. [L. *scutum*, shield]. Of the scutum.

SCUTATE. [L. *scutum*, shield]. Being protected by large scales or horny plates.

SCUTATEIFORM. [L. *scutum*, shield; *forma*, shape]. Shield-shaped.

SCUTCHEON. [OF. *escusson*, shield]. The scutellum.

SCUTE. [L. *scutum*, shield]. Any scale-like structure. See also Scutum.

SCUTELLA, SCUTEL. [L. *scutellum*, little shield]. See Scutellum.

SCUTELLATE (SCUTELLIFORM). [L. *scutellum*, little shield]. Shaped like a small shield.

SCUTELLATION. [L. *scutellum*, little shield]. The arrangement of scales.

SCUTELLIGEROUS. [L. *scutellum*, little shield; *gerere*, to bear]. Having small scutes, or a scutellum.

SCUTELLUM, SCUTELLA, SCUTULIS. [L. *scutellum*, little shield]. Any shield-shape structure.

SCUTIFORM. [L. *scutum*, shield; *forma*, shape]. Shield-shaped.

SCUTIGEROUS (SCUTIFEROUS). [L. *scutum*, shield; *gerere*, to bear]. Having a shield-like structure.

SCUTUM. [L. *scutum*, shield]. A horny, bony or chitinous shield-shaped plate that develops in the integument. In ticks: the dorsal shield.

SCYPHIFORM (SCYPHOID). [L. *scyphus*, drinking-cup; *forma*, shape]. Cup-shaped.

SCYPHULUS. [LL. *scyphula*, little cup]. Any small cup-shaped structure.

SCYTODIDAE. [Gr. σκυτώδης, like leather]. The family of spitting spiders (infraorder Araneomorphae, superfamily Haplogynae). They have a very characteristic domed carapace which houses a pair of enormously enlarged two-lobed glands: the front lobe producing a poison and the rear lobe producing an adhesive substance. These glands are connected to holes near the tip of each fang, and by the sudden contraction of muscles, these glands are compressed and their contents sprayed out. During the discharge the fangs are oscillated rapidly to produce a zigzag pattern of dispersal. They have six eyes arranged in three groups, some species occupy a web, others are nocturnal, and the female carries her egg bundle under the body.

SCYTODOIDEA. [Gr. σκυτώδης, like leather]. In a previous classification, a superfamily of leaf-litter spiders, brown recluse spiders, six-eyed sand spiders and spitting spiders (infraorder Araneomorphae) that united the families **Sicariidae (Loxoscelidae)**, **Periegopidae**, **Scytodidae**, and **Drymusidae**. These families are now placed in the superfamily Haplogynae

se. In the Prostigmata: the external scapular seta (sce, sc2, s2) on the prodorsum.

226

SEARCH-LIGHT EYES. The enormously enlarged rear eyes (PME - Posterior Median Eyes) of the net-casting 'ogre-eyes spiders' *Deinopis* (**Deinopidae**). Their large, curved, compound lenses face forward, have a wide field of view and gather available light very efficiently. Each night a large area of light sensitive membrane is manufactured within these eyes and broken down again at dawn.

SEASONAL ISOLATION. A form of reproductive isolation in which different species become reproductively active at different times of the year.

SEBACEOUS. [L. *sebum*, tallow; *-aceous*, of the nature of]. Fatty or oily: applied to glands secreting such substances.

SEBIFEROUS. [L. *sebum*, tallow; *ferre*, to carry]. Transporting fatty material.

SEBIFIC. [L. *sebum*, tallow]. Oily: sebaceous: somewhat sticky.

SEBIFIC DUCT. [L. *sebum*, tallow; *ducere*, to lead]. A duct that carries the excretions of the collateral gland to the bursa copulatrix.

SECONDARY. [L. *secundus*, second]. Second in importance or position. Generally applied to structures which have been greatly reduced or lost during evolution.

SECONDARY CHARACTERS. [L. *secundus*, second]. The specialized features which are off the main line of evolution and represent particular adaptations to a way of life.

SECONDARY EYES. [L. *secundus*, second]. All the eyes other than the anterior median eyes; which may have a tapetum layer.

SECONDARY SEX RATIO. See Sex Ratio.

SECONDARY SEXUAL CHARACTERISTICS. [L. *secundus*, second]. The differences between the sexes other than the gonads and associated ducts and glands.

SECONDARY SPECIATION. See Speciation.

SECOND TROCHANTER. [L. *secundus*, second; Gr. τροχαντηρ, runner]. The second segment of the leg, between the coxa (coxapodite) and the femur. See Limb.

SECRETA. [L. *secernere*, to separate]. Any or all the products of a secretory process.

SECRETION. [L. *secretio*, separation]. The discharge of useful material, as opposed to the elimination of waste material (excretion). The material secreted (itself called a secretion) is usually complex and has a special function for the organism.

SECTORIAL. [L. *sector*, cutter]. Formed or adapted for cutting, e.g. teeth.

SECURIFORM. [L. *securis*, axe; *forma*, shape]. Hatchet-shaped.

SEGESTRIIDAE. [Gr. σεγεστρον, blanket]. A cosmopolitan family of tube-dwelling spiders (infraorder Araneomorphae, superfamily Haplogynae). They construct tubular retreats with radiating trigger threads and wait near the entrance with the front legs on the rim of the opening: then rush out to seize prey when the threads are disturbed. They have six eyes arranged in a semicircle, the abdomen is elongate and cylindrical and the first three pairs of legs are directed forward, which is thought be an adaptation for living in tubes.

SEGMENT. [L. *segmentum*, a strip or piece cut off]. One of a series of ring-like divisions into which the body or an appendage is divided.

SEGMENTATE. [L. *segmentum*, a strip or piece cut off]. Made up of rings or segments.

SEGMENTATION. [L. *segmentum*, a strip or piece cut off; *-ation*, ending of some nouns of action]. The division or splitting into portions. In general: the formation of a series of segments arranged along the length of the body, with repetition of the principle organs in each segment. In arachnids, distinct external segments have been lost but remnants of segmentation may be represented by hysterosomal folds or transverse arrays of setae and other cuticular sense organs. Theoretically, all chelicerates have a prosoma composed of six segments (cheliceral, pedipalpal, and four leg-bearing segments = body segments I-VI). Ventrally the positions of the prosomal segments can be identified by the insertions of their appendages, but dorsally they are obscured. The opisthosoma is thought to comprise an additional 12-13 segments (body segments VII-XVIII or XIX), but appears to be somewhat—to much, reduced in most mites, except possibly Opilioacarida. See also Metameric Segmentation.

227

SEISMAESTHESIA. [Gr. σεισμος, shaking; αισθησις, sense-perception]. The perception of mechanical vibrations.

SEISMOTAXIS. [Gr. σεισμος, shaking; ταξις, an arranging]. Movement in response to mechanical vibrations.

SEJIDA (SEJINA). [L. *Seius*, fictitious name/supporter of Caesar]. A suborder of predatory or scavenging mites (superorder Parasitiformes, order Mesostigmata) that are mainly associated with tree holes, nests and patchy habitats. Most have deutonymphs that are phoretic on insects. Superfamilies: Heterozerconoidea, Sejoidea.

SEJOIDEA. [L. *seius*, fictitious name/supporter of Caesar]. A superfamily of carnivorous mites (order Mesostigmata, suborder Sejida). Families: **Ichthyostomatogasteridae, Reginacharlottiidae, Sejidae, Uropodellidae.**

SEJUGAL. [L. *seiugo*, separate]. Indicating the furrow or interval separating divisions or segments of an invertebrate body.

SEJUGAL SUTURE/PLANE. [L. *seiugo*, separate; *sutura*, seam]. In acariform mites: a division dissecting the idiosoma between legs II-III.

SEJUNCTUS. [L. *sejunctus*, separate]. Separated.

SELECTION. [L. *selectionem*, choice]. The non-random process by which different genotypes come to represent different proportions of a population. Their relative probability of surviving to the next generation being their adaptive value. **Disruptive selection**: a selective process which changes the frequency of the alleles in a divergent manner such that some alleles may become fixed in some individuals of the population. After several generations of selection two divergent phenotypes may be observed, each tending to an extreme. This process may be the foundation of sympatric speciation. See also Speciation.

SELENIFORM. [Gr. σεληνη, the moon; L. *forma*, shape]. In the shape of a full moon.

SELENOID. [Gr. σεληνοειδης, crescent-shaped]. Crescent-shaped, crescentic.

SELENOPIDAE. [Gr. Σεληνη, the moon goddess; ωψ, the eye]. A cosmopolitan family of spiders (infraorder Araneomorphae, superfamily Entelegynae) which are very flat dorsoventrally, have two tarsal claws, and laterigrade legs. They have eight eyes arranged in one row with six and one with two. Their running and striking speeds place them among the world's fastest animals. Previously in the monotypic superfamily Selenopoidea.

SELLATE, SELLAEFORM (SELLIFORM). [L. *sella*, saddle; *forma*, shape]. Saddle-shaped.

SELVA. [L. *silva*, wood]. A tropical rain forest.

SEMATIC. [Gr. σημα, sign]. Of some coloration, odor, behavior or structure that acts as a danger or warning signal. **Allosematic.** Having protective coloration resembling that of dangerous or inedible species. **Antiaposematic.** Of coloration that disguises a predator. **Aposematic (Synaposematic).** Having a warning device that tells a potential predator that an animal is distasteful or poisonous. **Proaposematic**: the warning is actually a warning. **Pseudaposematic**: the warning is a bluff (protective mimicry). **Synaposematic**: a warning that is shared in common with other, usually more powerful, species. See also Mimicry. **Episematic.** Of characters or traits that aid recognition, e.g. colors, markings, behavior etc. **Antepisematic**: implies a threat. **Proepisematic**: indicates social recognition. **Pseudepisematic**: involves deception; i.e. having false coloration or markings, either for aggressive or alluring purposes. **Parasematic.** Of markings, structures or behavior that tend to mislead or deflect attack. **Pseudaposematic.** A warning coloration or other protective feature indicating a harmful or distasteful animal, that is shown by a non-harmful species, which thus obtains a degree of protection from predators who tend to avoid both the real harmful species and the mimic i.e. showing Batesian Mimicry. **Pseudosematic.** Having false colors or markings, as in protective mimicry or for aggressive or alluring purposes. See also Mimicry.

SEMATOPHORE. [L. *semen*, seed; Gr. -φορα, carrying]. See Spermatophore.

SEMELPARITY. [L. *semel*, once only; *parere*, to give birth]. Having only one brood during the life-time.

SEMEN. [L. *semen*, seed]. The biochemically complex fluid composed of the secretions of the testes and accessory glands plus the spermatozoa.

228

SEMICORDATE. [L. *semi*, half; *cor*, heart]. Half or partly heart-shaped.

SEMICORONATE. [L. *semi*, half; *corona*, crown]. Partly surrounded by a margin of spines or hooks.

SEMICORONET. [L. *semi*, half; *coronatus*, crown]. A margin of spines or hooks partly surrounding a structure or process.

SEMICYLINDRICAL. [L. *semi*, half; *cylindrus*, cylinder]. Round on one side and flat on the other.

SEMIDIXIAL. [L. *semi*, half; Gr. δι-, two; αξων, axis]. Of the chelicerae of spiders that are intermediate between the diaxial condition of araneomorphs and the paraxial of mygalomorphs, as in the **Hypochilidae** (Opisthothelae).

SEMIGEOGRAPHIC SPECIATION. See Parapatric Speciation under Speciation.

SEMIHYALINE. [L. *semi*, half; Gr. υαλος, glass]. Hyaline in part only. Not completely transparent.

SEMILUNAR. [L. *semi*, half; *luna*, moon]. Halfmoon-shaped.

SEMINAL DUCTS. See Vasa Deferentia.

SEMINAL RECEPTACLE. [L. *semen*, seed; *recipere*, to receive]. See Spermatheca.

SEMINAL VESICLE. [L. *semen*, seed; *vesicula*, little bladder]. An organ for storing sperm.

SEMINAL. [L. *semen*, seed]. Of the fluid, ducts and vesicles associated with semen production and transportation.

SEMINATION. [L. *seminatio*, sowing]. The discharge of spermatozoa.

SEMINIFEROUS. [L. *semen*, seed; *ferre*, to carry]. Secreting or transporting semen.

SEMIORBICULAR. [L. *semi*, half; *orbis*, orb]. Hemispherical, half-rounded.

SEMIOTICS. [Gr. σημαινω, to show by a sign; (σημειωσις, visible sign)]. The scientific study of communication.

SEMIOVATE (SEMIOVOID). [L. *semi*, half; *ovum*, egg]. Half-oval. More-or-less oval.

SEMIOVIPAROUS. [L. *semi*, half; *ovum*, egg; *parere*, to beget]. Somewhere between oviparous and viviparous.

SEMIPARASITE. [L. *semi*, half; Gr. παρασιτος, one who eats at the table of another]. A partial parasite. See Parasite.

SEMIPENNIFORM. [L. *semi*, half; *penna*, feather; *forma*, shape]. Of muscles that bear a resemblance to a lateral half of a feather.

SEMIRECONDITE. [L. *semi*, half; *recondere*, to conceal]. Half concealed.

SEMISAGITTATE. [L. *semi*, half; *sagitta*, arrow]. Shaped like half an arrow head.

SEMISPECIES. [L. *semi*, half; *species*, particular kind]. A vague taxonomic grouping somewhere between species and subspecies or race. There is reduced outbreeding and gene flow, and such a group may represent an advanced stage of speciation. See also Nomenclature.

SENESCENCE. [L. *senescere*, to grow old]. The ageing process that leads to death.

SENILITY. [L. *senilis*, senile]. Degeneration due to old age.

SENOCULIDAE. [L. *senio*, gropu of six; *oculus*, eye]. A monospecific family of spiders (infraorder Araneomorphae, superfamily Entelegynae) from South America, as far north as Mexico.

SENSEIFEROUS (SENSIGEROUS). [L. *sensus*, sense; *ferre*, to carry; *gerere*, to bear]. Receiving or conveying sensory data.

SENSILE. [L. *sensilis*, sensitive]. Of something capable of affecting a sense.

SENSILLA. [L. *sensus*, sense]. See Sensillum.

SENSILLA AMPULLACEA. [L. *sensus*, sense; *ampulla*, a flask]. A general term for any pit-shaped, flask-shaped, mushroom-shaped, etc. sensory structure bearing small sensory hairs. For example in the Solifugae and some other arachnids.

SENSILLUM (SENSILLIUM, pl. SENSILLA). [L. dim. of *sensus*, sense]. 1. A receptor complex composed of a sense cell or groups of sense cells plus their associated structures, such as innervated hairs, flat sensory plates, or sensory pits. 2. A small epithelial sense organ or nerve ending. A simple receptor complex. There are several types of sensilla: chemosensilla, mechanosensilla, photosensilla, thermosensilla and multifunctional sensilla which may be combinations. Many sensilla are dispersed over the body and appendages while others are clustered in specialized organs such as Haller's Organ, the palpal organ on palpal article IV, the sensilla on the cheliceral digits, the eyes, etc.

SENSILLUM AMPULLACEUM (AMPULLACEOUS SENSILLUM). [L. dim. of *sensus*, sense; *ampulla*, a flask]. A sense organ in which the sense cone is a flask or pouch-shaped cavity with no external structure evident.

SENSILLUM AURIFORME. [L. dim. of *sensus*, sense; *auris*, ear; *forma*, shape]. In ticks and mites: a sense organ with flattened disks, similar to sensillum campaniformium.

SENSILLUM BASICONICUM (BASICONIC SENSILLUM). [L. dim. of *sensus*, sense; Gr. βασις, base; κονος, cone]. A sense organ with an external process in the form of a minute cone or peg.

SENSILLUM CAMPANIFORMIUM (UMBRELLA ORGAN). [L. dim. of *sensus*, sense; LL. *campana*, bell; *forma*, shape]. A thin, flexible, dome-shaped sense organ that has no pore or opening. They respond to strains on the cuticle, as opposed to individual muscle movement, and sometimes occur in groups.

SENSILLUM CHAETICUM. [L. dim. of *sensus*, sense; Gr. χαιτη, hair]. A tactile sense organ with an external process in the form of a spine or bristle-like seta.

SENSILLUM COELOCONICUM (COELOCONIC SENSILLUM). [L. dim. of *sensus*, sense; Gr. κοιλος, hollow; κωνος, cone]. A sense organ with an external process in the form of a thin walled conical or peg-like projection in a shallow pit below the surface of the body wall.

SENSILLUM COLEUM. [L. dim. of *sensus*, sense; *colere*, to inhabit]. A sense organ that is completely covered with a sheath except for the internal canal.

SENSILLUM INSITICUM. [L. dim. of *sensus*, sense; *insitus*, inserted]. A sense organ that shows no evidence of an external structure or pore, but the ciliary process or modified cilia are embedded in the cuticle.

SENSILLUM OPTICUM. [L. dim. of *sensus*, sense; Gr. οψις, sight]. A light perceiving sense organ.

SENSILLUM PLACODEUM. [L. dim. of *sensus*, sense; Gr. πλαξ, plate; οδος, a way]. A possibly olfactory sense organ in the form of a flat plate-like external membranous cover over an enlarged pore tubule, with the outer surface continuous with the general surface.

SENSILLUM SCOLOPOPHORUM. See Scolopidium.

SENSILLUM SQUAMIFORMIUM (SENSORY SCALES). [L. dim. of *sensus*, sense; *squama*, scale; *forma*, shape]. A sense organ with a scale-like external appearance with nerve fiber endings at its base.

SENSILLUM STYLOCONICUM. [L. dim. of *sensus*, sense; Gr. στυλος, pillar; κωνος, cone]. A sense organ having a terminal sensory cone, usually in a pit in the cuticle. It is innervated by nerve fibers running to its tip.

SENSILLUM TRICHODEUM (TRICHOID SENSILLUM). [L. dim. of *sensus*, sense; Gr. τριχο-, hair; οδος, way]. A sense organ bearing an elongate seta which is articulated with the body wall by a membranous socket so that it is free to move. It may be a mechanoreceptor or less often, a chemoreceptor.

SENSITIVE. [MedL. *sensitivus*, sensitive]. Capable of receiving external stimulation, or capable of reacting to a stimulus.

SENSITIVITY. [MedL. *sensitivus*, sensitive]. See Irritability.

SENSITIZATION. [MedL. *sensitivus*, sensitive]. 1. The increase in the probability that repeated exposure to a particular stimulus will produce a response in an animal. 2. The process of increasing an animal's reaction to an antigen.

SENSOMOBILE. [L. *sensus*, sense; *mobilis*, moveable]. Responding to irritable stimulation with movement.

SENSORIUM. [L. *sensus*, sense; *-arium*, a place were something is kept]. The location of sensation or consciousness; the complete nervous system.

SENSORY. [L. *sensus*, sense; *-arium*, a place were something is kept]. Of some structure (usually a nerve fiber) having direct contact with any region of the sensorium.

SENSORY ADAPTATION. See Adaptation.

SENSORY PITTINGS. [L. *sensus*, sense; *-arium*, a place were something is kept]. Deep pits or punctures through the surface, which may or may not bear pegs, bristles or setae and may be open or covered by a membrane.

SENSU AMPLIFICATO (S. AMPL.). [L. *sensus*, sense; *amplificatio*, an enlarging]. In the enlarged sense.

SENSU LATO (S. L.). [L. *sensus*, sense; *latus*, broad]. In the broad, or widest sense.

SENSU PROPRIO (S. Pr.). [L. *sensus*, sense; *proprius*, individual]. In the original sense.

SENSU STRICTO (S. STR.). [L. *sensus*, sense; *strictus*, severe]. In the narrow sense.

SENTIENT. [L. *sentire*, to feel]. Of life forms which are sensitive and perceptive.

SEPICOLOUS. [L. *saepes*, a hedge; *colere*, to inhabit]. Living in hedges.

SEPIMENT. [L. *saepimentum*, hedge]. A partition.

SEPTAL. [L. *septum*, partition]. Pertaining to a septum.

SEPTATE. [L. *septum*, partition]. Divided by partitions.

SEPTIFORM. [L. *septum*, partition; *forma*, shape]. Having the shape of an enclosure or septum.

SEPTULUM. [L. *septulum*, little partition]. A small or secondary septum.

SEPTUM, SEPTA. [L. *septum*, partition]. A partition separating two chambers, cavities or masses of tissue.

SERIATE, SERIATIM. [L. *serere*, join/bind together]. Arranged in rows or series.

SERICATE (SERICEOUS). [L. *sericus*, silken]. Covered with fine, closely pressed, silky hairs.

SERICIN. [L. *sericus*, silken; *-in*, chem. suf. used for neutral substances]. A water-soluble, gelatinous protein which forms the outer layer of the silk threads of spiders and insects.

SERIFIC. [L. *sericum*, silk; *facere*, to make]. Silk-producing.

SERIFIC GLANDS. [L. *sericum*, silk; *facere*, to make]. Silk production glands that secrete a viscous fluid that solidifies as it passes through the orifice of the spinneret, emerging as two semicrystalline threads.

SERODEME. [L. *serum*, whey; Gr. δημος, a people]. A local population of animals (a deme), commonly parasites, that differ from others in their immunological characteristics.

SEROTINAL. [L. *serus*, late]. 1. One of the terms for the six part division of the year commonly used in ecology, especially with reference to terrestrial and fresh-water communities. The six parts are: prevernal (early spring), vernal (late spring), aestival (early summer), serotinal (late summer), autumnal (autumn) and hibernal (winter). 2. Of animals that are active in the late evening.

SEROUS. [L. *serum*, serum]. Of serum or other similar watery fluid.

SEROUS FLUIDS. [L. *serum*, serum]. Any watery secretion. The watery constituent of saliva, etc.

SEROUS GLANDS. [L. *serum*, serum]. Any glands which secrete a watery fluid.

SERPENTINOUS. [OF. *serpentine*, greenish mineral]. A dark green.

SERRA. [L. *serra*, saw]. Any saw-like structure.

SERRATE (SERRATIFORM). [L. *serratus*, toothed like a saw]. Notched like a saw.

231

SERRATODENTATE. [L. *serra*, saw; *dens*, tooth]. Toothed, with the tooth edges themselves saw-toothed.

SERRATULATE. [L. *serrula*, small saw]. Having little teeth or serrations.

SERRATURE. [L. *serra*, saw]. A single saw-like notch.

SERRIFEROUS. [L. *serra*, saw; *ferre*, to carry]. Bearing a saw-like organ.

SERRIFORM. [L. *serra*, saw; *forma*, shape]. Saw-shaped.

SERRIPED. [L. *serra*, saw; *pes*, foot]. Having notched feet.

SERRULA. [L. *serrula*, little saw]. In some spiders: a comb-like ridge on the chelicerae.

SERRULATE (SERRATULATE). [L. *serrula*, little saw]. Finely notched.

SERRULATION. [L. *serrula*, little saw]. A small notch.

SESQUIOCELLUS. [L. *sesqui*, one and one half; *oculus*, little eye]. A large ocellate spot including a smaller one.

SESQUITERTIAL. [L. *sesqui*, more by half; *tertianus*, belonging to the third]. Occupying a fourth part.

SETA. [L. *seta*, bristle]. A hair, bristle or scale. An extension of the exocuticle which is produced by a trichogen. It may be filled with a refractive material and may be hair-like, spine-like, branched or a variously expanded structure on the surface of the legs and body. Most setae are mechanoreceptors or chemoreceptors but some have unknown or ambiguous functions. See also Grandjean System.

SETACEOUS. [L. *seta*, bristle; *-aceous*, of the nature of]. Bristle-like.

SETATE. [L. *seta*, bristle]. Provided with bristles.

SETATION. [L. *seta*, bristle]. See Chaetotaxy.

SETIFEROUS (SETIGEROUS, CHAETIFEROUS). [L. *seta*, bristle; *ferre*, to carry, *gerere*, to bear]. Bearing bristles or setae.

SETIFORM. [L. *seta*, bristle; *forma*, shape]. Bristle-shaped.

SETIGENOUS. [L. *seta*, bristle; Gr. -γενης, producing]. Giving rise to setae.

SETIPAROUS. [L. *seta*, bristle; *parere*, to beget]. Producing setae or bristles.

SETIREME. [L. *seta*, bristle; *remus*, oar]. In aquatic forms: a hairy, oar-like leg.

SETOSE. [L. *seta*, bristle]. Having bristles, bristly.

SETULA (SETULAE). [L. *setula*, little bristle]. A thread-like or hair-like bristle.

SETULE. [L. *setula*, little bristle]. In ticks and mites: a small, seta-like cuticular process, typically on the pretarsal empodia or claws.

SETULIFORM. [L. *setula*, little bristle; *forma*, shape]. Thread-like.

SETULOSE. [L. *setula*, little bristle]. Having small bristles.

SEX. [L. *sexus*, sex]. 1. The totality of the characteristic structures and functions of an individual which determine its classification as either male or female. In general; an individual producing numerous, small, motile, nutrient-poor gametes is male while one producing few (or fewer), large (or larger) non-motile, nutrient-rich gametes is female. In some organisms the gametes are morphologically indistinguishable isogametes, in which case the sexes are arbitrarily designated 'plus' and 'minus'. 2. In the broad sense: any process which recombines in a single organism the genes derived from more than a single source.

SEX CHROMOSOME. [L. *sexus*, sex; Gr. χρωμα, color; σωμα, body]. The chromosome whose presence or absence, or particular form, determines the sex of the individual. They are present in all sexually reproducing, diploid plants and animals. The gender which has a homologous pair of sex chromosomes (generally termed XX) being the homogamitic sex while the gender with a non-homologous pair or with an unpaired chromosome is the heterogamitic sex (XY). The homogamitic sex, therefore, produces gametes that are identical in their chromosome set, all having one X chromosome; while the heterogamitic sex produces equal numbers of two different type of gametes, one that carries an X and one without, that may carry a Y-chromosome or none at all. In respect of sex chromosomes, every mating is between a homozygote and a heterozygote and therefore produces an equal number of offspring of both sexes (although this may be modified by other factors).

SEX DETERMINATION. [L. *sexus*, sex]. Any strategy by which the sex of an individual is established. In many species this is controlled at the time of fertilization by the nature of the male gamete, e.g. being X or Y and combining with the female X to produce XX (female) or XY (male). In some species the gender may change depending on circumstances. **Maternal Sex Determination:** the condition in which the sex of the offspring is determined by the genotype of the female gamete. **Metagamic Sex Determination:** the sex of the offspring is conditional, to a greater or lesser extent, on external environmental influences. **Phenotypic Sex Determination:** the sex of an individual is determined by external environmental factors and not directly by karyogamy. **Progamic Sex Determination:** the sex of the offspring is determined in the egg prior to fertilization. **Sex Digamety:** the ability of the heterogamitic sex to produce male or female determining gametes by means of a sex-chromosome mechanism. **Sex Monogamety:** the ability of an hermaphrodite or parthenogenetic individual, or population to produce gametes of only one sex. **Sex Polygamety:** the ability of an individual to produce gametes of many different types by means of the integrated action of multiple independent genes (polyfactorial sex determination). **Syngamic Sex Determination:** the determination of gender as a result of the fusion of two gametic nuclei with the consequent interchange of nuclear material (karyogamy). **Environmental Sex Determination:** sex determination as a result of environmental factors, commonly temperature.

SEXFID. [L. *sex*, six; *findere*, to cleave]. Divided into six.

SEX GLAND. [L. *sexus*, sex]. A gonad.

SEX HORMONES. [L. *sexus*, sex; Gr. ορμαω, rouse]. Any hormone produced by, or affecting, the activity of the gonads.

SEX LINKED CHARACTER. [L. *sexus*, sex]. Any character controlled by a gene located on a sex chromosome.

SEX MOSAIC. [L. *sexus*, sex]. A Gynandromorph.

SEX POLYGAMETY. [L. *sexus*, sex; Gr. πολυς, many; γαμετης, spouse]. See Sex Determination.

SEX RATIO. [L. *sexus*, sex]. The percentage of males in a population; i.e. the ratio of the number of males per 100 females or per 100 births. This measure is usually given within the context of an age group; the primary sex ratio being the ratio immediately after fertilization, the secondary ratio being that at birth or hatching and the tertiary being that at maturity.

SEXUAL BIMATURISM. [L. *sexus*, sex; *bis*, twice, *maturus*, timely]. Deferred male maturity.

SEXUAL CONGRESS. [L. *sexus*, sex; *congressio*, meeting]. The association of males and females for sexually reproductive purposes.

SEXUAL DIMORPHISM. [L. *sexus*, sex; Gr. δι-, two; μορφη, shape]. The differences in structure, shape, size, color, etc. (other than primary sexual characters) between males and females of the same species.

SEXUAL PORE. See Gonopore.

SEXUAL REPRODUCTION. [L. *sexus*, sex]. Any reproductive strategy that involves fusion of two gametes to form a zygote. During gamete formation (meiosis) the number of chromosomes is halved (haploid) and thus when two gametes combine the original (diploid) number is restored. The important advantage of sexual reproduction is that different gene combinations can arise, so facilitating adaptation to changing environments.

SEXUAL SELECTION. [L. *sexus*, sex]. A mate-selection strategy adopted by either males or females (depending on the species) by which a choice of mate is made based on certain characteristics which are then inherited by the progeny. Such characters could be used in display (intersexual selection, e.g. the appropriate courtship dance in male spiders) or in combat between rival males.

SHAFT. [AS. *sceaft*, shaft]. The cylindrical part of a limb or structure.

SHAGREENED (CHAGRINED). [Turk. *saghri*, back of a horse - like rough-surfaced horse leather]. Having numerous tooth-like projections.

SHANNON-WIENER INDEX OF DIVERSITY (INFORMATION INDEX). The ratio of the number of species to their importance value (biomass or productivity) within a trophic level or community. The index (D) = $-\sum_{i=1}^{R} pi \ln pi$ where R is the total number of species in the sample, i is the total number of individuals in one species and pi is the number of individuals of one species in relation to the number of individuals in the population. This measure is generally used when a system contains too many individuals for each to be identified and examined.

SHARD. [OE. *sceard*, fragment]. A chitinous sheath or elytron.

SHEATH. [AS. *sceth*, shell or pod]. A enclosing cover.

SHEET-WEB SPIDERS. See **Agelenidae.**

SHELL. [AS. *scell*, shell]. The thick membranous or calcareous covering of an egg.

SHELL GLAND. [AS. *scell*, shell]. Any glands in the wall of, or opening into, an oviduct that secrete substances which on hardening form the shell of an egg.

SHELL MEMBRANE. [AS. *scell*, shell]. The membrane immediately inside the shell.

SHIELD. [AS. *scyld*, shield]. Any protective plate. See Carapace, Clypeus, Scutellum, Scutum.

SHOULDER. [AS. *sculdor*, shoulder]. Any obtuse angulation.

si. In the Prostigmata: the internal scapular seta (sci, scl, s1) on the prodorsum. See Vertical-Scapular System.

SIALADEN. [Gr. σιαλον, saliva; αδενα, a gland]. See Salivary Glands.

SIALIC. [Gr. σιαλον, saliva]. Of saliva.

SIALISTERIUM. [Gr. σιαλον, saliva; στερεωμα, a solid body]. A salivary gland.

SIALOID. [Gr. σιαλον, saliva; ειδος, form]. Saliva-like.

SIB MATING. [OE. *sibling*, relative]. Mating between siblings, i.e. between the progeny of the same parents.

SIBLINGS (SIBS). [OE. *sibling*, relative]. Offspring which have one or both parents in common.

SICARIIDAE (LOXOSCELIDAE). [Gr. λοξος, slanting; σκελος, the leg]. The family of the brown recluse spiders (infraorder Araneomorphae, superfamily Haplogynae) from north and South America. They are rather delicate, reclusive spiders whose hemolytic venom produces a necrotic wound that is difficult to heal.

SICCOCOLOUS. [L. *siccus*, dry; *colere*, to inhabit]. Living in dry, arid habitats.

SIENNA. [It. *terra di Sienna*, earth of Siena]. A brownish orange.

SIEVE PLATE (SIEVE DISC). [OE. *sife*, sieve]. In spiders: a region of the coxal lobe of the pedipalp that bears the openings of the salivary ducts.

SIEVE PORE. [OE. *sife*, sieve]. One of the perforations of a sieve plate.

SIEVE TRACHEAE. [OE. *sife*, sieve; LL. *trachia*, windpipe]. In the Ricinulei: the bundles of tracheae that arise from a tubule of an ectodermal invagination on the 8th somite. See also Tube Tracheae.

SIGILLUM. [L. *sigillum*; embossed figure]. In some spiders (Araneae): the impressed, suboval, clear areas on the sternum. In ticks and mites: the external mark of a muscle insertion.

SIGILLA. [L. *sigilla*, seal]. The depressed and/or striate cuticular regions that are visual indication of muscle insertions. They may be oval or irregular in shape and are often in clusters.

SIGILLOTAXY. [L. *sigilla*, seal; Gr. ταξις, arrangement]. The use of cuticular muscle insertions as taxonomic characters (designation = sg).

SIGLA. [ML. *sigila*, a seal]. Designations for setae.

σ **Σ** (Sigma). In the Acariformes: a designation for the solenidion of the genu. φ (phi) on the tibia; ω (omega) on the tarsus.

SIGMOID. [Gr. Σ, sigma; ειδος, form]. Of some structure that is curved in two directions.

SIGMOID FLEXURE. [Gr. Σ, sigma; L. *flexus*, bending]. An S-shaped double curve.

SIGNATE, SIGNATUS (NOTATE). [L. *signum*, sign]. Bearing marks or spots.

SIGNATURE. [ML. *signatura*, sign]. A colored blotch of any size or shape.

SIGN STIMULUS. [L. *signare*, to mark out/designate; *stimulus*, a goad]. A stimulus or group of stimuli which activate an intrinsic behavior pattern. See also Releaser.

SILIQUIFORM. [L. *siliqua*, a pod; *forma*, shape]. Being long, tubular and narrow like a pod. Having the shape of a silique (which is the pod shape peculiar to the plant family Cruciferae (or Brassicaceae)).

SILK. [Gr. σηρικπς, silken, from Σηρες, the oriental people from whom silk was first obtained]. A soft, strong, lustrous fiber consisting of extremely fine threads composed of a central strand of strong elastic protein (fibroin) surrounded by a layer of a more gelatinous protein (sericin). It is produced by spiders (and many insects). The silk-like threads of spiders are produced from the spinnerets on the hind region of the abdomen. Acariform mites produce silk to form a molting chamber (cocoon) or protect or attach eggs. In the silkworm larvae (*Bombyx*) it is produced by modified salivary glands; in the web-spinners (Embioptera) it is produced from tarsal glands on the front legs.

SILK GLANDS. [Gr. σηρικπς, silken]. Glands that secrete the liquids that produce silk on exposure to the air.

SILVICOLOUS. [L. *silvicola*, forest inhabitant]. Inhabiting woodlands.

SIMPLE, SIMPLEX. [L. *simplex*, simple]. Without embellishment. Not modified, forked, toothed, branched or divided.

SIMPLE EYES. See Eye.

SIMULATION. [L. *simulare*, to simulate]. The development of structures intended to deceive enemies, such as the body forms seen in stick insects (**Phasmatidae**) and leaf insects (**Phylliidae**) and all forms of coloration and mimicry. See also Mimicry.

SIMULTANEOUS POLYANDRY. See Polyandry.

SINCIPUT (SYNCIPUT). [L. *sinciput*, half a head]. The upper or fore region of the head.

SINISTRAL, SINISTRAD. [L. *sinister*, left]. On, or belonging to the left side of the body. Opposite = dextral.

SINISTROCAUDAD. [L. *sinister*, left; *cauda*, tail]. Extending obliquely from the left toward the tail.

SINISTROCEPHALAD. [L. *sinister*, left; Gr. κεφαλη, head]. Extending obliquely from the left toward the head.

SINISTRON. [L. *sinistra*, left]. The left side of the body.

SINISTROSE. [L. *sinister*, left; *vertere*, to turn]. Growing in a spiral which curves from right to left, anticlockwise from the point of view of an observer. Opp. - Dextrorse.

SINOPIMOIDAE. See **Linyphiidae.**

SINUATE. [L. *sinus*, curve]. Curved. Having a curved or wavy margin.

SINUATOCONVEX. [L. *sinus*, curve; *convexus*, arched outward]. Sinuate and convex.

SINUATOLOBATE. [L. *sinus*, curve; Gr. λοβος, lobe]. Sinuate and lobed.

SINUATOTRUNCATE. [L. *sinus*, curve; *truncatus*, cut off]. Truncated, with the margin sinuate.

SINUOSITY. [L. *sinus*, curve]. A series of curves or bends.

SINUOUS. [L. *sinus*, curve]. Undulating. Curved in and out.

SINUS (LACUNA). [L. *sinus*, curve or fold]. Any cavity, depression, dilatation or recess.

SIPHON. [Gr. σιφων, tube or reed]. Any tubular structure through which water passes.

SIPHONOSTOMATOUS. [Gr. σιφων, tube; στομα, mouth]. Having a tubular mouth.

SIRONIDAE. [river *Ciron* in SW France]. A family of harvestmen (suborder Cyphophthalmi, infraorder Boreophthalmi) with a mainly Laurasian distribution, plus one species found in Japan.

SIRONOIDEA. [river *Ciron* in SW France]. In a previous classification: a superfamily of harvestmen (order Opilones, suborder Cyphophthalmi) that united the families **Pettalidae**, **Sironidae** and **Troglosironidae**.

SITOTROPISM. [Gr. σιτος, food; τροπη, turn]. The tendency to turn in the direction of food.

SITUS. [L. *situs*, place]. A locality.

SKELETON. [Gr. σκελετος, dried, body]. The hardened framework of an organism that supplies support and protection for the softer parts. It may be external or internal and solid or jointed.

SKIOPHILOUS. [Gr. σκια, shade; φιλος, loving]. Living in shaded habitats.

SKOTOTAXIS. [Gr. σκοτος, darkness; ταξις, an arranging]. A positive orientation or movement towards dark objects against a light background. Not the same as negative phototaxis.

SLATY, SLATEY. [OE. *slat*, slate]. The color of slate. Very dark blackish grey with a reddish tinge. The color of slate.

SLIT SENSE ORGANS. See Lyrifissure, Lyriform Organs.

SMALTINUS. [OHG. *smalz*, grease]. A dull greyish blue.

SMARAGDINUS. [L. *smaragdinus*, resembling emerald]. Emerald green.

SNOUT MITE. Any mite with a well developed projecting gnathosoma, but commonly members of the **Bdellidae** and **Cunaxidae** (Prostigmata).

SOCIAL. [L. *sociare*, to associate]. Living in organized groups or colonies.

SOCIAL GROUP. [L. *sociare*, to associate]. A co-operative grouping of individuals of the same species.

SOCIAL RELEASER. [L. *sociare*, to associate]. Any stimulus provided by an individual which elicits an instinctive response in another individual, either of the same or different species. See also Releaser.

SOCIOHORMONE. [L. *sociare*, to associate; hor*mone* (Gr. ορμαω, rouse)]. See Pheromone.

SOIL MITE. Any mite found in the soil-litter.

SOLEA. [L. *solea*, sandal]. In some arachnids: a modified area with a high concentration of sensory setae.

SOLENIDION (SOLENIDIA). [Gr. σωληνιδιον, small pipe]. In acariform mites: a hollow, optically inactive, blunt, seta associated with a sensory cell. They are often bulbous or otherwise modified and sometimes associated with a companion seta. Solenidia are designated with Greek letters by leg segment: Ω (omega) on the tarsus, Φ (phi) on the tibia, and Σ (sigma) on the genu.

SOLENIFORM. [Gr. σωλην, pipe; L. *forma*, shape]. Shaped like a razor handle.

SOLENOSTOME. [Gr. σωληv, pipe; στομα, mouth]. The external opening of a gland or gland-like internal structure.

SOLID. Of an organ that is usually jointed when these joints form into one mass.

SOLIFUGAE (SOLPUGIDA). [LL. *solifuga*, a venomous ant or spider, from L. *sol*, the sun; *fuga*, running away]. An order of about 900 species of arachnids (class Euchelicerata, subclass Arachnida) known as sun spiders, wind scorpions, sun scorpions, camel spiders, false spiders and gerrymanders. Many species live in the desert regions of southern Asia, Africa, the

Mediterranean, central and southern USA, Mexico and the West Indies. Large arachnids in which the prosoma is divided into a large anterior carapace (proterosoma) and a short posterior section. There are a pair of closely placed eyes on the anterior median border of the anterior carapace and in some, vestigial lateral eyes may be present. The abdomen is large, broadly joined to the prosoma and visibly segmented. The entire body is covered with long, sensory hairs. Characteristically, the chelicerae are enormously enlarged, chelate and armed with teeth; the pedipalps are leg-like, sensory and terminate in an adhesive organ used in the capture of prey. Only six legs are used for walking, the first pair having become slender, reduced and used as tactile organs. The terminal region of the last pair of walking legs contains racket organs (sensory function). There is a highly developed tracheal system similar to that of insects, rather than to other arachnids. Most species are crepuscular or nocturnal; some hide under stones and in crevices but most construct burrows and may gather together in areas of high prey density. Prey (arthropods, small vertebrates (e.g. lizards)) are caught by chase or ambush and crushed by the chelicerae, there being no poison glands. Courtship behavior is generally simple, relying on pacifying the female for a few moments while sperm transfer takes place; between 50 and 200 eggs are laid in burrows. Families: **Ammotrechidae, Ceromidae, Daesiidae, Eremobatidae, Galeodidae, Gylippidae, Hexisopodidae, Karschiidae, Melanoblossidae, Mummuciidae, Rhagodidae, Solpugidae.** †**Protosolpugidae**, a Pennsylvanian fossil.

SOLITARY/SOLITARIUS. [L. *solus/solitarius*, alone]. Occurring singly or in pairs: not in groups or colonies.

SOLPUGIDA. See Solifugae.

SOLPUGIDAE. [L. *solpuga* a kind of venomous spider]. A large family of sun spiders (subclass Arachnida, order Solifugae) from Africa and Iraq. Solpugs have clusters of papillae on their pedipalps which project from sockets and are thought to have a mechanoreceptor and contact chemoreceptor function.

SOMA, SOMATIC. [Gr. σωμα, body]. The body of a plant or animal.

SOMAESTHESIS. [Gr. σωμα, body; αισθησις, a sensation]. Sensation due to stimuli from the skin, muscle or internal organs.

SOMATIC. [Gr. σωμα, body]. Of the body cells or structures, but not the gametic cells.

SOMATIC CELL. [Gr. σωμα, body]. A body cell, i.e. any cell that is not destined to become a gamete and will not, therefore, pass on its genes to future generations.

SOMATIC CHAETAE. [Gr. σωμα, body; χαιτη, hair]. See Somatic Setae.

SOMATIC MUSCULATURE. [Gr. σωμα, body]. The muscles of the body.

SOMATIC PARTHENOGENESIS. See Parthenogenesis.

SOMATIC SETAE. [Gr. σωμα, body; L. *seta*, bristle]. Any setae on the body.

SOMATIC TISSUES. [Gr. σωμα, body]. The tissues of the body-wall.

SOMATOINTESTINAL MUSCLES. [Gr. σωμα, body; L. *intestinus*, intestine]. Muscles found in the region of the intestine, extending from the body wall.

SOMITE (SOMATOME). [Gr. σωμα, body]. A division of the body of an animal.

SONIFACTION. [L. *sonus*, sound; *facere*, to make]. The production of sound.

SONIFEROUS, SONORIFIC. [L. *sonus*, sound; *ferre*, to carry]. Capable of producing sound.

SONORAN REGION. [*Sonora*, Mexican state]. The zoogeographical region between the Nearctic and the Neotropical regions, i.e. encompassing southern North America and northern Mexico.

SOUTH AFRICAN REGION. A subdivision of the African subkingdom of the Palaeotropical kingdom.

SP./SPP. Species, singular/plural.

SPADICEOUS. [L. *spadix*, date-brown/nut-brown]. Of a bright clear brown or chestnut color.

SPANANDRY. [Gr. σπανος, rare; ανηρ, male]. A scarcity of, or a progressive decrease in the number of males.

SPANOGYNY (SPANOGAMY). [Gr. σπανος, rare; γυνη, a woman]. A scarcity of, or a progressive decrease in the number of females.

SPARASSIDAE (syn. **HETEROPODIDAE**). [Gr. σπαρασσω, to rend]. The tropical and subtropical family of mainly nocturnal fast moving spiders (infraorder Araneomorphae, superfamily Entelegynae) known as huntsman spiders. The body is often flattened, the legs are held sideways; crab-like, and they run to catch their prey. Usually with only four silk glands. They were previously in the monotypic superfamily Sparassoidea.

SPASM. [Gr. σπασμος, tension]. An involuntary contraction of muscles. A spastic contraction of muscle fibers.

SPATIA. [L. *spatium*, space]. Spaces.

SPATIAL SUMMATION. See Summation.

SPATULA. [L. *spatula*, spoon]. Any spoon-shape structure.

SPATULATE (SPATHULATE). [L. *spatula*, spoon]. Spatula-like. Flattened, while broad apically and narrow basally.

SPEAR. See Stylet.

SPECIALIST. [L. *specialis*, special]. A species which has a very narrow range of habitats or food preferences.

SPECIALIZATION. [L. *specialis*, special]. The adaptations for a particular mode of life or habitat that occur during the course of evolution.

SPECIALIZED. [L. *specialis*, special]. Being highly modified from the ancestral condition.

SPECIATION. [L. *species*, particular kind]. A theory to account for the evolution of species as a consequence of populations becoming divided and geographically isolated as a result of, for example, geological events such as mountain building (orogeny) or sea incursions. Such separation, over time, may lead to the acquisition of reproductive isolating mechanisms between populations which originally belonged to the same species. **Abrupt Speciation**: the formation of a species as the result of sudden viable chromosome changes. **Allochronic Speciation**: 1. Speciation due to the sequential replacement of species through time. 2. Speciation without geographical separation but with temporal separation, such as different breeding seasons. **Alloparapatric Speciation**: speciation in which the initial segregation of the diverging populations takes place in disjunction, complete reproductive isolation only being attained after range adjustment so that the populations become self-contained but contiguous. **Allopatric Speciation**: the attainment of reproductive isolation in populations which are completely separated geographically. **Area Effect Speciation**: speciation that is associated with increasing differentiation between two subspecies that have incompatible gene complexes. Thus the hybrids are strongly selected against. **Centrifugal Speciation**: the principle that speciation is more likely to occur near the center of the range rather than towards the periphery. It has been observed that the more primitive species are distributed towards the edge of the range of a species-group or genus. There may, of course, be other explanations. **Clinal Speciation**: a form of allopatric speciation in which a geographic barrier develops across a cline and thus divides a species (which may already have some variation) into two segments that then diverge (See also Cline). **Dichopatric Speciation**: of populations or species that are geographically separated to such an extent that individuals from each would never meet and gene flow is impossible. **Parapatric (Semigeographic) Speciation**: speciation that occurs regardless of minor gene flow between populations that overlap in a very narrow zone. **Phyletic Speciation**: the gradual evolution within a phyletic lineage of one species from another. **Quantum Speciation**: see Quantum Evolution. **Quasisympatric Speciation**: the separation of one species into two due to adaptation to different niches by different subpopulations. **Secondary Speciation**: hybridization between two distinct evolutionary lineages (species or subspecies) which were formerly isolated geographically, followed by the establishment of an adaptive norm through natural selection. **Stasimorphic Speciation**: the formation of new species without morphological differentiation. **Stasipatric Speciation**: speciation as a result of chromosomal rearrangements producing homozygotes which are adaptively more robust in a particular region of the environment or geographical range of the ancestral species. **Sympatric Speciation**: speciation in populations which are not geographically isolated and thus have overlapping ranges. This mode depends on assortative mating.

SPECIENT. [L. *species*, particular kind]. An individual member of a species.

SPECIES. [L. *species*, particular kind]. A group of interbreeding animals that produce viable offspring. A species includes geographical races and varieties. See Cline, Speciation and also Nomenclature.

SPECIES AGGREGATE (SPECIES GROUP). [L. *species*, particular kind]. A group of very closely related species, usually with partially overlapping ranges, and which therefore have more in common with each other than with other species.

SPECIES NAME. See Nomenclature.

SPECIES RECOGNITION. [L. *species*, particular kind]. The exchange of appropriate stimuli and responses between individuals, especially as part of courting behavior.

SPECIES-SPECIFIC BEHAVIOR (INBORN BEHAVIOR). [L. *species*, particular kind]. Behavior patterns that are intrinsic to a species and performed by all members of that species under the same conditions and which are not modified by learning.

SPECIES SWARM. [L. *species*, particular kind]. A large number of closely related species found in the same geographical region and derived from the same ancestral stock.

SPECIFIC. [L. *species*, particular kind]. Of characters, behaviors, etc. that distinguish a species.

SPECIFIC EPITHET (SPECIFIC NAME). [L. *species*, particular kind]. The second name in a binomial. See Nomenclature.

SPERCHONTOIDEA. [Gr. σπερχω, to be in haste]. In a previous classification; a monotypic superfamily of mites. Family: **Sperchontidae**. This family is now in the superfamily Lebertioidea (suborder Prostigmata, infraorder Anystina).

SPERM. [Gr. σπερμα, seed]. Any male gamete.

SPERM ACCESS SYSTEM. [Gr. σπερμα, seed]. A term used for the complex secondary insemination system in female mites in which more than simple sperm storage occurs. In the Dermanyssiae (Gamasina), two basic types of sperm access systems are known: Laelapid Type Of Sperm Access System, Phytoseiid Type Of Sperm Access System.

SPERMADACTYL. See Spermatodactyl.

SPERMADUCT. [Gr. σπερμα, seed; L. *ducere*. to lead]. A duct for conveying spermatozoa from the testis to the exterior.

SPERMARIUM (SPERMARY). [Gr. σπερμα, seed; L. *-arium*, a place where something is kept]. Any organ in which sperm are produced.

SPERMATHECA (SPERMOTHECA, RECEPTACULUM SEMINIS, SEMINAL RECEPTACLE). [Gr. σπερμα, seed; θηκη, case]. In females: a sac connected to the genital tract for storing the spermatozoa received during copulation. It is of ectodermal origin, lined with cuticle and often contains glandular cells which are thought to nourish the spermatozoa.

SPERMATHECAL DUCTS. [Gr. σπερμα, seed; θηκη, case; L. *ducere*, to lead]. The paired tubes that receive the embolus of the male in copulation and lead inwards from the copulatory openings to the spermathecae.

SPERMATHECAL GLAND. [Gr. σπερμα, seed; θηκη, case]. A special gland opening into the duct of the spermatheca, or near the junction of the latter with the vagina.

SPERMATHECAL ORGAN. [Gr. σπερμα, seed; θηκη, case]. A small prominence at or near the junction of the copulatory tube and spermatheca.

SPERMATHECAL TUBE. [Gr. σπερμα, seed; θηκη, case]. Any duct or other tubular structure that is part of a sperm storage structure. In some it is poorly defined while in others it may be distinct and long.

SPERMATOCYST. [Gr. σπερμα, seed; κυστις, bladder]. A seminal sac.

SPERMATODACTYL. [Gr. σπερμα, seed; δακτυλος, finger]. In ticks and mites: a modification of the chelicera used to transfer sperm from the male's gonopore to the female's copulatory receptacles. They may take various forms, from simple finger-like processes to very long, contorted structures.

SPERMATOGENESIS (SPERMOGENESIS). [Gr. σπερμα, seed; γενεσις, descent]. Sperm formation.

SPERMATOID. [Gr. σπερμα, seed; ειδος, form]. Sperm-like.

SPERMATOPHORE. [Gr. σπερμα, seed; -φορα, -carrying]. A packet or capsule of spermatozoa for transfer from male to female.

SPERMATOPHORY. [Gr. σπερμα, seed; -φορα, -carrying]. A type of fertilization strategy in which stalked spermatophores are placed on the substrate for the females to take up into her genital tract. See also Gonopody, Podospermia, Tocospermia.

SPERMATOPOSITOR. [Gr. σπερμα, seed; L. ponere, to lay]. In ticks and mites: a small evaginable male organ for depositing spermatophores. A penis.

SPERMATOTHECA. See Spermatheca.

SPERMATOTREME. [Gr. σπερμα, seed; τρημα, opening]. In the male **Parasitidae**: a slit-like opening on the movable digit of the chela that seizes the neck of the spermatophore during sperm transfer.

SPERMATOZOA. [Gr. σπερμα, seed; ζωον, animal]. The male gametes (singular = spermatozoon). They usually consist of a head region containing the nucleus, a mid-section containing mitochondria and a tail section, which is a locomotory flagellum.

SPERM CELL. [Gr. σπερμα, seed]. A small, usually motile, gamete.

SPERM COMPETITION. [Gr. σπερμα, seed]. The competition for successful fertilization that occurs among sperm when a female is inseminated by more than one male during one mating period. Competition may be by increased sperm size, increased activity, the creation of sperm plugs (to block later, rival sperm), etc.

SPERM CYST. [Gr. κυστις, bladder]. A cellular capsule within the testis containing the spermatocytes.

SPERM INDUCTION. [Med.L. inductivus, leading to]. In the Arachnida: the passage of spermatozoa from the genital orifice beneath the base of the abdomen into the receptacle in the male palpus.

SPERMIDUCTS. [Gr. σπερμα, seed; L. ducere, to lead]. The male gonoducts, spermaducts, sperm ducts, spermoducts, vas deferens.

SPERMIOGENESIS (SPERMATELEOSIS). [Gr. σπερμα, seed; γενεσις, descent]. The complete developmental process of spermatozoa.

SPERMOZEUGMA. [Gr. σπερμα, seed; ζευγμα, a bond]. The mass of regularly aggregated spermatozoa prior to placing into a spermatheca.

SPERM SAC. [Gr. σπερμα, seed; σακκος, a bag]. Any sac in which mature sperm is stored. It may be formed from a diverticulum of the seminal vesicle or from the vas deferens.

SPERM WEB. In the Arachnida; a web on which male spiders deposit the semen before taking it into the palpus.

SPHAEROLICHIDA. [Gr. σφαιρα, globe; λιχος, greedy]. A suborder of rounded soft-bodied white, yellow, yellow-brown, pink or red mites (superorder Acariformes, order Trombidiformes) in which the prodorsum bears two pairs of filamentous trichobothria. A median eye may be present on the underside of the naso. Superfamily Lordalycoidea, family **Lordalychidae**. Superfamily Sphaerolichoidea, family **Sphaerolichidae**.

SPHAGNOPHILOUS/SPHAGNICOLOUS. [Gr. σφαγνος, a kind of moss; φιλος, loving/L. colere, to inhabit]. Thriving in, or inhabiting, moss.

SPHERULA. [L. sphaerula, small globe]. A small sphere.

SPHERULATE. [L. *sphaerula*, small globe]. Having one or more rows of minute tubercles.

SPHERULE. [L. *sphaerula*, small globe]. A minute sphere or globule.

SPHIGMOID. [Gr. σφυγμωδης, like a pulse]. Pulsating.

SPHINCTER. [Gr. σφιγκτηρ, that which binds tight]. See Muscle Terminology.

SPICATE. [L. *spica*, spike]. Arranged in spikes.

SPICIFORM. [L. *spica*, spike; *forma*, shape]. Spike-shaped.

SPICULA. [L. *spicula*, little spike]. A small spike, a needle-like body.

SPICULATE. [L. *spicula*, little spike]. Divided into small spikes.

SPICULE. [L. *spicula*, little spike]. A minute needle-like body or a minute pointed process.

SPICULIFORM. [L. *spicula*, little spike; *forma*, shape]. Spicule-shaped.

SPICULOSE. [L. *spicula*, small spike]. Bearing spicules.

SPICULUM. [L. *spiculum*, a dart]. A small spicule or thin, pointed process.

SPIDER. [OE. *spiþra*, spider]. See Araneae.

SPIDERLING. [OE. *spiþra*, from PGmc. *spenthro*, from *spenwanan*, to spin; OE. *–ling*, dim. suffix]. The nymphal or immature stage of a spider when it is able to move about and is not dependent on the yolk for nourishment.

SPIDER MITE. Any member of the family **Tetranychidae** (Eleutherengona).

SPIGOT. [L. *spica*, spike]. In spiders: the large form of a fusulus; the cylindrical projections of the spinnerets, each of which contains numerous minute tubules from which the silk is secreted.

SPINA. [L. *spina*, thorn]. A spine.

SPINAE ADNATAE. [L. *spina*, thorn; *adnatus*, swim towards]. In the **Damaeidae** (Oribatida): a pair of tooth-like projections on the anterior margin of the notogaster.

SPINATE. [L. *spina*, thorn]. Bearing spines.

SPINATION. [L. *spina*, thorn]. The development or arrangement of spines.

SPINDLE-SHAPED (FUSIFORM). [AS. *spinnan*, to spin]. Cylindrical and elongate, being thicker in the middle and tapering to each end.

SPINE. [L. *spina*, thorn]. A pointed process or outgrowth. Thorn-like.

SPINESCENT. [L. *spinescere*, to become spiny]. Tapering, becoming spiny.

SPINIFEROUS (SPINIGEROUS). [L. *spina*, thorn; *ferre*, to carry; *gerere*, to bear]. Bearing spines.

SPINIFORM. [L. *spina*, thorn]. Resembling a spine.

SPINIGEROUS. [L. *spina*, thorn; *gerere*, to carry]. Spine-bearing.

SPINNERET. [AS. *spinnan*, to spin]. In spiders: the movable, sclerotized, conical tubes of variable size, composed of several segments, through which the liquid silk (fibroin) is extruded via many tiny spigots (fusulae) on the ends and ventral sides. Polymerization occurring as a consequence of tension rather than being an oxidative or evaporative process. In general there are four pairs of spinnerets, two on the tenth abdominal segment and two on the eleventh although the pair on the tenth abdominal segment is often lost in the adult stage. In some the anterior median pair fuse during development to form an oval plate covered with thousands of minute spigots (the cribellum). **ALS**: Anterior Lateral Spinnerets. **AMS**: Anterior Median Spinnerets. **MS**: Median Spinnerets. **PLS**: Posterior Lateral Spinnerets. **PMS**: Posterior Median Spinnerets. **PS**. Posterior Spinnerets.

SPINNERS. [AS. *spinnan*, to spin]. The paired appendages at the rear end of the spider abdomen, below the anal tubercle. Silk strands are extruded from the spigots which are located here.

SPINNERULE. [AS. *spinnan*, to spin]. In spiders: a tube through which the silk secretions are discharged.

SPINOSE. [L. *spina*, thorn]. Bearing many spines.

SPINOUS. [L. *spinosus*, prickly]. Spiny or spine-like.

SPINOUSRADIATE. [L. *spinosus*, prickly; *radius*, ray]. Having spines in a circle, either concatenate, united at their bases, or setaceous, like bristles.

SPINULATE. [L. *spinula*, small spine]. Covered with small spines.

SPINULE. [L. *spinula*, small spine]. A small spine.

SPINULIFEROUS. [L. *spinula*, small spine; *ferre*, to carry]. Bearing small spines.

SPINULOSE, SPINULOUS. [L. *spinula*, small spine]. Having small spines.

SPIRACLE (SPIRACULUM). [L. *spiraculum*, air hole]. An opening of the book lungs. In spiders (Araneae) an opening (breathing pore) of the tracheae on the ventral side of the body. Also known as a spiracular plate, or peritreme in gamasids, or stigmal plate. In ticks and mites (Parasitiformes) the spiracle is a respiratory organ situated ventrolaterally posterior to coxa IV. It may be circular, oval or comma-shaped. In all ixodid ticks the spiracular plate has a more-or-less central macula adjacent to a small, often slit-like, ostium which is the opening to the respiratory system. The surface is punctate, representing semi-transparent goblets, which in turn represent aeropyles (internal spaces). The number and arrangement of these goblets vary greatly and occasionally provide characters for species separation within the **Ixodidae**. The spiracles open into the atrium, a large sinus-like structure from which the tracheal trunks arise. The structure of the spiracle is useful in classification.

SPIRACULAR MUSCLES. [L. *spiraculum*, air hole]. The occlusor and dilator. See Muscle Terminology.

SPIRACULAR PLATE. See Peritreme. Spiracle.

SPIRACULAR SIEVE PLATE. [L. *spiraculum*, air hole]. A plate-like sclerite covering a spiracle that functions to exclude entry of dust or water into the tracheal system.

SPIRACULATE. [L. *spirare*, to breathe]. With spiracles.

SPIRACULIFEROUS / SPIRACULATE. [L. *spiraculum*, air hole; *ferre*, to carry]. Having spiracles.

SPIRACULIFORM. [L. *spiraculum*, air hole; *forma*, shape]. Shaped like a spiracle.

SPIRACULUM. [L. *spiraculum*, air hole]. See Spiracle.

SPIRAL THREAD / FILAMENT. See Taenidium.

SPIRIFEROUS. [L. *spira*, coil; *ferre*, to carry]. Having a spiral structure.

SPIROID. [L. *spira*, coil; Gr. ειδος form]. Spiral-shaped.

SPIRULATE. [L. *spira*, coil]. Of any coiled arrangement or spiral structure.

SPITTING SPIDERS. See **Scytodidae**.

SPLANCHNIC. [Gr. σπλαγχνον, entrails]. Of the viscera.

SPLANCHNIC LAYER (SPLANCHNOPLEURE). [Gr. σπλαγχνον, entrails]. The inner layer of the mesoderm applied to the wall of the alimentary canal.

SPLENDENT, SPLENDENS. [L. *splendens*, shining]. Shining; glossy; reflecting light intensely.

SPLIT SENSE ORGANS. The cuticular sense organs of spiders that respond to cuticular stress and vibrations.

SPONGIOSE. [L. *spongia*, sponge]. Spongy, full of small holes.

SPOOLS. See Fusulus.

SPOROTHECA (SPOROTHECAE). [Gr. σπορος, seed; θηκη, case]. In the Eleutherengona (Prostigmata): the typically paired, eversible, sack-like structures used to carry fungal spores.

SPRAING. [Scot. of Scand. origin, *sprang*, stripe]. A bright streak or stripe.

SPUR. [AS. *spora*, spur]. A calcar. A movable spine-like process.

SPURIOUS. [L. *spurius*, false]. Seemingly true but morphologically false.

242

SPURIOUS CLAW. [L. *spurius*, false]. A false claw. A claw-like stout bristle.

SPURIOUS DISSEPIMENTS. [L. *spurius*, false; *dissaepire*, to separate]. False partitions.

SQUAMA, SQUAMAE. [L. *squama*, scale]. Any structure shaped or arranged like a scale.

SQUAMATE. [L. *squamatus*, scaly]. Scaly.

SQUAMELLIFORM. [L. *squama*, scale, *forma*, shape]. Resembling a small scale.

SQUAMIFEROUS. [L. *squama*, scale; *ferre*, to bear]. Having scales.

SQUAMIFORM. [L. *squama*, scale; *forma*, shape]. Scale-like.

SQUAMOUS. [L. *squamosus*, of the nature of a scale]. Consisting of scales.

SQUAMULA. [L. *squamula*, little scale]. A small scale.

SQUAMULATE/SQUAMULOSE. [L. *squamula*, little scale]. Having minute scales.

SQUARROUS, SQUARROSE. [LL. *squarrosus*, scurfy]. Rough with projecting scales. Covered with rough scales differing in direction, standing upright, or not parallel to the surface.

S. STR. Sensu Stricto. [L. *sensus*, sense; *strictus*, severe]. In the narrow sense.

st. In the Mesostigmata: sternal setal sigla; st1-5.

st4 (MS). In the Mesostigmata: the metasternal seta.

stp. In the Mesostigmata: the sternal lyrifissure sigla; stp1-3 (iv 1-3).

STABILAMENTUM, STABILIMENTUM. [L. *stabilis*, firm; *amentum*, strap]. In the Arachnida: one of a series of obvious zigzag lines at the hub of certain orb spider webs that warn birds to avoid them.

STADIUM. [L. *stare*, to stand]. The stage between two successive ecdyses. The interval between larval molts.

STARLING MITE. See Fowl Mite

STAGE. In some arthropods: a distinct developmental form such as the egg, larval, nymphal and adult. In ticks and mites: as instars are usually morphologically distinct, they are also stages (but see Stase). However, some authorities suggest that an instar should be determined from apolysis to apolysis while a stage should be from ecdysis to ecdysis. Since apolysis can be a discontinuous process that is difficult to determine, in practice the difference between a stage and an instar is somewhat abstract.

STASE. [Gr. στασις, standing]. 1. In the Chelicerata: one of the successive instars of the postembryonic development of a specific species. 2. In ticks and mites: an instar, independent of growing molts, that is distinct within a species and can be homologized with the corresponding instars of other species.

STASIMOPIDAE. [Gr. στασιμος, stable; ωψ, the eye]. A monospecific family of trap door spiders (infraorder Mygalomorphae, superfamily Avicularioidea) from southern Africa.

STASIPATRIC SPECIATION. See Speciation.

STASIS. [Gr. στασις, standing]. A stoppage or retardation. A period of little evolutionary change.

STASOID. [Gr. στασις, standing; ειδος, like]. In the Chelicerata: the life cycles of some instars that cannot be homologized with corresponding instars of other species of the same group.

STATOKINETIC. [Gr. στατος, standing; κινητικος, putting in motion]. Of reflexes and the associated movements which maintain equilibrium.

STEGASIMOUS (STEGASIME). [Gr. στηγη, roof]. In ticks and mites: having the prodorsal sclerite project over the chelicerae. See also Astegasimous.

STELLIFORM. [L. *stella*, a star; *forma*, shape]. Star-shaped.

243

STENARTHRIC. [Gr. στενος, narrow; αρθρον, joint]. In the Acariformes; a subcapitulum with a triangular mentum and oblique labiogenal sutures. This is thought to be a primitive condition. See also Anarthric, Diarthric.

STENOCHILIDAE. [Gr. στενος, narrow; χειλος, a lip]. A small family of spiders (infraorder Araneomorphae, superfamily Palpimanoidea) from southeast Asia.

STENOECIOUS. [Gr. στενος, narrow; οικος, dwelling]. Of animals which have a narrow range of habitats. Opposite - Euryoecious.

STENOGAMY. [Gr. στενος, narrow; γαμος, marriage]. The ability to mate in a confined space.

STENOGASTRIC. [Gr. στενος, narrow; γαστηρ, stomach]. With a shortened abdomen or gaster.

STENOHYGRIC. [Gr. στενος, narrow; υγρος, moist]. Of an organism tolerating only a narrow atmospheric humidity range.

STENOHYGROBIA. [Gr. στενος, narrow; υγροβιος, living in the wet]. Of animals which are tolerant to only a narrow range of humidity.

STENOMORPHIC. [Gr. στενος, narrow; μορφα, form]. Dwarfed or smaller than normal due to a cramped habitat.

STENOPHAGOUS (STENOPHAGIC). [Gr. στενος, narrow; -φαγος, -eating]. Existing on a very limited range of foods. Opposite Euryphagous. See also Monophagous, Polyphagous.

STENORHYNCHAN. [Gr. στενος, narrow; ρυγχος, a snout]. Narrow beaked or snouted.

STENOSIS. [Gr. στενος, narrow; -οσις, suf. of condition]. A narrowing or constriction of a tubular vessel or structure.

STENOSTOMATOUS. [Gr. στενος, narrow; στομα, mouth]. Narrow-mouthed.

STENOTHERMOUS, STENOTHERMAL. [Gr. στενος, narrow; θερμη, heat]. Of animals that are adaptable to a narrow range of environmental temperatures. Opposite - Eurythermous.

STENOTOPIC. [Gr. στενος, narrow; τοπος, place]. Having a restricted geographical distribution or range of environments. Opposite - Eurytopic.

STENOTROPIC. [Gr. στενος, narrow; τροπη, a change]. Having a very limited ability to adapt to varying conditions.

STENOVALENT. [Gr. στενος, narrow; L. valens, strong]. Of an organism restricted to few types of environmental conditions. See also Euryvalent.

STENOXENOUS. [Gr. στενος, narrow; ξενος, guest]. Of a parasite able to tolerate only a small range of host species.

STERCORAL. [L. stercus, dung]. Of feces; and applied to a dorsal sac of the hind-gut (proctodaeum) in spiders.

STERCORAL POCKET. [L. stercus, dung]. A dilated portion of the proctodeum of certain spiders in which fecal matter and excreta temporarily accumulate.

STEREOGNOSTIC SENSE. [Gr. στερεος, solid; γνωστος, knowable]. A sense or ability which enables an animal to appreciate size, shape and weight.

STEREOKINESIS. [Gr. στερεος, solid; κινησις, movement]. See Thigmokinesis.

STEREOTAXIS. [Gr. στερεος, solid; ταξις, an arranging]. See Thigmotaxis.

STEREOTROPISM. [Gr. στερεος, solid; τροπος, turn]. A movement in a direction determined by contact with a solid body. **Positive stereotropism**: toward contact. **Negative stereotropism**: away from contact.

STERILE. [L. sterilis, barren]. Incapable of propagation or reproduction. Incapable of conveying an infection. Devoid of living organisms.

STERNAL. [Gr. στερνον, chest]. Of the sternum or of a sternite.

STERNAL PLASTRON. See Sternum.

STERNAL PLATES. [Gr. στερνον, chest]. The exoskeletal plates which form the ventral covering of each segment.

STERNAL PORES (stp or iv). [Gr. στερνον, chest]. In the Mesostigmata: the lyrifissures in the intercoxal region.

STERNAL TAENIDIUM. [Gr. στερνον, chest; ταινια, a ribbon; -ιδιον, dim. suf]. In the Opilioacariformes: a surface canal in the sternal region of the podosoma that extends from the coxal gland orifice, between coxae I and II, to the subcapitular gutter.

STERNAL SETAE. [Gr. στερνον, chest]. In the Mesostigmata: the five pairs of setae in the intercoxal region, designated st1-5. st1-3 are present in the larvae; st4, the metasternal setae, are added in the deutonymph; st5, the genital setae, are added in the protonymph.

STERNAL SHIELD. [Gr. στερνον, chest]. In the Parasitiformes: a shield in the anterior intercoxal region that bears one or more pairs of sternal setae.

STERNAL VERRUCAE. [Gr. στερνον, chest; L. *verruca*, wart]. In the Opilioacariformes: the paired wart-like structures in the sternal region.

STERNAPOPHYSIS. [Gr. στερνον, chest; απο, separate; φυσειν, to grow]. In ticks and mites: protuberances (single, paired or three) in the sternal region of leg I.

STERNOGENITAL/STERNITOGENITAL/STERNITIGENITAL SHIELD. [Gr. στερνον, chest; L. *genitalis*, of generation or birth]. See Intercoxal.

STERNOGYNUM (STERNOGYNAL/STERNOGYNIAL SHIELD). [Gr. στερνον, chest; γυνη, woman]. In female Trigynaspida (Mesostigmata): a shield in the pregenital position that bears a pair of lyrifissures. See also Pseudosternogynum.

STERNOPHOROIDEA. [Gr στερνον, chest; -φορα, -carrying]. A monotypic superfamily of venomous false scorpions (order Pseudoscorpiones, suborder Iocheirata). Family: **Sternophoridae.**

STERNOPHTHALMI. [Gr. στερνον, chest; οφθαλμος, the eye]. An infraorder of harvestmen (order Opiliones, suborder Cyphophthalmi). Families: **Neogoveidae, Ogoveidae, Troglosironidae.**

STERNOVAGINAL SCLERITES. [Gr. στερνον, chest; L. *vagina*, sheath]. In female Aenictequoidea (Antennophorina): a pair of posterior internal processes in the pregenital region.

STERNUM. [Gr. στερνον, chest]. A ventral plate of a typical segment. The often heart-shaped or oval exoskeletal shield that forms the middle portion of the under surface of the thorax, between the coxal cavities and marking the floor of the cephalothorax.

STETHIDIUM. [Gr. στηθος, breast; -ιδιον, dim. suf.]. The thorax and its appendages. In ticks and mites: the nonsclerotized prodorsum.

STETHOSOMA. [Gr. στηθος, breast; σωμα, body]. In ticks and mites: that part of the body from the circumcapitular furrow to the disjugal furrow. The prosoma without the gnathosoma.

STICHIC. [Gr. στιχος, row]. In a row parallel to the long axis.

STIGMA (STIGMATA). [Gr. στιγμη, mark]. A mark, eyespot, spot, etc.

STIGMATIFEROUS. [Gr. στιγμη, mark; L. *ferre*, to carry]. Bearing a stigma or stigmata.

STIGMATIFORM. [Gr. στιγμη, mark; L. *forma*, shape]. In the form of a stigma or stigmata.

STIMULATION. [L. *stimulare*, to incite]. The excitation or irritation of an organism by either internal or external stimuli.

STIMULUS. [L. *stimulus*, goad]. Any agent which causes a reaction or change in an organism or in any of its parts.

STIPE. [L. *stipes*, a stem]. Any stalk-like or stem-like structure.

STIPHIDIIDAE. [Gr. στιφος, compact body; -ιδιον, dim. suf.]. A family of sheet-web spiders (infraorder Araneomorphae, superfamily Entelegynae). Medium sized (ca. 8 mm) spiders with long legs. Except for *Asmea*, which is from Papua New Guinea, most members of this family occur in New Zealand and Australia.

STIPIFORM. [L. *stipes*, a stem; *forma*, shape]. Resembling a stalk.

STIPITATE. [L. *stipes*, tree trunk]. Having a stipe or stalk.

STIPPLE. [Du. *stippelen*, to spot]. Numerous circles or dots. The shading effects produced by dots, circles or small marks.

STOMATE. [Gr. στομα, mouth]. Bearing a mouth.

STOMATODEUM. See Stomodeum.

STOMATOGENESIS. [Gr. στομα, mouth; γενεσις, origin]. The process of mouth formation.

STOMODEUM (STOMODAEUM). [Gr. στομα, mouth; οδος, a way]. The anterior region of the gut.

STORAGE MITES. See Astigmata.

stp. In the Mesostigmata: sternal lyrifissure (pore) sigla; stp1-3 (also iv 1-3)

STRAMINEOUS. [L. *stramineus*, made of straw]. Straw-colored.

STRANGULATE. [L. *strangulatus*, strangled]. Constricted, as if by bands or cords.

STRATIFIED. [L. *stratum*, layer]. Arranged in layers.

STRATIFORM/STRATOSE. [L. *stratum*, layer; *forma*, shape]. Layered.

STRAW-ITCH MITE. Any member of the genus *Pyemotes* (Eleutherengona: Pyemotidae). Their bites cause large itchy wheals on humans.

STRESS. Any environmental factor which restricts the growth and reproduction of an organism.

STRESS HYPOTHESIS. A hypothesis concerning self regulation of population size in which the mutual interactions in an increasing population lead to physiological changes that cause a reduction in the number of births and an increase in the number of deaths.

STRETCHER. In some **Linyphiidae**: a pit at the tip of the epigynal scape.

STRETCH RECEPTOR. A receptor neuron which senses muscle length. A weak stretch initiates a steady stream of impulses, the frequency of impulses depending on the amount of stretch. A stronger stretch produces a larger potential. See also Receptor.

STRIA (STRIAE). [L. *stria*, groove]. A band, channel, groove, narrow streak, etc. Part of the stridulating system or marks radiating from the central fovea on the carapace.

STRIATE(D). [L. *striatus*, grooved]. Marked by narrow lines or grooves, which are commonly parallel.

STRIATED MUSCLE. [L. *striatus*, grooved]. Voluntary muscle, striped muscle. See Muscle.

STRIATION. [L. *stria*, furrow]. A longitudinal ridge or furrow.

STRICTURE. [L. *stringere*, to bind tight]. A binding or contraction.

STRIDULATING ORGANS. [L. *stridere*, to make a harsh noise or animal noise]. The sound producing organs of arthropods. There are a wide variety of methods of sound production, but basically, a file is rubbed across a membrane. In some arachnids: an area with many sclerotized parallel striae which are rubbed by hairs or a tooth on an opposing structure. They may be located on the palps, legs, chelicerae, abdomen or the carapace.

STRIDULATION. [L. *stridere*, to make a harsh noise or animal noise]. The production of sound by rubbing particular parts of the body together. Most arachnids are silent, but some tarantula species are known to stridulate. When disturbed, *Theraphosa blondi*, can produce a hissing noise by rubbing together the bristles on its legs, and the wolf spider, *Schizocosa stridulans*, can produce a low-frequency sound by flexing its abdomen (tremulation) or a high-frequency stridulation by using the cymbia on the ends of its pedipalps.

STRIDULATORY FILE. [L. *stridere*, to make a harsh noise or animal noise]. A series of fine grooves used in conjunction with small thick pointed setae (thorns) to produce sound. They are commonly located along the ectal margin of the chelicera, or along the anteroventral margin of the abdomen.

STRIGA. [L. *striga*, ridge/furrow]. A band of upright, stiff, pointed hair or bristles. A bristle-like scale.

STRIGATE. [L. *striga*, ridge]. Bearing strigae.

STRIGILE, STRIGILIS. [L. *strigilis*, scraper]. Maculation that consists of parallel longitudinal lines.

STRIGILLOSE. [L. *strigilla*, small ridge/furrow]. Minutely strigose.

STRIGOSE. [L. *striga*, ridge]. Covered with stiff hairs. Marked by small furrows or ridges.

STRIGULA. [L. *striga*, furrow]. A fine, short transverse mark or line.

STRIGULATED. Having numerous strigulae.

STRIOLA. [L. *striola*, small channel]. A narrow line or streak.

STRIOLATE, STRIOLATUS. [L. *striola*, small channel]. Having finely impressed parallel lines.

STRIPED MUSCLE. Voluntary muscle. See Muscle.

STROMBULIFEROUS. [L. *strombula*; little spiral shell; *ferre*, to carry]. Having spirally coiled organs or structures.

STROMBULIFORM. [L. *strombula*; little spiral shell; *forma*, shape]. Spirally coiled.

STRUCTURAL COLORS. Colors that are a consequence of the fine structure of a surface rather than pigmentation. See Interference Colors, Iridescence.

STUPEOUS. [L. *stupa*, coarse flax]. Covered with fiber-like filaments.

STUPULOSE. [L. *stupa*, coarse flax]. Covered with coarse decumbent hairs.

STYGNIDAE. [Gr. στυγνος, abhorred]. A family of neotropical harvestmen or daddy longlegs (suborder Laniatores, superfamily Gonyleptoidea). Most species live in the Amazonian rainforest, but their distribution is poorly known.

STYGNOMMATIDAE. [*Stygnus* (Stygnidae); ομμα, eye (poet.)]. A small family of neotropical harvestmen or daddy longlegs (suborder Laniatores, superfamily Samooidea).

STYGNOPSIDAE. [*Stygnus* (Stygnidae); –οψ, appearance]. A small family of harvestmen or daddy longlegs (suborder Laniatores, superfamily Gonyleptoidea), mainly from Mexico. Some are cave-dwellers.

STYGOPHALANGIIDAE. [Gr. Στυγιος, Stygian - of the nether world; + Phalangiidae]. A monospecific family of harvestmen or daddy longlegs (suborder Eupnoi, superfamily Phalangioidea). The affinities of this species are uncertain, it may in fact be a species of mite (Acari).

STYGOPHILIC. [Gr. Στυγιος, Stygian - of the nether world; φιλος, loving]. Thriving in caves or subterranean passages.

STYGOTHROMBIOIDEA. [Gr. Στυγιος, Stygian - of the nether world; Gr. θρομβος, clot]. A superfamily of mites (suborder Prostigmata, infraorder Anystina). Family: **Stygothrombiidae.**

STYGOXENOUS. [Gr. Στυγιος, Stygian - of the nether world; ξενος, stranger]. Found only occasionally in caves or subterranean passages.

STYLE. [Gr. στυλος, pillar; L. *stylus*, pricker]. The embolus of spiders.

STYLET. [L. *stylus*, pricker]. Any small, pointed, bristle-like appendage. In some ticks and mites: the needle-like chelicerae.

STYLET EXTENSION. See Odontophore.

STYLET-LIKE (STYLETTIFORM, STYLIFORM). [L. *stylus*, pricker]. Chelicerae or movable digits that are slender, elongate, and usually acuminate. They may be composed of the entire chelicera (as in some parasitic Dermanyssoidea or the *Bimichaelia*) or only the movable digits (as in many Prostigmata). Elongate cheliceral stylets may be known as whip-like stylets (e.g. in spider mites and their relatives).

STYLET SHEATH (CHELICERAL SHEATH, ROSTRAL GUTTER). [L. *stylus*, pricker]. In the Eriophyoidea (Prostigmata): the median anterior process of the capitulum, in the form of a paired membranous U-shaped sheath/gutter, that attaches the chelicera to the cheliceral frame, so as to allow extension and retraction.

STYLIFEROUS. [L. *stylus*, pricker; *ferre*, to bear]. Having a style or bristly appendages.

STYLIFORM (STYLETTIFORM). [L. *stylus*, pricker; *forma*, shape]. Prickle-shaped, bristle-shaped. See Stylet-Like.

STYLOCELLIDAE. [Gr. στυλος, pillar; L. *ocellus*, eye]. A small family of harvestmen (suborder Cyphophthalmi, infraorder Boreophthalmi) from India to New Guinea. *Stylocellus* species have eyes, but they are absent from the other two known genera.

STYLOCELLOIDEA. [Gr. στυλος, pillar; L. *ocellus*, eye]. In a previous classification: a monotypic superfamily of harvestmen (order Opilones, suborder Cyphophthalmi) that contained the family **Stylocellidae**. This family in now in the infraorder Boreophthalmi.

STYLOID. [Gr. στυλος, pillar; ειδος, like]. Long and slender.

STYLOPHORE. [L. *stylus*, pricker; Gr. -φορα, -carrying]. The type of chelicerae formed from fused cheliceral bases. They bear stylet-like movable digits and in the predatory and parasitic Cheyletoidea (Prostigmata) the stylophore and subcapitulum are fused into a gnathosomal capsule.

STYLOSE. [Gr. στυλος, pillar/L. *stylus*, pricker]. Bearing a style or several styli.

STYLOSTOME. [L. *stylus*, pricker; Gr. στομα, mouth]. In mites: a tube in the skin of the host or victim which is produced in reaction to the insertion of the mite chelicerae.

SUB-. [L. *sub-*, under]. A prefix meaning below, nearly, not quite, somewhat, etc. In classification it is used to denote a taxon intermediate between two levels; e.g. subclass, suborder, subfamily. See Nomenclature.

SUBADULT. Almost adult; the last instar before maturity.

SUBADUNCATE. [L. *sub-*, somewhat, *aduncus*, bent inwards]. Somewhat hooked or curved.

SUBALPINE. [L. *sub-*, under; *alpinus*, alpine]. Of organisms that live below the timber line.

SUBALTERNATE. [L. *sub-*, under; *alternus*, alternate]. Not quite opposite, yet not regularly alternate.

SUBARBORESCENT. [L. *sub-*, somewhat; *arborescens*, growing into a tree]. Somewhat tree-like.

SUB-BASAL. [L. *sub-*, under; Gr. βασις, foundations]. Situated near the base.

SUBCAPITULAR. [L. *sub-*, under; *caput*, head]. In ticks and mites: of the ventral surface of the infracapitulum.

SUBCAPITULAR APODEME. [L. *sub-*, under; *caput*, head; Gr. απο, down from; δεμας, the living body]. In ticks and mites: a sclerotized continuation of the mentum internally, to which several tendons are attached.

SUBCAPITULAR GROOVE. See Deutosternal Gutter.

SUBCAPITULAR GUTTER. [L. *sub-*, under; *caput*, head]. In the anactinotrichid mites: the median taenidium on the ventral surface of the infracapitulum.

SUBCAPITULAR PLATE. [L. *sub-*, under; *caput*, head]. In ticks and mites: an apodeme that supports the chelicerae ventrally and to which the muscles of the labrum are anchored.

SUBCAPITULUM (INFRACAPITULUM). [L. *sub-*, under; *caput*, head]. In ticks and mites: the venter of the capitulum. The ventral faces of the fused palpcoxae.

SUBCARINATE. [L. *sub-*, somewhat; *carina*, keel]. Somewhat keel-shaped.

SUBCEPHALIC. [L. *sub-*, under; Gr. κεφαλη, head]. Located posterior to the cephalic region.

SUBCHELICERAL PLATE. [L. *sub-*, under; + Chelicerae]. The internal sclerotized plate on which the chelicerae rest.

SUBCLASS. [L. *sub-*, under; *classis*, division]. In classification: a major subdivision of a class, comprised of related orders.

SUBCLAVATE. [L. *sub-*, somewhat; *clava*, a club]. Somewhat thickened toward the tip, but not quite club-shaped.

SUBCORIACEOUS. [L. *corium*, leather; *-aceous*, of the nature of]. Somewhat leathery.

SUBCUTANEOUS. [L. *sub-*, under; *cutis*, skin]. Under the skin. Usually of structures or fat bodies just below the skin's surface or of parasites which live just below the skin.

SUBDENTATE. [L. *sub-*, somewhat; *dens*, tooth]. Slightly toothed.

SUBDERMAL. [L. *sub-*, under; Gr. δερμα, the skin]. Under the skin.

SUBDORSAL. [L. *sub-*, below; *dorsum*, back]. Situated more-or-less on the dorsal surface.

SUBDORSAL SETA. [L. *sub-*, below; *dorsum*, back; *seta*, bristle]. In the Eriophyoidea: the opisthosomal seta c1.

SUBEQUAL. [L. *sub-*, below; *aequalis*, equal]. Similar, but not quite equal in size, form or other characters.

SUBFAMILY. [L. *sub-*, under; *familia*, family]. A category below the level of family. The standard suffix is -inae. E.g. the Salticinae, are a subfamily of the family **Salticidae** (jumping spiders). See also Nomenclature.

SUBFOSSORIAL. [L. *sub-*, under; *fossor*, digger]. Adapted for digging.

SUBFRONTAL. [L. *sub-*, below; *frons*, forehead]. Close to the front or immediately behind the front margin.

SUBFUSIFORM. [L. *fusus*, spindle; *forma*, shape]. Somewhat spindle-shaped.

SUBGENERIC NAME. See Subgenus.

SUBGENICULATE. [L. *sub-*, somewhat; *geniculum*, little knee]. Somewhat bent.

SUBGENITAL. [L. *sub-*, below; *genitalis*, genital]. In general: below the reproductive organs.

SUBGENUS, SUBGENERA. [L. *sub-*, under; *genus*, tribe]. The name of an optional category between genus and species.

SUBMARGINAL. [L. *sub*; below; *margo*, margin]. Very near the margin.

SUBOCELLATE. [L. *sub*; below; *ocellus*, little eye]. An ocellate spot that is blind or without a pupil.

SUBOCULAR. [L. *sub*; below; *oculus*, eye]. Beneath or below the eyes.

SUBOPTIC. [L. *sub-*, below; Gr. οπτικος, of sight]. Below the eye.

SUBORAL. [L. *sub-*, below; *os*, mouth]. Near to or below the mouth.

SUBOVATE. [L. *sub-*, somewhat; *ovum*, egg]. Somewhat oval.

SUBPECTINATE. [L. *sub-*, somewhat; *pecten*, comb]. More-or-less comb-like or tending to become comb-like.

SUBPEDUNCULATE. [L. *sub-*, somewhat; LL. *pedunculus*, little foot]. Having or resting on a very short stalk.

SUBPHYLUM. [L. *sub-*, under; Gr. φυλη, tribe, race]. A major subdivision in classification between phylum and class.

SUBPOLAR. [L. *sub-*, below; Gr. πολος, pole]. Situated near the pole.

SUBPOPULATION. A particular breeding group within a larger population or species and in which migration in or out of the breeding group is restricted.

SUBSELLATE. [L. *sub-*, somewhat; *sella*, saddle]. Nearly like or approaching the form of a saddle.

SUBSESSILE. [L. *sub-*, nearly; *sedere*, to sit]. Almost sessile; having almost no stalk.

249

SUBSOCIAL. [L. *sub-*, under; *socius*, companion]. Applied to adults caring for their young for some period of time. See also Parasocial.

SUBSPECIES. [L. *sub-*, below; *species*, particular type]. Within a species: a group of individuals having certain characteristics that separate them from other members of the species and which form a breeding group. They are normally considered to be a race and are given a Latin name. As phenotypic and systematic variations will occur within species, there are no clear rules for defining a subspecies except that they must be geographically distinct populations and differ to some degree from other geographically distinct populations. See Nomenclature.

SUBTEGULUM. [L. *sub-*, under; *tegula*, tile]. In some arachnids: a chitinous structure that protects the haematodocha. It forms the proximal of the three divisions of the male palpal bulb. It is often a ring or cup-like structure and is attached to the cymbium by the proximal haematodocha.

SUBTERES. [L. *sub-*, nearly; *teres*, smooth/tapering]. Nearly cylindrical.

SUBTERMINAL. [L. *sub-*, nearly; *terminus*, end]. Located near the end.

SUBTERMINAL APOPHYSIS. [L. *sub-*, nearly; *terminus*, end; Gr. αποφυσις, an offshoot]. A sclerotized section in the apical division of the bulb of the male palpus.

SUBTIDAL (SUBLITTORAL) ZONE. See Intertidal Zone.

SUBTILE, SUBTILIS. [L. *subtilis*, fine-spun/fine/slender]. Slightly, feebly, graceful.

SUBTUS. [L. *subtus*, below/underneath]. Beneath. At the under surface.

SUBTRIBE. [L. *sub-*, under; *tribus*, tribe]. In classification: a rank below the tribe and above the genus.

SUBTROPICAL ZONE. [L. *sub-*, beneath; Gr. τροπικος, tropical; ζωνη, girdle]. The region between 23.5° and 34° of latitude in either hemisphere.

SUBTYPICAL. [L. *sub-*, somewhat; Gr. τυπος, pattern]. Deviating just a little from the type.

SUBULATE, SUBULIFORM. [L. *subula*, awl; *forma*, shape]. Shaped like an awl. With convex sides, slender and tapering to a point.

SUBUMBONATE. [L. *sub-*, under; *umbo*, boss]. Being slightly convex or having a low rounded protuberance.

SUBUNCINATE. [L. *sub-*, somewhat; *uncus*, hook]. Being somewhat hook-shaped.

SUBUNGUINAL SETA. [L. *sub-*, under; *unguis*, nail; *seta*, bristle]. In acariform mites: an unpaired seta between the unguinal and anterolateral pairs on the tarsi.

SUBXERIC. [L. *sub-*, somewhat; Gr. ξηρος, dry]. Dry conditions with only a little water available.

SUCCESSION. [L. *successio*, succession]. A sequence of events. A sequence of species either geological, ecological or seasonal. A sequential (chronological) distribution of organisms in a given region. The development of a plant community from first invaders to the climax community.

SUCCESSIVE POLYANDRY. See Polyandry.

SUCCINEOUS. [L. *succinum* amber]. Resembling amber in either color or appearance.

SUCKER. [AS. *sucan*, to suck]. Organs variously adapted for creating a vacuum for the purpose of drawing in food particles, or assisting in locomotion or maintaining attachment.

SUCKER PLATE. [AS. *sucan*, to suck]. In the Astigmata: an array of modified setae in the anal region of the hypopi.

SUCTORIAL. [L. *sugere*, to suck]. 1. Adapted for sucking. 2. Furnished with suckers.

SUFFUSED. [L. *suffusus*, overspread]. Clouded or obscured by a darker color.

SUGENT, SUGESCENT. [L. *sugere*, to suck]. Suctorial.

SULCATE. [L. *sulcus*, furrow]. Grooved. Furrowed.

SULCATION. [L. *sulcatio*, ploughing]. The formation of ridges or furrows.

SULCI. [L. *sulcus*, furrow]. Grooves of a functional nature, such as the strengthening ridges of the head.

SULCIFORM. [L. *sulcus*, furrow; *forma*, shape]. Being groove-like or groove-shaped.

SULCUS (SULCULUS, FISSURE). [L. *sulcus*, furrow]. A groove or furrow.

SULPHUREOUS, SULPHUREUS. [L. *sulfur*, brimstone]. Bright, Sulfur yellow.

SUN SPIDERS. See Solifugae.

SUNBATHING. A strategy for regulating or maintaining body temperature in those animals whose body temperature varies with that of the surrounding medium, i.e. poikilothermic. This strategy is also taken by animals resting and thereby conserving metabolic energy that would otherwise be needed to maintain body temperature.

SUNDALAND. [*Sunda*, a local region in SE Asia]. A geographical region comprising Borneo, Java, Malaya, Sumatra and all the intervening islands which are linked by shallow water (less than 200 m deep). The Sunda shelf was exposed during Pleistocene times and thus the fauna is basically homogeneous and differs slightly from that of the regions further northwest.

SUPER-. [L. *supero*, over/above]. In classification: a taxon just above the level of the preceding taxon, e.g. superclass, superfamily. In many cases a supertaxon is (more-or-less) equivalent to a subtaxon of the next higher category, thus a superorder may be (more-or-less) equivalent to a subclass. See Nomenclature.

SUPERANS. [L. *superans*, surmounting]. Exceeding in size and length.

SUPERCILIARY. [L. *superans*, surmounting; *cilium*, eyelid]. Placed above the eyes.

SUPERCILIUM. [L. *superans*, surmounting; *cilium*, eyelid]. An arched line over an ocellate spot.

SUPERFICIAL EPICUTICULAR LAYER. See Cerotegument.

SUPERFICIAL. [L. *super*, over; *facies*, face]. On, or near, the surface.

SUPERFICIES. [L. *facies*, face]. The upper surface.

SUPERIOR. [L. *superior*, upper]. Higher, upper, anterior, of one structure above another.

SUPERIOR CLAWS (LATERAL CLAWS). [L. *superior*, upper]. In all spiders: the claws found at the tip of the leg.

SUPERNE. [L. *superne*, at or to a higher level]. Of all those parts belonging to the upper surface.

SUPERNUMERARY. [LL. *supernumerarius*, added after completion]. Additional or added. Of cells, veins or other structures.

SUPEROVULATION. [L. *super*, over; *ovum*, egg; *latum*, borne away]. The production of an unusually large number of eggs at any one time.

SUPERPARASITE. A hyperparasite. See Parasite.

SUPERPOSED. [L. *superponere*, to superpose]. Placed one above the other.

SUPERSPECIES. [L. *super*, over; *species*, particular type]. A grouping of closely related species (allopatric species) on the basis of morphological similarities.

SUPERSTITIONIIDAE. [*Superstition* Mountains, Arizona]. A monospecific family of scorpions (order Scorpiones, superfamily Chactoidea). *Superstitionia donensis*.

SUPINATE. [L. *supinus*, bent backwards]. Inclined or leaning backwards.

SUPRA. [L. *supra*, above]. A prefix used to indicate, above or higher; on the dorsal side; opposite to infra.

SUPRA-ANAL. [L. *supra*, above; *anus*, anus]. Above the anal region.

SUPRA-CHELICERAL LIMBUS. [L. *supra*, above; Gr. χηλη, claw; κερας, horn; L. *limbus*, border]. In the Mesostigmata (Parasitiformes): an extension of part of the tegulum above the chelicera.

SUPRA-COXAL FOLD. [L. *supra*, above; *coxa*, hip]. In argasid ticks: a prominent fold on the lateral ventral margin of the body, lateral to the legs; this fold bears the spiracles and, when present, the eyes.

SUPRA-COXAL SETA. [L. *supra*, above; *coxa*, hip; *seta*, bristle]. In astigmatans: an often inflated or otherwise elaborated dorsal coxal seta associated with the supracoxal gland opening.

SUPRA-ORBITAL. [L. *supra*, above; *orbis*, eye socket]. Situated above the eye.

SUPRA-LITORAL (SUPRA-LITTORAL). [L. *supra*, above; *litus*, seashore]. Of the seashore above the high-water line or the spray zone.

SUPRA-OCULAR. [L. *supra*, above; *oculus*, eye]. Over or above the eye.

SUPRA-OESOPHAGEAL (SUPRAPHARYNGEAL, HYPERPHARYNGEAL, CEREBRAL) GANGLION. [L. *supra*, above; Gr. οισοφαγος, gullet; γαγγλιον, little tumor]. The nerve mass above the esophagus. Occasionally it may become sufficiently complex to be regarded as a brain.

SUPRA-SPECIFIC. [L. *supra*, above; *species*, kind]. Applied to a category or evolutionary phenomenon above the species level.

SUPRA-STIGMAL. [L. *supra*, above; *stigma*, mark]. Above the spiracles.

SUPRA-TEGULUM. [L. *supra*, above; *tegula*, tile]. In male **Linyphiidae**: a sclerotized structure that arises from the tegulum.

SUPRA-TIDAL (SUPRA-LITTORAL) ZONE. [L. *supra*, above; OE, *tid*, portion of time]. Above the high-water mark. See Intertidal Zone.

SURANAL. [L. *supra*, above; anus]. Above the anus. Supra-anal.

SURFACE PHEROMONE. [Gr. φερειν, to bear; hor*mone* (Gr. ορμαινω, excite)]. A pheromone active only on or very close to the body. Contact or near contact must be made.

SURSUM. [L. *sursum* up/on high]. Directed upwardly.

SUSPENSORIA. [L. *suspendere*, to hang up]. Those muscles or ligaments that hold the viscera and other internal organs in place.

SUSPENSORIUM. [L. *suspendere*, to hang up]. Anything that suspends a structure.

SUSTENTACULAR. [L. *sustentaculum*, prop/support]. Supporting. Of the connective tissue that acts as a supportive framework for an organ.

SUSTENTACULAR CELLS. [L. *sustentaculum*, prop/support]. The supporting cells of an organ as opposed to the functional cells.

SUTURE. [L. *sutura*, seam]. A groove in the body wall. An inflexible junction between two body parts. A line of fusion between two formerly separate body parts or regions.

SUTURIFORM. [L. *sutura*, seam; *forma*, shape]. An articulation united in such a way that only a slight impressed line is visible.

SWARM (SYNHESMIA). [AS. *swearm*, swarm]. A large number of small motile organisms when considered collectively; particularly bees (**Apidae**) and locusts (**Acrididae**).

SWEEP NET. A net of very fine mesh, usually with a large round mouth, that is used for sampling the fauna dispersed in the upper regions of tall vegetation.

SWEEPSTAKE DISPERSAL ROUTE. A possible route for faunal interchange which is unlikely to be used by most animals but, by random chance, will be used by some. For example, animals blown far out to sea by a storm may accidentally land on an oceanic island and colonize it, but it is unlikely that this will happen a second time for that species. This concept was first described by G. G. Simpson in 1940.

Sx. In the Mesostigmata: the designation for an extra seta in the S-series on the opisthonotum, i.e. not assignable to setae S1-5 in the Lindquist-Evans system.

SYARINIDAE. [derive.uncert.]. A small family of false scorpions (suborder Iocheirata, superfamily Neobisioidea).

SYLVAN/SYLVESTRAL/SYLVICOLOUS. [L. *silva*, a wood; *colere*, to inhabit]. Pertaining to, or inhabiting, woods.

SYMBASIS. [Gr. συμβασις, agreement]. The common evolutionary trend in an interbreeding association of organisms.

SYMBIOGENESIS. [Gr. συμβιωναι, to live with; γενεσις, birth/descent]. The evolutionary origins of symbiotic relationships between organisms.

SYMBIONT (SYMBIOTE). [Gr. συμβιωναι, to live with]. One of the partners in a symbiotic relationship.

SYMBIOSIS (SYMBIOTIC). [Gr. συμβιωναι, to live with]. The living together of two different organisms; which may or may not be for mutual benefit (mutualism). The interactive association between two different species or populations. E.g. the bacteria which inhabit the gut, symbiotic protozoa in the termite gut, the fungi attached to the roots of trees, the micro-algae in the body of a hydra, etc., etc. **Calobiosis**. A symbiosis in which one species lives in the nest of another, to the general detriment of the host. Either temporary or permanent. **Kleptobiosis**. An interspecific association in which one species steals from the food store of another without living in the food store, but living or nesting in close proximity. The following forms of symbiosis are not related to arachnids. Social symbiosis exists among ants in its most highly developed form and distinctive terms have been proposed for the various types of relations: **Dulosis**. Slavery amongst ants. E.g. the brown ant *Formica fusca* living in the same nest as, and working for, the red ant *Polyergus rufescens*. Most of the slave-making ant species are so specialized as raiders that they starve to death if deprived of their slaves. **Hamabiosis (Neutralism)**. A situation in which two species or populations coexist with neither being affected by the other. **Lestobiosis**. Brigandage by ants. A form of symbiosis in which a group of physically small 'thief ants' nest in or near the chambers of termites and larger ants, consuming their stored food, larvae and pupae unnoticed by their benefactors. **Parabiosis**. The utilization of the same nest by colonies of different species of social insects which use inosculating galleries and thus intermingle, but nevertheless keep separate. **Phylacobiosis**. A mutual or unilateral protective behavior. E.g. the relation existing between ants and termites (their inquilines) in which the ants live in the entrances of the termite mounds and function as guards. **Synclerobiosis**. An association between two species of social insect that normally inhabit separate colonies. **Trophibiosis**. The relationship between ants and the species they attend for their own benefit. E.g. aphids and coccids. These species are actively sought, protected and 'herded' by the ants. **Xenobiosis**. Hospitality in ant colonies. A symbiosis in which one species of ant lives as a guest in the nest of another, maintaining its own household, and mingling freely with the host species, the two living on terms of mutual toleration. See also Parasitism, Commensal.

SYMMETRICAL. [Gr. συμ-, with; μετρον, measure]. Being divisible into similar halves: regular in form; structurally similar on each side of an axis. See also Bilaterally Symmetrical.

SYMPARASITISM. [Gr. συμ-, together; παρασιτος, parasite]. The development of several competing species of parasite within or on one host. See also Parasite.

SYMPATHETIC NERVOUS SYSTEM. [Gr συμπαθητικος; having sympathy]. Of the nerves and ganglia of the alimentary canal and other viscera which they innervate.

SYMPATRIC. [Gr. συμ-, together; πατρη, native land]. Of a distribution of two or more populations in which there is an overlapping of their geographical range. See also Allopatric, Parapatric, Speciation.

SYMPATRIC HYBRIDIZATION. [Gr. συμ-, together; πατρη, native land; L. *hibrida*, cross]. The production of hybrid individuals between two sympatric species.

SYMPATRIC INTROGRESSION. See Introgression.

SYMPATRIC SPECIATION. See Speciation.

SYMPHORESIS. [Gr. συμφορησις, bringing together]. Moving collectively.

SYMPHYSIS. [Gr. συμφυσις, a growing together]. The growing together of two parts.

SYMPHYTOGNATHIDAE. [Gr. συμ- with; φυτον, a plant; γναθος, jaw]. A small family of spiders (infraorder Araneomorphae, superfamily Entelegynae). *Patu digua* is possibly the smallest spider in the world, with a body size of 0.37 millimeters.

SYMPLESIOMORPH. [Gr. συν-, with; πλησιος, near; μορφη, form]. Of characters which are seen as primitive (plesiomorphic) and shared between two or more taxa. See also Phylogenetic Classification.

SYNANTHROPIC (SYNANTHROPISM). [Gr. συν-, with; ανθρωπος, man]. Associated with human dwellings.

SYNAPHRIDAE. [Gr. συν-, with; αφρος, foam]. A small family of spiders (infraorder Araneomorphae, superfamily Entelegynae). They were previously a subfamily (Synaphrinae) of the **Anapidae.**

SYNAPOMORPHIC. [Gr. συν-, with; απο, away from; μορφη, shape]. Of apomorphic characters that are shared by two or more taxa. See also Apomorphic Characters, Autapomorphic Character, Phylogenetic Classification, Plesiomorphic Characters.

SYNAPORIUM. [Gr. συναπορεω, suffer poverty together]. An association of animals formed due to unfavorable environmental conditions.

SYNAPOSEMATIC. [Gr. συν-, with; απο, away from; σημα, signal]. See Sematic.

SYNARTHROSIS. [Gr. συναψις, contact; αρθρον, joint]. See Joint.

SYNCEREBRUM. [Gr. συν-, with; L. *cerebrum*, brain]. A secondary brain formed by a union of the brain with one or more ventral cord ganglia. A compound brain.

SYNCHEIMADIA. [Gr. συν-, with; χειμαδιον, winter dwelling]. Animal societies over-wintering together.

SYNCHOROLOGY. [Gr. συν-, with; χωρος, place]. The scientific study of the geographical distribution of plant or animal communities.

SYNCHRONIC. [Gr. συν-, with; χρονος, time]. Contemporary.

SYNCHRONIZATION. [Gr. συν-, with; χρονος, time]. The expression of the same behavior in the same species at the same time. This may be under hormonal control, pheromonal control or as a result of synchronized circadian rhythms (sensitivity to changes in light intensity, lunar periods, etc.).

SYNCHRONIZER (ZEITGEBER). [Gr. συν-, with; χρονος, time]. Any environmental factor which acts as a stimulus to an endogenous circadian rhythm causing it to become precisely synchronized (entrained) to a 24 hour cycle, rather than free-running. Such factors are light intensity, temperature, etc.

SYNCHRONOUS. [Gr. συν-, with; χρονος, time]. Happening at the same time.

SYNCIPUT. See Sinciput.

SYNCRYPTIC. [Gr. συν-, with; κρυπτος, hidden]. Of animals which are morphologically similar yet are unrelated. This similarity may evolve due to the development of a protective resemblance to their surroundings. See also Syntechnic.

SYNDESIS. [Gr. συνδεσις, binding together]. The form of articulation in which two parts are connected by a membrane which permits of considerable motion between them.

SYNECOLOGY. [Gr. συν-, together; οικος, household; λογος, discourse]. The ecology of the totality of animal (or plant) communities.

SYNERGIC. [Gr. συνεργος, working together]. Operating together. Of muscles / nerve systems which combine to affect a particular movement. Also of some hormones.

SYNERGISM. [Gr. συνεργος, working together]. The phenomenon where substances, such as hormones, combine to provide a greater effect that either would individually, i.e. the effect of both together is greater than the sum of their individual parts or actions.

SYNGAMIC SEX DETERMINATION. [Gr. συν-, together; γαμετης, spouse]. See Sex Determination.

SYNGENETIC. [Gr. συν-, with; γενεσις, descent]. Being descended from the same ancestors.

254

SYNOECY. [Gr. συνοικος, living in the same house]. An association between two species where one is benefited without harm to the other.

SYNOMONE. [Gr. συν-, together; hormone (Gr. ορμαινω, excite)]. A mutually beneficial signal chemical: a chemical released by members of one species that affects the behavior of another species and benefits both parties. See also Allelochemic.

SYNONYM. [Gr. συνωνυμεω, to have the same name]. In taxonomy: a different name for the same taxon. Usually the first validly published name takes precedence. For example, the mite family Atopochthoniidae (Grandjean, 1949) has previously been known as the Pterochthoniidae (Grandjean, 1950) and Phyllochthoniidae (Travé, 1967). The first validly published name (Atopochthoniidae) taking precedence. Synonyms may occur when the same taxon is described and named more than once, either independently or in error. They may also occur when two taxa are joined to become one, or a taxon is moved to a different group, or if the codes of nomenclature change such that older names are no longer acceptable. **Junior synonym**: the later synonym, the first being the **senior synonym**.

SYNOTAXIDAE. [Gr. συν-, with; ταξις, arrangement]. A family of long-legged tangle-web spiders (infraorder Araneomorphae, superfamily Entelegynae) with a large southern-temperate distribution.

SYNSCLERITOUS. [Gr. συν-, with; σκληρος, hard]. The joining of a tergite and a sternite to form a complete ring. See also Discleritous.

SYNSPERMIATA. See Haplogynae.

SYNTAGMA. See Tagma.

SYNTECHNIC. [Gr. συν-, with; τεχνη, art]. A resemblance between unrelated animals due to a similar response to the environment. See also Syncryptic, Convergence.

SYNTHETONYCHIDAE. [Gr. συνθετος, composite; ονυξ, talon]. A family of harvestmen or daddy longlegs (suborder Laniatores, superfamily Triaenonychoidea) that are endemic to New Zealand.

SYNTROPHY. [Gr. συν-, together; τροφη, nourishment]. Nutritional interdependence; a cross-feeding between two individuals in which each derives essential nutrient(s) from the other.

SYNTROPIC. [Gr. συν-, together; τροπη, a turn]. Arranged in the same direction. Turning in the same direction.

SYNZOOCHOROUS. [Gr. συν-, together; ζωον, animal; χωρεω, to disperse]. Dispersed by animals.

SYRINGOPHILIDAE. [Gr. συριγξ, pipe; φιλος, loving]. A family of quill mites (suborder Eleutherengona, superfamily Cheyletoidea). Parasitic mites, of largely unknown economic importance, that are restricted to living in the quills of bird's feathers. Very little is known of this family but nearly all described species seem to be monospecific, so there may be as many species of these mites as there are species of birds.

SYSTALTIC. [Gr. συστελλω, draw together]. Contractile. Alternately contracting and dilating.

SYSTEMATICS. [Gr. συστημα, organized whole]. The classification of organisms into a hierarchical series of groups on the basis of their perceived phylogenetic relationships. See also Taxonomy.

SYSTEMIC. [Gr. συστημα, organized whole]. Belonging to, supplying, or affecting the system or body as a whole.

SZIDAT'S RULE. See Host-Parasite Associations.

T

TA. See Tibial Apophysi.

TACHYAUXESIS. [Gr. ταχυς, quick; αυξησις, growth]. Relative quick growth, especially of one part at a faster rate than the whole. See also Bradyauxesis, Heterauxesis, Isauxesis.

TACHYBLASTIC. [Gr. ταχυς, quick; βλαστος, growth]. Of some quickly hatching eggs which undergo cleavage immediately after oviposition. See also Opsiblastic.

TACHYGEN. [Gr. ταχυς, quick; γεννναειν, to produce]. An evolutionary structure of abrupt origin.

TACHYGENESIS. [Gr. ταχυς, quick; γενεσις, descent]. A form of development in which some stages are missing, thus, development is accelerated.

TACTILE. [L. tactilis, that which can be touched]. Of structures, such as hairs, bristles, end organs, etc. associated with the sense of touch.

TACTILE CORPUSCLE. [L. tactilis, that which can be touched; corpusculum, small body]. The sensory ending of a nerve, surrounded by a bulbous swelling of the perineurium.

TACTILE RECEPTORS. [L. tactilis, that which can be touched; recipere, to receive]. Any sensory receptors able to detect pressure or touch.

TACTILE SENSILLUM. See Sensillum Trichodeum.

TACTORECEPTORS. [L. tactus, touch; receptor, receiver]. Hairs, bristles, or other epidermal structures that have a role in touch where the organism comes in contact with the substratum, vibration of the substratum or high intensity airborne sounds.

TAENIA. [L. taenia, ribbon]. A broad longitudinal stripe. A nerve or muscle band.

TAENIATE. [L. taenia, ribbon]. Ribbon-like. Striped.

TAENIDIUM. [Gr. ταινια, a ribbon; -ιδιον, dim. suf.]. A spiral ridge of cuticle (larger tracheae) or annular rings (smaller tracheae and tracheoles) which strengthens the chitinous layer and prevents the collapse of the trachea if the pressure within is reduced.

TAENIOID. [Gr. ταινιοειδης, ribbon-like]. Ribbon-like.

TAGMA (pl. **TAGMATA**). [Gr. ταγμα, corpse]. In a segmented animal: the regions formed by fusion of similar somites or segments. For example, the tagmata of spiders are the prosoma (or cephalothorax) and opisthosoma (or abdomen) [those of insects are head, thorax and abdomen]. See also Pseudotagma.

TAGMOSIS. [Gr. ταγμα, corpse; -οσις, suf. of condition]. The functional specialization that occurs within metamerically segmented animals, producing a subdivision of the body into distinct regions (tagmata).

TAIGA. [Rus. taiga, rocky]. The ecosystem adjacent to the arctic tundra; i.e. the northern coniferous forest biome.

TAIL. [OE. tæg(e)l, rope's end]. The hindmost region of any animal, especially when it extends beyond the rest of the body.

TAIL-LESS WHIP SCORPIONS. See Amblypygi.

TAILPIECE. In male **Linyphiidae**: a linear structure attached to the radix which usually points towards the proximal end of the unexpanded palp.

TALON. [L. talus, heel]. Shaped like a claw. Unguiculate.

TANAUPODOIDEA. [Gr. ταναυπους, long-striding/long-shanked]. A monotypic superfamily of mites (suborder Prostigmata, infraorder Anystina). Family: **Tanaupodidae**.

TANGORECEPTOR. [L. tangere, to touch; receptor, receiver]. A receptor sensitive to slight pressure.

TARACIDAE. [Taharqa, an Egyptian king of the twenty-fifth dynasty]. A small family of long-jawed harvestmen (suborder Dyspnoi, superfamily Ischyropsalidoidea).

TAPETUM (TAPETUM LUCIDUM). [L. *tapete*, tapestry; *lucidum*, bright/shining]. A light reflecting surface within the indirect eyes (ALE, PLE, PME) of arachnids (and other animals' eyes) which increases visual sensitivity by reflecting light back through the retina, thus increasing the light available to the photoreceptors.

TARANTULA. [MedL. *tarantula*, from Taranto, S. Italy, where it is commonly found]. The common name for any of about 800 species of large, hairy spiders belonging to the family **Theraphosidae**. In the USA the name tarantula is applied to related families (e.g. such as the trapdoor, purse-web, and funnel-web spiders) in the infraorder Mygalomorphae. See **Theraphosidae**.

TARSAL. [Gr. ταρσος, sole of foot]. Of the foot or tarsus.

TARSAL APOTELE (PRETARSUS). [Gr. ταρσος, sole of foot; απο, away; τελος, end]. In ticks and mites: the most distal segments of the legs and palps, which bear the claws and empodium.

TARSAL APPENDAGES. [Gr. ταρσος, sole of foot]. The tarsal apoteles.

TARSAL CLAW. [Gr. ταρσος, sole of foot]. The claw borne on the final tarsal segment.

TARSAL COMB. [Gr. ταρσος, sole of foot]. See Calamistrum.

TARSAL ORGANS. [Gr. ταρσος, sole of foot]. In spiders: the cup-like or pit-like structures located near the tips of the legs. They are probably olfactory receptors.

TARSATION. [Gr. ταρσος, sole of foot]. Communication by touching with the tarsi.

TARSOCHEYLOIDEA. [Gr. ταρσος, sole of foot; χελωνη, tortoise/turtle]. A monotypic superfamily of mites (suborder Prostigmata, infraorder Eleutherengona). Family: **Tarsocheylidae**.

TARSOMERES. [Gr. ταρσος, sole of foot; μερος, part]. In arachnids: the basistarsus and telotarsus, i.e. the two parts of the dactylopodite.

TARSONEMOIDEA. [Gr. ταρσος, wicker crate, νεμος, forest]. A superfamily of mites (suborder Prostigmata, infraorder Eleutherengona). Families: **Podapolipidae (Podapolipodidae), Tarsonemidae**.

TARSUS. [Gr. ταρσος, sole of foot]. The segment of the leg distal to the tibia. It is usually divided into a number of segments (tarsomeres). See also Limb.

TASTE CUPS. [OFr. *tast*, sense of touch]. Specialized pits or cups, with or without a peg or hair, that are connected to ganglionated nerve cells. They occur on the mouth structures.

TASTE PORE. [OFr. *tast*, sense of touch]. An opening in the epithelium that leads to the terminal hairs of sensory cells in a taste bud.

TAXA. See Taxon.

TAXIS. [Gr. ταξις, an arranging]. A locomotory movement towards (positive) or away from (negative) a particular stimulus. See also Kinesis, Klinokinesis, Klinotaxis.

TAXON. [Gr. ταξις, an arranging]. Any definite unit of classification. A taxonomic group of any level (e.g. family, genus, species).

TAXONOMIC HEIRARCHY. [Gr. ταξις, an arranging]. A hierarchical system of taxonomic categories arranged in an ascending series of ranks. In zoology there are seven main ranks: species, genus, family, order, class, phylum, kingdom. Additional divisions can be introduced by the use of the prefixes super-, sub-, infra-. See also Nomenclature.

TAXONOMY. [Gr. ταξις, an arranging; νομος, law]. The study of the rules and principles governing the classification of plants and animals. Sometimes synonymous with Systematics

TECNOPHAGOUS. [Gr. τεκνον, child; -φαγος, -eating]. Feeding on one's own eggs.

TECTALS (tc). [L. *tectum*, roof]. In acariform mites: a pair of dorsal tarsal setae between the iterals and the fastigals.

TECTIFORM. [L. *tectum*, roof; *forma*, shape]. Roof-like. Sloping.

TECTOCEPHEOIDEA. [Gr. τεκτων, builder; κηφευς, name of a constellation]. A superfamily of mites (suborder Oribatida, infraorder Brachypylina - section Pycnonoticae). Families: **Tectocepheidae, Tegeocranellidae.**

TECTOLOGY. [Gr. τεκτων, builder; λογος, discourse]. A study of morphology in which the individual is regarded as a group of morphological units, as distinct from physiological units.

TECTOPEDIUM (TECTOPEDIA). [L. tectum, roof; pes, foot]. See Pedotectum.

TECTOSTRACUM. [L. tectus, covered; Gr. οστρακον, shell]. A thin, waxy covering of an exoskeleton, as in ticks and mites. See also Cerotegument.

TECTUM. [L. tectum, roof]. Any roof-like structure.

TECTUM CAPITULI. [L. tectum, roof; capitulum, little head]. In the Mesostigmata: the tectum or epistome.

TEETH (CHELICERAL TEETH). [AS. toth, tooth]. The conical rigid outgrowths of the margins of the cheliceral furrow.

TEGES. [L. teges, mat]. See Seta.

TEGMEN (TEGMINA). [L. tegmen, covering]. In some Prostigmata: a term sometimes used for the gnathosomal capsule.

TEGULA. [L. tegula, tile]. A small sclerite. In general: any tile-shaped structure.

TEGULUM. [L. tegulum, roof]. In ticks and mites: the dorsal region of the cheliceral frame extending from the cheliceral base to the rostrum. The sclerite that unites with the medium apophysis, to form the middle of the three divisions of the male palpal bulb. It is often a broad ring-like structure.

TEGUMENT. [L. tegumentum, a covering]. A covering surface or skin.

TEGUMENTARY GLANDS. [L. tegumentum, a covering]. In ticks and mites: specialized secretory glands located in, or immediately beneath, the hypodermis.

TELA. [L. tela, web]. Any web-like tissue.

TELARIAN. [L. tela, web]. Web-spinning.

TELEGAMIC. [Gr. τηλε, far; γαμος, marriage]. Attracting females from a distance; usually by pheromones.

TELEGONY. [Gr. τηλε, far; γονος, offspring]. A supposed influence that one male parent has on offspring, subsequent to his own, from the same female but by another male.

TELEIOCHRYSALIS. [Gr. τελειος, complete; χρυσαλλις, gold-colored sheath of butterflies]. In some mites: the nymph during the resting stage which precedes the adult form.

TELEMIDAE. [Gr. τελειος, perfect]. A family of long-legged cave spiders (suborder Opisthothelae, infraorder Araneomorphae) in which there are no book lungs but instead two pairs of tracheal spiracles. Most species have six eyes, but eyes are absent in some; and *Telema* only lays a single egg at a time.

TELEONOMY. [Gr. τελειος, complete; νομος, law]. The hypothesis that a structure exists in an organism due to having conferred an evolutionary advantage on that organism.

TELEOTYPIC CHARACTER. [Gr. τελος, end; τυπος, pattern]. Any unique distinguishing character of a species.

TELESCOPE. [Gr. τηλε, far; σκοπεω, view]. To have the ability to evert and invert a body part.

TELIODERMA. [Gr. τελειος, complete; δερμα, skin]. In ticks and mites: the cuticle of the previous stage nymph (apoderma) covering the tritonymph.

TELIOPHAN. See Tritonymph.

TELMOPHAGE (POOL FEEDER). [Gr. τελμα, pond; φαγειν, to eat]. A blood-feeder which consumes blood from a blood-pool created by laceration, rather than by piercing.

TELOFEMUR. [Gr. τελος, end; L. *femur*, thigh]. In some ticks and mites: a distal segment of the femur, between the basifemur and genu.

TELOLECITHAL. [Gr. τελος, end; λεκιθος, yolk]. An egg cell with abundant yolk concentrated towards the lower side of the cell. See also Alecithal, Centrolecithal, Heterolecithal, Macrolecithal, Mediolecithal, Meiolecithal, Mesolecithal, Microlecithal, Oligolecithal, Polylecithal.

TELOTARSUS (TARSUS). [Gr. τελος, end; ταρσος, sole of foot]. In spiders: the distal tarsomere of the dactylopodite.

TELOTAXIS. [Gr. τελος, end; ταξις, an arranging]. The direct-line movement between an animal and the source of the stimulus which elicits that movement.

TELSON. [Gr. τελσον, extremity/boundary]. The terminal region of an arthropod body (not considered a true somite) and usually containing the anus. In scorpions: the curved caudal spine or sting.

TELUM. [Gr. τελος, end]. The last abdominal segment.

TEMPERATURE REGULATION. Temperature regulation depends on the balance between the rate of heat production and the rate of heat loss. Heat production is a function of the general rate of metabolism and particularly the rate of oxidation of foodstuffs. Heat loss is a function of the total surface area of the body and the nature of the skin. The volume of an animal varies with the cube of its linear dimensions, thus the larger the animal, the less is the surface area in proportion to its volume. A large animal, therefore, loses heat less quickly than a smaller animal (all else being equal) and consequently needs proportionally less food. See also Eccritic Temperature, Ectotherm, Poikilotherm.

TEMPLE, TEMPORA. [OFr. *temple*, side of the forehead]. The posterior part of the gena; behind, before or beneath the eye.

TEMPORAL ISOLATION. [L. *temporalis*, temporary]. A mechanism that tends to keep populations of related species or races distinct by time related phenomena (e.g. mating cycles, gamete-releasing times) and so provide the opportunity for divergence to become more prevalent during the course of evolution.

TEMPORARY PARASITE. A parasite which only makes contact with its host for feeding.

TENANT HAIR. See Tenent Hair.

TENDON. [L. *tendere*, to stretch]. The slender, chitinous plates, bands, strap or cup-shaped pieces, to which muscles are attached for moving appendages. See also Apodemes.

TENENT HAIR. [L. *tenere*, to hold fast]. On the tarsus of spiders: of the hairs which secrete an adhesive fluid.

TENERAL. [L. *tener*, tender]. Immature.

TENGELLIDAE. [L. *tenere*, to hold fast; *-ella*, dim. suf.]. In a previous classification: a family of eight-eyed araneomorph spiders (infraorder Araneomorphae, superfamily Tengelloidea), mainly confined to the New World but with two monospecific genera in Madagascar and New Zealand. This family has recently been merged into the **Zoropsidae** (superfamily Entelegynae).

TENORECEPTOR. [Gr. τενων, tendon; L. *recipere*, to receive]. A proprioceptor in a tendon that responds to contraction.

TENSION RECEPTORS. [L. *tensionem* a stretching; *recipere*, to receive]. The sensory receptors which respond to stretching or pulling of the cuticle.

TENSOR. [L. *tendere*, to stretch]. Of muscles which stretch parts of the body.

TENTIFORM. [ML. *tenta*, a tent]. Shaped like a tent.

TENUOUS, TENUIS. [L. *tenuis*, thin]. Thin, slender, delicate.

TEREBRATE. [L. *terebra*, borer]. Adapted for boring; bearing an organ for boring.

TERES, TERETE. [L. *teres*, rounded]. Nearly cylindrical. A smoothly tapering cylinder.

TERGAL. [L. *tergum*, back]. Located at the back.

TERGITES. [L. *tergum*, back]. The transverse sclerites on the abdominal dorsum in Mesothelae and some Mygalomorphae. They are often flanked by strong setae and represent the primitive segmented condition.

TERGOPLEURAL. [L. *tergum*, back; Gr. πλευρον, side]. Referring to the upper and lateral portion of a segment.

TERGORHABDITES. [L. *tergum*, back; Gr. ραβδος, rod]. Plates on the inner dorsal surface of the abdominal wall.

TERGOSTERNAL. [L. *tergum*, back; Gr. σταρνον, chest]. Of the muscles which connect a tergite to its corresponding sternite.

TERGUM / TERGA. [L. *tergum*, back]. In general: the back. The dorsal wall of a body segment.

TERMINAL. [L. *terminus*, end]. Of, or situated at, the end.

TERMINAL APOPHYSIS. [L. *terminus*, end; Gr. αποφυσις, an offshoot]. In the male palpus: a variously shaped sclerite of the apical region of the genital bulb.

TERMINATION STIMULUS. [L. *terminationem*, determining, *stimulus*, goad]. An external or internal stimulus which causes cessation of a behavior, for example, the visual stimulus that a web is complete causes web-building behavior to terminate.

TERNATE. [L. *terni*, three in a group]. Divided into three parts.

TERRESTRIAL. [L. *terra*, earth]. Living on land.

TERRICOLOUS. [L. *terra*, earth; *colere*, to inhabit]. Inhabiting the soil.

TERRITORIALITY. [L. *territorium*, domain]. A form of social system or behavior in which an animal marks out an area or volume and defends it against others of the same species, and usually the same gender; commonly during a mating ritual. Once a territory has been established the animals can usually exist without conflict. A member of a territorial species that lacks a territory is unlikely to breed. This behavior has been found in all major groups.

TERRITORY. [L. *territorium*, domain]. An area or volume marked out and defended by an individual against members of the same species; usually just before and during the mating season. This area is perceived as being able to supply sufficient resources and may be defended by overt defense, display or advertisement.

TERTIARY CONSUMER. [L. *tertius*, third]. A carnivore which eats other carnivores (which are the secondary consumers and eat herbivores which are the primary consumers).

TERTIARY PARASITE. [L. *tertius*, third; Gr. παρασιτος, parasite]. A hyperparasite's parasite.

TERTIARY SEX RATIO. [L. *tertius*, third]. See Sex Ratio.

TESSELLATE. [L. *tessellatus*, mosaic]. Marked or colored in a pattern of squares, or oblong areas. Chess-board-like.

TEST. [L. *testa*, shell]. A shell or hardened outer covering.

TESTATE. [L. *testa*, shell]. Having a shell or 'test'.

TESTES, TESTIS. [L. *testis*, testicle]. The male sperm-producing glands or organs.

TESTICULAR (ORCHITIC). [L. *testicle*, little testis]. Testicle-shaped.

TESTICULAR FEMINIZATION. [L. *testicle*, little testis]. A condition in which an individual male develops as a female and spermatogenesis fails to occur.

TESTICULAR FOLLICLES. [L. *testicle*, little testis]. Those structures which, in the adult, form the tubes composing the testes. In the adult applied also to the tubes forming the testes.

TETHYS (TETHYIAN) SEA. [Gr. Τεθυς, a sea Goddess]. The shallow, tropical sea that existed between the supercontinents of Laurasia (to the north) and Gondwana (south) during the Mesozoic: reaching from what is now Mexico across the Atlantic and Mediterranean to central Asia. The remnants of this ocean are now the Mediterranean, Black Sea, Aral Sea, Lake Baikal (world's deepest lake) and others.

TETRABLEMMIDAE. [Gr. τετρα-, four; βλεμμα, the eye]. A family of armored spiders (infraorder Araneomorphae, superfamily Haplogynae) with a wide southern hemisphere distribution. Some species are cave-dwellers and consequently show typical adaptations, such as loss of eyes and weak sclerotization. Others have only four eyes. There are many extinct genera known from Burmese amber.

TETRACEROUS. [Gr. τετρα-, four; κερας, horn]. Four-horned.

TETRADACTYLE. [Gr. τετρα-, four; δακτυλος, finger]. With four fingers or finger-like processes.

TETRAGNATHIDAE. [Gr. τετρα-, four; γναθος, jaw]. A cosmopolitan family of spiders (infraorder Araneomorphae, superfamily Entelegynae) known as horizontal orb-weavers. Most species spin orb-webs with a small hole in the hub, but some have abandoned web-spinning and hunt at ground level. Some are elongate with long chelicerae, others are of more 'normal' proportions but have large chelicerae which are elongate in males. The males of some species are long-legged. In all the maxillae are longer than broad and the epigynes are simple. In some classifications the genus *Meta* has been placed in its own family, the **Metidae**.

TETRAMEROS. [Gr. τετρα-, four; μερος, part]. Composed of four parts.

TETRANYCHIDAE. [Gr. τετρα-, four; αγχι, close by]. A family of spider mites (infraorder Eleutherengona, superfamily Tetranychoidea) which are plant-parasites and have the chelicerae modified as needle-like stylets with which they pierce the plants and suck out the fluids. They construct protective webs from silk glands which open near the base of the chelicerae.

TETRANYCHOIDEA. [Gr. τετρα-, four; αγχι, close by]. A superfamily of mites (suborder Prostigmata, infraorder Eleutherengona). Families: **Allochaetophoridae, Linotetranidae, Tenuipalpidae, Tetranychidae, Tuckerellidae.**

TETRAPLOID. [Gr. τετραπλη, fourfold]. See Ploidy.

TETRAPNEUMONOUS. [Gr. τετρα-, four; πνευμων, lung]. Of spiders which have four book lungs. See also Dipneumonous.

TETRAPODILI. [Gr. τετρα-, four; πους, foot]. In some classifications: a suborder of minute gall mites which are plant-parasites and have stylet-shaped chelicerae. See Eriophyoidea.

TETRAPTEROUS. [Gr. τετρα-, four; πτερον, wing]. Having four wings or wing-like processes.

TETRASTERNUM. [Gr. τετρα-, four; στερνον, chest]. In ticks and mites: the sternite of the fourth segment of the prosoma or the second segment of the podosoma.

TETRASTICHOUS. [Gr. τετρα-, four; στιχος, row]. Arranged in four rows.

TETRASTIGMATA. [Gr. τετρα-, four; στιγμη, a mark]. See Holothyrida.

TETRATOSTERNUM. [Gr. τετρα-, four; στερνον, chest]. See Jugularia.

TETROPHTHALMI. [Gr. τετρα-, four; οφθαλμος, the eye]. A small suborder of extinct harvestmen or daddy longlegs (subclass Arachnida, order Opiliones) containing two species; *Hastocularis argus* and *Eophalangium sheari*. They had both median and lateral eyes.

THALPOSIS. [Gr. θαλπος, warmth]. The sensation of warmth.

THAMNOPHILOUS. [Gr. θαμνος, shrub; φιλος, loving]. Inhabiting thickets or dense shrubbery.

THANATOSIS. [Gr. θανατος, death]. See Death Feigning. Letisimulation.

THECA. [Gr. θηκη, case]. A structure which serves as a protective covering for an organ or organism.

THECACYST. [Gr. θηκη, case; κυστις, bladder]. The sperm envelope (or spermatophore) formed by the spermatheca.

THECAL. [Gr. θηκη, case]. Surrounded by a protective membrane.

THECAPHORE. [Gr. θηκη; case; -φορα, -carrying]. The structure on which a theca is borne.

THELEPHOROUS. [Gr. θηλη, teat; φορειν, to bear]. Having nipples or nipple-like projections.

THELYBLAST. [Gr. θηλυς, female; βλαστος, bud]. A mature female gamete.

THELYGENIC. [Gr. θηλυς, female; -γενης, producing]. Producing offspring that are mainly or entirely female. See also Arrhenogenic.

THELYPHONIDA. See Uropygi.

THELYPHONOIDEA. [Gr. θηλυφωνος, with a woman's voice]. The monospecific superfamily of the Uropygi *sensu stricto* (subclass Arachnida, order Uropygi) containing the whip scorpions or vinegaroons (vinegarroons or vinegarones). Family: **Thelyphonidae** (syn. **Geralinuridae**). See Uropygi.

THELYTOKY. [Gr. θηλυς, female; τοκος, offspring]. See Parthenogenesis.

THERAPHOSIDAE. [Gr. θηρα, metaph. eager pursuit; φως, light]. The family of bird spiders and monkey spiders (infraorder Mygalomorphae, superfamily Avicularioidea), that are also known (incorrectly) as tarantulas in the USA. Large, hairy, non-social spiders which have claw tufts, four spinnerets, and eight closely grouped eyes. They feed on large insects and occasionally reptiles, amphibians and nestling birds. Most species chew their prey, sometimes dipping them into water. Defensive postures include raising the chelicerae, pedipalps and first walking legs and some species stridulate. The larger forms become mature in 2-3 years but the males only live for a few months while the females may live up to 20 years (in captivity). The north American species live in deep burrows and some Amazonian species are arboreal. None of the American species are dangerous to man, although they have barbed urticating setae on the abdomen. About 1,236 species in 147 genera.

THERAPHOSOIDEA. [Gr. θηρα, metaph. eager pursuit; φως, light]. In a previous classification: a superfamily of spiders (suborder Opisthothelae, infraorder Mygalomorphae) that united the **Paratropididae** and **Theraphosidae**. These families are now separately in the superfamily Avicularioidea.

THERIDIIDAE. [Gr. θηριδιον, little wild animal]. The family of cobweb spiders and comb-footed spiders (infraorder Araneomorphae, superfamily Entelegynae). Medium to small web-making spiders in which there are vertical combs of serrated bristles on the tarsi of the fourth legs which are used to cast threads of silk over prey, although in the smaller species these combs may be reduced or absent. They exhibit a great variety of shape and coloration but in general they are glossy, have large protuberant eyes and most construct tangled three dimensional webs with adhesive threads on the periphery, although some have abandoned web-spinning altogether. Within this family is the black widow spider (*Latrodectus mactans*) whose venom is toxic to mammals.

THERIDIOSOMATIDAE. [Gr. θηριδιον, little wild animal; σωμα, the body]. A family of orb-web spiders (infraorder Araneomorphae, superfamily Entelegynae). A single spine is present on femur I and the claw is lacking on the female palp. Their small orb-web has the radii joined in groups of two or three before meeting at the center. The spider sits at the center, facing away from the web and holding a thread which runs to adjacent vegetation. This thread is pulled taut and the web assumes the shape of an inverted umbrella. When prey is snared the tensing thread is slackened and the prey becomes more entangled.

THERMAESTHESIA. [Gr. θερμη, heat; αισθησις, sense-perception]. Sensitivity to heat stimuli.

THERMOGENESIS. [Gr. θερμη, heat; -γενης, producing]. The production of body heat by oxidation or the action of bacteria.

THERMOLYSIS. [Gr. θερμη, heat; λυσις, setting free]. The loss of body heat.

THERMOPERIODICITY. [Gr. θερμη, heat; περιοδος, period of time]. The response of organisms to regular changes in temperature, either daily or seasonal.

THERMOPHIL. [Gr. θερμη, heat; φιλος, loving]. Thriving at relatively high temperatures.

THERMOPHOBIC. [Gr. θερμη, heat; φοβος, fear]. Of organisms able to live only at relatively low temperatures.

THERMORECEPTORS. [Gr. θερμη, heat; L. *recipere*, to receive]. Receptor cells which are specialized for detecting and signaling temperature changes. Some are in the skin and respond to the external environment, others are located internally and monitor the temperature of internal organs. See also Receptor.

THERMOREGULATION. [Gr. θερμη, heat; LL. *regulare*, to rule]. The maintenance or regulation of body temperature. See Temperature Regulation.

THERMOTAXIS. [Gr. θερμη, heat; ταξις, an arranging]. A locomotor response to a temperature stimulus.

THIGMAESTHESIA. [Gr. θιγημα, touch; αισθησις, sense-perception]. The sense of touch.

THIGMOKINESIS. [Gr. θιγημα, touch; κινησις, motion]. The initiation or inhibition of movement in response to contact stimuli.

THIGMOTACTIC. [Gr. θιγημα, touch; L. *tactilis*, that which can be touched]. Adhesive.

THIGMOTAXIS (STEREOTAXIS). [Gr. θιγημα, touch; ταξις, an arranging]. Movement, or sometimes an inhibition of movement, in response to touch which causes many animals to cling to surfaces with which they come into contact.

THIGMOTROPISM (STEROTROPISM). [Gr. θιγημα, touch; τροπος, turn]. Movement in response to contact with a solid body.

THINOZERCONOIDEA. [Gr. θινος, the beach; Ger. *Zirkon*, high-quality diamond-like gemstones]. A superfamily of mites (suborder Monogynaspida, infraorder Uropodina). Families: **Protodinychidae, Thinozerconidae**.

THOMISIDAE. [Gr. θωμιξω, cord/bind]. The family of crab-spiders (infraorder Araneomorphae, superfamily Entelegynae) in which the legs bear only two claws and the anterior legs are held laterally, not forwards. Somewhat crab-like, broad-bodied spiders with the first two pairs of legs being more robust and longer than the posterior two pairs: they can walk sideways as well as forwards and backwards. The spinnerets are small and inconspicuous and none spin a web: the majority (Misumeninae) sit and wait for prey which they grab with the front pair of legs, other (Philodrominae) are more active hunters. Some species live on bark and all have a potent arthropod venom. There is a great diversity of form and color related to their wide range of habitats and often remarkable capacity for camouflage; e.g. *Misumena vatia* being able to change color to match the yellow or white flowers on which it lies in wait. In some species there is a great disparity in size and markings between the males and females. In *Xysticus* species, the male strokes the female to induce a torpid state and then walks over and around her cephalothorax and flexed legs, trailing silk to bind up her front end prior to mating. In some classifications this family is split into the two families **Thomisidae** (Misumeninae) and **Philodromidae**.

THOMISOIDEA. [Gr. θωμιξω, cord/bind]. In a previous classification, a superfamily of eight-eyed araneomorph spiders (order Araneae, suborder Araneomorphae) that united the families: **Philodromidae, Thomisidae**.

THON'S ORGAN. [*K. Thon*, German Arachnologist]. In the Holothyrida: a gland that opens on the lateral dorsal shield, posterior to the peritreme.

THORACIC. [Gr. θωραξ, breastplate]. Of, or in the region of, the chest.

THORACIC GROOVE. [Gr. θωραξ, breastplate]. A short median groove on the thoracic region of the carapace. It is situated just above the internal attachment of the gastric muscles.

THORACICOABDOMINAL. [Gr. θωραξ, breastplate; L. *abdomen*, belly]. Of the first segment of the abdomen when united with the thorax so as to form part of it.

THORAX. [Gr. θωραξ, breastplate]. In arachnids the head and thorax are fused to form the cephalothorax (prosoma). Otherwise, that part of the cephalothorax behind the head region and separated from it by a shallow groove.

THORN. [OE. *þorn*, sharp point on a stem or branch]. A small thick pointed seta used with stridulatory file to produce sound.

263

THREAT. [OE. þreat, coercion/menace]. A defensive strategy by which an animal communicates its aggression to rivals, or deters potentially dangerous animals without actually coming to blows and thus risking damage which would leave it disadvantaged in the next contest. Threat displays can be exposure of warning colors, body inflation, tail waving, jaw gaping and many species-specific actions.

THUMB-CLAW (PALP THUMB-CLAW COMPLEX). In some Prostigmata: a hypertrophied claw-like seta on the dorsodistal margin of the palptibia. It forms a pincer with the palptarsus.

THYLACOGENS. [Gr. θυλαξ, sac; γενναω, produce]. A general name of various substances produced by parasites which cause reactive hypertrophy of the host's tissue at the site of infection.

THYRSUS. [Gr. θυρσος, the Bacchic wand]. A cluster.

TIARATE, TIARATUS. [Gr. τιαρα, a Persian head-dress]. Turban or tiara-like.

TIBIA. [L. *tibia*, shin]. The segment of the leg between the patella and the basitarsus. The tibia anchors the musculature that controls the tarsi; the muscles controlling the tibia are anchored in the femur. See also Limb.

TIBIAL APOPHYSIS (TA). [L. *tibia*, shin; Gr. αποφυσις, an offshoot]. In male spiders (Araneae): an outgrowth or process (apophysis) on the palpal tibia, most commonly retrolateral, but may occur on other surfaces. See also Retrolateral Tibial Apophysis, Ventral Tibial Apophysis.

TIBIAL SPINE FORMULA. [L. *tibia*, shin; *spina*, thorn]. A formula for the number of dorsal spines (1 or 2) on the tibia of legs I and IV, from front to back, (example 2-2-1-1) and is used in identification of the **Linyphiidae.**

TIBIAL SPUR. [L. *tibia*, shin]. A large spine usually located on the distal end of the tibia.

TIBIALE. [L. *tibia*, shin]. See Tarsus.

TIBIOTARSUS. [L. *tibia*, shin; Gr. ταρσος, sole of foot]. The combined tarsus and tibia.

TIBOVIRUS. [**ti**ck **bo**rne **virus**]. A virus transmitted by ticks, such as Tick-borne encephalitis.

TICKS. [OE. *ticia*, tick]. Any small parasitic arachnids of the families **Ixodidae** (hard ticks) and **Argasidae** (soft ticks) that typical live on the skin of warm blooded animals, feeding on the blood and tissues of their hosts; plus certain other arachnids of the superorders Acariformes, Opilioacariformes, and Parasitiformes. See also See Acari.

TINE. [AS. *tind*, spike]. Any slender, pointed, projecting part.

TIPHOPHILOUS. [Gr. τιφος, pond; φιλος, loving]. Thriving in ponds.

TITANOECIDAE. [Gr. Τιταν, myth. one of the gods; οικια, house]. A family of cribellate spiders (infraorder Araneomorphae, superfamily Entelegynae) in which the calamistrum is on metatarsus IV and comprises a single row of bristles which extends along most of its length. They usually have a retreat under stones, in leaf-litter or on low vegetation in which the female remains with her egg sac; the open-meshed cribellate web extending around the opening.

TITHAEIDAE. [Gr. Τιθαιος, a cavalry officer in Xerxes' army.]. A family of harvestmen or daddy longlegs (suborder Laniatores, superfamily Epedanoidea) from the Indo-Malayan region.

TITANOECOIDEA. [Gr. Τιταν, myth. one of the gods; οικια, house]. In a previous classification, a cosmopolitan superfamily of eight-eyed araneomorph spiders (order Araneae, suborder Araneomorphae) that united the families **Phyxelididae** and **Titanoecidae.**

TM1. A formula to represent the relative position of the trichobothrium along the length of the metatarsus 1, expressed as a decimal fraction. This, plus the presence or absence of a trichobothrium on the forth metatarsus (TmIV), is used in identification.

TOCOSPERMAL. [Gr. τοκος, birth; σπερμα, seed]. Direct transfer of sperm between male and female.

TOCOSPERMIA. [Gr. τοκος, birth; σπερμα, seed]. In the Chelicerata: a sperm transfer system where the spermatophore is deposited directly into the female genital opening. See also Gonopody, Podospermia.

TOCOSTOME, TOKOSTOME. [Gr. τοκος, birth; στομα, mouth]. In ticks and mites: the female genital aperture.

TOKOSTOME. [Gr. τοκος, offspring; στομα, mouth]. In mites: the female genital aperture.

TOMENTOSE. [L. tomentum, the stuffing in a pillow]. Woolly. Covered with a fine mesh of hairs.

TONG-LIKE. [OE. tange, tongs/pincers/forceps]. Of chelicerae that resemble opposed hooks, usually edentate or at most with small teeth.

TONIC IMMOBILITY. [Gr. τονος, tension]. See Death Feigning.

TOOTH. [AS. toth, tooth]. Any acute angulation. A short pointed process from an appendage or margin. A spine on the chelicerae which assists in feeding. A small outgrowth on the paired claws of the leg in many spiders.

TOPOCHEMICAL. [Gr. τοπος, place; χημεια, transmutation]. Of the perception of odors in relation to a track or place.

TOPODEME. [Gr. τοπος, place; δεμος, people]. A deme occupying a particular geographical region.

TOPOGAMODEME. [Gr. τοπος, place; γαμος, marriage; δεμος, people]. Collectively, the individuals which occupy a precise locality and which form a natural breeding unit.

TOPOMORPH. [Gr. τοπος, place; μορφη, form]. An environmental variant. A geographic form, variety or subspecies.

TOPOTAXIS. [Gr. τοπος, place; ταξις, an arranging]. Orientation followed by movement either towards or away from the stimulus.

TOROSE. [L. torus, a swelling]. Having fleshy swellings.

TORPID. [L. torpidus, benumbed]. Dormant.

TORQUEATE (TORQUATE). [L. torquatus, wearing a metal collar or neck chain]. Having a ring or collar.

TORQUES. [L. torques, necklace]. Any necklace-like arrangement of scales, etc.

TORTICONE. [L. torquere, to twist; conus, cone]. A turreted, spirally twisted shell.

TORTILIS. [L. tortilis, twisted]. Twisted.

TORTOISE MITE. Any member of the Uropodoidea (Uropodina) with recesses into which the head and legs (pedofossae) can be tucked. See also Turtle Mite.

TORTUOSE. [L. torquere, to twist]. Twisting. Winding. Irregularly curved.

TORULOSE, TORTULOSEUS. [L. torulus, little bulge]. Having knoblike swellings. Moniliform.

TOTIDEM. [L. totidem, as many]. In the all parts: entirely.

TOXICOPHOROUS, TOXIFEROUS. [Gr. τοξικον, poison; -φορα, -carrying]. Holding or carrying poison.

TOXIGNATHS. [Gr. τοξικον, poison; γναθος, jaw]. In general: poison-bearing jaws.

TOXIN. [Gr. τοξικον, poison]. Any poison derived from a plant or animal, usually proteinaceous.

TOXOPIDAE. [Gr. τοξικον, poison; -οψ, appearance]. A small family of spiders (infraorder Araneomorphae, superfamily Entelegynae). Previously a subfamily of the **Desidae**.

TRACHEA. [LL. trachia, windpipe]. In arachnids: the respiratory tubes which open via spiracles arranged along the sides of the body and ramify throughout the body, bringing air directly to the tissues; the finest branches being the tracheoles.

TRACHEAL MITE. See Honeybee Tracheal Mite.

TRACHEAL SPIRACLE. [LL. *trachia*, windpipe; L. *spiraculum*, air hole]. In spiders: one of the two forms of respiratory organ (see also Book Lungs). They are located just anterior to the spinnerets and the faster moving species have two pairs.

TRACHEATE. [LL. *trachia*, windpipe]. Having trachea. Applied to all those animals which take in oxygen by a system of tracheal tubes.

TRACHEATION. [LL. *trachia*, windpipe]. The arrangement or system of distribution of trachea.

TRACHELATE. [Gr. τραχηλος, neck]. Narrowed like a neck.

TRACHELIDAE. [Gr. τραχηλος, gristle about the neck]. A family of spiders (infraorder Araneomorphae, superfamily Entelegynae) known as 'ground sac spiders'. They have a characteristic red cephalothorax and a yellow/tan abdomen. They bear inward-pointing chelicerae; and thus are thought to be more recently evolved.

TRACHEOBLAST. [L. *trachia*, windpipe; Gr. βλαστος, bud]. Cells which are derived from the epidermal cells lining the trachea, and that give rise to the tracheoles.

TRACHEOLES. [LL. *trachia*, windpipe]. The minute branching tubes that lead from the trachea to all parts of the body.

TRACT. [L. *tractus*, region]. A system when considered as a whole, e.g. the digestive tract. A band or bundle of nerve fibers.

TRÄGÅRDH'S ORGAN (ONCOPHYSIS). [*I. Trägårdh*; Swedish Arachnologist]. A flat, finger-like paraxial projection on the chelicerae of some oribatid mites (Oribatida).

TRAIL PHEROMONE. [Gr. φερειν, to bear; hor*mone* (Gr. ορμαω, rouse)]. A chemical laid down as a trail by one individual and followed by another of the same species.

TRAIT. [L. *tractus*, drawing]. Any character or property of an organism.

TRAMP SPECIES. Species that have been spread inadvertently by human commerce.

TRANSAD. [L. *trans*, across; *ad*, to]. A species, or pair of closely related species, that have become separated by an environmental barrier. See also Vicariation.

TRANSCOXA. [L. *trans*, across; coxa, hip]. In some Chelicerata: a term used instead of coxa. See Limb

TRANSCURRENT. [L. *trans*, across; *currens*, running]. Extending transversely.

TRANSECT. [L. *trans*, across; *secare*, to cut]. In ecology: a line marked within an area to provide a means of measuring and representing graphically the distribution of organisms, especially when arranged in a linear sequence.

TRANSECTION. [L. *trans*, across; *secare*, to cut]. A transverse section. A cut across at right angles to the body.

TRANSIENT POLYMORPHISM. [L. *transire*, to pass by; Gr. πολυμορφος, multiform]. The co-existence of two or more distinct morphological types in the same breeding population for a short period. One type ultimately replacing the other(s).

TRANSLAMELLA. [L. *trans*, across; *lamella*, thin plate]. In some oribatid mites: a transverse ridge joining the lamellae on the prodorsum.

TRANSLUCENT. [L. *translucere*, to shine through]. Semi-transparent. Allowing the passage of light but not of images.

TRANSLUCID. [L. *translucere*, to shine through]. Clear. Transparent enough to be seen through.

TRANSMEDIAN. [L. *trans*, across; *medius*, middle]. Of, or crossing the middle plane.

TRANS-STADIAL. [L. *trans*, across; *stadium*, stage]. The retention of microorganisms from one stage of the host to the next. This may be part or all of the host's life cycle.

TRANSVERSE. [L. *transversare*, to cross/throw across]. Crossing at right angles to the longitudinal axis.

TRANSVERSE PLANE. [L. *transversare*, to cross/throw across]. A plane or section perpendicular to the longitudinal axis.

TRANSVERSE STRIATION. [L. *transversare*, to cross/throw across; *stria*, furrow]. A circular groove or arc whose plane is perpendicular to the longitudinal axis.

TRAPDOOR SPIDERS. Generally, mainly nocturnal spiders which live in a silk-lined tube dug into the ground, and provided with a with a hinged trapdoor made of soil, vegetation and silk. They attack with great rapidity and drag passing insects into their lair. Most species have three tarsal claws, and a rastellum on the chelicerae. See **Actinopodidae, Antrodiaetidae, Barychelidae, Ctenizidae, Cyrtaucheniidae, Migidae.**

TRAPEZIFORM. [Gr. τραπεζιον, small table; L. *forma*, shape]. Trapezium-shaped (i.e. a four-sided structure with at least one pair of parallel sides).

TRAVUNIIDAE. [L. *Travunia*, city of Trabinje, in Bosnia & Herzegovina]. A family of harvestmen or daddy longlegs (suborder Laniatores, superfamily Travunioidea) from Europe, Japan and the United States. They have slender, unarmed legs and robust, strongly spined pedipalps.

TRAVUNIOIDEA. [L. *Travunia*, city of Trabinje, in Bosnia & Herzegovina]. A superfamily of harvestmen (order Opiliones, suborder Laniatores). Families: **Nippononychidae, Paranonychidae, Travuniidae** (syn **Cladonychiidae, Pentanychidae**).

TRENCHANT. [OF. *trenchier*, to cut]. Having a sharp edge.

TRIAD. [Gr. τρια, three]. An arrangement of three; a trinity. A group of three contiguous eyes.

TRIAENONYCHIDAE. [Gr. τριαινα, trident; ονυξ, talon]. A large family of mainly small harvestmen or daddy longlegs (suborder Laniatores, superfamily Triaenonychoidea) in which the armed pedipalps are large, and much stronger than the (almost always) short legs.

TRIAENONYCHOIDEA. [Gr. τριαινα, trident; ονυξ, talon]. A superfamily of harvestmen (order Opiliones, suborder Laniatores). Families: **Synthetonychidae, Triaenonychidae.**

TRIARTICULATE. [L. *tres*, three; *articulus*, joint]. Three-jointed.

TRIAXIAL SYMMETRY. [Gr. τρια, three;. L. *axis*, axis]. A type of symmetry with three axes, known as sagittal, longitudinal, and transverse.

TRIBE. [L. *tribus*, tribe]. In classification: a subdivision of a family, below the level of subfamily. See also Nomenclature.

TRICARINATE. [L. *tres*, three; *carina*, keel]. With three keels or carinae.

TRICHOBOTHRIOTAXY. [Gr. τριχο-, hair; βοθρος, pit; ταξις an arrangement]. The location and arrangement of the trichobothria, particularly in relation to classification.

TRICHOBOTHRIUM. [Gr. τριχο-, hair; βοθρος, pit]. In some spiders: a long, fine, sensory hair or setula which is inserted into a flexible membrane. It detects air vibration and currents. See also Bothridial Sensillum.

TRICHOCERCOUS (erron. Trichocerous). [Gr. τριχο-, hair; κερκος, the tail]. Spiny-tailed.

TRICHOGEN. [Gr. τριχο-, hair; -γενης, producing]. A seta-producing cell.

TRICHOID. [Gr. τριχο-, hair; ειδος, form]. Hair-like. Of a type of sensilla.

TRICHOIDY. [Gr. τριχη, in three parts; ειδος, form]. Having a body divided into three regions, as in some oribatids, by a protero-hysterosomatic and a podo-opisthosomatic articulation. See also Dichoidy, Holoid, Ptychoidy.

TRICHOMES. [Gr. τριχοομαι, to be furnished with hair]. The modified tufts of hair that assist in the dispersion of pheromones.

TRICHOPORE (NEUROPORE). [Gr. τριχο-, hair; πορος, channel]. An opening for an emerging hair or bristle; as in spiders.

TRICHOTOMOUS. [Gr. τριχη, in three parts; τομη, a cutting]. Divided into three parts; three-forked.

TRICHROIC (TRICHROISM). [Gr. τρια, three; χρως, color]. Having three different colors when viewed from three different directions.

TRICHROMATIC. [Gr. τρια, three; χρωμα, color]. Of, or able to perceive, the three primary colors.

TRICOMMATIDAE. [Gr. τρια, three; κομματος, stamp or impression of a coin]. A family of short-legged harvestmen or daddy longlegs (suborder Laniatores, superfamily Gonyleptoidea) from southern Brazil and Paraguay.

TRICOSTATE. [Gr. τρια, three; L. *costa*, rib]. Having three ribs or ridges.

TRICUSPID, TRICUSPIDATE. [Gr. τρια, three; L. *cuspis*, a point]. Divided into three cusps or points.

TRIDACTYL. [Gr. τρια, three; δακτυλος, finger]. Of an appendage, ambulacrum, or claw with three ungues. See also Bidactyl, Heterodactyl, Homodactyl, Monodactyl.

TRIDENCHTHONIIDAE. [Gr. τρι- ; L. *dens*, tooth; Gr. χθονιος, beneath the earth]. A family of false scorpions (suborder Heterosphyronida, superfamily Chthonioidea). All tridenchthoniid nymphs bear three blades on the galea (the horn-like processes on the moveable part of the chelicerae).

TRIDENT (TRIDENTATE. [L. *tridentem*, three-pronged / three-toothed]. Having three teeth. Three-pronged.

TRIFID. [L. *trifidus*, three-forked]. Divided into three lobes. Three-pronged.

TRIFURCATE. [L. *trifurcatus*, three-forked]. Having three forks or branches.

TRIGENETIC. [Gr. τρια, three; γενεσις, origin]. Requiring three different hosts during the course of a life cycle.

TRIGONAL. [Gr. τρια, three; γωνια, an angle]. Of, or in the form of, a triangle.

TRIGONATE. [Gr. τρια, three; γωνια, an angle]. Three-cornered: approximately triangular.

TRIGONEUTISM. [Gr. τρια, three; γονος, offspring]. The production of three broods in one season.

TRIGONOUS. [Gr. τριγωνον, triangle]. Triangular in cross section.

TRIGYNASPIDA. [Gr. τρια, three; γυνη, woman]. A suborder of mites (superorder Parasitiformes, order Mesostigmata) Infraorders: Antennophorina, Cercomegistina.

TRILABIATE. [L. *tri-*, three; labium, lip]. Having three lips.

TRILATERAL. [L. *tri-*, three; *latus*, side]. Three-sided.

TRILOBATE. [Gr. τρια, three; λοβος, lobe]. Having three lobes.

TRILOCULAR. [L. *tri-*, three; *loculus*, small place]. With three cavities or cells.

TRIMEROUS. [Gr. τρια, three; μερος, part]. Having three parts.

TRIMORPHIC. [Gr. τρια, three; μορφη, form]. Having three different forms.

TRINOMIAL. [Gr. τρια, three; L. *nomen*, name]. Consisting of three terms, as for example in the scientific naming of subspecies, e.g. the pseudoscorpion *Acanthocreagris granulata granulata*, *Acanthocreagris granulata parva* (**Neobisiidae**). See Nomenclature.

TRIONYCHA. [Gr. τρια, three; ονυξ, a claw]. A grouping of spiders in which there are three claws on the end of the tarsus. Members of this group are usually web-builders, the extra claw being used for holding silk threads. See also Dionycha, Scopula.

TRIPARTITE. [L. *tri-*, three; *partitus*, divided]. Divided into three parts, divisions or segments.

TRIPECTINATE. [L. *tri-*, three; *pecten*, comb]. Having three rows of comb-like branches.

TRIPLOID. [Gr. τριπλοος, threefold]. See Ploidy.

TRIPLOSTICHOUS. [Gr. τριπλοος, threefold; στιχος, row]. Arranged in three rows; as in the eyes of larval scorpions which have preretinal, retinal and postretinal layers.

TRIQUETRAL, TRIQUETROUS. [L. *triquetrus*, three sided]. Having three angles or arms. Triangular in section.

TRISTICHOUS. [Gr. τρια, three; στιχος, row]. Arranged in three vertical rows.

TRITONYMPH. [Gr. τριτος, third; νυμφη, chrysalis]. In ticks and mites: the developmental stage following the deutonymph stage.

TRITORAL. [L. *tritor*, grinder]. Adapted for grinding.

TRITOSTERNAL BASE. [Gr. τριτος, third; στερνον, chest]. The columnar basal part of the tritosternum. It may be expanded and rectangular or otherwise altered.

TRITOSTERNUM. [Gr. τριτος, third; στερνον, chest]. In ticks and mites: a sternite of the third segment of the prosoma or the first segment of the podosoma.

TRIUNDULATE. [L. *tres*, three; LL. *undulatus*, wavy]. Having three waves or undulations.

TRIVIAL NAME. [L. *trivialis*, trivial]. The name of a taxon in any language other than the language of zoological nomenclature. A popular name.

TRIVITTATE. [L. *vitta*, band / ribbon]. Having three stripes or vitta.

TRIVOLTINE. [L. *tres*, three; It. *volta*, time]. Having three broods in one year. See also Voltine.

TRIZETOIDEA. [Gr. τρια, three; ζητες seeking]. A superfamily of mites (suborder Oribatida, infraorder Brachypylina - section Pycnonoticae). Families: **Cuneoppiidae, Rhynchoribatidae, Suctobelbidae, Trizetidae.**

TROCHAL. [Gr. τροχος, wheel]. Wheel-shaped.

TROCHANTER. [Gr. τροχαντηρ, runner]. A small segment of the leg between the coxa and the femur. See also Limb.

TROCHANTERELLUS. [Gr. τροχαντηρ, runner; L. *-ellus*, dim. suf.]. See Apophysis.

TROCHANTERIIDAE. [Gr. τροχαντηρ, runner]. A small family of secretive spiders (infraorder Araneomorphae, superfamily Entelegynae) that live underneath tree bark or rocks. The trochanter in spiders is the second segment of the leg or palp. between the coxa and the femur. Some **Trochanteriidae** have a greatly elongated trochanter IV, which is at least 1.5 times longer than trochanter III, an unusual character.

TROCHANTIN(E) (ROTULE). [Gr. τροχαντηρ, runner]. The basal part of the trochanter when it is two-jointed.

TROCHATE. [Gr. τροχος, wheel]. Wheel-shaped. Having a wheel-like structure.

TROCHLEA. [Gr. τροχιλια, pulley]. A pulley-like structure.

TROCHLEARIS. [Gr. τροχιλια, pulley]. Pulley-shaped. Like a cylinder contracted medially.

TROCHOID. [Gr. τροχοειδης, wheel-like]. Wheel-shaped. Able to rotate, such as a pivot joint.

TROCHOMETRIDIOIDEA. [Gr. τροχος, wheel; μητριδιος fruitful; -ιδιον, dim. suf.]. A superfamily of mites (suborder Prostigmata, infraorder Eleutherengona). Families: **Athyreacaridae, Trochometridiidae.**

TROCHUS. [Gr. τροχος, wheel]. The part of an articulated body inserted between the joints.

TROGLOBIONT. [Gr. τρωγλη, hole; βιωναι, to live]. Any organism that lives only in caves.

TROGLODYTIC. [Gr. τρωγλοδυτης, one who creeps into holes]. Living underground only.

TROGLOMORPHIC. [Gr. τρωγλη, hole; μοργη, form]. Of animals that live in caves and consequently have reduced pigmentation and often lack eyes.

TROGLOPHILE. [Gr. τρωγλη, hole; φιλος, loving]. An animal frequently found in caves but not confined to them.

TROGLORAPTORIDAE. [Gr. τρωγλοδυτης, one who creeps into holes; L. *raptoris*, a plunderer]. A small monospecific family of large spiders (infraorder Araneomorphae, superfamily Haplogynae) from deep inside caves in Oregon (USA). The body length is 7-10 mm but with outstretched legs they can reach up to 7.6 cm. These spiders are unique in having flexible toothed hook-like claws on the tarsus.

TROGLOSIRONIDAE. [Gr. τρωγλοδυτης, one who creeps into holes + Sironidae]. A small family of eyeless harvestmen (suborder Cyphophthalmi, infraorder Sternophthalmi) exclusively from the leaf litter on the island of New Caledonia.

TROGLOTAYOSICIDAE. [Gr. τρωγλοδυτης, one who creeps into holes; Los *Tayos* region of Ecuador; Gr. -ισκος, dim. suf.]. A small family of scorpions (order Scorpiones, superfamily Chactoidea) that are either cavernicolous or live just outside caves. All have a loss or reduction of eyes, depigmentation and appendage attenuation. The taxonomy is in a state of flux as they were previously in the **Chactidae**, then in the **Superstitioniidae**.

TROGLOXENE. [Gr. τρωγλη, hole; ξενος, guest]. An animal occasionally found in caves.

TROGULIDAE. [Gr. τρωγειν, gnawing]. A small family of harvestmen (suborder Dyspnoi, superfamily Troguloidea) from western and southern Europe, western North Africa and the Levant, the Caucasus and northern Iran. *Trogulus tricarinatus*, a predator of terrestrial snails (Gastropoda).

TROGULOIDEA. [Gr. τρωγειν, gnawing]. A superfamily of harvestmen (order Opiliones, suborder Dyspnoi). Families: **Dicranolasmatidae, †Eotrogulidae, Nemastomatidae, †Nemastomoididae, Nipponopsalididae, Trogulidae.**

TROMBICULIDAE. [NL. *trombid*, a little timid one; -*culus*, -little]. A family of ticks (infraorder Anystina, superfamily Trombiculoidea) known as harvest mites, chiggers or red-bugs, in which only the larval stage is parasitic. They attach to the skin and inject a mixture of digestive enzymes which cause the cellular contents to breakdown. The skin of the host hardens to form a tube (stylostome) through which the mite engorges. *Leptotrombidium* larvae are vectors of *Rickettsia tsutsugamushi*, which causes scrub typhus in humans. This family includes the giant velvet (or desert) mite (*Dinothrombium*).

TROMBICULOIDEA. [NL. *trombid*, a little timid one; -*culus*, -little]. A superfamily of mites (suborder Prostigmata, infraorder Anystina). Families: **Audyanidae, Johnstonianidae, Leeuwenhoekiidae, Neotrombidiidae, Trombellidae, Trombiculidae, (?Vatacaridae), Walchiidae.**

TROMBIDIFORMES. [NL. *trombid*, a little timid one; L. *forma*, shape]. An order of mites (subclass Arachnida, superorder Acariformes) that contains many plant parasite species, although many species are also predators, fungivores and animal parasites. Some of the most conspicuous species of free-living mites are the relatively large and bright red velvet mites (**Trombidiidae**). A recent classification describes 151 families and around 25,821 species in 2,235 genera. Suborders: Prostigmata, Sphaerolichida.

TROMBIDIIDAE. [NL. *trombid*, a little timid one]. The cosmopolitan family of velvet mites or chiggers (infraorder Anystina, superfamily Trombidioidea). Predatory mites that feed on spider mites, thrips, and whiteflies. Most are fairly generalist feeders but some specialize on groups of pests or seek prey in certain environments.

TROMBIDIINA. [NL. *trombid*, a little timid one; L. -*ina*, dim.suf.]. In a previous classification: a clade (or subcohort) of short-legged velvet mites and water mites (suborder Prostigmata, infraorder Anystina) that united the terrestrial superfamilies Allotanaupodoidea, Amphotrombioidea, Chyzerioidea, Tanaupodoidea, Trombiculoidea, Trombidioidea; and the aquatic superfamilies Arrenuroidea, Eylaoidea, Hydrachnoidea, Hydrovolzioidea, Hydryphantoidea, Hygrobatoidea, Lebertioidea, Sperchontoidea, Stygothrombioidea

TROMBIDIOIDEA. [NL. *trombid*, a little timid one; Gr. ειδος, form]. A superfamily of ticks (suborder Prostigmata, infraorder Anystina). Families: **Achaemenothrombiidae, Microtrombidiidae** (syn. **Eutrombidiidae**), **Neothrombiidae, Trombidiidae.**

TROMBIDIOSIS. [Trombiculidae + Gr. -οσις, suf. of condition]. Dermatitis caused by infestation by larval trombiculoid mites (**Trombiculidae**); also called scrub-itch. See Chigger.

270

TROPEIC. [Gr. τροπις, keel]. Resembling a keel. Cariniform.

TROPHAGONES. [Gr. τροφη, nourishment; αγω, lead]. Specific substances produced by live parasites whose action on the host results in the carriage of food substances towards the parasite's habitat. See also Xenagones.

TROPHIC. [Gr. τροφη, nourishment]. 1. Of, or connected with nutrition. 2. Of hormones that influence the activity of the endocrine glands and growth.

TROPHOTAXIS. [Gr. τροφη, nourishment; ταξις, an arranging]. Response to stimulation by something which may serve as food.

TROPIC. [Gr. τροπικος, pert. turn]. Of movement in response to stimulation.

TROPICAL FOWL MITE. *Ornithonyssus bursa*, **Macronyssidae**: Mesostigmata.

TROPICAL RAT MITE. *Ornithonyssus bacoti*, **Macronyssidae**: Mesostigmata.

TROPICOPOLITAN. [Gr. τροπικος, pert. turn; πολιτης, citizen]. Of an organism which is widely distributed in tropical regions.

-TROPISM. [Gr. τροπη, turn]. Suffix meaning 'turn'. Of the movement or orientation of an organism in response to a stimulus.

TROPOPARASITE. [Gr. τροπος, guise; παρασιτος, parasite]. An organism which lives for only part of its life as a parasite.

TROPOPHILOUS. [Gr. τροπος, turn; φιλος, loving]. Adapted to seasonal changes and thus tolerating alternating periods of cold and warmth or moisture and dryness.

TROPOTAXIS. [Gr. τροπος, turn; ταξις, an arranging]. A movement in which an animal orients itself in relation to a source of stimulation by simultaneously comparing the amount of stimulation received on either side by symmetrically placed sense organs. E.g. locating the source of a sound.

TRUNCATE. [L. *truncatus*, cut off]. Ending abruptly, as if cut off.

TRUNK. [Fr. *tronc*, from L. *truncus*, stem of a tree]. 1. The body exclusive of the head and limbs. 2. The main stem of a vessel or nerve.

TUBERCULATE. [L. *tuberculum*, small hump]. Having tubercles.

TUBERCULE. [L. *tuberculum*, small hump]. Any small, rounded prominence.

TUBERCULOSE. [L. *tuberculum*, small hump]. Having many tubercles.

TUBERCULUM. [L. *tuberculum*, small hump]. Any small, rounded protuberance or swelling.

TUBERIFEROUS. [L. *tuberculum*, small hump; *ferre*, to bear]. Bearing tubercles.

TUBE TRACHEAE. [L. *tubus*, pipe; LL. *trachia*, windpipe]. In the Opiliones, Solifugae and most spiders: the tube-like tracheae. They are usually unbranched ectodermal invaginations. See also Sieve Tracheae.

TUBICOLOUS. [L. *tubus*, tube; *colere*, to inhabit]. Inhabiting tubes.

TUBIFACIENT. [L. *tubus*, tube; *faciens*, making]. Tube-making.

TUBULE. [L. *tubulus*, little tube]. A minute tube.

TUBULUS ANNULATUS. [L. *tubulus*, little tube; L. *annulatus*, furnished with a ring]. In those mesostigmatans with a laelapid-type sperm access system: the long tube running from the base of the sacculus vestibulus to the ramus sacculus.

TUCKERELLIDAE. [*Richard William Ethelbert Tucker*, South African Arachnologist; L. *-ella*, dim.suf.]. The monospecific family (infraorder Eleutherengona, superfamily Tetranychoidea) of the peacock mite. They bear feather-like (or leaf-like) setae, and long hair-like caudal setae that may be used as defensive whips. They are a significant herbivorous pest in the tropics.

TULLGREN FUNNEL. [*H. Tullgren*, the inventor]. A device for collecting small invertebrates from dry soil samples. The sample is placed in a container with a base made from gauze with a mesh designed to hold the soil particles but permit the small animals to pass. The container is placed over a funnel, with a light above. Over time the heat from the light drives the animals away from the top of the sample through the gauze sheet and into the funnel, from where they are collected.

TUMESCENCE. [L. *tumescere*, to swell]. A swelling.

TUMID. [L. *tumere*, to swell]. Swollen. Enlarged. Abnormally distended.

TUNDRA. [Rus. *tundra*, arctic hill]. A treeless region with permanently frozen subsoil.

TUNIC. [L. *tunica*, a garment]. An investing membrane.

TUNICA. [L. *tunica*, a garment]. A covering or enveloping membrane or tissue.

TUNICA ADVENTITIA. [L. *tunica*, a garment; *adventitius*, extraordinary]. The outermost fibro-elastic layer of various tubular organs.

TUNICA INTIMA. [L. *tunica*, a garment; *intimus*, innermost]. An inner lining or membrane. The inner layer of the silk glands.

TUNICA PROPRIA. [L. *tunica*, a garment; *proprius*, one's own]. A layer of epithelial cells and connective tissue lining the interior of the hind gut. The outer layer of the silk glands. Any covering or investing membrane.

TUNICARY. [L. *tunica*, a garment]. Pertaining to a covering membrane or a tunic.

TURBINATE. [L. *turbo*, whirl]. Shaped like a top.

TURGID. [L. *turgidus*, swollen]. Swollen. Distended.

TURRETED. [L. *turris*, a tower]. Tower-shaped.

TURRITUS. [L. *turritus*, tower-shaped]. Towering. Of a surface rising cone-like.

TURTLE MITE. Any member of the family **Scutacaridae** (Eleutherengona). See also Tortoise Mite.

TUTAMEN/TUTAMINA. [L. *tutamen*, protection]. A means of protection.

TUTORIUM (TUTORIA). [L. *tutor*, protector]. In oribatid mites: a ridge on the lateral prodorsum, ventral and more or less parallel to the lamella and which offers protection for legs I when retracted.

TWITCH. [OE. *twiccian*, to pluck]. The very brief contraction of a muscle under the influence of a single short stimulus.

TYCHOPARTHENOGENESIS. [Gr. τυχη, chance; παρθενος, virgin; γενεσις, birth]. Parthenogenesis which occurs in species which are normally sexually reproducing. See Parthenogenesis.

TYCHOPOTAMIC. [Gr. τυχη, chance; ποταμος, river]. Thriving only in still backwaters.

TYDEOIDEA. [Gr. Τυδυες, a Greek hero]. A superfamily of mites (suborder Prostigmata, infraorder Eupodina). Families: **Ereynetidae, Iolinidae, Triophtydeidae, Tydeidae.**

TYLOSIS. [Gr. τυλος, a knot/callus]. A hardening or thickening. A callous.

TYMPANOID. [Gr. τυμπανον, drum; ειδος, form]. Shaped like a flat drum.

TYNDALL COLORS OR SCATTERING. [*John Tyndall*; Irish Scientist]. The color that results from the interference of light reflected from granules and illuminating an absorbing layer of dark pigment beneath a more or less transparent cuticle. This structure produces blue, green or white, depending upon the size of granules.

TYPHLOCHACTIDAE. [Gr. τυφλος, blind' + Chactidae]. A small family of troglomorphic scorpions (order Scorpiones, superfamily Chactoidea) that is endemic to eastern Mexico. They were previously in the **Superstitioniidae.**

TYPHLOSOLE. [Gr. τυφλος, blind; σωλην, a channel]. A longitudinal infolding of the dorsal intestinal wall into the intestinal lumen.

TYPOSTASIS. [Gr. τυπος, pattern; στασις, standing]. A static phase in evolution.

U

UBIQUITOUS. [Mod.L. *ubiquitas*, everywhere]. Having a world-wide distribution.

UDUBIDAE (incl. part **ZOROCRATIDAE**). [deriv.uncert.]. A small family of spiders (infraorder Araneomorphae, superfamily Entelegynae) from central Africa and Madagascar.

ULIGINOUS. [L. *uliginosus*, wetness]. Inhabiting swampy or muddy environments.

ULOBORIDAE. [Gr. ουλος, woolly; βορος, devouring/greedy]. A family of cribellate spiders (infraorder Araneomorphae, superfamily Entelegynae) known as hackled orb weavers. Uniquely, venom glands are lacking. To immobilize prey they rely entirely on their cribellate (hackled) silk (a lace-like composite) and a very elaborate wrapping process.

ULOBOROIDEA. [Gr. ουλος, woolly; βορος, devouring/greedy]. In a previous classification, a superfamily of eight-eyed, cribellate, araneomorph spiders (order Araneae, suborder Araneomorphae) that united the families **Deinopidae** and **Uloboridae**.

ULOID. [Gr. ουλη, scar, ειδος, form]. Resembling a scar.

ULOTRICHOUS. [Gr. ουλος, woolly; θριξ, hair]. Having woolly or curly hair.

ULTRAMARINE. [Sp. *ultramarino*, from beyond the sea]. An intense deep blue.

UMBEL. [L. *umbella*, a sunshade]. An arrangement in which a number of processes, more-or-less equal in length, radiate from a common center.

UMBELLIFORM. [L. *umbella*, sunshade; *forma*, shape]. Shaped like an umbel.

UMBILICATED. [L. *umbilicus*, navel]. Having a central depression; navel-like.

UMBILICUS, UMBILICI. [L. *umbilicus*, navel]. A navel, or navel-like depression. A basal depression.

UMBO, UMBONE. [L. *umbo*, shield boss]. Any convex protuberance like the boss of a shield.

UMBONATE. [L. *umbo*, shield boss]. Umbo-like.

UMBRACULATE, UMBRACULIFEROUS. [L. *umbraculum*, sunshade]. Bearing an umbrella-like structure or organ.

UMBRACULUM. [L. *umbraculum*, sunshade]. In general: any umbrella-like structure.

UMBRATICOLOUS. [L. *umbraculum*, sunshade; *colere*, to inhabit]. Living in shaded habitats.

UMBRELLA ORGAN. See Sensillum Campaniformium.

UMBROPHILIC. [L. *umbra*, a shade; Gr. φιλος, loving]. Thriving in shaded habitats.

UMBROSA. [L. *umbrosa*, shady/shadowy]. Shaded or clouded.

UNARMED. Without spurs, spines or armature of any kind.

UNARTICULATE. [AS. *un*, not; L. *articulosus*, jointed]. Not jointed nor segmented.

UNCATE. [L. *uncus*, hook]. Hooked. Hamate.

UNCIFEROUS. [L. *uncus*; hook; *ferre*, to carry]. Bearing hooks or hook-like projections.

UNCIFORM. [L. *uncus*; hook; *forma*, shape]. Hook- or barbed-shaped.

UNCINATE, UNCINNATE. [L. *uncinatus*; furnished with a hook]. Hook-like. Hooked at the end.

UNCINUS. [L. *uncinus*; hook]. Any small hooked or hook-like structure.

UNCONDITIONED REFLEX. An inborn reflex, i.e. one that is not learnt or acquired.

UNDATE, UNDULATE. [L. *unda*, undulate]. Wavy, undulating.

UNDIFFERENTIATED. [AS. *un*, not; L. *differe*, to differ]. In immature form. Still embryonic.

UNDOSE. [L. *undosus*, billowy]. Having undulating and more-or-less parallel depressions which resemble ripple marks and run into one another.

UNDULATED. [L. *undulatus*, wavy]. Obtusely waved in segments of circles.

UNDULORIBATOIDEA (EREMAEOZETOIDEA). [L. *undulatus*, wavy; Gr. ορεοβατες, mountain-ranging]. A superfamily of mites (suborder Oribatida, infraorder Brachypylina - section Poronoticae). Families: **Eremaeozetidae** (syn. **Idiozetidae**), **Unduloribatidae**.

UNGUAL. [L. *unguis*, claw]. Of the ungues or claws.

UNGUICULATE. [L. *unguiculi*, lesser nail/claw]. Armed with a hook, nail or claw.

UNGUICULUS, UNGUICULI. [L. *unguiculi*, lesser nail/claw]. A small terminal claw or nail-like process.

UNGUIFER. [L. *unguis*, nail; *ferre*, to bear]. A median process of the last tarsomere with which the claws articulate.

UNGUIFLEXOR. [L. *unguis*, claw; *flectere*, to bend]. The muscles responsible for moving or extending the ungues.

UNGUIFORM. [L. *unguis*, claw; *forma*, shape]. Shaped like a claw.

UNGUINALS (u). [L. *unguis*, nail]. In acariform mites: the most distal, ventral pair of setae at the base of the ambulacrum on the tarsi.

UNGUIS, UNGULA. [L. *unguis*, nail]. A nail or claw. In arachnids: the crochet of the fang of the chelicerae.

UNGUITRACTOR. [L. *unguis*, nail; *tractus*, pull]. A median plate for attachment of the retractor or flexor muscles of the claw.

UNGUITRACTOR TENDON. [L. *unguis*, nail; *tractus*, pull]. The tendon that attaches the unguitractor to the pretarsal depressor muscle.

UNGULA. See Unguis.

UNI-. [L. *unus*, alone/a single]. One, a combining form.

UNIAURICULATE. [L. *unus*, one; *auricula*, outer ear]. Having a single ear-like process.

UNIAXIAL. [L. *unus*, one; *axis*, axis]. Movement in only one plane.

UNICAMERATE, UNICAMERAL. [L. *unus*, one; *camera*, vault]. One-chambered.

UNICAPSULAR. [L. *unus*, one; *capsula*, little box]. Having a single capsule.

UNICARINATE. [L. *unus*, one; *carina*, keel]. Having a single ridge or keel.

UNICOLOUR (MONOCHROMATIC). [L. *unicolour*, of one color]. Having only one color, or being the same color throughout.

UNICORNOUS. [L. *unus*, one; *cornu*, horn]. Having one horn.

UNIDEFICIENT. [L. *unus*, one; *deficere*, to fail]. Lacking one seta from the assumed holotrichous condition.

UNIDENTATE. [L. *unus*, one; *dens*, tooth]. Having one tooth.

UNIDIVERTICULATE. [L. *unus*, one; *diverticulum*, a bypath]. Having one diverticulum.

UNIFOLLICULAR. [L. *unus*, one; *folliculus*, small bag]. Having one follicle.

UNIGEMINAL. [L. *unus*, one; *geminus*, twin]. With one pair.

UNILABIATE. [L. *unus*, one; *labium*, lip]. Having one lip.

UNILATERAL. [L. *unus*, one; *latus*, side]. On one side only.

UNIMUCRONATE. [L. *unus*, one; *mucro*, sharp point]. Having a single sharp tip.

UNIONICOLIDAE. [Gr. υνιον, little plough-share; L. *colere*, to inhabit]. A family of freshwater mites (infraorder Anystina, superfamily Hygrobatoidea) in which the larval stages are ectoparasites of aquatic insects and clams, but the adult stages are free-living.

UNIPARENTAL INHERITANCE. [L. *unus*, one; *parens*, parent; OFr. *enheriter*, make heir]. The phenomenon in which the off-spring of a particular mating seem to have inherited certain phenotypes from only one parent regardless of the other parent's phenotype.

UNIPLICATE. [L. *unus*, one; *plicare*, to fold]. Having a single fold or line of folding.

274

UNISERIAL, UNISERIATE. [L. *unus*, one; *series*, rank]. Arranged in one row or series.

UNISERRATE. [L. *unus*, one; *serra*, saw]. One row of serrations.

UNISETOSE. [L. *unus*, one; *seta*, bristle]. Possessing only one seta or bristle.

UNISEXUAL. [L. *unus*, one; *sexus*, sex]. Distinctly male or female.

UNISPIRE. [L. *unus*, one; *spira*, coil]. A single turn of a spiral.

UNIVOLTINE. [L. *unus*, one; It. *volta*, time]. Producing only one brood per year. See also Voltine.

UNIVOROUS. [L. *unus*, one; *vorare*, to devour]. Feeding on only one type of food.

UNSPECIALIZED. [AS. *un*, not; L. *species*, a particular kind]. Lacking modifications for any special function or purpose.

UNSTRIATED MUSCLE (UNSTRIPED MUSCLE). Involuntary or smooth muscle. See Muscle.

UR series. In the Acari: the posterior submarginal row of setae in the Lindquist-Evans system.

URCEOLATE. [L. *urceolus*, small pitcher]. Pitcher-shaped.

UREA. [Gr. ουρον, urine]. A simple organic compound, $CO(NH_2)_2$, a major nitrogenous waste product.

UROMERE (URITE). [Gr. ουρα, tail; μερος, part]. An abdominal segment.

UROMORPHIC. [Gr. ουρα, tail; μορφη, shape]. Tail-like.

UROPODINA. [Gr. ουρα, tail; πους, foot]. An infraorder of mites (order Mesostigmata, suborder Monogynaspida). Superfamilies: Diarthrophalloidea, Microgynioidea, Thinozerconoidea, Uropodoidea.

UROPODOIDEA. [Gr. ουρα, tail; πους, foot]. A superfamily of mites (suborder Monogynaspida, infraorder Uropodina) which are tortoise-like and encased in armor dorsally and ventrally. Thirty families.

UROPORE. [Gr. ουρον, urine; πορος, channel]. In ticks and mites: an opening of the excretory duct.

UROPYGI (THELYPHONIDA). [Gr. ουρα, tail; πυγη, rump]. The small monotypic order of whip scorpions or vinegaroons (class Euchelicerata, subclass Arachnida) from tropical and subtropical regions. Small to medium sized, nocturnal arachnids which bear a pair of powerful pincers (pedipalpi) that are held flexed and parallel to the ground. The long antenniform first pair of legs are not used in locomotion but have a sensory-tactile function. On the terminal segment (twelfth segment) of the abdomen there is a long, jointed, multi-segmented, whip-like flagellum from which, when disturbed, they elevate and eject a stream of noxious fluid (mainly acetic and caprylic acid) from anal glands. The prosoma is covered by a dorsal carapace that carries a simple pair of anterior eyes and on either side a cluster of three to four eyes. They are commonly brownish and flat and live under stones, stump bark, and litter, preying on small arthropods (commonly crickets) and small toads. Uropygids have elaborate courtship behavior and the female produces from seven to 35 large eggs in a burrow or retreat. She remains in the shelter with the eggs attached to her body until they have hatched and undergone several molts. The female dies shortly after the young disperse. The schizomids (Schizomida) were previously included here. See also Holopeltida. Family: **Thelyphonidae.**

UROPYGIUM. [Gr. ουρα, tail; πυγη, rump]. The ovipositor when it is only an extension of the abdominal segments.

UROSOME. [Gr. ουρα, tail; σωμα, body]. The abdomen.

UROSTERNITE. [Gr. ουρα, tail; στερνον, chest]. The ventral plate of the abdominal segment.

UROTERGITE. [Gr. ουρα, tail; L. *tergum*, back]. An abdominal tergite.

URSTIGMA, URSTIGMATA. [Ger. *ur-*, pref. earliest; Gr. στιγμα, mark]. In ticks and mites: the sense organs between the coxae of the first and second pairs of legs. They are thought to be humidity receptors. See also Claparède's Organ.

URTICATE, URTICATION. [L. *urtica*, nettle]. To sting or burn.

URTICATING HAIRS. [L. *urtica*, nettle]. Bristles with minute lateral points producing irritation upon contact; whether due to mechanical action or the presence of poisonous secretions.

URTICATING SETAE. [L. *urtica*, nettle; *seta*, bristle]. On many New World tarantulas (**Theraphosidae**): barbed and irritating defensive setae on the abdomen which can readily penetrate the skin of an attacker or predator, such as a small mammal which enters the spider's burrow. In man they can cause a rash.

USTULATE, USTULATUS. [L. *ustulatus*, scorch or burn]. Brownish. Having the appearance of being scorched or burned.

UTERUS, UTERINE. [L. *uterus*, womb]. An enlargement of the lower end of the oviduct in which eggs are retained temporarily or in which the embryo develops.

UTRICLE. [L. *utriculus*, wine skin/leather bottle]. A small bag or bladder.

UTRICULUS. [L. *utriculus*, wine skin/leather bottle]. A little bag or hollow vesicle. See also Lageniform.

UTRIFORM. [L. *uter*, wine skin/leather bottle; *forma*, shape]. Bladder-shaped.

V

v1. In the Prostigmata: the internal vertical seta (vi) on the prodorsum.

v2. In the Prostigmata: the external vertical seta (ve) on the prodorsum.

VACUOLAR. [L. *vacuus*, empty]. Like a vacuole.

VACUOLATE VACUOLATED. [L. *vacuus*, empty]. With vacuoles or small cavities, empty or filled with a watery fluid.

VACUOLE. [L. *vacuus*, empty]. One of the spaces in the cell cytoplasm containing air, water, partially digested food or other materials.

VAEJOVIDAE. [L. *uae*, a cry of pain: *iouis* (= iuppter) Jupiter]. A large family of scorpions (order Scorpiones, superfamily Chactoidea) from Guatemala, Mexico, the Southern and South-western United States and one species from Canada (thus cold-adapted).

VAGIFORM. [L. *vagus*, indefinite; *forma*, shape]. Indefinite, indeterminate, amorphous.

VAGILE. [L. *vagus*, wandering]. Freely motile; free-moving; able to migrate.

VAGINA. [L. *vagina*, sheath]. The terminal portion of the female reproductive tract. The tubular structure formed by the union of the oviducts in the female, opening externally to allow passage of the egg to the ovipositor.

VAGINAL SCLERITES. [L. *vagina*, sheath; Gr. σκληρος, hard]. In the Mesostigmata: a pair of internal sclerites in the genital region.

VAGINATE/VAGINIFEROUS. [L. *vagina*, sheath; *ferre*, to bear]. Invested by a sheath.

VAGRANT. [L. *vagari*, wander]. Unattached. Of organisms that are wind-blown or move under their own volition.

VALGATE. [L. *valga*, knock-kneed]. Enlarged at the bottom. Clubfooted.

VALLECULA. [LL. *vallecula*, little valley]. A depression or a groove.

VALLECULATE. [LL. *vallecula*, little valley]. Grooved.

VALVES. [L. *valva*, folding door]. Any of many various structures which permit flow in only one direction and are capable of closing and preventing backflow. See also Corniculus.

VALVELET. [L. *valvula*, small fold]. A small fold or valve.

VALVULA. [L. *valvula*, little valve]. A small valve.

VALVULAR. [L. *valvula*, small folding door]. Of or pertaining to a small valve or valvula.

VALVULE. [L. *valvula*, small fold]. Any small valve-like process.

VAN DER HAMMEN'S ORGAN. [L. *van der Hammen*, Dutch Arachnologist]. In some intertidal Oribatida: a respiratory organ composed of cuticular tubercles and the overlying cerotegument (e.g. *Fortuynia*: **Fortuyniidae**).

VARIABLE CHARACTER. [L. *varians*, changing]. Any characteristic that exhibits many different degrees of expression in individuals of the same population, species, or some other specified group.

VARIANT. [L. *varians*, changing]. An individual or species which deviates in some character from the (arbitrary) standard type.

VARIATION. [L. *varians*, changing]. The degree of divergence among individuals of a group, specifically the difference between an individual and others of the same species that cannot be attributed to a difference in age, sex, or position in life cycle.

VARIEGATED. [L. *variegatus*, of different sorts]. Marked by different shades or colors.

VARIETY. [L. *varietas*, variety]. A taxonomic group below the species level. It is used in different ways by different authors, but in general it is equivalent to subspecies, race, geographical race, breed or strain.

VARIOLE, VARIOLA. [LL. *variola*, smallpox]. A small pit-like marking which may be found on various parts of the body. A rounded impression with defined edges.

VARIOLATE, VARIOSE. [L. *varius*, spotted]. With large rounded impressions, like pockmarks.

VAS. [L. *vas*, vessel]. A small vessel, duct, canal or blind tube.

VASA DEFERENTIA, VAS DEFERENS. [L. *vas*, vessel; *deferre*, convey]. Sperm ducts leading away from a testis. They usually unite into a single ductus ejaculatorius that conducts the semen from the interior of the male palpus to the embolus.

VASA VARICOSA. [L. *vas*, vessel; *varicosa*, full of dilated veins]. The malpighian tubules.

VASCULAR. [L. *vasculum*, small vessel]. Of some structure which consists of, or contains vessels which are adapted for the transmission or circulation of fluids.

VAS DEFERENS, VASA DEFERENTIA. [L. *vas*, vessel; *deferre*, convey]. A sperm duct leading away from a testis.

VAS EFFERENS, VASA EFFERENTIA. [L. *vas*, vessel; *efferre*, bring out]. A tubule leading from the testis to the vas deferens.

VASIFORM. [L. *vas*, vessel; *forma*, shape]. Resembling, or functioning as a duct.

ve. In the Prostigmata: the external vertical seta (v2, z2) on the prodorsum.

VECTOR. [L. *vector*, bearer]. Any carrier of (for example) pathogens, parasites, fragments of DNA, etc.

VEGETATIVE FUNCTIONS. [L. *vegetare*, to animate]. All the natural functions of living organisms that maintain life.

VEIGAIOIDEA. [L. *veia* (*ueho*), to carry; Gr. γαια the earth/one's country]. A monotypic superfamily of free-living and predatory mites (suborder Monogynaspida, infraorder Gamasina) that, distinctively, have a hyaline appendage on the tarsus of the pedipalp. They can be found in soil and decaying organic matter and some species inhabit rocky shorelines. Family: **Veigaiidae**. In some classifications this superfamily may be included in the sub-cohort Dermanyssiae.

VELUTINOUS. [It. *velluto*, velvet]. Velvety.

VELVET MITE. [L. *villutus*, shaggy cloth]. - The nymphal or adult stage of a terrestrial member of the Trombidiformes that feed on small arthropods and their eggs.

VENTOSE. [L. *ventosus*, puffed up]. Inflated. Puffed out.

VENOM. [L. *venenum*, poison]. A poison produced by animals.

VENOM GLAND. [L. *venenum*, poison]. Any gland secreting an irritating or lethal substance. In true spiders: a pair of glands situated in the cephalothorax; in others, on the chelicerae with ducts traversing each claw with an oval slit opening near the tip.

VENOMOUS. [L. *venenum*, poison]. Having poison-producing glands, or being able to inflict a poisonous wound.

VENT. [VL. *exventare*, release wind]. The anus.

VENTER. [L. *venter*, belly]. The abdomen. The lower abdominal surface.

VENTILATION TRACHEAE. [LL. *trachia*, windpipe]. Tracheae that respond to variations in the surrounding air pressure and may collapse. See also Diffusion Tracheae.

VENTRAD. [L. *venter*, belly, *ad*, to]. Towards the lower or abdominal surface.

VENTRAL. [L. *venter*, belly]. Located on the lower, abdominal or under-surface.

VENTRAL PLATE. [L. *venter*, belly]. Any plate in the ventral region. In the Brachypylina (Oribatida): a sclerotized plate covering the ventral region of the opisthosoma and separated from the notogaster by the circumgastric scissure.

VENTRAL REGION. [L. *venter*, belly]. In the Mesostigmata: the area between the genital and anal regions.

VENTRAL SETA I (1ST VENTRAL SETA). [L. *venter*, belly; *seta* bristle]. In the Eriophyoidea: the opisthosomal seta d.

VENTRAL SETA II (2ND VENTRAL SETA). [L. *venter*, belly; *seta* bristle]. In the Eriophyoidea: the opisthosomal seta e.

VENTRAL SETA III (3RD VENTRAL SETA). [L. *venter*, belly; *seta* bristle]. In the Eriophyoidea: the opisthosomal seta f.

VENTRAL SETAE. [L. *venter*, belly; *seta* bristle]. In the Mesostigmata: the three longitudinal rows of setae in the ventral region, designated (Jv, Zv, Lv) in the Lindquist-Evans system.

VENTRAL SHIELD. [L. *venter*, belly]. In the Mesostigmata: any shield in the ventral region. It may often be fused with the anal shield to form a ventrianal shield.

VENTRAL TIBIAL APOPHYSIS (VTiA). [L. *venter*, belly; *tibia*, shin; Gr. αποφυσις, an offshoot]. In male spiders (Araneae), an outgrowth or process (apophysis) on the lower surface of a tibia. See also Retrolateral Tibial Apophysis, Tibial Apophysis.

VENTRIANAL. [L. *venter*, belly; *anus*, anus]. In some ticks and mites: of a plate formed by the fused ventral and anal sclerites.

VENTRIANAL SHIELD. [L. *venter*, belly; *anus*, anus]. In the Mesostigmata: a ventral shield bearing the anal opening, circumanal setae, and one or more pairs of ventral setae or lyrifissures. See also Anal Shield.

VENTRICLE. [L. *ventriculus*, little belly]. A cavity or chamber.

VENTRICOSE. [L. *venter*, belly]. Swelling out in the middle.

VENTRICULAR. [L. *ventriculus*, ventricle]. In the heart: of the ligaments, septa and valves.

VENTRICULUS. [L. *ventriculus*, ventricle]. A small ventricle.

VENTRIMESON. [L. *venter*, belly; Gr. μεσος, middle]. The middle line of the ventral surface of the body.

VENTRITE. [L. *venter*, belly]. A ventral segment. The ventral aspect of annular rings.

VENTROCEPHALAD. [L. *venter*, belly; Gr. κεφαλη, head]. Toward the lower side and anteriorly.

VENTRODORSAL. [L. *venter*, belly; *dorsum*, back]. Extending from the ventral to the dorsal surface.

VENTROLATERAL (ANTEROLATERAL). [L. *venter*, belly; *latus*, side]. Located at the side of the ventral region.

VENTROMEDIAL. [L. *venter*, belly; *medius*, median]. Of the median ventral line.

VERMIAN. [L. *vermis*, worm]. Worm-like.

278

VERMICULAR. [L. *vermicula*, little worm]. Resembling a worm in either appearance or movement.

VERMICULATE. [L. *vermicula*, little worm]. Having numerous fine sinuate bands of color or being marked by numerous fine sinuate irregular depressed lines.

VERMICULATION. [L. *vermicula*, little worm]. Peristaltic, or worm-like movement.

VERMICULE. [L. *vermicula*, little worm]. A small worm-like structure.

VERMIFORM (HELMINTHOID). [L. *vermis*, worm; *forma*, shape]. Worm-shaped.

VERNACULAR NAME. [L. *vernaculus*, indigenous]. The common name for a species or other group. See also Scientific Name, Nomenclature.

VERNANTIA. [L. *vernalis*, of the spring]. Molting or shedding of the skin.

VERNAL. [L. *vernalis*, of the spring]. One of the terms for the six part division of the year commonly used in ecology, especially with reference to terrestrial and fresh-water communities. The six parts are: prevernal (early spring), vernal (late spring), aestival (early summer), serotinal (late summer), autumnal (autumn) and hibernal (winter).

VERNICOSE. [Fr. *vernis*, varnished]. Having a varnished or glossy appearance.

VERRICULE, VERRICULATE. [L. *verriculum*, net]. A dense tuft of nearly parallel upright hairs.

VERRUCIFORM. [L. *verruca*, wart; *forma*, shape]. Wart-shaped.

VERRUCOSE. [L. *verruca*, wart]. Warty.

VERRUCULOSE. [L. *vermicula*, little worm]. Being covered with minute wart-like excrescences.

VERSATILE. [L. *versatilis*, mobile/changeable]. Moving freely.

VERSICOLOUR. [L. *versicolour*, having colors that change]. Having many colors; changeable in color.

VERSON'S GLANDS (DERMAL GLANDS). [*Enrico Verson*, Italian Entomologist]. The molting glands. Epidermal glands which secrete a fluid (or in some species a gel) into the space between the cuticle and the epidermis. This fluid contains enzymes, a proteinase and a chitinase, which digests the endocuticle. Secretion continues until the cuticulin layer of the new cuticle is complete. See also Ecdysis.

VERTEX. [L. *vertex*, top]. The top of the head.

VERTEXAL. [L. *vertex*, top]. Occurring on or near the vertex, or directed toward it.

VERTICAL. [L. *vertex*, top]. The vertex – the highest point. See also Reclivous.

VERTICAL-SCAPULAR SYSTEM. [L. *vertex*, top; L. *scapula*, shoulder]. In the Acariformes and especially in the Endeostigmata and Prostigmata: a system of designations for the prodorsal setae.

VERTICAL SETAE. [L. *vertex*, top; *seta*, bristle]. In the Mesostigmata: the most anterior pair of median setae in the j-series, setae j1. They usually project over the gnathosoma, are often modified and inserted across a lyrifissure from the paravertical setae z1.

VERTICIL. [L. *verticillus*, a whorl]. A whorl of setae around a region of a leg segment. It is used in determining setal designations.

VERTICILLATE. [L. *verticillus*, a whorl]. Arranged in a whorl or whorls.

VESICA. [L. *vesica*, bladder]. The urinary bladder, or any bladder.

VESICANT. [L. *vesica*, bladder]. Blistering. Able to produce a blister.

VESICATING. [L. *vesica*, blister, bladder]. Blister-like.

VESICLE. [L. *vesica*, bladder]. Any small cavity, sac or membrane-bound sphere containing fluid. In scorpions: the base of the postanal segment.

VESICULA. [L. *vesicula*, small bladder]. A small bladder-like sac or cyst.

VESICULAR. [L. *vesica*, bladder/blister]. Containing small cavities or vesicles.

VESICULA SEMINALIS. [L. *vesicula*, small bladder; *semen*, seed]. A sac in which spermatozoans are stored and complete their development. See also Seminal Vesicle.

VESPERTINE. [L. *vespertinus*, of the evening]. Being active in the evening.

VESSEL. [L. *vascellum*, little vessel]. Any tube or canal with defined walls in which a fluid (blood, lymph, etc.) moves.

VESTIBULAR SYSTEM. [L. *vestibulum*, porch]. The sensory system which provides information about the position and movement of the head.

VESTIBULE/VESTIBULUM. [L. *vestibulum*, porch]. A cavity which leads into another cavity or passage.

VESTIGIAL/VESTIGE. [L. *vestigium*, trace]. A small imperfectly formed or degenerate part, limb or organ. Usually a part which was at one time in the past a fully functioning part, limb or organ. For example, the vestigial eyes in many cave-dwelling species. Such features give the creationists a hard time.

VESTITURE. [L. *vestire*, to clothe]. A body covering, e.g. of scales, hair, fur, etc.

vi. In the Prostigmata: the internal vertical seta (v1) on the prodorsum.

VIABILITY. [Fr. *vie*, live]. Under specified environmental conditions: a measure of the probability that a fertilized egg will survive and develop into an adult.

VIABLE. [Fr. *vie*, live]. Capable of life. Capable of developing.

VIBRATILE. [L. *vibrare*, to quiver]. Vibrating, oscillating.

VIBROTAXIS. [L. *vibrare*, to vibrate; Gr. ταξις, an arranging]. An organism's response to mechanical vibrations.

VICARIANCE BIOGEOGRAPHY. [L. *vicarius*, deputy]. The concept that the distribution of organisms depends on their normal means of dispersal and so disjunctions are accounted for in terms of new barriers such as rivers, rises in sea level etc. This school of thought rejects the concept of 'sweepstake dispersal routes' and similar proposals, postulating instead former land bridges and, where there is sufficient coincident plant and animal distribution, even vanished continents.

VICARIANCE EVENT. See Vicariation.

VICARIANTS. [L. *vicarius*, deputy]. The closely related taxa that are separated geographically by a vicariance event. See Vicariation.

VICARIATION. [L. *vicarius*, deputy]. The occurrence of closely related taxa in corresponding but separate environments. See also Transad.

VICARIOUS. [L. *vicarius*, deputy/substitute]. Taking the place of. Of closely related taxa in corresponding but separate environments.

VICARIOUS DISTRIBUTION. [L. *vicarius*, deputy]. The geographic distribution that results from the replacement of one member of a species pair (two closely related species derived from a common ancestor) by the other. In zoology, subspecies are conspecific vicariants. See also Vicariation.

VICARIOUS SPECIES. [L. *vicarius*, deputy]. See Vicariation, Vicarious Distribution.

VICINAL. [L. *vicinus*, neighbor]. Neighboring.

VICINISM. [L. *vicinus*, neighbor]. The propensity to variation due to proximity of related organisms.

VILLOSE/VILLOUS. [L. *villus*, shaggy hair]. Pubescent, shaggy, covered with villi.

VILLI (VILLUS). [L. *villus*, tuft of hair]. Soft flexible hairs or papillate processes on the surface of some absorbent and sensory organs. See also Microvilli.

VINOUS, VINACEOUS. [L. *vinum*, wine; -*aceous*, of the nature of]. Wine-colored.

VIOLACEOUS. [L. *viola*, violet; -*aceous*, of the nature of]. Violet. A mixture of blue and red.

VIRESCENT or **VIRIDESCENT.** [L. *virescere*, to grow green]. Greenish or becoming green.

VIRGATE. [L. *virga*, rod]. Rod-shaped.

VIRGIN. [L. *virgo*, virgin]. Of native habitat, fauna or flora that is untouched by humans or human activity.

VIRGIN BIRTH. [L. *virgo*, virgin]. See Parthenogenesis.

VIRGINIPAROUS. [L. *virgo*, virgin; *parere*, to bring forth]. Of organisms that reproduce only by parthenogenesis.

VIRIDANT. [L. *viridare*, to make green]. Becoming or being green.

VIRIDASIIDAE. [L. *viridis*, green]. A small family of spiders (infraorder Araneomorphae, superfamily Entelegynae), known as 'zebra spiders'; from Madagascar and Brazil. This family was previously in the **Ctenidae**

VIRIDIS, VIRIDESCENT. [L. *viridis*, green]. Green. Greenish.

VIRULENCE. [L. *virulentus*, full-of-poison]. The state of being pathogenic.

VISCERA. [L. *viscera*, bowels]. The internal organs contained in various body cavities.

VISCERAL SEGMENTS. [L. *viscera*, bowels]. All the abdominal segments anterior to the genital segments.

VISCID. [L. *viscum*, mistletoe]. Sticky.

VISCOTAXIS. [LL. *viscum*, bird-lime; Gr. ταξις, an arranging]. A change in direction as a result of the organism encountering a change in the viscosity of its environment.

VISCOUS. [LL. *viscosus*, sticky]. Thick, sticky or semiliquid.

VISION. [L. *visio*, sight]. See Eye.

VISIOPERCEPTIVE AREA. [L. *visio*, sight; *perceptio*, a gathering together]. The sensitive area of the retina.

VISUAL ACUITY. [L. *visio*, sight]. Sharpness of vision: the ability to see small objects clearly.

VISUAL AXIS. [L. *visio*, sight]. A straight line between the point at which the eye is directed and the fovea centralis.

VITELLINE MEMBRANE (PRIMARY EGG MEMBRANE). [L. *vitellus*, yolk; *membrana*, membrane]. A membrane that is secreted by and surrounds the ovum. A secondary membrane is secreted by the ovary and tertiary membranes are secreted by the oviduct.

VITREOUS. [L. *vitreus*, glassy]. Transparent, hyaline.

VITTA. [L. *vitta*, band/ribbon]. A broad stripe or band.

VITTATE. [L. *vittatus*, carrying a band/ribbon]. Striped.

VIVIPAROUS (ZOOGONOUS). [L. *vivus*, living; *parere*, to beget]. A reproductive strategy in which there is maximum development within the maternal body and the young are thus born well developed and in many cases able to assimilate their surroundings and react appropriately. Of an animal which produces live young, rather than eggs. See also Oviparous, Ovoviviparous.

VIXIGREGARIOUS. [L. *vix*, with difficulty; *grex*, flock; *-arius*, connected with]. Sparsely distributed or occurring only in small, poorly defined groups.

VOLTINE. [It. *volta*, time]. Of the number of broods per year. One per year, monovoltine or univoltine; two, bivoltine; three, trivoltine; four, quadrivoltine; several, polyvoltine; many, multivoltine.

VOLUNTARY BEHAVIOR. [L. *voluntas*, will]. Behavior that is non-habitual and associated with the somatic nervous system or with operant control of the autonomic nervous system.

VOLUNTARY MUSCLE. See Muscle.

VOLUTE. [L. *voluta*, rolled]. Spirally twisted, rolled up.

-VOROUS, -VORE. [L. *vorare*, to devour]. Suffixes meaning 'feeding upon'.

VULGAR. [L. *vulgaris*, common]. Common. Not conspicuous. Obscure in appearance and abundant in number.

VULTUS. [L. *vultus*, face/expression]. The face. The part of head below in front and between the eyes.

VULVA. [L. *vulva*, vulva]. The external female genitalia.

W

WALKING DANDRUFF. See Cheyletiosis.

WANDERNYMPH. [Ger. *wander*, walk + *nymph*]. A German term for a phoretic nymph, especially in the Uropodina and Sejida.

WARNING COLORATION. The conspicuous coloration an animal uses to warn potential predators of its noxious, unpalatable or otherwise harmful properties. See also Mimicry.

WATER MITE. Any member of the Hydracarina (Prostigmata)—now a convenience grouping. They are often large, brightly colored, and the larval stages are usually parasitic on aquatic insects. See also **Halacaridae**.

WATER SPIDERS. See **Argyronetidae**.

WAX. [AS. *weax*, wax]. Esters of alcohols higher than glycerol which are insoluble in water and difficult to hydrolyse. They form a protective waterproof covering for cuticle, etc. The composition varies from species to species.

WAX GLANDS. [AS. *weax*, wax]. Any gland in various parts of the body that secrete a waxy product in the form of a scale, string or powder.

WAX LAYER. [AS. *weax*, wax]. The wax secreted at or near the surface or incorporated into the inner layers of the cuticle. It is responsible for waterproofing the cuticle.

WAX-PLATE. [AS. *weax*, wax]. A plate where the secretions of the wax glands are deposited.

WEB. [AS. *webbe*, web]. The network of threads spun by a spider.

WESTERN PREDATORY MITES. **Phytoseiida**e mites *Galendromus*, *Metaseiulus*, *Typhlodromus*, that are use as biocontrol agents for spider mites.

WHIP-LIKE STYLETS. See Stylet-Like.

WHIP SCORPIONS. See Amblypygi, Uropygi.

WHORL. [OE. *whorvil*, the whirl of a spindle]. In acariform mites: the whorls or verticils of birefringent setae on the leg segments. Setae are named based on their segment, position on the segment, position relative to the body axis and relationship to other setae in the whorl.

WILD TYPE. The arbitrarily designated typical genotype of an organism. The most frequently observed type.

WIND SCORPIONS, WIND SPIDERS. See Solifugae.

WINGS OF THE HEART. The series of diagonal and other muscular fibers above the diaphragm in the pericardial cavity. See Pericardial Diaphragm.

WITH'S ORGANS. [*Carl Johannes With*, Danish Arachnologist]. In ticks and mites: a pair of large hypertrophied setae towards the side of the hypostome on the venter of the gnathosoma. A pair of robust sclerotized rutella flank these organs and may aid the mite in cleaning its chelicerae or holding its food.

WITHIIDAE. [*Carl Johannes With*, Danish Arachnologist]. A large family of false scorpions (suborder Iocheirata, superfamily Cheliferoidea) with a distribution covering Africa, America, Asia and Oceania.

WOLF SPIDERS. See **Lycosidae**.

X

XANTHIC. [Gr. ξανθος, yellow]. Yellowish.

XANTHODERMIC. [Gr. ξανθος, yellow; δερμα, skin]. Having a yellowish skin.

XANTHOPHANE. [Gr. ξανθος, yellow; φαινειν, to show]. See Chromophanes.

XANTHOPSIN. [Gr. ξανθος, yellow; οψις, sight]. Visual yellow, a yellow pigment from an arthropod's eye

X-CHROMOSOME. [Gr. χρωμα, color; σωμα, body]. The sex chromosome, present in single dose in the heterogamitic sex and paired in the homogamitic sex. See Sex Chromosome.

XENAGONES. [Gr. ξενος, host; αγω, lead towards]. Specific substances produced by live parasites which act on the host; sometimes causing changes in behavior. See also Trophagones.

XENAUTOGAMOUS. [Gr. ξενος, host; αυτος, self; γαμος, marriage]. Of organisms in which cross fertilization normally occurs, but in which self fertilization is also possible.

XENOCTENIDAE. [Gr. ξενος, strange; κτενος, a comb]. A small family of spiders (infraorder Araneomorphae, superfamily Entelegynae), that were previously included in the Miturgidae

XENODEME. [Gr. ξενος, host; δημος, people]. A local population of parasites differing from others in host specificity.

XENOECIC. [Gr. ξενος, host; οικος, house]. Living in the empty shell of another organism.

XENOGAMY. [Gr. ξενος, strange; γαμος, marriage]. Cross fertilization.

XENOGENOUS. [Gr. ξενος, strange; γενος, descent]. Originating outside the organism; of some thing caused by external stimuli.

XENOLOGY. [Gr. ξενος, host; λογος, discourse]. The scientific study of hosts in relation to the life history of their parasites.

XENOMIXIS. [Gr. ξενος, strange; μιξις, mingling]. The union of gametes from different sources.

XENOMONE. [Gr. ξενος, strange, hor*mone* (Gr. ορμαινω, excite)]. See Allelochemic.

XENOPARASITE. [Gr. ξενος, a stranger; παρασιτος, parasite]. A parasite which is infecting an organism which is not its normal host.

XERIC. [Gr. ξηρος, dry]. Tolerating or adapted to arid conditions.

XEROCOLE. [Gr. ξηρος, dry; L. *colere*, to dwell]. An animal which lives in a dry or arid place.

XEROPHILOUS. [Gr. ξηρος, dry; φιλος, loving]. Adapted to living in a dry climate.

XEROPHOBOUS. [Gr. ξηρος, dry; φοβος, fear]. Intolerant of arid conditions.

XEROTHERMAL. [Gr. ξηρος, dry; θερμη, heat]. Of organisms which tolerate or thrive in hot, dry environments.

XIPHIFORM. [Gr. ξιφος, sword; L. *forma*, shape]. Sword-shaped.

XIPHOID. [Gr. ξιφοειδης, sword-shaped]. Sword-shaped.

XYLOID. [Gr. ξυλον, wood; ειδος, like]. Resembling wood. Ligneous.

XYLOPHAGE. [Gr. ξυλον, wood; φαγειν, to eat]. Feeding on wood.

Y

Y-CHROMOSOME. The sex chromosome which pairs with the X-chromosome in the heterogamitic sex. See Sex Chromosome.

YOLK. [AS. *geoloca*, yellow part]. The nutritive material in an ovum. It consists mainly of proteins and fats and is normally produced within the egg cell and contained by the viteline membrane.

YOLK CELLS. [AS. *geoloca*, yellow part]. Primary yolk cells that take no part in the blastoderm formation.

YOLK DUCT. [AS. *geoloca*, yellow part]. See Vitelline Duct.

YOLK EPITHELIUM. [AS. *geoloca*, yellow part]. The epithelium which surrounds the yolk sac.

YUREBILLOIDEA. [*Yurebilla*, derived from aboriginal (Kaurna) name for Mt Lofty, South Australia]. A monotypic superfamily of mites (suborder Prostigmata, infraorder Anystina). Family: **Yurebilldae.**

Z

z2. In the Prostigmata: the external vertical seta (v2, ve) on the prodorsum, especially in spider mites.

ZALMOXIDAE. [Gr. Ζαλμοξις, Thracian Dacian god]. A family of harvestmen or daddy longlegs (suborder Laniatores, superfamily Zalmoxoidea) with a wide tropical distribution, but not Africa or Madagascar.

ZALMOXOIDEA. [Gr. Ζαλμοξις, Thracian Dacian god]. A superfamily of small harvestmen (suborder Laniatores, infraorder Grassatores) that are dark brown to dark yellow with varied darker mottling. The males of some species bear sexually dimorphic and embellished armature, mainly on the fourth walking leg. Families: **Escadabiidae, Fissiphalliidae, Guasiniidae, Icaleptidae, Kimulidae, Zalmoxidae.**

Z-CHROMOSOME. The equivalent of the Y-chromosome when the female is the heterogamitic sex.

ZEITGEBER. [Ger. *Zeit*, time; *Geber*, giver]. See Synchronizer.

ZERCONOIDEA. [Ger. *Zirkon*, high-quality diamond-like gemstones]. A superfamily of mites (suborder Monogynaspida, infraorder Gamasina). Families: **Coprozerconidae, Zerconidae.**

ZETA. [Gr. ζ, zeta]. A designation for eupathidia on the legs of acariform mites.

ZETOMOTRICHOIDEA. [Gr. ζητες seeking; θριξ, hair.]. A monotypic superfamily of mites (suborder Oribatida, infraorder Brachypylina - section Poronoticae). Family: **Zetomotrichidae.**

ZETORCHESTOIDEA. [Gr. ζητες seeking; ορχηστης, a dancer]. A monotypic superfamily of mites (suborder Oribatida, infraorder Brachypylina - section Pycnonoticae). Family: **Zetorchestidae.**

ZODARIIDAE. [Gr. ζωδαριον, little animal]. A family (infraorder Araneomorphae, superfamily Entelegynae) of small to medium-sized, eight-eyed, fast-moving, ground-hunting spiders that feed exclusively on ants. The abdomen is shiny black on the upper surface and pale yellow beneath; the legs are slender and mainly devoid of spines; the anterior spinners arise from a cylindrical projection and both the median and posterior spinners are much reduced. Previously in the monotypic superfamily Zodarioidea.

ZOETIC. [Gr. ζωη, life]. Pertaining to life.

ZOIC. [Gr. ζωικος, of life]. Containing the remains of organisms.

ZONA. [L. *zona*, girdle]. A belt or zone.

ZONATE. [L. *zona*, girdle]. Zoned, or marked with rings.

ZONATION. [L. *zona*, girdle]. The spatial distribution of species in association with variations in their environment.

ZONE. [Gr. ζωνη, girdle]. A region characterized by a similar fauna or flora. A region to which certain species are limited. A rock stratum characterized by typical fossils.

ZONITE. [Gr. ζωνη, girdle]. An arthromere or somite.

ZONOID. [Gr. ζωνη, girdle; ειδος, form]. Like a zone.

ZONULE. [L. *zonaula*, little girdle]. A little zone, belt or girdle.

ZOO- is derived from Gr. ζωον (animal) and should really be written zoö. Conventionally the diaeresis/umlaut (¨) is dropped but the pronunciation remains, as in Zoo-ology.

ZOOAPOCRISIS. [Gr. ζωον, animal; αποκρισις, answer]. The total responses of an animal to its environment.

ZOOBENTHOS. [Gr. ζωον, animal; βενθος, depths of the sea]. The fauna of the sea floor, or of the bottom of inland waterways.

ZOOBIOTIC. [Gr. ζωον, animal; βιωτικος, of life]. Of some animal parasitic on, or living on, another animal.

ZOOCENOSE. [Gr. ζωον, animal; κοινος, common]. An animal community.

ZOOCHORIC. [Gr. ζωον, animal; χωρειν, to disperse]. Dispersed by animals.

ZOOCOENOSIS (ZOOCENOSIS). [Gr. ζωον, animal; κοινος, in common]. An animal community.

ZOODYNAMICS. [Gr. ζωον, animal; δυναμις, power]. The physiology of animals.

ZOOECOLOGY. [Gr. ζωον, animal; οικος, household; λογος, discourse]. The scientific study of the relationships between animals and their environment.

ZOOGAMETE (PLANOGAMETE). [Gr. ζωον, animal; γαμος, marriage]. A motile gamete.

ZOOGAMY. [Gr. ζωον, animal; γαμετης, spouse]. Sexual reproduction in animals.

ZOOGENESIS. [Gr. ζωον, animal; γενεσις, descent]. The ontogeny and phylogeny of animals.

ZOOGENETICS. [Gr. ζωον, animal; γενεσις, descent]. Animal genetics.

ZOOGENOUS. [Gr. ζωον, animal; γενναω, produce]. Of something produced or caused by animals.

ZOOGEOGRAPHICAL REGIONS. [Gr. ζωον, animal; γη, earth; γραφειν, to write]. Any of the major geographical regions of the Earth, characterized by a particular faunal composition and separated by natural barriers such as mountain ranges and oceans. The nine major regions are: **Australasian** (Australia, New Guinea and islands southeast of Wallace's line), **Ethiopian** (Africa, Arabia), **Madagascan** (Madagascar), **Nearctic** (north America, Greenland, etc.), **Neotropical** (Mexico, central and southern America), **New Zealand** (New Zealand and neighbouring islands), **Oriental** (India, Burma, southeast Asia west of Wallace's line), **Palearctic** (central and northern Asia and Europe) and **Polynesian** (various Pacific islands of volcanic origin which have no obvious connection with a land mass).

ZOOGEOGRAPHICAL SPECIES. [Gr. ζωον, animal; γη, earth; γραφειν, to write]. A species or group of closely related allopatric species (super-species) which may be treated as a single unit for the purposes of zoogeographical analysis.

ZOOGEOGRAPHY. [Gr. ζωον, animal; γη, earth; γραφειν, to write]. The scientific study of the distribution of animals.

ZOOGONOUS. [Gr. ζωον, animal; γονος, offspring]. See Viviparous.

ZOOLOGY. [Gr. ζωον, animal; λογος, discourse]. The scientific study of the structure, function, behavior, classification and distribution of animals.

ZOOMETRY. [Gr. ζωον, animal; μετρον, measure]. The application of statistical methods to the study of animals.

ZOON. [Gr. ζωον, animal]. An individual that has developed from an egg.

ZOONEUSTON. [Gr. ζωον, animal; ναυστος, swimming]. Collectively, those animals associated with the water surface and influenced by surface tension; those associated with the upper surface being epineustic and those associated with the lower surface being hyponeustic. See also Neuston.

ZOONITE. [Gr. ζωον, animal; -ιτης, belonging to]. The body segment of an articulated animal.

ZOONOMY. [Gr. ζωον, animal; νομος, law]. Animal physiology.

ZOOPARASITE. [Gr. ζωον, animal; παρασιτος, parasite]. Any parasitic animal.

ZOOPHAGOUS. [Gr. ζωον, animal; -φαγος, -eating]. Feeding on animals or animal matter.

ZOORHRIA. [Gr. ζωον, animal; ρεω, to run]. the use of animals for migration. See Phoresy.

ZOOSEMIOTICS. [Gr. ζωον, animal; σημειωσις, visible sign]. The scientific study of animal communications.

ZOOSPERM. [Gr. ζωον, animal; σπερμα, seed]. See Spermatozoa.

ZOOTAXY. [Gr. ζωον, animal; ταξις, an arranging]. The classification of animals.

ZOOTOXIN. [Gr. ζωον, animal; τοξικον, poison]. Any toxin produced by animals.

ZORIDAE. [Gr. ζωρος, strong (undiluted)]. A family of wandering ghost spiders (infraorder Araneomorphae, superfamily Entelegynae); hunting spiders mainly from the topics, that are active during the day on low vegetation and at ground level. The eyes have a characteristic arrangement and the body is yellowish with distinctive brown markings. The female stands guard directly over her white flat egg sac, which is typically attached to a stone or leaf. In some classifications they may be included as a subfamily (Zorinae) of the **Miturgidae.**

ZOROPSIDAE. [Gr. ζωρος, pure; οψις, appearance]. The family of false wolf-spiders (infraorder Araneomorphae, superfamily Entelegynae). Cribellate spiders that can be distinguished from wolf-spiders by having two rows of eyes that are more equal than those of the **Lycosidae.** In some classifications, some of the **Tengellidae** and part of **Zorocratidae** are included here.

Z.P.G. Zero Population Growth. The population status in which births equal deaths.

z-series. [Ger. *zwischen*, between]. In the Mesostigmata: a designation for the longitudinal row of prodorsal setae between the j-series and the s-series which runs from the anterior paravertical setae z1 to setae z6 at or near the posterior margin of the pronotal region. See Lindquist-Evans System.

Z-series. [Ger. *zwischen*, between]. In the Mesostigmata: a designation for the longitudinal row of opisthodorsal setae between the J-series and the S-series which runs from the setae Z1 to setae Z5 at or near the posterior margin of the opisthonotal region. See Lindquist-Evans System.

ZUGSCHEIDE. [Ger. *zugscheide*, separate course/boundary]. A term sometimes used to describe a migratory divide, i.e. a line or narrow zone on either side of which the breeding populations migrate in different, divergent directions.

Zx. An the Mesostigmata: a designation for an extra seta in the Z-series on the opisthonotum, i.e. not assignable to setae Z1-5 in the Lindquist-Evans system.

ZYGOID PARTHENOGENESIS. [Gr. ζυγωδης, yoke-like]. See Parthenogenesis.

ZYGOMELOUS. [Gr. ζυγον, yoke; μελος, limb]. Having paired appendages.

ZYGOMORPHIC (MONOSYMMETRICAL). [Gr. ζυγον, yoke; μορφη, shape]. Bilaterally symmetrical; i.e. with only one plane of symmetry.

ZYGOPLEURAL. [Gr. ζυγον, yoke; πλευρον, side]. Bilaterally symmetrical.

ZYGOTAXIS. [Gr. ζυγον, yoke; ταξις, an arranging]. The mutual attraction between male and female gametes.

ZYGOTE. [Gr. ζυγωτος, yoked]. A fertilized ovum. A cell formed by the union of two gametes or reproductive cells.

APPENDIX ONE

Synopsis and Outline Classification of the Subclass Arachnida

One of the great problems, if not the greatest in any classification system, is that we are dealing with a continuum of forms of which only a small fraction is extant and an even smaller fraction is preserved as fossil material. Furthermore the continuum is multidimensional in that we measure or observe many varying physiological traits as well as biochemical and gross genetic characters; sometimes even behaviors. But, with the recent advent of molecular genetic analysis and an ever growing comprehension of what, exactly, genetic differences mean, we should soon reach a sounder understanding of relationships.

Splitters and **Lumpers**.   Casual terms for taxonomists who prefer a nomenclature that recognizes either fine distinctions (splitters) or broad groupings (lumpers). Here, I have tended towards splitting in order to include more rather than less groupings, as I prefer a nomenclature that recognizes finer distinctions, although in some areas a lumper's approach has been adopted. Thus I have no doubt exposed myself to the wroth of both camps. However, I also feel it is easier to start with a large field and reduce it as more knowledge becomes available, rather than the opposite. This is only my personal preference and ultimately, of course, it is unlikely that there will ever be a consensus; such is the nature of taxonomy.

This classification does not intend to be definitive, it is merely a list of what seems to be the most popularly accepted arrangement at the moment. It has been compiled from a number of authorities and sources, which may be found in the bibliography. This taxonomy is based on the latest scientific consensus (2021) and is provided as a general reference source. While every effort has been made to provide the most reliable and up-to-date information available, ultimately one will have to perform one's own research to confirm these data. Especially so as classification progresses in the light of continuous developments.
Synonyms and common but abandoned names are in parentheses.

SUBCLASS	ARACHNIDA	Extremely diverse, mostly terrestrial chelicerates that are mainly predatory. They have book lungs or tracheae derived from gills, and the body divided into two distinct regions; a prosoma (or cephalothorax), which bears two pairs of prehensile and sensory appendages and four pairs of walking legs; and an opisthosoma which contains most of the internal organs and glands. The two regions may be broadly jointed or narrowly connected by a pedicel.
SUPERORDER	ACARIFORMES	A large and biologically diverse chelicerate superorder of plant parasites, chiggers, hair follicle mites, velvet mites, water mites, fur, feather, dust and human itch mites, etc. This is the largest and most diverse group of mites, in terms of both morphology and ecological diversity. Over 300 families are recognized, containing over 30,000 described species. They range in size from less than 1 mm up to 10 mm and are distinguished from other arachnids by: the body not being divided into a cephalothorax and abdomen, and the basal leg segment (coxa) being internalized and thus leaving the next segment (trochanter) as the first functional leg segment. The mouthparts and associated sensory structures form a gnathosoma, and the legs, central nervous system, ocelli (where present), reproductive and digestive systems are all fused into a single unsegmented structure (opisthosoma). Most acariform mites also possess osmoregulatory

		organs known as genital papillae. Unique to this group are specialized setae. Some setae have a layer of optically active chitin (actinochitin) that is birefringent under polarized light. Other, unique, sensory setae include trichobothria (detect airborne vibrations and currents), solenidia (on the legs and detect vibrations and/or scent) and eupathidia (on the palptarsus or first leg tarsus and may be chemoreceptors).
ORDER	SARCOPTIFORMES	Micro-herbivores, fungivores and detritivores. Some have become associated with vertebrates and nest-building insects. These include the well known house dust mites, scab mites and mange mites, stored product mites, feather mites and some fur mites.
SUBORDER	ASTIGMATA (Astigmatina)	A very diverse group of mites in which the tracheal system is absent. This suborder includes many species which are parasites of vertebrates, e.g. the mange and scab-producing mites (Sarcoptidae and Psoroptidae) and the storage mites (Acaridae).
Superfamily	Acaroidea	Families: Acaridae, Gaudiellidae (syn. Platyglyphidae), Glycacaridae, Lardoglyphidae, Sapracaridae, Scatoglyphidae, Suidasiidae.
Superfamily	Analgoidea	Families: Alloptidae, Analgidae, Apionacaridae, Avenzoariidae, Cytoditidae, Dermationidae, Dermoglyphidae, Epidermoptidae, Laminosioptidae, Proctophyllodidae, Psoroptoididae, Pteronyssidae, Ptyssalgidae, Pyroglyphidae, Thysanocercidae, Trouessartiidae, Turbinoptidae, Xolalgidae, (incertae sedis) Heteropsoridae.
Superfamily	Canestrinioidea	Family: Canestriniidae, (incertae sedis) Lophonotacaridae.
Superfamily	Glycyphagoidea	Families: Aeroglyphidae, Chortoglyphidae, Echimyopodidae, Euglycyphagidae, Glycyphagidae, Pedetropodidae, Rosensteiniidae.
Superfamily	Hemisarcoptoidea	Families: Algophagidae, Carpoglyphidae, Chaetodactylidae, Hemisarcoptidae, Hyadesiidae, Meliponocoptidae, Winterschmidtiidae.
Superfamily	Histiostomatoidea	Families: Guanolichidae, Histiostomatidae.
Superfamily	Hypoderoidea	Family: Hypoderidae.
Superfamily	Pterolichoidea	Families: Ascouracaridae, Caudiferidae, Cheylabididae, Crypturoptidae, Eustathiidae, Falculiferidae, Freyanidae, Gabuciniidae, Kiwilichidae, Kramerellidae, Ochrolichidae, Oconnoriidae, Pterolichidae, Ptiloxenidae, Rectijanuidae, Syringobiidae, Thoracosathesidae, Vexillariidae.
Superfamily	Sarcoptoidea (Psoroptoidea)	Families: Atopomelidae, Chirodiscidae, Chirorhynchobiidae, Gastronyssidae, Lemurnyssidae, Listrophoridae, Lobalgidae, Myocoptidae, Pneumocoptidae, Psoroptidae, Rhyncoptidae, Sarcoptidae.

Superfamily	Schizoglyphoidea	Family: Schizoglyphidae.
Unassigned families		Chetochelacaridae, Heterocoptidae, Lemanniellidae.
SUBORDER	**ENDEOSTIGMATA**	Mites that are mainly fungivores, algivores or prey on minute soft-bodied invertebrates such as nematodes. The taxonomy of this group is in a state of confusion.
Infraorder	**Alicorhagiida**	
Superfamily	Alicorhagioidea	Family: Alicorhagiidae.
Infraorder	**Bimichaeliida**	
Superfamily	Alycoidea	Families: Alycidae, Nanorchestidae, Proterorhagiidae.
Infraorder	**Nematalycina**	
Superfamily	Nematalycoidea	Families: Micropsammidae, Nematalycidae, Proteonematalycidae.
Infraorder	**Terpnacarida**	
Superfamily	Oehserchestoidea	Families: Grandjeanicidae, Oehserchestidae.
Superfamily	Terpnacaroidea	Family: Terpnacaridae.
SUBORDER	**ORIBATIDA**	Soil-living mites known as beetle mites or armoured mites. Five postembryonic instars: larva, three nymphal instars and adult. All stages feed on a variety of material including living and dead plant and fungal material, lichens and carrion, some are predaceous, none are parasitic.
Infraorder	**Brachypylina**	
Section	**Poronoticae**	
Superfamily	Achipterioidea	Families: Achipteriidae (Austrachipteriidae), Epactozetidae, Tegoribatidae.
Superfamily	Ceratozetoidea (Limnozetoidea)	Families: Ceratozetidae (Heterozetidae), Chamobatidae, Humerobatidae, Limnozetidae, Maudheimiidae, Punctoribatidae (Mycobatidae).
Superfamily	Galumnoidea	Families: Galumnellidae, Galumnidae.
Superfamily	Licneremaeoidea	Families: Dendroeremaeidae, Lamellareidae, Licneremaeidae, Micreremidae, Passalozetidae, Scutoverticidae.
Superfamily	Microzetoidea	Family: Microzetidae.
Superfamily	Oribatelloidea	Families: Ceratokalummidae, Oribatellidae.
Superfamily	Oripodoidea (Oribatuloidea)	Families: Caloppiidae (Neotrichozetidae), Drymobatidae, Haplozetidae (Nasobatidae), Hemileiidae, Liebstadiidae, Mochlozetidae, Nesozetidae, Oribatulidae, Oripodidae (Parapirnodidae), Parakalummidae, Pirnodidae, Protoribatidae, Pseudoppiidae, Scheloribatidae, Symbioribatidae, Tubulozetidae.
Superfamily	Phenopelopoidea	Family: Phenopelopidea.
Superfamily	Unduloribatoidea (Eremaeozetoidea)	Families: Eremaeozetidae (syn. Idiozetidae), Unduloribatidae.
Superfamily	Zetomotrichoidea	Family: Zetomotrichidae.

Section	Pycnonoticae	
Superfamily	Amerobelboidea (Ameroidea)	Families: Ameridae, Amerobelbidae, Basilobelbidae, Ctenobelbidae, Damaeolidae, Eremobelbidae, Eremulidae, Heterobelbidae, Oxyameridae, Platyameridae, Spinozetidae, Staurobatidae.
Superfamily	Ameronothroidea	Families: Ameronothridae, Fortuyniidae, Selenoribatidae.
Superfamily	Carabodoidea	Families: Carabodidae, Nippobodidae.
Superfamily	Charassobatoidea	Families: Charassobatidae, Nosybeidae.
Superfamily	Cymbaeremaeoidea (Eremelloidea)	Families: Adhaesozetidae, Ametroproctidae, Cymbaeremaeidae, Eremellidae.
Superfamily	Damaeoidea	Families: Damaeidea, Hungarobelbidae.
Superfamily	Eremaeoidea	Families: Aribatidae, Caleremaeidae (incl. Megeremaeidae), Eremaeidae, Kodiakellidae, Oribellidae.
Superfamily	Eutegaeoidea (Cepheoidea)	Families: Cerocepheidae, Compactozetidae (syn. Cepheidae), Eutegaeidae, Microtegeidae, Nodocepheidae, Salvidae (syn. Pterobatidae), Tumerozetidae.
Superfamily	Gustavioidea	Families: Astegistidae, Ceratoppiidae, Gustaviidae, Liacaridae, Multoribulidae, Peloppiidae (syn. Metrioppiidae), Tenuialidae, Xenillidae.
Superfamily	Gymnodamaeoidea	Families: Aleurodamaeidae, Gymnodamaeidae.
Superfamily	Hermannielloidea	Families: Hermanniellidae, Plasmobatidae.
Superfamily	Hermannioidea	Family: Hermanniidae (Galapagacaridae).
Superfamily	Hydrozetoidea	Family: Hydrozetidae.
Superfamily	Nanhermannioidea	Family: Nanhermanniidae.
Superfamily	Neoliodoidea	Family: Neoliodidea.
Superfamily	Niphocepheoidea	Family: Niphocepheidae.
Superfamily	Oppioidea	Families: Arceremaeidae, Autognetidae, Decoroppiidae, Epimerellidae, Granuloppiidae, Lyroppiidae, Machadobelbidae, Machuellidae, Oppiidae, Papillonotidae, Quadroppiidae, Rioppiidae, Sternoppiidae, Teratoppiidae, Thyrisomidae, Tuparezetidae.
Superfamily	Otocepheoidea	Families: Dampfiellidae, Otocepheidae, Tetracondylidae, Tokunocepheidae.
Superfamily	Plateremaeoidea	Families: Licnobelbidae, Licnodamaeidae, Pheroliodidae, Plateremaeidae.
Superfamily	Polypterozetoidea	Families: Podopterotegaeidae, Polypterozetidae.
Superfamily	Tectocepheoidea	Families: Tectocepheidae, Tegeocranellidae.
Superfamily	Trizetoidea	Families: Cuneoppiidae, Rhynchoribatidae, Suctobelbidae, Trizetidae.
Superfamily	Zetorchestoidea	Family: Zetorchestidae.

Infraorder	Enarthronota	
Superfamily	Atopochthonioidea	Families: Atopochthoniidae (Phyllochthoniidae, Pterochthoniidae).
Superfamily	Brachychthonioidea	Family: Brachychthoniidae.
Superfamily	Cosmochthonioidea	Families: Cosmochthoniidae, Haplochthoniidae, Pediculochelidae, Sphaerochthoniidae.
Superfamily	Heterochthonioidea	Families: Arborichthoniidae, Heterochthoniidae, Nanohystricidae, Trichthoniidae.
Superfamily	Hypochthonioidea	Families: Eniochthoniidae, Hypochthoniidae, Psammochthoniidae.
Superfamily	Lohmannioidea	Family: Lohmanniidae.
Superfamily	Mesoplophoroidea	Family: Mesoplophoridae.
Superfamily	Protoplophoroidea	Family: Protoplophoroidae.
Infraorder	Holosomata (Desmonomata, Nothronata)	
Superfamily	Crotonioidea	Families: Crotoniidae (Camisiidae), Malaconothridae, Nothridae, Trhypochthoniidae.
Infraorder	Mixonomata	
Section	Dichosomata	
Superfamily	Epilohmannioidea	Family: Epilohmanniidae.
Superfamily	Eulohmannioidea	Family: Eulohmanniidae.
Superfamily	Nehypochthonioidea	Family: Nehypochthoniidae.
Superfamily	Perlohmannioidea	Families: Collohmanniidae, Perlohmaniidae.
Section	Euptyctima	
Superfamily	Euphthiracaroidea	Families: Euphthiracaridae, Oribotritiidae, Synichotritiidae.
Superfamily	Phthiracaroidea	Family: Phthiracaridae (Steganacaridae).
Infraorder	Palaeosomata	
Superfamily	Acaronychoidea	Family: Acaronychidae.
Superfamily	Palaeacaroidea (Ctenacaroidea)	Families: Aphelacaridae, Ctenacaridae, Palaeacaridae.
Infraorder	Parhyposomata	
Superfamily	Parhypochthonioidea	Families: Elliptochthoniidae, Gehypochthoniidae, Parhypochthoniidae.
ORDER	TROMBIDIFORMES	A large grouping of many plant parasite species, although many species are also predators, fungivores and animal parasites.
SUBORDER	PROSTIGMATA	The most diverse of the major mite groups. There is a single pair of spiracles located anteriorly near the mouth parts, and many species are pests on plants, parasites on vertebrates and invertebrates or predators of small invertebrates. Others have a more varied lifestyle or switch their food sources as they mature. Currently, the prostigmata are divided into four infraorders. However, the demarcation and interrelationships of these groups are entirely unclear.

Infraorder	Anystina	Many of the superfamilies included here are disputed.
Superfamily	Adamystoidea	Family: Adamystidae.
Superfamily	Allotanaupodoidea	Family: Allotanaupodidae.
Superfamily	Amphotrombioidea	Family: Amphotrombiidae.
Superfamily	Anystoidea	Families: Anystidae, Chulacaridae, Pseudocheylidae, Teneriffiidae.
Superfamily	Arrenuroidea	Families: Acalyptonotidae, Amoenacaridae, Arenohydracaridae, Arrenuridae, Athienemanniidae, Bogatiidae, Chappuisididae, Gretacaridae, Harpagopalpidae, Hungarohydracaridae, Kantacaridae, Krendowskiidae, Laversiidae, Mideidae, Mideopsidae, Momoniidae, Neoacaridae, Nipponacaridae, Nudomideopsidae, Uchidastygacaridae.
Superfamily	Caeculoidea	Family: Caeculidae.
Superfamily	Calyptostomatoidea	Family: Calyptostomatidea.
Superfamily	Chyzerioidea	Family: Chyzeriidae.
Superfamily	Erythraeoidea	Family: Erythraeidae, Smarididae.
Superfamily	Eylaoidea	Families: Apheviderulicidae, Eylaidae, Limnocharidae, Piersigiidae.
Superfamily	Hydrachnoidea	Family: Hydrachnidae.
Superfamily	Hydrovolzioidea	Family: Acherontacaridae, Hydrovolziidae.
Superfamily	Hydryphantoidea	Families: Ctenothyadidae, Hydrodromidae, Hydryphantidae (incl. Eupatrellidae), Malgasacaridae, Rhynchohydracaridae, Teratothyadidae, Thermacaridae, Zelandothyadidae.
Superfamily	Hygrobatoidea	Families: Astacocrotonidae, Aturidae, Feltriidae, Ferradasiidae, Frontipodopsidae, Hygrobatidae, Lethaxonidae, Limnesiidae, Omartacaridae, Pionidae, Pontarachnidae, Unionicolidae, Wettinidae.
Superfamily	Lebertioidea	Families: Acucapitidae, Anisitsiellidae (Nilotoniidae), Bandakiopsidae, Lebertiidae, Oxidae, Rutripalpidae, Sperchontidae, Stygotoniidae, Teutoniidae, Torrenticolidae.
Superfamily	Paratydeoidea	Families: Paratydeidae, Stigmocheylidae.
Superfamily	Pomerantzioidea	Family: Pomerantziidae.
Superfamily	Stygothrombioidea	Family: Stygothrombiidae.
Superfamily	Tanaupodoidea	Family: Tanaupodidae.
Superfamily	Trombiculoidea	Families: Audyanidae, Johnstonianidae, Leeuwenhoekiidae, Neotrombidiidae, Trombellidae, Trombiculidae, ?Vatacaridae, Walchiidae.

Superfamily	Trombidioidea	Families: Achaemenothrombiidae, , Microtrombidiidae (syn. Eutrombidiidae), Neotrombiidae, Podothrombiidae, Trombidiidae.
Superfamily	Yurebilloidea	Family: Yurebillidae.
Infraorder	**Eleutherengona**	
Superfamily	Cheyletoidea	Families: Cheyletidae, Demodecidae, Epimyodicidae, Harpyrhynchidae, Ophioptidae, Psorergatidae, Syringophilidae.
Superfamily	Cloacaroidea	Family: Cloacaridae.
Superfamily	Dolichocyboidea	Families: Crotalomorphidae, Dolichocybidae.
Superfamily	Heterocheyloidea	Family: Heterocheylidae.
Superfamily	Myobioidea	Family: Myobiidae.
Superfamily	Pterygosomatoidea	Family: Pterygosomatidae.
Superfamily	Pyemotoidea	Families: Acarophenacidae, ?Bembidiacaridae Caraboacaridae, Pyemotidae, Resinacaridae.
Superfamily	Raphignathoidea	Families: Barbutiidae, Caligonellidae, Camerobiidae, Cryptognathidae, Dasythyreidae, Eupalopsellidae, Homocaligidae, Mecognathidae, Raphignathidae, Stigmaeidae, Xenocaligonellididae.
Superfamily	Scutacaroidea	Families: Microdispidae, Neopygmephoridae, Pygmephoridae (syn Siteroptidae), Scutacaridae.
Superfamily	Tarsocheyloidea	Family: Tarsocheylidae.
Superfamily	Tarsonemoidea	Families: Podapolipidae (Podapolipodidae), Tarsonemidae.
Superfamily	Tetranychoidea	Families: Allochaetophoridae, Linotetranidae, Tenuipalpidae, Tetranychidae, Tuckerellidae.
Superfamily	Trochometridioidea	Families: Athyreacaridae, Trochometridiidae.
Infraorder	**Eupodina**	
Superfamily	Bdelloidea	Families: Bdellidae, Cunaxidae.
Superfamily	Eriophyoidea	Families: Diptilomiopidae, Eriophyidae, Nalepellidae, Pentasetacidae, Phytoptidae.
Superfamily	Eupodoidea	Families: Cocceupodidae, Dendrochaetidae, Eriorhynchidae, Eupodidae, Pentapalpidae, Penthaleidae, Penthalodidae, Rhagidiidae, Strandtmanniidae.
Superfamily	Halacaroidea	Families: Halacaridae, Pezidae.
Superfamily	Tydeoidea	Families: Ereynetidae, Iolinidae, Triophtydeidae, Tydeidae.
Infraorder	**Labidostommatina**	
Superfamily	Labidostommatoidea	Family: Labidostommatidae.
SUBORDER	**SPHAEROLICHIDA**	A small grouping of rounded soft-bodied white, yellow, yellow-brown, pink or red mites in which the prodorsum bears two pairs of filamentous trichobothria. A median eye may be present on the underside of the naso.

Superfamily	Lordalycoidea	<u>Family</u>: Lordalycidae.
Superfamily	Sphaerolichoidea	<u>Family</u>: Sphaerolichidae.
SUPERORDER	OPILIOACARIFORMES (syn. NOTOSTIGMATA)	Primitive, brightly colored mites that have a segmented abdomen and four pairs of spiracles located behind the fourth coxa.
ORDER	OPILIOACARIDA	<u>Family</u>: Opilioacaridae.
SUPERORDER	PARASITIFORMES	Soft-bodied, white, yellow, yellow-brown, pink or red mites; many are parasitic.
ORDER	HOLOTHYRIDA	Large, predatory mites from Australia, New Zealand and the Indo-Pacific region. <u>Families</u>: Allothyridae, Holothyridae, Neothyridae.
ORDER	IXODIDA	Haematophagous ticks that are ectoparasites of mammals, birds and occasionally reptiles and amphibians.
Superfamily	Ixodoidea	<u>Families</u>: Argasidae, Ixodidae, Nuttalliellidae.
ORDER	MESOSTIGMATA	Parasitic, free-living and predatory mites that can be recognized by the single pair of lateral spiracles.
SUBORDER	MONOGYNASPIDA	Free-living predatory mites associated with soil and leaf litter.
Infraorder	**Gamasina**	
Sub-cohort (in some classifications) **Dermanyssiae**		Superfamilies: Ascoidea, Dermanyssoidea, Eviphidoidea, Rhodacaroidea, Veigaioidea.
Superfamily	Arctacaroidea	<u>Family</u>: Arctacaridae
Superfamily	Ascoidea	<u>Families</u>: Ameroseiidae, Antennochelidae, Ascidae, Melicharidae.
Superfamily	Dermanyssoidea	<u>Families</u>: Dasyponyssidae, Dermanyssidae, Entonyssidae, Haemogamasidae, Halarachnidae, Hystrichonyssidae, Iphiopsididae, Ixodourhynchidae, Laelapidae (incl. Hirstionyssidae), Larvamimidae, Macronyssidae, Manitherionyssidae, Omentolaelapidae, Pneumophionyssidae, Raillietiidae, Rhinonyssidae, Spelaeorhynchidae, Spinturnicidae, Trichoaspididae, Varroidae.
Superfamily	Epicrioidea	<u>Families</u>: Dwigubskyiidae, Epicriidae.
Superfamily	Eviphidoidea	<u>Families</u>: Eviphididae, Leptolaelapidae, Macrochelidae, Megalolaelapidae, Pachylaelapidae, Parholaspididae.
Superfamily	Heatherelloidea	<u>Family</u>: Heatherellidae.
Superfamily	Parasitoidea	<u>Family</u>: Parasitidae.
Superfamily	Phytoseioidea	<u>Families</u>: Blattisociidae, Otopheidomenidae, Phytoseiidae, Podocinidae.
Superfamily	Rhodacaroidea	<u>Families</u>: Digamasellidae, Euryparasitidae, Halolaelapidae, Laelaptonyssidae, Ologamasidae, Rhodacaridae, Teranyssidae.
Superfamily	Veigaioidea	<u>Family</u>: Veigaiidae.

Superfamily	Zerconoidea	Families: Coprozercxonidae, Zerconidae.
Infraorder	**Uropodina**	
Superfamily	Diarthrophalloidea	Family: Diarthrophallidae.
Superfamily	Microgynioidea	Families: Nothogynidae, Microgyniidae.
Superfamily	Thinozerconoidea	Families: Protodinychidae, Thinozerconidae.
Superfamily	Uropodoidea	Families: Baloghjkaszabiidae, Brasiluropodidae, Cillibidae, Clausiadinychidae, Cyllibulidae, Deraiophoridae, Dinychidae, Discourellidae, Eutrachytidae, Hutufeideriidae, Kaszabjbaloghiidae, Macrodinychidae, Metagynuridae, Nenteriidae, Oplitidae, Phymatodiscidae, Polyaspididae, Prodinychidae, Rotundabaloghiidae, Tetrasejaspidae, Trachytidae, Trachyuropodidae, Trematuridae, Trichocyllibidae, Trichouropodellidae, Trigonuropodidae, Uroactiniidae, Urodiaspididae, Urodinychidae, Uropodidae.
SUBORDER	**SEJIDA (Sejina)**	
Superfamily	Heterozerconoidea	Families: Discozerconidae, Heterozerconidae.
Superfamily	Sejoidea	Families: Ichthyostomatogasteridae, Reginacharlottiidae, Sejidae, Uropodellidae.
SUBORDER	**TRIGYNASPIDA**	
Infraorder	**Antennophorina**	
Superfamily	Aenictequoidea	Families: Aenictequidae, Euphysalozerconidae , Messoracaridae, Ptochacaridae.
Superfamily	Antennophoroidea	Family: Antennophoridae.
Superfamily	Celaenopsoidea	Families: Celaenopsidae, Costacaridae, Diplogyniidae, Euzerconidae, Megacelaenopsida, Neotenogyniidae, Schizogyniidae, Triplogyniidae.
Superfamily	Fedrizzioidea	Families: Fedrizziidae, Klinckowstroemiidae.
Superfamily	Megisthanoidea	Families: Hoplomegistidae, Megisthanidae.
Superfamily	Paramegistoidea	Paramegistidae.
Superfamily	Parantennuloidea	Parantennulidae, Philodanidae, Promegistidae.
Infraorder	**Cercomegistina**	
Superfamily	Cercomegistoidea	Families: Asternoseiidae, Cercomegistidae, Davacaridae, Pyrosejidae, Saltiseiidae, Seiodidae, Vitzthumegistidae.
ORDER	**AMBLYPYGI**	Nocturnal, secretive, tropical and semi-tropical arachnids known as 'tail-less whip scorpions' or 'whip spiders'. They have a flattened body and a pair of powerful raptorial pedipalps. The first pair of legs are modified as long whip-like appendages. They walk with a crab-like gait and one of the long tactile legs is always pointed towards the direction of movement.
SUBORDER	**EUAMBLYPYGI**	
Superfamily	Charinoidea	Family: Charinidae.
Superfamily	Charontoidea	Family: Charontidae.

Superfamily	Phrynoidea	Families: Phrynichidae, Phrynidae.
SUBORDER	PALEOAMBLYPYGI	Family: Paracharontidae.
ORDER	ARANEAE	Spiders, ranging in size from 0.5 mm to about 9 cm and typically with a prosoma (cephalothorax) which is separated by a waist from the opisthosoma (abdomen) which is soft, unsegmented and bears several pairs of silk-producing spinnerets. Almost all species use their eight legs for walking and some jump by means of a sudden extension of the legs resulting from a very rapid rise in blood pressure. The convex carapace usually bears eight eyes anteriorly. Most spiders are carnivorous, they bite their prey with chelicerae, which uniquely bear poison glands and with which they may also hold and macerate the tissue during digestion. Approximately 131 families containing around 45,000 species, but more are being discovered every month.
SUBORDER	MESOTHELAE	Families: †Arthrolycosidae, †Arthromygalidae, Liphistiidae.
SUBORDER	OPISTHOTHELAE	
Infraorder	Mygalomorphae (Orthognatha)	In all species the plane of articulation of the fangs is the same as the long axis of the body; thus at rest they are folded along this axis, and many species use them for digging burrows.
Superfamily	Atypoidea	Families: Antrodiaetidae, Atypidae, Hexurellidae, Mecicobothriidae, Megahexuridae.
Superfamily	Avicularioidea	Families: Actinopodidae, Anamidae, Atracidae, Barychelidae, Bemmeridae, Ctenizidae, Cyrtaucheniidae, Dipluridae, Entypesidae, Euagridae, Euctenizidae, Halonoproctidae, Hexathelidae, Idiopidae, Ischnothelidae, Macrothelidae, Microhexuridae, Microstigmatidae, Migidae, Nemesiidae, Paratropididae, Porrhothelidae, Pycnothelidae, Stasimopidae, Theraphosidae.
Infraorder	Araneomorphae	In all species the plane of articulation of the chelicerae is at right angles to the long axis of the body and thus chelicerae act in a pincer-like fashion.
		Families: Filistatidae, Hypochilidae (may be in separate superfamily: Hypochiloidea), Leptonetida, Telemidae.
Superfamily	Austrochiloidea	Families: Austrochilidae, Gradungulidae.
Superfamily	Entelegynae	Families: Agelenidae, Amaurobiidae (incl. Chummidae), Ammoxenidae, Anapidae (incl. Holarchaeidae, Micropholcommatidae), Anyphaenidae, Araneidae (incl. Nephilidae), Argyronetidae, Arkyidae, Cheiracanthiidae (syn. Eutichuridae), Cithaeronidae, Clubionidae, Corinnidae, Ctenidae, Cyatholipidae, Cybaeidae, Cycloctenidae, Deinopidae, Desidae (Amphinectidae), Dictynidae, Eresidae, Gallieniellidae, Gnaphosidae (incl. Prodidomidae), Hahniidae, Hersiliidae,

		Homalonychidae, Lamponidae, Linyphiidae (incl. Sinopimoidae), Liocranidae, Lycosidae, Malkaridae (Pararchaeidae), Megadictynidae, Mimetidae, Miturgidae (incl. Zoridae), Mysmenidae, Nesticidae, Nicodamidae, Oecobiidae, Oxyopidae, Penestomidae, Philodromidae, Phrurolithidae, Physoglenidae, Phyxelididae, Pimoidae, Pisauridae, Psechridae, Salticidae, Selenopidae, Senoculidae, Sparassidae (Heteropodidae), Stiphidiidae, Symphytognathidae, Synaphridae , Synotaxidae, Tetragnathidae, Theridiidae, Theridiosomatidae, Thomisidae, Titanoecidae, Toxopidae, Trachelidae, Trechaleidae, Trochanteriidae, Udubidae (incl. part Zorocratidae), Uloboridae, Viridasiidae, Xenoctenidae, Zodariidae, Zoropsidae (incl. Tengellidae & part Zorocratidae).
Superfamily	Haplogynae (Synspermiata)	Caponiidae, Diguetidae, Drymusidae, Dysderidae, Ochyroceratidae, Oonopidae Orsolobidae, Pacullidae, Periegopidae, Pholcidae, †Pholcochyroceridae, Plectreuridae, Scytodidae, Segestriidae, Sicariidae (Loxoscelidae), Tetrablemmidae, Trogloraptoridae.
Superfamily	Hypochiloidea	Hypochilidae (may be included in the Haplogynae).
Superfamily	Palpimanoidea	Archaeidae, Huttoniidae, Mecysmaucheniidae, Palpimanidae, Stenochilidae.
Infraorder	**Mygalomorphae** (**Orthognatha**)	In all species the plane of articulation of the fangs is the same as the long axis of the body; thus at rest they are folded along this axis, and many species use them for digging burrows.
Superfamily	Atypoidea	Families: Antrodiaetidae, Atypidae, Hexurellidae, Mecicobothriidae, Megahexuridae.
Superfamily	Avicularioidea	Families: Actinopodidae, Anamidae, Atracidae, Barychelidae, Bemmeridae, Ctenizidae, Cyrtaucheniidae, Dipluridae, Entypesidae, Euagridae, Euctenizidae, Halonoproctidae, Hexathelidae, Idiopidae, Ischnothelidae, Macrothelidae, Microhexuridae, Microstigmatidae, Migidae, Nemesiidae, Paratropididae, Porrhothelidae, Pycnothelidae, Stasimopidae, Theraphosidae.
ORDER	**OPILIONES** (**PHALANGIDA**)	Temperate and tropical long-legged spiders in which the prosoma is broadly jointed to the short, externally segmented abdomen but without a constriction between the two divisions. Silk glands lacking, chelicerae are three-jointed and bear pincers, pedipalps are leg-like. Leg autotomy is an important means of defence but regeneration is lacking. The taxonomy of this order is in a state of flux and some confusion.
SUBORDER	**CYPHOPHTHALMI**	
Infraorder	**Boreophthalmi**	Families: Sironidae, Stylocellidae.
Infraorder	**Scopulophthalmi**	Family: Pettalidae

Infraorder	**Sternophthalmi**	Families: Neogoveidae, Ogoveidae, Troglosironidae.
SUBORDER	**DYSPNOI**	
Superfamily	Acropsopilionidae	Family: Acropsopilionidae
Superfamily	Ischyropsalidoidea	Families: Ischyropsalididae (incl Ceratolasmatidae), Sabaconidae, Taracidae.
Superfamily	Troguloidea	Families: Dicranolasmatidae, †Eotrogulidae, Nemastomatidae, †Nemastomoididae, Nipponopsalididae, Trogulidae.
SUBORDER	**EUPNOI**	
Superfamily	Caddoidea	Family: Caddidae.
Superfamily	Phalangioidea	Families: Monoscutidae, Neopilionidae, Phalangiidae, Protolophidae, Sclerosomatidae, Stygophalangiidae.
SUBORDER	**LANIATORES** (INSIDIATORES)	
Superfamily	Travunioidea	Families: Nippononychidae, Paranonychidae, Travuniidae (syn Cladonychiidae, Pentanychidae).
Superfamily	Triaenonychoidea	Families: Synthetonychidae, Triaenonychidae.
Infraorder	**Grassatores**	
Superfamily	Assamioidea	Families: Assamiidae, Pyramidopidae.
Superfamily	Epedanoidea	Families: Epedanidae, Petrobunidae, Podoctidae, Sandokanidae (incl Oncopodidae), Tithaeidae.
Superfamily	Gonyleptoidea	Families: Agoristenidae, Cosmetidae, Cranaidae, Gonyleptidae, Manaosbiidae, Metasarcidae, Stygnidae, Stygnopsidae, Tricommatidae.
Superfamily	Phalangodoidea	Family: Phalangodidae.
Superfamily	Samooidea	Families: Biantidae, Samoidae, Stygnommatidae.
Superfamily	Zalmoxoidea	Families: Escadabiidae, Fissiphalliidae, Guasiniidae, Icaleptidae, Kimulidae, Zalmoxidae.
	Genera *incertae sedis*	Alpazia, Anamota, Arulla, Ausulus, Babrius, Bebedoura, Belemarua, Biconibunus, Bindoona, Bissopius, Caecobunus, Caribula, Cleombrotus, Contuor, Costabrimma, Detlefilus, Gjellerupia, Gunturius, Heterobabrius, Ignacianulus, Isaeolus, Jimeneziella, Johorella, Kokoda, Liomma, Manuelangelia, Metaconomma, Metapellobunus, Micrisaeus, Microconomma, Mirda, Munis, Neoparalus, Neoscotolemon, Octophthalmus, Ortizia, Ostracidium, Parabupares, Paraconomma, Paraphalangodus, Pegulius, Peltamma, Pentos, Phalangodinus, Philacarus, Proscotolemon, Pseudomitraceras, Pucallpana, Seblatus, Sergitius, Siryseus, Spalicus, Spinolatum, Stygnomimus, Tarmaops, Turquinia, Tweedielus, Valifema.
SUBORDER	**TETROPHTHALMI**	*Hastocularis argus, Eophalangium sheari.*

ORDER	PALPIGRADI	Microwhip scorpions. Segmented abdomen is broadly joined to the prosoma and bears a long, jointed, mobile, whip-like terminal flagellum. Pedipalps undifferentiated and used as a pair of walking legs, however, the first pair of legs appear to have a sensory function and are held off the ground during locomotion. Eyes are absent. Families: Eukoeneniidae, Prokoeneniidae.
ORDER	PSEUDOSCORPIONES	Minute, flattened arachnids which resemble scorpions but do not possess a stinging organ. There are two pairs of tracheae ventrally on the third and fourth abdominal segments and one or two pairs of eyes at each anterior lateral corner of the rectangular carapace. Within the small chelicerae are several ducts leading from a pair of silk glands in the prosoma, the silk being used for constructing over-wintering, moulting and brood chambers.
SUBORDER	ATOPOSPHYRONIDA	
Superfamily	Feaelloidea	Families: Feaellidae, Pseudogarypidae.
SUBORDER	HETEROSPHYRONIDA (EPIOCHEIRATA)	
Superfamily	Chthonioidea	Families: Chthoniidae, †Dracochelidae (Devonian fossil), Lechytiidae, Pseudotyrannochthoniidae, Tridenchthoniidae.
SUBORDER	IOCHEIRATA	
Superfamily	Cheiridioidea	Families: Cheiridiidae (maybe in Garypoidea), Pseudochiridiidae (maybe in Garypoidea).
Superfamily	Cheliferoidea	Families: Atemnidae, Cheliferidae, Chernetidae, Withiidae.
Superfamily	Garypinoidea	Families: Garypinidae, Larcidae.
Superfamily	Garypoidea	Families: Garypidae, Geogarypidae, Hesperolpiidae, Menthidae, Olpiidae.
Superfamily	Neobisioidea	Families: Bochicidae, Gymnobisiidae, Hyidae, Ideoroncidae, Neobisiidae, Parahyidae, Syarinidae.
Superfamily	Sternophoroidea	Family: Sternophoridae.
ORDER	RICINULEI (PODOGONA)	Slow-moving, eyeless arachnids that inhabit leaf mould and caves in tropical Africa and America. On hatching the spiderling is a six-legged 'larva' similar to that of ticks and mites.
SUBORDER	NEORICINULEI	
Superfamily	Ricinoidoidea	Family: Ricinoididae.
ORDER	SCHIZOMIDA (SCHIZOPELTIDA, TARTARIDAE)	Small tropical arachnids in which the prosoma is divided into three regions, each covered dorsally by thin separate plates of chitin.
Superfamily	Hubbardioidea	†Calcitronidae, Hubbardiidae (Schizomidae), ProtoSchizomidae.

ORDER	SCORPIONES	Scorpions. Large, primitive, secretive, nocturnal arachnids that have changed little from their aquatic ancestors of the Silurian. The prosoma is covered by a single carapace and broadly joins the abdomen, which is divided into a wide, seven-segmented preabdomen (anterior mesosoma) and a long, postabdomen (posterior metasoma) consisting of five, narrow, ring-shaped segments terminating in a telson with a venomous sting. The chelicerae are very small but the pedipals are greatly enlarged to form a pair of large pincers. There is a pair of median eyes (except in some cave-dwelling species) and two to five pairs of lateral eyes on the carapace margin. There is very little sexual dimorphism and a high degree of parental care.
Superfamily	Buthoidea	Families: †Archaeobuthidae, Buthidae, Microcharmidae, †Palaeoburmesebuthidae, †Protobuthidae.
Superfamily	Chactoidea	Families: Chactidae, Euscorpiidae, Superstitioniidae, Troglotayosicidae, Typhlochactidae, Vaejovidae.
Superfamily	Chaeriloidea	Family: Chaerilidae.
Superfamily	Iuroidea	Families: Caraboctonidae, Iuridae.
Superfamily	Pseudochactoidea	Family: Pseudochactidae.
Superfamily	Scorpionoidea	Families: Bothriuridae, Diplocentridae (or subfamily of Scorpionidae), Hemiscorpiidae (syn. Ischnuridae/Liochelidae), Heteroscorpionidae (contentious), Scorpionidae.

ORDER	SOLIFUGAE (SOLPUGIDA)	Sun spiders, wind scorpions, sun scorpions, camel spiders, false spiders and gerrymanders. Large arachnids in which the prosoma is divided into a large anterior carapace (proterosoma) and a short posterior section. The abdomen is large, broadly joined to the prosoma and visibly segmented. The entire body is covered with long, sensory hairs. The chelicerae are enormously enlarged, chelate and armed with teeth. The pedipalps are leg-like, sensory and terminate in an adhesive organ used in the capture of prey. Only six legs are used for walking, the first pair having become slender, reduced and used as tactile organs. Families: Ammotrechidae, Ceromidae, Daesiidae, Eremobatidae, Galeodidae, Gylippidae, Hexisopodidae, Karschiidae, Melanoblossiidae, Mummuciidae, †Protosolpugidae, Rhagodidae, Solpugidae.
ORDER	UROPYGI (THELYPHONIDA)	Whip scorpions. Small to medium sized, nocturnal arachnids which bear a pair of powerful pincers (pedipalpi) that are held flexed and parallel to the ground. The long antenniform first pair of legs are not used in locomotion but have a sensory-tactile function. On the terminal segment is a long, whip-like flagellum which, when disturbed, they elevate and eject a stream of noxious fluid from anal glands. The prosoma is covered by a dorsal carapace that carries a simple pair of anterior eyes and on either side a cluster of three to four eyes. The female dies shortly after the young disperse. Family: Thelyphonidae.

APPENDIX TWO
Alphabetical List of 789 Families

Family	In the sequence, where these categories exist: Superfamily : Infraorder : Suborder : **Order** : Superorder
Acalyptonotidae	Arrenuroidea : Anystina : Prostigmata : **Trombidiformes** : Acariformes
Acaridae	Acaroidea : - : Astigmata : **Sarcoptiformes** : Acariformes
Acaronychidae	Acaronychoidea : Palaeosomata : Oribatida : **Sarcoptiformes** : Acariformes
Acarophenacidae	Pyemotoidea : Eleutherengona : Prostigmata : **Trombidiformes** : Acariformes
Achaemenothrombiidae	Trombidioidea : Anystina : Prostigmata : **Trombidiformes** : Acariformes
Acherontacaridae	Hydrovolzioidea : Anystina : Prostigmata : **Trombidiformes** : Acariformes
Achipteriidae (Austrachipteriidae)	Achipterioidea : Brachypylina sec. Poronoticae : Oribatida : **Sarcoptiformes** : Acariformes
Acropsopilionidae	Acropsopilionoidea : - : Dyspnoi : **Opiliones**
Actinopodidae	Avicularioidea : Mygalomorphae (Orthognatha) : Opisthothelae : **Araneae**
Acucapitidae	Lebertioidea : Anystina : Prostigmata : **Trombidiformes** : Acariformes
Adamystidae	Adamystoidea : Anystina : Prostigmata : **Trombidiformes** : Acariformes
Adelphacaridae	Palaeacaroidea (Ctenacaroidea) : Palaeosomata : Oribatida : **Sarcoptiformes** : Acariformes
Adhaesozetidae	Cymbaeremaeoidea (Eremelloidea) : Brachypylina sec. Pycnonoticae : Oribatida : **Sarcoptiformes** : Acariformes
Aenictequidae	Aenictequoidea : Antennophorina : Trigynaspida : **Mesostigmata** : Parasitiformes
Aeroglyphidae	Glycyphagoidea : - : Astigmata : **Sarcoptiformes** : Acariformes
Agelenidae	Entelegynae : Araneomorphae (Labidognatha) : Opisthothelae : **Araneae**
Agoristenidae	Gonyleptoidea : Grassatores : Laniatores : **Opiliones**
Aleurodamaeidae	Gymnodamaeoidea : Brachypylina sec. Pycnonoticae : Oribatida : **Sarcoptiformes** : Acariformes
Algophagidae	Hemisarcoptoidea : - : Astigmata : **Sarcoptiformes** : Acariformes
Alicorhagiidae	Alicorhagioidea : Alicorhagiida : Endeostigmata : **Sarcoptiformes** : Acariformes
Allochaetophoridae	Tetranychoidea : Eleutherengona : Prostigmata : **Trombidiformes** : Acariformes

Alloptidae	Analgoidea : - : Astigmata : **Sarcoptiformes** : Acariformes
Allotanaupodidae	Allotanaupodoidea : Anystina : Prostigmata : **Trombidiformes** : Acariformes
Allothyridae	- : - : - : **Holothyrida** (Tetrastigmata) : Parasitiformes
Alycidae	Alycoidea : Bimichaeliida : Endeostigmata : **Sarcoptiformes** : Acariformes
Amaurobiidae (incl. Chummidae)	Entelegynae : Araneomorphae (Labidognatha) : Opisthothelae : **Araneae**
Ameridae	Amerobelboidea (Ameroidea) : Brachypylina sec. Pycnonoticae : Oribatida : **Sarcoptiformes** : Acariformes
Amerobelbidae	Amerobelboidea (Ameroidea) : Brachypylina sec. Pycnonoticae : Oribatida : **Sarcoptiformes** : Acariformes
Ameronothridae	Ameronothroidea : Brachypylina sec. Pycnonoticae : Oribatida : **Sarcoptiformes** : Acariformes
Ameroseiidae	Ascoidea : Gamasina : Monogynaspida : **Mesostigmata** : Parasitiformes
Ametroproctidae	Cymbaeremaeoidea (Eremelloidea) : Brachypylina sec. Pycnonoticae : Oribatida : **Sarcoptiformes** : Acariformes
Ammotrechidae	- : - : - : **Solifugae**
Ammoxenidae	Entelegynae : Araneomorphae (Labidognatha) : Opisthothelae : **Araneae**
Amoenacaridae	Arrenuroidea : Anystina : Prostigmata : **Trombidiformes** : Acariformes
Amphotrombiidae	Amphotrombioidea : Anystina : Prostigmata : **Trombidiformes** : Acariformes
Analgidae	Analgoidea : - : Astigmata : **Sarcoptiformes** : Acariformes
Anamidae	Avicularioidea : Mygalomorphae (Orthognatha) : Opisthothelae : **Araneae**
Anapidae (incl. Holarchaeidae, Micropholcommatidae)	Entelegynae : Araneomorphae (Labidognatha) : Opisthothelae : **Araneae**
Anisitsiellidae (Nilotoniidae)	Lebertioidea : Anystina : Prostigmata : **Trombidiformes** : Acariformes
Antennochelidae	Ascoidea : Gamasina : Monogynaspida : **Mesostigmata** : Parasitiformes
Antennophoridae	Antennophoroidea : Antennophorina : Trigynaspida : **Mesostigmata** : Parasitiformes
Antrodiaetidae	Atypoidea : Mygalomorphae (Orthognatha) : Opisthothelae : **Araneae**
Anyphaenidae	Entelegynae : Araneomorphae (Labidognatha) : Opisthothelae : **Araneae**
Anystidae	Anystoidea : Anystina : Prostigmata : **Trombidiformes** : Acariformes

303

Apheviderulicidae	Eylaoidea : Anystina : Prostigmata : **Trombidiformes** : Acariformes
Apionacaridae	Analgoidea : - : Astigmata : **Sarcoptiformes** : Acariformes
Araneidae	Entelegynae : Araneomorphae (Labidognatha) : Opisthothelae : **Araneae**
Arborichthoniidae	Heterochthonioidea : Enarthronota : Oribatida : **Sarcoptiformes** : Acariformes
Arceremaeidae	Oppioidea : Brachypylina sec. Pycnonoticae : Oribatida : **Sarcoptiformes** : Acariformes
Archaeidae	Palpimanoidea : Araneomorphae (Labidognatha) : Opisthothelae : **Araneae**
Archaeobuthidae †	Buthoidea : - : - : **Scorpiones**
Arctacaridae	Arctacaroidea : Gamasina : Monogynaspida : **Mesostigmata** : Parasitiformes
Arenohydracaridae	Arrenuroidea : Anystina : Prostigmata : **Trombidiformes** : Acariformes
Argasidae	Ixodoidea : - : - : **Ixodida** : Parasitiformes
Argyronetidae	Entelegynae : Araneomorphae (Labidognatha) : Opisthothelae : **Araneae**
Aribatidae	Eremaeoidea : Brachypylina sec. Pycnonoticae : Oribatida : **Sarcoptiformes** : Acariformes
Arkyidae	Entelegynae : Araneomorphae (Labidognatha) : Opisthothelae : **Araneae**
Arrenuridae	Arrenuroidea : Anystina : Prostigmata : **Trombidiformes** : Acariformes
Arthrolycosidae †	- : - : Mesothelae : **Araneae**
Arthromygalidae †	- : - : Mesothelae : **Araneae**
Ascidae	Ascoidea : Gamasina : Monogynaspida : **Mesostigmata** : Parasitiformes
Ascouracaridae	Pterolichoidea : - : Astigmata : **Sarcoptiformes** : Acariformes
Assamiidae	Assamioidea : Grassatores : Laniatores : **Opiliones**
Astacocrotonidae	Hygrobatoidea : Anystina : Prostigmata : **Trombidiformes** : Acariformes
Astegistidae	Gustavioidea (Liacaroidea) : Brachypylina sec. Pycnonoticae : Oribatida : **Sarcoptiformes** : Acariformes
Asternoseiidae	Cercomegistoidea : Cercomegistina : Trigynaspida : **Mesostigmata** : Parasitiformes
Atemnidae	Cheliferoidea : - : Iocheirata : **Pseudoscorpiones** (Chelonethida Pseudoscorpionida)
Athienemanniidae	Arrenuroidea : Anystina : Prostigmata : **Trombidiformes** : Acariformes
Athyreacaridae	Trochometridioidea : Eleutherengona : Prostigmata : **Trombidiformes** : Acariformes
Atopochthoniidae (Phyllochthoniidae, Pterochthoniidae)	Zetorchestoidea : Enarthronota : Oribatida : **Sarcoptiformes** : Acariformes

Atopomelidae	Sarcoptoidea : - : Astigmata : **Sarcoptiformes** : Acariformes
Atracidae	Avicularioidea : Mygalomorphae (Orthognatha) : Opisthothelae : **Araneae**
Aturidae	Hygrobatoidea : Anystina : Prostigmata : **Trombidiformes** : Acariformes
Atypidae	Atypoidea : Mygalomorphae (Orthognatha) : Opisthothelae : **Araneae**
Audyanidae	Trombiculoidea : Anystina : Prostigmata : **Trombidiformes** : Acariformes
Austrochilidae	Austrochiloidea : Araneomorphae (Labidognatha) : Opisthothelae : **Araneae**
Autognetidae	Oppioidea : Brachypylina sec. Pycnonoticae : Oribatida : **Sarcoptiformes** : Acariformes
Avenzoariidae	Analgoidea : - : Astigmata : **Sarcoptiformes** : Acariformes
Baloghjkaszabiidae	Uropodoidea : Uropodina : Monogynaspida : **Mesostigmata** : Parasitiformes
Bandakiopsidae	Lebertioidea : Anystina : Prostigmata : **Trombidiformes** : Acariformes
Barbutiidae	Raphignathoidea : Eleutherengona : Prostigmata : **Trombidiformes** : Acariformes
Barychelidae	Avicularioidea : Mygalomorphae (Orthognatha) : Opisthothelae : **Araneae**
Basilobelbidae	Amerobelboidea (Ameroidea) : Brachypylina sec. Pycnonoticae : Oribatida : **Sarcoptiformes** : Acariformes
Bdellidae	Bdelloidea : Eupodina : Prostigmata : **Trombidiformes** : Acariformes
Bembidiacaridae	Pyemotoidea : Eleutherengona : Prostigmata : **Trombidiformes** : Acariformes
Bemmeridae	Avicularioidea : Mygalomorphae (Orthognatha) : Opisthothelae : **Araneae**
Biantidae	Samooidea : Grassatores : Laniatores : **Opiliones**
Blattisociidae	Phytoseioidea : Gamasina : Monogynaspida : **Mesostigmata** : Parasitiformes
Bochicidae	Neobisioidea : - : Iocheirata : **Pseudoscorpiones** (Chelonethida Pseudoscorpionida)
Bogatiidae	Arrenuroidea : Anystina : Prostigmata : **Trombidiformes** : Acariformes
Bothriuridae	Scorpionoidea (Bothriuroidea) : - : - : **Scorpiones**
Brachychthoniidae	Brachychthonioidea : Enarthronota : Oribatida : **Sarcoptiformes** : Acariformes
Brasiluropodidae	Uropodoidea : Uropodina : Monogynaspida : **Mesostigmata** : Parasitiformes
Buthidae	Buthoidea : - : - : **Scorpiones**
Caddidae	Caddoidea : - : Eupnoi : **Opiliones**
Caeculidae	Caeculoidea : Anystina : Prostigmata : **Trombidiformes** : Acariformes
Calcitronidae †	Hubbardioidea : - : - : **Schizomida**

305

Caleremaeidae (incl. Megeremaeidae)	Eremaeoidea : Brachypylina sec. Pycnonoticae : Oribatida : **Sarcoptiformes** : Acariformes
Caligonellidae	Raphignathoidea : Eleutherengona : Prostigmata : **Trombidiformes** : Acariformes
Caloppiidae (Neotrichozetidae)	Oripodoidea (Oribatuloidea) : Brachypylina sec. Poronoticae : Oribatida : **Sarcoptiformes** : Acariformes
Calyptostomatidae	Calyptostomatoidea : Anystina : Prostigmata : **Trombidiformes** : Acariformes
Camerobiidae	Raphignathoidea : Eleutherengona : Prostigmata : **Trombidiformes** : Acariformes
Canestriniidae	Canestrinioidea : - : Astigmata : **Sarcoptiformes** : Acariformes
Caponiidae	Haplogynae (Synspermiata) : Araneomorphae (Labidognatha) : Opisthothelae : **Araneae**
Caraboacaridae	Pyemotoidea : Eleutherengona : Prostigmata : **Trombidiformes** : Acariformes
Caraboctonidae	Iuroidea : - : - : **Scorpiones**
Carabodidae	Carabodoidea : Brachypylina sec. Pycnonoticae : Oribatida : **Sarcoptiformes** : Acariformes
Carpoglyphidae	Hemisarcoptoidea : - : Astigmata : **Sarcoptiformes** : Acariformes
Caudiferidae	Pterolichoidea : - : Astigmata : **Sarcoptiformes** : Acariformes
Celaenopsidae	Celaenopsoidea : Antennophorina : Trigynaspida : **Mesostigmata** : Parasitiformes
Ceratokalummidae	Oribatelloidea : Brachypylina sec. Poronoticae : Oribatida : **Sarcoptiformes** : Acariformes
Ceratoppiidae	Gustavioidea (Liacaroidea) : Brachypylina sec. Pycnonoticae : Oribatida : **Sarcoptiformes** : Acariformes
Ceratozetidae (Heterozetidae)	Ceratozetoidea (Limnozetoidea) : Brachypylina sec. Poronoticae : Oribatida : **Sarcoptiformes** : Acariformes
Cercomegistidae	Cercomegistoidea : Cercomegistina : Trigynaspida : **Mesostigmata** : Parasitiformes
Cerocepheidae	Eutegaeoidea (Cepheoidea) : Brachypylina sec. Pycnonoticae : Oribatida : **Sarcoptiformes** : Acariformes
Ceromidae	- : - : - : **Solifugae**
Chactidae	Chactoidea (Vaejovoidea) : - : - : **Scorpiones**
Chaerilidae	Chaeriloidea : - : - : **Scorpiones**
Chaetodactylidae	Hemisarcoptoidea : - : Astigmata : **Sarcoptiformes** : Acariformes
Chamobatidae	Ceratozetoidea (Limnozetoidea) : Brachypylina sec. Poronoticae : Oribatida : **Sarcoptiformes** : Acariformes
Chappuisididae	Arrenuroidea : Anystina : Prostigmata : **Trombidiformes** : Acariformes

Charassobatidae	Charassobatoidea : Brachypylina sec. Pycnonoticae : Oribatida : **Sarcoptiformes** : Acariformes
Charinidae	Charinoidea : - : Euamblypygi : **Amblypygi**
Charontidae	Charontoidea : - : Euamblypygi : **Amblypygi**
Cheiracanthiidae (Eutichuridae)	Entelegynae : Araneomorphae (Labidognatha) : Opisthothelae : **Araneae**
Cheiridiidae	Cheiridioidea : - : Iocheirata : **Pseudoscorpiones** (Chelonethida Pseudoscorpionida)
Cheliferidae	Cheliferoidea : - : Iocheirata : **Pseudoscorpiones** (Chelonethida Pseudoscorpionida)
Chernetidae	Cheliferoidea : - : Iocheirata : **Pseudoscorpiones** (Chelonethida Pseudoscorpionida)
Chetochelacaridae	- : - : Astigmata : **Sarcoptiformes** : Acariformes
Cheylabididae	Pterolichoidea : - : Astigmata : **Sarcoptiformes** : Acariformes
Cheyletidae	Cheyletoidea : Eleutherengona : Prostigmata : **Trombidiformes** : Acariformes
Chirodiscidae	Sarcoptoidea : - : Astigmata : **Sarcoptiformes** : Acariformes
Chirorhynchobiidae	Sarcoptoidea : - : Astigmata : **Sarcoptiformes** : Acariformes
Chortoglyphidae	Glycyphagoidea : - : Astigmata : **Sarcoptiformes** : Acariformes
Chthoniidae	Chthonioidea : - : Heterosphyronida (Epiocheirata) : **Pseudoscorpiones** (Chelonethida Pseudoscorpionida)
Chulacaridae	Anystoidea : Anystina : Prostigmata : **Trombidiformes** : Acariformes
Chyzeriidae	Chyzerioidea : Anystina : Prostigmata : **Trombidiformes** : Acariformes
Cillibidae	Uropodoidea : Uropodina : Monogynaspida : **Mesostigmata** : Parasitiformes
Cithaeronidae	Entelegynae : Araneomorphae (Labidognatha) : Opisthothelae : **Araneae**
Clausiadinychidae	Uropodoidea : Uropodina : Monogynaspida : **Mesostigmata** : Parasitiformes
Cloacaridae	Cloacaroidea : Eleutherengona : Prostigmata : **Trombidiformes** : Acariformes
Clubionidae	Entelegynae : Araneomorphae (Labidognatha) : Opisthothelae : **Araneae**
Cocceupodidae	Eupodoidea : Eupodina : Prostigmata : **Trombidiformes** : Acariformes
Collohmanniidae	Perlohmannioidea : Mixonomata sec. Dichosomata : Oribatida : **Sarcoptiformes** : Acariformes
Compactozetidae (Cepheidae)	Eutegaeoidea (Cepheoidea) : Brachypylina sec. Pycnonoticae : Oribatida : **Sarcoptiformes** : Acariformes
Coprozerconidae	Zerconoidea : Gamasina : Monogynaspida : **Mesostigmata** : Parasitiformes

Corinnidae	Entelegynae : Araneomorphae (Labidognatha) : Opisthothelae : **Araneae**
Cosmetidae	Gonyleptoidea : Grassatores : Laniatores : **Opiliones**
Cosmochthoniidae	Cosmochthonioidea : Enarthronota : Oribatida : **Sarcoptiformes** : Acariformes
Costacaridae	Celaenopsoidea : Antennophorina : Trigynaspida : **Mesostigmata** : Parasitiformes
Cranaidae	Gonyleptoidea : Grassatores : Laniatores : **Opiliones**
Crotalomorphidae	Dolichocyboidea : Eleutherengona : Prostigmata : **Trombidiformes** : Acariformes
Crotoniidae (Camisiidae)	Crotonioidea (Nothroidea) : Holosomata (Desmonomata, Nothronata) : Oribatida : **Sarcoptiformes** : Acariformes
Cryptognathidae	Raphignathoidea : Eleutherengona : Prostigmata : **Trombidiformes** : Acariformes
Crypturoptidae	Pterolichoidea : - : Astigmata : **Sarcoptiformes** : Acariformes
Ctenacaridae	Palaeacaroidea (Ctenacaroidea) : Palaeosomata : Oribatida : **Sarcoptiformes** : Acariformes
Ctenidae	Entelegynae : Araneomorphae (Labidognatha) : Opisthothelae : **Araneae**
Ctenizidae	Avicularioidea : Mygalomorphae (Orthognatha) : Opisthothelae : **Araneae**
Ctenobelbidae	Amerobelboidea (Ameroidea) : Brachypylina sec. Pycnonotica : Oribatida : **Sarcoptiformes** : Acariformes
Ctenothyadidae	Hydryphantoidea : Anystina : Prostigmata : **Trombidiformes** : Acariformes
Cunaxidae	Bdelloidea : Eupodina : Prostigmata : **Trombidiformes** : Acariformes
Cuneoppiidae	Trizetoidea : Brachypylina sec. Pycnonoticae : Oribatida : **Sarcoptiformes** : Acariformes
Cyatholipidae	Entelegynae : Araneomorphae (Labidognatha) : Opisthothelae : **Araneae**
Cybaeidae	Entelegynae : Araneomorphae (Labidognatha) : Opisthothelae : **Araneae**
Cycloctenidae	Entelegynae : Araneomorphae (Labidognatha) : Opisthothelae : **Araneae**
Cyllibulidae	Uropodoidea : Uropodina : Monogynaspida : **Mesostigmata** : Parasitiformes
Cymbaeremaeidae	Cymbaeremaeoidea (Eremelloidea) : Brachypylina sec. Pycnonoticae : Oribatida : **Sarcoptiformes** : Acariformes
Cyrtaucheniidae	Avicularioidea : Mygalomorphae (Orthognatha) : Opisthothelae : **Araneae**
Cytoditidae	Analgoidea : - : Astigmata : **Sarcoptiformes** : Acariformes
Daesiidae	- : - : - : **Solifugae**

Damaeidae	Damaeoidea : Brachypylina sec. Pycnonoticae : Oribatida : **Sarcoptiformes** : Acariformes
Damaeolidae	Amerobelboidea (Ameroidea) : Brachypylina sec. Pycnonoticae : Oribatida : **Sarcoptiformes** : Acariformes
Dampfiellidae	Otocepheoidea : Brachypylina sec. Pycnonoticae : Oribatida : **Sarcoptiformes** : Acariformes
Dasyponyssidae	Dermanyssoidea : Gamasina : Monogynaspida : **Mesostigmata** : Parasitiformes
Dasythyreidae	Raphignathoidea : Eleutherengona : Prostigmata : **Trombidiformes** : Acariformes
Davacaridae	Cercomegistoidea : Cercomegistina : Trigynaspida : **Mesostigmata** : Parasitiformes
Decoroppiidae	Oppioidea : Brachypylina sec. Pycnonoticae : Oribatida : **Sarcoptiformes** : Acariformes
Deinopidae	Entelegynae : Araneomorphae (Labidognatha) : Opisthothelae : **Araneae**
Demodicidae	Cheyletoidea : Eleutherengona : Prostigmata : **Trombidiformes** : Acariformes
Dendrochaetidae	Eupodoidea : Eupodina : Prostigmata : **Trombidiformes** : Acariformes
Dendroeremaeidae	Licneremaeoidea : Brachypylina sec. Poronoticae : Oribatida : **Sarcoptiformes** : Acariformes
Deraiophoridae	Uropodoidea : Uropodina : Monogynaspida : **Mesostigmata** : Parasitiformes
Dermanyssidae	Dermanyssoidea : Gamasina : Monogynaspida : **Mesostigmata** : Parasitiformes
Dermationidae	Analgoidea : - : Astigmata : **Sarcoptiformes** : Acariformes
Dermoglyphidae (incl. Gaudoglyphidae)	Analgoidea : - : Astigmata : **Sarcoptiformes** : Acariformes
Desidae (Amphinectidae)	Entelegynae : Araneomorphae (Labidognatha) : Opisthothelae : **Araneae**
Diarthrophallidae	Diarthrophalloidea : Uropodina : Monogynaspida : **Mesostigmata** : Parasitiformes
Dicranolasmatidae	Troguloidea : - : Dyspnoi : **Opiliones**
Dictynidae	Entelegynae : Araneomorphae (Labidognatha) : Opisthothelae : **Araneae**
Digamasellidae	Rhodacaroidea : Gamasina : Monogynaspida : **Mesostigmata** : Parasitiformes
Diguetidae	Haplogynae (Synspermiata) : Araneomorphae (Labidognatha) : Opisthothelae : **Araneae**
Dinychidae	Uropodoidea : Uropodina : Monogynaspida : **Mesostigmata** : Parasitiformes
Diplocentridae	Scorpionoidea (Bothriuroidea) : - : - : **Scorpiones**
Diplogyniidae	Celaenopsoidea : Antennophorina : Trigynaspida : **Mesostigmata** : Parasitiformes
Dipluridae	Avicularioidea : Mygalomorphae (Orthognatha) : Opisthothelae : **Araneae**

Diptilomiopidae	Eriophyoidea : Eupodina : Prostigmata : **Trombidiformes** : Acariformes
Discourellidae	Uropodoidea : Uropodina : Monogynaspida : **Mesostigmata** : Parasitiformes
Discozerconidae	Heterozerconoidea : Uropodina : Sejida (Sejina) : **Mesostigmata** : Parasitiformes
Dolichocybidae	Dolichocyboidea : Eleutherengona : Prostigmata : **Trombidiformes** : Acariformes
Dracochelidae †	Chthonioidea : - : Heterosphyronida (Epiocheirata) : **Pseudoscorpiones** (Chelonethida Pseudoscorpionida)
Drymobatidae	Oripodoidea (Oribatuloidea) : Brachypylina sec. Poronoticae : Oribatida : **Sarcoptiformes** : Acariformes
Drymusidae	Haplogynae (Synspermiata) : Araneomorphae (Labidognatha) : Opisthothelae : **Araneae**
Dwigubskyiidae	Epicrioidea : Gamasina : Monogynaspida : **Mesostigmata** : Parasitiformes
Dysderidae	Haplogynae (Synspermiata) : Araneomorphae (Labidognatha) : Opisthothelae : **Araneae**
Echimyopodidae	Glycyphagoidea : - : Astigmata : **Sarcoptiformes** : Acariformes
Elliptochthoniidae	Parhypochthonioidea : Parhyposomata : Oribatida : **Sarcoptiformes** : Acariformes
Eniochthoniidae	Hypochthonioidea : Enarthronota : Oribatida : **Sarcoptiformes** : Acariformes
Entonyssidae	Dermanyssoidea : Gamasina : Monogynaspida : **Mesostigmata** : Parasitiformes
Entypesidae	Avicularioidea : Mygalomorphae (Orthognatha) : Opisthothelae : **Araneae**
Epactozetidae	Achipterioidea : Brachypylina sec. Poronoticae : Oribatida : **Sarcoptiformes** : Acariformes
Epedanidae	Epedanoidea : Grassatores : Laniatores : **Opiliones**
Epicriidae	Epicrioidea : Gamasina : Monogynaspida : **Mesostigmata** : Parasitiformes
Epidermoptidae	Analgoidea : - : Astigmata : **Sarcoptiformes** : Acariformes
Epilohmanniidae	Epilohmannioidea : Mixonomata sec. Dichosomata : Oribatida : **Sarcoptiformes** : Acariformes
Epimerellidae	Oppioidea : Brachypylina sec. Pycnonoticae : Oribatida : **Sarcoptiformes** : Acariformes
Epimyodicidae	Cheyletoidea : Eleutherengona : Prostigmata : **Trombidiformes** : Acariformes
Eremaeidae	Eremaeoidea : Brachypylina sec. Pycnonoticae : Oribatida : **Sarcoptiformes** : Acariformes
Eremaeozetidae (Idiozetidae)	Unduloribatoidea (Eremaeozetoidea) : Brachypylina sec. Poronoticae : Oribatida : **Sarcoptiformes** : Acariformes
Eremellidae	Cymbaeremaeoidea (Eremelloidea) : Brachypylina sec. Pycnonoticae : Oribatida : **Sarcoptiformes** : Acariformes

Eremobatidae	- : - : - : **Solifugae**
Eremobelbidae	Amerobelboidea (Ameroidea) : Brachypylina sec. Pycnonoticae : Oribatida : **Sarcoptiformes** : Acariformes
Eremulidae	Amerobelboidea (Ameroidea) : Brachypylina sec. Pycnonoticae : Oribatida : **Sarcoptiformes** : Acariformes
Eresidae	Entelegynae : Araneomorphae (Labidognatha) : Opisthothelae : **Araneae**
Ereynetidae	Tydeoidea : Eupodina : Prostigmata : **Trombidiformes** : Acariformes
Eriophyidae	Eriophyoidea : Eupodina : Prostigmata : **Trombidiformes** : Acariformes
Eriorhynchidae	Eupodoidea : Eupodina : Prostigmata : **Trombidiformes** : Acariformes
Erythraeidae	Erythraeoidea : Anystina : Prostigmata : **Trombidiformes** : Acariformes
Escadabiidae	Zalmoxoidea : Grassatores : Laniatores : **Opiliones**
Euagridae	Avicularioidea : Mygalomorphae (Orthognatha) : Opisthothelae : **Araneae**
Euctenizidae	Avicularioidea : Mygalomorphae (Orthognatha) : Opisthothelae : **Araneae**
Euglycyphagidae	Glycyphagoidea : - : Astigmata : **Sarcoptiformes** : Acariformes
Eukoeneniidae	Eukoenenioidea : - : - : **Palpigradi**
Eulohmanniidae	Eulohmannioidea : Mixonomata sec. Dichosomata : Oribatida : **Sarcoptiformes** : Acariformes
Eupalopsellidae	Raphignathoidea : Eleutherengona : Prostigmata : **Trombidiformes** : Acariformes
Euphthiracaridae	Euphthiracaroidea : Mixonomata sec. Dichosomata : Oribatida : **Sarcoptiformes** : Acariformes
Euphysalozerconidae	Aenictequoidea : Antennophorina : Trigynaspida : **Mesostigmata** : Parasitiformes
Eupodidae	Eupodoidea : Eupodina : Prostigmata : **Trombidiformes** : Acariformes
Euscorpiidae	Chactoidea (Vaejovoidea) : - : - : **Scorpiones**
Eustathiidae	Pterolichoidea : - : Astigmata : **Sarcoptiformes** : Acariformes
Eutegaeidae	Eutegaeoidea (Cepheoidea) : Brachypylina sec. Pycnonoticae : Oribatida : **Sarcoptiformes** : Acariformes
Eutrachytidae	Uropodoidea : Uropodina : Monogynaspida : **Mesostigmata** : Parasitiformes
Euzerconidae	Celaenopsoidea : Antennophorina : Trigynaspida : **Mesostigmata** : Parasitiformes
Eviphididae	Eviphidoidea : Gamasina : Monogynaspida : **Mesostigmata** : Parasitiformes
Eylaidae	Eylaoidea : Anystina : Prostigmata : **Trombidiformes** : Acariformes

Falculiferidae	Pterolichoidea : - : Astigmata : **Sarcoptiformes** : Acariformes
Feaellidae	Feaelloidea : - : Atoposphyronida : **Pseudoscorpiones** (Chelonethida Pseudoscorpionida)
Fedrizziidae	Fedrizzioidea : Antennophorina : Trigynaspida : **Mesostigmata** : Parasitiformes
Feltriidae	Hygrobatoidea : Anystina : Prostigmata : **Trombidiformes** : Acariformes
Ferradasiidae	Hygrobatoidea : Anystina : Prostigmata : **Trombidiformes** : Acariformes
Filistatidae	- : Araneomorphae (Labidognatha) : Opisthothelae : **Araneae**
Fissiphalliidae	Zalmoxoidea : Grassatores : Laniatores : **Opiliones**
Fortuyniidae	Ameronothroidea : Brachypylina sec. Pycnonoticae : Oribatida : **Sarcoptiformes** : Acariformes
Freyanidae	Pterolichoidea : - : Astigmata : **Sarcoptiformes** : Acariformes
Frontipodopsidae	Hygrobatoidea : Anystina : Prostigmata : **Trombidiformes** : Acariformes
Gabuciniidae	Pterolichoidea : - : Astigmata : **Sarcoptiformes** : Acariformes
Galeodidae	- : - : - : **Solifugae**
Gallieniellidae	Entelegynae : Araneomorphae (Labidognatha) : Opisthothelae : **Araneae**
Galumnellidae	Galumnoidea : Brachypylina sec. Poronoticae : Oribatida : **Sarcoptiformes** : Acariformes
Galumnidae	Galumnoidea : Brachypylina sec. Poronoticae : Oribatida : **Sarcoptiformes** : Acariformes
Garypidae	Garypoidea : - : Iocheirata : **Pseudoscorpiones** (Chelonethida Pseudoscorpionida)
Garypinidae	Garypinoidea : - : Iocheirata : **Pseudoscorpiones** (Chelonethida Pseudoscorpionida)
Gastronyssidae	Sarcoptoidea : - : Astigmata : **Sarcoptiformes** : Acariformes
Gaudiellidae (Platyglyphidae)	Acaroidea : - : Astigmata : **Sarcoptiformes** : Acariformes
Gehypochthoniidae	Parhypochthonioidea : Parhyposomata : Oribatida : **Sarcoptiformes** : Acariformes
Geogarypidae	Garypoidea : - : Iocheirata : **Pseudoscorpiones** (Chelonethida Pseudoscorpionida)
Glycacaridae	Acaroidea : - : Astigmata : **Sarcoptiformes** : Acariformes
Glycyphagidae	Glycyphagoidea : - : Astigmata : **Sarcoptiformes** : Acariformes
Gnaphosidae	Entelegynae : Araneomorphae (Labidognatha) : Opisthothelae : **Araneae**
Gonyleptidae	Gonyleptoidea : Grassatores : Laniatores : **Opiliones**

Gradungulidae	Austrochiloidea : Araneomorphae (Labidognatha) : Opisthothelae : **Araneae**
Grandjeanicidae	Oehserchestoidea : Terpnacarida : Endeostigmata : **Sarcoptiformes** : Acariformes
Granuloppiidae	Oppioidea : Brachypylina sec. Pycnonoticae : Oribatida : **Sarcoptiformes** : Acariformes
Gretacaridae	Arrenuroidea : Anystina : Prostigmata : **Trombidiformes** : Acariformes
Guanolichidae	Histiostomatoidea : - : Astigmata : **Sarcoptiformes** : Acariformes
Guasiniidae	Zalmoxoidea : Grassatores : Laniatores : **Opiliones**
Gustaviidae	Gustavioidea (Liacaroidea) : Brachypylina sec. Pycnonoticae : Oribatida : **Sarcoptiformes** : Acariformes
Gylippidae	- : - : - : **Solifugae**
Gymnobisiidae	Neobisioidea : - : Iocheirata : **Pseudoscorpiones** (Chelonethida Pseudoscorpionida)
Gymnodamaeidae	Gymnodamaeoidea : Brachypylina sec. Pycnonoticae : Oribatida : **Sarcoptiformes** : Acariformes
Haemogamasidae	Dermanyssoidea : Gamasina : Monogynaspida : **Mesostigmata** : Parasitiformes
Hahniidae	Entelegynae : Araneomorphae (Labidognatha) : Opisthothelae : **Araneae**
Halacaridae	Halacaroidea : Eupodina : Prostigmata : **Trombidiformes** : Acariformes
Halarachnidae	Dermanyssoidea : Gamasina : Monogynaspida : **Mesostigmata** : Parasitiformes
Halolaelapidae	Rhodacaroidea : Gamasina : Monogynaspida : **Mesostigmata** : Parasitiformes
Halonoproctidae	Avicularioidea : Mygalomorphae (Orthognatha) : Opisthothelae : **Araneae**
Haplochthoniidae	Cosmochthonioidea : Enarthronota : Oribatida : **Sarcoptiformes** : Acariformes
Haplozetidae (Nasobatidae)	Oripodoidea (Oribatuloidea) : Brachypylina sec. Poronoticae : Oribatida : **Sarcoptiformes** : Acariformes
Harpagopalpidae	Arrenuroidea : Anystina : Prostigmata : **Trombidiformes** : Acariformes
Harpirhynchidae	Cheyletoidea : Eleutherengona : Prostigmata : **Trombidiformes** : Acariformes
Heatherellidae	Heatherelloidea : Gamasina : Monogynaspida : **Mesostigmata** : Parasitiformes
Hemileiidae	Oripodoidea (Oribatuloidea) : Brachypylina sec. Poronoticae : Oribatida : **Sarcoptiformes** : Acariformes
Hemisarcoptidae	Hemisarcoptoidea : - : Astigmata : **Sarcoptiformes** : Acariformes

Hemiscorpiidae (Ischnuridae, Liochelidae)	Scorpionoidea (Bothriuroidea) : - : - : **Scorpiones**
Hermanniellidae	Hermannielloidea : Brachypylina sec. Pycnonoticae : Oribatida : **Sarcoptiformes** : Acariformes
Hermanniidae (Galapagacaridae)	Hermannioidea : Brachypylina sec. Pycnonoticae : Oribatida : **Sarcoptiformes** : Acariformes
Hersiliidae	Entelegynae : Araneomorphae (Labidognatha) : Opisthothelae : **Araneae**
Hesperolpiidae	Garypoidea : - : Iocheirata : **Pseudoscorpiones** (Chelonethida Pseudoscorpionida)
Heterobelbidae	Amerobelboidea (Ameroidea) : Brachypylina sec. Pycnonoticae : Oribatida : **Sarcoptiformes** : Acariformes
Heterocheylidae	Heterocheyloidea : Eleutherengona : Prostigmata : **Trombidiformes** : Acariformes
Heterochthoniidae	Heterochthonioidea : Enarthronota : Oribatida : **Sarcoptiformes** : Acariformes
Heterocoptidae	- : - : Astigmata : **Sarcoptiformes** : Acariformes
Heteropsoridae	Analgoidea : - : Astigmata : **Sarcoptiformes** : Acariformes
Heteroscorpionidae (contentious)	Scorpionoidea (Bothriuroidea) : - : - : **Scorpiones**
Heterozerconidae	Heterozerconoidea : Uropodina : Sejida (Sejina) : **Mesostigmata** : Parasitiformes
Hexathelidae	Avicularioidea : Mygalomorphae (Orthognatha) : Opisthothelae : **Araneae**
Hexisopodidae	- : - : - : **Solifugae**
Hexurellidae	Atypoidea : Mygalomorphae (Orthognatha) : Opisthothelae : **Araneae**
Histiostomatidae	Histiostomatoidea : - : Astigmata : **Sarcoptiformes** : Acariformes
Holothyridae	- : - : - : **Holothyrida** (Tetrastigmata) : Parasitiformes
Homalonychidae	Entelegynae : Araneomorphae (Labidognatha) : Opisthothelae : **Araneae**
Homocaligidae	Raphignathoidea : Eleutherengona : Prostigmata : **Trombidiformes** : Acariformes
Hoplomegistidae	Megisthanoidea : Antennophorina : Trigynaspida : **Mesostigmata** : Parasitiformes
Hubbardiidae (**Schizomidae**)	Hubbardioidea : - : - : **Schizomida**
Humerobatidae	Ceratozetoidea (Limnozetoidea) : Brachypylina sec. Poronoticae : Oribatida : **Sarcoptiformes** : Acariformes
Hungarobelbidae	Damaeoidea : Brachypylina sec. Pycnonoticae : Oribatida : **Sarcoptiformes** : Acariformes
Hungarohydracaridae	Arrenuroidea : Anystina : Prostigmata : **Trombidiformes** : Acariformes
Huttoniidae	Palpimanoidea : Araneomorphae (Labidognatha) : Opisthothelae : **Araneae**

Hutufeideriidae	Uropodoidea : Uropodina : Monogynaspida : **Mesostigmata** : Parasitiformes
Hyadesiidae	Hemisarcoptoidea : - : Astigmata : **Sarcoptiformes** : Acariformes
Hydrachnidae	Hydrachnoidea : Anystina : Prostigmata : **Trombidiformes** : Acariformes
Hydrodromidae	Hydryphantoidea : Anystina : Prostigmata : **Trombidiformes** : Acariformes
Hydrovolziidae	Hydrovolzioidea : Anystina : Prostigmata : **Trombidiformes** : Acariformes
Hydrozetidae	Hydrozetoidea : Brachypylina sec. Pycnonoticae : Oribatida : **Sarcoptiformes** : Acariformes
Hydryphantidae (incl. Eupatrellidae)	Hydryphantoidea : Anystina : Prostigmata : **Trombidiformes** : Acariformes
Hygrobatidae	Hygrobatoidea : Anystina : Prostigmata : **Trombidiformes** : Acariformes
Hyidae	Neobisioidea : - : Iocheirata : **Pseudoscorpiones** (Chelonethida Pseudoscorpionida)
Hypochilidae	Hypochiloidea : Araneomorphae (Labidognatha) : Opisthothelae : **Araneae**
Hypochilidae	- : Araneomorphae (Labidognatha) : Opisthothelae : **Araneae**
Hypochthoniidae	Hypochthonioidea : Enarthronota : Oribatida : **Sarcoptiformes** : Acariformes
Hypoderidae	Hypoderoidea : - : Astigmata : **Sarcoptiformes** : Acariformes
Hystrichonyssidae	Dermanyssoidea : Gamasina : Monogynaspida : **Mesostigmata** : Parasitiformes
Icaleptidae	Zalmoxoidea : Grassatores : Laniatores : **Opiliones**
Ichthyostomatogasteridae	Sejoidea : Uropodina : Sejida (Sejina) : **Mesostigmata** : Parasitiformes
Ideoroncidae	Neobisioidea : - : Iocheirata : **Pseudoscorpiones** (Chelonethida Pseudoscorpionida)
Idiopidae	Avicularioidea : Mygalomorphae (Orthognatha) : Opisthothelae : **Araneae**
Iolinidae	Tydeoidea : Eupodina : Prostigmata : **Trombidiformes** : Acariformes
Iphiopsididae	Dermanyssoidea : Gamasina : Monogynaspida : **Mesostigmata** : Parasitiformes
Ischnothelidae	Avicularioidea : Mygalomorphae (Orthognatha) : Opisthothelae : **Araneae**
Ischyropsalididae	Ischyropsalidoidea : - : Dyspnoi : **Opiliones**
Iuridae	Iuroidea : - : - : **Scorpiones**
Ixodidae	Ixodoidea : - : - : **Ixodida** : Parasitiformes
Ixodorhynchidae	Dermanyssoidea : Gamasina : Monogynaspida : **Mesostigmata** : Parasitiformes
Johnstonianidae	Trombiculoidea : Anystina : Prostigmata : **Trombidiformes** : Acariformes
Kantacaridae	Arrenuroidea : Anystina : Prostigmata : **Trombidiformes** : Acariformes

315

Karschiidae	- : - : - : **Solifugae**
Kaszabjbaloghiidae	Uropodoidea : Uropodina : Monogynaspida : **Mesostigmata** : Parasitiformes
Kimulidae	Zalmoxoidea : Grassatores : Laniatores : **Opiliones**
Kiwilichidae	Pterolichoidea : - : Astigmata : **Sarcoptiformes** : Acariformes
Klinckowstroemiidae	Fedrizzioidea : Antennophorina : Trigynaspida : **Mesostigmata** : Parasitiformes
Kodiakellidae	Eremaeoidea : Brachypylina sec. Pycnonoticae : Oribatida : **Sarcoptiformes** : Acariformes
Kramerellidae	Pterolichoidea : - : Astigmata : **Sarcoptiformes** : Acariformes
Krendowskiidae	Arrenuroidea : Anystina : Prostigmata : **Trombidiformes** : Acariformes
Labidostommatidae	Labidostommatoidea : Labidostommatina : Prostigmata : **Trombidiformes** : Acariformes
Laelapidae (incl. Hirstionyssidae)	Dermanyssoidea : Gamasina : Monogynaspida : **Mesostigmata** : Parasitiformes
Laelaptonyssidae	Rhodacaroidea : Gamasina : Monogynaspida : **Mesostigmata** : Parasitiformes
Lamellareidae	Licneremaeoidea : Brachypylina sec. Poronoticae : Oribatida : **Sarcoptiformes** : Acariformes
Laminosioptidae	Analgoidea : - : Astigmata : **Sarcoptiformes** : Acariformes
Lamponidae	Entelegynae : Araneomorphae (Labidognatha) : Opisthothelae : **Araneae**
Larcidae	Garypinoidea : - : Iocheirata : **Pseudoscorpiones** (Chelonethida Pseudoscorpionida)
Lardoglyphidae	Acaroidea : - : Astigmata : **Sarcoptiformes** : Acariformes
Larvamimidae	Dermanyssoidea : Gamasina : Monogynaspida : **Mesostigmata** : Parasitiformes
Laversiidae	Arrenuroidea : Anystina : Prostigmata : **Trombidiformes** : Acariformes
Lebertiidae	Lebertioidea : Anystina : Prostigmata : **Trombidiformes** : Acariformes
Lechytiidae	Chthonioidea : - : Heterosphyronida (Epiocheirata) : **Pseudoscorpiones** (Chelonethida Pseudoscorpionida)
Leeuwenhoekiidae	Trombiculoidea : Anystina : Prostigmata : **Trombidiformes** : Acariformes
Lemanniellidae	- : - : Astigmata : **Sarcoptiformes** : Acariformes
Lemurnyssidae	Sarcoptoidea : - : Astigmata : **Sarcoptiformes** : Acariformes
Leptolaelapidae	Eviphidoidea : Gamasina : Monogynaspida : **Mesostigmata** : Parasitiformes
Leptonetidae	- : Araneomorphae (Labidognatha) : Opisthothelae : **Araneae**
Lethaxonidae	Hygrobatoidea : Anystina : Prostigmata : **Trombidiformes** : Acariformes

Liacaridae	Gustavioidea (Liacaroidea) : Brachypylina sec. Pycnonoticae : Oribatida : **Sarcoptiformes** : Acariformes
Licneremaeidae	Licneremaeoidea : Brachypylina sec. Poronoticae : Oribatida : **Sarcoptiformes** : Acariformes
Licnobelbidae	Plateremaeoidea : Brachypylina sec. Pycnonoticae : Oribatida : **Sarcoptiformes** : Acariformes
Licnodamaeidae	Plateremaeoidea : Brachypylina sec. Pycnonoticae : Oribatida : **Sarcoptiformes** : Acariformes
Liebstadiidae	Oripodoidea (Oribatuloidea) : Brachypylina sec. Poronoticae : Oribatida : **Sarcoptiformes** : Acariformes
Limnesiidae	Hygrobatoidea : Anystina : Prostigmata : **Trombidiformes** : Acariformes
Limnocharidae	Eylaoidea : Anystina : Prostigmata : **Trombidiformes** : Acariformes
Limnozetidae	Ceratozetoidea (Limnozetoidea) : Brachypylina sec. Poronoticae : Oribatida : **Sarcoptiformes** : Acariformes
Linotetranidae	Tetranychoidea : Eleutherengona : Prostigmata : **Trombidiformes** : Acariformes
Linyphiidae (incl. Sinopimoidae)	Entelegynae : Araneomorphae (Labidognatha) : Opisthothelae : **Araneae**
Liocranidae	Entelegynae : Araneomorphae (Labidognatha) : Opisthothelae : **Araneae**
Liphistiidae	- : - : Mesothelae : **Araneae**
Listrophoridae	Sarcoptoidea : - : Astigmata : **Sarcoptiformes** : Acariformes
Lobalgidae	Sarcoptoidea : - : Astigmata : **Sarcoptiformes** : Acariformes
Lohmanniidae	Lohmannioidea : Enarthronota : Oribatida : **Sarcoptiformes** : Acariformes
Lophonotacaridae (*incertae sedis*)	Canestrinioidea : - : Astigmata : **Sarcoptiformes** : Acariformes
Lordalycidae	Lordalycoidea : - : Sphaerolichida : **Trombidiformes** : Acariformes
Lycosidae	Entelegynae : Araneomorphae (Labidognatha) : Opisthothelae : **Araneae**
Lyroppiidae	Oppioidea : Brachypylina sec. Pycnonoticae : Oribatida : **Sarcoptiformes** : Acariformes
Machadobelbidae	Oppioidea : Brachypylina sec. Pycnonoticae : Oribatida : **Sarcoptiformes** : Acariformes
Machuellidae	Oppioidea : Brachypylina sec. Pycnonoticae : Oribatida : **Sarcoptiformes** : Acariformes
Macrochelidae	Eviphidoidea : Gamasina : Monogynaspida : **Mesostigmata** : Parasitiformes
Macrodinychidae	Uropodoidea : Uropodina : Monogynaspida : **Mesostigmata** : Parasitiformes
Macronyssidae	Dermanyssoidea : Gamasina : Monogynaspida : **Mesostigmata** : Parasitiformes

317

Macrothelidae	Avicularioidea : Mygalomorphae (Orthognatha) : Opisthothelae : **Araneae**
Malaconothridae	Crotonioidea (Nothroidea) : Holosomata (Desmonomata, Nothronata) : Oribatida : **Sarcoptiformes** : Acariformes
Malgasacaridae	Hydryphantoidea : Anystina : Prostigmata : **Trombidiformes** : Acariformes
Malkaridae (Pararchaeidae)	Entelegynae : Araneomorphae (Labidognatha) : Opisthothelae : **Araneae**
Manaosbiidae	Gonyleptoidea : Grassatores : Laniatores : **Opiliones**
Manitherionyssidae	Dermanyssoidea : Gamasina : Monogynaspida : **Mesostigmata** : Parasitiformes
Maudheimiidae	Ceratozetoidea (Limnozetoidea) : Brachypylina sec. Poronoticae : Oribatida : **Sarcoptiformes** : Acariformes
Mecicobothriidae	Atypoidea : Mygalomorphae (Orthognatha) : Opisthothelae : **Araneae**
Mecognathidae	Raphignathoidea : Eleutherengona : Prostigmata : **Trombidiformes** : Acariformes
Mecysmaucheniidae	Palpimanoidea : Araneomorphae (Labidognatha) : Opisthothelae : **Araneae**
Megacelaenopsidae	Celaenopsoidea : Antennophorina : Trigynaspida : **Mesostigmata** : Parasitiformes
Megadictynidae	Entelegynae : Araneomorphae (Labidognatha) : Opisthothelae : **Araneae**
Megahexuridae	Atypoidea : Mygalomorphae (Orthognatha) : Opisthothelae : **Araneae**
Megalolaelapidae	Eviphidoidea : Gamasina : Monogynaspida : **Mesostigmata** : Parasitiformes
Megisthanidae	Megisthanoidea : Antennophorina : Trigynaspida : **Mesostigmata** : Parasitiformes
Melanoblossiidae	- : - : - : **Solifugae**
Melicharidae	Ascoidea : Gamasina : Monogynaspida : **Mesostigmata** : Parasitiformes
Meliponocoptidae	Hemisarcoptoidea : - : Astigmata : **Sarcoptiformes** : Acariformes
Menthidae	Garypoidea : - : Iocheirata : **Pseudoscorpiones** (Chelonethida Pseudoscorpionida)
Mesoplophoridae	Mesoplophoroidea : Enarthronota : Oribatida : **Sarcoptiformes** : Acariformes
Messoracaridae	Aenictequoidea : Antennophorina : Trigynaspida : **Mesostigmata** : Parasitiformes
Metagynuridae	Uropodoidea : Uropodina : Monogynaspida : **Mesostigmata** : Parasitiformes
Metasarcidae	Gonyleptoidea : Grassatores : Laniatores : **Opiliones**
Micreremidae	Licneremaeoidea : Brachypylina sec. Poronoticae : Oribatida : **Sarcoptiformes** : Acariformes
Microcharmidae	Buthoidea : - : - : **Scorpiones**

Microdispidae	Scutacaroidea (Pygmephoroidea) : Eleutherengona : Prostigmata : **Trombidiformes** : Acariformes
Microgyniidae	Microgynioidea : Uropodina : Monogynaspida : **Mesostigmata** : Parasitiformes
Microhexuridae	Avicularioidea : Mygalomorphae (Orthognatha) : Opisthothelae : **Araneae**
Micropsammidae	Nematalycoidea : Nematalycina : Endeostigmata : **Sarcoptiformes** : Acariformes
Microstigmatidae	Avicularioidea : Mygalomorphae (Orthognatha) : Opisthothelae : **Araneae**
Microtegeidae	Eutegaeoidea (Cepheoidea) : Brachypylina sec. Pycnonoticae : Oribatida : **Sarcoptiformes** : Acariformes
Microtrombidiidae (Eutrombidiidae)	Trombidioidea : Anystina : Prostigmata : **Trombidiformes** : Acariformes
Microzetidae	Microzetoidea : Brachypylina sec. Poronoticae : Oribatida : **Sarcoptiformes** : Acariformes
Mideidae	Arrenuroidea : Anystina : Prostigmata : **Trombidiformes** : Acariformes
Mideopsidae	Arrenuroidea : Anystina : Prostigmata : **Trombidiformes** : Acariformes
Migidae	Avicularioidea : Mygalomorphae (Orthognatha) : Opisthothelae : **Araneae**
Mimetidae	Entelegynae : Araneomorphae (Labidognatha) : Opisthothelae : **Araneae**
Miturgidae (incl. Zoridae)	Entelegynae : Araneomorphae (Labidognatha) : Opisthothelae : **Araneae**
Mochlozetidae	Oripodoidea (Oribatuloidea) : Brachypylina sec. Poronoticae : Oribatida : **Sarcoptiformes** : Acariformes
Momoniidae	Arrenuroidea : Anystina : Prostigmata : **Trombidiformes** : Acariformes
Monoscutidae	Phalangioidea : - : Eupnoi : **Opiliones**
Multoribulidae	Gustavioidea (Liacaroidea) : Brachypylina sec. Pycnonoticae : Oribatida : **Sarcoptiformes** : Acariformes
Mummuciidae	- : - : - : **Solifugae**
Myobiidae	Myobioidea : Eleutherengona : Prostigmata : **Trombidiformes** : Acariformes
Myocoptidae	Sarcoptoidea : - : Astigmata : **Sarcoptiformes** : Acariformes
Mysmenidae	Entelegynae : Araneomorphae (Labidognatha) : Opisthothelae : **Araneae**
Nalepellidae	Eriophyoidea : Eupodina : Prostigmata : **Trombidiformes** : Acariformes
Nanhermanniidae	Nanhermannioidea : Brachypylina sec. Pycnonoticae : Oribatida : **Sarcoptiformes** : Acariformes
Nanohystricidae	Heterochthonioidea : Enarthronota : Oribatida : **Sarcoptiformes** : Acariformes

Nanorchestidae	Alycoidea : Bimichaeliida : Endeostigmata : **Sarcoptiformes** : Acariformes
Nehypochthoniidae	Nehypochthonioidea : Mixonomata sec. Dichosomata : Oribatida : **Sarcoptiformes** : Acariformes
Nemastomatidae	Troguloidea : - : Dyspnoi : **Opiliones**
Nematalycidae	Nematalycoidea : Nematalycina : Endeostigmata : **Sarcoptiformes** : Acariformes
Nemesiidae	Avicularioidea : Mygalomorphae (Orthognatha) : Opisthothelae : **Araneae**
Nenteriidae	Uropodoidea : Uropodina : Monogynaspida : **Mesostigmata** : Parasitiformes
Neoacaridae	Arrenuroidea : Anystina : Prostigmata : **Trombidiformes** : Acariformes
Neobisiidae	Neobisioidea : - : Iocheirata : **Pseudoscorpiones** (Chelonethida Pseudoscorpionida)
Neogoveidae	- : Sternophthalmi : Cyphophthalmi : **Opiliones**
Neoliodidae	Neoliodoidea : Brachypylina sec. Pycnonoticae : Oribatida : **Sarcoptiformes** : Acariformes
Neopilionidae	Phalangioidea : - : Eupnoi : **Opiliones**
Neopygmephoridae	Scutacaroidea (Pygmephoroidea) : Eleutherengona : Prostigmata : **Trombidiformes** : Acariformes
Neotenogyniidae	Celaenopsoidea : Antennophorina : Trigynaspida : **Mesostigmata** : Parasitiformes
Neothrombiidae	Trombidioidea : Anystina : Prostigmata : **Trombidiformes** : Acariformes
Neothyridae	- : - : - : **Holothyrida** (Tetrastigmata) : Parasitiformes
Neotrombidiidae	Trombiculoidea : Anystina : Prostigmata : **Trombidiformes** : Acariformes
Nesozetidae	Oripodoidea (Oribatuloidea) : Brachypylina sec. Poronoticae : Oribatida : **Sarcoptiformes** : Acariformes
Nesticidae	Entelegynae : Araneomorphae (Labidognatha) : Opisthothelae : **Araneae**
Nicodamidae	Entelegynae : Araneomorphae (Labidognatha) : Opisthothelae : **Araneae**
Niphocepheidae	Niphocepheoidea : Brachypylina sec. Pycnonoticae : Oribatida : **Sarcoptiformes** : Acariformes
Nippobodidae	Carabodoidea : Brachypylina sec. Pycnonoticae : Oribatida : **Sarcoptiformes** : Acariformes
Nipponacaridae	Arrenuroidea : Anystina : Prostigmata : **Trombidiformes** : Acariformes
Nippononychidae	Travunioidea : - : Laniatores : **Opiliones**
Nipponopsalididae	Troguloidea : - : Dyspnoi : **Opiliones**
Nodocepheidae	Eutegaeoidea (Cepheoidea) : Brachypylina sec. Pycnonoticae : Oribatida : **Sarcoptiformes** : Acariformes

Nosybeidae	Charassobatoidea : Brachypylina sec. Pycnonoticae : Oribatida : **Sarcoptiformes** : Acariformes
Nothogynidae	Microgynioidea : Uropodina : Monogynaspida : **Mesostigmata** : Parasitiformes
Nothridae	Crotonioidea (Nothroidea) : Holosomata (Desmonomata, Nothronata) : Oribatida : **Sarcoptiformes** : Acariformes
Nudomideopsidae	Arrenuroidea : Anystina : Prostigmata : **Trombidiformes** : Acariformes
Nuttalliellidae	Ixodoidea : - : - : **Ixodida** : Parasitiformes
Ochrolichidae	Pterolichoidea : - : Astigmata : **Sarcoptiformes** : Acariformes
Ochyroceratidae	Haplogynae (Synspermiata) : Araneomorphae (Labidognatha) : Opisthothelae : **Araneae**
Oconnoriidae	Pterolichoidea : - : Astigmata : **Sarcoptiformes** : Acariformes
Oecobiidae	Entelegynae : Araneomorphae (Labidognatha) : Opisthothelae : **Araneae**
Oehserchestidae	Oehserchestoidea : Terpnacarida : Endeostigmata : **Sarcoptiformes** : Acariformes
Ogoveidae	- : Sternophthalmi : Cyphophthalmi : **Opiliones**
Ologamasidae	Rhodacaroidea : Gamasina : Monogynaspida : **Mesostigmata** : Parasitiformes
Olpiidae	Garypoidea : - : Iocheirata : **Pseudoscorpiones** (Chelonethida Pseudoscorpionida)
Omartacaridae	Hygrobatoidea : Anystina : Prostigmata : **Trombidiformes** : Acariformes
Omentolaelapidae	Dermanyssoidea : Gamasina : Monogynaspida : **Mesostigmata** : Parasitiformes
Oonopidae	Haplogynae (Synspermiata) : Araneomorphae (Labidognatha) : Opisthothelae : **Araneae**
Ophioptidae	Cheyletoidea : Eleutherengona : Prostigmata : **Trombidiformes** : Acariformes
Opilioacaridae	- : - : - : **Opilioacarida** (Notostigmat, **Opilioacarida**) : Opilioacariformes
Oplitidae	Uropodoidea : Uropodina : Monogynaspida : **Mesostigmata** : Parasitiformes
Oppiidae	Oppioidea : Brachypylina sec. Pycnonoticae : Oribatida : **Sarcoptiformes** : Acariformes
Oribatellidae	Oribatelloidea : Brachypylina sec. Poronoticae : Oribatida : **Sarcoptiformes** : Acariformes
Oribatulidae	Oripodoidea (Oribatuloidea) : Brachypylina sec. Poronoticae : Oribatida : **Sarcoptiformes** : Acariformes
Oribellidae	Eremaeoidea : Brachypylina sec. Pycnonoticae : Oribatida : **Sarcoptiformes** : Acariformes
Oribotritiidae	Euphthiracaroidea : Mixonomata sec. Euptyctima : Oribatida : **Sarcoptiformes** : Acariformes

321

Oripodidae (Parapirnodidae)	Oripodoidea (Oribatuloidea) : Brachypylina sec. Poronoticae : Oribatida : **Sarcoptiformes** : Acariformes
Orsolobidae	Haplogynae (Synspermiata) : Araneomorphae (Labidognatha) : Opisthothelae : **Araneae**
Otocepheidae	Otocepheoidea : Brachypylina sec. Pycnonoticae : Oribatida : **Sarcoptiformes** : Acariformes
Otopheidomenidae	Phytoseioidea : Gamasina : Monogynaspida : **Mesostigmata** : Parasitiformes
Oxidae	Lebertioidea : Anystina : Prostigmata : **Trombidiformes** : Acariformes
Oxyameridae	Amerobelboidea (Ameroidea) : Brachypylina sec. Pycnonoticae : Oribatida : **Sarcoptiformes** : Acariformes
Oxyopidae	Entelegynae : Araneomorphae (Labidognatha) : Opisthothelae : **Araneae**
Pachylaelapidae	Eviphidoidea : Gamasina : Monogynaspida : **Mesostigmata** : Parasitiformes
Pacullidae	Haplogynae (Synspermiata) : Araneomorphae (Labidognatha) : Opisthothelae : **Araneae**
Palaeacaridae	Palaeacaroidea (Ctenacaroidea) : Palaeosomata : Oribatida : **Sarcoptiformes** : Acariformes
Palaeoburmesebuthidae †	Buthoidea : - : - : **Scorpiones**
Palpimanidae	Palpimanoidea : Araneomorphae (Labidognatha) : Opisthothelae : **Araneae**
Papillonotidae	Oppioidea : Brachypylina sec. Pycnonoticae : Oribatida : **Sarcoptiformes** : Acariformes
Paracharontidae	- : - : Paleoamblypygi : **Amblypygi**
Parahyidae	Neobisioidea : - : Iocheirata : **Pseudoscorpiones** (Chelonethida Pseudoscorpionida)
Parakalummidae	Oripodoidea (Oribatuloidea) : Brachypylina sec. Poronoticae : Oribatida : **Sarcoptiformes** : Acariformes
Paramegistidae	Paramegistoidea : Antennophorina : Trigynaspida : **Mesostigmata** : Parasitiformes
Paranonychidae	Travunioidea : - : Laniatores : **Opiliones**
Parantennulidae	Parantennuloidea : Antennophorina : Trigynaspida : **Mesostigmata** : Parasitiformes
Parasitidae	Parasitoidea : Gamasina : Monogynaspida : **Mesostigmata** : Parasitiformes
Paratropididae	Avicularioidea : Mygalomorphae (Orthognatha) : Opisthothelae : **Araneae**
Paratydeidae	Paratydeoidea : Anystina : Prostigmata : **Trombidiformes** : Acariformes
Parholaspididae	Eviphidoidea : Gamasina : Monogynaspida : **Mesostigmata** : Parasitiformes
Parhypochthoniidae	Parhypochthonioidea : Parhyposomata : Oribatida : **Sarcoptiformes** : Acariformes
Passalozetidae	Licneremaeoidea : Brachypylina sec. Poronoticae : Oribatida : **Sarcoptiformes** : Acariformes

Pedetopodidae	Glycyphagoidea : - : Astigmata : **Sarcoptiformes** : Acariformes
Pediculochelidae	Cosmochthonioidea : Enarthronota : Oribatida : **Sarcoptiformes** : Acariformes
Peloppiidae (Metrioppiidae)	Gustavioidea (Liacaroidea) : Brachypylina sec. Pycnonoticae : Oribatida : **Sarcoptiformes** : Acariformes
Penestomidae	Entelegynae : Araneomorphae (Labidognatha) : Opisthothelae : **Araneae**
Pentapalpidae	Eupodoidea : Eupodina : Prostigmata : **Trombidiformes** : Acariformes
Pentasetacidae	Eriophyoidea : Eupodina : Prostigmata : **Trombidiformes** : Acariformes
Penthaleidae	Eupodoidea : Eupodina : Prostigmata : **Trombidiformes** : Acariformes
Penthalodidae	Eupodoidea : Eupodina : Prostigmata : **Trombidiformes** : Acariformes
Periegopidae	Haplogynae (Synspermiata) : Araneomorphae (Labidognatha) : Opisthothelae : **Araneae**
Perlohmanniidae	Perlohmannioidea : Mixonomata sec. Dichosomata : Oribatida : **Sarcoptiformes** : Acariformes
Petrobunidae	Epedanoidea : Grassatores : Laniatores : **Opiliones**
Pettalidae	- : Scopulophthalmi : Cyphophthalmi : **Opiliones**
Pezidae	Halacaroidea : Eupodina : Prostigmata : **Trombidiformes** : Acariformes
Phalangiidae	Phalangioidea : - : Eupnoi : **Opiliones**
Phalangodidae	Phalangodoidea : Grassatores : Laniatores : **Opiliones**
Phenopelopidae	Phenopelopoidea : Brachypylina sec. Poronoticae : Oribatida : **Sarcoptiformes** : Acariformes
Pheroliodidae	Plateremaeoidea : Brachypylina sec. Pycnonoticae : Oribatida : **Sarcoptiformes** : Acariformes
Philodanidae	Parantennuloidea : Antennophorina : Trigynaspida : **Mesostigmata** : Parasitiformes
Philodromidae	Entelegynae : Araneomorphae (Labidognatha) : Opisthothelae : **Araneae**
Pholcidae	Haplogynae (Synspermiata) : Araneomorphae (Labidognatha) : Opisthothelae : **Araneae**
Pholcochyroceridae †	Haplogynae (Synspermiata) : Araneomorphae (Labidognatha) : Opisthothelae : **Araneae**
Phrurolithidae	Entelegynae : Araneomorphae (Labidognatha) : Opisthothelae : **Araneae**
Phrynichidae	Phrynoidea : - : Euamblypygi : **Amblypygi**
Phrynidae	Phrynoidea : - : Euamblypygi : **Amblypygi**
Phthiracaroidae (Steganacaridae)	Phthiracaroidea : Mixonomata sec. Euptyctima : Oribatida : **Sarcoptiformes** : Acariformes
Phymatodiscidae	Uropodoidea : Uropodina : Monogynaspida : **Mesostigmata** : Parasitiformes
Physoglenidae	Entelegynae : Araneomorphae (Labidognatha) : Opisthothelae : **Araneae**

Phytoptidae	Eriophyoidea : Eupodina : Prostigmata : **Trombidiformes** : Acariformes
Phytoseiidae	Phytoseioidea : Gamasina : Monogynaspida : **Mesostigmata** : Parasitiformes
Phyxelididae	Entelegynae : Araneomorphae (Labidognatha) : Opisthothelae : **Araneae**
Piersigiidae	Eylaoidea : Anystina : Prostigmata : **Trombidiformes** : Acariformes
Pimoidae	Entelegynae : Araneomorphae (Labidognatha) : Opisthothelae : **Araneae**
Pionidae	Hygrobatoidea : Anystina : Prostigmata : **Trombidiformes** : Acariformes
Pirnodidae	Oripodoidea (Oribatuloidea) : Brachypylina sec. Poronoticae : Oribatida : **Sarcoptiformes** : Acariformes
Pisauridae	Entelegynae : Araneomorphae (Labidognatha) : Opisthothelae : **Araneae**
Plasmobatidae	Hermannielloidea : Brachypylina sec. Pycnonoticae : Oribatida : **Sarcoptiformes** : Acariformes
Plateremaeidae	Plateremaeoidea : Brachypylina sec. Pycnonoticae : Oribatida : **Sarcoptiformes** : Acariformes
Platyameridae	Amerobelboidea (Ameroidea) : Brachypylina sec. Pycnonoticae : Oribatida : **Sarcoptiformes** : Acariformes
Plectreuridae	Haplogynae (Synspermiata) : Araneomorphae (Labidognatha) : Opisthothelae : **Araneae**
Pneumocoptidae	Sarcoptoidea : - : Astigmata : **Sarcoptiformes** : Acariformes
Pneumophionyssidae	Dermanyssoidea : Gamasina : Monogynaspida : **Mesostigmata** : Parasitiformes
Podapolipidae (Podapolipodidae)	Tarsonemoidea : Eleutherengona : Prostigmata : **Trombidiformes** : Acariformes
Podocinidae	Phytoseioidea : Gamasina : Monogynaspida : **Mesostigmata** : Parasitiformes
Podoctidae	Epedanoidea : Grassatores : Laniatores : **Opiliones**
Podopterotegaeidae	Polypterozetoidea : Brachypylina sec. Pycnonoticae : Oribatida : **Sarcoptiformes** : Acariformes
Podothrombiidae	Trombidioidea : Anystina : Prostigmata : **Trombidiformes** : Acariformes
Polyaspididae	Uropodoidea : Uropodina : Monogynaspida : **Mesostigmata** : Parasitiformes
Polypterozetidae	Polypterozetoidea : Brachypylina sec. Pycnonoticae : Oribatida : **Sarcoptiformes** : Acariformes
Pomerantziidae	Pomerantzioidea : Anystina : Prostigmata : **Trombidiformes** : Acariformes
Pontarachnidae	Hygrobatoidea : Anystina : Prostigmata : **Trombidiformes** : Acariformes

Porrhothelidae	Avicularioidea : Mygalomorphae (Orthognatha) : Opisthothelae : **Araneae**
Proctophyllodidae	Analgoidea : - : Astigmata : **Sarcoptiformes** : Acariformes
Prodinychidae	Uropodoidea : Uropodina : Monogynaspida : **Mesostigmata** : Parasitiformes
Prokoeneniidae	Eukoenenioidea : - : - : **Palpigradi**
Promegistidae	Parantennuloidea : Antennophorina : Trigynaspida : **Mesostigmata** : Parasitiformes
Proteonematalycidae	Nematalycoidea : Nematalycina : Endeostigmata : **Sarcoptiformes** : Acariformes
Proterorhagiidae	Alycoidea : Bimichaeliida : Endeostigmata : **Sarcoptiformes** : Acariformes
Protobuthidae †	Buthoidea : - : - : **Scorpiones**
Protodinychidae	Thinozerconoidea : Uropodina : Monogynaspida : **Mesostigmata** : Parasitiformes
Protolophidae	Phalangioidea : - : Eupnoi : **Opiliones**
Protoplophoroidae	Protoplophoroidea : Enarthronota : Oribatida : **Sarcoptiformes** : Acariformes
Protoribatidae	Oripodoidea (Oribatuloidea) : Brachypylina sec. Poronoticae : Oribatida : **Sarcoptiformes** : Acariformes
Proto**Schizomidae**	Hubbardioidea : - : - : **Schizomida**
Protosolpugidae †	- : - : - : - : **Solifugae**
Psammochthoniidae	Hypochthonioidea : Enarthronota : Oribatida : **Sarcoptiformes** : Acariformes
Psechridae	Entelegynae : Araneomorphae (Labidognatha) : Opisthothelae : **Araneae**
Pseudochactidae	Iuroidea : - : - : **Scorpiones**
Pseudocheylidae	Anystoidea : Anystina : Prostigmata : **Trombidiformes** : Acariformes
Pseudochiridiidae	Cheiridioidea : - : Iocheirata : **Pseudoscorpiones** (Chelonethida Pseudoscorpionida)
Pseudogarypidae	Feaelloidea : - : Atoposphyronida : **Pseudoscorpiones** (Chelonethida Pseudoscorpionida)
Pseudoppiidae	Oripodoidea (Oribatuloidea) : Brachypylina sec. Poronoticae : Oribatida : **Sarcoptiformes** : Acariformes
Pseudotyrannochthoniidae	Chthonioidea : - : Heterosphyronida (Epiocheirata) : **Pseudoscorpiones** (Chelonethida Pseudoscorpionida)
Psorergatidae	Cheyletoidea : Eleutherengona : Prostigmata : **Trombidiformes** : Acariformes
Psoroptidae	Sarcoptoidea : - : Astigmata : **Sarcoptiformes** : Acariformes
Psoroptoididae	Analgoidea : - : Astigmata : **Sarcoptiformes** : Acariformes
Pterolichidae	Pterolichoidea : - : Astigmata : **Sarcoptiformes** : Acariformes

Pteronyssidae	Analgoidea : - : Astigmata : **Sarcoptiformes** : Acariformes
Pterygosomatidae	Pterygosomatoidea : Eleutherengona : Prostigmata : **Trombidiformes** : Acariformes
Ptiloxenidae	Pterolichoidea : - : Astigmata : **Sarcoptiformes** : Acariformes
Ptochacaridae	Aenictequoidea : Antennophorina : Trigynaspida : **Mesostigmata** : Parasitiformes
Ptyssalgidae	Analgoidea : - : Astigmata : **Sarcoptiformes** : Acariformes
Punctoribatidae (Mycobatidae)	Ceratozetoidea (Limnozetoidea) : Brachypylina sec. Poronoticae : Oribatida : **Sarcoptiformes** : Acariformes
Pycnothelidae	Avicularioidea : Mygalomorphae (Orthognatha) : Opisthothelae : **Araneae**
Pyemotidae	Pyemotoidea : Eleutherengona : Prostigmata : **Trombidiformes** : Acariformes
Pygmephoridae (Siteroptidae)	Scutacaroidea (Pygmephoroidea) : Eleutherengona : Prostigmata : **Trombidiformes** : Acariformes
Pyramidopidae	Assamioidea : Grassatores : Laniatores : **Opiliones**
Pyroglyphidae	Analgoidea : - : Astigmata : **Sarcoptiformes** : Acariformes
Pyrosejidae	Cercomegistoidea : Cercomegistina : Trigynaspida : **Mesostigmata** : Parasitiformes
Quadroppiidae	Oppioidea : Brachypylina sec. Pycnonoticae : Oribatida : **Sarcoptiformes** : Acariformes
Raillietiidae	Dermanyssoidea : Gamasina : Monogynaspida : **Mesostigmata** : Parasitiformes
Raphignathidae	Raphignathoidea : Eleutherengona : Prostigmata : **Trombidiformes** : Acariformes
Rectijanuidae	Pterolichoidea : - : Astigmata : **Sarcoptiformes** : Acariformes
Reginacharlottiidae	Sejoidea : Uropodina : Sejida (Sejina) : **Mesostigmata** : Parasitiformes
Resinacaridae	Pyemotoidea : Eleutherengona : Prostigmata : **Trombidiformes** : Acariformes
Rhagidiidae	Eupodoidea : Eupodina : Prostigmata : **Trombidiformes** : Acariformes
Rhagodidae	- : - : - : **Solifugae**
Rhinonyssidae	Dermanyssoidea : Gamasina : Monogynaspida : **Mesostigmata** : Parasitiformes
Rhodacaridae	Rhodacaroidea : Gamasina : Monogynaspida : **Mesostigmata** : Parasitiformes
Rhynchohydracaridae	Hydryphantoidea : Anystina : Prostigmata : **Trombidiformes** : Acariformes
Rhynchoribatidae	Trizetoidea : Brachypylina sec. Pycnonoticae : Oribatida : **Sarcoptiformes** : Acariformes
Rhyncoptidae	Sarcoptoidea : - : Astigmata : **Sarcoptiformes** : Acariformes
Ricinoididae	Ricinoidoidea : - : Neoricinulei : **Ricinulei**

Rioppiidae	Oppioidea : Brachypylina sec. Pycnonoticae : Oribatida : **Sarcoptiformes** : Acariformes
Rosensteiniidae	Glycyphagoidea : - : Astigmata : **Sarcoptiformes** : Acariformes
Rotundabaloghiidae	Uropodoidea : Uropodina : Monogynaspida : **Mesostigmata** : Parasitiformes
Rutripalpidae	Lebertioidea : Anystina : Prostigmata : **Trombidiformes** : Acariformes
Sabaconidae	Ischyropsalidoidea : - : Dyspnoi : **Opiliones**
Salticidae	Entelegynae : Araneomorphae (Labidognatha) : Opisthothelae : **Araneae**
Saltiseiidae	Cercomegistoidea : Cercomegistina : Trigynaspida : **Mesostigmata** : Parasitiformes
Salvidae (Pterobatidae)	Eutegaeoidea (Cepheoidea) : Brachypylina sec. Pycnonoticae : Oribatida : **Sarcoptiformes** : Acariformes
Samoidae	Samooidea : Grassatores : Laniatores : **Opiliones**
Sandokanidae	Epedanoidea : Grassatores : Laniatores : **Opiliones**
Sapracaridae	Acaroidea : - : Astigmata : **Sarcoptiformes** : Acariformes
Sarcoptidae	Sarcoptoidea : - : Astigmata : **Sarcoptiformes** : Acariformes
Scatoglyphidae	Acaroidea : - : Astigmata : **Sarcoptiformes** : Acariformes
Scheloribatidae	Oripodoidea (Oribatuloidea) : Brachypylina sec. Poronoticae : Oribatida : **Sarcoptiformes** : Acariformes
Schizoglyphidae	Schizoglyphoidea : - : Astigmata : **Sarcoptiformes** : Acariformes
Schizogyniidae	Celaenopsoidea : Antennophorina : Trigynaspida : **Mesostigmata** : Parasitiformes
Sclerosomatidae	Phalangioidea : - : Eupnoi : **Opiliones**
Scorpionidae	Scorpionoidea (Bothriuroidea) : - : - : **Scorpiones**
Scutacaridae	Scutacaroidea (Pygmephoroidea) : Eleutherengona : Prostigmata : **Trombidiformes** : Acariformes
Scutoverticidae	Licneremaeoidea : Brachypylina sec. Poronoticae : Oribatida : **Sarcoptiformes** : Acariformes
Scytodidae	Haplogynae (Synspermiata) : Araneomorphae (Labidognatha) : Opisthothelae : **Araneae**
Segestriidae	Haplogynae (Synspermiata) : Araneomorphae (Labidognatha) : Opisthothelae : **Araneae**
Seiodidae	Cercomegistoidea : Cercomegistina : Trigynaspida : **Mesostigmata** : Parasitiformes
Sejidae	Sejoidea : Uropodina : Sejida (Sejina) : **Mesostigmata** : Parasitiformes
Selenopidae	Entelegynae : Araneomorphae (Labidognatha) : Opisthothelae : **Araneae**
Selenoribatidae	Ameronothroidea : Brachypylina sec. Pycnonoticae : Oribatida : **Sarcoptiformes** : Acariformes

Senoculidae	Entelegynae : Araneomorphae (Labidognatha) : Opisthothelae : **Araneae**
Sicariidae (Loxoscelidae)	Haplogynae (Synspermiata) : Araneomorphae (Labidognatha) : Opisthothelae : **Araneae**
Sironidae	- : Boreophthalmi : Cyphophthalmi : **Opiliones**
Smarididae	Erythraeoidea : Anystina : Prostigmata : **Trombidiformes** : Acariformes
Solpugidae	- : - : - : **Solifugae**
Sparassidae (Heteropodidae)	Entelegynae : Araneomorphae (Labidognatha) : Opisthothelae : **Araneae**
Spelaeorhynchidae	Dermanyssoidea : Gamasina : Monogynaspida : **Mesostigmata** : Parasitiformes
Sperchontidae	Lebertioidea : Anystina : Prostigmata : **Trombidiformes** : Acariformes
Sphaerochthoniidae	Cosmochthonioidea : Enarthronota : Oribatida : **Sarcoptiformes** : Acariformes
Sphaerolichidae	Sphaerolichoidea : - : Sphaerolichida : **Trombidiformes** : Acariformes
Spinozetidae	Amerobelboidea (Ameroidea) : Brachypylina sec. Pycnonoticae : Oribatida : **Sarcoptiformes** : Acariformes
Spinturnicidae	Dermanyssoidea : Gamasina : Monogynaspida : **Mesostigmata** : Parasitiformes
Stasimopidae	Avicularioidea : Mygalomorphae (Orthognatha) : Opisthothelae : **Araneae**
Staurobatidae	Amerobelboidea (Ameroidea) : Brachypylina sec. Pycnonoticae : Oribatida : **Sarcoptiformes** : Acariformes
Stenochilidae	Palpimanoidea : Araneomorphae (Labidognatha) : Opisthothelae : **Araneae**
Sternophoridae	Sternophoroidea : - : Iocheirata : **Pseudoscorpiones** (Chelonethida Pseudoscorpionida)
Sternoppiidae	Oppioidea : Brachypylina sec. Pycnonoticae : Oribatida : **Sarcoptiformes** : Acariformes
Stigmaeidae	Raphignathoidea : Eleutherengona : Prostigmata : **Trombidiformes** : Acariformes
Stigmocheylidae	Paratydeoidea : Anystina : Prostigmata : **Trombidiformes** : Acariformes
Stiphidiidae	Entelegynae : Araneomorphae (Labidognatha) : Opisthothelae : **Araneae**
Strandtmanniidae	Eupodoidea : Eupodina : Prostigmata : **Trombidiformes** : Acariformes
Stygnidae	Gonyleptoidea : Grassatores : Laniatores : **Opiliones**
Stygnommatidae	Samooidea : Grassatores : Laniatores : **Opiliones**
Stygnopsidae	Gonyleptoidea : Grassatores : Laniatores : **Opiliones**
Stygophalangiidae	Phalangioidea : - : Eupnoi : **Opiliones**

Stygothrombiidae	Stygothrombioidea : Anystina : Prostigmata : **Trombidiformes** : Acariformes
Stygotoniidae	Lebertioidea : Anystina : Prostigmata : **Trombidiformes** : Acariformes
Stylocellidae	- : Boreophthalmi : Cyphophthalmi : **Opiliones**
Suctobelbidae	Trizetoidea : Brachypylina sec. Pycnonoticae : Oribatida : **Sarcoptiformes** : Acariformes
Suidasiidae	Acaroidea : - : Astigmata : **Sarcoptiformes** : Acariformes
Superstitioniidae	Chactoidea (Vaejovoidea) : - : - : **Scorpiones**
Syarinidae	Neobisioidea : - : Iocheirata : **Pseudoscorpiones** (Chelonethida Pseudoscorpionida)
Symbioribatidae	Oripodoidea (Oribatuloidea) : Brachypylina sec. Poronoticae : Oribatida : **Sarcoptiformes** : Acariformes
Symphytognathidae	Entelegynae : Araneomorphae (Labidognatha) : Opisthothelae : **Araneae**
Synaphridae	Entelegynae : Araneomorphae (Labidognatha) : Opisthothelae : **Araneae**
Synichotritiidae	Euphthiracaroidea : Mixonomata sec. Euptyctima : Oribatida : **Sarcoptiformes** : Acariformes
Synotaxidae	Entelegynae : Araneomorphae (Labidognatha) : Opisthothelae : **Araneae**
Synthetonychiidae	Triaenonychoidea : - : Laniatores : **Opiliones**
Syringobiidae	Pterolichoidea : - : Astigmata : **Sarcoptiformes** : Acariformes
Syringophilidae	Cheyletoidea : Eleutherengona : Prostigmata : **Trombidiformes** : Acariformes
Tanaupodidae	Tanaupodoidea : Anystina : Prostigmata : **Trombidiformes** : Acariformes
Taracidae	Ischyropsalidoidea : - : Dyspnoi : **Opiliones**
Tarsocheylidae	Tarsocheyloidea : Eleutherengona : Prostigmata : **Trombidiformes** : Acariformes
Tarsonemidae	Tarsonemoidea : Eleutherengona : Prostigmata : **Trombidiformes** : Acariformes
Tectocepheidae	Tectocepheoidea : Brachypylina sec. Pycnonoticae : Oribatida : **Sarcoptiformes** : Acariformes
Tegeocranellidae	Tectocepheoidea : Brachypylina sec. Pycnonoticae : Oribatida : **Sarcoptiformes** : Acariformes
Tegoribatidae	Achipterioidea : Brachypylina sec. Poronoticae : Oribatida : **Sarcoptiformes** : Acariformes
Telemidae	- : Araneomorphae (Labidognatha) : Opisthothelae : **Araneae**
Teneriffiidae	Anystoidea : Anystina : Prostigmata : **Trombidiformes** : Acariformes
Tenuialidae	Gustavioidea (Liacaroidea) : Brachypylina sec. Pycnonoticae : Oribatida : **Sarcoptiformes** : Acariformes
Tenuipalpidae	Tetranychoidea : Eleutherengona : Prostigmata : **Trombidiformes** : Acariformes

Teranyssidae	Rhodacaroidea : Gamasina : Monogynaspida : **Mesostigmata** : Parasitiformes
Teratoppiidae	Oppioidea : Brachypylina sec. Pycnonoticae : Oribatida : **Sarcoptiformes** : Acariformes
Teratothyadidae	Hydryphantoidea : Anystina : Prostigmata : **Trombidiformes** : Acariformes
Terpnacaridae	Terpnacaroidea : Terpnacarida : Endeostigmata : **Sarcoptiformes** : Acariformes
Tetrablemmidae	Haplogynae (Synspermiata) : Araneomorphae (Labidognatha) : Opisthothelae : **Araneae**
Tetracondylidae	Otocepheoidea : Brachypylina sec. Pycnonoticae : Oribatida : **Sarcoptiformes** : Acariformes
Tetragnathidae	Entelegynae : Araneomorphae (Labidognatha) : Opisthothelae : **Araneae**
Tetranychidae	Tetranychoidea : Eleutherengona : Prostigmata : **Trombidiformes** : Acariformes
Tetrasejaspidae	Uropodoidea : Uropodina : Monogynaspida : **Mesostigmata** : Parasitiformes
Teutoniidae	Lebertioidea : Anystina : Prostigmata : **Trombidiformes** : Acariformes
Thelyphonidae	Thelyphonoidea : - : - : **Uropygi**
Theraphosidae	Avicularioidea : Mygalomorphae (Orthognatha) : Opisthothelae : **Araneae**
Theridiidae	Entelegynae : Araneomorphae (Labidognatha) : Opisthothelae : **Araneae**
Theridiosomatidae	Entelegynae : Araneomorphae (Labidognatha) : Opisthothelae : **Araneae**
Thermacaridae	Hydryphantoidea : Anystina : Prostigmata : **Trombidiformes** : Acariformes
Thinozerconidae	Thinozerconoidea : Uropodina : Monogynaspida : **Mesostigmata** : Parasitiformes
Thomisidae	Entelegynae : Araneomorphae (Labidognatha) : Opisthothelae : **Araneae**
Thoracosathesidae	Pterolichoidea : - : Astigmata : **Sarcoptiformes** : Acariformes
Thyrisomidae	Oppioidea : Brachypylina sec. Pycnonoticae : Oribatida : **Sarcoptiformes** : Acariformes
Thysanocercidae	Analgoidea : - : Astigmata : **Sarcoptiformes** : Acariformes
Titanoecidae	Entelegynae : Araneomorphae (Labidognatha) : Opisthothelae : **Araneae**
Tithaeidae	Epedanoidea : Grassatores : Laniatores : **Opiliones**
Tokunocepheidae	Otocepheoidea : Brachypylina sec. Pycnonoticae : Oribatida : **Sarcoptiformes** : Acariformes
Torrenticolidae	Lebertioidea : Anystina : Prostigmata : **Trombidiformes** : Acariformes
Toxopidae	Entelegynae : Araneomorphae (Labidognatha) : Opisthothelae : **Araneae**
Trachelidae	Entelegynae : Araneomorphae (Labidognatha) : Opisthothelae : **Araneae**

Trachytidae	Uropodoidea : Uropodina : Monogynaspida : **Mesostigmata** : Parasitiformes
Trachyuropodidae	Uropodoidea : Uropodina : Monogynaspida : **Mesostigmata** : Parasitiformes
Travuniidae	Travunioidea : - : Laniatores : **Opiliones**
Trechaleidae	Entelegynae : Araneomorphae (Labidognatha) : Opisthothelae : **Araneae**
Trematuridae	Uropodoidea : Uropodina : Monogynaspida : **Mesostigmata** : Parasitiformes
Trhypochthoniidae	Crotonioidea (Nothroidea) : Holosomata (Desmonomata, Nothronata) : Oribatida : **Sarcoptiformes** : Acariformes
Triaenonychidae	Triaenonychoidea : - : Laniatores : **Opiliones**
Trichoaspididae	Dermanyssoidea : Gamasina : Monogynaspida : **Mesostigmata** : Parasitiformes
Trichocyllibidae	Uropodoidea : Uropodina : Monogynaspida : **Mesostigmata** : Parasitiformes
Trichouropodellidae	Uropodoidea : Uropodina : Monogynaspida : **Mesostigmata** : Parasitiformes
Trichthoniidae	Heterochthonioidea : Enarthronota : Oribatida : **Sarcoptiformes** : Acariformes
Tricommatidae	Gonyleptoidea : Grassatores : Laniatores : **Opiliones**
Tridenchthoniidae	Chthonioidea : - : Heterosphyronida (Epiocheirata) : **Pseudoscorpiones** (Chelonethida Pseudoscorpionida)
Trigonuropodidae	Uropodoidea : Uropodina : Monogynaspida : **Mesostigmata** : Parasitiformes
Triophtydeidae	Tydeoidea : Eupodina : Prostigmata : **Trombidiformes** : Acariformes
Triplogyniidae	Celaenopsoidea : Antennophorina : Trigynaspida : **Mesostigmata** : Parasitiformes
Trizetidae	Trizetoidea : Brachypylina sec. Pycnonoticae : Oribatida : **Sarcoptiformes** : Acariformes
Trochanteriidae	Entelegynae : Araneomorphae (Labidognatha) : Opisthothelae : **Araneae**
Trochometridiidae	Trochometridioidea : Eleutherengona : Prostigmata : **Trombidiformes** : Acariformes
Trogloraptoridae	Haplogynae (Synspermiata) : Araneomorphae (Labidognatha) : Opisthothelae : **Araneae**
Troglosironidae	- : Sternophthalmi : Cyphophthalmi : **Opiliones**
Troglotayosicidae	Chactoidea (Vaejovoidea) : - : - : **Scorpiones**
Trogulidae	Troguloidea : - : Dyspnoi : **Opiliones**
Trombellidae	Trombiculoidea : Anystina : Prostigmata : **Trombidiformes** : Acariformes
Trombiculidae	Trombiculoidea : Anystina : Prostigmata : **Trombidiformes** : Acariformes
Trombidiidae	Trombidioidea : Anystina : Prostigmata : **Trombidiformes** : Acariformes

Trouessartiidae	Analgoidea : - : Astigmata : **Sarcoptiformes** : Acariformes
Tubulozetidae	Oripodoidea (Oribatuloidea) : Brachypylina sec. Poronoticae : Oribatida : **Sarcoptiformes** : Acariformes
Tuckerellidae	Tetranychoidea : Eleutherengona : Prostigmata : **Trombidiformes** : Acariformes
Tumerozetidae	Eutegaeoidea (Cepheoidea) : Brachypylina sec. Pycnonoticae : Oribatida : **Sarcoptiformes** : Acariformes
Tuparezetidae	Oppioidea : Brachypylina sec. Pycnonoticae : Oribatida : **Sarcoptiformes** : Acariformes
Turbinoptidae	Analgoidea : - : Astigmata : **Sarcoptiformes** : Acariformes
Tydeidae	Tydeoidea : Eupodina : Prostigmata : **Trombidiformes** : Acariformes
Typhlochactidae	Chactoidea (Vaejovoidea) : - : - : **Scorpiones**
Uchidastygacaridae	Arrenuroidea : Anystina : Prostigmata : **Trombidiformes** : Acariformes
Udubidae (incl. part Zorocratidae)	Entelegynae : Araneomorphae (Labidognatha) : Opisthothelae : **Araneae**
Uloboridae	Entelegynae : Araneomorphae (Labidognatha) : Opisthothelae : **Araneae**
Unduloribatidae	Unduloribatoidea (Eremaeozetoidea) : Brachypylina sec. Poronoticae : Oribatida : **Sarcoptiformes** : Acariformes
Unionicolidae	Hygrobatoidea : Anystina : Prostigmata : **Trombidiformes** : Acariformes
Uroactiniidae	Uropodoidea : Uropodina : Monogynaspida : **Mesostigmata** : Parasitiformes
Urodiaspididae	Uropodoidea : Uropodina : Monogynaspida : **Mesostigmata** : Parasitiformes
Urodinychidae	Uropodoidea : Uropodina : Monogynaspida : **Mesostigmata** : Parasitiformes
Uropodellidae	Sejoidea : Uropodina : Sejida (Sejina) : **Mesostigmata** : Parasitiformes
Uropodidae	Uropodoidea : Uropodina : Monogynaspida : **Mesostigmata** : Parasitiformes
Vaejovidae	Chactoidea (Vaejovoidea) : - : - : **Scorpiones**
Varroidae	Dermanyssoidea : Gamasina : Monogynaspida : **Mesostigmata** : Parasitiformes
Vatacaridae	Trombiculoidea : Anystina : Prostigmata : **Trombidiformes** : Acariformes
Veigaiidae	Veigaioidea : Gamasina : Monogynaspida : **Mesostigmata** : Parasitiformes
Vexillariidae	Pterolichoidea : - : Astigmata : **Sarcoptiformes** : Acariformes
Viridasiidae	Entelegynae : Araneomorphae (Labidognatha) : Opisthothelae : **Araneae**
Vitzthumegistidae	Cercomegistoidea : Cercomegistina : Trigynaspida : **Mesostigmata** : Parasitiformes

Walchiidae	Trombiculoidea : Anystina : Prostigmata : **Trombidiformes** : Acariformes
Wettinidae	Hygrobatoidea : Anystina : Prostigmata : **Trombidiformes** : Acariformes
Winterschmidtiidae	Hemisarcoptoidea : - : Astigmata : **Sarcoptiformes** : Acariformes
Withiidae	Cheliferoidea : - : Iocheirata : **Pseudoscorpiones** (Chelonethida Pseudoscorpionida)
Xenillidae	Gustavioidea (Liacaroidea) : Brachypylina sec. Pycnonoticae : Oribatida : **Sarcoptiformes** : Acariformes
Xenocaligonellididae	Raphignathoidea : Eleutherengona : Prostigmata : **Trombidiformes** : Acariformes
Xenoctenidae	Entelegynae : Araneomorphae (Labidognatha) : Opisthothelae : **Araneae**
Xolalgidae	Analgoidea : - : Astigmata : **Sarcoptiformes** : Acariformes
Yurebillidae	Yurebilloidea : Anystina : Prostigmata : **Trombidiformes** : Acariformes
Zalmoxidae	Zalmoxoidea : Grassatores : Laniatores : **Opiliones**
Zelandothyadidae	Hydryphantoidea : Anystina : Prostigmata : **Trombidiformes** : Acariformes
Zerconidae	Zerconoidea : Gamasina : Monogynaspida : **Mesostigmata** : Parasitiformes
Zetomotrichidae	Zetomotrichoidea : Brachypylina sec. Poronoticae : Oribatida : **Sarcoptiformes** : Acariformes
Zetorchestidae	Zetorchestoidea : Brachypylina sec. Pycnonoticae : Oribatida : **Sarcoptiformes** : Acariformes
Zodariidae	Entelegynae : Araneomorphae (Labidognatha) : Opisthothelae : **Araneae**
Zoropsidae (incl. Tengellidae & part Zorocratidae)	Entelegynae : Araneomorphae (Labidognatha) : Opisthothelae : **Araneae**

Genera Incertae Sedis

Hastocularis argus	Zalmoxoidea : Grassatores : Tetrophthalmi : **Opiliones**
Eophalangium sheari	Zalmoxoidea : Grassatores : Tetrophthalmi : **Opiliones**
Alpazia	*Genera Incertae sedis* : : : **Opiliones**
Anamota	*Genera Incertae sedis* : : : **Opiliones**
Arulla	*Genera Incertae sedis* : : : **Opiliones**
Ausulus	*Genera Incertae sedis* : : : **Opiliones**
Babrius	*Genera Incertae sedis* : : : **Opiliones**
Bebedoura	*Genera Incertae sedis* : : : **Opiliones**
Belemarua	*Genera Incertae sedis* : : : **Opiliones**
Biconibunus	*Genera Incertae sedis* : : : **Opiliones**
Bindoona	*Genera Incertae sedis* : : : **Opiliones**

333

Bissopius	*Genera Incertae sedis* : : : **Opiliones**
Caecobunus	*Genera Incertae sedis* : : : **Opiliones**
Caribula	*Genera Incertae sedis* : : : **Opiliones**
Cleombrotus	*Genera Incertae sedis* : : : **Opiliones**
Contuor	*Genera Incertae sedis* : : : **Opiliones**
Costabrimma	*Genera Incertae sedis* : : : **Opiliones**
Detlefilus	*Genera Incertae sedis* : : : **Opiliones**
Gjellerupia	*Genera Incertae sedis* : : : **Opiliones**
Gunturius	*Genera Incertae sedis* : : : **Opiliones**
Heterobabrius	*Genera Incertae sedis* : : : **Opiliones**
Ignacianulus	*Genera Incertae sedis* : : : **Opiliones**
Isaeolus	*Genera Incertae sedis* : : : **Opiliones**
Jimeneziella	*Genera Incertae sedis* : : : **Opiliones**
Johorella	*Genera Incertae sedis* : : : **Opiliones**
Kokoda	*Genera Incertae sedis* : : : **Opiliones**
Liomma	*Genera Incertae sedis* : : : **Opiliones**
Manuelangelia	*Genera Incertae sedis* : : : **Opiliones**
Metaconomma	*Genera Incertae sedis* : : : **Opiliones**
Metapellobunus	*Genera Incertae sedis* : : : **Opiliones**
Micrisaeus	*Genera Incertae sedis* : : : **Opiliones**
Microconomma	*Genera Incertae sedis* : : : **Opiliones**
Mirda	*Genera Incertae sedis* : : : **Opiliones**
Munis	*Genera Incertae sedis* : : : **Opiliones**
Neoparalus	*Genera Incertae sedis* : : : **Opiliones**
Neoscotolemon	*Genera Incertae sedis* : : : **Opiliones**
Octophthalmus	*Genera Incertae sedis* : : : **Opiliones**
Ortizia	*Genera Incertae sedis* : : : **Opiliones**
Ostracidium	*Genera Incertae sedis* : : : **Opiliones**
Parabupares	*Genera Incertae sedis* : : : **Opiliones**
Paraconomma	*Genera Incertae sedis* : : : **Opiliones**
Paraphalangodus	*Genera Incertae sedis* : : : **Opiliones**
Pegulius	*Genera Incertae sedis* : : : **Opiliones**
Peltamma	*Genera Incertae sedis* : : : **Opiliones**
Pentos	*Genera Incertae sedis* : : : **Opiliones**
Phalangodinus	*Genera Incertae sedis* : : : **Opiliones**
Philacarus	*Genera Incertae sedis* : : : **Opiliones**
Proscotolemon	*Genera Incertae sedis* : : : **Opiliones**
Pseudomitraceras	*Genera Incertae sedis* : : : **Opiliones**
Pucallpana	*Genera Incertae sedis* : : : **Opiliones**
Seblatus	*Genera Incertae sedis* : : : **Opiliones**
Sergitius	*Genera Incertae sedis* : : : **Opiliones**
Siryseus	*Genera Incertae sedis* : : : **Opiliones**

Spalicus	*Genera Incertae sedis* : : : **Opiliones**
Spinolatum	*Genera Incertae sedis* : : : **Opiliones**
Stygnomimus	*Genera Incertae sedis* : : : **Opiliones**
Tarmaops	*Genera Incertae sedis* : : : **Opiliones**
Turquinia	*Genera Incertae sedis* : : : **Opiliones**
Tweedielus	*Genera Incertae sedis* : : : **Opiliones**
Valifema	*Genera Incertae sedis* : : : **Opiliones**

APPENDIX THREE
Biogeographical Regions and Subregions

AFRICO-TROPICAL (ETHIOPIAN, AETHIOPIAN) REALM. [L. *Africa*, Africa; Gr. τροπικος, tropic]. Sub-Saharan Africa including the mid-Atlantic islands of Ascension and St. Helena, the continental shelf islands, Madagascar, the mid-Atlantic islands of Ascension and St. Helena; and some islands of the Indian Ocean. It is one of the six major biogeographic areas and is subdivided into twenty-nine provinces.

ANTARCTIC REALM. [Gr. αντι-, opposite; αρκτικος, northern; OFr. *reaume*, kingdom]. Antarctica and surrounding islands including southernmost archipelago of Tierra del Fuego, the Falklands etc., and New Zealand and associated shelf islands. It is one of the six major biogeographic areas and is divided into four provinces.

AUSTRAL KINGDOM. [L. *australis*, southern]. See Biogeographical Kingdoms.

AUSTRALASIA. [Fr. *Australasie*, Australia and neighboring islands]. Including Australia, New Guinea, New Zealand, and the neighbouring islands. The northern boundary of this zone is known as the Wallace Line. It is one of the six major biogeographic areas of the world.

AUSTRALIAN REALM. [L. *australis*, southern;]. The islands of Australia, Tasmania and continental shelf islands. It is one of the six major biogeographic areas and is subdivided into thirteen provinces.

BIOGEOGRAPHICAL BARRIER. [Gr. βιος, life; γεο-, the earth; γραφιεν, to sketch]. A barrier that prevents the migration of species. Such barriers may be climatic, or consist of geographical features.

BIOGEOGRAPHICAL KINGDOMS. [Gr. βιος, life; γεο-, the earth; γραφιεν, to sketch]. According to the International Code of Area Nomenclature, there are four Biogeographical Kingdoms: the **Holarctic**, comprised of the Nearctic and Palearctic regions. The **Holotropical**, comprised of the Neotropical, Ethiopian, and Oriental regions. The **Austral**, comprised of the Cape region, the Andean region, the Australian region; and the **Antarctic** region. There are also several transition zones: Mexican transition zone (Nearctic to Neotropical transition), Saharo-Arabian transition zone (Palearctic to Ethiopian transition), Chinese transition zone (Palearctic to Oriental transition zone), Indo-Malayan, Indonesian or Wallace's transition zone (Oriental to Australian transition), South American transition zone (Neotropical to Andean transition). Not all biogeographers agree with this scheme.

BIOGEOGRAPHICAL PROVINCE. [Gr. βιος, life; γεο-, the earth; γραφιεν, to sketch]. A biological subdivision of the earth's surface, considering both fauna and flora, and usually based on taxonomic as opposed to ecological criteria.

BIOGEOGRAPHICAL REGION/REALM. [Gr. βιος, life; γεο-, the earth; γραφιεν, to sketch; OFr. *reaume*, kingdom]. Any geographical region characterized by a distinctive flora and or fauna. Biogeographical regions are composed of groups of biogeographical provinces; of which the following nine are generally recognized; Afrotropical (Ethiopian), Antarctic, Australian, Indomalayan, Nearctic, Neotropical, Oceania, Oriental, Palearctic.

BOREAL. [L. *boreas*, north wind]. The northern biogeographical region; the Holarctic except the Sonoran (southern north America including northern Mexico).

DENDROGAEA. [Gr. δενδρον, tree; γαια, earth]. The biogeographical region that includes all the neotropical region except temperate South America.

DINOMIC. [Gr. δι-, two; νομος, region]. Of species restricted to two different biogeographical regions.

EAST ASIAN REGION. A division of the Palearctic Realm consisting of China, Korea and Japan, in which the temperate coniferous, broadleaf, and mixed forests are now mostly limited to mountainous areas. In the subtropical region of southern China and the southern edge of the Himalayas, the Palearctic temperate forests transition to the subtropical and tropical forests of the Indomalayan region.

ETHIOPIAN, AETHIOPIAN. [Gr. αιθιοψ, burnt-face; L *Æthiopia*, generally, central Africa]. See Afrotropical Realm.

EURO-SIBERIAN REGION. [Gr. myth. Ευρωπη, daughter of Oceanos; *Sibir*, ancient Tatar fortress]. A division of the Palearctic Realm. The largest biogeographic region in the Palearctic; stretching from the tundra in the northern reaches of Russia and Scandinavia to the taiga—the boreal coniferous forests which run across the continent. South of the taiga are a belt of temperate coniferous, broadleaf, and mixed forests. The Palearctic and Nearctic share numerous plant species (the Arcto-Tertiary Geoflora), and many zoologists consider the Palearctic and Nearctic to be a single Holarctic realm.

EUROPEAN SUBREGIONS. **Alpine**: Austria, Bulgaria, Germany, Spain, Finland, France, Italy, Poland, Romania, Sweden, Slovenia, Slovakia, Ukraine, Russia, Georgia, Armenia (Alps, Pyrenees, Carpathians, Dinaric Alps, Balkans, Rhodopes, Sondes, Urals, Caucasia). **Anatolian**: Turkey. **Arctic**: Iceland, Norway, Russia. **Atlantic**: Belgium, Germany, Denmark, Spain, France, Ireland, Portugal, Netherlands, United Kingdom. **Black Sea**: Bulgaria, Romania, Turkey, Georgia. **Boreal**: Estonia, Finland, Latvia, Lithuania, Sweden, Belarus, Russia. **Continental**: Austria, Belgium, Bulgaria, Czech Republic, Germany, Denmark, France, Italy, Luxembourg, Poland, Romania, Sweden, Slovenia, Belarus, Ukraine, Russia, Moldova, Serbia. **Macaronesian**: Spain, Portugal (Azores, Madeira, Canaries islands). **Mediterranean**: Cyprus, Spain, France, Greece, Italy, Malta, Portugal, Turkey. **Pannonia**: Czech Republic, Hungary, Romania, Serbia, Slovakia, Ukraine. **Steppic**: Romania, Moldova, Ukraine, Russia.

HOLARCTIC KINGDOM. [Gr. ολος, entire; αρκτικος, northern]. See Biogeographical Kingdoms.

HOLOTROPICAL KINGDOM. [Gr. ολος, entire; τροπικος, of the tropics]. See Biogeographical Kingdoms.

INDO-MALAYAN REALM. [*India* + *Malaya*]. Including the Indian subcontinent, Southeast Asia south of the Himalayas chain, southern China (approximately south of the Qinling–Huaihe Line), Sumatra, Java, Borneo, the Philippines and Taiwan. It is one of the six major biogeographic areas and is subdivided into twenty-seven provinces.

LIFE ZONE CONCEPT. A biogeographical region that has a characteristic fauna and flora.

MACARONESIA. [Gr. μακαρ, blessed; νησος, island]. A biogeographical region composed of the islands off the coast of northwest Africa and Europe (Azores, Canaries, Cape Verde Islands, Madeira).

MAMMAL REGIONS. Four biogeographic regions suggest by CH. Smith on the basis of statistical analysis. They are; Afro-Tethyan, Holarctic, Island and Latin American.

MANCHURIAN SUBREGION. [*Manchuria*, a region of northeast China]. One of four biogeographical subregions of the Palearctic, as defined by Alfred Russel Wallace. This region encompasses Mongolia, Korea, Manchuria, and Japan. The other three regions being the European, Mediterranean and Siberian.

MEDITERRANEAN REGION. [L. *mediterraneus*, 'the sea in the middle of the earth']. A division of the Palearctic Realm. The lands of southern Europe, north Africa, and western Asia form the Mediterranean Basin ecoregion, with generally mild, rainy winters and hot, dry summers. The region was previously mainly covered with forests and woodlands, but human use has reduced most of the region to the sclerophyll shrublands known as chaparral, matorral, maquis, or garrigue

MELANESIA. [Gr. μελας, black; νησος, island]. A geographical region comprising the continental islands of the western Pacific south of the equator. Sometimes considered to be a distinct biogeographical unit and sometimes considered to be part of Polynesia.

NEARCTIC REALM. [Gr. νεα, new; αρκτικος, northern]. North America including parts of northern Mexico, continental shelf islands (except those on the southeast Atlantic coastal shelf), and Greenland (but not Iceland). It is one of the six major biogeographic areas and is subdivided into forty-four provinces.

NEOTROPICAL FAUNAL REGION (NEOTROPICS, NEOGAEA). [Gr. νεα, new; τροπικος, of the tropics; L. *Faunus*, god of the woods]. The zoogeographical region comprising southern Mexico, Central and South America, the West Indies and the Galapagos Islands. It is one of the six major biogeographic areas and is divided into four provinces.

NEOTROPICAL REALM. [Gr. νεα, new; τροπικος, of the tropics; OFr. *reaume*, kingdom]. South from the coastal area of Baja California and Sinaloa flanking the Gulf of California, to Tierra del Fuego (except the southernmost archipelago), including all the continental shelf islands, the West Indies and the Galapagos Islands. It is one of the six major biogeographic areas and is divided into forty-seven provinces.

OCEANIAN REALM. [Gr. ωκεανος, the great river or sea surrounding the disk of the Earth]. Including Polynesia (except New Zealand), Micronesia, the Hawaiian and Fijian Islands. It is one of the six major biogeographic areas of the world. This realm is subdivided into seven provinces.

ORIENTAL (SINO-INDIAN) REGION. [L. *orientalis*, of the east]. A biogeographical region extending eastward from India to include the mainland and many of the islands of Southeast Asia.

PALEARCTIC REALM. [Gr. παλαιος, ancient; αρκτικος, northern]. It has mainly boreal to subarctic-climate to temperate-climate, and extends from North Africa, across all of Eurasia north of the foothills of the Himalayas, to the Bering Sea. It consists of the ecoregions: Euro-Siberian, Mediterranean Basin, Sahara and Arabian Deserts, Western and Central Asia, and East Asian. It is one of the six major biogeographic areas of the world and the largest of the eight realms. This realm is divided into twenty-two provinces.

PALAEOTROPICAL KINGDOM. [Gr. παλαιος, ancient; τροπικος, of the tropics]. A floristic region that includes the African, Indo-Malaysian, and Polynesian subkingdom.

SAHARA AND ARABIAN DESERT REGION. [Ar. Çahra, desert (pl. çahara); Gr. Αραβια, Arabia). A division of the Palearctic Realm. The great deserts of the African Atlantic coast, the Sahara desert, and the Arabian desert separate the Palearctic and Afrotropic ecoregions.

WESTERN AND CENTRAL ASIAN REGION. A division of the Palearctic Realm, bordered on the west by the Caucasus mountains, which run between the Black Sea and the Caspian Sea, across the Central Asian and Iranian plateaux, to the plateau of Tibet. The southern boundary between Palearctic Realm and the Indomalaya region is formed by foothills of the Himalaya between about 2000–2500 m.

BIBLIOGRAPHY

Specific internet references have not been included due to many websites disappearing or changing their address. However some government, museum and university websites, and a few others are more reliable. A few general ones are noted below, others are in the references.

https://www.itis.gov/ (Integrated Taxonomic Information System on-line database)

http://www.marinespecies.org/

http://www.arachne.org.au/

https://www.biodiversitylibrary.org/

http://taxondiversity.fieldofscience.com/search/label/Arachnida

https://bugguide.net/node/view/15740

André, H.M. (1992). Calyptostases As Indicators Of Developmental Constraints In Mites And Other Arthropods. Acarologia, t. XXXIII, fasc. 3, 1992.

Baker, E.W. (1949). A review of the mites of the family Cheyletidae in the United States National Museum. Proceedings of the United States National Museum. 99(3238): 267-320.

Baker, G.T. (1997). Spiracular Plate of Nymphal and Adult Hard Ticks (Acarina: Ixodidae): Morphology and Cuticular Ultrastructure. Invertebrate Biology, 116:4. 341-347

Barker, S.C. & Walker, A.R. (2014). Ticks of Australia. The species that infest domestic animals and humans. Zootaxa 3816 (1): 001-144. Magnolia Press.

Barnes, R.D (1980). Invertebrate Zoology. 4th Edition. Saunders College, Philadelphia.

Bennett, R.G. (1989). Emmerit's glands in *Cybaeota* (Araneae, Agelenidea). J. Arachno., 17:225-235.

Bochkov, A., Fain, A. (2001). Phylogeny and system of the Cheyletidae (Acari: Prostigmata) with special reference to their host-parasite associations. Bulletin de l'Institut royal des sciences naturelles de Belgique. Entomologie. 71: 5-36.

Breene, R.G. (Chairman) (2003). Common Names of Arachnids. 5th Edn. The American Arachnological Society Committee on Common Names of Arachnids.

Brown, R.W. (1956). Composition of Scientific Words. Smithsonian Institute Press.

Brusca, R.C., & Brusca, G.J. (2002). Invertebrates. 2nd edn. Sinauer Associates, Sunderland, MA. USA.

Buchsbaum, R. (1948). Animals Without Backbones Vols I & II. Penguin.

Burn, D.M. (1980). The Complete Encyclopedia of the Animal World. Octopus Books.

Coleman, D.C., Crossley, D.A. & Hendrix, P.F. (2004). Fundamentals of Soil Ecology. 2nd Edition, Academic Press.

Domrow, R. (1991). Acari Prostigmata (excluding Trombiculidae) parasitic on Australian vertebrates: an annotated checklist, keys and bibliography. Invertebrate Taxonomy 4, 1238-1376.

Dunlop, J.A., Penney, D. & Jekel, D. (2016). A summary list of fossil spiders and their relatives. In World Spider Catalogue, Natural History Museum Bern, online at http://wsc.nmbe.ch, version 17.5, accessed on Jan 2021.

Evans, G.O. 1992. Principles of Acarology. CAB International, Cambridge.

Fet, V. & Soleglad, M.E. (2005). Contributions to Scorpion Systematics. I. On Recent Changes in High-Level Taxonomy. Euscoprius @ Marshall University, Huntington, WV 25755-2510, USA.http://www.science.marshall.edu/fet/euscorpius/

Goodnight, C.J. & Goodnight, M.L (1942). Phalangids From Central America And The West Indies American Museum Novitiates No. 1184.

Grandjean, F. (1952). Au sujet de l'ectosquelette du podosoma chez les Oribates supérieurs et de sa terminologie. Bull. Soc. zool. France, 77:13-36.

Harvey, M.S. (1992). The Phylogeny and Classification of the Pseudoscorpionida (Chelicerata : Arachnida). Invertebr. Taxon., 1992, 6, 1373-435.

Haupt, J. & Song, D. (1996). Revision of East Asian whip scorpions (Arachnida, Uropygi, Thelyphonida). I. China and Japan". Arthropoda Selecta, 5:43–52.

Hickman, C., Roberts L., Keen S., Larson A., Eisenhour D. (2006) Animal Diversity (4th ed.). New York: Mc Graw Hill.

Hoff, C.C. (1958). List of the Pseudoscorpions of North America North of Mexico. American Museum Novitiates No. 1875.

Huntingford, F. (1984). The Study of Animal Behavior. Chapman & Hall.

Huxley, J. (1944). Evolution: The Modern Synthesis. Geoge Allen & Unwin.

Hynes, H.B.N. (1993). Adults and Nymphs of British Stoneflies. Freshwater Biological Association.

Jackson, R.R., Pollard, S.D., Nelson, X.J., Edwards, B.G. & Barion, A.T. (2001). Jumping spiders (Araneae: Salticidae) that feed on nectar. J. Zool. Lond. 255: 25–29.

Johnston, D.E. & Moraza, M.L. (1991). The idiosomal adenotaxy and poroidotaxy of Zerconidae (Mesostigmata: Zerconina). in Dusabek & Bukva (eds) Modern Acarology Vol. 2. pp. 349-356.

Khaustov A.A. (2000). Bembidiacaridae, a new family of mites (Acari: Heterostigmata) associated with carabid beetles of the genus *Bembidion* (Coleoptera: Carabidae). Acarina. Vol.8. No.1: 3–8.

Klompen, H. (2010). Holothyrids and ticks: new insights from larval morphology and DNA sequencing, with the description of a new species of *Diplothyrus* (Parasitiformes: Neothyridae). Acarologia 50(2): 269–285.

Klompen, J.S.H., Oliver, J.H., Keirans, J.E. & Homsher, P.J. (1997). A re-evaluation of relationships in the Metastriata (Acari: Parasitiformes: Ixodidae). Systematic Parasitology 38(1):1-24

Krantz, G.W. & Redmond. (1987). Identification of glandular and poroidal idionotal systems in Macrocheles perglaber (Acari: Macrochelidae). Exp. Appl. Acarol. 3: 243-253.

Krantz, G.W. (1978). A Manual of Acarology. 2nd Edition. Oregon State University Bookstores, Corvallis.

Lees, A.D. (1948). The sensory physiology of the sheep tick, *Ixodes ricinus* L. Journal of Experimental Biology 1948 25: 145-207.

Lehtinen, P.T. (1995). Revision of the old world Holothyridae (Arachnida : Anactinotrichida : Holothyrina). Invertebrate Taxonomy 9(4): 767-826.

Lewis, T. & Taylor, L.R. (1967). Introduction to Experimental Ecology. Academic Press.

Liddell, H.G. & Scott, R. (1996). Greek-English Lexicon. 9th Edition. Clarendon Press, Oxford.

Lindquist, E.E. & Evans, G.O. (1965). Taxonomic concepts in the Ascidae, with a modified setal nomenclature for the idiosoma of the Gamasina (Acarina : Mesostigmata). Memoirs of the Entomological Society of Canada 47: 1-64.

Lourenço, W.R. (1981). Scorpions cavernicoles de l'Equa teur: *Tityus demangei* n. sp. et *Ananteris ashmolei* n. sp. (Buthidae); *Troglotayosicus vachoni* n. gen., n. sp. (Chactidae), Scorpion troglobie. Bull. Mus. natn. Hist. nat., Paris, 4e ser., 3, 1981, section A, n° 2 : 635-662.

Mayr. E. (1963). Animal Species and Evolution. The Belknap Press of Harvard University. Cambridge, Massachusetts.

Mcdermott, A. (1975). Cytogenetics of Man and Other Animals. Chapman and Hall.

Mclver, J.D. & Stonedahl, G. (1993). Myrmecomorphy: Morphological and Behavioral Mimicry of Ants. Annual Review of Entomology 38: 351–377

Meehan, C,J., Olson, E.J. & Curry, R.L. (2008). Exploitation of the Pseudomyrmex–Acacia mutualism by a predominantly vegetarian jumping spider (Bagheera kiplingi). The 93rd ESA Annual Meeting.

Milne, L. & Milne, M. (1980). National Audubon Society Field Guide to Insects and Spiders. Knopf.

Morrone, J.J. (2015). Biogeographical regionalisation of the world: a reappraisal. Australian Systematic Botany 28: 81-90

O'Toole, C. (1986). Firefly Encyclopedia of Insects and Spiders. Firefly Books.

Ortega-Escobar, J. & Muñoz-Cuevas, A. (1999). Anterior median eyes of lycosa tarentula (Araneae, Lycosidae) detect polarized light: Behavioral experiments and Electroretinographic analysis. The Journal of Arachnology 27:663–671.

Parkin, D.T. (1979). An Introduction to Evolutionary Genetics. Edward Arnold.

Pechenik, J. A. (2005). Biology of the Invertebrates. Boston: McGraw-Hill, Higher Education. pp. 178.

Pepato, A.R. & Klimov, P.B. (2015). Origin and higher-level diversification of acariform mites – evidence from nuclear ribosomal genes, extensive taxon sampling, and secondary structure alignment. BMC Evolutionary Biology (2015) 15:178

Phillipson, J. (1966). Ecological Energetics. Studies in Biology No. 1 Edward Arnold.

Platnick, N.I. (2008). The world spider catalog. version 8.5. American Museum of Natural History.

Pritchard, A.E. & Baker, E.W. (1955). A revision of the spider mite family Tetranychidae. Mem. Pac. Coast Entomol. Soc. 2: 1-472.

Rees, H. & Jones, R.N. (1977). Chromosome Genetics. Edward Arnold.

Roberts, M.J. (1995). Spiders of Britain and Northern Europe. Collins.

Rowland, J.M. & Cooke, J.A.L. (1973). Systematics of the arachnid order Uropygida (5 Thelyphonida). The Journal of Arachnology, 1:55–71.

Seedman, O. (2019). The megisthanid mites (Mesostigmata: Megisthanidae) of Australia. Zootaxa 4563 (1): 001–040

Sharma P.P., & Gonzalo G. (2011). The evolutionary and biogeographic history of the armored harvestmen – Laniatores phylogeny based on ten molecular markers, with the description of two new families of Opiliones (Arachnida). Invertebrate Systematics, 2011, 25, 106–142

Shultz, J.W. (2001), Chelicerata (Arachnids, Including Spiders, Mites and Scorpions). Encyclopedia of Life Sciences, John Wiley & Sons, Ltd.

Simon, E. (1892). Historire Naturelle des Araignées. Paris 1892.

Simpson, D.P. (1994). Cassell's Latin Dictionary. 5th Edition. Cassell.

Simpson, G.G. (1940). Mammals and land bridges. Journal of the Washington [D. C.] Academy of Science, vol. 30, p. 137-163.

Smith, I.M., Lindquist, E.E. & Behan-Pelletier, V. (2009). Assessment Of Species Diversity In The Mixedwood Plains Ecozone: Mites.

Subías, L.S (2004-2011). Listado Sistemático, Sinonímico Y Biogeográfico De Los Ácaros Oribátidos (Acariformes: Oribatida) Del Mundo. Publicado originalmente en Graellsia, 60 (número extraordinario): 3-305 (2004). Actualizado en junio de 2006, en abril de 2007, en mayo de 2008, en abril de 2009, en julio de 2010 y en febrero de 2011).

Udvardy, M.D.F. (1975). A classification of the biogeographical provinces of the world. IUCN Occasional Paper No. 18. Morges, Switzerland: IUCN.

Walter, D.E. & Proctor H.C. (1998). Feeding behavior and phylogeny: observations on early derivative Acari. Experimental and Applied Acarology 22, 39-50.

Walter, D.A. (2001). Endemism and cryptogenesis in 'segmented' mites: A review of Australian Alicorhagiidae, Terpnacaridae, Oehserchestidae and Grandjeanicidae (Acari: Sarcoptiformes). Australian Journal of Entomology. 40:3 207-218

Whitehouse, H.L.K. (1973). Towards an Understanding of the Mechanism of Heredity. 3rd Edition. Edward Arnold.

Williams, T.R. (2005). A Dictionary of the Roots and Combining Forms of Scientific Words. Squirrox Press, Fakenham, England.

Williams, T.R. (2009). A Dictionary for Entomology. Lulu.com

Williams, T.R. (2009). A Dictionary for Invertebrate Zoology. Lulu.com

Wunderlich, J. (ed.) (2012). Fifteen papers on extant and fossil Spiders (Araneae). Beiträge Zur Araneologie, 7 (2012)

Sakunwarin, S., Baker, G.T. & Chandrapatya, A. (2004). Structure of sensilla on the palptarsus and the tarsus I of Tetranychus truncatus Ehara (Acari: Tetranychidae). Systematic and Applied Acarology, pp. 133-140, July 2004. ISSN 1362-1971.

Zhang, Z.-Q., Fan, Q.-H., Pesic, V., Smit, H., et al. (2011). Order Trombidiformes Reuter, 1909. In: Zhang, Z-Q. (ed.) Animal biodiversity: an outline of higher-level classification and survey of taxonomic richness. Zootaxa. 3148.

Made in United States
North Haven, CT
16 April 2022

18337018R00196